# Human Rights and Conflict

# Human Rights and Conflict

## Exploring the Links between Rights, Law, and Peacebuilding

Edited by Julie Mertus and Jeffrey W. Helsing

UNITED STATES INSTITUTE OF PEACE PRESS
Washington, D.C.

UNITED STATES INSTITUTE OF PEACE
1200 17th Street NW, Suite 200
Washington, DC 20036-3011

First published 2006

Printed in the United States of America

The paper used in this publication meets the minimum requirements of American National Standards for Information Science—Permanence of Paper for Printed Library Materials, ANSI Z39.48-1984.

**Library of Congress Cataloging-in-Publication Data**
    Human rights and conflict : exploring the links between rights, law, and peacebuilding / edited by Julie Mertus and Jeffrey W. Helsing.
      p. cm.
    Includes bibliographical references and index.
    ISBN-13: 978-1-929223-76-3 (softcover : alk. paper) ISBN-10: 1-929223-76-5 (softcover : alk. paper) ISBN-13: 978-1-929223-77-0 (hardcover : alk. paper) ISBN-10: 1-929223-77-3 (hardcover : alk. paper)
    1. Human rights. 2. Conflict management. 3. Humanitarian intervention.
  I. Mertus, Julie, 1963- II. Helsing, Jeffrey W.
    JC571.C68727 2006
    323—dc22
                                      2006008569

# Contents

# Foreword

Newcomers to the field of international relations may be surprised to learn that efforts to advance human rights are often at odds with attempts to halt violent conflicts. In the experience of practitioners, however, it is unfortunately a commonplace that the promotion of human rights and the practice of conflict resolution, while both admirable endeavors in themselves, are by no means necessarily complementary objectives.

The international landscape is littered with episodes in which advocates of the two objectives have pointed accusing fingers at one another, charging that their own best efforts have been undermined, ignored, or counteracted by actions taken by counterparts from the other camp. In Bosnia, for instance, human rights activists spent years pressing NATO's Stabilization Force to arrest indicted war criminals, a move that many diplomats and soldiers felt would only further destabilize an already volatile situation. In Pakistan, U.S. policymakers have had to contend with charges that they have turned a blind eye to torture and other human rights abuses of the government in return for cooperation of the regime in Islamabad in the fight against al Qaeda. In a host of cases, from the Middle East to the Balkans to West Africa, would-be peacemakers have seen their best efforts to reach negotiated settlements challenged, if not undermined, by groups protesting the inclusion in peace talks of leaders who have used terror, genocide, and ethnic cleansing to advance their political goals.

Such clashes have not, of course, passed unnoticed. Throughout the past decade, human rights and conflict resolution scholars and practitioners have vigorously debated the differences and tensions between the two approaches. Much public discussion has also occurred in forums where representatives of the two camps have met to argue for the primacy of their concerns and activities. Heat, however, does not always generate light, and our understanding of the relationship between the two approaches has not always been illuminated by such exchanges.

The chief ambition of this volume is to improve that level of understanding by turning an analytical spotlight on the relationship between human rights promotion and conflict management—or, more precisely, by turning a series of spotlights on different facets of the relationship. The volume's origins lie in May 2001, when the Education Program of the United States Institute of Peace and the Joan B. Kroc Institute for International Peace Studies at the University of Notre Dame organized a symposium to examine not only where human rights and conflict resolution diverge but also where they converge. Inspired by the discussions at that and similar gatherings, the volume's editors—Julie Mertus, who was then a senior fellow at the United States Institute of Peace, and Jeffrey Helsing of the Institute's Education Program—recruited a wide range of scholars and practitioners to explore subjects and themes that elicited significant interest during the symposium. The results of their work are evident in the chapters that comprise this volume.

As those chapters attest, the relationship between conflict management and resolution on the one hand, and human rights promotion on the other, is multifaceted, intricate, and fluid, evolving in response not only to changes in the nature of contemporary violent conflict but also to the two camps' growing experience in working as partners instead of competitors. The volume also makes clear that to see the relationship as two-sided distorts reality, for there are in fact *three* camps involved: conflict resolution, human rights, and international humanitarian law. The last of these—which seeks to regulate the conduct of war and to protect civilians during armed conflict, and which is championed not least by humanitarian relief agencies —can serve as a bridge between peace negotiators and human rights advocates because it is a human rights and legal tool that can strengthen a peace process or agreement by helping to reduce suffering and creating legitimacy for a settlement.

I will leave it to the reader to discover in the following chapters the richness of the interaction among these three approaches, the ways in which they can reinforce and complement, and not just undercut, one another's efforts. I will, however, draw attention here to a point made several times in the volume, namely, that the triadic nature of the relationship seems to be particularly conspicuous, and particularly important, in efforts to create sustainable peace. In light of the challenges presented today in countries such as Afghanistan, Bosnia, Iraq, and Sierra Leone, the United States Institute of Peace is devoting substantial effort to the task of determining the critical components of a stable and sustainable peace. Many of the ideas raised in *Human Rights and Conflict* merit serious consideration by everyone working to build sustainable settlements in societies emerging from conflict.

This volume also accords with the Institute's principles and priorities in offering food for thought both to those who work with soldiers, civilians, and politicians in the field and to those who wrestle with policy options and ideas in government offices, think tanks, and universities. *Human Rights and Conflict* introduces the reader to many of the practical, concrete issues that practitioners and policymakers confront today in responding to violent conflict. At the same time, however, it is also intended as a teaching tool, providing multiple perspectives on the ways in which human rights, conflict resolution, and humanitarian law complement one another. This breadth of appeal is more than matched by the diversity of the cast of contributing authors, who include practitioners, scholars, and other experts from each of the three camps.

Encouragingly, to speak of "camps," with all that that term implies about exclusivity and mutual distrust, may one day be inappropriate. Already, as *Human Rights and Conflict* illustrates, proponents of each of the three approaches are discovering that their activities can be mutually supportive and that their goals, especially when viewed over the mid- to long term, are often mutually reinforcing. If *Human Rights and Conflict* achieves its own goals, this awareness of the holistic nature of building and sustaining peace will become clearer and more prevalent.

Over the course of more than twenty years, the United States Institute of Peace has supported groundbreaking work in all three areas of endeavor highlighted in this volume. It has been especially active in funding and disseminating cutting-edge research in the field of conflict resolution, but it has also contributed significantly to the debate and the literature on the role of international law in conflict management. In recent years, it has enhanced its work in the area of human rights promotion in various ways, including, for example, publishing Debra Liang-Fenton's edited volume *Implementing U.S. Human Rights Policy*. Given the breadth of our interest in and commitment to these issues, it should be evident that the Institute is very pleased to publish *Human Rights and Conflict*. This volume does not shy away from the differences, real and imagined, that separate conflict resolution, human rights, and international law; indeed, it explores those differences and recognizes the obstacles to closer cooperation between conflict managers and other practitioners and activists. But this book also investigates the complementarities, acknowledged and unacknowledged, that link the three approaches and that, if exploited, promise greater success in producing sustainable peace in states wracked by conflict.

Richard H. Solomon, President
UNITED STATES INSTITUTE OF PEACE

 # Preface and Acknowledgments

This project was born from a desire to provide educators and scholars in the fields of human rights and conflict resolution with a resource that would enable them to analyze and teach about the growing intersection between human rights and the field known variously as conflict resolution, conflict transformation, and conflict management. Learning about conflict resolution and human rights will make a positive contribution to understanding in both fields because there is a complementarity between the two disciplines, and practitioners of both often end up working in the same conflict arenas.

We wanted to produce a book that presented and analyzed the key underlying ideas, assumptions, and objectives of human rights as they relate to conflict management. In addition, we felt that it was critical to incorporate practitioners and scholars of international humanitarian law into the volume because they combine a human rights focus with an application in arenas of violent conflict. We began to develop this project with the idea that each chapter should be balanced with a responding commentary from someone with a different perspective and from a different discipline. It is our belief that student audiences appreciate different viewpoints as a way to flesh out essential elements of a topic.

As we sought out contributors, we thought it was particularly useful to ask the following questions:

- What are some of the key human rights issues that the military forces, humanitarian relief agencies, and local NGOs face today?
- To what extent are competing conceptions of human rights and different priorities and strategies for addressing human rights a source of tension?

- What ethical dilemmas regarding human rights and peacebuilding do diplomats, advocates, security forces and relief organizations face?
- How are such basic goals as peace, stability, justice, and rule of law prioritized and how should they be sequenced?

After receiving the contributions for the book, we realized that some commentaries deserved their own status as independent chapters. This delayed the production of the book for a while and it must be acknowledged that some of the initial drafts were written well over two years ago. They have been updated and brought current as much as is possible. As with any book that deals with ongoing peace and conflict issues, however, new themes, events, and policy decisions may have emerged since the final copyediting has been concluded. Nonetheless, the main themes we have examined here remain of significance to future developments.

There are a number of people to thank directly for their help on this book. We are grateful to the entire education program of the United States Institute of Peace, in particular Pamela Aall, who has strongly encouraged this project from its inception. Raina Kim was, as always, very helpful with all administrative matters. The Institute's publications staff was very helpful and always supportive of the project. The editorial assistance of Nigel Quinney has been essential in helping us bring together the many contributions into a coherent whole. Nigel is a superb editor and makes the process very easy and productive.

The editors benefited greatly from two workshops sponsored by the United States Institute of Peace. The first was in May 2001 at Notre Dame University's Joan B. Kroc Center for International Peace Studies. The workshop was titled "Do Good Things *Really* Go Together? Assessing Human Rights and Peace in the Contemporary World." A second symposium took place in September 2002 at the University of Dayton and was titled "No Peace without Justice" and cosponsored by the International Human Rights Education Consortium. Both workshops raised questions and explored issues that have been raised in this book. We are indebted in particular to Professors George Lopez of the Kroc Center and Mark Ensalaco of the University of Dayton for conceiving and developing the two respective workshops.

In addition, we benefited from a roundtable discussion at the United States Institute of Peace in July 2003 on the relationship between human rights and peacebuilding in Iraq. The contributions of Dawn Calabia, Reuben Brigety, Jeff Walker, and Sanam Anderlini were particularly valuable, as were those of the roundtable chair, Louis Goodman, dean of the School of

International Service at American University. The editors also benefited considerably from meetings of conflict resolution and human rights practitioners initiated and sponsored by Hurst Hannum and Eileen Babbitt of the Center for Human Rights and Conflict at the Fletcher School of Law and Diplomacy.

Julie Mertus would like to dedicate this book to Professor Abdul Aziz Said for his inspiration and leadership in the field of human rights. She would also like to thank the students of American University's human rights and conflict courses in the spring of 2004 and 2005 for their feedback on earlier versions of these chapters, American University PhD students Eve Bratman and Maia Carter Hallward for their research support, and last, but certainly not least, Janet Lord for her editing, substantive suggestions, and ongoing encouragement and support. Jeffrey Helsing would like to thank his family for their patience and support when manuscripts were brought home nights and weekends and also his colleagues in the United States Institute of Peace education program for their terrific support and collegiality.

Finally, we have to thank each of the contributors to the book for their hard work, excellent analysis, and patience (particularly in some cases). This was not always an easy project, but we feel that it has paid off handsomely in the end.

# Contributors

**Julie A. Mertus** is an associate professor of international relations at American University, where she is also codirector of the Ethics, Peace, and Global Affairs Program. A graduate of Cornell University and Yale Law School, she is a frequent consultant on human rights and humanitarian issues to a number of organizations, including the United Nations High Commissioner for Refugees, the Humanitarianism and War Project, Women Waging Peace, and Oxfam. Her previous appointments include senior fellow, United States Institute of Peace; human rights fellow, Harvard Law School; writing fellow, MacArthur Foundation; Fulbright fellow (Romania); law and religion fellow, Emory University; and counsel, Human Rights Watch (Helsinki Watch). Her book *Bait and Switch: Human Rights & U.S. Foreign Policy* was named "Human Rights Book of the Year" by the American Political Science Association. Her other books include *United Nations Human Rights Mechanisms* (2004); *Kosovo: How Myths and Truths Started a War* (1999); *War's Offensive against Women: The Humanitarian Challenge in Bosnia, Kosovo, and Afghanistan* (2000); *The Suitcase: Refugees' Voices from Bosnia and Croatia* (1999); and (with Mallika Dutt and Nancy Flowers) *Local Action/Global Change* (1999), which was translated into more than ten languages.

**Jeffrey W. Helsing,** deputy director for education at the United States Institute of Peace, is responsible for many of the Institute's faculty and teacher workshops as well as for curriculum development. He often leads workshops on teaching about war and peace. Helsing also works with many groups in Israel and the Palestinian Authority to train educators, NGO workers, students, and young leaders in developing their skills in conflict resolution, nonviolence, human rights, communication, and facilitation. He has fifteen years of experience as an educator, having taught courses in a broad range of international relations subjects, including conflict resolution, international relations theory, and foreign policy analysis; he currently teaches a graduate course on human rights and conflict resolution at Georgetown University. Helsing has written numerous articles and book chapters on U.S. policy in the Middle East and on Middle East conflicts. He holds a PhD in political science from Columbia University and a BA from Stanford University.

■    ■    ■

**Mohammed Abu-Nimer** is an associate professor in the International Peace and Conflict Resolution (IPCR) program and director of the Peacebuilding and Development Institute at American University. His recent publications include *Nonviolence and Peacebuilding in Islam: Theory and Practice* (2003) and *Reconciliation, Justice, and Coexistence: Theory and Practice* (2001).

**Kevin Avruch** is Professor of Conflict Resolution and Anthropology in the Institute for Conflict Analysis and Resolution, and faculty and senior fellow in the Peace Operations Policy Program (School of Public Policy), at George Mason University. Professor Avruch has published more than fifty articles and essays and is author or editor of five books, most recently *Critical Essays on Israeli Society, Religion, and Government* (1997), *Culture and Conflict Resolution* (1998) and *Information Campaigns for Peace Operations* (2000).

**Christine Bell** is director of the Transitional Justice Institute and professor of public international law at the University of Ulster (Magee Campus). Her previous positions include director of the Centre for International and Comparative Human Rights Law, Queen's University of Belfast, and chairperson of the Committee on the Administration of Justice. She was a founding member of the Northern Ireland Human Rights Commission, established under the terms of the Belfast Agreement. Her publications include *Peace Agreements and Human Rights* (2000) and *The Role of Human Rights in Peace Agreements* (2006).

**John Cerone** is director of the Center for International Law and Policy at the New England School of Law. He has worked for a range of intergovernmental and nongovernmental organizations and has extensive field experience in conflict and postconflict environments, including Afghanistan, Kosovo, Sierra Leone, and East Timor.

**Jack Donnelly** is the Andrew Mellon Professor at the Graduate School of International Studies, University of Denver. He has written widely in the field of human rights—his books include *Universal Human Rights in Theory* *and Practice* (2nd edition, 2003)—as well as on political realism and international relations theory.

**Richard Falk** is Milbank Professor of International Law Emeritus at Princeton University and since 2001 has been a visiting professor of global studies at the University of California at Santa Barbara. He is chair of the board of the Nuclear Age Peace Foundation. His most recent books are *The Great Terror War* (2003) and *The Declining World Order* (2004).

**Nancy Flowers** consults and writes on human rights education. Her most recent publications include (with Julie Mertus and Mallika Dutt) *Local Action/Global Change: Learning about the Human Rights of Women and Girls* (2nd edition, forthcoming 2006) and *Human Rights Education Handbook.* She edits the University of Minnesota's Human Rights Education Series.

**Maia Carter Hallward** has worked for four years in the Middle East, teaching and researching at the Ramallah Friends School and the United Nations University International Leadership Academy, as well as working with local Israeli and Palestinian Jerusalem-based organizations. She is active in the work of the Religious Society of Friends (Quakers) and is assistant editor of the *Journal of Peacebuilding and Development.* She is a PhD candidate at American University.

**Edward (Edy) Kaufman** has served as director of the Center for International Development and Conflict Management at the University of Maryland and as executive director of the Truman Institute for Peace at the Hebrew University in Jerusalem. He has done extensive work in facilitating track-two meetings, strengthening civil society, and peacebuilding. He has taught, researched, and written about human rights in world politics, and has helped train law enforcement agencies.

**Alan Keenan** is a Visiting Scholar at the University of Pennsylvania's Solomon Asch Center for Study of Ethnopolitical Conflict. He is the author of *Democracy in Question: Democratic Openness in a Time of Political Closure* (2003), as well as articles in a number of academic journals and edited volumes.

**Charles O. Lerche** is associate program director for the Master's in Diplomacy Program at Norwich University, Vermont. His research interests include international relations, the politics of the Global South, world order, and peace and conflict studies. He has coauthored *Concepts of International Politics in Global Perspective,* edited three volumes of essays on world order studies, and published articles in several academic journals. He is consulting editor for the *International Journal of Peace Studies.*

**Janet E. Lord** is director of the Amnesty International/AU Summer Human Rights Institute at American University and a human rights lawyer in the Washington, D.C.–based firm of BlueLaw LLC. She has served as advocacy director at Landmine Survivors Network and as an attorney with the World Bank. She earned an LLB and LLM from the University of Edinburgh and an LLM in international law from George Washington University.

**Michael S. Lund** is senior associate for conflict and peacebuilding at Management Systems International, Inc. The author of *Preventing Violent Conflicts* (1996) and founding director of the United States Institute of Peace's Jennings Randolph Fellows Program, he has published and consulted widely on intrastate conflicts and the effectiveness of conflict prevention programs and multilateral efforts. He has a PhD in political science from the University of Chicago.

**Ellen L. Lutz** is the executive director of Cultural Survival. She previously ran the Center for Human Rights and Conflict Resolution at Tufts University's Fletcher School, where she also taught international human rights law and international criminal law. From 1989 to 1994 she was the California director for Human Rights Watch. An experienced mediator, arbitrator, and facilitator, she has written widely on human rights and conflict resolution and on international and transnational accountability for human rights violations.

**Ram Manikkalingam** served until recently as senior adviser to President Kumaratunga of Sri Lanka, advising the president on a range of policy issues related to the peace process with the Tamil Tigers. He was closely associated with designing a joint mechanism between the government and rebels for relief and reconstruction after the tsunami of 2005. Previously, he was an adviser on peace and security to the Rockefeller Foundation and led the foundation's work in this area.

**Susan Martin** is director of Georgetown University's Institute for the Study of International Migration. She previously served as executive director of the U.S. Commission on Immigration Reform and research director at the Refugee Policy Group. Her publications include *Refugee Women* and *The Uprooted: Improving Humanitarian Responses to Forced Migration.*

**Jonathan Moore** is at the Kennedy School at Harvard University. He works on relief and development programs in countries such as Somalia, Haiti, Rwanda, and Sri Lanka. He was U.S. coordinator for refugees and ambassador to the United Nations. He is the editor of *Hard Choices: Moral Dilemmas in Humanitarian Intervention* (1998).

**Vasuki Nesiah** is a senior associate at the International Center for Transitional Justice, where she heads up the center's work in South Africa, Ghana, and Sri Lanka. She also leads its work on gender and nonstate actors in transitional justice and coleads the project "Innovations in Justice." Originally from Sri Lanka, she has published and lectured on international and comparative law, feminist theory, law and development, postcolonial studies, constitutionalism, and governance in plural societies.

**Jordan J. Paust** is the Mike and Teresa Baker Law Center Professor of International Law at the Law Center of the University of Houston. He has served as the chair of the Section on International Law of the Association of American Law Schools and on the executive council and the president's committee of the American Society of International Law. He has authored or coauthored *International Law and Litigation in the U.S.* (2005), *International Law as Law of the United States* (2003), and *International Criminal Law: Cases and Materials* (2000).

**Abdul Aziz Said** is the senior ranking professor and the Mohammed Said Farsi Chair of Islamic Peace at American University. He is a founder and director of the Center for Global Peace and of the International Peace and Conflict Resolution Program. He has written, coauthored, or edited sixteen books, including *Peace and Conflict Resolution in Islam: Precept and Practice, Concepts of International Politics in a Global Perspective, Human Rights and World Order,* and *Ethnicity in an International Context.*

**Lisa Schirch** is an associate professor of peacebuilding at Eastern Mennonite University, specializing in security, human rights, the arts, and development. A former African Fulbright fellow, she is the author of four books: *Strategic Peacebuilding, Ritual and Symbol in Peacebuilding, Civilian Peacekeeping,* and *Women in Peacebuilding Resource and Training Manual.*

**Andrew I. Schoenholtz** is the deputy director of Georgetown University's Institute for the Study of International Migration and visiting professor at the Georgetown University Law Center and School of Foreign Service. His publications include *The Uprooted: Improving Humanitarian Responses to Forced Migration* and numerous articles on asylum and refugee protection.

**Hugo Slim** is chief scholar at the Centre for Humanitarian Dialogue in Geneva, leading its work on the protection of civilians. Previously, he was reader in international humanitarianism at Oxford Brookes University, served as a trustee of Oxfam GB, and worked with Save the Children and the United Nations in Africa and the Middle East.

**David P. Stewart** is assistant legal adviser at the U.S. Department of State. He is a graduate of Princeton University and the Yale Law and Graduate Schools and received an LLM in international law from New York University. He teaches as an adjunct professor of law at the Georgetown University Law Center.

**Thomas G. Weiss** is Presidential Professor at the CUNY Graduate Center and director of the Ralph Bunche Institute for International Studies, where he is codirector of the United Nations Intellectual History Project. He has written extensively about multilateral approaches to peace and security, humanitarian action, and sustainable development.

**Richard Ashby Wilson** is the Gladstein Distinguished Chair of Human Rights and director of the Human Rights Institute at the University of Connecticut. His recent books include *The Politics of Truth and Reconciliation in South Africa* (2001) and *Human Rights and the "War on Terror"* (2005).

# Human Rights and Conflict

# Introduction

## Exploring the Intersection between Human Rights and Conflict

Julie A. Mertus and Jeffrey W. Helsing

## A Complex, Dynamic Relationship

Every day our newspapers and broadcasters convey stories about violent conflict. We hear of civilians murdered by suicide bombers, states erupting into genocidal violence, beleaguered humanitarian relief agencies struggling to cope with the most basic needs of enormous refugee populations, failed states collapsing in chaos, the torture of prisoners captured during wartime—and the list goes on. All these calamitous situations point up the complex relationship between international human rights and conflict. This book explores that relationship, examining its powerful dynamics and multiple facets from several angles.

Our aims are twofold. The first is to provide an accurate account of the relationship between human rights and conflict by making in-depth analyses of particular facets and presenting a composite picture of the overall relationship. We also lay out the differences of opinion among scholars, activists, diplomats, and policymakers on how best to interpret and respond to the sometimes competing issues of human rights, humanitarian law, and conflict resolution while also encouraging the reader to think about how those different approaches can complement one another.

The notion that deprivation of human rights contributes to protracted social conflict draws from the theory of basic human needs. Human needs theory is closely identified with the seminal work of John Burton, who theorized in *Deviance, Terrorism and War: The Process of Solving Unsolved Social and Political Problems*[1] that unsatisfied human needs are the root cause of many of the most violent conflicts. Human rights abuses, like unmet human needs, threaten the security of individuals and social groups and, in so doing, create cycles of dehumanization based on fear. Politicians and militaries can use that fear to stoke their campaigns and further their agendas. Such was the case in Rwanda in 1994, as Tutsis in exile violated the rights of Hutu leaders even as Hutus in power dehumanized and slaughtered Tutsis at home.

Not only do human rights abuses lead to the onset of conflict, but also, as Louis Kriesberg notes, "inhumane treatment deepens the antagonism and the desire to continue the struggle and even to seek revenge. The callous and indiscriminate use of violence, intended to intimidate and suppress the enemy, is frequently counterproductive, prolonging a struggle and making an enduring peace more difficult to attain."[2] Some ideologies use dehumanizing imagery to exclude "enemy" groups, describing other peoples as "animals," "vermin," or "evil incarnate" and thereby setting the stage for future human rights abuses. Leaders who emphasize ends over means are not likely to hesitate before violating human rights in pursuit of their goals. Memories can likewise evoke violent responses, since old resentments and distrust can keep tensions higher between groups or countries. For example, Rwanda's history of social tensions, widespread killings, and long-standing human rights abuses fueled the genocidal massacres of the 1990s.

While the *denial* of human rights can thus engender and intensify conflict, so, too, can the *demand* for those same rights. The state's inability or unwillingness to protect basic human rights and provide mechanisms for the civil resolution of conflict may prompt groups to use force in pressing their demands for such rights, resulting in violent conflict both within and between states.[3] Violent conflicts have grown out of the quest for self-determination, demands for fair access to resources, resistance to forced acculturation and discrimination, and—most often—a combination of such factors. For example, the ongoing conflict in Nigeria's delta region is fueled not only by the petroleum industry's pollution of the traditional living areas of the Ogoni people but also by extrajudicial killings of Ogoni and by that ethnic minority's demands for increased rights. Rights abuses also motivated the uprising, in eastern Zaire in 1996, of the Banyamulenge Tutsi minority, who eventually overthrew Zaire's president, Mobutu Sese Seko. These abuses included discrimination at the hands of Mobutu's regime over three decades, the decision of a provincial governor to expel the Banyamulenge from Zaire—where they had lived for two hundred years—and Mobutu's support for the Hutu Interahamwe, a militia that had taken part in the Rwandan genocide.

States that neglect human rights do so at their own peril. Neglect or dismissal of human rights demands can raise the stakes from low-intensity conflict to high-intensity conflict. Especially in ethnically divided societies, domestic policies that ignore the rights of minorities can increase social and political tensions until a full-blown conflict erupts. The daily abuses that are part of systematic government oppression may initially leave citizens feeling insecure and powerless, but at some point those same citizens may conclude that the only possible response to a violent system is violence. Human rights abuses are the legacy of violent regimes, such as that of General Augusto Pinochet in Chile,[4] and such cultures of domination often lead to other manifestations of social violence, including domestic violence and differential standards of justice.

Table 1 summarizes the various ways in which violations of, and demands for, human rights can be symptoms as well as causes of conflict. Policymakers, diplomats, human rights activists, humanitarian aid workers, and peacekeepers as well as scholars all acknowledge that a relationship exists between human rights and conflict. The complexities of the relationship, however, are not as well understood. In determining which side of the relationship is more influential or more important, and especially when deciding what should be done to shape or manage the relationship, stark differences of opinion emerge.

## What to Do about the Relationship: Three Different Approaches

The range of views on the relationship between human rights and conflict is quite diverse, but three distinct schools of thought stand out. The "human rights" approach is dominant among individuals and organizations that work to promote respect for human dignity and that stress the importance of exposing the truth about governmental abuses and bringing an end to injustices. A second approach, the "conflict resolution" perspective, is commonly espoused by those who focus on resolving, managing, preventing, or transforming violent conflict, whether through negotiation and mediation or through the threat or use of military force and other coercive measures. The third approach, inspired by the corpus of international humanitarian law concerning the conduct of war and the protection of civilians during armed conflict, is the "humanitarian law" approach. It is characteristic of relief agencies and other organizations, especially those administered by the United Nations, that work in the field to assist populations hit by violent conflict.

**Table 1.** The Relationship between Human Rights and Conflict

| | Description | Stage of Conflict[a] | Examples | Chapter |
|---|---|---|---|---|
| **Demand for human rights as a cause of conflict** | Demands—for self-determination, fair access to resources, an end to forced acculturation and discrimination—involve violent conflict between groups. | Stage 1 (possibly Stage 3) | Tiananmen Square protests in China, 1989; Papua New Guinea | Chapters 1, 2, 4, 14 |
| **State's inability or unwillingness to protect rights as a cause of conflict** | Domestic policies (especially in ethnically divided societies) that ignore minority rights increase social and political tensions until conflict erupts. Even in stable polities, structural oppression increases the danger of future confrontation and violence. | Stage 1 (possibly Stage 3) | Ogoni in Nigeria; Tutsis in Zaire, 1996 | Chapters 1, 3, 5, 6 |
| **Instrumental use of human rights violations by politicians** | Politicians manipulate collective memories of human rights abuses to create a sense of entitlement for revenge. | Stages 1 and 2 (possibly Stage 3) | Rwanda, Yugoslavia | Chapters 10, 13 |

| | | | | |
|---|---|---|---|---|
| **Human rights violations as a conflict escalator** | The sustained denial of human rights causes repressed/oppressed groups to react and may prompt intervention, intensifying the conflict. | Stages 1 and 2 | South Africa, Northern Ireland | Chapters 2, 6, 7, 11, 16 |
| **Human rights violations as direct symptoms of violent conflict** | Warring parties torture, rape, mutilate, and summarily execute both combatants and noncombatants. | Stage 2 | Liberia, Guatemala, Sri Lanka | Chapters 8, 11 |
| **Human rights violations as a direct or indirect consequence of violent conflict** | War adversely affects such things as the environment and the ability of people to work, thereby affecting related human rights. Cease-fires and peace agreements that ignore human rights often perpetuate inequities and denial of human rights, leading to greater suffering and violence. Sustainable peace depends on the assurance of human rights. | All stages | Sierra Leone, Israel-Palestine, Nicaragua, Kosovo | Chapters 1, 3, 5, 7, 8, 9, 10, 12, 15 |

a. Stage 1 = conflict intensification/mitigation; Stage 2 = armed conflict; Stage 3 = postconflict/postcrisis.

These three approaches have traditionally been treated separately, at least as they are studied formally. For instance, human rights have largely remained a separate field, not only from security studies and humanitarian law but also from conflict resolution. In practice, however, all three approaches are blended. The "peace and justice" wing of the conflict resolution field tends to define peace to mean, among other things, the assurance of rights and justice. And the conflict resolution field as a whole has embraced a wide-ranging notion of security—including political, economic and social, cultural, and environmental security—that incorporates human rights norms and also includes nongovernmental actors. Still, these broad categories are recognizable to most people who work in one or another of the three fields.

The differences in outlook have much to do with the setting of priorities. For many in the conflict resolution field, the first goal in tackling an ongoing conflict must be to end wholesale violence. This may sometimes entail working with people who are guilty of violating human rights, because without them a peace agreement would be hard to implement. According to many conflict resolution specialists, only after the violence has stopped will there be any possibility for advocacy for human rights—hostilities must cease before peace with justice can become a viable objective. In contrast, for human rights advocates there can be no peace without justice, and thus, no agreement to end violence or war can be sustained without accountability for human rights violations. At the same time, for many people who work in the field of humanitarian relief, the foremost priority is to address *how* the conflict is conducted and how that affects the immediate needs of people living in the conflict zone. Much of the tension among professionals working in these three areas stems from this difference in priorities.

The turbulent years since the end of the Cold War—years in which we have seen internal wars proliferate, ethnic tensions intensify, and impassioned debate rage over questions of if, when, and how the international community should respond to intrastate violence—have prompted many people to look for ways to break down the barriers between human rights, humanitarian law, and conflict resolution. And indeed all three schools of thought have moved closer together, propelled by the recognition that despite their very different origins and favored mechanisms, they share more in common than anyone previously acknowledged: namely, a fundamental commitment to maximizing human dignity and minimizing civilian harm. There is also a growing recognition that proponents of the three approaches can work well together, with their differences complementing rather than undermining one another.

This convergence is greatly to be welcomed. The challenge now is to integrate these perspectives in a manner that best responds to the nature of conflict in today's world. If human rights violations are viewed merely as a symptom of conflict, the primary objective of the international community should be to put an end to violence and protect people from further abuses, thus creating "negative peace," that is, the absence of violent conflict. International humanitarian law is an important instrument for negative peace, because it seeks to limit the excesses of war and protect civilians and other vulnerable groups. On the other hand, if human rights violations are viewed as causing violent conflict, the main objective of the international community should be to transform the structural and systemic conditions that give rise to violence. This perspective seeks to achieve more than the mere absence of war, working toward "positive peace" via the long-term process of transforming attitudes and institutions to create and sustain a society that is both peaceful and just. Reality, however, is rarely so clear-cut. As the authors in this book demonstrate, the relationship between human rights and conflict is complex and shifting, demanding policies, actions, and solutions that integrate both negative and positive peace.

Some texts examine the connection between human rights and conflict from a relatively narrow angle. For instance, to the extent that human rights books discuss conflict, they largely confine their analysis to humanitarian law and international mechanisms for its enforcement. This does not jibe with the reality of the human rights field, which relies heavily on extralegal mechanisms and on the promotion of human rights norms through diplomacy, the building of human rights institutions, education, and post-conflict reconstruction and reconciliation. Similarly, while conflict resolution books may mention human rights, they usually treat them as a peripheral issue, so that the human rights dimensions of conflict resolution are never adequately explored. Often human rights are viewed as a by-product of peace, not as a major component for building peace.

We have sought to correct such analytical "tunnel vision" in this volume by assembling a cast of authors who together present a panoramic view of the field. The authors chosen for this collection are practitioners and scholars working on the various aspects of the human rights and conflict dynamic. To ensure diversity of views and a balance between scholars and practitioners, some chapters are supplemented by short responses from additional commentators. In particular, if a chapter has been written by an expert whose work is primarily in the field of human rights or humanitarian law, we have asked for commentary from someone who has worked mostly in the field of conflict resolution, and vice versa. In gathering their work together in a single volume, this book encourages a more integrated approach to understanding the relationship between human rights and conflict.

## The Structure of This Book: Three Stages of Conflict

The chapters in this book are organized around the notion of stages of conflict. Human rights considerations are important factors throughout the course of a violent conflict, and every conflict can be depicted as passing through any number of different stages. For analytical purposes, however, we identify three—inevitably overlapping—stages.

- *The conflict intensification stage:* Communal conflicts turn violent; human rights violations are often a root cause of conflict, and the ability of perpetrators to act with impunity contributes to the intensification of conflict; the failure to address human rights issues hinders conflict prevention efforts.

- *The armed conflict stage:* Violent conflict intensifies as competing factions take up arms; human rights abuses are both a common by-product of the violence and a component of wartime strategy; international human rights norms inform standards for international intervention in conflicts, evaluation of the conduct of armed forces, and wartime protection of civilians.

- *The postconflict/postcrisis stage:* Violent conflict ceases, and efforts at rebuilding begin; human rights considerations play a role in peace agreements, the treatment of refugees, civil society–building efforts, human rights education campaigns, and the creation of truth commissions and other efforts to hold perpetrators of human rights abuses accountable; if patterns of destructive relationships are not transformed into healthier patterns of interaction, this third stage can lead to a new round of intensified conflict.

This book examines the ethical and operational issues confronting policymakers, diplomats, human rights and humanitarian aid workers, soldiers, police officers, and others in responding to each of these stages. The following outline seeks not to summarize each chapter but rather to situate the chapters of this book within the context of the three stages of conflict.

### Stage One: Conflict Intensification

The first part of this book addresses the many ways in which human rights considerations either intensify or mitigate conflict. These chapters bring to

bear distinct sets of analytical tools, drawing from the fields of peace studies, international conflict resolution, and sociology (cultural studies), that
may prove useful in the analysis of problems presented in later chapters.
These contributions will help to frame the relationship between human
rights and conflict. At the end of part I is a discussion on whether the logic
of linking peace and human rights extends to the consideration of peace
itself as a basic human right.

Human rights violations can be both symptom and cause of conflict.
As Ellen Lutz points out, human rights are often at the core of a conflict or
war. Human rights or human security have often been cited in more recent
examples of humanitarian intervention. Human rights have also been cited
as one reason for armed intervention or preemptive war, including the military intervention by the U.S.-led coalition in Iraq. Lutz notes that the differences between human rights and conflict management approaches play
out among the parties in actual conflict situations, as they have in Rwanda,
Nigeria, and Sri Lanka. There are also many examples of human rights
claims being manipulated by aggressive powers in order to justify intervention. But as many of the authors in this book emphasize, human rights
are not only significant factors in the conduct of war or the justification for
war but also critical sources of conflicts that devolve into war. Often both
sides of a conflict compete in proclaiming themselves victims of human
rights violations.

In the next chapter Michael Lund explains that past and present violations of human rights can lead to outbreaks of violence. He also explores
the theory that the spread of human rights may create additional potential
points of contention and renewed violence. There are competing claims
regarding not only assurances of rights but also the definition of rights.
This situation reflects the ongoing conflict between haves and have-nots or
between the status quo and a new order, which is the basis of many violent
conflicts. Lund argues that human rights cannot be "revered as a moral absolute." Instead, human rights must be interwoven with efforts to produce
a "more productive economy; a more legitimate and effective government;
ultimately more democratic politics; and a more humane society." In order
for human rights and conflict resolution to complement each other, those
interested in building a stable peace must be practical and must not focus
solely on securing respect for human rights while ignoring the need to end
violent conflict.

In her contribution to this volume, Lisa Schirch proposes how conflict resolution practitioners and human rights advocates might begin to
coordinate and synthesize their ideas and practice with the common goal
of building peace. Human rights cannot be dismissed without endangering

stability in the future and creating a significant threat to peace. Nor can human rights be mere empty rhetoric spouted in the service of realist, interest-based foreign policy goals. Human rights and conflict resolution will best be able to work together when those committed to building peace adopt a needs-based approach to conflict resolution and work to address structural sources of conflict and promote restorative justice. For Schirch, only when human rights are an integrated, genuine component of conflict resolution, will it be possible to move into conflict transformation, which is essential to sustainable peace.

In the next chapter in this part, Kevin Avruch brings culture into the mix. His chapter (which could have been included in any part in this book, since it is relevant throughout) explains the concept of human rights as perceived and acted on by different cultures. Different cultures may have very different perceptions of human rights and how human rights are perceived will have a major impact on how they are embraced, adopted, and implemented. How we view others and how we view ourselves is reflected in how we perceive human rights. It matters greatly whether we view human rights as something inalienable that humankind merely had to discover or as something that has been created or constructed by humans. Indeed, these very differences in the understanding of human rights can themselves be sources of conflict.

In his comment on Avruch, Ram Manikkalingam argues that there is a need for universality in terms of rights and that differences in definition and interpretation of human rights can actually contribute to conflict: "Some of the most egregious forms of human cruelty to other humans, such as genocide, ethnic cleansing, and discrimination, have stemmed from the refusal to treat others as we would our own. So HR activists are confident that insisting that we do, and finding the common standards that will enable us to, will, on the whole, improve the condition of humans everywhere." Manikkalingam warns that universal human rights must be accepted as legitimate and not viewed as illegitimately imposed from outside. The existence of human rights as a set of values derived from political motives and processes may risk "becoming a coercive project" in the eyes of different communities and then can only fuel conflict.

In the final chapter in this part, Abdul Aziz Said and Charles Lerche go beyond the previous contributions to argue that peace is itself a fundamental right and must be accorded status as a universal right for individuals as an extension of the idea of positive peace and human needs theory. Their argument reflects to some degree the case that the international community must go beyond national security and promote or ensure human security. They argue, in effect, that peace cannot be just the absence of war and that recognition of a right to peace reinforces all other human rights. But as Jack Donnelly notes, such an argument may be problematic if it is more than just an ideal. Peace cannot be viewed as a precondition for human rights, since the protection of human rights is critically important in the absence of peace.

## Stage Two: Armed Conflict

Part II of the book addresses many of the human rights issues arising during armed conflict and other forms of violent conflict (including terrorist attacks). In some cases, human rights abuses may be deemed an "accidental" by-product of warfare and extreme violence. In other cases, such as those involving ethnic or communal conflict or terrorist activity, the forced deportation or other abuse of civilians is an integral part of the attack strategy. Increasingly, states acting in coalition, often through international institutions and invoking norms of global governance, assert their responsibility to respond to human rights violations; however, whether, when, and how third parties should respond to human rights abuses in times of conflict is hotly contested.

Hugo Slim notes that the rise in civil wars and humanitarian intervention has raised the question of the duty to respond to suffering. Governmental and nongovernmental responses to humanitarian crisis must be guided by certain principles and imperatives, Slim suggests. Donor efforts are counterproductive when they ignore local coping mechanisms in favor of plans conceived of, and implemented by, outsiders. The dependency relationship that emerges in such situations creates new sources of tension and instability. The decolonization of humanitarianism can come about only if the duty to respond to suffering is matched with another duty. This corollary obligation is the duty to help develop the capacity of local institutions and governments to provide and deliver humanitarian relief and protect (and value) human rights.

At the same time, as Jonathan Moore notes in his commentary, when one moves from theory to practice in humanitarian relief, there are choices to be made and consequences to be faced as a result of those choices. Neutrality may not be possible or even desirable in order to deliver humanitarian relief and protect human rights: "It is obvious that human rights suffer in so-called peace operations, and it is true that protecting those rights may require some measure of departure from neutrality. When human rights protections are aggressively pursued, someone's ox is inevitably gored, and other initiatives with urgent humanitarian portent may be interrupted. In the fulfillment of humanitarian duty, the protection and advancement of human rights must be a constant devotion but not a mindless juggernaut."

Richard Falk argues for restraint in using armed force to respond to humanitarian crises and human rights violations. Above all, he urges, the "humanitarian" quality and objectives of humanitarian intervention must be maintained. This is akin to the development of a "just war" theory or a "just humanitarian intervention" theory. Thus, intervention by the international community to mitigate, manage, or prevent conflict must have a strong humanitarian imperative as well as an expectation of effectiveness and success. A rights-based approach provides much greater credibility and justification for conflict resolution and conflict prevention efforts than do interest-based or results-based approaches.

Responding to Falk, Thomas Weiss says that there has been far too little humanitarian intervention rather than too much. The motives of intervenors are rarely pure, Weiss concedes, but still, strong moral arguments may exist for intervening on human rights grounds. Force can be an effective means of preventing genocide or stemming massive human rights violations. As research director for the United Nations' International Commission on Intervention and State Sovereignty (ICISS), Weiss strongly argued that "we should be less preoccupied that military action will be taken too often for insufficient humanitarian reasons, and more that it will be taken too rarely for the right ones."[5] Weiss reflects the views of many humanitarian and human rights NGOs, such as Human Rights Watch, that advocated military intervention in Rwanda and Bosnia and those that have more recently called for stronger intervention, though short of an all-out military effort, in western Sudan.

Weiss encourages policymakers to consider one kind of "what if" question focusing on the potential impact of humanitarian interventions on likely victims of abuse: What if the failure to respond with force to stem human rights violations leads to even greater abuses and costs thousands (and, in some cases, tens or hundreds of thousands) of lives? Falk addresses another set of "what if" questions, focusing on the potential impact of humanitarian intervention on larger questions of power and justice in international relations. His analysis encourages policymakers to consider the implications if powerful states, acting unilaterally or jointly, should continue to intervene selectively in human rights crises throughout the world. Who and what will serve as a check on the behavior of powerful states? What will this mean for the system of international relations and international law? These provocative questions emphasize the potential outcomes of a wide range of humanitarian intervention scenarios.

There is a critical ethical dilemma here, as many of the authors note: Humanitarian intervention can both prevent and cause deaths. At the same time, human rights may be violated in the name of humanitarian intervention. In his contribution, John Cerone surveys the international human rights and humanitarian law standards that apply in times of armed conflict. One particularly interesting aspect of his chapter is his discussion of the application of international law to nonstate actors, such as paramilitary troops. John Cerone notes, "By 1949, humanitarian law had begun to recognize the increasing relevance of nonstate actors and to embrace the language of rights." As the nature of conflict and combatants has changed, so, too, has international law.

Additional considerations come into play when the violence to which states are responding is terrorist in nature. Terrorism directly disrupts and involves a denial of human rights and thus poses particular problems for establishing justice and addressing terrorism-based violence. The gravity of the acts committed against civilians may encourage extreme responses, but as Jordan Paust explains, human rights norms still apply to the treatment of suspected terrorists. As David Stewart emphasizes in his response to Paust, "It is impermissible, as well as counterproductive, to fight terrorism with terrorism." The best response to terrorism, Paust and Stewart both suggest, is one that not only is in line with international law but also promotes human rights and reduces the various deprivations, real or perceived, that frequently spawn terrorism. This is not just because, as the argument goes, the terrorists win whenever states ignore or undermine those principles that most represent their own core values, but because it is a strategic mistake to create conditions that allow terror as a political tactic to take root.

In the Israeli-Palestinian conflict, as Mohammed Abu-Nimer and Edy Kaufman note, the conditions of security and rights are intrinsically linked to the cycle of violence between the two communities. For many Israelis and Palestinians, human rights and peacemaking are not just separate but diametrically opposed. Among Israelis, the language of human rights is often viewed as a threat, and among Palestinians the notion of peace is condemned if it is not accompanied by the concept of a "just" peace or one that embraces rights (especially the right of return). Kaufman and Abu-Nimer underscore that an emphasis on conflict resolution is embraced mostly by Israelis and a rights-based approach by Palestinians. Such a divide can create a formidable barrier to reaching a stable peace during processes of reconciliation.

Julie Mertus and Maia Carter Hallward then discuss Iraq as a way to explore how a human rights framework can factor into decision making on whether and how to respond to gross human rights abuses. Had a human rights framework been employed before the U.S. military incursion into Iraq, Mertus and Carter Hallward contend, alternatives to violence would have been exposed and the legality and legitimacy of the attacks called into question. "If human rights concerns are invoked as a justification for military intervention," they argue, "the human rights framework should remain at the forefront of political and social planning throughout the reconstruction process and should be used as a compass when formulating decisions and taking actions on a range of issues, from the formation of a representative democratic government to empowering local educational institutions and creating a social and economic infrastructure that meets the needs of local people." The chapter also suggests that had a human rights framework been employed, there is far less likelihood that the controversies surrounding the treatment of Iraqi prisoners would have arisen.

## Stage Three: Postconflict/Postcrisis

The last part of the book addresses the stage that occurs after "hot conflict" ends and the society begins to rebuild and restabilize. This stage may also be coterminous with the first stage, since it can also be a time for conflict intensification.

A considerable body of scholarship argues that peace negotiations must pay attention to issues of human rights and restorative justice and their careful implementation. In her chapter on the peace process in Northern Ireland, Christine Bell argues that human rights must be taken into account when addressing the roots of violent conflict and creating the kinds of institutions that may promote long-term peace and justice. But she goes further and concludes that the application of human rights principles can help facilitate negotiation about the structure of government and other general issues beyond matters pertaining specifically to rights. At the same time, she asserts that the introduction of human rights at the negotiation stage may become a critical mechanism of conflict prevention.

Ultimately, adversaries must "have reason to believe they can look forward to living together without threatening each other, perhaps even in harmony and unity."[6] In the case outlined by Bell, this belief did not exist, nor could it be imposed by outsiders. This does not mean, however, that outsiders do not play a crucial role in peacemaking. In addition to promoting peaceful solutions, the international community may address underlying structural and cultural divisions that lead to human rights violations. Many of the authors in this book provide specific examples of the form this kind of assistance could take, including civil society institution building, the development of justice mechanisms, and the funding of human rights education programs.

If injustice and human rights abuses are merely buried, conflict resolution and reconciliation will be undermined. Vasuki Nesiah encourages us to consider the ways that truth and reconciliation commissions can contribute to the strengthening of societies by providing an accounting of the past and determining what happened. While courts are more focused on guilt and innocence as well as on punishment, truth and reconciliation commissions offer greater possibilities for divided societies to reunite. Nesiah shows that the pursuit of truth and the pursuit of justice can be complementary. Institutions and processes can be established, and communication fostered, that promote both interests: that of exposing the truth, and that of levying justice. Nesiah also points out the importance of understanding the context and unique circumstances of each specific conflict, an approach that many in the conflict resolution field promote.

In his response to Nesiah, Richard Wilson notes the degrees to which truth commissions and courts can have a political purpose as well as a peacebuilding one. Over time, truth commissions may advance the goal of nation building, assist in the writing and documenting of the history of a conflict, or create legitimacy for the state or state institutions. Truth and justice need not be incompatible, nor should peace and justice. But as Roy Licklider cautions, "we simply do not know whether transitional justice makes future violence more or less likely. Reconciliation, after all, is likely to take generations."[7] Thus, because building peace and human rights regimes is a long-term investment, proponents of conflict management and of human rights will need to work together to ensure a stable and just peace.

War-affected populations, especially forced migrants (refugees and internally displaced persons), are particularly susceptible to human rights abuses. Refugees can destabilize an entire region, opening the door to new human rights atrocities, as was the case with Rwanda and Burundi. The spread of refugees creates conflicts by upsetting social balances and changing economic and demographic distributions. The status of forced migrants is becoming an increasingly critical factor both in protecting human rights and in reducing sources of conflict. As Susan Martin and Andrew Schoenholtz note, refugees are not just the victims of conflict, and the need to protect their human rights is not just an outgrowth of the conflict; rather, the reasons for their forced migration and their continued status often continue to fuel conflict. The security issues posed by large refugee flows, as well as the moral imperative to aid those who are suffering, support calls for "saving strangers" and humanitarian intervention.[8]

Human rights organizations have been crucial in creating a demand for and expertise in monitoring. Monitoring is necessary to achieving adherence to peace agreements and to the prevention of future conflicts. But education programs also can play a critical role in building peace in post-conflict situations. Janet Lord and Nancy Flowers point to the role of human rights education in both human rights promotion and conflict management. As with the two fields in general, there is not much coordination of the peace and human rights curricula or pedagogy. Many peace programs do not incorporate human rights elements, and many human rights programs do not incorporate much, if anything, from the conflict resolution field. As Lord and Flowers explain, both human rights education and peace education are expanding their scope and, as they do so, increasingly integrating key elements of each other's main teachings.

The final chapter addresses the difficulties of adopting a human rights approach in a highly conflicted society. In the case of Sri Lanka, Alan Keenan observes that efforts to ensure effective human rights protections during the peace process may run counter to the conflict resolution strategy. Keenan points out that human rights can become a tool—a battleground, even—in a peace process or a conflict between groups competing for political power. He reiterates Michael Lund's point that human rights principles are often the very thing that violent international conflicts are about. But human rights can also be a fertile area for cooperation. The Sri Lanka case study demonstrates that protection of human rights is not a zero-sum game. Ensuring the rights of Tamils can more firmly strengthen those of Sinhalese. Recognition of this by many whites in South Africa helped ease the transitional political path to a multiracial state as well as helping in the process of reconciliation. As Keenan notes, finding common ground on human rights has helped Tamils, Sinhalese, and other groups in Sri Lanka begin to find common ground for a shared future.

## Toward a More Integrated Approach?

We conclude by identifying the overarching themes that frame the debate within this volume—and within the wider academic, practitioner, and policymaking communities—on the relationship between human rights and conflict. We then point to common threads from the contributors' analyses, focusing in particular on those issues and factors that seem always to play a part in the dynamic interaction between the assertion of rights, the pursuit of justice, and the quest for peace. In so doing, we look toward the future and, more particularly, toward the prospects for integrating the approaches typically associated with the human rights, humanitarian law, and conflict resolution constituencies. The signs are encouraging. For example, human rights and humanitarian law advocates are increasingly interested in conflict prevention. The growing emphasis given to "conflict transformation" in the conflict management field means that justice and peace are increasingly seen as overlapping values, and the inclusion of human rights provisions in peace agreements and in conflict resolution and prevention initiatives is growing more common. The increased focus on the protection of civilians in all stages of conflict blurs the lines between human rights, humanitarian law, and conflict resolution, bringing actors from all three approaches together in a common cause. However, while the common ground shared by the three approaches is gaining greater recognition, the tensions between them cannot be ignored. The priorities and baseline orientations of the three approaches differ. When hard choices must be made, these differences become evident: The human rights approach opts for whatever will best promote individual human dignity, the humanitarian law approach makes humane conduct in wartime the priority, and the conflict resolution approach focuses on the promotion of peace.

The diverse contributions to this book suggest that there is no single blueprint for resolving such tradeoffs and dilemmas. But opportunities do exist—and have been taken—for members of the different fields to work together cooperatively and effectively. This book seeks not only to enhance understanding of how human rights and conflict interact but also to stimulate interaction among scholars, practitioners, and policymakers. All these groups have important roles to play in contributing to the quest for a world in which peace and human rights are equally respected.

## Notes

1. John Burton, *Deviance, Terrorism and War: The Process of Solving Unsolved Social and Political Problems* (New York: St. Martin's Press, 1979).

2. Louis Kriesberg, *Constructive Conflicts: From Escalation to Resolution* (Lanham, MD: Rowman and Littlefield, 2003), 372.

3. Michelle Parlevliet, "Bridging the Divide: Exploring the Relationship between Human Rights and Conflict Management," *Track Two* 11, no. 1 (March 2002): 28.

4. David Lorey and William Beezley, eds., *Genocide, Collective Violence, and Popular Memory* (Wilmington, DE: Scholarly Resources, 2002), xii.

5. International Commission on Intervention and State Sovereignty (ICISS), *Intervention and State Sovereignty, the Responsibility to Protect* (Ottawa:

International Development Research Center, 2001), xi; see also Thomas G. Weiss et al., *Political Gain and Civilian Pain* (Oxford: Oxford University Press, 1997), 105.

6. Kriesberg, *Constructive Conflicts*, 329.

7. Roy Licklider, "Obstacles to Peace Settlements," in *Turbulent Peace: The Challenges of Managing International Conflict*, ed. Chester A. Crocker, Fen Osler Hampson, and Pamela Aall (Washington, DC: United States Institute of Peace Press, 2001), 712.

8. See Nicholas Wheeler, *Saving Strangers; Humanitarian Intervention in International Society* (New York: Oxford University Press, 2000).

# PART I
# The Role of Human Rights in Conflict Intensification

# 1

# Understanding Human Rights Violations in Armed Conflict

Ellen L. Lutz

From an international law perspective, human rights are those norms embedded in treaties and other forms of international law that require states or other actors to protect, ensure, or recognize certain rights possessed equally by all people. But those involved in violent conflict—whether as parties to the conflict, victims of deliberate or accidental abuses, or intervenors advocating on behalf of victims or working at conflict resolution or peacebuilding—all have their own subjective view of human rights. To understand the human rights dimension of a violent conflict, and the prospects for achieving sustainable peace, both international norms and the subjective views about human rights held by internal and external actors must be explored.

This article provides a template for reaching such an understanding. It begins by providing an overview of the origin, content, and means of implementing international human rights law. It then surveys the typical (though by no means comprehensive) views of human rights of both internal and external actors involved in or concerned with a violent conflict, and some of the reasons they hold those views. Finally, it looks at some common scenarios in which differing perspectives on human rights, particularly those held by intervenors, complicate efforts to end the violence or build peace.

## The International Human Rights Legal Framework

Underpinning international human rights law are the premises that every state has a duty to respect the human rights of its citizens and that other nations and the international community may challenge any state that fails to do so. Contemporary international human rights law is a legacy of worldwide horror at the atrocities inflicted on innocent civilians during World War II. Before then, international law exclusively governed the relations between states. While individuals may have been the subject about which states made agreements, only sovereign states enjoyed the prerogative of enforcing that law vis-à-vis another state. Thus if State X harmed a citizen of State Y, only State Y, and not the harmed individual, could lodge a protest or demand compensation. If paid, that compensation went to State Y, which international law deemed to be the aggrieved party. The individual had no right independent of her state to seek redress. Within their own territories, governments of sovereign states could do as they wished to their citizens without fear of outside intervention.

The United Nations Charter, which was drafted during the summer of 1945, declares that saving "succeeding generations from the scourge of war . . . , [and] . . . reaffirm[ing] faith in fundamental human rights" are among the highest purposes of the organization. The Universal Declaration of Human Rights (UDHR), which was adopted by the UN General Assembly just three years later, declares that human rights are the foundation of freedom, justice, and peace. Everyone is entitled to all the rights and freedoms set forth, without distinction of any kind, such as race, color, sex, language, religion, political or other opinion, national or social origin, property, birth, or other status. The fundamental rights in the UDHR can be grouped into five categories: security of the person,[1] equality before the law,[2] nationality and the rights to leave and return to one's state,[3] political rights,[4] and economic, social, and cultural rights.[5] Since 1948, the United Nations and other intergovernmental organizations have codified almost all the norms in the UDHR in multiple international treaties, including the widely ratified International Covenant on Civil and Political Rights and the International Covenant on Economic, Social, and Cultural Rights.

International human rights law is an odd species of law. Most domestic law, and even much international law, is created by memorializing, regulating, and creating mechanisms for enforcement of already widely accepted social norms. In other words, law arrives on the scene after social agreement about the content of the law and practices that demonstrate commitment to social agreement are already in place. In contrast, international human rights law was born of wishful thinking by a hopeful world confronting the evils of its immediate past. Indeed, the UDHR declares itself to be not a legal document but "a common standard of achievement for all peoples and all nations." Even decades later, as the two covenants were adopted by the UN General Assembly, many of the states that drafted and ratified them continued to engage in practices that violated terms of those treaties. For those states, ratification was an expression of solidarity with international good intent—a means of demonstrating to other states that they were among the "good guys"—rather than a set of legal standards that constrained their conduct at home. Pre–World War II ideas about sovereignty and the duty of states to refrain from interfering in the domestic affairs of other sovereign states led them to resist mechanisms or practices of policing their own compliance with their treaty obligations.

Because the United Nations and other intergovernmental bodies possess only the authority that member states delegate to them, international human rights law enforcement has lagged far behind the articulation of norms. In the absence of effective formal enforcement mechanisms, international human rights advocates formed nongovernmental organizations (NGOs) to promote human rights and developed an array of advocacy strategies for pressuring governments to conform their behavior with international human rights law. These organizations investigate human rights abuses wherever they occur, including in places enduring armed conflict. Because of their reputation for accuracy, their findings are relied on by the news media, many governments, and most intergovernmental institutions. While these NGOs hope their reports will bring about a change in the behavior of the government or other entity whose abuses they spotlight, their main targets are the policymakers who are in a more powerful position to put pressure on human rights violators. They lobby other governments to take human rights into account in their foreign aid and press the United Nations and other intergovernmental organizations to put pressure on rights abusers.

International human rights law defines the rights that citizens possess under their own governments. But in cases of international armed conflict it may be the government of another state that is inflicting suffering on civilians. In many situations involving internal armed conflict, the rebel group or other party responsible for abusing civilians' rights is not a state and therefore not a party to the international human rights conventions. Thus, even in the absence of enforcement mechanisms, the rights enshrined in human rights treaties have limited applicability in most armed conflicts.

Beginning in the 1980s, when bloody and destructive Cold War–era proxy wars in Central America and other parts of the world dominated world news, human rights activists turned increasingly to international humanitarian law as the legal foundation for their advocacy in situations involving armed conflict. This body of law, the origins of which predate international human rights law by centuries, was crafted to protect civilians and others not taking part in armed conflict, such as sick or wounded soldiers or prisoners of war, from the ravages of war. Its prohibitions include mass killing, mass expulsion, using food as a weapon of war, hostage taking, murder, torture, rape, and the mistreatment of persons held in displaced-person or detention facilities. International humanitarian law is articulated in the almost universally ratified Geneva Conventions of 1949 and numerous other international treaties. Crimes of genocide and crimes against humanity, which, like international human rights law, entered international jurisprudence in the wake of World War II, are part of international humanitarian as well as international human rights law.

With the end of the Cold War and the beginning of an era of greater UN receptivity to institutional activism, human rights activists turned their attention to strengthening international enforcement measures. Although activists are often at odds in determining at what point the United Nations should send troops to intervene in armed conflicts with serious human rights consequences, they quickly unite in pressing for judicial sanctions against those who commit or are responsible for human rights atrocities in the context of armed conflict. Human rights activists were the creative force behind the UN Security Council's decision to establish the International Tribunal for the former Yugoslavia, and its cousin, the International Tribunal for Rwanda. And to universalize the probability that perpetrators of human rights atrocities would be held to account in a court of law, they spearheaded the drive for the establishment of the International Criminal Court.

## Human Rights from the Perspective of Parties to Violent Conflict

Human rights violations are an integral part of every armed conflict. Sometimes they are among the principal reasons for the conflict, as was true in the American Civil War, in which one of the Union's major objectives was ending Southern black slavery. Abuses of human rights also spawned many wars of national liberation against colonial powers, and wars waged by leftist guerrilla insurgents against corrupt or dictatorial governing regimes.

Even where leaders of a society are motivated to go to war as a means to attain or retain their power or wealth, they typically manipulate long-held human rights grievances as a means to exhort the populace to join them in their warring adventure. This was the case in the wars in the former Yugoslavia, in which Serbian political leaders incited Serbs to join them in their nationalist territorial claims by reminding them of unredressed ancient and World War II–era human rights violations against Serbs, and blaming that suffering on other Yugoslav national groups.

Human rights are often invoked even when they have little or no connection with the real reason for the war. For example, when President George H. Bush sought to win American popular support for armed efforts to repel the Iraqi invasion of Kuwait, he cited an Amnesty International report alleging that Iraqi soldiers had invaded Kuwaiti hospitals, thrown babies out of incubators and onto the floor, and taken the incubators back to Baghdad. In fact, the incubator story was false, invented and promulgated by a public relations firm and paid for by the government of Kuwait as part of its campaign to lure the United States into war with Iraq. While Amnesty International acknowledged that it had been duped, the first Bush administration made no attempt to correct the mistake, even after American involvement was well under way.[6]

Germany's Nazi regime first invented and then manipulated rights grievances as part of its strategy to win the support and participation of the German people in their conquest of Europe and murderous crusade against European Jewry and other ethnic groups. They injected virulent anti-Jewish propaganda into a political environment in which freedoms of speech, association, and the press were squelched. As a result, most Germans had little or no access to sources of information that could counteract the racist propaganda blitz. In that propaganda the Nazis falsely "reminded" Germans that they had been the target of vast crimes and other harms perpetrated against them by Jews and that a destructive response to Europe's Jews was not outside the bounds of morality, because Jews were not "human."[7]

Human rights are central concerns even in cases in which the motive for a conflict has no connection to human rights, or in which human rights are not invoked as a rationale for a conflict. This is because in every modern war innocent civilians suffer human rights abuses as a consequence of the conflict. In some cases that suffering is accidental, as when civilians step on land mines, are killed or maimed by bombs that land off target, or, in guerrilla war contexts, are mistakenly assumed to be fighters. But in contemporary wars, which are fought around population centers and not on defined battlefields, civilians are frequently the targets of war. Every contemporary war brings us images and news accounts of vast suffering by innocent civilians: refugees streaming out of Bosnian or Kosovar villages; mountains of bones of genocide victims in Cambodia and Rwanda; orphanages filled with child amputees in Sierra Leone; besieged communities in Sarajevo, Ethiopia, and Sudan, where hunger was used as a weapon of war; unspeakable mistreatment of prisoners of war in Afghanistan, where Northern Alliance opposition forces sealed hundreds of captured Taliban troops in shipping containers, leaving them to die from lack of air, water, and food; and, universally, the rape of women on a mass scale.

If rights abuses are not addressed in the context of the resolution of the current conflict, they can set the stage for future conflicts because unredressed past grievances are so easy to manipulate. The formula has been applied over and over again. Leaders remind their people of the time when THEY did something terrible to US, and of OUR powerlessness at that past time to redress the grievance. If the "us" group simultaneously is made to feel vulnerable (politically, economically, or in any other way) or threatened, or lacks access to alternative perspectives such as those provided by a free press, emotions can easily become charged. People seldom act rationally in the midst of such charged emotions and often embark on a course of conduct that, at a more secure or politically open time, they would find abominable. Once strongly held views about respecting the rights of others give way to revised views about the importance of protecting US from future abuse by THEM or finally getting what is rightfully OURS. All sensitivity to the possibility that THEY have legitimate grievances of their own evaporates. At that point, violence makes more sense than dialogue.

Once people have joined the ranks of those committing new rights violations, moral reflection on their own conduct becomes even more difficult. They obey orders that under other circumstances they know to be immoral and illegal. They replace moral qualms with greater fervor for the cause, or some sort of alternative morality such as "How can I be disloyal to my comrades in arms, who have sacrificed so much?" They avoid or destroy anyone who challenges their revised worldview. When both (or all) sides involved in a conflict are motivated by similar stimuli and charged emotions, and where the balance of power is relatively even, the conflict is likely to become intractable; the underlying motivations for fighting are likely to be redefined with the passage of time or changing internal or external circumstances.

## Victims' Perspectives on Human Rights

Victims, depending on their level of education and political sophistication, may be familiar with international human rights law, but it is their subjective experience that most colors their understanding of human rights. Most people spend most of their lives occupied with matters that are immediately important to them, their families, and their local communities. When rights concerns arise for them, it is usually in reaction to something that has happened: the murder, disappearance, or arrest of someone they know; an experience with discrimination; or any of the range of atrocities associated with armed conflict.

When other human beings deliberately inflict human rights abuses on them or their loved ones, victims feel aggrieved. Their response is to want the violence and abuse to stop and their suffering to end. They also want to make sure it does not happen to anyone else, and to restore their dignity and other losses resulting from the abuse. When victims cannot stop the abuse, when they see it happening to others, and when they have no place to turn for justice or other types of help, they feel powerless. The combination of the abuse they have suffered, their sense of grievance, and their feelings of powerlessness may lead to despair and depression; it may also lead to a desire for revenge.

Most human rights abuses also cause victims to suffer some degree of psychological trauma. Deliberate human-induced suffering rattles the foundations of the victim's worldview and transforms his or her experience of trusting others. How could my neighbor, my government, any other human being, do this to me? The internalization of this trauma leads to a range of psychological and psychosomatic responses that, where full-blown, fit the psychiatric diagnoses of post-traumatic stress disorder (PTSD) and on depression. Even in cases in which a victim's responses do not meet these diagnoses, most people who have suffered human-induced trauma satisfy at least some of the PTSD criteria. Moreover, if untreated, these symptoms may last a lifetime. Aspects may be passed on to others in the victims' immediate environment, particularly their children. The interrelated experience of grievance, powerlessness, and psychic trauma leaves victims and those close to them susceptible to unscrupulous leaders who would exploit their past to achieve the leaders' own self-serving ends.

International human rights law and the international network of human rights NGOs provide victims with an alternative, cycle-breaking response to this potentiality. The legal framework afforded by international law provides victims who have access to it with an objective means to identify and measure the magnitude of the wrongs they have suffered. Although modest, and not consistent from one part of the world to the next, international human rights enforcement mechanisms provide victims with a venue for raising complaints that are superior to the co-opted judicial or political institutions that exist in the place where the harm occurred. International human rights investigators validate victims' stories by listening carefully, independently verifying them where possible, and publishing them in the international domain, which may result in at least embarrassment to, if not sanctions against, the responsible parties.

Many victims become active in domestic human rights organizations or victims' groups that document abuses, identify means for putting pressure on responsible parties to end those abuses, and provide mutual support should the victims become targets of renewed rights violations. Through these various means, victims reduce their sense of powerlessness, increase the likelihood that their grievances will be addressed, and provide themselves with some insulation from being drawn into a perpetrator role in the future.

## Intervenors' Perspectives on Human Rights

We already have observed that international human rights advocates view human rights largely through the lens of international human rights law. At the same time, they tend to be highly sensitive to the suffering of victims and perceive themselves to be advocates or agents on victims' behalf.

Those who are involved in conflict resolution, whether as diplomats mediating peace negotiations (track-1 conflict resolvers) or nongovernmental facilitators of dialogue between groups involved in a conflict (track-2 conflict resolvers), usually are unequivocal about human rights violations, but their focus is different. They understand that conflict is normal but abhor the associated violence and loss of life. Their principal aim is to help the parties to a conflict achieve a settlement while decreasing the overall level of violence. Over the long term they try to facilitate improved relations between the parties to a conflict so that those parties will be in a better position to resolve or de-escalate future conflict before it turns violent.

Because their focuses are different, human rights advocates and conflict resolvers may find themselves at odds. At a recent joint meeting of leading international human rights advocates and conflict resolution professionals, participants were divided by profession into two groups and asked to reflect on the question "What values motivate the other group's work?"

With respect to the values of conflict resolvers, the human rights advocates described them as nonadversarial, value neutral, expedient professionals who prefer quiet diplomacy over confrontation, are prepared to put everything on the table, believe that every individual is redeemable or capable of change, view the world in shades of gray instead of in black and white, and put peace above all other interests, including justice. The conflict resolvers described the human rights advocates as adversarial, believers in the power of shame, outcome directed with little concern for process, "bleeding hearts," absolutist (based on universal principles), judgmental, unwilling to consider non–human rights issues, and "conversation stoppers."

Both disciplines recognized aspects of their own values in the other group's descriptions of them, though both groups were quick to clarify that these attitudes were not universally held and that there were great differences among individual diplomats, activists, and NGOs in their field.[8]

## Ways in Which Differing Perspectives on Human Rights Complicate Efforts to End Violence or Build Peace

### Perceptions of Bias

Because victims in armed conflict want the violence and abuse to stop and their suffering to end, they welcome the assistance of professional outside intervenors who can genuinely help. These include human rights advocates, who can draw worldwide attention to their plight, and conflict resolvers, who can help the parties to end the violence. Yet charges of lack of impartiality can undermine the capacity of these intervenors to assist effectively.

While most international human rights NGOs think of themselves as impartial—they report evenhandedly about human rights and humanitarian law violations by all parties to an armed conflict, and they investigate human rights violations in all parts of the world without regard for the political orientation of the responsible regime—they often are seen by one or more of the parties to a conflict as biased. Conflict resolvers also tend to think of human rights NGOs as parties themselves, or at least stakeholders, in a conflict. This is because human rights advocates openly advocate for victims and for the strict application and enforcement of international human rights and humanitarian law.

Where the aim of one of the parties to a conflict is to end severe or long-standing human rights violations such as injustice, discrimination, or repression, human rights advocates are likely to sympathize with that party's cause. In such cases, even where these advocates have reported objectively on abuses by all parties, they are likely to be perceived as biased by those in power and by those members of society who benefit from the social order that existed before the conflict or who prefer it to war. Opposition forces may interpret activists' human rights advocacy as a form of "solidarity" with their cause. Once labeled as biased, human rights advocates have a difficult time shedding their partisan mantle. Thus, in cases where an armed conflict was motivated initially by political or socioeconomic rights violations even though the rationale for fighting has subsequently changed to greed or deep-seated hatred and inability to trust the other side, the legitimacy of human rights advocates is often suspect.

Human rights advocates also may be accused of partiality to parties who have claims with which they sympathize. Like all nonprofit organizations, human rights NGOs must marshal their resources and set priorities for reporting to maximize the impact of their work. Massive or dramatic violations involving loss of life and intense human misery typically draw greater resources and command greater media attention then grinding socioeconomic conditions or long-standing repression or discriminatory practices. Those involved in fighting what they believe to be a "just war" to end these latter types of abuses may feel that human rights advocates are biased or hypocritical because they failed to adequately publicize the underlying abuses that occurred before a resort to arms was perceived to be necessary.

Like their human rights counterparts, conflict resolvers involved in mediating the settlement of an armed conflict may be subjected to charges of partiality. For the sake of neutrality and to maintain their acceptability to all parties as outside intervenors, conflict resolvers involved in settlement talks typically take no position with respect to the conflict. But conflict resolvers tend not to be neutral about the violence and suffering associated with the conflict, which they openly deplore. Parties who depend on continuing violence to retain power may see conflict resolvers as agents of their opponents. On the other hand, in cases where one or more of the parties have turned to violence because they believe that all peaceful means for resolving underlying structural human rights violations have been barred, those parties may perceive conflict resolvers' efforts to end the violence— particularly in the short term, when there is not adequate opportunity to address all the underlying issues—as merely a sop to those in power. For these parties, loss of life and other human suffering caused by armed conflict are an acceptable price to pay to ensure that those underlying structural issues are resolved in their favor.

### The Interplay between Human Rights Investigations and the Conduct and Settlement of Armed Conflict

Human rights reports, although written to draw attention to ongoing violence and suffering, sometimes contribute to the escalation of a conflict. In conflicts between ethnically divided groups, human rights reports directed against members of a group can inflame the anger of already emotionally charged troops and their civilian supporters and can provoke those who were otherwise reluctant to take part in the violence to take up arms. For example, in Macedonia, human rights reports of abuses by the Macedonian security forces inflamed emotions in the Albanian community, while reports of violations by Albanian fighters had the same effect on Macedonians.[9]

Accounts of suffering by members of one's own group can reduce or further numb moral reflection and thus make it easier for fighters to take out their anger on, or seek revenge against, members of the other group, including those who bear no responsibility for the original suffering.

Also, when sensitive conflict resolution negotiations are contemplated or ongoing, independent human rights reports may impact conflict resolvers' ability to bring the parties together or keep them at the negotiating table. And the reports can serve to harden parties' positions, thereby making it more difficult for them to explore their real interests. For example, at a critical early moment in the Salvadoran peace negotiation process, a leading international human rights NGO released a report documenting, for the first time, abductions and killings by the FMLN rebel forces. The report stung the rebel leadership and caused them to reexamine their relationship with the international human rights community, among which they included the United Nations. This made it more difficult for the UN mediator in El Salvador to win the rebels' confidence and persuade them to negotiate. To avoid repetition of the problem, the mediator conferred with the NGO and asked it to inform him when a report would soon be released. This enabled him to avoid surprise and provided him with useful knowledge that he converted into a mediation tool. By strategically using his advance knowledge, he was able to put discreet pressure on the party that was the target of an upcoming human rights report to adopt measures that simultaneously improved rights conditions and its prospects at the negotiating table.[10]

## Peace Agreements and the Amnesty Problem

Virtually every time conflict resolvers intervene to assist the parties in negotiating an end to armed conflict, they encounter the problem of how to deal with those individuals who are responsible for violations of human rights or the laws of war. Both international human rights and humanitarian law impose a duty on states to prosecute those who have committed the most egregious human rights violations, war crimes, and crimes against humanity. In past decades, criminal prosecution for such violations was an academic concern for most peace process participants who had committed international crimes; they had confidence that if they could not negotiate an amnesty or other form of immunity from prosecution, another state would afford them comfortable refuge. As international human rights advocates have placed increasing emphasis on criminal justice responses to human rights violations, criminal prosecution has increasingly become a real possibility.[11] For some necessary parties to peace processes, the potential for

criminal prosecution has been a barrier to serious—or indeed any—participation in negotiations. Thus, for example, General Raoul Cedras was prepared to negotiate the restoration of democracy in Haiti only after he had
been assured of asylum in Panama. In Mozambique, amnesty was a necessary precondition for both parties to come to the negotiating table.

Parties with clean hands also may be leery of confronting the issue
of prosecuting war criminals during the peace negotiation process. While
their formal position may be that war criminals must be brought to justice,
interests such as creating or restoring democracy, maintaining order during
the transition period, placating a restive military or other armed fighters, or
staving off economic collapse may be of much higher immediate priority.
Thus, it is not surprising that redressing the past usually does not figure prominently in settlement agreements but is left for the postagreement implementation phase, if it is undertaken at all.[12]

Demands for amnesty, on the other hand, are a frequent subject in
peace negotiations. Human rights advocates and conflict resolvers often are
divided on how to respond to such demands, especially when those seeking amnesty are seated at the negotiating table. Former president Jimmy
Carter and his negotiating partners, General Colin Powell and Senator Sam
Nunn, faced rebuke from the human rights community for including an
amnesty for General Raoul Cedras and his cohorts as a condition in the settlement that led to the restoration of Haiti's democratically elected government. For their part, the negotiating team, who were given only twenty-
four hours to mediate a solution, defended the amnesty as necessary to
achieve a negotiated settlement and stave off an imminent military attack by
U.S. troops.[13]

When the parties to the Bosnian conflict met in Dayton, Ohio, to negotiate an end to the violence, impunity also was on the table. From the outset of the talks, there was speculation among human rights advocates that
the International Criminal Tribunal for the Former Yugoslavia (ICTY) would
find itself on the Dayton chopping block. Even after it became clear that the
tribunal was secure, reports from Dayton suggested that the parties and
NATO were reluctant to make cooperation with the tribunal a "show stop-
per" to the larger peace.[14] Ultimately the Dayton Accords included language that required the parties to cooperate in the prosecution of offenders
before the ICTY but did not define the limits of such cooperation. Moreover,
the Dayton Accords made no mention of what role NATO troops were to
play in apprehending indicted war criminals. NATO subsequently took the
position that it did not have the authority to track down indictees, though
it could arrest those it came across while carrying out other duties.[15]

In Sierra Leone, the parties to the Lome peace negotiations were prepared to address a broad range of human rights issues but resisted human rights advocates' efforts to insert themselves into debate about a proposed amnesty provision. Even the UN Secretary-General's Special Representative Francis Okelo's efforts to propose amendments that would narrow the broad sweep of the proposed provision and specifically omit international crimes were rebuffed. The Lome Agreement granted "absolute and free pardon and reprieve to all combatants and collaborators in respect of anything done by them in pursuit of their objectives, up to the signing of the present Agreement." This provoked an instruction from UN secretary-general Kofi Annan to Okelo to dissociate the United Nations from the provision by appending to his signature to the agreement the words "The United Nations holds the understanding that the amnesty and pardon . . . shall not apply to international crimes of genocide, crimes against humanity, war crimes and other serious violations of international law."[16]

## Postsettlement Peacebuilding and the Relative Priority of Justice and Reconciliation

In postsettlement contexts, human rights advocates and conflict resolvers share the goals of developing and strengthening civil society and preventing backsliding that could cause renewed human rights abuses or violence; however, their priorities for reaching these goals differ. Human rights NGOs typically emphasize achieving justice through the prosecution and punishment of those responsible as the highest priority. Conflict resolution NGOs focus their attention on promoting dialogue and reconciliation among previously warring parties.

These priorities often appear to collide and may even be absorbed or manipulated by the parties in ways that contribute to undermining the postsettlement aims of both disciplines. This occurred in Rwanda, where the distortion of NGO priorities increased the postconflict polarization of the two communities. Because most of the genocide victims were Tutsi, justice came to be identified as a "Tutsi issue." Hutus, on the other hand, including perpetrators of the genocide, their family members and supporters, and those who had no involvement in the violence but were subjected to blame solely as a result of their ethnicity, came to be identified with the issue of reconciliation.[17] This sort of division has been reported elsewhere, including Nigeria and Sri Lanka. According to a senior Sri Lankan peace activist, most human rights NGOs operating in the area of ethnic conflict comprise Tamils, whereas most domestic conflict resolvers are Sinhalese.[18]

Human rights advocates and conflict resolvers have honed their skills and gained the most experience intervening in situations in which serious atrocities are ongoing and an end to violence is most urgently needed. Thus, it is not surprising that afterward both tend to place a high priority on the lingering issues resulting from the conflict. The approaches and methods the two groups of intervenors use when tensions are at their highest, however, are not always well suited to a postconflict milieu characterized by political insecurity, a dearth of institutions able to maintain order, and massive resettlement or reconstruction needs. Enforcement approaches to human rights are ill suited to the early stages of peace implementation, during which enforcement mechanisms are nonexistent.[19] Facilitated dialogue is not sufficient in and of itself to promote coexistence, let alone reconciliation. Coexistence interventions are necessarily long-term processes that involve changing parties' perceptions and attitudes. Intervenors must be prepared to devote a lot of time to training, launching, and overseeing coexistence activities, and even then, in the absence of structural changes at the societal level to ensure the safety and security of citizens, they should not be overconfident that such activities will be a bulwark against future violence.[20]

Achieving justice for past wrongs and bringing about the reconciliation of previously warring groups are needs that any postconflict society that seeks a peaceful, rights-respecting future must address. But that future necessarily also includes the full range of postsettlement societal needs such as political stabilization, economic development, institution building, physical reconstruction, education, and health care, as well as truth, justice, and reconciliation. A society in transition from war to peace must decide for itself the relative order for addressing these needs. That is not to say that human rights and conflict resolution intervenors have no role to play in the nation-building process. On the contrary, human rights-advocates have the potential to contribute significantly toward promoting rights respecting law enforcement, administrative, and judicial institutions; developing and monitoring processes that protect individuals against discrimination; and promoting economic and social rights. Conflict resolvers are needed to foster dialogue and cooperation among members of previously warring groups so that they can work together to set priorities and meet societal needs. When they adopt this shared forward-looking approach, both groups of professionals diminish the likelihood that they will be identified with an issue that gives relief or support to only one party to the conflict. This, in turn, reduces the possibility that intervenors will fuel societal divisions that could then flare into renewed violence.

# Notes

**1.** These rights include life, liberty and security of the person, the right not to be held in slavery, the right not to be subjected to torture or cruel, inhuman, or degrading treatment or punishment, and the right not to be subjected to arbitrary arrest or detention.

**2.** These rights include fair and impartial hearings, due process in criminal proceedings, and effective remedies for violations of fundamental rights.

**3.** These rights include freedom of movement, the right to leave and return to one's country, and the right to seek asylum.

**4.** These rights include freedom of thought, conscience, and religion; freedom of expression; peaceful assembly; the right to participate in government; and the right to vote in periodic, genuine elections.

**5.** These include the rights to food, to health care, to education, to work, to found a family, to own property, and to participate in cultural life.

**6.** See Robert L. Koenig, "Testimony of Kuwaiti Envoy's Child Assailed," *St. Louis Post-Dispatch*, January 9, 1992, 1-C; Jim Dwyer, "Desert Mirage of Dead Babies," *Newsday*, July 3, 1992, 2.

**7.** See, e.g., Lucy S. Dawidowicz, *The War against the Jews: 1933–1945* (New York: Bantam Books, 1986).

**8.** Joint meeting of International Human Rights Advocates and Conflict Resolution Professionals, Fletcher School of Law and Diplomacy, Tufts University, December 1, 2000.

**9.** Sarah Broughton, "Macedonia" (conference paper, Carnegie Council on Ethics and International Affairs, "Bridging Human Rights and Conflict Resolution: A Dialogue between Critical Communities," July 16–17, 2001), 11.

**10.** Ambassador Alvaro de Soto (presentation, Fletcher School of Law and Diplomacy, Tufts University, April 21, 2001).

**11.** See Ellen Lutz and Kathryn Sikkink, "The Justice Cascade: The Evolution and Impact of Foreign Human Rights Trials in Latin America," *Chicago Journal of International Law* 2, no. 1 (Spring 2001).

**12.** Christine Bell, *Peace Agreements and Human Rights* (New York: Oxford University Press, 2000), 273.

**13.** Robert A. Pastor, "More and Less Than It Seemed: The Carter, Nunn, Powell Mediation in Haiti, 1994," in *Herding Cats: Multiparty Mediation in a Complex World*, ed. Chester A. Crocker, Fen Osler Hampson, and Pamela Aall (Washington, DC: United States Institute of Peace Press, 1999), 505–25.

**14.** Michael Scharf, "The Amnesty Exception to the Jurisdiction of the International Criminal Court," *Cornell International Law Journal* 32, no. 3 (1999): 507.

**15.** Human Rights Watch, "Good Neighbors: NATO and Indicted War Crimes Suspects in Bosnia and Hercegovina" (press release, November 12, 1997).

**16.** Michael O'Flaherty, "Sierra Leone's Peace Process: The Role of the Human Rights Community, 1998–2000," in *Human Rights and Conflict Resolution in Context: Reflections on Practice in Colombia, Sierra Leone, and Northern Ireland,* ed. Ellen L. Lutz and Eileen Babbitt (forthcoming).

**17.** Hizkias Assefa, interview by Ellen L. Lutz, June 7, 2001.

**18.** Carnegie Council on Ethics and International Affairs, "Integrating Human Rights and Peace Work: Perspectives from Sri Lanka, South Africa, Northern Ireland, and Nigeria," *Human Rights Dialogue* (Winter 2002).

**19.** See Tonya L. Putnam, "Human Rights and Sustainable Peace," in *Ending Civil Wars: The Implementation of Peace Agreements,* ed. Stephen John Stedman, Donald Rothchild, and Elizabeth M. Cousens (Boulder, CO: International Peace Academy and Lynne Rienner, 2002), 237–71.

**20.** Eileen F. Babbitt et al., "Imagine Coexistence: Findings and Recommendations for the UNHCR" (July 2002), http://Fletcher.tufts.edu/chrcr/pdf/imagine.pdf.

# 2

# Human Rights
## A Source of Conflict, State Making, and State Breaking

Michael S. Lund

When the George W. Bush administration justified its invasion of Iraq by appealing, belatedly, to the need to liberate the Iraqi people from the oppression of Saddam Hussein, it was making a normative argument based implicitly on universal human rights. This was a dramatic recent occasion when rights arguments have been used to legitimize the use of arms by the United States or other nations and movements. Much of this book focuses on the problem of trying to enforce contemporary international legal standards for human rights during the course of intrastate violent conflicts, in which the combatants usually and often deliberately inflict violence on noncombatants. The volume also deals with the problem of bringing past violators to justice after a war. The practitioners who must deal with these problems are obviously correct to seek ways to mitigate them. Ellen Lutz's chapter presents an excellent starting point. However, these problems are embedded in a much larger and more fundamental global-historical process, whereby human rights principles themselves and the values that they seek to legalize often contribute to conflicts over state making and state breaking. Differing human rights come into conflict with one another, and the principles and discourse of human rights themselves can contribute to violent conflict. Human rights are not simply something that may or may not be abridged or enforced amid or after a conflict; they are often what the conflict is about.

By arguing that human rights can be part of the problem and not always a solution, I do not mean only that gross human rights violations by oppressors often trigger violent reactions from the oppressed. That is one way in which conflicts arise. More fundamentally, interstate as well as intrastate conflicts often have been *clashes between differing societal and international normative orders*—between a status quo order and a rival new order—and thus between the competing entitlements and rights that the antagonists each claim are inalienable under these respective contending orders. Conflicts frequently arise when major changes in the prevailing political rules that govern the social, economic, and political relationships in a society are occurring but are also contested and resisted. Conflicts are waged not simply between forces promoting rights and forces denying rights, but between differing notions of right and of rights.

This reality requires focusing on a broader challenge for U.S. and international policy and practice, one that goes beyond promoting current human rights standards within violent contexts. The challenge involves the reconciling and balancing of competing notions of rights when old orders are giving way to new ones in the *first* place, so that the tensions and disputes that arise do not lead to the outbreak of violent conflict but instead result in peaceful change. Put another way, it involves deciding whether our priority in other peoples' countries is to safeguard one of the most fundamental human rights, the right to life—security against physical threats due to social conflict—or to promote civil or other rights, which can lead to disorder and death if the social change is not managed. Thus, although this book focuses mostly on situations of active armed conflict or postconflict reconstruction and thus to the "middle" stages or "back end" of conflicts, the tensions between contending notions of rights, such as between peace and justice, also arise at the "front end," whenever a society's social and political disputes and tensions initially have the potential to erupt into violent forms. The problem thus involves not only postconflict societies but also those where no armed conflicts have occurred recently but where they might erupt in the future. The conflict early-warning lists that are being set up by the United States, other governments, the United Nations, regional organizations, and nongovernmental organizations seek to identify where such violent escalations of hostilities, and state collapses, are most likely to occur. These are the places where more attention needs to focus proactively on managing the tensions that arise between old and new normative orders and their competing sets of rights.

In her passages about the differing perspectives on human rights held by conflict protagonists, intervenors, and victims, and about the American Civil War and recent conflicts, Lutz recognizes that human rights can drive conflicts. But that discussion can be usefully nested within the broader perspective of globalization and state and nation building that is developed in the following section.

This argument that human rights can cause conflicts may sound like a gratuitously provocative, theoretical diversion from the more operational concerns of this book. But applying this perspective has very timely and practical implications for how the United States and other major international actors ought to approach the now-forming future conflicts and for the current concern about potential "failed states," including the problem of dealing with "rogue" regimes such as Iraq under Saddam Hussein. The chapter's later sections develop these policy implications.

## The Globalization of Liberal Human Rights, 1500 to the Post–Cold War Era

To put in this wider perspective the contemporary dilemma of bringing a human rights agenda to intrastate conflict, it is useful to start by reviewing the role of human rights in past conflicts and, in particular, tracing the spread of the principles of liberal democracy as a basis for state making and world order.

Universal rights inhering in the members of a society go back at least to the Greek city-states and Roman law, but these ideas began to gain wide and lasting political influence after the Reformation of the 1500s and the subsequent formation of national states. Many of the violent conflicts of the next five centuries came about because new beliefs in the universal political, economic, or social rights of some aggrieved or awakening people—usually articulated by intellectuals, political and religious leaders, or other visionaries—were juxtaposed with their status in an existing order. Wars were clashes between the putatively superior principles of a new order and the reigning principles of the prevailing order, fought because the aggrieved group often sought to overturn the existing order through violence.[1]

The religious wars of the early 1600s, fueled by the Protestant doctrine that the relationship between individual believers and God can be mediated only by Scripture and not by the Church, were fought over whether local rulers had the right to choose which Christian persuasion their subjects would follow, or whether they would remain under the Holy Roman Empire. The Treaty of Westphalia in 1648 confirmed the victory of the former right and established a new order, expressed in the principle of *cuis regio, eius religio*. In the next four hundred years, as absolutist monarchs and nationalist leaders extended military control over certain territories, the major western European states began to take the form we know today. The most powerful European states of the time—Portugal, Spain, England, France, and the Netherlands—also exerted mercantilist dominion over far-flung colonial territories.

Within some of these powers, the Lockean notion was also emerging that the rulers who had unified their territories and established a central government had obligations to the national citizenry they thus created, and that those citizens had certain rights.[2] A government's right to rule existed, not by the prerogatives and power of a king or nobility, but solely through the freely given consent of the governed or some portion thereof, to whom the governors were accountable. Thus, the English civil war in the 1640s asserted the rights of citizens, through Parliament, to reject hereditary monarchs and their claims to embody the interests of the nation. In the "Age of the Democratic Revolution" of the late 1700s, revolts swept much of continental Europe and America (of which the American and French revolutions were the most significant), advocating the inalienable liberty and equality of all mankind.[3] Notwithstanding his personal imperial fantasies, Napoleon's military campaigns against the other European powers were justified as liberating the common man from the depredations of aristocracies. About the same time, almost all the Latin American countries achieved independence from their colonial masters. Similarly, nationalist uprisings in the nineteenth century against the Ottoman and Habsburg empires appealed to the awakening desires of newly conscious ethnic and regional communities in eastern Europe and the Balkans to rule themselves.

As successive waves of conflict were fought, the notion of inalienable rights influenced and was adopted by leaders of later struggles and in other lands. Baronial rebellions against domineering kings, which gave rise to the Magna Carta, influenced the principles behind the English civil war. The American Revolution was influenced by political philosophers who had challenged rule by divine right of kings. In turn, the American Declaration of Independence influenced the French Revolution's Declaration of the Rights of Man. These revolutions' principles also shaped later populist movements within the independent states, such as workers' protests against the social dislocations produced by industrialization and, eventually, women's suffrage. In the mid-twentieth century, indigenous leaders in Africa and Asia who advocated independence for the remaining and newly colonized societies there—leaders such as Kwame Nkrumah and Jomo Kenyatta—appealed to an assumed right of self-determination. Ho Chi Minh paraphrased the Declaration of Independence as he sought to oust the French from Vietnam in the 1950s.

All these political struggles or policy changes were animated by some notion of a popular will that embodies the aspirations of ordinary people and that must be served by political authorities. But as major powers experienced differing degrees, forms, and rates of industrialization and democratization through the nineteenth and twentieth centuries, they varied greatly in how that popular will was voiced and where decision-making prerogative and power were vested for moving societies toward achieving it. In societies such as Great Britain and the United States, where constitutionalism became most firmly rooted, greater emphasis was placed on the rights of the individual to liberty and freedom from the restraints of the state. These nations' bodies of law continued to widen and deepen the individual rights that came along with being a citizen. Roughly speaking, civil rights, such as the right to assembly, were established in the eighteenth century; political rights, such as suffrage, were achieved in the nineteenth century; and social rights, such as social security, came about in the twentieth century.[4] Sometimes these rights came about through the peaceful means of political demonstrations, elections, judicial decisions, and legislative action, but often they were pursued through violent agitation or even civil war.[5]

In contrast, late-industrializing states such as Japan, Prussia/Germany, and Russia experienced political takeovers that gave the state the major role in achieving social change, and these revolutions stressed collective rights, such as the spirit of a nation, embodied in the people as a whole or in a classless society.[6] The Russian and Chinese Communist revolutions were guided by Marxist notions of rights of the working class being undermined through exploitation by industrial capitalism. Although launched in peasant societies against aristocracies, they advocated workers' rights over those of the aristocracy and bourgeoisie, delegating the pursuit of those rights to a vanguard of party leaders. Later, Marxist principles influenced Cold War–era insurgencies against landed oligarchies, such as those in Cuba, Nicaragua, Guatemala, and El Salvador. Though the Communist regimes established after revolutions emphasized social and economic rights rather than political and civil rights, they varied greatly in how much they actually benefited their populations' material conditions. Some impoverished rather than bettered their societies, doing worse economically than their capitalist counterparts. As seen in Stalin's gulag and in Ethiopia under Haile Mariam Mengistu's Dergue, such regimes often became more politically oppressive of the populace than the anciens régimes they had overthrown. Nonetheless, violent social revolution was advocated in the name of the people's universal rights to economic and social justice.[7]

By the 1930s, three divergent ideologies for organizing a society and the state to serve the rights of the people had taken concrete form in particular states and were vying for global influence: liberal democracy, national socialism, and communism. Among these competing models, liberal democracy was to become the most powerful influence around the world.

The set of rights associated with political liberalism that were shaping the Western societies began to gain dominance globally, to a great extent because of these states' neo-imperialism in the late nineteenth century, the fact that their alliances won the two world wars over other aspiring empires, and the increasing industrial and military power of the United States in particular. The United States' entry into World War I to help defeat an authoritarian government and "make the world safe for democracy" enabled President Woodrow Wilson to promulgate his Fourteen Principles as a vision for domestic societies after the war. The Versailles Conference applied some of these principles by carving the boundaries of self-governing new states out of old empires, based on the push for self-governance by various eastern and southern European ethnic populations who saw themselves as "nations." The early twentieth century also witnessed the coming into being of international bodies such as the League of Nations. In addition to setting up numerous international agreements such as customs unions and multilateral and bilateral arms control and other treaties, these bodies endorsed popular sovereignty and even extended the notion of sacred government obligations to the people in "protectorates" and "trust territories."[8] Most dramatically, after their World War II alliance with Soviet communism to defeat Nazism, the Allies applied their postwar power to establish global and regional international policies and institutions, such as the Marshall Plan, the UN agencies, and the Bretton Woods institutions. The principles affirmed in the UN Charter were inspired in part by President Franklin Roosevelt's wartime articulation of the Four Freedoms. The principles underlying these institutions' policies were based on the Allies' own domestic— and thus liberal—principles and policies.

Since World War II, as Ellen Lutz enumerates, a wide array of human rights have been codified as international norms, in such agreements as the Universal Declaration of Human Rights and other conventions, which are expected to be followed by the signatory states. These agreements elevated to international status many human rights that the United States and other victorious liberal democracies had established as the ordering principles for their own societies.[9] The norm of democratic self-governance obviously shaped the independence movements and decolonization process that started in the 1950s.

These international entities, accords, and norms also codified the increasing reality of an international system whose principal constituent part was the sovereign state.[10] Despite the vastly different geographies and cultural makeup of humanity's social groupings, the almost universal form of organization that human societies were taking was not empires or local communities but individual legally sovereign states, in which form the Western societies had crystallized. The UN Charter and its various bodies conferred equal status and often voting rights within an emerging global community on the states that were its members, whatever their relative size, wealth, or power.[11] As this state system was established, particular peoples and societies increasingly could benefit from relationships with other societies by constituting themselves as a state, being recognized as such by other states and international bodies, and interacting with them as members of multilateral forums and treaties. The United Nations and other international organizations thus reinforced the state-centered basis of a world society and the rules of this emerging international, and liberal, order. The value of being recognized as a sovereign state explains why millions of people have been quite literally dying to get into those clubs by fighting for their own recognized governments, and the number of states has grown considerably. Simultaneously, the members' behavior has been influenced at least in part by the agreed-on international norms, treaties, and laws to which they were subscribing, such as the now generally respected prohibition against aggression.

## Post–Cold War Conflicts:
## The Liberal Solution as Part of the Problem

The armed intrastate conflicts of the post–Cold War era, and potential future ones, are also usefully viewed through the lens of the global-historical process in which new rights are espoused to challenge existing orders, with such appeals motivating some parties to take up arms. What clashing systems of social order and rights have led to the bloodshed of post–Cold War intrastate conflicts?

At the level of principle, the Cold War had pitted against each other the liberal and communist ideologies for governing, led by the two superpowers. In principle, political rights were stressed by the Western bloc and social and economic rights were stressed by the Eastern bloc. In practice, however, neither the United States nor the Soviet Union vigorously promulgated its particular canon of human rights. The West's inclination to extend liberal human rights was abridged because the global competition between the Soviet- and U.S.-led blocs put a premium on the two superpowers' lining up and maintaining proxy regimes on their respective sides. Both Soviet- and American-supported client governments often committed major human rights violations in the name of domestic stability. However, with the end of the Cold War, the opportunity opened up for the West to promulgate liberal democracy and the existing body of internationally recognized human rights. By default, the collapse of the Soviet Union and other communist regimes, and the consequent wide discrediting of their domestic socialist policies, rapidly led to liberal principles becoming the dominant global ideology for governing societies domestically. Although these norms are obviously still far from being fully respected, liberal values assumed the preeminent normative position from which the behavior of all states was increasingly judged.

However, that liberalism had won a global battle among the alternative governing ideologies did not solve the practical problem of dealing with the gross underdevelopment and chronic instability of the many developing societies in Africa and Latin America, now independent but still poor. To achieve loyalty and cohesion among their often disparate populations, Cold War–era postcolonial polities usually were ruled by various forms of personal rulership, cliques, interclan alliances, oligarchies, single-party systems, and military juntas. Emerging from often vicious postindependence and recurrent power struggles among their postcolonial political elites, these countries had been held together by various ethnic- or religious-based institutions and corresponding patronage networks, as well as by force. In these systems, the assets and instruments of the state, including the foreign assistance it received, represented the principal source of influence to reward followers, maintain social cohesion, and provide for the society's welfare. But many of these societies also had been highly dependent on their patron states for trade, subsidies, and military aid, and when that support was suddenly removed, they were left to fend for themselves. As the authoritarian regimes that had received military and political support during the Cold War began losing this support, the ethnic, clan, or regionally organized social compacts and entitlement systems they had set up to maintain a political base through various kinds of clientelist patronage began to weaken, leaving little in the way of a state structure to replace them. Similarly, the entirely new states in eastern Europe and central Asia that had made up the former Soviet bloc were suddenly deprived of their subsidies and trade markets and let go onto a competitive global economy. The globalization that has intensified since the end of the Cold War also has brought pressures—from within as well as from outside—essentially to remake the economies and polities of developing societies along liberal lines by creating more open markets, enlarging political pluralism and participation, redressing existing social hierarchies, and, in some cases, tolerating unconventional beliefs and lifestyles, including new understandings of the social roles of men and women and the rights of women.

During this tumultuous post–Cold War era of liberalism's ascendancy, in the place of the patronage-based regimes, the more pluralistic, though not always individualistic, principles and policies of liberalism provided the most influential alternative formula for organizing the state—which by now was universally accepted as a priority in order to belong to the international community—and for building a nation. Just as in the past, many proponents in the recent conflicts advanced notions of popular rights such as democracy. In cases such as Somalia and Yugoslavia, regional movements sought more self-determination through autonomy or full independence vis-à-vis an existing regime. The Yugoslav secessionist republics appealed to democratic rights to rule themselves, notwithstanding that ethnic nationalist appeals enabled the republics' leaders to mobilize mono-ethnic movements. In cases such as the genocide in Rwanda and the civil wars in Burundi and Zaire (later the Democratic Republic of the Congo), the conflicts have been interethnic, interregional, or interfactional power struggles over control of the existing state, but again in the name of democracy.[12] A populist argument appealing to the will and interests of the people also motivated the earlier Islamic revolution in Iran and the Islamist FLN movement in Algeria.

Yet the new liberal principles and corresponding policies that were promoted by the International Monetary Fund, the World Bank, and other development bodies for these new states, such as privatization and reduced government spending, were unable to act as a ready solvent for contending interests by automatically alleviating the intergroup tensions and new power struggles within these societies. In fact, they had an opposite effect of weakening the ability of public authorities to maintain order. Instead, in many developing societies the new post–Cold War liberal order created enormous new strains and stresses in maintaining stability while the states still sought to make social progress.[13] In other words, the post–Cold War era has seen many of the developing countries engulfed, not in a regionally based clash of civilizations, but in a global conflict between the governing principles of political and economic patrimonialism, including new forms of populism such as in Venezuela, on the one hand, and greater pluralism, though not fully liberal individualism, on the other. The animus behind global terrorism also reflects the tension within Islamic cultures in response to the expansion of Western economic, political, social, and cultural liberalism.

Despite these strains, fortunately, most developing and post-Soviet societies experiencing this uncertain period of extraordinary economic and political upheaval—even those with significant ethnic or sectarian divisions—actually have handled the pressures to democratize and devolve economic power more or less peacefully, and have done so to a greater extent than is generally appreciated. Diverse intrastate examples include the Czech Republic and Slovakia, Hungary in its ethnic relations with neighbors such as Slovakia and Romania, most of the new countries of the former USSR, Russia itself, Macedonia, the Baltic states, Ukraine (Crimea), and, of course, South Africa. Little-discussed examples of relatively successful post-independence transitions to more liberal and pluralist systems have occurred even in postcolonial sub-Saharan Africa, in places as diverse as Botswana, Ghana, Nigeria, and Tanzania. Other societies have postponed the conflict with liberalism by remaining statist, as in Uzbekistan, reverting to neo-authoritarianism, as in Myanmar, or developing token quasi democracies or "illiberal democracies," as in Belarus. Mixed systems are manifesting the tensions between these value systems, such as in Iran and other regimes in the Middle East. China has accepted some parts of the liberal package big time, but not others.

In sum, a wide spectrum of developing and "in-transition" countries from Azerbaijan to Zimbabwe that fall short of being full liberal democracies are in one stage or another of evolving from relatively centralized and statist political orders based on clientelism (e.g., autocratic or authoritarian regimes, Communist or other one-party states, executive-dominated oligarchies, military governments, neo-authoritarian regimes) to some more individualistic, more pluralistic, or more popularly directed order in which political and economic power are more devolved and in which control over governance and public policy is subject to electoral competition. In Zimbabwe, for example, President Robert Mugabe, the country's liberation leader, and his autocratically run, increasingly repressive ZANU-PF party claim to represent the rights of self-rule by black Africans against "neocolonialist" Western powers. They have been under pressure from the opposition MDC party, which claims a mandate based on the results of general elections that implement the voting rights of individual citizens.

Nevertheless, unfortunately, many new post–Cold War destructive armed conflicts have also arisen over these changes, the vast majority of which have been intrastate in nature, such as in several parts of the former Yugoslavia (Croatia, Bosnia, Kosovo), Georgia, Tajikistan, Rwanda, Burundi, the DRC, Sierra Leone, Mozambique, Afghanistan, Liberia, and East Timor (with Indonesia). These outbreaks of devastating violence occurred in cases where the change from the existing system of rules and regulations to a more pluralistic one could not be managed through the existing or emerging institutions and political processes. But whether these recent intrastate conflicts have been peaceful or violent, and whether the violent conflicts are called ethnic wars, self-determination struggles, Islamic fundamentalist clashes, or genocide, these post–Cold War conflicts have been, fundamentally, *conflicts over liberalization.*

The weaknesses of the postcolonial and post–Cold War institutions in the countries succumbing to conflict can be traced in part to a precipitous and often chaotic adoption of democratic and economic institutions and policies—a relatively drastic, wrenching set of changes compared to those that evolved over several centuries in the established Western powers, but without the latter states' accumulated financial and coercive power. In the established powers, historically, "war made the state, and the state made war." The achievement of strong central authority occurring mainly through conquest generally preceded democratization and economic development.[14] In contrast, many of the territories that have become states since the two world wars are "juridical" rather than "empirical" states.[15] They achieved statehood, to a great extent not through their own extension of central authority over given territories, or even always through armed struggles for independence that had the unequivocal support of the population, but through the unilateral policy decisions of more powerful states, such as the decisions at Versailles and Yalta, or because colonizers simply decided to let their colonies go since their empires were already collapsing. Moreover, many of these states came into being during the heyday of liberal neo-orthodox structural-adjustment economic policies that pressured existing governments to shrink and reduce their taxation powers. Hampered by debt burdens, high oil prices, and lack of competitive exports, they lacked the resources for governing through providing public services to their populations. And yet, the new postcolonial states entering a world of sovereign states were barred by international law and established norms from invading other states to capture needed resources, an option their Western predecessors had exercised during their own period of state making.

In this sense, many developing nations that are now being called "fragile" or "failed" states have never really been states in the first place. Although members of the United Nations, with the accompanying privileges, they have never been fully functioning states in the Weberian sense of possessing a monopoly on the legitimate use of force and governing through legal-rational authority, nor have they been well-integrated nations, at all. Rather, they are incomplete states and unformed nations, for they have not developed the dense variety of operating principles, enforceable laws, constitutionally based institutions, national markets, and internalized cultural incentives for cross-societal cooperation that have been established over many decades or even centuries in the older, industrialized, more prosperous economies and now fully liberal democratic countries.

## Surviving Liberalism

Because of the inherent challenge of managing liberalization peacefully, the international policymakers in the major powers and multilateral organizations, and thus their policies toward human rights and democracy, now face a serious but still largely ignored problem posed by the dominant liberal creed. The current liberal consensus regarding governance and the economy that mainly prevails among the major Western powers is now deeply ensconced not only in the Western countries' bilateral aid agencies but throughout the UN system, including the World Bank and IMF, in the European Union, in the Organization for Security and Cooperation in Europe (OSCE), and, increasingly, among other regional organizations, such as the African Union (AU) and the Organization of American States (OAS), as well as some increasingly vigorous subregional organizations, such as the Economic Community of West African States (ECOWAS).[16] Although most public protests over market-oriented and other neo-orthodox economic principles in international institutions tend to be directed against the IMF, WTO, and World Bank, the liberal doctrines out of which the so-called Washington Consensus springs are not being enforced only in organizations in which the United States either enjoys preponderant voting rights on the bodies' boards of directors or wields veto power. Most of these international organizations, as well as the many nongovernmental organizations they contract as their "partners" to implement programs in developing countries, have for some time widely endorsed and sought to promote market-oriented economic reform, democratization, individual human rights, rule of law, civil society, "good governance," and transparency.[17]

Because of the pervasive liberal perspective, most officials and professionals within these international organizations tend to assume that any and all liberal values and policies advance not only economic development but peace as well and, further, prevent conflict—ipso facto, in any context, form, or increment in which they are applied.[18] The liberal model that drives most international development activities in developing societies is being grafted onto societies most conspicuously by the international agencies involved in postconflict peace operations and reconstruction, where the destruction of many economic and political institutions has often left a vacuum. In that sense, this activity is accurately described, not as *reconstruction* of *failed* states, but as *construction* of *liberal* states, for the first time.

The problem arises because of the potentially destabilizing effects of liberal policies, as mentioned earlier. In the long run, there is considerable statistical evidence that measures of liberalization such as free trade are highly correlated with lower levels of both poverty and conflict, brought about through improving political stability.[19] The liberal ideal model for national and international order may be the best single governing model for prevention of interstate and intrastate violent conflict.

But those who mention this finding are referring to liberalism *once it is achieved.* Though liberal policies and polities may eventually be beneficial, in the short run the shift toward more political and economic openness can—and has—contributed to the intrastate instabilities in which violent conflicts have arisen. During the period in which particular authoritarian or other nonliberal systems are shifting to democratic policies and structures, the risk of conflict rises.[20] Of course, specific liberalizing measures to expand rights that may be enacted in the short run, such as elections and granting territorial autonomy, have under certain circumstances helped to manage change peacefully by appeasing restive elements that otherwise might have resorted to violence. But depending on the context and their specific design, such measures can also alter the existing balance of power in such a threatening way as to provoke backlash from those fearing a loss of their power and, thus, violent conflict. Burundi has seen many more people killed in the civil war that erupted after its first truly multiparty election, in 1993, than in all its earlier recurrent interethnic massacres since independence. Thus, the unfolding global liberal revolution creates a serious potential for even further destabilizing many of the poorest and politically weakest states and divided societies.[21]

Regrettably, this dilemma of effecting peaceful change in poor, politically immature societies is not sufficiently recognized by discussion of the tension between achieving peace versus achieving justice in midconflict and postconflict situations.[22] The conflict between "mere peace" and political justice, or so-called negative versus positive peace—that is, between an old and a new, more progressive order—also arises in potential conflict situations, and thus has critical implications for international economic policy and development assistance programs. Societies in transition face the tensions, discussed above, between maintaining stability and achieving more social improvement. In such settings, international aid and foreign policies can have unintended effects of fostering conflict or collapse—just the opposite of what they assume they are doing.

Specifically, if international programs provide unqualified and singular political support for rapid democratization and respect for human rights, such as by championing existing minorities *alone,* whatever the context—

even at the expense of creating serious political and economic insecurity for status quo interests—they can contribute to the breakdown of a state and help to precipitate violence or armed challenges. However oppressive of minorities and other citizens the existing preliberal orders have been under many noxious regimes, they provided in many instances a kind of public order and sometimes a measure of physical and economic security for large numbers of people. However, if a rapid or radical shift to a new and uncertain order, albeit in the name of social or political justice, actually brings widespread violence and destruction and, thus, greater human suffering, the overall price that has been paid in pursuit of these progressive values— assuming that progressive change actually follows the extensive violence that instead has broken out—is exceedingly high.[23]

In fact, it could be argued that this pattern has characterized the international responses to Croatia, Bosnia, and Rwanda in 1993–94; Burundi in 1993; Kosovo in 1992–98; East Timor in 1999; and possibly other cases of what became violent conflicts. The international community's sympathetic political championing of the rights of an ethnic minority or political opposition, such as through honoring unofficial referendums and denouncing the human rights violations of their oppressors, may tend to polarize the local political relations further by demonizing and isolating the perpetrators, and thus help to catalyze preemptive crackdowns—unless robust preventive diplomacy and protective deterrent measures are also taken. The forces of potential violent backlash, which often have the military upper hand in such settings, may be encouraged to act coercively to forestall the impending threat of political change that they see facing them, and the international community is usually not prepared to deter their reaction. Consequently, well-intentioned advocacy for human rights, provision of humanitarian aid, or other international measures that are advanced on behalf of a vulnerable group may actually put that group at greater risk by tempting more powerful and better-armed forces of reaction to strike while they can still defeat the forces of change, because adequate international provision is not made to protect the victims of this reaction. What is presumed to be violence *prevention* actually becomes violence *precipitation*.[24]

## Policy Implications: Fostering Peaceful Transformations

If, in the long term, liberal economies, polities, and societies yield tremendous benefits and help to guarantee human rights, and yet destructive, violent conflicts can occur on the road to such a system, what is the best strategy for countries that face such transitions in this era of increasing globalization? Whereas not long ago observers were blithely predicting the demise of the state in favor of regionalism, multinational corporations, and subnational entities, now policymakers are worriedly searching for ways to prevent state collapse. Must international policies choose between, on the one hand, passively condoning political and economic stagnation or human rights repression and, on the other, witnessing violent backlash or revolt take place and then intervening (maybe), after those forces have already ripped societies apart?

The current clash of conflicting values and social orders needs to be faced consciously, viewed more dispassionately and less moralistically, and approached more deliberately and consistently. This can be done by using trade, diplomatic, development, and security instruments more vigorously behind a global strategy that aggressively fosters peaceful transitions toward strong liberal states but through adroit violence prevention initiatives and robust conflict-sensitive policies. This gradualist yet activist approach to liberalization would require investing more money behind smart forms of economic and political development, but it would be much less costly than the current ad hoc and naive applications of blanket liberal reforms that can destabilize societies, and of fitful military interventions after conflicts have arisen.

Despite the rhetorical contrast that is often drawn between tyranny and freedom, liberal states did not and do not emerge spontaneously with the simple decline of authoritarianism, as American and Iraqi families and U.S. policymakers have been learning very painfully since the military intervention in Iraq. Liberalism cannot be approached simplistically as an inherent human instinct and a pent-up urge for freedom that requires only the removal of tyranny in order to flourish. The liberal state is a distinct form of social order, just as authoritarianism and totalitarianism are forms of social order, and thus, it needs to be built up over time through engendering deliberate government policies and cultivating politically astute civic action.

First, liberal policymakers would be in a more defensible position if they were to candidly embrace the underlying global competition going on between liberalism and patrimonialism in the building of nations and should thereby recognize that serious conflict is being risked when poor societies with weak states undertake rapid, wholesale transitions to liberal openness. Frankly acknowledging the reality of the clash of liberalism with existing normative orders and dealing with it proactively at the early stages of transition will be much less troublesome and difficult than assuming the burdens of humanitarian intervention or postconflict reconstruction and peace-building after state collapse has occurred,[25] or—more morally dubious—than zealously promoting democratization at any price, including waging preemptive war to topple repressive regimes. A more effective strategy sees the policy challenge as one of advancing liberalism, *but only through peaceful means,* thus increasing the chances that the current conflict of basic values will lead to desirable evolutionary social and political changes and not turn into bloody and destructive intrastate wars.[26]

Second, we need to dispel various sentimentalisms that view intrastate conflicts as morality plays rather than as symptoms of fundamental global-historical processes of change. One of these misconceptions is that such conflicts are simply random events that, unfortunately, happen because certain bad rulers inflict cruelties on their fellow citizens. Policies on conflicts will be better served if the moralistic discourse portraying good guys versus bad guys is discarded, notwithstanding that atrocities committed under some regimes often are truly horrible. Another misleading imagery is that of these conflicts as heroic popular struggles. Perhaps because of the legacy of the United States' own founding revolution, the defeat of the scourge of Nazism in World War II, or the recent freeing of Communist societies from the yoke of Soviet-imposed communism, many Americans seem to hold on to a romantic notion about recent conflicts that views them all as general popular rebellions against tyrannical regimes. Thus, the remedy is assumed to be some kind of libertarian fantasy that unleashes the forces of "freedom" by destroying state authority, rather than a problem of ensuring social order and security while governments and societies are in transition, and weakening the state may lead only to chaos or various forms of warlordism.

To illustrate, the venal and debilitating regime of Joseph Mobutu Sese Seko in Zaire was finally overturned not by a popular uprising but by an armed movement instigated by the entrepreneurial Laurent Kabila in a stateless, remote area. Kabila then repeated Mobutu's ways when he assumed office, thanks to the continuing absence of strong state institutions and a vital civil society, bringing on a regionwide war. In that sense, Mobutu was at least empirically right in his caution "Mobutu or chaos," even though such statements by such figures are obviously also often rationalizations for nepotism and corruption that fail to husband the available human and natural resources of their societies in order to build effective and legitimate states.

This example points up a similarly uncritical current assumption in the policy discourse, that states suddenly "fail" because of unforeseen circumstances. Rather, political regimes are gradually undermined by global forces and nonadaptive policies over many years until they are utterly unable to cope with their changing international environment. Fortunately, through the empirical work of conflict researchers, the recent spate of violent intrastate conflicts and state failures is being demythologized, and the sources and perpetuation of these problems through competition for resources and power in permissive environments of weakening governments are being understood more clearly.

In this more clinical perspective, the eruption of destructive intrastate conflict is not simply a random calamity that suddenly befalls societies at various unpredictable moments. It tends to arise in specific historical moments when larger global forces are threatening to change a given society's status quo, thus harming some interests but benefiting others. Conflicts are basically clashes of interests, but they can be pursued through nonviolent or violent means. Much of the time, no matter what particular political systems and cultural values prevail, the conflicts among the various interests in a society are regulated through its prevailing customs, rules, and governing arrangements. Societies normally maintain stability through a whole host of accepted and partially imposed understandings that govern the relationships of individuals and groups and thus foster basic order and some degree of functional harmony. Minor and small-scale violent conflicts may be tolerated but regulated to be kept within certain bounds, as with the role of cattle rustling used to be in the rites of passage within nomadic tribes in rural east Africa.

But the chances of major intrastate violent conflicts increase when global forces begin to require large-scale changes in the existing distribution of power and privilege, and these pressures are unmanageable within the existing rules for handling differences between interests, so the state can no longer play an effective intermediating role. Destructive and violent conflicts that depart from the normally ordered relationships occur when forces from within or outside these societies threaten to change the existing distribution of advantages that characterize the status quo, and raise such a serious challenge that they meet substantial opposition. Groups sharing common interests may form and consider the use of physical coercion to achieve gains that they aspire to, or to keep hold of the interests they enjoy.

Third, a deliberate, explicit, and coherent strategy to promote liberalism peacefully needs to be undertaken with U.S. allies through the United Nations and other intergovernmental organizations at the level of particular countries that are developing or in transition. The overarching goal of this strategy should be to achieve peaceful transformation toward home-grown, rule-governed societies and increasingly liberal states. This departs from the current practice of simply pursuing each discrete liberal objective of human rights, democracy, or marketization everywhere as an end in itself, lockstep, posthaste, regardless of the possible negative fallout. None of these values should be revered and pursued as a moral absolute, whatever the consequences. Instead, multidimensional but country-specific strategies should concentrate on effecting a relatively stable transition process that moves each particular illiberal society toward these values over time—that is, toward an increasingly more productive economy, a more humane society, a more legitimate and effective government, and a more responsive politics. Serving ordinary economic improvement may be more effective than guaranteeing all political liberties—that is, prioritizing social and economic rights or needs and the protection of human life over the imperative of full democracy, especially if the latter means violent upheaval. Such a strategy thus requires an appropriate balance between the "supply side" of building on, but also transforming institutions and forces that preserve stability, and the "demand side" that is pushing for socioeconomic and political overhaul, between continuities and change.[27] As long as regimes do not threaten their neighbors' security and are not massacring their own citizens, the application of vigorous inducements, positive more than negative, for evolutionary change is likely to be more effective than either forceful intervention or laissez-faire. This change will produce creative tensions and perhaps low-level violence, but it need not countenance either stagnant authoritarianism or significant violence and state breakdown.

It follows that rather than a "one-size-fits-all" approach in foreign policies and aid strategies, which presses for the same liberalizing reforms everywhere all the time, individual countries need to be assessed in detail so as to be differentiated according to their capacity to absorb disruptive shifts in unregulated power, and the consequent instability, without erupting into violent conflict or prompting regression into neo-authoritarianism. A specific step toward democratization, such as an election, may be one of the adaptive, stabilizing mechanisms that help to ensure peaceful change in a particular context. But this judgment can be reached only by an assessment of each particular country's vulnerability to violent conflict and its ability to manage peaceful transformation, or "conflict-carrying capacity." Tailored and conflict-sensitive development and trade policies are needed that (a) at a minimum "do no harm," by taking great care, when influencing vulnerable societies, not to inadvertently increase the risks of destructive conflict; and (b) "do some good" by deliberately and sensitively fostering peaceful and constructive political conflict and avoiding violent destructive expression of the inevitable clashes between interests during a period of strife.

This more balanced, contextualized approach is needed to foster desirable changes and can draw on many available but underused carrots and sticks among the tools of diplomacy, development, and deterrence, as well as democracy assistance. This more measured approach rules out military intervention with the aim of imposing human rights ideals and democracy, in favor of containment. Instead, that immensely problematic act would be restricted to situations where there are clearly imminent security threats to other countries, impending domestic massacres, or massive devastating humanitarian emergencies—and even then would be taken only after robust diplomatic and other options that push the limits of multilateral action had been exhausted. The latter circumstances may become rarer as resources are diverted from ever more sophisticated and costly military hardware to preventive strategies that are more cost-effective.

In sum, the risk of intrastate conflict needs to be approached in a more dispassionate, deliberate, contextualized, and multidimensional way that places a higher priority on the desire for improved livelihood and the need for security than on instant democracy and civil and political rights.

Unfortunately, however, such differentiated, multifaceted, nonheroic strategies have been little considered, because of the remarkable narrowness with which the question of America's involvement in developing countries is still discussed. The post–Cold War international experience with Somalia, Rwanda, Bosnia, and other troubled countries toward which military action was taken has sparked intense debate over the grounds on which intervention into a state's affairs can be justified. The criteria for legitimate humanitarian intervention actually have been expanding, as in the notion of the "responsibility to protect."

But in this debate, "intervention" is still assumed to mean only through military force, as if the choice were simply between military action at the last minute or hands-off. With the exception of the considerable attention focused on economic and diplomatic sanctions, the prevailing discourse of think tanks and policy institutes and in the U.S. Congress has failed utterly to bring into the discussion the wide range of peaceful positive inducements that exist—and are quietly already being used, sometimes to good effect, in effecting peaceful change. Such peaceful interventions include, for example, conditional aid, "track-two diplomacy," muscular mediation, human rights capacity building, political development programs, civil society training in nonviolent mobilization, and the setting of norms by regional institutions. Active consideration of these multiple peaceful means for achieving social and international change has been going on for years at organizations such as the United States Institute of Peace and, especially recently, among many UN agencies, the European Union, and multilateral and bilateral development agencies, including the World Bank. And yet, the elementary concepts and policy tools of such long-established fields as conflict resolution and negotiations, as well as the lesson learned from recent prevention and postconflict peacebuilding efforts, still seem to have had no impact on the thinking of high-level U.S. policymakers.

In the absence of applying grounded country strategies, particular crises arise and are reacted to in reflexive, one-dimensional ways. When conflicts reach critical or more escalated and thus emotional stages of violence, a typical default response is to evoke high moral principles to back one's cause. But if the outside parties, not only the protagonists and their respective supporters, view conflicts only as a clash of right versus wrong rather than as competing conceptions of rights under one order versus those under another in a larger global process of modernization, the erroneous assumption is easily made that the use of violence to resolve these conflicts is the only way, and thus inevitable and justified. The difference between violent and nonviolent ways to pursue conflicts becomes ignored or obscured. For example, recent commentators have confused the post-9/11 U.S. priorities of antiterrorism and of vigorously transforming societies toward liberalism with the adoption by the United States of an overbearing imperial role, and of military force as the means to ensure peace, as if no peaceful means to promote democracy existed.[28] But this solely combative approach can become a self-fulfilling prophecy.

The George W. Bush administration follows in a long tradition of the United States' seeking to export its democratic and market values. The Bush policy rashly discarded much Cold War realist wisdom about how regime change can take place peacefully, through containment, placed a utopian faith in the self-generating power of mass democracy in all settings, and took a radical unilateralist stance regarding the grounds for military invasion and occupation. Suddenly, a whole decade of extensive debate about when humanitarian intervention can legitimately override state sovereignty and about the burdens of nation-building was tossed aside by a costly military occupation that was quickly rationalized, not by the need to stop imminent genocide or starvation, as in a Darfur or Somalia, but by the lack of democracy and full human rights. But this was simply the latest major example of how absolutist approaches to principles of human rights have often themselves animated international and intrastate conflicts. Perhaps a significant segment of those who influence U.S. foreign policy might still be persuaded that peaceful transformations of clientelist and authoritarian regimes can be achieved at a substantially lower cost than the various forbidding alternatives of chaos, repeated midconflict and postconflict peacekeeping missions, or preemptive invasion, leading to possible quagmires or trusteeships. If so, future American foreign and defense policy might be significantly more effective and less risky, and the world's states and regime opponents could achieve a wider range of human rights more consistently and ultimately more quickly, without violence.

## Notes

1. Not all conflicts arise in this way, and conflicts are obviously admixtures of principles with other interests, some more legitimate than others. The argument would be trivial if any deluded, casual, or cynical justification that one side or the other invoked was deemed to constitute a bona fide argument for certain rights. And internal conflicts that start from genuine grievances may evolve into mere struggles over power and gain, as illustrated by the drug-fed war in Colombia.

2. A classic is Reinhard Bendix, *Nation-Building and Citizenship* (Berkeley: University of California Press, 1977).

3. R. R. Palmer, *The Age of the Democratic Revolution*, vol. 1, *The Challenge* (Princeton, NJ: Princeton University Press, 1957).

4. See T. H. Marshall, "Citizenship and Social Class," in *Class, Citizenship and Social Development* (Garden City, NJ: Doubleday, 1964). Despite differing emphases on individual rights such as ownership of property, all the industrialized democracies, including the United States, extended social protection and economic regulation, or the so-called welfare state, in response to the social dislocations of industrialization and urbanization. See Karl Polanyi, *The Great Transformation: The Political and Economic Origins of Our Time* (Boston: Beacon Press, 1944).

5. The historical process by which aristocratically ruled Western empires broke apart into sovereign states and then experienced industrialization, economic growth, urbanization, and representative institutions is summarized in much social science literature as "modernization." This overall process has taken different forms in different eras, but it constitutes one of the major background influences that can contribute to ethnic and other violent conflicts. See, e.g., Saul Newman, "Does Modernization Breed Ethnic Conflict?" *World Politics* 43, no. 3 (April 1991): 451–78.

6. On why some states, such as Prussia, adopted more militaristic and nationalistic domestic and foreign policies residing in the central state, while other countries, such as England, placed constraints on the state, see Robert Solo, "The Formation and Transformation of States," in *An International Political Economy*, ed. W. Ladd Hollist and F. LaMond Tullis (Boulder, CO: Westview Press, 1985), 72–80.

7. Also, though their leaders often were ruthless, many of these regimes' egalitarian ideologies and nominally populist bases of power did lead them to introduce fairly comprehensive programs in health; nutrition; literacy; education; and road, railroad, and electrification infrastructure that improved the standard of living of many in their populations and raised the status of minorities such as women.

**8.** Lisa Anderson, "Antiquated before They Ossify: States That Fail before They Form," *Journal of International Affairs* 58, no. 1 (Fall 2004): 6–7. This recent article parallels several of the points developed here.

**9.** Stephen Krasner, *Structural Conflict: The Third World against Global Liberalism* (Berkeley: University of California Press, 1985), 279.

**10.** See Charles Tilly, ed., *The Formation of National States in Western Europe* (Princeton, NJ: Princeton University Press, 1975), 7, 636–38.

**11.** Krasner, *Structural Conflict,* 8.

**12.** Although advancing religious or ideological causes, some recent conflicts were mainly power struggles between regional groups or political factions for control of the state, such as in Tajikistan. The Tutsi junior army officers who, in October 1993, assassinated Burundi's newly elected Hutu president may have had in their heads an aristocratic notion of the Tutsis' right to rule, but they were also fearful of a Hutu deluge.

**13.** Mohammed Ayoob, "State Making, State Breaking, and State Failure," in *Managing Global Chaos: Sources of and Responses to International Conflict,* ed. Chester Crocker, Fen Osler Hampson, and Pamela Aall (Washington, DC: United States Institute of Peace Press, 1996).

**14.** Tilly, *The Formation of National States.*

**15.** Robert Jackson and Carl Rosberg, "Why Africa's Weak States Persist," *World Politics* 35, no. 1 (October 1982), cited in Anderson, "Antiquated before They Ossify," 23.

**16.** However, east Asian states and regional bodies are less receptive to international pressure to apply liberal political norms within the members' sovereign states.

**17.** Theodore H. Von Laue, *The World Revolution of Westernization: The Twentieth Century in Global Perspective* (Oxford: Oxford University Press, 1989). In this light, the current administration's antipathy toward the United Nations and other international bodies and toward multilateral approaches to international problems is ironic, not only because the United States was so instrumental in setting up these bodies in the first place, but because they are already actively promulgating Washington's values.

**18.** This tendency may reflect in part the fact that the outsider organizations that carry out the liberal menu of programs in developing countries are bureaucratically structured predominantly in a "stovepipe" fashion, along sectoral or functional lines, rather than along more decentralized, geographically focused lines.

**19.** Havard Hegre et al., "Globalization and Internal Conflict," in *Globalization and Armed Conflict,* ed. Gerald Schneider et al. (Lanham, MD: Rowman and Littlefield, 2003).

**20.** Jack Goldstone, Ted Robert Gurr, Monty Marshall, and Jay Ulfelder, "Beyond Democracy" (unpublished paper, 2003). In methodological terms, studies that look cross-sectionally at a "large N" of countries to identify the societal factors that are most highly correlated statistically with levels of conflict or development do not capture the actual historical processes through which particular countries either produced those correlations or took other paths. Those processes need to be examined longitudinally. To deduce policy solutions directly from such correlates can be ineffective or risky.

**21.** Krasner argues that the leaders of small and weak developing countries generally have resisted the pressure to adopt liberal international regimes with domestic policy implications such as free-trade agreements, because of the potential for domestic unrest, and so they seek international agreements that protect them from global market forces. Krasner, *Structural Conflict*, 4–7.

**22.** See, e.g., Pauline H. Baker, "Conflict Resolution versus Democratic Governance: Divergent Paths to Peace?" in *Managing Global Chaos*, ed. Crocker et al.

**23.** This observation was written several years before the U.S. war and occupation in Iraq.

**24.** Some analysts argue that international concern for the human rights of minorities creates a serious moral hazard in which the minorities, although weaker than their oppressors, deliberately try to trigger international armed intervention on their behalf by picking a fight with their oppressors. See Alan J. Kuperman, *The Limits of Humanitarian Intervention: Genocide in Rwanda* (Washington, DC: Brookings Institution Press, 2001), viii.

**25.** As Pierre Sane, secretary general of Amnesty International, states, "We call for human rights concerns to be central at all stages of conflict resolution, peacekeeping, and peacebuilding. . . . Prevention of human rights crises is the correct course. The problem is not early warning but lack of early action . . . [which would otherwise] render the debate over humanitarian intervention obsolete." *Amnesty International Report 2000*, 8–9.

**26.** So-called neoconservatives who lately have supported coercive policies to achieve democratization in authoritarian regimes seem to have forgotten conservative thinkers such as Edmund Burke and Michael Oakeshott, who cautioned against rapid social change and ambitious social schemes in the Western societies. A still-pertinent corrective to ideologically driven, messianic approaches toward developing societies is found in Peter Berger, *Pyramids of Sacrifice: Political Ethics and Social Change* (Garden City, NJ: Doubleday, 1976).

**27.** For a fuller analysis, see Roland Paris, *At War's End: Building Peace after Civil Conflict* (Cambridge: Cambridge University Press, 2004).

**28.** Robert Kaplan, "Supremacy by Stealth: Ten Rules for Managing the World," *Atlantic Monthly*, July–August 2003, 66–83.

# 3

# Linking Human Rights and Conflict Transformation
## A Peacebuilding Framework

Lisa Schirch

A variety of metaphors provide insight into the relationship between the fields of human rights and conflict transformation, a term now widely used to describe strategies for building effective relationships and communication patterns between groups in conflict.[1] At times the relationship looks like quarreling siblings named Justice and Peace, battling for primacy and status at each other's expense. At other times the relationship between human rights and conflict transformation looks more like pieces of a puzzle that complement each other. During violent conflict, human rights groups can act like a sheepdog, rounding up groups in conflict and herding them into the structured pen where conflict transformation experts can work their facilitative magic. Or maybe human rights workers lay the roads to peace, and conflict transformation workers build the bridges over the canyons and rivers that obstruct the path. In the minds of some, conflict transformation and human rights advocacy are simply recent children of the liberal left, with its "bleeding hearts" and naive idealism.

My graduate students in the Summer Peacebuilding Institute at Eastern Mennonite University come from around the world. While most of our courses focus on skills and practices related to the field of conflict transformation, many of our students are human rights activists coming from such diverse places as Zimbabwe; Nagaland, India; and Nicaragua. At the community level, many of these practitioners see no contradiction between human rights advocacy and conflict transformation in working for social change, and thus blend the two approaches. However, in North America and Europe, where large organizations in both fields compete for money and use differing theories of change, the fields seem to have little contact with each other and at times show open disdain for each other's tools for addressing conflict.

This book details many of these differences, synopsized in Mertus's comparative chart in the introduction. This chapter proposes that human rights and conflict transformation are pieces of a much larger peacebuilding puzzle. While discussions between the two fields are often locked in a debate over priorities or in either-or thinking, a focus on peacebuilding looks at the need for a "both-and" approach: both peace and justice, both human rights and conflict transformation.

This chapter begins with a peacebuilding framework that helps locate human rights advocacy and conflict transformation practices within a wider array of social-change disciplines. Next we explore four reasons why the human rights and conflict transformation fields are so frequently linked: They share a moral call, they share similar analytical tools for understanding conflict and violence, they pose a similar challenge to state structures, and their strategies for addressing conflict offer strategic alternatives to war. The third section of the chapter explores the different but complementary functions played by conflict transformation and human rights actors in peacebuilding processes. Following this exploration, the fourth section examines the tensions between the two fields, and specifically the challenges, faced in the postwar context, involving peace settlements and amnesty programs. This section of the chapter offers readers two peacebuilding frameworks for addressing these tensions: a theory of how to coordinate coercive and persuasive strategies, and a restorative justice plan for linking offender accountability, victim needs, and the urgent desire for cease-fires and peace settlements in order to end the fighting. Finally, the chapter lays out a number of concrete steps for joint action for conflict transformation and human rights practitioners.

## A Peacebuilding Framework

Peacebuilding prevents, reduces, transforms, and helps people to recover from violence in all forms while at the same time empowering people to foster relationships at all levels to create structural justice. It both nurtures the capacity within societies to prevent violence and provides healing and help in the midst of war or in postwar societies. Peacebuilding pursues a just peace. The concept of just peace recognizes that justice pursued violently contributes to further injustice and human rights violations, and that peace without justice is unlikely to be sustainable or to meet people's basic needs. Just peace exists where a sustainable set of structures and processes allows people to meet their basic human needs and protects their human rights with an absence of either direct or structural violence. Peacebuilding recognizes the importance of efforts to reduce direct violence while pursuing a deeper transformation of structures, paradigms, cultures, and values over a longer time frame. Distributive justice, where people share both resources and decision making, is required for sustainable peace.

Peacebuilding coordinates the activities of a wide range of actors at all levels of society over a period of months, years, and decades, and requires a combination of approaches to peace through a nexus for collaboration. Human rights and conflict transformation are just two of many different approaches to peacebuilding, as shown in figure 1.

Peacebuilding is a relatively new idea, though the term "peacebuilding" is now widely used to refer to the linking of different approaches to social change.[2] As illustrated in the center of the figure, peacebuilding synthesizes the values, relational skills, analytical frameworks, and processes used in each of these fields. The next section looks at some important similarities in the values, analysis, and approaches used by conflict transformation, human rights, and other peacebuilding fields.

## A Moral Call

Peacebuilding approaches such as conflict transformation and human rights advocacy follow a moral call to improve the *human security* for all people, not just for one group. Human security exists when governments adequately protect people's rights to meet their basic needs, including food, health care, education, participation in community life, cultural expression, identity, and religion.

The idea of human security bridges the concepts of human rights and human needs. Building on a long tradition of human needs theory in the conflict transformation field, conflict scholar John Burton argues that all humans have innate needs.[3] Human rights and human needs are inextricably related: People have a right to what they need.[4]

People articulate their human needs and human rights in a variety of ways. In workshops, I often conduct a human needs and human rights exercise at the beginning. I put my children (or their picture) on a chair in the middle of the room and ask the group to list what these children need to live a life free from violence. The answers are always very similar, regard-

**Figure 1.** The Peacebuilding Nexus

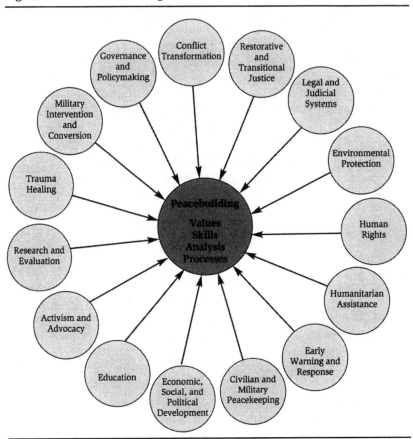

*Source:* Lisa Schirch, *The Little Book of Strategic Peacebuilding* (Intercourse, PA: Good Books, 2004), 12.

less of whether the workshop is in Senegal, Japan, or the United States, or whether the participants have only a grade school education or a PhD. At the community level around the world, people think children require food, shelter, health care, education, peace and security, freedom from repression, democratic participation in decisions that affect their lives, and the ability to express their cultural and religious identity. These same answers apply equally to all human beings; all humans have a right to live without violence.

It is helpful to divide this list of needs and rights into three categories: material, social, and cultural.

- Material needs and rights include food, shelter, health care, and the basic economic resources to survive physically. They require governments to protect economic rights through distributive justice, or a fair distribution of wealth, education, and employment opportunities for all people.

- Social needs and rights include a sense of human dignity, security from attack, predictability in relationships with others, and a sense of participation and self-determination in decision making. They require societies to protect social, civil, and political rights through procedural justice, to ensure democratic civil structures, to enforce the rule of law, and to foster social justice and cross-cultural understanding.

- Cultural needs and rights include the ability to give life meaning through belief systems and a sense of identity, culture, and religion. They require societies to protect religious freedoms, minority rights, and other social and civil rights.

In human rights language, material needs are called economic rights, social needs are called political and civil rights (such as freedom of speech, freedom of movement, and so on), and cultural needs refer to the freedom to practice one's own religion, the ability to choose how to identify oneself, and so on.

## Unmet Human Needs and Human Rights Violations Cause Conflict and Violence

The fields of human rights and conflict transformation share similar analytical tools for understanding conflict and violence. Both fields argue that the deprivation of human rights and human needs is the major cause of conflict, and that when conflicts turn violent, they deny people's need for security and lead to further human rights abuses. If people perceive that their needs are not met, they may engage in conflict, crime, or violence to pursue their needs and rights at any cost. People are willing to fight and die for their identity and culture, for their ability to control or have an impact on the world around them, and for basic material needs such as food and water. The drive to satisfy these needs controls human behavior; people who have their needs met act in "good" or peaceful ways, while those who do not often act in bad, evil, criminal, or violent ways.

Levels of violence are determined less by natural or innate aggression and greed and more by the degree to which cultural, political, economic, and social structures support human needs and protect human rights. The human capacity to act in cooperative ways to meet mutual needs and rights is evident in the great disparity in levels of violence in various cities and regions of the world. While some places are extremely violent, other places experience greater communal cooperation, sharing of resources, and relative peace. Humans often recognize that their own needs and rights are ultimately tied together with the needs and rights of others. Many families cooperate and share resources because they can see directly how these behaviors contribute to the greater good. Unfortunately, the calculation of whose needs and rights are tied together often ends at the edge of one's identity group or at the border of the state.

Cultural, social, economic, political, and other structures create an architecture for relationships and help determine whether resources will be shared relatively equally. Some structures disable or threaten people and increase disparities in need satisfaction and rights protections between groups of people. When societies are structured in ways that deprive people or fail to protect their rights, people may behave in ways that cause destruction to themselves and others. Structural violence begins a cycle of violence. Secondary forms of violence, such as crime, terrorism, and revolutionary movements, are responses to structural violence. Both violent social movements such as al Qaeda and nonviolent social movements such as the U.S. civil rights movement channel frustration against structural violence. If social movements do not exist, people may express their frustration through self-destructive behaviors such as alcoholism or drug abuse, or through destructive behaviors such as crime and interpersonal violence in their homes and communities.[5] Figure 2 provides a visual comparison of types of secondary violence and their relationship to structural violence.

Human needs and human rights analytical frameworks are useful in understanding, for example, the ever-increasing tide of terrorism committed by small, decentralized groups whose members are prepared to die for their cause and have nothing to lose in terms of territory or wealth. While it is important to condemn terrorist violence, it is also important to understand the perceptions of those who commit and support terrorist acts. In his "Letter to America," Osama bin Laden detailed his perception that unmet human needs and human rights abuses in many places in the world result directly from the policies, institutions, and decisions of the United States and other Western countries.[6] Al Qaeda perceives its use of terrorism as a response to structural violence. Representatives from the human rights and conflict transformation communities argue that addressing structural violence by increasing aid to the developing world to meet

**Figure 2.** Cycle of Violence Map

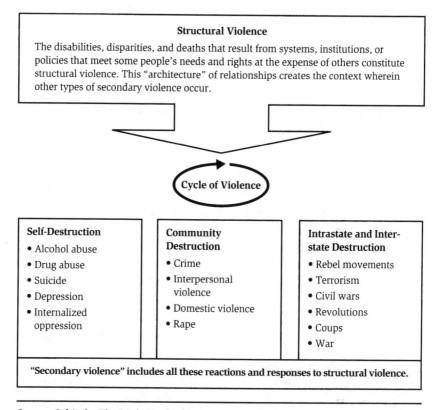

**Structural Violence**

The disabilities, disparities, and deaths that result from systems, institutions, or policies that meet some people's needs and rights at the expense of others constitute structural violence. This "architecture" of relationships creates the context wherein other types of secondary violence occur.

Cycle of Violence

**Self-Destruction**
- Alcohol abuse
- Drug abuse
- Suicide
- Depression
- Internalized oppression

**Community Destruction**
- Crime
- Interpersonal violence
- Domestic violence
- Rape

**Intrastate and Inter-state Destruction**
- Rebel movements
- Terrorism
- Civil wars
- Revolutions
- Coups
- War

"**Secondary violence**" includes all these reactions and responses to structural violence.

*Source:* Schirch, *The Little Book of Strategic Peacebuilding,* 24.

basic material needs, fostering greater democratic discussion of key global issues at all levels of every society, and focusing on human rights laws are essential to American security.[7]

While human needs and human rights analytical frameworks are helpful in identifying ways to address conflict, there are some conceptual challenges.[8] First of all, both human rights and human needs are difficult to measure. At what level of deprivation or relative deprivation do people engage in conflict? A wide array of researchers have conclusively linked structural violence to a variety of violent responses, including increased crime, domestic violence, terrorism, and war. Some research points to the finding that relative deprivation, or the ability to compare unequal levels of needs and rights between people, leads to far greater levels of violence than does isolated deprivation.[9] The most powerful predictor of the homicide rate in a city, state, or country is not the degree of poverty but the size of the disparities in income and wealth between the rich and the poor.[10] Also, there is less violence in those areas where poor people do not have regular contact with images of the wealth and luxury consumed by other people.

Another problem with a needs-and-rights-based analysis is distinguishing between legitimate grievances over unmet needs and illegitimate greed. There are different ways to satisfy basic needs: All people need shelter, but not everyone can own a five-bedroom house. Some people want to satisfy their needs at the expense of others, particularly when, for example, one ethnic or religious group has dehumanized another group. When people are able to profit from mobilizing other people around their perceived grievances, violent conflict is likelier.[11] The greed-versus-grievance debate falsely poses these two motivations as opposite, when in fact they are more a matter of *perception*. The theory that conflict is caused by greed relies on an overly simplistic understanding of human nature. While it is true that some people's grievances and perceptions of their deprivation of needs are more accurate and just than others', a psychologically complex understanding of how people perceive justice and develop a sense of deprivation and grievance provides a richer understanding of the causes of conflict and violence.

For example, even within an armed movement such as the one in Chechnya, some will articulate their struggle for identity and self-determination more earnestly than others. The Chechen fighting for power and resources may look greedy to an outsider but likely sees him- or herself as fighting for legitimate grievances in the way power and resources are distributed. Humans generally tend to see their own actions and motivations as "good." The greed-versus-grievance debate can help us talk about these different motivations, but perhaps it is more accurate to discuss them as part of a spectrum.

The psychodynamic of "internalized superiority" allows people to believe that their lives and experiences are more valuable than others'. Groups that have been oppressed historically and are socialized into their inferior roles, such as many women around the world, often behave in ways that demonstrate a sense of "internalized inferiority" and an acceptance of fewer rights. People who have internalized inferiority may respond to their unmet needs and rights through the inward violence of depression and lack of self-esteem rather than through outward violence against others. In either case, human needs and human rights are distorted. Those who have internalized superiority greedily proclaim the "need" for, and "right" to, more and more resources, while those who have internalized inferiority try to convince themselves that having fewer needs and rights is somehow in the natural order of life.

This needs-and-rights-based analysis of violent conflict is very different from the paradigm that sees human nature as essentially evil. Many people in the world see violence as the ultimate solution when all else fails. Yet military solutions to many security problems, for example, often fail because they decrease levels of need satisfaction and therefore prompt rather than quell people's desire to fight or engage in crime. A needs-and-rights-based analysis of the causes of violence and its cyclical nature affects the strategies that each field chooses to address conflict.

## Challenging State Structures

Peacebuilding is a process of constructing or reconstructing state structures to foster just peace and human security.[12] The human rights and conflict transformation fields favor strategies that protect individual human needs and rights while challenging structures that violate human rights or fail to create an environment wherein people can meet their basic needs. The human rights field challenges the idea that the concept of sovereignty allows states to violate the rights of individuals.[13] Conflict transformation poses a less direct challenge to states. First, it advocates that nongovernmental actors such as academics and community mediators can play significant roles in transforming public conflicts, a task some consider reserved for government actors. Second, it takes an impartial stance when mediating between state and nonstate actors. It takes the positions, interests, and needs of all groups seriously and looks for solutions that meet human needs rather than protecting existing structures. In other words, conflict transformation sees the state itself as negotiable.

Both fields face challenges when actually trying to transform state structures. Peace settlements in Guatemala and South Africa brought an end to intrastate violence in those countries. However, levels of structural violence, including the level of disparity between ethnic groups and between rich and poor people, are relatively unchanged. The levels of individual and community forms of secondary violence have actually increased. In South Africa, for example, the rate of homicides increased drastically after the African National Congress and the de Klerk government made "peace": from 9,913 in 1986 to 23,823 in 2000.[14] South Africa also has some of the highest rates of rape and domestic violence in the world.[15]

In Guatemala, many of the state-sanctioned perpetrators and organizers of the genocidal violence that killed 200,000 people in the 1980s are now back in political office. Local human rights workers and others are again facing death threats and disappearance as the culture of impunity takes root. In both these cases, peace settlements failed to make adequate structural changes. The international community, and in particular the consultative group of major donor countries, have failed to adequately apply persuasive and coercive pressure on the officials refusing to enact human rights commitments made in the peace accord. Sustainable peace requires holding those responsible for the violence accountable to victims and making real structural changes that protect human rights and democracy.[16]

National and international structures pose major obstacles to both conflict transformation and human rights workers. Structural violence results in far more deaths than direct or secondary forms of violence, since people without food, housing, or health care suffer and die because their governments have discriminated against them or failed to provide basic services. Research by Kohler and Alcock shows that 18 million people die every year from structural violence, compared to roughly 100,000 deaths per year from armed conflict.[17]

Structural violence is pervasive: Two billion people in the world today live in desperate poverty that stems directly from national and international policies. Desperation provides fertile ground for revolution, civil war, genocide, and terrorism. Terrorist groups find their base of support in poor communities and from elite groups tired of seeing "their people" humiliated by poverty in a world where others have so much. Structural violence that obstructs people's ability to satisfy their basic needs coupled with the media engine of globalization, whose television and billboard ads display the vast disparity in wealth, creates a steady fuel of shame and humiliation, prompting secondary violence.

The field of peacebuilding, including both conflict transformation and human rights advocates, aims to address these structural challenges. It encourages good governance so that state actors may gain legitimacy through policies and structures that help people satisfy their basic needs and that maintain order through the practice of democracy and human rights protection rather than through the use of violence.

## Strategic Alternatives to War

Human rights and conflict transformation scholars also stand at the other end of the spectrum from realist scholars who advocate "any means necessary" for the protection of state interests. The ideology of "realism" or realpolitik shapes most governments' policies and their responses to conflict. Realists are correct when they describe the world as a place where some people seek power over others so that they can further their own interests. The question is not whether selfish, greedy, or criminal behavior exists. Rather, it is how to respond to a world with many "offenders"—people and groups violating laws and the rights of others. While the fields of human rights and conflict transformation are both well acquainted with the prevalence of violence, they generally reject the realists' prescriptive solution of exerting power through overwhelming violence as the best or only strategy for combating the violence of others.

Within the United States there is an ongoing debate about whether realism or human rights should prescribe U.S. policy. Robert Kaplan's book *Warrior Politics: Why Leadership Demands a Pagan Ethos,* for example, articulates a *prescriptive realist* U.S. foreign policy, that is, one that prescribes the use of "any means necessary" in order to protect national interests.[18] In the logic of power politics, might makes right, even at the expense of the human needs and human rights of a state's own citizens or of people in other countries. Guided by this prescriptive realism, the U.S. military, for example, was willing to risk the lives of thousands, if not hundreds of thousands, of innocent Afghan people in its pursuit of security for U.S. citizens from al Qaeda terrorism.

People working in the fields of human rights and conflict transformation tend to side with those in the U.S. government who argue that while realists accurately *describe* the challenges of working in a world of violence, there are often strategies that provide effective alternatives to war, contributing more both to American security and to global human security. A human rights–centered foreign policy acknowledges how American interests and security are interdependent with global security concerns. The security of people in other regions of the world is tied to U.S. security. Unfortunately, many experts now agree that the war in Iraq is increasing the number of al Qaeda recruits around the world and increasing the risk of future terrorist attacks rather than decreasing them.[19] William F. Schulz, the executive director of Amnesty International USA, and author of *In Our Own Best Interest: How Defending Human Rights Benefits Us All,* makes the case that a U.S. foreign policy based on human rights values would be both morally and strategically superior to the prevailing realist paradigm.[20] Protecting the human rights of all people is an effective security strategy for preventing terrorism.

Both human rights and conflict transformation actors generally denounce war as a tool for foreign policy and find themselves on the same side of the political debate about what to do with the Saddam Husseins of the world. Using war to depose a dictator or destroy terrorist cells hidden throughout the countryside puts innocent civilians at risk for massive human rights violations and is often used before sufficient sophisticated diplomatic initiatives and "smart" sanctions are exhausted.[21] Both human rights and conflict transformation scholars opposed the preemptive war on Iraq and advocated a much larger toolbox for addressing the conflict than did prescriptive realists.

## Human Rights and Conflict Transformation in Peacebuilding Practice

In practice, human rights and conflict transformation practitioners play different but complementary roles. The four main categories of peacebuilding are waging conflict nonviolently, reducing direct violence, transforming relationships, and building the capacity for just peace. Human rights and conflict transformation approaches are found in each category. While many actors engage in multiple categories of peacebuilding, each approach to peacebuilding has unique goals, as illustrated in figure 3. Each of these categories can feed into an ongoing cycle of peacebuilding, where different peacebuilding processes complement and build on one another.

Human rights and conflict transformation skills and processes are useful in each category. However, human rights practitioners spend most of their time *waging conflict nonviolently,* trying to *reduce direct violence,* and creating a human rights culture through education, training, and other *capacity-building* programs. Conflict transformation practitioners, on the other hand, spend most of their time *transforming relationships* with processes such as dialogue, negotiation, and mediation.

A description of actors and activities in each category of peacebuilding highlights the complementary aspects of human rights and conflict transformation practice.

### Waging Conflict Nonviolently

In conflicts where power is unbalanced and there is little public awareness of the issues, it is often difficult or impossible to get to the negotiation table. Those groups that are able to find space for dialogue in this context often find it unsatisfying, since groups with more power may not negotiate in good faith.[22] Many groups resort to violence to help motivate others to address their needs or to resist oppression by other groups. Strategic nonviolent action, that is, waging conflict nonviolently, is an alternative. It can

**Figure 3.** A Map of Peacebuilding

Source: Schirch, *The Little Book of Strategic Peacebuilding*, 26.

help balance power, raise public awareness of and sympathy for injustice, increase an understanding of how the groups in conflict are interdependent, and convince or coerce a group in power to negotiate with less powerful groups who perceive a violation of their human rights.

Human rights workers play important roles in this category of peacebuilding. They have pioneered creative ways of coercing human rights offenders to change their behavior or to come to the negotiation table. Amnesty International uses the phrase "the mobilization of shame" to capture the dynamic that occurs when nations experience pressure from other countries to change behavior that is perceived to be degrading, humiliating, and shameful.[23] Citizens of a country committing human rights abuses can "mobilize" shame through advocacy and direct action to increase the power of the victims and raise public awareness of the abrogation of their human rights. Human rights organizations around the world translate human rights abuses into vivid descriptions of the stories and experiences of real people. Their reports become testimonies to the truth as they see it. Victims of human rights abuses gain sympathy and support from others who read the reports while experiencing the satisfaction and healing power of seeing their stories added to a historical record so they will not be forgotten. Research on South Africa's Truth and Reconciliation Commission attests to the relief some victims feel in seeing their truths exposed.[24]

Some victims have the satisfaction of seeing hundreds or thousands of protesters take to the streets in response to the abuse of their human rights. In Guatemala, Colombia, and Argentina, for example, mothers' organizations protested the disappearance and murders of their husbands, sons, and fathers by the state. Protesters aim to draw attention to abuses and to gain the sympathy and support of people within the country, and possibly in the international community, through media coverage. By mobilizing shame against offending governments, protesters increase their power and raise awareness of human rights abuses. Nonviolent action can no longer be dismissed as unrealistic or ineffective, because its track record in bringing about sustainable change in even the most repressive governments appears to be as good as or better than those of groups who have sought social change through violence.[25]

Human rights activists need conflict transformation skills to build effective relationships and communicate their causes in diplomatic ways. Relationships between activist groups are often antagonistic and competitive, and groups can find it difficult to work together on areas of common ground and are often sidetracked by internal conflicts. Building a movement to wage conflict nonviolently therefore requires forming coalitions between groups with different goals and experiences. The communication and relational skills used in conflict transformation also help human rights activists frame or articulate issues in assertive but diplomatic ways so that others are most likely to hear and understand them. In framing their campaigns, activists often use language that alienates potential supporters. For example, many of the various groups concerned with World Bank and IMF policies often call for the "destruction" of the World Bank. Many commentators have noted that the language of "transformation" and "accountability" would win the World Bank's detractors more support in furthering their goals.

While the skills and processes of waging conflict nonviolently are important tools in building peace, other peacebuilding processes are needed to reduce direct violence and build relationships across the lines of conflict.

## Reducing Direct Violence

Efforts to reduce direct forms of violence are also part of peacebuilding. Peacebuilding organizations need to find ways to stop or reduce the violence, create safe spaces for dialogue or negotiations between conflicting groups, address people's physical needs, restrain offenders, and limit the amount and level of trauma experienced by people in conflict situations. Processes that aim to reduce direct violence include legal and judicial systems that apply human rights and international humanitarian law; civilian or military peacekeeping operations; peace zones, relief aid, and refugee camps for displaced people and victims of violence; and human rights observers and monitors. It may also include cease-fire agreements that bring a temporary end to fighting.

Human rights workers and organizations help prevent or reduce violence in the midst of violent crises by the threat of mobilizing the international community in response to human rights abuses. They work with armed groups, for example, to encourage commitments to international humanitarian law that limits harm to civilians during war. Human rights groups can deter or prevent violence just by their presence and their documentation of human rights violations.

A single North American human rights worker in a village in Nicaragua, for example, was able to prevent an attack on the entire village by the U.S.-backed Contra forces during the 1980s. Contra forces became aware that human rights groups such as Witness for Peace had established a rapid-response network that would send stories and photos of Contra attacks on civilians to U.S. policymakers, and that this publicity threatened the Contras' ongoing U.S. support.[26] In Colombia, civilian peacekeepers and human rights groups are currently monitoring the ongoing abuse of the human rights of the Colombian people by both rebel and government-supported armed groups. In other parts of the world, international human rights organizations provide accompaniment for local human rights workers who might otherwise be threatened or killed because of their work. In Sri Lanka, Peace Brigades International (PBI) provides accompaniment for any civilians who are afraid they may be killed because of their work. PBI workers accompany these threatened civilians twenty-four hours a day, sending a continuous message that "the world is watching."[27] Human rights efforts to reduce direct violence make the space for conflict transformation practitioners to bring conflicting groups together in order to reduce direct violence and pursue justice.

## Transforming Relationships

Transforming conflictual relationships requires healing trauma, addressing the roots of the conflict, and pursuing justice. Relationships are the foundation of peacebuilding; they create motivation for working together to solve the shared problem of unmet needs and rights. Conflict transformation processes work in coordination with the fields of trauma healing, restorative justice, and transitional justice to bring people together to analyze the roots of conflict, build relationships across lines of conflict, and find creative ideas for mutually satisfying human needs. Processes that transform relationships include mediation, dialogue, negotiation, restorative justice processes, legal and judicial processes, amnesty programs, truth and reconciliation processes, and processes that reintegrate combatants into civil society.

Human rights ideas and documents support conflict transformation processes that aim to transform relationships in at least three ways. First, human rights declarations set standards for official diplomatic conflict transformation efforts, such as peace negotiations. Reflecting on the role of human rights work in Northern Ireland, Christine Bell argues that human rights documents provide a way of measuring the legitimacy of negotiation claims.[28]

Second, human rights abuse reports provide a relatively objective version of the past. It is not easy to move forward and build peace without a realistic appraisal of the past and its human rights abuses. Verifying actual stories and events of human rights abuses by witnesses and others involved establishes a history that can be used in future truth and reconciliation transitional justice processes.

Third, human rights reports can create an atmosphere in which offending groups feel pressure to accept compromises at the negotiation table. A United Nations mediator in El Salvador found it useful to time the release of human rights abuse reports by monitoring organizations in order to strategically apply pressure on groups at the negotiation table to include "significant human rights protection" within formal peace negotiations.[29]

## Building Capacity

Building a capacity for peace is a long-term effort and requires a focus on sustainability. Training and education, sustainable social, economic, and political development, institution building, conversion of military structures to focus on human security, and research and evaluation are all part of capacity building. Human rights and conflict transformation training and education programs, for example, give people the values, skills, analytical tools, and knowledge of processes required for building a just peace. Knowledge of the existence and content of the Universal Declaration of Human Rights or local human rights charters may empower people to have the courage to become agents of change in situations where abuses take place. Training programs on conflict transformation skills give people the needed tools to build relationships, networks, and coalitions that have the power and capacity to bring about change. Creating and strengthening peacebuilding organizations also help communities sustain a culture of peace.

None of these peacebuilding processes alone can bring about peace; the tasks of peacebuilding are too complex. While human rights and conflict transformation are complementary in many ways, there are also real differences and challenges.

## Addressing Tensions between Human Rights and Conflict Transformation

The tensions between human rights and conflict transformation approaches center on how to treat human rights violators. Should they be involved in cease-fire negotiations and peace settlements? Should they be reintegrated into civil society? Should they be given amnesty to induce truth-telling and reconciliation in postwar contexts? Or should they be imprisoned?

In the design of peace settlements, conflict transformation practitioners help decide who comes to the negotiation table and what the final settlement looks like. Some human rights activists express concern or object when human rights violators are allowed to take part in peace settlements, since it appears to reward their brutality and legitimize their tenuous authority, which may have been achieved in the first place through violent means rather than community support. Conflict transformation practitioners argue that the extremists and "spoilers" are necessary elements in peace settlements since they have the potential to destabilize or spoil a peace settlement.[30]

In the recent Liberian cease-fire negotiations, for example, representatives of both government and armed groups were the main negotiators, even though most of these people had committed human rights violations. It would have been impossible to try to hold a peace negotiation without representatives from these groups, however, for they were the ones doing the fighting. At the same time, the negotiations themselves gave legitimacy to the representatives, even though many of them have little popular support.

Peacebuilding requires both condemning human rights violations and, at the same time, acknowledging that human rights violators often perceive that they are fighting for justice. Regardless of whether their perceptions are justified, they must be acknowledged because to ignore their concerns or needs leaves the possibility of ongoing violence as they seek to pursue a solution that they see as just.

The difference between human rights and conflict transformation approaches stems in part from their differing interpretations of conflict and crime. Conflict transformation approaches focus on the "conflict," while human rights and restorative justice approaches focus on the "crime." Figure 4 illustrates how these two different approaches create different paths.

There are tensions between these different paths. The concept of "crime" requires the establishment of the identity of the "offender" and "victim." Restorative justice processes (described more fully below) identify victims' needs and offenders' obligations. Human rights work takes an advocacy stance in conflicts and seeks to identify and punish those who commit human rights violations. Naming terrorist behavior and identifying perpetrators is a key human rights strategy. Yet human rights workers tend to focus on state-based violations of human rights rather than on those of nonstate actors such as al Qaeda. Human rights workers aim to hold states to objective standards for behavior, such as the Universal Declaration of Human Rights, and use the legal system in the pursuit of justice, wherein offenders are punished for their actions. In human rights literature, people in conflict are not equally culpable for the abuse of human rights. There are clear victims and offenders.

In a conflict, the victimhood of all sides is given credence, and all sides are given mutual responsibility for the task of addressing the problem. In many cases of conflict and violence, its not clear who plays the role of victim or offender, for a variety of reasons. There may not be laws or a criminal justice body that defines behavior deemed an offense. In civil war and international conflicts in particular, there is often no cultural or political authority to define what is "illegal." In conflict transformation practices there is an underlying assumption that each individual or group takes part in developing the conflict, so each is responsible or guilty.

Conflict transformation values impartial approaches to the parties in conflict. Conflict transformation practitioners relish the freedom to focus on the process of bringing people in conflict together without issuing judgments declaring victims and offenders, as these terms may inhibit groups in conflict from fully participating in the process. Conflict transformation practitioners' goal of being a mediating "bridge" between groups in conflict, helping each

**Figure 4.** Contrasting "Conflict" and "Crime"

| Crime | Conflict |
|---|---|
| Laws and legal authorities define an event as a "crime" or "human rights violation." It is possible to identify victims and offenders. | No laws or legal authorities exist to address the "conflict." It is not possible or deemed necessary to identify offenders and victims. |

| Criminal Justice | Restorative Justice | Amnesty | Negotiation or Mediation |
|---|---|---|---|
| Crime is seen as a violation of the law and the state. Justice requires the state to identify offenders, determine blame, and impose pain through punishment of the offender. | Crime is seen as a violation of people and relationships. Victims, communities, and offenders work collaboratively to define ways to identify and address harms, needs, and obligations of offenders to their victims. | State laws and institutions may not be able to process everyone who engaged in war crimes. Holding offenders accountable may jeopardize peace settlements in a fragile political environment. Offenders may be offered amnesty in exchange for telling the truth. | Armed groups identify the causes of the conflict and key issues and develop mutually satisfactory solutions. Impunity or amnesty for war crimes is seen as a necessary sacrifice for creating political stability. |

to empathize with the other, to share perspectives on "truth," and to work together to find ways of moving forward is often seen as incompatible with the goal of raising awareness and naming injustices. The term "terrorist" or "criminal" does not show up frequently in conflict transformation literature, as these types of labels create barriers to communication.

There are growing concerns in both the human rights and conflict transformation fields over addressing injustices that occur during war while not jeopardizing the fragile attempts to build relationships between groups in conflict. Another area of tension arises out of the flurry of amnesty programs, truth and reconciliation commissions, and reintegration efforts that generally offer human rights violators forgiveness in exchange for the admission of guilt. In amnesty processes, offenders are not held accountable to the state and are not punished for their acts. Victims often voice the need for truth and public accountability in the justice process, and amnesty programs can help meet these goals by making the process of exposing the truth of human rights violations less threatening to the offenders. Yet human rights advocates raise the issue of the victims' need for offenders to be punished. Some human rights scholars criticized the South African Truth and Reconciliation Commission (TRC) for contributing to a "culture of impunity" by not doing enough to punish perpetrators.[31]

Both groups have valid points in these arguments. Rather than pose an either-or solution to these tensions, peacebuilding frameworks can help coordinate coercive and persuasive strategies for change and show how to use restorative justice principles to make offender accountability, truth telling, and victim healing compatible in transitional justice processes.

## Using Restorative Justice

The philosophy and practice of restorative justice can help bridge the tensions between human rights and conflict transformation concerns in the postwar context. The Western legal model, advocated by human rights groups, is useful in detailing agreements about what constitutes crime, identifying what laws have been broken, discovering who committed them, and deciding how the state should punish criminals. Yet there are several problems with relying only on this legal model.[32] First, victims' needs get left out, and the process of justice may actually feel like a revictimization if victims' stories are questioned or put on trial. Second, the focus on punishment makes it more difficult to gain the cooperation, confession, and commitment of human rights violators to participate in the justice process. It also fails to provide a context whereby offenders may feel empathy for their victims and take responsibility for their crimes. Third, punishment tends to stimulate even more criminal behavior,[33] since prison culture reinforces a worldview of using violence as a tool for addressing conflict.

Perhaps the major failure of Western legal systems is that these systems fail to understand that offenders view their own crimes as a struggle for justice. Citing many years of work with the most violent criminals in U.S. prisons, Harvard psychologist James Gilligan claims that all offenders justify their own violence as a search for justice or an attempt to undo injustice.[34] As discussed earlier in the "Cycle of Violence" map (figure 2), secondary forms of violence, such as crime and human rights violations during war, are often perceived by perpetrators as responses to some structural injustice. The legal system fails to understand the wider context of criminal acts and takes little interest in addressing the conditions that led perpetrators to choose crime rather than other methods to pursue their interests. Offenders are often unwilling to confess their crimes, because they see their actions through the lens of self-defense or as an effort to meet their own needs and rights. Punishment does little to deter people who perceive their crimes as a way of meeting their own, in their eyes legitimate, human needs and rights. While some offenders, particularly in a war context, openly express that they are fighting for profit or power, many of them talk about their use of violence as a struggle for justice and see themselves as victims.

In Nepal, for example, Maoist guerrillas use violence in an attempt to overthrow a system they perceive as unjust. The government, on the other hand, uses the global war on terror to frame the Maoists as terrorists having no legitimate concerns. Any justice process to address Maoist violence and human rights violations must also address the Maoist perception that the Nepalese government also violates the rights of its citizens.

The Western legal system is necessary but not sufficient. Threats of tribunals and imprisonment are important forms of coercive pressure to place on human rights violators, but justice requires both holding offenders accountable and providing a context in which their perceptions of justice and the legitimacy of their claims can be discussed. Addressing offenders' perceptions of injustice is essential to stopping the cycle of violence and building structures that meet everyone's needs. In peace settlements, then, it is important to include human rights offenders and to provide space for them to talk about their perception of what is fair while at the same time using human rights standards to define and condemn criminal behavior. It is also important for offenders to take responsibility for their crimes in public and to give restitution to their victims.

The philosophy and practice of restorative justice can help build a bridge from the coercive power of the legal system toward the persuasive processes of conflict transformation and its goal of reconciliation. Restorative justice processes may bring a new lens to the tensions in postwar contexts of addressing injustices that occur during war, without jeopardizing the fragile attempts to put an end to direct violence and build relationships between groups in conflict. Restorative justice provides a way of talking about offenders' accountability to victims that moves toward a needs-based orientation to justice. Restorative justice understands crime as a violation that creates needs for victims and their communities. Howard Zehr identifies a number of victim needs, including information about justice processes and options, truth-telling in a ritualized public setting, a sense of empowerment to make choices in the justice process, real and symbolic restitution for victims' losses in the crimes, and vindication from any feeling that they were somehow responsible for the crimes against them.[35] Restorative justice processes encourage offenders to understand the consequences of their actions and to empathize with victims, which, as research shows, is necessary to prevent a return to criminal behavior.[36]

Restorative justice principles are not new; they build on and expand indigenous justice systems still in practice in many areas of the world. Restorative justice does not require forgiveness or reconciliation, although these come more easily for participants in restorative justice processes. While some victims request victim-offender conferences, restorative justice does not require direct encounters, either. Restorative justice processes are not necessarily a replacement for the criminal justice system or prison; rather, they are now widely used as a supplement to, rather than a substitute for, the Western legal model.[37]

In conflict transformation processes, groups are encouraged to identify their BATNA, or "best alternative to a negotiated agreement," in order to evaluate their incentives for engaging in negotiation.[38] Groups are more likely to reach a negotiated agreement if they believe it is better than alternatives, such as continuing fighting. In the postwar context, a similar concept might be "BATARJ," or the "best alternative to a restorative justice." Individuals or groups facing prosecution in a war tribunal, for example, may assume that their BATARJ is worse than participating in a restorative process in which they will need to take responsibility for their crimes and be accountable to their victims and the larger community and state.

Although it depends on Western justice systems as a backup, restorative justice holds a number of advantages. First, its processes can be used to address the needs and issues raised by both victims and offenders. It is important to have everyone at the negotiating table, even human rights violators. Restorative justice condemns crime and violence but gives a voice to the offender. It recognizes the long-term importance of ensuring that offenders' sense of justice is also treated seriously. This provides an incentive for key actors in violent conflicts to submit to a restorative justice process. Second, a justice process focused on holding offenders accountable to victims' needs is quite different from a process in which the state only deals out physical punishment to offenders. Some offenders may be more likely to take responsibility for their crimes if their accountability comes through real and symbolic restitution directly to victims rather than through punishment by the state. Changing the way offenders are held accountable seems preferable to total amnesties that imply that offenders are not responsible for their crimes.

Third, restorative justice processes are logistically easier than Western legal processes. In a postwar situation, most offenders will necessarily need to be reintegrated back into society rather than assigned a jail cell, because many countries are unable to incarcerate large numbers of people. Restorative justice processes can be run at the local level by facilitators who bring together victims and community members to determine how to repair the harm done through crime or violence. Restorative justice is essential to peacebuilding because it assumes that crimes take place in a social environment where both victim and offender will need to relate to each other in the future.

Restorative justice is practiced widely at the level of individual crimes in many parts of the world, and there is a growing interest in including it in transitional justice processes required in postwar societies. Critical test cases that experimented with restorative justice principles and practices, such as South Africa's TRC, have come under premature yet heavy criticism.[39] Victims' needs for truth were taken seriously, yet the justice system failed to hold offenders accountable for restitution to victims. It also failed in many cases to use the legal system against offenders who did not use the TRC process, as mandated by the TRC regulations. The TRC was neither a complete success nor a complete failure. Rather, it was an experiment in transitional justice that provides an opportunity for learning.

## Timing the Coordination of Coercive and Persuasive Strategies

Human rights activists are more likely to rely on coercive strategies to bring about change, whereas conflict transformation actors are more likely to use persuasive strategies. Conflict transformation processes aim to persuade people in conflict to change their worldviews and behaviors by humanizing opposing groups and recognizing that the mutual satisfaction of the needs of all groups in conflict is the best way of achieving individual and group goals. When people voluntarily make their own choices as a result of learning through negotiation or dialogue, they are more likely to feel good about these choices, and the change in their behavior is more likely to be lasting. Conflict transformation workers are often hesitant to use coercion as the basis for change, arguing that change brought about through persuasive dialogue and negotiation leads to real understanding and sustainable changes.

However, the field of conflict transformation has little theory and few tools to address situations where groups in conflict are unwilling to meet

**Figure 5.** Coordination of Coercive and Persuasive Strategies

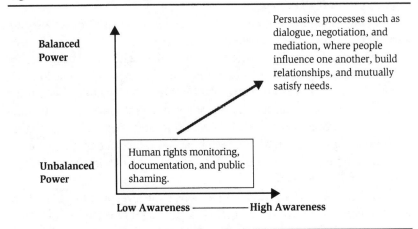

*Source:* Adam Curle, *Making Peace* (London: Tavistock Press, 1971); adapted by Schirch.

with or talk to the opposing sides. Persuasion is not always possible. Adam Curle's model (figure 5) illustrates that conflict transformation methods are often not useful where perceived power is unbalanced and public sympathy for and awareness of about the conflict or perceived injustice are low. Nonviolent coercive force can raise public awareness and balance power between groups in conflict. In many cases, coercive means are necessary to move groups in conflict toward the negotiating table, where creative problem solving can occur. Human rights strategies such as monitoring, documentation, and public shaming of human rights violators use coercive pressure to move groups toward the upper-right quadrant, where conflict transformation practitioners can bring people together to address the roots of conflict.

The U.S. civil rights movement, for example, began with sit-ins, demonstrations, and other forms of nonviolent coercive pressure on the white community to change. Nonviolent action aimed to make people uncomfortable—to create tension that would force people to look at the structural violence inflicted on African Americans through segregation. These coercive acts led to a willingness on the part of some white leaders to sit down with the African American leadership of the civil rights movement in order to design a more equal society.

This model blends coercive and persuasive tactics to force those with more power to see that it is in their interest to negotiate with others, but recognizes that ultimately coercion alone cannot solve problems. Peace-building requires the use of both coercive force, to compel groups to come to the negotiation table, and persuasive processes, for building relationships and jointly solving problems. Coercive human rights strategies such as nam-ing offenders in media reports and boycotting economic goods such as dia-monds or wood products used to buy arms, for example, put pressure on armed movements to follow international humanitarian law and can en-courage armed groups to identify violators within their own ranks.

In the Democratic Republic of the Congo, for example, conflict trans-formation efforts at peace settlements or grassroots dialogue have had lit-tle effect, because there appear to be vested economic interests in perpetu-ating the ethnic hatred and genocidal violence. Human rights groups are searching for a clear connection between Western economic interests in both logging and the mining of coltan (columbite-tantalite), a mineral used in cell phones, and the outside forces arming groups and fueling ethnic hatreds. If the people orchestrating the violence for their own economic in-terests could be identified, it would be easier to apply coercive pressure on them through media shaming or boycotts. This coercion would help balance power between groups, decreasing the power of armed groups and increas-ing the power of those advocating peace. It could give those interested in peace a chance to create fair resource distribution and democratic govern-ing structures.

While there are challenges for human rights and conflict transforma-tion practitioners in working together in conflict situations, this section illustrates how taking a broader peacebuilding perspective can address key tensions between the two fields. The peacebuilding frameworks offered here demonstrate the complementarity of coercive and persuasive approaches, and the utility of including other fields, such as restorative justice, to bridge the gulf between human rights and conflict transformation principles.

## Agenda for Coordinated Action

The last section of this chapter details an agenda for human rights and conflict transformation practitioners to enable a more successful synthesis of ideas and synergy of practice in the wider field of peacebuilding.

### Coordination Networks

The two fields need a broad-based effort to create institutionalized coordi-nation networks for joint funding, planning, and implementation of a variety of different approaches to peacebuilding, including conflict transformation and human rights. Groups working for peace and justice are often unaware of potential partners involved in similar work, which weakens their capacity to fulfill their own goals. Rather than competing for resources and a claim to independent success, organizations doing different kinds of work need to go to funders with a comprehensive framework. Coordinating bodies need to be created to help foster cooperation between these different approaches, and funders need to require grantees to link with groups using other approaches.

The West African Network for Peacebuilding (WANEP) is an example of a coordinating body that brings together human rights, development, education, and other organizations in an effort to coordinate peacebuilding actors. In Nigeria, for example, WANEP works on planning and coordination with a wide variety of actors concerned about interreligious violence. Rather than using only dialogue or human rights pressure to address violence, WANEP brings together conflict transformation and human rights actors to work together to coordinate their programs for maximum effect.

## Exchange Training and Increase Dialogue

Perhaps the first step toward the establishment of these coordination networks could be an exchange of training and increased opportunities for dialogue between human rights and conflict transformation scholars and practitioners. Michelle Parlevliet of the South African–based Centre for Conflict Resolution's human rights program advocates an exchange of training between the fields of human rights and conflict resolution in order to infuse the language of human rights documents into conflict transformation practice and infuse conflict transformation skills into human rights advocacy.[40] Conflict transformation practitioners can benefit from learning how to use human rights advocacy in order to pressure groups in conflict to negotiate and incorporate human rights documents in the agendas of peace settlements. Human rights workers can benefit from practicing conflict transformation skills within their own organizations and using dialogue and negotiation processes to build coalitions with other groups seeking change. Conflict transformation's communication skills and the language of human needs can also help groups communicate about human rights in a way that is less threatening and more easily heard by groups in conflict.

## Use the Language of "Needs" and "Rights" Strategically

When is the use of "needs" or "rights" language appropriate? As noted earlier in this chapter, the field of conflict transformation relies more heavily on "needs" language, while human rights actors, obviously, speak of "rights." Victoria Rader argues that the language and concept of "rights" are preferable to those of "needs" because the idea of needs can too easily lead to blaming the victims for having needs that they are unable to satisfy on their own, thus placing them in a dependent relationship with someone who can meet those needs.[41] Rights language creates the possibility of using the power of legal tools to enforce and protect. For example, rights language may assist in bolstering a community's claim to government policies that support job opportunities, freedom of religion, or the equality of all people under the law. Rights language brings along with it the force and power of laws and judicial institutions, as well as the power that comes with belonging to the international community and following its agreed-upon laws.

Many development organizations are moving from using "needs" language to using "rights" language. This shift is due in part to the increasing criticism of state structures and policies as a major source of poverty, inequality, disease, and other development problems. By adopting rights-based language and approaches, the field of development is in essence seeking to empower people to advocate for structural changes rather than requesting external aid or assistance in meeting their needs.

There are also arguments that support the use of "needs" language. Michelle Parlevliet argues that "needs" language is preferable to "rights" language in some types of peacebuilding practice. She argues that in mediation of a conflict where rights have been violated, offending groups are more open to listening to an opposing group articulate its needs than to being accused of violating that group's rights.[42] Needs language may facilitate a dialogue that gets beyond people's "positions" or fixed statements about what they "demand," toward an exploration of their deeper interests and needs. A needs-based dialogue may reveal, for example, that a group's demand for a piece of territory is rooted in its need for respect, self-determination, or participation in decisions that affect the lives of its members. A variety of creative solutions to address these deeper needs could help break an impasse in negotiation over competing demands for land.

The choice of whether to use the language of needs or that of rights will likely depend on context, since the two words conjure up different images and associations. It would be helpful if scholars from both fields conducted research on the use of "needs" and "rights" language to determine a set of guidelines for their use.

## Coordinate the Use of Persuasion and Coercion against Human Rights Offenders

The previous section of this chapter detailed the need for coordinating persuasive and coercive strategies. Without significant pressure from the international community to hold offenders accountable to victims in postwar contexts, peace accords are unlikely to succeed. Human rights advocates and conflict transformation practitioners can coordinate their actions in a sort of "good cop, bad cop" routine to maximize the chances for creating sustainable solutions in which groups feel compelled to negotiate rather than fight. This coordination of coercive and persuasive strategies for change would benefit from further discussion and research by the human rights and conflict transformation fields to determine how they can coordinate use of the carrot and the stick in peacebuilding strategies.

## Incorporate Restorative Justice

Human rights and conflict transformation scholars and practitioners also need to learn more about, and incorporate the concept and practice of, restorative justice to address postwar tensions. They could begin with a series of conferences that include human rights, conflict transformation, and restorative justice scholars and practitioners in creating new transitional justice mechanisms that offer alternatives to amnesty or state-based punishment.

## Localize the Articulation of Needs and Rights

The exercise of including people in naming their human needs and human rights is also an important step. Elicitive and participatory forms of education are widely recognized as superior to the "banking" method of teaching, in which an authority or expert hands over a list of knowledge to students.[43] For example, human rights education programs that rely on externally defined human rights are less likely to be effective in building a strong human rights culture. The introduction of the Universal Declaration of Human Rights, for example, can be introduced after local communities have gone through their own process of articulating how they understand the basic needs and rights of all people. Human rights education programs may actually do harm if they ignore or do not nurture a local human rights culture. Julie Mertus provides compelling testimony to the ways in which Western peacebuilders undermined human rights culture in Kosovo during the early 1990s by importing and imposing external human rights standards rather than exploring and nurturing the human rights traditions within the various cultures there.[44]

If human rights principles are to be embraced widely, they will need to be owned and implemented by people in every community. The Asian Human Rights Charter, for example, developed out of a grassroots dialogue between thousands of Asians and over two hundred Asian nongovernmental organizations.[45] The very process of local or regional groups articulating human rights through the lens of their own cultures and experiences is essential. Conflict transformation and human rights groups could jointly facilitate local efforts around the world to develop indigenous human rights charters.

## Unmask Human Rights Discourse That Hides the Goals of National Interests

The final three steps include working together to change structures. In his article "Liberal Talk, Realist Thinking," realist advocate John Mearsheimer argues that governments increasingly cover up their realist, national interest–based policies with a liberal human rights discourse that is an easier "sell" to the public.[46] Julie Mertus documents this increasingly blatant trend in her book *Bait and Switch: Human Rights and U.S. Foreign Policy.*[47] Many Americans, for example, supported the war on Iraq because U.S. politicians justified it with a human rights agenda. The fields of human rights and conflict transformation need to work together to unmask language that uses human rights discourse to gloss over national interests. The war on terror, the threat of weapons of mass destruction, and the presence of oil were much more pressing reasons for U.S. political leaders to begin the war on Iraq than were their concerns over the Hussein regime's oppression of its people. The field of peacebuilding needs to challenge the insincere use of human rights language, in this case creating awareness of how the war endangered the human rights and lives of American and British soldiers as well as thousands of Iraqi citizens.[48]

## Market Alternative Values and Strategies

People from the conflict transformation, human rights, development, and other peacebuilding fields can work together to more clearly articulate and market the human security and peacebuilding approach to domestic and foreign policy. While the moral arguments for human rights and conflict transformation are relatively well known, the strategic utility of these approaches is not widely recognized. Human rights and conflict transformation advocates need to find more engaging and creative ways to communicate their philosophy, values, analysis, and experience in ways that people outside these fields can understand.

## Address Structural Violence

Finally, the field of peacebuilding as a whole needs to create a long-term coordinated plan for addressing structural violence. The global community is lacking the *will* rather than the means to address issues of structural violence. The world currently has enough material resources to meet their human needs and rights of all its citizens. Four percent of the combined wealth of the 225 richest people in the world could provide the additional $40 billion of aid per year needed to create a world where everyone has access to food, shelter, education, safe water, sanitation, and health care.[49] Forty billion dollars could lead to vast increases in human needs satisfaction and violence prevention around the globe. This amount is only a small fraction of the over $400 billion U.S. military budget for 2005.

Development expert Jeffrey Sachs beckons the U.S. government to use "weapons of mass salvation" to address structural violence.[50] Efforts to institutionalize just economic policies that give developing countries a fair chance in the world economy will reduce Western profits in the short run but will likely lead to vast improvements in the quality of life in the developing world, which in turn affects global population levels and the environment and reduces the likelihood of people's feeling so much desperation and frustration that they will join or support terrorist movements that threaten Western security. Peacebuilding fields could join together to mobilize the political will for creating a regulatory framework for global and economic institutions and decision making in order to safeguard human rights, as suggested by human rights scholar Richard Falk.[51]

## Conclusion

The growing awareness of the sense of competition and the potential for coordination between human rights and conflict transformation practitioners is a good sign of growth for both fields. Each field needs the challenging questions raised by the other, for frustration and challenge are the mothers of innovation and improvisation. This chapter lays out a peacebuilding framework for understanding how the similarities and tensions between human rights and conflict transformation can be harnessed for maximum synergy. The ideas outlined in the last section are the stepping-stones toward a day when the competitive metaphors used to describe the two fields are no longer appropriate and are widely replaced with images of two friends supporting each other along a bumpy road.

## Notes

1. Unlike conflict resolution, the field of conflict transformation has situated itself within a long-term peacebuilding framework that fosters complementarity and coordination among various social change strategies. On my use of the term

"conflict transformation" throughout the chapter, see also John Paul Lederach, *The Little Book of Conflict Transformation* (Intercourse, PA: Good Books, 2003).

2. Luc Reychler and Thania Paffenholz, eds., *Peacebuilding: A Field Guide* (Boulder, CO: Lynne Rienner, 2001). European Centre for Conflict Prevention, ed., *People Building Peace* (Utrecht, Netherlands: European Centre for Conflict Prevention, 1999).

3. John W. Burton, ed., *Conflict: Human Needs Theory* (New York: St. Martin's Press, 1990).

4. Christian Bay, "Taking the Universality of Human Needs Seriously," in *Conflict: Human Needs Theory,* ed. John Burton (New York: St. Martin's Press, 1990), 235–56.

5. For details about the connection between structural and secondary forms of violence, see James Gilligan, *Violence: Reflections on a National Epidemic* (New York: Vintage Books, 1996), and Gilligan, *Preventing Violence* (New York: Thames and Hudson, 2001).

6. Osama bin Laden, "Full Text: Bin Laden's 'Letter to America,'" *Guardian Unlimited* (London), November 24, 2002.

7. Jayne Docherty and Lisa Schirch, *A Long-Term Strategy for American Security,* Eastern Mennonite University, www.emu.edu/ctp/bse-longterm.html (accessed October 2001). Nobel laureates, *Statement of 100 Nobel Laureates,* Eastern Mennonite University, www.emu.edu/ctp/bse-100nobel.html.

8. Christopher Mitchell, "Necessitous Man and Conflict Resolution: More Basic Questions about Basic Human Needs Theory," in Burton, *Conflict: Human Needs Theory,* 149–76.

9. Ted Gurr, *Why Men Rebel* (Princeton, NJ: Princeton University Press, 1970).

10. Gilligan, *Preventing Violence,* 40.

11. Paul Collier and Ankee Hoeffler, *Greed or Grievance in Civil War* (Washington, DC: World Bank, 2001).

12. Kathleen Hill Hawk, *Constructing the Stable State: Goals for Intervention and Peacebuilding* (Westport, CT: Praeger, 2002).

13. Richard Falk, *Human Rights Horizons: The Pursuit of Justice in a Globalizing World* (New York: Routledge, 2000).

14. Richard Wilson, "Challenging Restorative Justice," *Human Rights Dialogue* 2, no. 7 (Winter 2002): 16.

15. Martin Schonteich and Antoinette Louw, "Crime Trends in South Africa, 1985–1998" (paper commissioned by the Center for the Study of Violence and Reconciliation, Johannesburg, South Africa, 1999).

16. Amnesty International, "Guatemala: Ballots or Bullets? Political Violence Must Be Addressed" (press release, News Service no. 154, June 28, 2003).

17. Gilligan, *Violence*, 193–209.

18. Robert D. Kaplan, *Warrior Politics: Why Leadership Demands a Pagan Ethos* (New York: Random House, 2002).

19. Dana Priest and Josh White, "War Helps Recruit Terrorists, Hill Told," *Washington Post*, February 17, 2005; and Kim Sengupta, "Occupation Made World Less Safe, Pro-War Institute Says," *Independent*, May 26, 2004.

20. William F. Schulz, *In Our Own Best Interest: How Defending Human Rights Benefits Us All* (Boston: Beacon Press, 2001).

21. David Cortright, Alistair Millar, and George A. Lopez, *Smart Sanctions: Restructuring UN Policy in Iraq* (South Bend, IN: Fourth Freedom Forum and Joan B. Kroc Institute of International Peace Studies, 2001).

22. Mohammed Abu-Nimer, *Dialogue, Conflict Resolution, and Change: Arab-Jewish Encounters in Israel* (New York: State University of New York, 1999).

23. Robert Drinan, *The Mobilization of Shame: A World View of Human Rights* (New Haven, CT: Yale University Press, 2001), 32.

24. Priscilla B. Hayner, *Unspeakable Truths: Confronting State Terror and Atrocity* (New York: Routledge, 2001).

25. Peter Ackerman and Jack Duvall, *A Force More Powerful: A Century of Nonviolent Conflict* (New York: St. Martin's Press, 2001).

26. Lisa Schirch, *Civilian Peacekeeping: Reducing Violence and Making Space for Democracy* (Uppsala, Sweden: Life and Peace Institute, 2005).

27. Liam Mahony and Luis Enrique Eguren, *Unarmed Bodyguards: International Accompaniment for the Protection of Human Rights* (Bloomfield, CT: Kumarian Press, 1997).

28. Christine Bell, "Principle versus Pragmatism," *Human Rights Dialogue* 2, no. 7 (Winter 2002): 6–8.

29. Ellen Lutz, "Troubleshooting Differences," *Human Rights Dialogue* 2, no. 7 (Winter 2002): 23–24.

30. S. J. Stedman, "Spoiler Problems in Peace Processes," in *International Conflict Resolution after the Cold War*, ed. P. Stern and D. Druckman (Washington, DC: National Academy Press, 2000).

31. Wilson, "Challenging Restorative Justice."

32. Howard Zehr, *Changing Lenses* (Scottsdale, PA: Herald Press, 1990).

33. Joan Petersilia, Susan Turner, and Joyce Peterson, *Prison versus Probation in California: Implications for Crime and Offender Recidivism* (Santa Monica, CA: RAND Corporation, 1986).

34. Gilligan, *Preventing Violence.*

35. Howard Zehr, *The Little Book of Restorative Justice* (Intercourse, PA: Good Books, 2002).

36. Zehr, *Changing Lenses.*

37. Zehr, *The Little Book of Restorative Justice.*

38. Roger Fisher and William Ury, *Getting to Yes* (New York: Penguin Books, 1991).

39. Wilson, "Challenging Restorative Justice."

40. Michelle Parlevliet, "Bridging the Divide: Exploring the Relationship between Human Rights and Conflict Management," *Track Two* 11, no. 1 (March 2002): 8–52.

41. Victoria Rader, "Human Needs and the Modernization of Poverty," *Conflict: Human Needs Theory,* ed. John Burton (New York: St. Martin's Press, 1990), 232.

42. Parlevliet, "Bridging the Divide," 28.

43. Jane Vella, *Training through Dialogue: Promoting Effective Learning and Change with Adults* (San Francisco: Jossey-Bass, 1995).

44 Julie Mertus, "The Undermining of Human Rights Culture in Kosovo," *Human Rights Dialogue* 2, no. 5 (Winter 2001): 8–9.

45. *Asian Human Rights Charter,* www.tahr.org.tw/data/ahrc/ (accessed March 22, 2002).

46. John J. Mearsheimer, "Liberal Talk, Realist Thinking," *University of Chicago* magazine, February 2002, 24–28.

47. Julie Mertus, *Bait and Switch: Human Rights and U.S. Foreign Policy* (New York: Routledge, 2004).

48. Lisa Schirch and William Goldberg, "Overview of the War on Iraq and Strategic Alternatives," Conflict Transformation Program, Eastern Mennonite University, Beyond September 11 Web site, www.emu.edu/ctp/bse-alternatives.html (accessed February 2003).

49. United Nations Development Programme, *United Nations Human Development Report* (New York: United Nations Development Programme, 1998).

50. Jeffrey Sachs, "Weapons of Mass Salvation," *Economist,* October 26, 2002, 101.

51. Falk, *Human Rights Horizons.*

# 4
# Culture, Relativism, and Human Rights

Kevin Avruch

The purpose of this chapter is to explore the many ways in which the concept of "culture" has affected our understanding of human rights, both their designation and their implementation, and in doing so expose the ways in which culture has created controversy and conflict within the field of human rights. This discussion points to one of the greatest controversies in the entire human rights field: the extent to which human rights are "universal" and transcultural, operating above parochial understandings, or are instead "relative" to culture—determined, and thus limited, by local cultural contexts that differ from society to society. The view of human rights as imperialistic and particular only to Western culture limits the utility of human rights in peacebuilding endeavors. Thus, the inquiry here is crucial to the entire undertaking of this book.

How should we understand universal and relative claims with respect to human rights? To answer this question we shall need to "unpack" different conceptions of culture, of universalism and relativism, and of human rights, including what it means to be "human." It is impossible in a work of this length to adequately sample all the world's cultures and discuss their conceptions of human rights in any detail. My aim, rather, is to show how the concept of culture has informed (and occasionally deformed) our approach to human rights, and to suggest ways to sharpen our understanding of the concept so that it can be used to make our discussion of human rights—and, beyond discussion, their implementation—more productive.

## In the Beginning: UN Philosophers, Human Rights, and Culture, 1947

Specialists in the study of culture, anthropologists, or others whose research or practice takes them to "exotic," non-Western places, especially those who work in the area of aid and development, often complain that culture is never taken seriously enough by the economists, agronomists, engineers, or planners, working for the World Bank or similar international institutions, who design and implement vast programs of social change for "others." A similar complaint is often heard when cultural specialists come into fleeting contact with the U.S. foreign policy establishment, for instance the State Department, in Washington. But in the area of human rights this was not always so.

At the very beginning of the human rights endeavor, in June 1947, while a newly formed United Nations committee was preparing first drafts of what would, in December 1948, become the Universal Declaration of Human Rights, a so-called philosophers' committee formed by UNESCO was busy analyzing the results of a questionnaire "asking for reflections on human rights from Chinese, Islamic, Hindu, and customary law perspectives, as well as from American, European, and socialist points of view."[1] More than seventy people responded, broadly corroborating the existence of human rights in their own cultural traditions, though many acknowledged the idea as being fairly recent and European in its articulation. Still, a few crucial reservations were noted at the time. Some Asian respondents, for example, including Mohandas Gandhi, emphasized that "duties" as well as "rights" mattered in their own traditions and should be featured strongly in whatever document was to emerge.

The work of the philosophers' committee was not without its flaws. Certainly it sampled only the elites of those various cultures, many of whom had been extensively educated in the West, and the fact remains that of the original fifty-one member states of the United Nations, only three were from Africa and eight from Asia. Today the work of the philosophers' committee has been, if not forgotten, certainly repudiated by some who argue that for these and other reasons the Universal Declaration of Human Rights— and the entire idea of human rights—is culturally bound by and limited to the West. Still, it is important to mention the work of the committee to show that unlike in the areas of aid, development, or the foreign policy world of *machtpolitik*, "culture" has been a concern for human rights thinkers from the very beginning of international efforts to articulate it. Meanwhile, human rights and their attendant complexities, in one form or another, can be discerned in history long before any efforts to articulate them.

## In the Kond Hills, India

Sometime in the 1830s in India, the British, still operating in the guise of the East India Company, pushed farther into what would become the Raj and learned of certain tribes in the Kond hills (in what is today the state of Orissa) who practiced human sacrifice meriah and female infanticide. "They were outraged," F. G. Bailey tells us, "at this affront to natural justice."[2] Despite the difficult terrain, the resistance of the tribes, and the depredations of endemic cerebral malaria, the company found itself embroiled for the next two decades in what became known as the Meriah Wars, aimed, normatively at least, at eradicating these unnatural practices while bringing the entire area under "civil" administration. One of the company's officers, a certain Captain Macpherson, thought that this was best accomplished through a sort of diplomacy, specifically by making the British into the de facto third party in mediating the many feuds and disputes that occurred among clans of the tribes, thus winning trust, gratitude, and influence among tribal leaders. He was replaced by General Campbell, Bailey writes, whose "method of bringing civilization was to hang the aged and infirm, who could not run fast enough, and to burn the crops and houses."[3]

Even though an articulated notion of "human rights" was undoubtedly missing from Macpherson's and Campbell's vocabulary, in this fragment of imperial history can be found most, if not quite all, of the themes relevant for a discussion of culture and human rights. First, one encounters the powerful notion of "natural justice," more commonly framed as "natural law," which the British invoked to judge human sacrifice and female infanticide wholly immoral and absolutely unacceptable—no further explanations are needed. Second, there is the idea that natural law provided for the British a *warrant* to act, specifically, to invade the hills and force the tribesmen to halt the practices. (And let us recall that the British action was costly for them, not to mention for the "objects" of their action, and took almost twenty years to accomplish.) Third, there was the tribal resistance to British action, which occurred at least in part, Bailey tells us elsewhere, because such practices and rituals were bound up with tribal beliefs and cosmology and with the maintenance of their material well-being. Fourth, there was not, at least initially, a single or monolithic British plan for action. Neither "British imperial culture" nor, more narrowly, East India Company "corporate culture" specified a clear script or scheme. In fact, the two options were more or less contradictory. Macpherson tried persuasion; Campbell relied on force. (Of course, force prevailed in the end: *sic semper imperium.*)

Finally, there is an unsettling moral paradox buried not all that deeply in this story. The British acted on their understanding of an absolute morality and natural law, whereby human sacrifice and female infanticide were unconditionally wrong and ought to bear a universal opprobrium. How could one be "relativistic" in judging such matters? And yet, at the very heart of one response aimed at eradicating these "affronts to natural justice"—Campbell's—the actions of the British made their own morality seem "relative" in the extreme: It depended on hanging noncombatants and burning crops and houses.

Ethicists, or moral philosophers, sometimes explain this phenomenon by making the distinction between a "consequentialist" ethics, whereby good or moral ends can justify the morally questionable means by which they are achieved, and a rather more restrictive "deontological" ethics, wherein ends, no matter how good or moral in themselves, can never justify immoral means. For the purposes of this chapter, however, the lesson is different: It is that universalism and absolutism can never entirely escape the complexities of relativism in the real world where men and women act, in part because judgments—assertions—of universalism and absolutism are, in the end, at least for someone somewhere, inevitably relative.

Clearly we need to unpack further the notions of universalism and relativism. But first we have to get a better sense of what is meant by "culture," in all its different senses.

## Culture as an Analytical and Political Concept

The first problem in defining culture is choosing which definition, among the literally hundreds that are available, to embrace. Culture is a concept that comes to us from the nineteenth century with several different senses (some of them mutually antagonistic) and a lot of political baggage.[4] One of the things that all contemporary social science definitions have in common is that for none of them is culture connected primarily to "high" art, refinement, or "taste." Indeed, this sense of culture is one of those nineteenth-century definitions (from Matthew Arnold, for instance) that confounds our colloquial usage today and carries political connotations (as it did in Arnold's time). For no anthropologist, certainly, is "culture" something possessed only by the educated and upper classes. Everyone has culture. In fact, everyone has potentially several cultures—this is one reason why using the concept can get so complicated.

At a minimum and very generally, culture is something that is widely shared by individuals in a society: "The socially learned ways of living found in human societies."[5] One can think of it in utilitarian or functionalist terms: "the socially inherited solutions to life's problems."[6] One can focus on the form culture takes: the "historically transmitted pattern of meanings, embodied in symbols . . . by means of which men communicate, perpetuate, and develop their knowledge about and attitudes toward life."[7] Notice that all three definitions stress the idea that culture is learned and passed down ("reproduced") in the context of social groups. Beyond this agreement, however, many questions can be and have been raised. For example, is culture *only* learned? Is no part of it innate? Are individuals merely passive recipients of cultural legacy—that which is passed down to them—or can they actively create new cultural understandings? Does culture refer *only* to how people symbolize or think about the world, or must it refer also to how people actually behave? How widely shared are cultural understandings, in any event? Referring to D'Andrade's definition, are solutions provided by culture for solving life's problems always the best possible ones? This question has particular resonance for human rights concerns, for if solutions differ from society to society, can we, or ought we, judge some of them better than others? And can it be that culture sometimes creates new problems in the course of presenting solutions to old ones? If so, how can such new problems be dealt with by the same culture that gave rise to them? (Here, certainly, we must return to the question, above, of individual creativity or agency.)

As theorists frame and answer these and other questions, they articulate more complex and comprehensive theories of culture than the ones offered in the simple definitions above. My own preference is for symbolic or cognitivist understandings of the idea: that culture provides for individuals cognitive and affective (emotional) frameworks, embodied in such representations as symbols, metaphors, schemas, or images, with which individuals perceive, interpret, and then act in, their social worlds. A good portion of these frameworks have to do with interpreting the behavior and motives of others, both those socially nearby and those more distant. Other parts are concerned with framing existential aspects of one's world. These include the nature of social conflict (What sorts of things are objects of dispute or in short supply: honor here, purity there, capital and profit somewhere else?) and how to manage it, concepts of rights and duties owed oneself and others, of dignity, concepts of right and wrong, of sin and its opposite, of liability.

Most contemporary understandings of culture, whatever their other theoretical differences may be, include the following characteristics:

- Cultures do not possess "agency to act"; individuals do.
- Cultures are not things ("nouns") but analytical categories.
- Individuals "carry" multiple cultures simultaneously, including ones rooted in religious, ethnic, racial, or national affiliations; gender; class; and occupation or profession.
- Individuals acquire their cultures as part of group membership *and* the experience of ongoing social life; specific cultures are neither

deep coded in the genome nor eternally inscribed in "the blood" or a mystical *Volksgeist*, the "spirit of a people" (more on this below).

- Cultures are "reproduced"—passed down to individuals—and in this sense one can speak of the force of "tradition"; but cultures (as acquired by individuals who can also act with *agency*) are also shaped, emergent, and responsive to environmental (social and physical) exigencies.

- Cultures are not monolithic, integrated, timeless, and stable wholes but are often fragmented, contestable, and contested.

- Cultures do not cause conflict; they are, however, "the lenses through which the causes of conflict are refracted"—and none the less crucial for that.[8]

In all of the ideas of culture noted above there is a sense that culture is an analytical, or "technical," term in the social sciences, and moreover, there has always been an intention on the part of anthropologists, sociologists, and political scientists to treat it this way. Indeed, this is one reason why theoretical arguments about culture have continued apace and why newer conceptions replace older ones. But I noted earlier that culture comes to us from the nineteenth century with a number of different meanings, only one of them developed by anthropology. Some of these other meanings reflect intense nineteenth-century conflicts of ideology around issues of group identity and social class—conflicts that are with us still. Already mentioned was the sense of culture advocated by Matthew Arnold or, later, by T. S. Eliot. Here, culture is the possession of an enlightened few, "the best which has been thought and said in the world."[9] It is a conservative and elitist concept, protective of English class divisions. More encompassing (and ultimately more dangerous) was the sense of culture developed by the German thinker Johann von Herder and his followers in the Romantic tradition. Here, culture refers to the unique (and eternal) spirit, ethos, or genius of "*a* people." In its time it was a counterrevolutionary idea, ranged against the revolution in thought and politics brought on by the French Enlightenment. More specifically, culture here supported an argument against the entire universalizing thrust of the Enlightenment, and in support of group—ethnic and nationalist—particularism, often expressed, as Michael Ignatieff put it, in the idiom of "blood and belonging."[10] Here, culture is very close to notions of race. And in the Romantic tradition, in literature, music, art, and politics, the word took on tremendous feelings of emotion, passion, and group pride. It was in no way an analytical, technical term, subject to discussion or debate. Certainly if, say, a Richard Wagner were to speak of "German culture," it is unlikely that he would have the contrast between high-context and low-context communicational styles in mind.

In fact, absent the passion and chauvinism, the Romantic's idea of culture was essentially the same as the early, inadequate ideas favored by many social scientists that used the term through the mid-twentieth century. The reason for this is that both meanings arose in the same German cultural matrix, though they eventually took on different characters. (The key figure for anthropology here is Franz Boas, educated in Germany, who emigrated to the United States and was central in establishing the study of culture as a scientific discipline in America from the early 1900s on.) In both understandings of the term, culture is presumed to be stable (resistant, at its core, to time and change), coherent, homogenous, and customary. It is *essentialized*. Possessing the force of custom (tradition), it determines (or, speaking politically, it *ought* to determine) virtually all the behavior of all individuals who carry it. It is *totalizing*. And in both senses, finally, culture points not to a universal identity for all people, but rather to uniqueness, to *difference,* and to particularisms of one sort or another, spiritual or racial (in Herder's world), or environmental or historical (in Boas's).

## Cultural Analysis and Culturalism

This last point underlines the important ways in which the two senses of culture, despite their similar intellectual history, diverged. First, as befitting a scientific term, Boas and his followers drained the affect, the Sturm und Drang, from the idea, and sought to make it analytical. We can't quite say, however, that Boas did away equally with all of its political content; but he did try to redirect it. Crucially, he decoupled "culture" from "race" and, he hoped, from mystical ideas of "blood." Membership in cultural groups (as in language communities) became contingencies, accidents of birth. Finally, although stressing the uniqueness of cultures with respect to one another, he sought to disentangle the whole notion of cultural difference from ideas of inferiority and superiority, from chauvinism or racism. Here, then, is the key difference between Boas and the Romantics. Both were reacting against universalism and in favor of some form of particularism, but they were not reacting against the same universalisms. For the Romantics, it was the universalism of the Enlightenment, embodied in the French Revolution and the Declaration of the Rights of Man and Citizen (1789), promising a new world of universal citizenship, equality, fraternity, and liberty. The Romantic counterthrust was for a world divided into cultural Self and Others, separated by language, custom, and eternal *geist,* or spirit. Boas, in contrast, was reacting to the nineteenth-century universalism of social evolutionists like Herbert Spencer and Sir James Frazier, who saw all of humankind ranged on a single evolutionary "ladder" from savagery, through barbarism, to civilization (that is, the Church of England, Oxbridge-educated English gentleman). Against this evolutionist's universalism, characterized by ideas of primitive and civilized, inferior and superior, Boas proposed a world composed of equally genuine and valid, but different, human cultures.

For the Romantics and their intellectual and political heirs, culture is part of a larger ideology we call "culturalism," that is, the use of culture to underwrite or legitimize ethnic, racial, or national differences—and their political consequences. For Boas (without denying his own liberal and antiracist political agenda) and the many anthropologists he trained, "culture" was first an analytical term, part of a larger project, aimed at the scientific understanding of difference, called "cultural analysis." As we saw in the preceding section, newer, less organic conceptions of culture have largely replaced the older ones proposed by Boas and other anthropologists; the latter are now seen as inadequate. Moreover, these newer understandings of the term have moved it even farther away from its "culturalist" roots, and in this manner cultural analysis has become even more critical of culturalism.

Once again, these distinctions are, for the human rights movement, more than academic. The Romantic sense of culture, "culturalism," opposing one form of universalism, has underwritten nationalism, both benign and malignant, as well as the ideology of ethnicity and, more recently and as a direct result of the human rights movement, "indigenism" or indigenous rights (see below). The Boasian sense, opposing another form of universalism entirely (but never the promise of the Enlightenment!), gave us "cultural analysis." But it came also to underwrite something called "relativism," a concept that has featured prominently in the debate on culture and human rights.

## Relativism and Universalism

Few ideas thrown up by the social sciences have generated as much controversy as that of "cultural relativism." In America it has become a dependable anathema for conservatives, many of them inheritors of Matthew Arnold's sense of culture, but battling now in a political world where "multiculturalism" denies from the outset a single standard for judging "the best which has been thought and said." For liberal supporters of human rights the same idea is viewed as a screen cynically or hypocritically held up by tyrants who abuse their people, to shield themselves from the disapprobation of the international community.

The idea of relativism became part of contemporary discussions of culture with the work of Franz Boas, but it was Boas's student, Melville Herskovits, who wrote most explicitly on it:

> Cultural relativism is in essence an approach to the question of the nature and role of values in culture. . . . [Its] principle . . . is as follows: Judgments are based on experience, and experience is interpreted by each individual in terms of his own enculturation.[11]

Herskovits's definition was influential in that it took the meaning of relativism directly to the level of values and judgments about it, rooting it in the life experience of individuals (which varies from culture to culture) and questioning the existence of any "absolute moral standards" that are separate from their cultural (and historical) context. Indeed, it is this meaning of relativism, opposed to the possibility of an absolute morality, that has been invoked in debates about the universality of human rights.

Some more recent discussions of relativism have pointed to three different senses of the term.[12] The first sense may be called "descriptive relativism," referring to the empirical fact of cultural variability in customs, beliefs, values, and so on. The *existence* of such variability is literally undeniable, part of what anthropologists call "the ethnographic record" (and what can also be called "the historical record"). Consider as an example food taboos or proscriptions. Hindus believe beef to be unclean; Muslims and Orthodox Jews, pork. Consider ideas about the afterlife: Christians, Muslims, and Jews believe in a single life to be lived; Buddhists and Hindus, in a round of rebirths and reincarnation.

The *fact* of cultural variability, of difference, may seem self-evident, but it is not, for our first impulse is often to see everyone else, as Clifford Geertz once put it, as "less well got up editions of ourselves."[13] Descriptive relativism is the acknowledgment of differences rooted in culture or, as Herskovits wrote, in the process by which individuals acquire their culture, "enculturation." For those who seek to learn about other cultures, descriptive relativism is also indispensable as a methodological guide. How can one hope to learn about or understand another culture if one does not, as a first principle, open oneself up to the possibilities of difference? One must be prepared to set aside ingrained ideas of what is appropriate, good, or true "back home." As a methodological principle, descriptive relativism calls "for the suspension of judgments in the service of understanding."[14]

The second sort of relativism is that propounded by Herskovits, called variously moral, ethical, or normative relativism. In its "weak" form it is merely the extension of descriptive relativism to the area of values, morals, or ethics: the recognition that moral systems may vary with culture. But the notion, especially when subjected to excoriation, is never understood in its weak form. Instead, the "strong" form of moral relativism is taken to mean the recognition of difference combined with a requirement to *tolerate* or even *approve of* such difference. Alternatively, one can say that the strong form of moral relativism carries with it a proscription against criticizing (or interfering with) a moral system different from one's own. In other words, in its strong form relativism gets linked to tolerance, and—in an even more stringent extension—tolerance forbids action or critique (aimed at changing the other moral system). It is precisely the ban against action or critique that has led some critics of relativism to accuse it of leading to "moral nihilism." And as far as human rights are concerned, it is the presumed ban against action or critique that is invoked by some who have denied the legitimacy of human rights instruments or regimes that have, so they argue, originated "in the West."

It is certainly the case that Boas and some of his followers linked the value of tolerance to the doctrine of relativism. For Boas, at the end of the nineteenth century and the first part of the twentieth, it was clearly part and parcel of his own politics, a move to counter the sometimes lethal intolerance espoused by racists and anti-Semites—Boas actively spoke and worked against lynchings in the southern United States—or the gathering clouds (throughout the 1930s) of fascism and Nazism in Europe.[15] But if we think even for a moment about the political roots of Boas's linkage of relativism to tolerance, we see that what drives it, far from moral nihilism, is a profound moral commitment to action and critique. This is one of the several paradoxes or contradictions at the heart of this understanding of relativism, namely, that demanding unconditional tolerance implies an absolute intolerance toward the intolerant. Furthermore, insofar as one recommends the *value* of tolerance in a world where all values are culturally relative, then one has to admit to the possibility of cultures wherein forms of intolerance are valued that then are (given moral relativism), of course, beyond critique or reformatory action. Finally, as the philosopher David Bidney noted long ago, by transmuting the fact of cultural difference (descriptive relativism) into the necessity for ("strong") moral relativism, relativists commit the "positivistic fallacy," deriving an "ought" from an "is."[16]

Before moving to consider the effects of these paradoxes or internal contradictions on the argument of relativism and human rights, I want to mention briefly the third form of relativism, called by Spiro "epistemological relativism."[17] In some ways it is, philosophically speaking, the strongest form that assertions about relativism can take. It holds that enculturation determines all reality. In its extreme form, epistemological relativism denies the existence of the "really real," an absolute reality over and above all the variant cultural constructions of it.[18] In the context of human rights I summarily dismiss the extreme form, wherein the "really real" ceases to exist, by pointing to the experience of thousands of human rights workers in the field: Examining and documenting the effects of fire, acid, truncheons, or electricity on the human body, every body, everywhere, they confront reality and make the denial of the "really real" existentially and morally quite simply insupportable.

The key is to keep in mind what moral relativism really does teach us: that values, morals, norms, and ethical standards do in fact differ from culture to culture, and that the differences may be significant. The doctrine of moral relativism cautions us to be aware that our own values and ethical standards are not necessarily universal or absolute. In this way it is a defense against moral tunnel vision or ethnocentric ignorance. But in no way does moral or ethical relativism necessarily commit us to avoid judging or tolerating all other ethical systems. What it does, quite explicitly, is to force us to focus attention on the nature of our own ethical or moral system—to be less smug about it, or, more positively, to make us articulate clearly the grounds for our "intolerance" toward others' practices, as well as the grounds for any possible interference in them.

The doctrine of moral relativism argues against moral universals or absolutes, perhaps even against a universal "human nature." But it holds no brief against political action or judgments of the "superiority" of our own morality. It is not the case, to twist around the French aphorism, that to understand all is to forgive everything. Such comprehensive understanding may lead us to the very opposite of forgiveness. The implications for human rights *activism* should be clear. Here is the philosopher Richard Rorty, a self-proclaimed relativist, on the reason why human rights advocates feel that they must reject moral relativism:

> [S]uch relativism seems to them incompatible with the fact that our human rights culture, the culture with which we in this democracy identify ourselves, is morally superior to other cultures. *I quite agree that ours is morally superior,* but I do not think this superiority counts in favor of the existence of a universal human nature. (Emphasis added)[19]

Rorty, the relativist, freely admits to his own judgment valuing democracy and human rights as "morally superior." What he denies is that he requires a transcultural, or metaphysical, doctrine of universal human nature to do so. Why do advocates of human rights seem to need such a *warrant* in order to justify themselves? Notice that we have moved from making relativism the problem for human rights to making universals problematic. We need to unpack the idea of universals and then return to the question of why their existence seems so crucial to theorists and activists seeking to advance the cause of human rights throughout the world.

## The Problem of Universals

If, in anthropology, the social science most enduringly concerned with understanding culture, the idea of cultural relativism had such supporters as Boas, Herskovits, and Ruth Benedict, it is also the case that there were, early on, severe critics of the idea and distinguished proponents of its seeming opposite: cultural universals. Clark Wissler, George P. Murdock, and Clyde Kluckhohn, to name three, all argued for the existence of traits, complexes, or patterns of behavior present (depending on the theorist) in all individuals, all societies, all cultures, or all languages—"provided that the trait or complex is not obviously anatomical or too remote from the higher mental functions."[20] Today the presumption of human universals, transcending cultural variation, strongly characterizes such academic fields as evolutionary psychology and Chomskyan linguistics. For many advocates of human rights, the existence of such universals is also presumed to be important for the establishment of a transculturally legitimate and effective human rights regime. But linguists, psychologists, and human rights advocates are not always talking about the same sort of "universals."

The search for human universals typically begins in the evolutionarily derived, psychobiologically composed set of human characteristics that laymen (or philosophers) call "human nature." These are somehow innate or intrinsic, and thus "precultural." They constitute the constants against (or within) which cultural variability takes place. It is not difficult—for me, at least—to agree that there exists some sort of psychobiological human nature under which all humankind is united. But this leaves most of the interesting or vexing questions about humankind (and almost all those that have to do with human rights) still unanswered. For example: Are these psychobiologically innate universals the only sort there are, or even the most important ones? How is invariant human nature modified by culture—can one, in fact, ever imagine a "complete," a functioning, social individual who is unmodified by culture (who lacks "enculturation," in Herskovits's words)? Why do we think that universals are so much more important in determining social life than culturally derived traits, complexes, or patterns? How can we get from the assertion of universals based on cognitive structures or neural architecture, which may well underlie linguistic functioning and a "universal grammar," to an assertion concerning a universal morality? And finally, what exactly do we *know* if we can assert the existence of such universals as, say, "family," "marriage," and "religion"? To declare religion as universal and then to define it as, say, humankind's "most fundamental orientation to reality," or to the "sacred," is to tell us very little about the different realities constituted and lived in by believers in Hinduism, Christianity, Islam, Aztecan, or traditional African religious systems.[21] Like the devil, the sacred is in the details, and it is in those details (not in abstractions or "least common denominators") that individuals live their lives and make sense of their worlds. We *speak* English, Arabic, Hopi, or Bantu—all, as they say, "mutually unintelligible"—*not* a universal grammar.

Some of these questions can be approached by first making a distinction between human universals and what some have called human "absolutes." Following Herskovits, absolutes (such as those derived from evolutionary human nature) are fixed and invariant, changeless from individual to individual, culture to culture, epoch to epoch. Universals "are those least common denominators to be extracted from the range of variation that all phenomena of the natural or cultural world manifest."[22] Leaving aside the notion of least common denominators for the moment, this distinction opens up a range of so-called universals that are in fact experientially, culturally, or historically variable and contingent. One can argue, for example, that because of shared human experience with the sight of blood, the color red is nearly universally taken as a sign of danger. Or that because of the universally shared experience of growing up in some sort of family, certain behavioral dynamics emergent from family life will be nearly universally shared. (This begs the question of the considerable variation in types of "families" found cross-culturally.) One can also argue that capitalism is today virtually universal in its scope and its ability to affect the lives of people in all societies in the world. Yet one may trace capitalism's development (from within "the West") historically, from the late sixteenth century onward—one can see it, that is, as an emergent and contingent universal. It is certainly a stretch to assert that capitalism is somehow encoded in the human genome or locatable in particular ganglia in the cerebral cortex.

Much like the idea of relativism discussed earlier, universalism, which appears at first glance to be a straightforward and monolithic concept rooted in something called "human nature," fractures into different types under closer examination. The most important fracture is that between the idea of invariant and fixed absolutes and other sorts of universals that are potentially emergent and contingent. In their own way such universals are also "relative" in the sense, for instance, that capitalism is relative to specific historical epochs and societies, *even as it undergoes movement toward "universalization."* The contingent ("relative") nature of such universals is what renders less supportable the usual, dichotomous conception of cultural universals and relativity as being unalterably mutually opposed. It also has important implications for the understanding of human rights—both their designation and implementation—considered cross-culturally.

## How to Understand Human Rights

In distinguishing universals from absolutes, Herskovits wrote of the need to search for "least common denominators," mostly constituted by human nature, which form the shared core or essence of all cultures everywhere. In fact, the search for such undergirding human commonalities in the area of morality has deeply influenced much writing, especially theorizing, on human rights and culture. In the main, these common denominators have been simply asserted, for instance in Kant's categorical imperatives or Rawls's "veil of ignorance" (the idea that when all culture and social identity is removed from individuals, a primordial conception of justice will emerge).[23]

In the social sciences some have tried empirically to ascertain, or "count," these least common denominators. A. D. Renteln's work is most germane to human rights.[24] After empirical investigation of the ethnographic record, she discovered one moral principle common (she says) to all societies: "retribution tied to proportionality," the *lex talionis*, or "eye for an eye," of the Old Testament. (Surely this principle can be as troublesome for advancing human rights as it is productive, for what constitutes "proportional"?) Consider the principle in terms of Article 5 of the Universal Declaration: "No one shall be subjected to torture or to cruel, inhuman or degrading treatment or punishment." What constitutes cruel, inhuman, or degrading punishment? And how do we tell the difference between them in a world where it is widely held by some that amputation is proportional to theft, and by others that persons defined by the United Nations as "children" may be put to death by the state for certain crimes? As for counting them at all, the anthropologist Donald Brown (a proponent of the existence of human universals) cautions:

> The first and most obvious point about the demonstration of universals is that it is never done by exhaustive enumeration, showing that a phenomenon exists and existed in each known individual, society, culture, or language. There are too many known people to make this feasible, and there are too many shortcomings in the descriptions of "known" peoples.

Thus all statements of universality are hypotheses or arguments based on various kinds of evidence.[25]

Given one empiricism that leaves us with *lex talionis* as a basis for human rights, and another that reduces all universals to research hypotheses, it is not surprising that those universals of the first sort, where a priori assertions are made about what, minimally speaking, universal human rights *must* be, have been far more influential than empirical investigations of human rights cross-culturally. Perhaps the best way to understand how such a priori assertions do their work is to consider two or three possible and different verbs that can be used to talk about how we "come to" and designate human rights.

If we believe that human rights (or some essential subset of them) are intrinsic to humans—just *there*, as "the rights that one has simply because one is a human being"[26]—then we might wish to explain why their formal articulation has occurred so late in human history and, arguably, originated in a particular human culture or civilization: the "West." On the assumption that human rights antedated their articulation, then the right verb to use is something on the order of "discovered," or, in the analogy of minerals or gems buried in the earth but awaiting the miners, "excavated" or "uncovered." In this case the question "Why so long?" is answerable by saying, "We were looking in the wrong place," or "We had to wait for a mining technology to develop to the point where we were able to excavate."

It is the second reason that some human rights advocates turn to when they invoke some variant of the "natural law" explanation for the existence of human rights (they were always there, waiting to be discovered and articulated) and combine it implicitly with an argument not for technological but for moral "advancement," "progress," or "development," or the "march of civilization through history" (from savagery to civilization), in order to explain why it is hard to find human rights expressed in the time of Attila the Hun but not so in that of Thomas Jefferson. But the first response (we'd been looking in the wrong place for a long time) has its advocates as well. Here, the verb of choice for finding the right place and uncovering that which was already there is closer to "revealed" than "excavated." And such revelations, about human rights, duties, dignity, and much more, are often brought by some special agent acting prophetically on behalf of a higher authority. The revelations, that is, come part and parcel with some local version of that human universal, religion.

To conceive of human rights as preexistent and then "discovered" is probably to refer to natural law. To think about them as immanent and "revealed" is probably to refer to some sacred text, tradition, or theology.

The verbs (and their referents) have more in common than not. Both natural law and theology, for example, ultimately prescribe universalist arguments about the way the world is (including morality) that seek to deny the legitimacy of relativism and difference by transcending culture. (Crucially, they also usually contain warrants for action in the world.) But culture is not so much transcended in such systems of belief as it is effaced or rendered invisible. Later on, when spokespersons for some religious traditions invoke them and seek to reject human rights as being "Western," "Christian," or "individualist," culture is made visible again, though now enlisted in its culturalist guise to provide a basis for rejection.

First, the effacement. Recall the British in the Kond hills in the 1830s. Bailey tells us that it was the "affronts to natural justice" (the violation of natural law) presented by human sacrifice and female infanticide that so incensed the British and moved them to act against the tribes. Yet how can we disentangle their judgments or their subsequent actions from the cultures of mercantilism and imperialism, of "the white man's burden" and militarism, that framed two decades of muscular "pacification" in the hills (and most of the rest of India)?

An even clearer example of effacing culture can be seen in that great document of natural law (and human rights), the American Declaration of Independence. Famously, Jefferson writes, "We hold these truths to be self-evident, that all men are created equal, that they are endowed by their Creator with certain unalienable Rights, that among these are Life, Liberty, and the pursuit of Happiness." What better example of uncovering that which is preexistent than by declaring its "self-evident" nature? Yet at the time these words were written the thirteen colonies held more than half a million persons of African descent, all but about one percent of them as chattel. The "truths" may be self-evident, but the definition of "all men"— *of what it is to be fully human, in fact*—seems contingent (and culturally constituted) in the extreme.

Where natural law effaces culture, sacred texts and theology do the same. The prophet Mohammed rejects human sacrifice as abominable before God in the Koran, but slavery remains. Lord Krishna instructs Arjuna in the meaning of dignity, the righteous life, and duty (*dharma*) in the Bhagavad Gita, but caste remains (indeed, is revalorized). The universal morality in these (and all other) sacred texts and theologies seeks to efface culture and reject relativism because they are founded on the revelation of (trans-cultural) absolutes. But, as is "self-evident" from looking around the world and at much of the conflict in it, there is no universal agreement in this matter; the precise nature of the absolutes is not agreed on universally, though many theologies promise a day to come when it will be.

Until that day comes we should remember what the doctrine of moral relativism, as discussed earlier, has to teach us: that standards of ethics or morality do indeed differ from culture to culture and epoch to epoch, sometimes significantly so; and that verbs that point us toward discovering preexistent and immanent human rights, or having them revealed to us, cannot in the end erase the effects of cultural difference, or the accompanying complexity of relativity. *Your* natural law and sacred theology may not be *mine,* and the way that you go about enforcing or propagating them may in any case appear to me immoral in the extreme.

Most of the thinking (especially from jurists or other legal scholars) on human rights has concerned itself, almost obsessively, with the nature of the "rights" themselves. From the perspective of cross-cultural analysis, however, an equally vexing question is directed toward the instability of the qualifier "human." It seems foolish to spend time and effort convincing a world to accept a universal definition, or list, of rights when what is so often at stake is the prior refusal of some to grant to others their full humanity. The drafters of the American Declaration of Independence who supported slavery believed that Africans, who could be owned as movable property, were not fully human. The notions of *dharma* (duty) and *varna* (caste) in Brahminical Hinduism in the Bhagavad Gita conceive of different species of inherently unequal beings.[27] Study after study of genocide and ethnic violence points to the inevitable dehumanization of the Other as a precursor and pretext for the worst human rights violations imaginable.[28] In all these cases, we should be careful to ensure that our interlocutors can agree first on extending a common humanity to all, before we move on to designating specific rights.

Earlier I wrote that such verbs as "discovered" and "uncovered" would lead to us to think of human rights in certain ways. But other verbs are possible. The alternative to seeing human rights as preexistent or immanent is to view them as "created" or "constructed." Such verbs locate human rights within history, not transcendental to it, and as arising from within particular social and cultural contexts. Such verbs also allow for human agency in the articulation of rights, including new ones, and, crucially, in social activism aimed at their propagation.

At first glance, to see rights as situated within culture and history seems to weaken them, first by allowing for the relativists' argument that since they may not have arisen from "our" history, they do not apply to "our" culture, and second by removing the metaphysical warrants for action provided by "natural" law or sacred beliefs and values. My own belief is that these concerns are exaggerated and, moreover, are based on the inadequate conceptions of culture—and recourse to culturalism—discussed earlier. Nevertheless, such concerns have affected the way scholars and others have approached the issue of human rights cross-culturally, with a mixture of apology, defensiveness, or, in reaction, chauvinism. Thus, the great majority of "theoretical" work that focuses on human rights cross-culturally has concerned itself with the task of finding least common denominators—commonalities, analogues, or counterparts—to admittedly Western conceptions of human rights, within the world's other major religions or ethical systems. Sometimes such analogues are found to exist;[29] other times their existence is doubted.[30] Occasionally, they are proclaimed not only to exist in other traditions but to do so in even historically earlier or purer forms than in the West, as in the Islamic Declaration of Human Rights.

What these works all share is the conviction that human rights, as found in the West, must also be immanent or preexistent in other cultures for such rights to enjoy legitimacy. If this is so, then it also means that should rights not be found, relativists could argue a priori for their nonlegitimacy in those cultures. But in both cases, the conception of culture used is inadequate in the senses I discussed earlier: It assumes culture's utter coherence, homogeneity, and stability; its totalizing effects on the behavior of individuals; and its essentialized, hermetic imperviousness to environment and change. This is the culturalism of romantic nationalism, framed now as anticolonial struggle, or in defense of sovereignty, and put in the service of an anti–human rights discourse.

To see rights, rather, as created or constructed is also to see them in line with the revised conception of culture that argues for its emergence and continuing invention in social worlds characterized by political and economic contestation and human agency. It is a conception of culture that is epistemologically hostile to absolutes—and in that sense "relativistic"—*but not to potential, constructed universals*. It is a conception of culture that denies the coherent holism of any cultural tradition in favor of more open, fragmentary, and contested traditions. Finally, it is a conception of culture that holds that no one "culture" speaks with a single and uncontested voice, nor can any one individual or entity, including the state, speak in one voice on behalf of the culture. This is the lesson on human rights that we get when we move away from the writing of theorists and go into the field, with cultural analysts on the one hand and human rights workers and activists on the other.

# Human Rights in Practice and the End of "Cultural Relativism"

If one is interested, it is possible to find surveys that review human rights by region, culture, or civilization.[31] But the further one moves from these macro levels, the closer one gets to rights "on the ground"—in a particular village or ward of a city, in a particular mosque, temple, or pulpit, or from the perspective of a particular women's NGO or journalist—the more varied and polyphonic people's talk about rights becomes. This is the sense we get from two recent collections containing work on human rights from mainly local, cross-cultural perspectives.[32] At the beginning of this chapter I said that space prevented my adequately sampling the world's cultures for their "positions" on human rights. But by now it should be clear that lack of space alone is not the only reason for this. Equally important is that any culture's "position" on human rights will depend on who, exactly, is given the privilege of articulating the position (and on the resources that agent has for disseminating and impressing it). An important work of the early 1990s that sought to capture as fully as possible Arab "voices on the human rights debate" demonstrated more than anything else what a variety of voices there were to be captured, and how diverse (and sometimes contradictory) were the conceptions of human rights within a Middle Eastern, mostly Islamic context at that time.[33]

Close to the ground (where most human rights workers are, as well) one sees human rights being actively constructed in the course of localized, ongoing political action: taking testimony, writing letters, organizing marches, demonstrations, and accompaniments. Wilson has argued that human rights are created as narratives of their violation (or vindication) are told and retold, more boldly that "the category of 'human rights violation' does not exist independently of its representation in human rights reports."[34] This is where the human rights worker, often famously impatient with the work of scholars and academics on these matters, gets to turn theory into practice, thereby remaking theory. Wilson is only partly right: Human rights are not created just via narratives, or "stories," but also by way of the many institutions, associations, and organizations that local activists have put together, funded, and staffed to get the work done in whatever currency or language is "native" to the area.

Whatever its original cultural or historical provenance, the discourse on human rights has become a universal one—even if only in opposition to it. It is easy to question the sincerity of regimes or states (or the individuals who speak for them) that oppose human rights on grounds of cultural relativism. Capitalism, originating in the West, finds an amenable enough home in some Asian, Confucian cultures (like that of Singapore), while Marxism-Leninism (also of the West) found, at least for a time, a home in another (China). But what is more telling for the future of human rights in the end is the plethora of human rights activists and groups *indigenous* to these and other non-Western cultures who reject the presumption that the leaders or party spokespersons speak for *them*.

The farther we move from culturalist accounts of human rights toward empirical cultural analytical ones, the less homogenous or integrated do the particular accounts appear. The closer we get to voices in the field, the more polyvocal, contested, even contradictory the descriptions of human rights become. In fact, aside from the writings of apologists, propagandists, and theologians, there is no single representation of what human rights are in any single cultural tradition. And this is potentially a very good thing for human rights. For if moral relativism teaches us that moral systems do differ significantly one from another, and that that of the Christian, democratic West is only one among many, then there are also other lessons to be learned: that cultures are open-ended and not hermetically sealed off, that change is possible (regardless of where the impetus for change originates), and that as the global discourse on human rights gets localized, what is relative is likely to become universalized.

## Conclusions: Culturalism Once Again

In a world of human rights where paradoxes abound, I should close by noting that in the so-called third generation of human rights (the first being political and civil ones, the second social and economic), that of indigenous rights or "cultural rights," culturalism returns (as if it ever left!), but this time "on the side" of human rights. Despite the reservations of many human rights advocates who see indigenous or cultural rights as endangering the all-important focus on the individual as the locus of rights,[35] the movement for protecting and enhancing such rights has grown tremendously since the late 1960s. (The key NGOs here include the International Working Group for Indigenous Affairs, based in Scandinavia, Cultural Survival, based in the United States, and Survival International, based in the United Kingdom.) In seeking to extend human rights protection to all members of a society based on their collective cultural identity, the movement for indigenous rights embraces what some have called a "strategic essentialism" with respect to culture.[36] The closer one gets to politics "on the ground," the more complicated (and occasionally abusive to particular individuals) such essentialism can appear.[37] But it does not appear that this (pro–human rights) use of culturalism in the service of indigenous rights will go away; and in the end it is perhaps only testimony to the protean appeal of culture in all its forms.

## Selected Readings in Culture, Relativism, and Human Rights

Abdullahi Ahmed An-Naim and Francis Deng, eds., *Human Rights in Africa: Cross-Cultural Perspectives* (Washington, DC: Brookings Institution, 1990). An important collection that reviews human rights in Africa from religious perspectives (Christianity, Islam, and traditional African religions) and from cultural and political (nation-state) points of view. Includes wide-ranging surveys and more focused studies of individual societies.

Kevin Avruch, *Culture and Conflict Resolution* (Washington, DC: United States Institute of Peace Press, 1998). This work extends the discussion of culture along the lines pursued in this chapter, relating different ideas of culture to ways of understanding social conflict and attempts to manage or resolve it.

Wm. Theodore de Bary and Tu Weiming, eds., *Confucianism and Human Rights* (New York: Columbia University Press, 1998). A collection of papers focused on the fit between Confucian and what the editors call "neo-Confucian" values for transcultural human rights. Most of the papers argue in favor of such a fit.

Jane K. Cowan, Marie-Benedicte Dembour, and Richard A. Wilson, eds., *Culture and Rights: Anthropological Perspectives* (Cambridge: Cambridge University Press, 2001). A collection of articles, mainly by field anthropologists, that examines human rights issues as they look "on the ground," to local individuals most affected by them.

Jack Donnelly, *Universal Human Rights in Theory and Practice* (Ithaca, NY: Cornell University Press, 1989). A comprehensive and strongly argued case for considering human rights as unconditionally due all individuals, everywhere, simply by virtue of their being human.

Kevin Dwyer, *Arab Voices: The Human Rights Debate in the Middle East* (Berkeley: University of California Press, 1991). Dwyer, an anthropologist who directed Amnesty International's Middle East Department for six years in the late 1980s, lets a variety of Arabs from a variety of backgrounds speak at length on their views of human rights, Arab culture, and Islam (with special attention to gender issues).

Richard A. Wilson, ed., *Human Rights, Culture, and Context: Anthropological Perspectives* (London: Pluto Press, 1997). This earlier volume is a companion to the Cowan collection, above. It, too, looks closely at human rights in their most localized cultural and social settings, including examining some of the occasionally unexpected or unintended effects of their implementation.

## Notes

I thank Fran Harbour, Lois Horton, Pushpa Iyer, and Zheng Wang for help on various aspects of this chapter.

**1.** M. A. Glendon, *A World Made New: Eleanor Roosevelt and the Universal Declaration of Human Rights* (New York: Random House, 2001), 73.

**2.** F. G. Bailey, *Stratagems and Spoils: A Social Anthropology of Politics* (Boulder, CO: Westview Press, 2001), 186.

**3.** Ibid.

**4.** See Kevin Avruch, *Culture and Conflict Resolution* (Washington, DC: United States Institute of Peace Press, 1998), 5–21.

**5.** Marvin Harris, *Theories of Culture in Postmodern Times* (Walnut Creek, CA: Alta Mira Press, 1999), 19.

**6.** Roy D'Andrade, *The Development of Cognitive Anthropology* (Cambridge: Cambridge University Press, 1995), 249.

**7.** Clifford Geertz, *The Interpretation of Cultures* (New York: Basic Books, 1973), 89.

**8.** Kevin Avruch and Peter W. Black, "Conflict Resolution in Intercultural Settings: Problems and Prospects," in *Conflict Resolution Theory and Practice: Integration and Application*, ed. D. Sandole and H. van der Merwe (Manchester, UK: Manchester University Press, 1993), 131–45.

**9.** Arnold, quoted in Chris Jenks, *Culture* (London: Routledge, 1993), 21.

**10.** Michael Ignatieff, *Blood and Belonging: Journeys into the New Nationalism* (New York: Farrar, Straus and Giroux, 1994).

**11.** Melville Herskovits, *Cultural Dynamics* (New York: Knopf, 1964), 49.

**12.** For example, Elmer Hatch, *Culture and Morality: The Relativity of Values in Anthropology* (New York: Columbia University Press, 1983); Melford E. Spiro, "Cultural Relativism and the Future of Anthropology," *Cultural Anthropology* 1 (1986): 254–86; and Peter W. Black and Kevin Avruch, "Cultural Relativism, Conflict Resolution, and Social Justice," *Peace and Conflict Studies* 6, no. 1 (1999): 21–36.

**13.** Clifford Geertz, *Local Knowledge* (New York: Basic Books, 1983), 16.

**14.** Black and Avruch, "Cultural Relativism," 26.

**15.** Herbert Lewis, "The Passion of Franz Boas," *American Anthropologist* 22 (1993): 221–45.

**16.** David Bidney, "On the Concept of Culture and Some Cultural Fallacies," *American Anthropologist* 46, no. 1 (1944): 30–44. See also A. D. Renteln, *International Human Rights: Universalism versus Relativism* (Newbury Park, CA: Sage,

1990); and E. Hatch, "The Good Side of Relativism," *Journal of Anthropological Research* 53 (1997): 371–81.

17. Spiro, "Cultural Relativism and the Future of Anthropology."

18. Black and Avruch, "Cultural Relativism," 29.

19. Richard Rorty, "Human Rights, Rationality, and Sentimentality," in *On Human Rights: The Oxford Amnesty Lectures*, ed. S. Shute and S. Hurley, (New York: Basic Books, 1993), 116.

20. Donald Brown, *Human Universals* (New York: McGrawHill, 1991), 42.

21. Geertz, *The Interpretation of Cultures*, 40.

22. Cited in Renteln, *International Human Rights*, 81.

23. John Rawls, *A Theory of Justice* (Cambridge, MA: Harvard University Press, 1971).

24. Renteln, *International Human Rights*.

25. Brown, *Human Universals*, 51.

26. Jack Donnelly, *Universal Human Rights in Theory and Practice* (Ithaca, NY: Cornell University Press, 1989), 12.

27. See A. Beteille, *The Idea of Inequality and Other Essays* (Delhi: Oxford University Press, 1983), for an outsider's view. For an insider's view, see K. Ilaiah, *Why I Am Not a Hindu: A Sudra Critique of Hindutva Philosophy, Culture, and Political Economy* (Calcutta: Samya, 1996).

28. For example, see Erwin Staub, *The Roots of Evil: The Origins of Genocide and Other Group Violence* (Cambridge: Cambridge University Press, 1989).

29. See, for example, T. de Bary and T. Weiming, eds., *Confucianism and Human Rights* (New York: Columbia University Press, 1998); and M. Meijer, ed., *Dealing with Human Rights: Asian and Western Views on the Value of Human Rights* (Bloomfield, CT: Kumarian Press, 2001).

30. For example, on Islam, see B. Tibi, "The European Tradition of Human Rights and the Culture of Islam," or J. Silk, "Traditional Culture and the Prospect for Human Rights in Africa," both in *Human Rights in Africa*, ed. A. A. An-Naim and F. Deng, (Washington, DC: Brookings Institution, 1990).

31. See, for example, Renteln, *International Human Rights*, 54–56; or E. Messer, "Anthropology and Human Rights," *Annual Review of Anthropology* 22 (1993): 227–32.

32. R. A. Wilson, ed., *Human Rights, Culture, and Context: Anthropological Perspectives* (London: Pluto Press, 1997); and J. K. Cowan, M-B Dembour, and R. A. Wilson, eds., *Culture and Rights: Anthropological Perspectives* (Cambridge: Cambridge University Press, 2001).

33. Kevin Dwyer, *Arab Voices: The Human Rights Debates in the Middle East* (Berkeley: University of California Press, 1991).

34. Wilson, *Human Rights, Culture, and Context*, 134.

**35.** For example, Donnelly, *Universal Human Rights in Theory and Practice.*

**36.** D. L. Hodgson, "Comparative Perspectives on the Indigenous Rights Movement in Africa and the Americas," *American Anthropologist* 104 (2002): 1037–45.

**37.** For example, D. Stoll, "To Whom Should We Listen? Human Rights Activism in Two Guatemalan Land Disputes," in Wilson, ed., *Human Rights, Culture, and Context,* 187–216; D. Gellner, "From Group Rights to Individual Rights and Back: Nepalese Struggles over Culture and Equality," in Cowan et al., eds., *Culture and Rights,* 177–200; and C. Samson, "Rights as the Reward for Simulated Cultural Sameness: The Innu in the Canadian Cultural Context," in Cowan et al., *Culture and Rights,* 226–48.

# Culture, Relativism, and Human Rights
## Commentary

Ram Manikkalingam

Human rights (HR) activists do not like cultural relativism. The success of the HR project, both philosophically and practically, depends on its commitment to universal human rights standards, that is, standards that apply to all humans, at all times, and in all situations. Cultural relativists who are ethnocentric reject the possibility that there are common standards that apply to all cultures. Philosophically, human rights activists are committed to the belief that all humans, whatever their situation, are endowed with a bundle of inalienable rights. This bundle of rights reflects the dignity as well as the equality of all humans. Taking away some of these rights, bargaining over when they should be applied, or acquiescing in not applying human rights to some individuals or groups not only disempowers and impoverishes those groups but also detracts from our common humanity.

Human rights activists also believe that the universalism of human rights is critical to its practical success as a tool for improving people's lives (not just as a philosophy about the universal standards for improvement). When the powerless or the dispossessed realize they have human rights because these rights are for everyone, they will be empowered to resist their oppressors and struggle for better conditions and improve their lives. And when the powerful realize that human rights apply to everyone, they will be shamed by a human rights report naming them as abusers of others' human rights.[1] So for human rights to work in practice as a way for improving people's lives, both the oppressed and the oppressors must know that human rights are universal. It is this link between human rights as a strategy to improve the lives of the vulnerable and human rights as a universal philosophy that applies to everyone that leads human rights activists to balk at any attempt by the ethnocentric to question the application of the same HR standards to culturally disparate situations.

In this brief comment on Kevin Avruch's useful paper, I will examine three ethnocentric objections to the HR project and universalist HR responses to these objections. Despite the importance of the challenge that cultural difference poses to the universality of human rights, the work of most human rights activists in practice can continue as it does. The support for resisting widespread forms of human cruelty and deprivation—from torture, imprisonment, and killings to lack of food, lack of medicine, and lack of housing—cuts across cultural differences. So, practically, one might ignore this critique and simply plow ahead, as many HR activists do. Still, engaging seriously with cultural relativists can have two important results: one philosophical, the other practical. First, it reminds HR activists of human finitude—they are, after all, only a subset of humanity and can sometimes be wrong. Second, it reminds them of our common humanity—we are all in this together, so we need to listen very carefully to what the cultural relativists are saying. And listening can have two important practical consequences. Where it is not possible to reasonably reject human rights standards, sincere listening can help human rights activists understand the basis of the opposition and find ways to address sincere misunderstanding. This will help in implementing universal human rights standards. Second, where human rights activists have come to mistaken conclusions about standards, listening can help the HR community think about how to alter those standards or specify them more clearly.

This will improve the possibility of human rights being accepted and implemented as a universal project. Either way, taking cultural relativists seriously—regardless of whether human rights standards are right or wrong —can have the paradoxical result of actually strengthening the universality of HR and the likelihood of its implementation, along with the commitment to a common humanity that is fundamental to its political success.

## 1. The First Ethnocentric Objection to Human Rights: "This Is How We Do Things around Here."

The first and most straightforward cultural relativist objection to the universality of human rights is that each community sets its own standards and that my community should be able to set its own. This objection is seen as adequate for two reasons. First, cultural relativists argue that human rights are culturally specific—developed and pushed by a subset of people and cultures (usually Western) onto others. They do not deny that some standards are common, only that the commonality is accidental, that is, that there is no deep truth about the shared values of humanity underlying the fact that some standards may be the same. The cultural relativists' key objection is that where central elements of a group's life come into conflict with other people's standards, the group has a right to pursue these elements. Where other people's standards are presented as universal, this is seen as simply reflecting a sincere ignorance of how a group actually lives, or as an invidious form of domination. By saying that your definition of rights is universal, so the argument goes, you impose your standards on me in order to dominate me.

Human rights activists rightly reject this cultural relativist objection, for two reasons. First, they deny the absence of a common humanity that is implied, if not stated, in the cultural relativist's view that "this is how we do things around here." HR activists do not consider this an adequate response to HR claims of universalism. It begs the question "So *why* do you do things like that around here?" which, in the HR activist's view, can lead to universal standards. But for the cultural relativist, "This is how we do things around here" is the conclusion of the conversation. It contains both the reasons and the conclusion: "We are different; that's why we do things differently."

But the unwillingness of the cultural relativist to enter into a conversation about the implications of our common humanity is not all that troubles the HR activist. If that were the case, it would at most be a philosophical distinction. Rather, what troubles the HR activist—particularly one who has covered genocide, ethnic cleansing, and racial discrimination—is that this unwillingness to treat members of other cultural groups as you would your own has been responsible for some of the nastiest forms of human cruelty and indifference. If indeed the standards we apply to our own are different from those we apply to others (and there is no reason for this other than the happenstance that they are our own), then there is nothing to stop us from disregarding others in ways that we would not disregard our own. So HR activists see this claim, at worst, as a blatant attempt by the dominant to retain their power, and, at best, as willful ignorance about human possibility.

Having rejected rightly the ethnocentrism of the powerful—those who can use their power to abuse others and who want to do so—HR activists then go on to lecture to the powerless or to the sincere who resort to ethnocentrism.[2] Against the ethnocentric view, they argue that cultures are internally diverse. This suggests that there will always be some member of a particular culture who will share the position of the HR activist rather than that of the representatives of the culture. And even when there may not be such diversity, the HR activist illustrates how the boundaries between cultures are blurred. It is hard to say where one culture begins and another ends, given the intermingling of cultures. To the HR activist, these facts about culture demonstrate an important political reality: that cultures are flexible and fluid, not fixed. Practically, HR activists point to cases where other cultures subsequently adopted practices that they initially considered alien; therefore, the HR activists confidently conclude that human rights standards are universal and that the ethnocentric critics who reject this out of ignorance (as opposed to those who do so out of a desire to hang on to privilege and power) just have not figured this out, although, with time, they will.

The self-righteous tone of HR activists' refusal to listen to, let alone respect, the argument "This is how we do things around here" may turn off many who sympathize with the HR community. But this self-righteousness does have a basis in historical reality. Some of the most egregious forms of human cruelty to other humans, such as genocide, ethnic cleansing, and discrimination, have stemmed from the refusal to treat others as we would our own. So HR activists are confident that insisting that we do, and finding the common standards that will enable us to, will, on the whole, improve the condition of humans everywhere.

## 2. The Second Ethnocentric Objection to Human Rights: "You Do Not Know Everything."

The second ethnocentric objection is that setting and implementing human rights standards is a politically charged task with no clear consensus, even within the HR community, on what these standards are. In short, HR is no less a political and historical invention than culture is. This objection stems from a claim about the limitations of human knowledge. It turns around the HR critique of culture as something flexible and fluid. While the HR activist may respond that upholding universal standards that apply to everyone will provide greater protection than not doing so, she is still vulnerable to the second ethnocentric objection about human finitude.

The strategy of this ethnocentric objection is to show how human rights standards and their applicability are open to interpretation and debate even among human rights activists, who share the premise of universal human rights standards. When human rights standards are applied to particular situations, people disagree. The very fact that we need courts, both international and domestic, to adjudicate between competing interpretations of HR is one indication of this. Consider the Universal Declaration of Human Rights (UDHR), widely considered the most fundamental international human rights document. This ethnocentric objection argues that the UDHR may have many desirable features and may even be the most universal rights document in existence, but that still, it was created and presented at a particular moment in history. It is easy to imagine a very different set of standards being enumerated by a different group of people with equal commitment to universal human rights. And the UDHR is just one particular manifestation of universal HR. To treat HR as if it were immutable and timeless is wrong. HR will change with time, and it may change with place. In short, at any particular moment HR activists cannot claim to have gotten human rights standards right; HR activists do not know everything.

This ethnocentric objection is not easy for the HR activists to refute without becoming fundamentalists, because to reject this criticism is to reject human finitude.[3] Sensible human rights activists cannot reject human finitude; that is to say, we are all ethnocentric in philosophical terms. Communities contribute to forming our ideals and our values, and how we analyze situations is often derived from our social experience.[4] But for HR activists, this fact does not refute either the desirability or the possibility of universally acceptable human rights standards. In fact, for HR activists it is precisely because we are all ethnocentric, in one way or another, that we need universal standards. We all live in this world and come across each other, and sometimes come up against each other. When we do, we may have differences that need to be resolved. One way of doing this is simply to assert our power, and our standards, over each other. But this can exacerbate rather than attenuate the possibility that our differences will lead to conflict. We need some transcultural standards to enable us to live more or less peaceably, if not peacefully, in this world. To the extent that many cultures will come across one another in the world—often simultaneously—common standards that cut across all these cultures will become important to our survival. And for us to adhere to these standards, we will need to relate to them, appreciate their importance, and commit to upholding them, that is, make them ours.

So for HR activists the case of universal standards is independent of the human capacity for knowledge. HR activists respond that they can simultaneously concede that they do not know everything while arguing that they need universal standards to enable them to live with others as equals in a common human society. In fact, it is precisely because they do not know everything that they will need these universal standards that are shared by all. Still, this HR response to the second ethnocentric objection concedes what the first response does not: the potential fluidity of HR standards, and therefore their potential fallibility. Unlike the first HR response to ethnocentrism, this one cannot be self-righteous.

## 3. The Third Ethnocentric Objection to Human Rights: "Treating Me as You Would Your Own Can Be Unfair."

HR standards are set by the more dominant—the richer, more powerful, or more articulate—who are likely to have a greater influence over these standards than are the oppressed. This is especially true at the international level. For small, relatively weak groups to have a political impact on international human rights standards is hard at best and impossible at worst. So universal standards and campaigns may be drawn up that inadequately consider the concerns of the very groups they apply to. This may lead to standards that are inappropriate for particular circumstances, however thoughtful or well intentioned they may be. Compelling adherence to these standards can disrupt the lives of people living in vulnerable communities. The sense that HR standards disrupt lives can also be shared by weaker subgroups such as women within a community, who may be the purported beneficiaries of these universal standards. If indeed groups as a whole reject standards that ought to apply to them, HR as a political project risks becoming a coercive project imposed on those it is meant to benefit. And if HR activists concede that "they do not know everything," they can never be sure what causes the resistance they face from a community when upholding a universal HR standard. Is it because people view the standard as an arbitrary imposition? Is this just a stubborn or ignorant rejection by those who simply refuse to uphold universal human rights? Or is it a play for power by the dominant?

Once HR activists concede human finitude, they cannot reject the possibility that the less powerful may be ignored in setting standards. And they must concede that those who reject the universality of human rights need not always be making a play for power to avoid doing what is just.[5] Conceding this possibility is not a compromise of human rights principles with the power of the dominant, but the consequence of accepting human finitude. To ensure that human rights standards are not arbitrary, HR activists must engage in a serious dialogue with groups that are sincere (even if sincerely wrong) in their rejection of particular universal human rights standards. This will improve the likelihood that human rights will be accepted and implemented as a universal project, along with the commitment to a common humanity that is fundamental to the project's political success.

# Notes

**1.** This is the "naming and shaming" on which the success of most international human rights activism depends.

**2.** By "sincere," I simply mean those who may be powerful but whose adherence to this ethnocentric objection does not stem from a desire to retain power.

**3.** Farid Abdel-Nour, "Liberalism and Ethnocentrism," *Journal of Political Philosophy* 8, no. 2 (2000): 207–26.

**4.** John Rawls, *Political Liberalism* (New York: Columbia University Press, 1993), 56–57.

**5.** See Salem Mekuria, "Female Genital Mutilation in Africa: Some African Views," *Association of Concerned African Scholars Bulletin,* nos. 44–45 (Winter–Spring 1995), www.prairienet.org/acas/bulletin/mekuria.html.

# 5

# Peace as a Human Right
## Toward an Integrated Understanding

Abdul Aziz Said and Charles O. Lerche

Fifteen years have passed since the extraordinary events that prompted the end of the Cold War and ushered in significant changes in the international community. For many people, these unexpected events renewed hope for a more peaceful world, but these hopes have not yet been realized. Our morning newspaper may trumpet the worldwide triumph of consumption-based capitalism or the emergence of Western-style democracy in unexpected places, but when we turn on the evening news, what we see looks like fanaticism or rampant nationalism. We must accept that we live in an era when the pace of change is accelerating, a fact that suggests that we can no longer use the past as a guide for the future. This means, among other things, that we have to do a lot of "inner work": reflection and reappraisal of received ideas. It means that our generation and those immediately to come have to innovate, to come up with ways of thinking and acting—individually and collectively—that are fundamentally new, holistic, and integrative. It is in this spirit and with this focus that we approach the relationship between "peace" and "human rights."

Human rights are inextricably linked with peace, and at first glance the relationship might seem straightforward. Starting from the premise that "all good things go together," we could simply conclude that human rights are conducive to peace and, as declared by Federico Mayor, then UNESCO director-general, that "lasting peace is a prerequisite for the exercise of all human rights and duties."[1] Beyond this, as long ago as 1984 the United Nations General Assembly "solemnly" declared "that the peoples of our

129

planet have a sacred right to peace."[2] So it could be argued that the status of peace as a human right is generally clear: We, the inhabitants of the earth, do have a right to peace, and since this is a right for all "peoples," then by definition it is a universal human right.

These passages are very significant because they make it clear that peace is a right of individuals, not just of states. However, even at a conceptual level, the argument cannot be left there. Though it may seem intuitively obvious that peace is what we want and that war and conflict are what we want to avoid or stop, several decades of analysis have shown that peace is anything but straightforward, that it is a multidimensional and significantly contested concept, and that in this regard different people use it for different purposes. Consider the following passage from Johan Galtung:

> The word "peace" is used both by the naïve who confuse absence of direct violence with peace and do not understand that the work to make and build peace is now just about to start, and by the less naïve who know this and do not want that work to get started. Thus the word "peace" becomes a very effective peace-blocker.[3]

Galtung's argument suggests that there are several approaches to peace: some that block what he would consider real peace, and others that would presumably enable or facilitate it. Galtung, whose arguments are presented in more detail below, has written extensively about the key difference between "positive" and "negative" peace, and Smoker and Groff, for example, suggest that peace has "a wide range of interpretations," of which they specify six.[4] If peace means so many things, we are obliged to ask, which approach to, or variety of, peace is it that should be seen as a prerequisite for human rights, and to what kind of peace *exactly* do we humans have a sacred right? These are challenging and significant questions, which, if taken seriously, rapidly bring the question of peace down from the sky of rhetoric and idealism to the real world of politics and policy. As we have seen in recent years, these questions are central to the conceptualization and implementation of a whole range of peacemaking initiatives, from humanitarian intervention to reconciliation, and therefore merit further consideration and careful analysis. This article is one attempt to explore the key issues they raise. In the discussion that follows, the concepts of both "peace" and "human rights" will be examined, and the argument put forth that there are a number of possible ways to understand each. The implications of some of the more prominent views are considered, and a case made in support of a transformative approach drawing on human needs theory—an approach that shows the extent to which the theory and practice of peace and of human rights interact dialectically and, over time, seem necessarily to be moving toward fusion. First, however, we must understand the similarities and differences in the emergence of both as issues on the agenda of world affairs.

## Background

Peace and human rights have different histories, and this may help to explain why they have remained conceptually distinct. A certain kind of peace has been part of international law at least since the Kellogg-Briand Pact of 1928, in which the signatories condemned "recourse to war for the solution of international controversies," and renounced it "as an instrument of national policy in their relations with one another." They also agreed that "the settlement or solution of all disputes or conflicts of whatever nature or of whatever origin they may be, which may arise among them, shall never be sought except by pacific means."[5] This was, as is well known, confirmed in Chapter VI of the United Nations Charter, wherein the member states are committed to peaceful settlement of disputes and the Security Council is given a clear role in promoting this approach to international conflict resolution.

This shows that a formal international legal commitment to "peace as the absence of war" predates and was, at least in a formal sense, an established fact before the international human rights regime, as we know it today, emerged. This second process, building on the brief mention of human rights in the charter's preamble, took on substance only with the Universal Declaration of Human Rights in 1948. The key difference here is that the Universal Declaration initially had no international legal standing (though it has acquired this with time), and human rights had to be given formal legal substance through various covenants—a process that continues today.

This distinction can be illustrated with an example from domestic politics. Most political systems, whether open or closed, have a prohibition against using force to settle personal disputes. Rather, citizens are expected to use juridical and other institutions of the state to settle conflicts nonviolently. Therefore, when a state wishes (for whatever reason) to establish the conditions of liberal democracy, whether in America in the late eighteenth century or in many transitional societies today, there is no need to include a civil right guaranteeing freedom from the infliction of violence on the individual person by other private persons, since this already exists in law. In the same vein, there was no need to include peace, at least in the narrow sense of the term, in the Universal Declaration, since it was already in the UN Charter.

This raises other questions, though. It seems that the only dimension of peace really reflected so far in international law is "negative" peace, and if the human rights agenda points in the direction of other kinds of peace, this may require a concomitant evolution of international law. However, as we will see later, developments in this direction are making the conceptual distinction between peace and human rights less and less clear or meaningful.

## A Closer Look at Peace

The discussion so far has considered only one aspect of peace. For instance, in the 1984 General Assembly declaration, peace is portrayed as "life without war,"[6] and states are enjoined to renounce the use of force. This is also the model of peace implicit in the charter formulation, since the UN was primarily created to "save future generations from the scourge of war."[7] While one should be sympathetic to the positive intentions in these documents and appreciate the historical contexts in which they were formulated—the aftermath of World War II, and the renewed Cold War of the 1980s—the study and analysis of peace have gone well beyond this understanding of the concept.

In the first decade of the twenty-first century there is increasing support for the idea that peace is more—much more, in fact—than the absence of war. Johan Galtung has led the way to this understanding by introducing the seminal distinction between "positive" and "negative" peace. The latter refers to the absence of violence as discussed above, but the former goes much farther in its implications. It can be defined as creating and maintaining equitable, participatory, and stable social institutions. Galtung's work cannot be adequately summarized here, but several of his insights are extremely useful for our purpose. For instance, at one point he actually defines peace as "the capacity to handle conflict creatively and nonviolently,"[8] which suggests that it is a social capacity, a form of social capital, which, to be truly effective, must inhere in institutions at all levels, from the family to the globe. Beyond this, he emphasizes that any social system is becoming either more peaceful or more violent over time, depending on how conflicts are handled. In this regard he first introduced the controversial but extremely helpful concept of "structural violence," meaning those social inequalities that create the desperation and resentment conducive to overt violence. Later he added the concept of "cultural" violence, referring to that "meta" layer of collective identity that fosters and underpins militarism through reference to quasi-mythologized historical injustices (often conveyed from one generation to the next through story and song) and that glorifies killing the "other."[9] The key point here is that peace as the absence of war may coexist at any given time with a significant degree of structural violence and cultural violence—forces that would, under the right enabling conditions, lead to further violent conflict over time. From this perspective the inadequacy of negative peace as either a process or an end state becomes obvious. Lasting peace is something more profound and more comprehensive.

If we look farther into the burgeoning literature on peace "praxis," or "peacebuilding," we find several themes that reinforce this perspective. Jan Øberg, for instance, describes peacebuilding as involving the reconstruction of "(1) human beings, soul and bodies, (2) social structure, (3) culture, (4) environment, and (5) . . . reconciliation, repentance, forgiveness, respect . . . and simultaneously moving toward a vision of peaceful coexistence,"[10] while Clements suggests that the keys to "development of more stable peaceful relationships between people lie in a deepening awareness of the key psychological, social and political processes which generate trusting communities within which individuals can realize their deepest sense of self."[11] The Carnegie Commission on Preventing Deadly Conflict (1997) goes even farther with this theme, suggesting that finding and implementing a more proactive model of peace represents a critical evolutionary threshold for our species:

> In our world of unprecedented levels of destructive weaponry and increased geographic and social proximity, competition between groups has become extremely dangerous. In the century to come, human survival may well depend on our ability to learn a new form of adaptation, one in which intergroup competition is largely replaced by mutual understanding and human cooperation. Curiously, a vital part of human experience—learning to live together—has been badly neglected throughout the world.[12]

This has far-reaching implications for our theme. First, though the Carnegie Commission does not explicitly state that there is a right to peace, many have argued that the most basic human right of all is the right to survival, and the passage states that survival itself depends on new levels of cooperation and, by implication, being freed from conflict and violence of various kinds at all levels of society. Only one of these levels, the interstate, is directly addressed in contemporary international law. Others, such as the domestic and the community levels, are addressed to some degree in national legal systems, and still others, if we use Øberg's list above as a guide, are hardly addressed at all. It is, rather, in the provisions of the human rights covenants that we find nascent international "legislation" in support of even a moderate formulation of positive peace.

To summarize, negative peace is, as indicated in the UN documents, only one human right among others, although it is certainly an essential one, since war destroys the possibilities for fuller life that the five areas of human rights seek to guarantee. However, once we try to specify characteristics of a peaceful society, this formulation is inadequate. While at first glance there seems to be no formal international covenant that explicitly guarantees the right to positive peace in the same way that the Kellogg-Briand Pact or the UN Charter promotes negative peace, we should bear in mind that positive peace is multidimensional. It involves, among other things, equitable, participatory, and stable political institutions, as well as economic, social, and cultural conditions that guarantee diversity and minimal standards of well-being and protection for the vulnerable. The human rights covenants are themselves the widely acknowledged source for such norms and standards. Still, as discussed in the next section, human rights are also a source of controversy and therefore in their contemporary form are neither an accurate reflection of international practice nor a fully adequate articulation of positive peace.

## A Closer Look at Human Rights

The diverse literature on human rights largely agrees on one point: Human rights are concerned with the dignity of the individual—that level of self-esteem that is secure and self-accepting. The Universal Declaration of Human Rights (1948), the (European) Convention for the Protection of Human Rights and Fundamental Freedoms (1950), the International Covenant on Economic, Social, and Cultural Rights (1966), and the International Covenant on Civil and Political Rights (1966) are part of the process of enlarging the dignity, freedom, opportunity for creativity, and welfare of individuals, and the development of an environment and the appropriate institutions to promote these goals.

Again, this formulation is not as straightforward as it looks. While the pursuit of human dignity is universal, it is defined by the culture of a people. Politics is a cultural activity and reflects tradition and environment. The global debate on human rights assumes that in spite of the differences that characterize the diversity of cultures, political conduct can be conceptualized by certain common norms and attitudes. In the modern global system, Westerners have concentrated on discovering common denominators rooted in the Judeo-Christian tradition, from which a calculus of human rights would emerge. This emphasis on Western common denominators has been criticized as a parochial view of human rights, neglecting the traditional cultures and present conditions of the global South.

Universality, in both conception and practice, is therefore the principal challenge of human rights, and the various conflicts between East and West, North and South, over human rights have been in large measure conflicts over whether the political, economic, or cultural diversity among states and peoples is compatible with worldwide standards of human rights. We suggest that any overt or subtle currents of Western cultural imperialism will undermine the further evolution of human rights. Furthermore, the principle of unlimited national sovereignty—the true conceptual foundation of the states system—continues to impede the evolution of a more effective, equitable, and authoritative human rights regime. Basically, there is a contradiction, in both theory and practice, between the need for universal norms and enforcement procedures and the reality of a decentralized and structurally anarchic world political system.

This can be better understood by considering a continuum of possible human rights regimes. Jack Donnelly, following Hedley Bull's three types of international society,[13] suggests three ideal type models of international human rights:

> *Statist:* "The traditional statist model sees human rights as principally a matter of sovereign national jurisdiction . . . statists . . . insist that human rights remain principally a matter of sovereign national jurisdiction and a largely peripheral concern of international (inter-state) relations."
>
> *Cosmopolitan:* "A cosmopolitan model starts with individuals, who are seen more as members of a single global political community (cosmopolis) than as citizens of states. . . Cosmopolitans often see international organizations and certain transnational NGOs as representatives of an inchoate global community of mankind."
>
> *Internationalist:* "Internationalists accept the centrality of states and sovereignty in international relations, but stress international social practices (such as international law and the rules and procedures of diplomacy) that regulate inter-state relations. This body of formal and informal restrictions on the original sovereignty of states creates an international social order, an anarchical society of states."[14]

It should be clear from the descriptions above that the statist and cosmopolitan models represent the two extremes on the continuum, and the internationalist model the center. Donnelly concludes that a relatively weak internationalist model, including only modest and primarily normative international societal constraints on state sovereignty, describes international human rights practices over the past half century, and is likely to continue to do so.[15]

He suggests further that the cosmopolitan model, beyond being purely prescriptive, is useful primarily as a prediction of the future of human rights.

Donnelly also provides an extensive overview of the human rights regime at both the global and regional levels and concludes, "Multilateral procedures for coercive intervention to enforce international human rights obligations simply do not exist. Recalcitrant states usually can violate human rights with impunity."[16] Elsewhere, Donnelly has simply concluded, "All international human rights issues are inherently problematic in a world structured around sovereign states."[17]

Moreover, in a world organized into sovereign states, there really is no authoritative spokesperson for the global public interest.[18] States are responsible for defining the public interest for their national communities, and a global public interest can only be defined as the overlap among their various national interests. Thus, despite the fact that human rights are by definition universal, the regime through which they are given effect will always remain piecemeal and uneven in the context of the state system. Governments decide according to their own particular priorities which rules and enforcement procedures to accept—and even these limited commitments are not necessarily binding for the long term, since nothing prevents a state from revising its commitments in light of changed circumstances. Finally, and perhaps most compelling, human rights, as mentioned earlier, are generally understood as a key element of democratic governance. The states system, however, does not function as a democracy either in theory or in practice, as demonstrated by such standard explanatory concepts in international relations as "realpolitik" and "hegemony." Even the United Nations Security Council, the most powerful international political institution, accords a special status to its permanent members and resembles as much the nineteenth-century Concert of Europe as it does the executive branch of a nascent democratic world government. Little wonder that the global human rights regime has been criticized (however self-interestedly) for imposing the values of the dominant powers on everyone else, since "might makes right" is fundamental to the practice of power politics, which still characterizes much of international relations.

Finally, it should be pointed out that the current prescribed international reform package of liberal democracy and liberal market reform does not in itself guarantee improvement in human rights practice around the world. Though human rights figure prominently in the rhetoric of demo-cratic and market reform, in the actual experience of reform to date there has been a reluctance for newly elected regimes to recognize the limits on their power implied by human rights, or to give sufficient attention to eco-nomic and social rights. It has to be borne in mind that human rights are nonmajoritarian, and therefore require more than just a commitment to the basic processes of democracy to become effective. In fact, a case can be made that the kinds of economic policies imposed on most states by global capitalism aggravate socioeconomic inequality and undermine many social and economic rights. Again, a commitment to more than free markets is necessary in this area if human rights are to become effective.

At least at a conceptual level the international community faces a basic choice between the states system and national sovereignty on the one hand and a more effective and meaningful human rights regime on the other. In certain respects national sovereignty, as currently understood and practiced, seems to be the problem and not the solution in regard to human rights, and there is a real need to find ways out of this impasse if the full potential for positive change latent in the contemporary human rights regime is ever to be released. In practice, one can imagine change both from "above," through a strengthened global human rights regime, and from "below," through education and public information passed on through international civil society, which continues to promote human rights as part of good gov-ernance. Thus, a change in international political culture in the direction of human rights may well precede and remain for some time ahead of the actual institutionalization of "enforcement" capabilities at the global level. In this regard, while we have seen the emergence of an "international" norm of humanitarian intervention, as a practice it currently seems limited to interventions by stronger countries in response to humanitarian emer-gencies in weaker ones. Though no doubt necessary, this can hardly be considered equitable.

## Toward Integration: A Human Needs Approach

From a number of angles, there is a striking parallel between the current global condition and the experience of an individual striving to overcome personal challenges in his or her life. With the individual, the first stage is a growing sense that something is not right. An introspective quest for more appropriate values follows, which may involve a systematic reexam-ination of old beliefs and habits, and a search for new ones. Once new value commitments are made, a constant effort is required to bring action into agreement with these values. From this perspective we can discover, amid the crises of contemporary global politics, a search for those values on which a viable future for our planet can be built. And indeed there is already a discernible convergence in efforts to formulate priorities for peace and human rights, and beyond these to the related areas of good governance and sustainable development. When evaluated in light of human needs theory, this convergence seems to provide a compelling direction for new thinking about the future of world order—thinking that increasingly suggests that we can, with a little effort, begin to discern the contours of, and criteria for, what might be called a "successful" global civilization.

John Burton developed human needs theory as a tool for studying social conflict, and his approach makes a distinction among needs, values, and interests. In trying to resolve disputes, it should be understood that only interests are negotiable in the short run, while values can change only over the long run, in an atmosphere of security and nondiscrimination, and needs cannot be negotiated away under any circumstances.[19] The implications of this formulation are far-reaching. For instance, it suggests "that there are limits to the extent to which the human person, acting separately or within a wider ethnic or national community, can be socialized or manipulated"; and "that there are human development needs that must be satisfied and catered for by institutions, if these institutions are to be stable, and if societies are to be significantly free of conflict."[20] While acknowledging that this is still a new and contested research area, Burton does present a plausible list of needs. First, human beings require a sense of security and identity. Second, since we have a generic drive to learn, we require a consistent response from the environment, without which learning is impossible. Third, from their social context people require both recognition and valued relationships, or bonding. Finally, and perhaps most important, individuals require (some) control over their environments in order to ensure that their needs are fulfilled.[21]

This approach has important implications for social institutions. If, on balance, needs are being met within an institution, the institution receives support and is consolidated and perpetuated. If, however, needs are not met, the institution loses support and legitimacy and confronts increasing opposition. In this latter case, authorities tend to react with repression and coercion, but if an institution is delegitimized for enough people, conflict cannot be resolved this way. Rather, the institutional structures have to evolve, sooner or later, to more fully accommodate the needs of the people they affect. If a particular social order is legitimized for only a portion of the society, one can expect, given enabling conditions, that those whose needs are not met will react. Burton goes so far as to assert that this has become the general condition in modern societies:

> Human needs are being frustrated on a large scale in all modern societies, and the more law and order is enforced to control frustration the more the frustration. *There is now a widespread concern regarding the legitimacy of even the most seemingly legitimized authorities.* The members of protest movements of many kinds in many different societies, and the terrorists who spring from relatively privileged classes, are demonstrating that there are features of societies, of all political types, unacceptable to a significant number of the people that comprise them.[22] (Emphasis added)

To Burton, *legitimacy* is a dynamic rather than a static condition, which "stresses the reciprocal nature of relations with authorities, the support given because of the services they render, and respect for legal norms when these are legitimized norms."[23] He contrasts this with a static notion of *legality*, which "has associated with it . . . loyalty to a sovereign or formal leader right or wrong, elitism, the common good and the national interest as interpreted by elites."[24] From this perspective, a peaceful society—or world, for that matter—is one in which the social and political order is popularly perceived as legitimate. Though such legitimacy is generally assumed to inhere in liberal democratic institutions, Burton has also argued that conventional representative democracy is only effective in a society with "relative ethnic homogeneity, classlessness and equality"; and this model alone is not able to guarantee institutional legitimacy "in a society that contains major income differences, and in which minorities are unrepresented but must observe the norms of a majority"[25]—conditions characteristic of many transitional countries. In summary, Burton's work indicates that social reform that goes farther than conventional Western models of governance to meet human needs, through promoting the full range of human rights, is necessary if today's deep-seated conflicts are to be transformed into peaceful and creative relations among the groups concerned.

Consider now the concept of "sustainable human development," defined here by the United Nations Development Programme as:

> expanding the choices for all people in society. This means that men and women—particularly the poor and vulnerable—are at the centre of the development process. It also means "protection of the life opportunities of future generations . . . and . . . the natural systems on which all life depends" (UNDP, Human Development Report 1996). This makes the central purpose of development the creation of an enabling environment in which all can enjoy long, healthy and creative lives.[26]

The UNDP's five aspects of sustainable human development are quite close to Burton's list of human needs:

> *Empowerment*—The expansion of men and women's capabilities and choices increases their ability to exercise those choices free of hunger, want, and deprivation. It also increases their opportunity to participate in, or endorse, decision making affecting their lives.

> *Co-operation*—With a sense of belonging important for personal fulfillment, well-being and a sense of purpose and meaning, human development is concerned with the ways in which people work together and interact.

> *Equity*—The expansion of capabilities and opportunities means more than income—it also means equity, such as an educational system to which everybody should have access.

> *Sustainability*—The needs of this generation must be met without compromising the right of future generations to be free of poverty and deprivation and to exercise their basic capabilities.

> *Security*—Particularly the security of livelihood. People need to be freed from threats, such as disease or repression and from sudden harmful disruption in their lives.[27]

The same UNDP document presents a list of characteristics of "good governance," which are also similar to Burton's needs, in both conception and implication. Here are some of the qualities they emphasize:

> *Participation*—All men and women should have a voice in decision making, either directly or through legitimate intermediate institutions that represent their interests. Such broad participation is built on freedom of association and speech, as well as capacities to participate constructively.

> *Rule of law*—Legal frameworks should be fair and enforced impartially, particularly the laws on human rights.

> *Transparency*—Transparency is built on the free flow of information. Processes, institutions and information are directly accessible to those concerned with them, and enough information is provided to understand and monitor them.

> *Responsiveness*—Institutions and processes try to serve all stakeholders.

> *Consensus orientation*—Good governance mediates differing interests to reach a broad consensus on what is in the best interests of the group and, where possible, on policies and procedures.

> *Equity*—All men and women have opportunities to improve or maintain their well-being.

*Effectiveness and efficiency*—Processes and institutions produce results that meet needs while making the best use of resources.

*Accountability*—Decision makers in government, the private sector, and civil society organisations are accountable to the public, as well as to institutional stakeholders. This accountability differs depending on the organisation and whether the decision is internal or external to an organisation.[28]

This could be considered a fairly comprehensive list of the elements of "positive peace," and also parallels advances in the theory and practice of human rights. The Cold War division between the capitalist camp's emphasis on civil and political rights and the socialist/Third World preference for social, economic, and cultural rights has now, fortunately, been recognized as unhelpful and unacceptable. Instead, in the wake of the first truly global conference on human rights, which met in Vienna in 1993, all five major areas of human rights have been acknowledged by the international community (however grudgingly in some cases) as an indivisible whole. Furthermore, the Vienna Declaration, the conference's key contribution to human rights thinking and practice, went farther, emphasizing women's rights, children's rights, the rights of indigenous peoples, and, significantly for our argument here, the right to development.

The emerging common perspective on needs, development, governance, and rights reflected here confirms the World Commission on Culture and Development's premise that there is indeed a nascent "global civic culture," from which important elements of global ethics can be derived.[29] However, putting such values into effect—essentially the process of promoting positive peace—will require far-reaching change, and it is not clear that the best way to give effect to all global core values is through lists of rights. As the World Commission on Culture and Development puts it,

Although the idea of human rights does obviously make use of the notion of rights, these rights may better be seen as general principles denoting the fundamental moral concern that in a social and political community ought to find adequate reflection. How exactly these principles should be implemented and what type of institutional arrangements they enjoin is a matter of political imagination and requires taking into account already existing traditions and institutions. Some of the concerns expressed in the idea of human rights are indeed best expressed in a system of individual legal rights. Yet others, such as the human right to the social and economic conditions necessary for minimally decent life, call for a complex mix of institutions and policies. And the right to fair treatment may involve, inter alia, educating police and security forces and making them familiar with due process and similar principles.[30]

In its own formulation, the commission puts forth five principal ideas that should form the core of global ethics:

- Human rights and responsibilities
- Democracy and the development of civil society
- Protection of minorities
- Peaceful conflict resolution
- Equity within and between generations

Although most governmental and nongovernmental groups concerned focus primarily on reform of existing national and international institutions, the promotion of peace, good governance, sustainable development, and human rights in an era of globalization raises more far-reaching questions. Ultimately, world order, at all levels, should be reconstructed to maximize these global core values. To put the matter another way, either we as human beings have to accept the oppression, violence, and injustice in the world as fundamental to the human condition and therefore irremediable, or we accept the premise of human needs theory that there are basic norms and needs that, when reflected in our institutions and processes of governance, should foster social peace, stability, and progress. The texts of the basic human rights instruments and the official reports and communiqués of recent UN-sponsored conferences on human rights, social development, and rights of indigenous peoples suggest that at the normative level the international community has officially accepted the second point of view. We are indeed moving away from the "statist" era of human rights, and governments now have to justify their policies in terms of international norms and are subject to public international scrutiny of their human rights practices. So the question becomes less one of *whether* such developments are necessary, and more one of *how* they can be effectively accomplished. Ultimately, national sovereignty as a foundation concept for international politics should be fundamentally questioned; however, in the short run we need to focus more on how it is exercised. States, and most obviously the great powers, shape the international political environment through their actions and motives. They can lay foundations for positive peace, or they can retard its advance, but Burton's work suggests that they may not ultimately be able to stop it, since peoples everywhere aspire to a better quality of life.

## Dialogue as Positive Peace Process

If we take a longer-term view, the current regime must become even more cosmopolitan in both theory and practice if it is to continue to provide the rationale and the foundation for positive peace. Perhaps more important for the immediate future is how the world approaches this task. Cultural imperialism, essentially the imposition of norms, is certainly not conducive to the emergence of positive peace. Rather, the current UNESCO-sponsored initiative of "dialogue of civilizations" presents a more promising prospect, which merits some consideration here.

The need for a dialogue among peoples is based on the recognition that our changing reality requires a new global ethic and a new perception of one another. Historically, unequal power relations, leaving the West arrogant and insensitive and the rest of the world largely defensive and insecure, have marred cultural contact among civilizations. All have much to gain from moving away from such postures. Attachment and commitment to these forms undermine the purpose of dialogue, keeping us estranged and unknown to one another. Today such relationships and the images they were built on are no longer sustainable.

Rather, it is only in a growing awareness of our diversity that we may come to discern our unity: our humanity and our common values and needs. Dialogue, as a new paradigm in global relations, is based on sharing knowledge in order to achieve new knowledge, to see each other with open and empathetic eyes under a different light, and to look together toward a shared future in a global community that will make our world safe for diversity. Dialogue is a key to effective communication that can help us to pierce through the walls of misperception and mistrust and gather valuable insights, lessons, and opportunities that enrich us all. A new and mutually rewarding relationship has the potential to emerge, where accumulated wisdom and insights for necessary progress provide the basis of a valued coexistence. Such a relationship would be premised not on ideas of cultural superiority but on mutual respect and openness to cultural eclecticism and, ultimately, synthesis; and only out of synthesis can the values of sustainable positive peace emerge.

This process of communication is key to transcending our historical accretion of deep subjectivity and ethnocentrism, and it requires active listening and a commitment to sustained dialogue: learning to understand how each communicates the shared concerns. In this way we can discover as well as create shared meanings and find our common ground while better understanding our own values and ideals as we are challenged to share them in a new way. Dialogue requires that we look on one another as moral equals and partners in creating a global community.

Effective dialogue implies active engagement. As cultural symbolism assumes greater significance in the relations of cultures, active engagement through sustained dialogue permits each participant to understand the deeper meanings, associations, and implications of the "other's" symbols, thus penetrating the "enigma of the external other" and defusing the dynamics of the clash of civilizations. Active engagement also permits us to understand and recognize the authentic expressions of human religiosity and protects us from the politics of manipulated symbolism. The confrontations we observe today feed on the need to address despair through actions predicated on—and intended to spread—fear. An understanding derived from active engagement would allow us to avoid being trapped in the system of confrontation, moving beyond immediate negative reactions (for instance, between the West and Islam) to discover human commonality and shared experiences and needs.

Dialogue as a tool for finding a desirable future demands the creation and development of a broad consensus of peoples and governments on an ever-wider range of issues. Consensus, the distinctive political tool in relations among equals, has already gone far (but not yet far enough) in replacing armed force as the preferred instrument of national policy. Positive peace requires, at the very least, a basic global agreement on priorities. The development of an agreement on priorities contributes to building a global community because different peoples feel they have a stake in the success of programs. When people agree on priorities they experience a common purpose. Then, through dialogue, they can begin to reach binding international decisions in those areas where they are essential. This is still a new and largely uncharted path, and mistakes will be made. But we have little choice: Either the emerging global order will learn to consult with all its members or it will not survive. Trial and error, seasoned by patience, will teach the elements of an operational code to govern the new process, and consensus building will become a more efficient and predictable instrument.

Each age has its appropriate metaphors, and civilizational dialogue should discover and bring forth the symbols that are appropriate to our contemporary condition. No worldview or tradition should be seen as closed; all have evolved over time. We must therefore begin to look deeply into our societies, our cultures, and ourselves to identify those principles and values that truly speak to our contemporary global experience. This is, in its essence, the true road to peace—not the negative imposed peace of unequal power relations, but an authentic peace in which everyone is a victor. As a UNESCO peace education training manual explains,

> The peace we endeavour to promote has no boundaries. It is a global human outlook which seeks for others what one seeks for oneself. It is not a national issue but a universal one. Peace encompasses an inner feeling of empathy and compassion to which all religions subscribe. It underlies the continuous effort needed to foster equitable economic and cultural relations of a given society and between States. Peace rejects power as the primary arbiter of human relations. Peace accepts the inevitability of change but does not resort to violence to change the process of events and redress inequalities.[31]

The same document argues, "Attitudes, values and identity are not fixed phenomena. They change and need to be oriented in harmony with the new local and global environment,"[32] and "Education, communication and co-operation are three vehicles through which changes can be brought about."[33] From these passages we see that peace is dialogue and dialogue is peace—or, to paraphrase Mahatma Gandhi, there is no *way* to dialogue; dialogue *is* the way.

Furthermore, this project requires both a *renewed* and a *new* spiritual consciousness; outer peace has always reflected and, at least to some extent, depended on inner peace. The emphasis on transcendence, the spirit's quest for ultimate reality, is one of the purest, oldest, and most mysterious dimensions of human experience and has always been a source of strength for humanity by connecting us with a larger meaning and purpose. Spirituality has always meant a shift in consciousness that sees the whole of existence contained in the parts, and from the parts the whole is understood. A spiritual framework that is world embracing would look beyond the us-versus-them dichotomies that no longer fit the neat conceptualizations of old systems of power and ways of thinking, and reveal these as fictions that can be upheld only through physical separation and deep existential anxiety. An emerging globalized ethic of spirituality embraces the unity we see in diversity, which finally gives us permission to celebrate both. In celebrating we find comfort in our individuality as one unique expression of a larger common reality.

## Conclusion

Human rights and peace have run on two separate but related tracks in international relations, but they can be seen to converge now in thinking about international relations. Peace is not only a right essential to the preservation of human dignity; it is equivalent to life itself. Negative peace is, however, only a space. The space must be filled with a process of positive peace—a process that, if it is to succeed, must in the end encompass the entire planet. Like human rights, positive peace is a universal need and aspiration, and also like human rights, it must find a universal expression.

In the converging thinking about global ethics, human needs, good governance, and sustainable development, which is reflected in the composite of international human rights documents, we can see the possibility and substance of a truly universal peace, which could serve as the normative foundation for the first global civilization. However, unless the bridge from the anarchic states system to a world order incorporating effective global governance is crossed, the promise for a more secure and fulfilling life embodied in the five dimensions of human rights will remain a chimera for large portions of the world's population.

Our discussion also highlights the point that peace is really more about changing attitudes and feelings than it is about finding acceptable ways to divide the material stakes of conflicts. In that sense it must be proactive. To move from a world of confrontation to a world of cooperation, an approach to peace is required that would help parties to transcend—literally, to "go beyond"—the limited perspective defined by their incompatible goals and negative experience. Furthermore, in our rapidly globalizing era, relevant models of peace must envision humanity as a collective whole rather than as contending parts, must be based on global ethics as described above, and must more fully incorporate the inward, spiritual dimensions of human experience—that source of inspiration where we find the strength to confront the dark side of our own and others' characters. Peace means, therefore, building new societies that are more just and more integrated, both internally and among themselves.

In practical terms, this is most directly an educational issue, as indicated by the earlier quotation from the Carnegie Commission: Children everywhere should learn the until-now-neglected skills necessary to live together in peace. As stated by the world's ministers of education in their declaration on the occasion of the forty-fourth session of the International Conference on Education (Geneva, October 1994):

> Education policies have to contribute to the development of understanding, solidarity and tolerance among individuals and among ethnic, social, cultural and religious groups and sovereign nations.

> Education should promote knowledge, values, attitudes and skills conducive to respect for human rights and to an active commitment to the

defence of such rights and to the building of a culture of peace and democracy.[34]

The declaration goes on to state that parents and society as a whole have the responsibility to

> work together with all those involved in the education system, and with non-governmental organizations, so as to achieve full implementation of the objectives of education for peace, human rights and democracy and to contribute in this way to sustainable development and to a culture of peace.[35]

As indicated here, UNESCO has done much during the past two decades to promote both the theory and practice of peace education. It remains, however, to systematically and comprehensively diffuse this information so that it is integrated into school curricula around the world. In a more general sense, positive peace, at any level, is a process, and efforts at peace and reconciliation, whether in workshops or through such means as truth commissions, are also steps in the right direction—though hopefully, such efforts can become more proactive and not come only in the wake of protracted and traumatic violent conflict. As Galtung has written, the many efforts at peacemaking in the world today should be seen as models of structural peace, that is, efforts to replace dysfunctional and violent patterns of behavior with alternative ways of dealing with conflict that are creative and nonviolent. Nongovernmental organizations have, again, led the way in this area, and if the history of peace and human rights until now is any guide, it will very likely remain their task for the foreseeable future to keep the relevant issues prominently on the global agenda. The "good" news is, they have made significant progress already; the "bad" news is, there is a very long way to go before the pattern of world order facilitates rather than, as so often happens, frustrates the emergence of truly peaceful societies.

Though many of these ideas are not new, in our time they have passed from the realm of ideals and aspirations into the realm of evolutionary challenge and necessity. If the world is indeed one system, then world order can only be a positive-sum game—in the long run we all either win or lose together. The challenge for all nations, states, and peoples is to put less emphasis on competing to win short-term, apparently zero-sum games and to start collaborating more effectively to win the only "game" that ultimately matters: establishing a solid foundation for this planet's long-term peace and prosperity.

# Notes

**1.** Federico Mayor, "The Human Right to Peace: Declaration by the Director-General of UNESCO," January 1997, www.unesco.org/general/eng/whatsnew/decl.eng.html (accessed October 17, 2002).

**2.** United Nations General Assembly, "Declaration on the Right of Peoples to Peace Approved by General Assembly Resolution 39/11 of 12 November 1984," www.unhchr.ch/html/menu3/b/73.htm (accessed October 27, 2002).

**3.** Johan Galtung, *After Violence: 3Rs, Reconstruction, Reconciliation, Resolution: Coping with Visible and Invisible Effects of War and Violence,* Transcend: A Peace and Development Network, July 1998, www.transcend.org/TRRECBAS.HTM (accessed October 27, 2002).

**4.** Paul Smoker and Linda Groff, "Creating Global-Local Cultures of Peace," *Peace and Conflict Studies* 3, no. 1 (June 1996). The authors mention specifically

- Peace as Absence of War
- Peace as Balance of Forces in the International System
- Peace as Negative Peace (No War) and Positive Peace (No Structural Violence)
- Feminist Peace: Macro and Micro Levels of Peace
- Holistic Gaia-Peace: Peace with the Environment
- Holistic Inner and Outer Peace

**5.** Kellogg-Briand Pact, 1928, www.yale.edu/lawweb/avalon/imt/kbpact.htm (accessed October 27, 2002).

**6.** United Nations General Assembly, "Declaration on the Right of Peoples to Peace."

**7.** "Preamble to the Charter of the United Nations," www.un.org/Overview/Charter/preamble.html (accessed October 27, 2002).

**8.** Johan Galtung, *Conflict Transformation by Peaceful Means (the TRANSCEND Method): A Manual Prepared for the United Nations Disaster Management Training Program,* Transcend: A Peace and Development Network, 1998, www.transcend.org/trmanpar.htm (accessed October 27, 2002).

**9.** Johan Galtung, *After Violence: 3Rs.*

**10.** Jan Øberg, "Conflict Mitigation in Reconstruction and Development," *Peace and Conflict Studies* 3, no. 2 (December 1996), www.gmu.edu/academic/pcs/oberg.htm (accessed October 27, 2002).

**11.** Kevin P. Clements, "Peace Building and Conflict Transformation," *Peace and Conflict Studies* 4, no. 1 (July 1997), www.gmu.edu/academic/pcs/clements.htm (accessed October 27, 2002).

**12.** Carnegie Commission on Preventing Deadly Conflict, "Toward a Culture of Prevention," chap. 7 in *Preventing Deadly Conflict: Final Report* (New York:

Carnegie Publications, 1997), www.ciaonet.org/book/ccp01/ccpdc07.html (accessed October 27, 2002).

13. Hedley Bull, *The Anarchical Society: A Study of Order in World Politics* (New York: Columbia University Press, 1977).

14. Jack Donnelly, "Human Rights and International Organizations: States, Sovereignty, and the International Community," in *International Organization: A Reader*, ed. Friedrich Kratochwil and Edward D. Mansfield (New York: Harper-Collins, 1994), 202–3.

15. Ibid., 203.

16. Ibid., 208.

17. Jack Donnelly, "Human Rights in the New World Order," *World Policy Journal* 9, no. 2 (Spring 1992): 268.

18. Bull, *The Anarchical Society*.

19. John Burton, *Conflict: Resolution and Prevention* (New York: St. Martin's Press, 1990), 36–41.

20. Ibid., 23.

21. Ibid., 47, 95.

22. Ibid., 98.

23. Ibid., 127.

24. Ibid.

25. John Burton, "Conflict Resolution: The Human Dimension," *International Journal of Peace Studies* 3, no. 1 (January 1998): 1–5.

26. United Nations Development Programme (UNDP), "Governance for Sustainable Development: A UNDP Policy Document," 1997, http://magnet.undp .org/policy/ (accessed October 27, 2002).

27. Ibid.

28. Ibid.

29. World Commission on Culture and Development, *Our Creative Diversity: Report of the World Commission on Culture and Development*, 1996, http://kvc .minbuza.nl/uk/archive/report/inleiding.html (accessed October 27, 2002).

30. Ibid.

31. International Peace Research Association, *Handbook Resource and Teaching Material in Conflict Resolution, Education for Human Rights, Peace and Democracy* (Paris: UNESCO, 1994).

32. Ibid.

33. Ibid.

34. UNESCO, Declaration of the 44th Session of the International Conference on Education, Geneva, Switzerland, October 1994, www.unesco.org/ human_rights/education.htm.

35. Ibid.

# Peace as a
# Human Right
## Commentary

Jack Donnelly

Said and Lerche, in the course of a wide-ranging discussion, suggest that, understood correctly, peace and human rights —along with many other good things, such as sustainable human development—are largely the same thing. Although I begin and end with these claims, my focus is on the narrower issue identified by their chapter title: peace as a human right. I will argue that a human right to peace not only is not currently recognized in positive international human rights law but should not be added to the list of internationally recognized human rights.

Let me begin, however, with definitions. By "human rights" I mean the equal and inalienable rights that each person has simply as a human being. For the purposes of this commentary I will take the 1948 Universal Declaration of Human Rights and the 1966 International Human Rights Covenants as an authoritative list.[1] By "peace" I mean the absence of interstate war. Said and Lerche canvass the limitations of this conception at considerable length. Nonetheless, it is the standard definition in both international law and international relations. And peace thus understood is an immensely valuable and, unfortunately, fragile condition that deserves careful attention.

Said and Lerche endorse "the premise that 'all good things go together'" (p. 129). This is true only in some ideal world (e.g., Augustine's "heavenly city"), not in the world we actually live in. It certainly is not the case, as they claim (p. 129), quoting Federico Mayor, that lasting peace is a prerequisite for the exercise of all human rights. Many human rights are protected and enjoyed even in times of war, let alone in the (sometimes rather lengthy) intervals of peace (understood as absence of war) we are able to enjoy.

If a human right to peace is not a matter of conceptual logic, it must rest on a moral, political, or (preferably) legal argument. Said and Lerche do advance as evidence the 1984 General Assembly Declaration on the Right of Peoples to Peace.[2] Unfortunately, the text of that document fails to support their position.

The fourth preliminary paragraph does assert that peace is a prerequisite to "the full implementation of the rights and fundamental human freedoms proclaimed by the United Nations." But this does not logically entail a human right to peace. Large sums of money are also essential, but this does not mean that there is a human right to large sums of money.

Particularly telling is the fact that the operative paragraphs of this declaration make no mention of *any* human right; the term "human rights" appears nowhere in the text. Only a right of *peoples*—collective groups, such as the French, Chinese, Guatemalans, Kenyans, or Egyptians—to peace is proclaimed. This studied avoidance of even the suggestion of an individual right clearly indicates its implicit denial.[3]

Said and Lerche, thus, are either mistaken or disingenuous when they claim that such passages "make it clear that peace is a right of individuals, not just of states" (p. 130). A right held by a collective group is not also held by each of its members. The United States, for example, has many rights that I as an individual American do not have.

Can we find a human right to peace elsewhere in international human rights law? It is mentioned in neither the Universal Declaration nor the International Human Rights Covenants. In fact, none of the approximately one hundred human rights instruments listed by the UN High Commissioner for Human Rights[4] asserts the existence of a human right to peace. The international community, as represented in the human rights standard-setting machinery of the United Nations, has chosen, quite consciously, not to recognize a human right to peace.

It would have been useful if Said and Lerche, rather than try to wish a human right to peace into existence, had mounted a case for recognizing such a right. But even without such an argument to react against, I want to defend the decision of the international community not to recognize a human right to peace.

Most people value peace as a political good of the highest order. They do not, however, feel that simply because they are human beings they are entitled to peace—which is what a human right to peace would mean. They do not see the presence of war anywhere in the world—as opposed to international violence directed against them or their state—as a violation of their basic rights. Peace, like love, is one of those good things that is not a matter of human rights.

This is not a merely semantic issue. War would have a very different moral, legal, and political meaning if every one of us, simply because we are human, were entitled to peace. Denying someone a good thing to which she is not entitled is a different kind of offense from denying her that same thing when she is entitled to it. It is a special kind of injustice that brings into play distinctive social practices.[5]

The fact that we have not yet recognized a human right to peace does not mean that it might not be done in the future. There is no logical reason why peace could not become an internationally recognized human right. To establish a human right to peace, however, would require major changes in our moral, legal, and political practices, and when it comes right down to it, most people—and certainly virtually all states—seem unwilling to do what would be necessary to make such changes.

Rights are held not merely by specified right-holders but against specific duty-bearers. In the case of internationally recognized human rights, the duty-bearer is the state of which one is a national.[6] More precisely, although all individuals, groups, and institutions may be bound not to deprive anyone of their human rights, international human rights law sees only states as having duties to protect, implement, and enforce these rights —and that only within their own territories.[7]

We might imagine a world in which other institutions—for example, firms, families, regional organizations, or the international community as a whole—had duties to implement and enforce internationally recognized human rights. That, however, is not the system established in contemporary international human rights law. With very few exceptions, one may claim one's human rights only from the state of which one is a national (or under whose jurisdiction one resides or temporarily falls). Moreover, sovereignty as we currently understand it prohibits other states and the international community—again, with very few exceptions[8]—from enforcing human rights within the territory of a sovereign state.

No less importantly, states do have a duty to protect their citizens from foreign invasion and international violence, and this ultimately may require war. International law recognizes the right of states to self-defense, not the right of states (let alone individuals) to peace.

I can imagine Said and Lerche responding that this is precisely the problem, that international law recognizes a right to defensive war rather than a right to peace. A human right to peace would mean instead that anyone anywhere would be entitled to demand, as a matter of right, that war anywhere be stopped.

Against whom, though, would such a right be asserted? Certainly we do not want to create a world in which any state that sees violence anywhere, when asked by any human being anywhere, has a right (let alone a duty) to intervene. The international community as a whole, however, has no institutional mechanism to respond to such claims. The Security Council, which does have a right, and perhaps even a duty, to protect international peace and security, is a political organ of the United Nations, an organization of sovereign states. It is not constituted to respond to claims of human rights.

A human right to peace, if it is to be more than an empty phrase, would require a radical restructuring of international politics. That might, in some abstract moral sense, be desirable. But I see no evidence that it is in fact widely desired by the citizenry of most states, let alone by governments. And exactly how we would get from here to there remains a mystery.

The states system does have war as one of its unfortunate consequences. Even today, despite the legal restriction of force to self-defense, interstate violence occurs occasionally, and "new wars" of various sorts have been a far-too-common phenomenon in the post–Cold War world. But the states system also has virtues, such as the protection of national self-determination and autonomy. Furthermore, the international society of states is our principal mechanism for assuring international order, however fragile and incomplete that order might be.[9] Before we start talking about dismantling this society, we should be confident not only that the alternative is practically realizable but also that we understand and are willing to bear the costs and unintended consequences of establishing it.

To be effective, a human right to peace would require, if not a world government, at least replacing the current system of individual and collective self-defense with a system of collective security managed by an international institution that not only had the authority (and power) to use force against any threat to, or breach of, the peace anywhere but could act without a veto by any state. That may or may not be preferable to what we have now, but it clearly is not in the offing. And until it is, talk of a human right to peace will be empty words or, at best, a pious aspiration.

None of this is to disparage the value of peace or of human rights. Both are of the utmost moral, legal, and political value. Both are worth struggling for with all our might. But they are very different things. And it does not help us to understand or achieve either goal by conflating their differences, let alone by dumping other things, such as development, into the same conceptual pot.

It may be the case that regimes that systematically protect, implement, and enforce the human rights of their citizens are more peaceful than those that do not. Reducing the threat of war may indeed allow states to do a better job implementing the rights of their citizens. But that does not make peace a human right, nor does it make peace and human rights different dimensions of the same thing.

The struggles for peace and for human rights may often intersect and even reinforce one another, but they are fundamentally different. Human rights are principally about getting states to respect the rights of their citizens. Peace is largely a matter of getting states to respect the rights of other states (and perhaps, indirectly, the rights of their citizens).

Nothing is to be gained, and much may be lost, conceptually and perhaps even practically, by conflating peace and human rights. They are different things that must be realized through (partly) different forms of political action in different arenas. Labeling peace a human right is not going to bring us any closer to realizing a world without war. Conversely, redirecting our human rights resources to the struggle for peace, even if that might make a more peaceful world, would still leave unaddressed most of the very serious human rights problems that, sadly, still plague us.

## Notes

**1.** These and most other international human rights instruments, as well as most of the available documents on the work of the United Nations human rights system, can be found at www.hchr.ch, the Web site of the United Nations High Commissioner for Human Rights. For an argument in defense of this definition and such a use of the Universal Declaration, see Jack Donnelly, *Universal Human Rights in Theory and Practice*, 2nd ed. (Ithaca, NY: Cornell University Press, 2003), chaps. 1–3.

**2.** I will set aside here the problem that such a declaration, being a resolution of the General Assembly, is in itself not legally binding.

**3.** In passing we can also note that this declaration conceptualizes peace as "life without war" and sees the goal of peace as a matter of eradicating war and eliminating the threat or use of force to resolve international disputes. In other words, the declaration supports my standard understanding of peace, not Said and Lerche's broader, prescriptive definition.

**4.** www.unhchr.ch/html/intlinst.htm (accessed October 28, 2003).

**5.** I examine these differences in Donnelly, *Universal Human Rights*, 7–13.

**6.** The one partial exception is the right of peoples to self-determination, recognized in Article 1 of both International Human Rights Covenants. This right, as it has come to be understood in international practice, is held against (Western) colonial powers, that is, not the state of which one is a national but the state that is illegitimately denying statehood to colonized peoples.

**7.** For a useful discussion of the types of duties correlative to rights, see Henry Shue, *Basic Rights: Subsistence, Affluence, and U.S. Foreign Policy,* 2nd ed. (Princeton, NJ: Princeton University Press, 1996), 51–64.

**8.** The 1984 Convention against Torture creates a system of universal jurisdiction. Genocide may also have emerged as an exception in recent years. For an argument to this conclusion, see Donnelly, *Universal Human Rights,* chap. 14.

**9.** The conception of the society of states and international order underlying this paragraph is best expressed in the work of the English School of international relations theory. See, for example, Hedley Bull, *The Anarchical Society* (New York: Columbia University Press, 1977) and, much more briefly, Andrew Linklater, "The English School," in *Theories of International Relations,* by Scott Burchill et al., 3rd ed. (New York: Palgrave, 2005).

**PART II**

# The Application of Human Rights in Armed Conflicts and Other Violent Conflicts

# 6

# Claiming a Humanitarian Imperative

## NGOs and the Cultivation of Humanitarian Duty

Hugo Slim

Reflecting on the turmoil of his age from his country estate in the late 1570s, the great French founder of the modern essay, Michel de Montaigne, observed how the number of people writing and the sheer volume of their output seems to increase inordinately at times of social and political crisis, when brutality, collapse, and change are on the rise. "Scribbling seems to be one of the symptoms of an age of excess," he wrote. "When did we ever write so much as since the beginnings of our Civil Wars?"[1]

The 1990s and the first five years of this new century have similarly been a time of deep political change, which in many parts of the world has resulted in the extreme violence of civil war. Within the humanitarian field, at least, Montaigne seems to have been proved right. The past ten years have indeed produced a mass of new "scribbling" about humanitarianism, reaching levels that may be unprecedented in the modern history of the humanitarian movement for restraint in war. This great wave of writing has swelled so large because so many people have found it so important to address the critical problem of the limits to human violence in armed conflict, and because the international community has frequently been in agreement about the need to intervene.

The greater part of this new humanitarian writing has grown out of an extraordinary confluence of different streams of academic study that have simultaneously converged on the question of war and international policy since the early 1990s.[2] Analysis of the causes of contemporary armed conflicts, and of urgent policymaking around international response to them, has led to a large new literature on war and humanitarian action. A small core group of scholars, international lawyers, and humanitarian practitioners has always written on the subject, but these writers have recently been joined by many more. The academic and professional context for the discussion of armed conflict and humanitarianism has widened dramatically. Scholars and policy analysts from the large and well-resourced fields of security studies, political science, economics, international law, international relations, and psychology have turned their attention to these questions. So, too, have military analysts, peace studies specialists, and human rights scholars, as well diplomats and NGO activists from a variety of traditions. In the past decade all these different disciplinary groups have found themselves attending conferences together, reading one another's journals, and contributing alongside one another in edited volumes. In this process, the fundamental values of the humanitarian ethic, and the principles of its practical application, have been rediscovered, held up to the light, scrutinized, and dismissed or reaffirmed.

## The Code of Conduct, Humanitarian Charter, and Sphere Standards

One very important part of this rewriting of humanitarianism has been led determinedly by the community of international NGOs concerned with humanitarian action. Since the early 1990s, while scholars have been theorizing and arguing, a core group of international NGO activists has sought to reaffirm the humanitarian ethic in three particularly important documents that have almost come to operate as "soft law" in the NGO community: the Code of Conduct, the Humanitarian Charter, and the Sphere Minimum Standards in Disaster Response. Although initially seen as a rigorous attempt to "put their house in order," this process of humanitarian writing has resulted in a deeper process of explicit recommitment to humanitarian values. The resulting documents remain contested within the NGO community itself, but they form an important—possibly vanguard—movement of a distinct interpretation of the humanitarian ethic based on rights and, as this chapter will argue, increasingly on duties.

Recognition of an explicitly rights-based expression of humanitarian values has been gaining ground in recent years.[3] But such debates are often preoccupied with arguing for or against rights rather than exploring their resulting duties. Analysis of the humanitarian ethic in terms of deontological (duty-based) and consequentialist (results-based) moral positions, in the British tradition, has also increasingly been made in recent years.[4] This chapter seeks to contribute further to these discussions by observing, on paper at least, the determination of international NGOs to emphasize universal rights-based and duty-making humanitarianism.

In some ways, these key NGO documents seem to have stolen a march on the rights debate by focusing, very practically, on duties. Starting with the Code of Conduct's idea of the "humanitarian imperative," the chapter will explore the emerging ideology of international humanitarian duty, obligation, and responsibility that lies at the heart of much of the current written confession of humanitarian values by NGOs.

In looking at this NGO writing or rewriting, it is important to recognize the perennial distinction between paper and practice. Writing things is not the same as doing those things; nor does writing about something mean that the things one writes about actually exist. As any human rights activist or humanitarian lawyer will testify, writing about rights and detailing duties is no shortcut to realizing those rights and meeting those duties. Yet the wonderful thing about writing is that it can sometimes be the beginning of things. In writing new formal documents about humanitarian duties and responsibilities in war, NGOs may just help to bring these obligations into political existence, or at least to ensure that the perpetually fragile sense of their moral reality is kept alive for a new generation.

## New Emphasis on Moral Imperative, Rights, and Duty

The first document to emerge from the international NGO community in the 1990s was the ten-point Code of Conduct.[5] This was prepared jointly by the International Federation of Red Cross and Red Crescent Societies and the International Committee of the Red Cross (ICRC), in consultation with the members of the Steering Committee for Humanitarian Response (SCHR).[6] Although the Code of Conduct was envisaged primarily as relating to relief in natural disasters, it has always been seen to apply to NGO humanitarian work in armed conflicts, too. In theory, the code's articles are now used as key criteria in the planning and evaluation of NGO programming in and around war. The code is also regarded as a central measure of NGO performance by the new Humanitarian Accountability Project.

The first four articles of the code are key restatements or reworkings of the first four principles of the Red Cross. The last six articles are more in the nature of statements of good practice in relief methodology. It is the first article of the code that is of particular interest in this chapter, emphasizing more than ever before the notion of humanitarian duty:

> The Humanitarian *imperative* comes first—the right to receive humanitarian assistance, and to offer it, is a fundamental humanitarian principle which should be enjoyed by all citizens of all countries. As members of the international community, we recognise our *obligation* to provide humanitarian assistance wherever it is needed. Hence the need for unimpeded access to affected populations is of fundamental importance in exercising that *responsibility.*[7] (Emphasis added)

Long before 1992, when the code began to be developed, the originally French tradition of *sans frontier* humanitarianism had advocated a *droit d'ingérence* (a right to intervene in order to save lives), but the new "imperative" form of humanitarian ethic, with its emphasis on compulsory obligation, burst on the ears of many humanitarians as strident and even extreme. Some of those who were used to delicately negotiating humanitarian access found it strangely imperious, while others, who were becoming increasingly aware of the ambiguity of humanitarian aid and its sometimes dangerous consequences, found it reckless and lacking in operational nuance.[8]

Those choosing the phrase "humanitarian imperative" were determined to reinstate emphatically the principle of humanity that they saw as being so undermined in practice around the world—first by the perpetrators of its violation, second by reluctant donor governments, and finally, perhaps, by more consequentialist observers emphasizing the potentially harmful effects of humanitarian aid in certain situations. But in their attempt to emphasize humanitarian values, these NGOs and the Red Cross may also have begun to transform the humanitarian ethic in a significant way. Their determination to revitalize humanitarianism with a sense of ethical imperative began a moral shift toward a categorical insistence on humanitarian aid and protection that affirmed it as a supreme duty as much as a right. In doing so, they also began to identify themselves and others as particular duty bearers. In the body of the code they identify their own "obligations" and "responsibilities" in universal and absolutist terms and then spell them out in principle in the following articles. In the three annexes of the code its authors identify other duty bearers (affected governments, donor governments, and intergovernmental organizations) and also spell out their duties in general terms.

In the Sphere minimum standards that followed, the same core group of international NGOs then canvassed many other NGO and academic personnel to produce precise and quantifiable standards for describing what their humanitarian duty would look like in practice. The resulting standards focus on the five key "life-sustaining" fields of water and sanitation, nutrition, food aid, shelter and site planning, and health. These standards seek not simply to ensure people's survival but to enable a "life with dignity."[9] The elaboration of these technical standards and their many "key indicators" served to develop the idea of humanitarian duty still further. It complemented the identification of key duty bearers in the process of humanitarian action by specifying the actual *content* of particular humanitarian duties. Sphere standards are not just the stuff of general moral obligation but present very precise, latrine-based ethics! As many have observed, this is an extraordinary attempt to specify rights and duties that is unprecedented in international law concerning human rights, humanitarian law, and refugee law.

If the Code of Conduct asserts the moral imperative of humanitarian duty and the Sphere standards specify the content of some of that duty, then the Humanitarian Charter underwrites both with rights and responsibilities set out in law—international law—so acknowledging the idea of legal duties.[10] The Humanitarian Charter (once again drafted by that same core group of international NGOs and then discussed with others across the NGO spectrum) is rooted firmly in human rights law, humanitarian law, and refugee law, which give explicit legal status to its humanitarian values of restraint and protection in "calamity or armed conflict." And while these values are expressed in terms of rights, there is, once again, a resounding emphasis on the notion of duty in its text. The Humanitarian Charter is

> based on agencies' appreciation of their own *ethical obligations,* and reflects the rights and *duties* enshrined in international law in respect of which states and other parties have established *obligations* . . . and reaffirms our belief in the humanitarian imperative and its primacy.[11] (Emphasis added)

The charter explicitly emphasizes "a corresponding duty on others" to take steps to preserve life where it is threatened. In Section 2, on "roles and responsibilities," the duties of states or warring parties are given primary status, and humanitarian agency duties only kick in when such parties either cannot or will not meet their humanitarian obligations under law.

## The Implications of Ethical Imperatives

The fundamental moral tone of these three NGO pronouncements on humanitarianism casts humanitarian values and humanitarian actions as morally absolute. The term "humanitarian imperative" reverberates with Immanuel Kant's famous idea of the "categorical imperative." As a result, it might be wise to look at what such imperatives mean in moral terms and to get a sense of the kind of ethical position with which many international NGOs are aligning themselves in their recent humanitarian statements.

Kant's view is that moral imperatives are necessary in human affairs because they are essential in guiding a wayward human nature that all too often tends toward something other than the good. Kant begins his theory of morality with the idea of the "will" and the "principle of volition."[12] Only those good actions that we really and unambiguously "will" have true moral worth. But not many of us have the kind of nature that is able to will good actions on a consistent basis. So, when what we *would* do is not always what we *should* do, we need the help of imperatives that tell us clearly what we *ought* to do. We need what Kant calls a "categorical imperative" to instruct us. But Kant's particular "oughts" are distinctive because they are absolute. They are what he calls "unconditioned oughts."

Kant's idea of duty determines that something is always good to do regardless of any conditions. These imperatives are supreme moral principles that make for absolute duties and obvious "oughts." Their goodness is not dependent on their outcomes. This is moral thinking governed by a categorical "must," not a hypothetical "if." Operating on categorical imperatives means that I do something because it is always good, not because I think that *if* I do it then good may come. Kant sums up the difference:

> Now all imperatives command either hypothetically or categorically. The former represent the practical necessity of a possible action as a means for attaining something else that one wants (or may possibly want). The categorical imperative would be one which represented an action as objectively necessary in itself, without reference to another end.[13]

From this brief encounter with Kant, it is fairly obvious how international NGOs who have signed these three documents understand humanitarian values today. They claim clearly that being humanitarian is a categorical imperative. It is an end in itself. It is an unconditioned "ought" and must never be subject to conditions. There are no "ifs" in the humanitarian imperative. From this moral reasoning flows the idea of humanitarian duties that always exist regardless of circumstances or of aspirations toward competing moral ends. In other words, a Kantian humanitarian would have a lot of problems with the suspension of a humanitarian program as a hypothetical means to leverage a good political outcome for democracy or women's rights. Equally, in the context of the new "war on terrorism," an imperative humanitarian would also find grave moral flaws in any strategy that stopped or compromised humanitarian action on the basis of some wider hypothetical arguments about counterterrorism benefits.

From this idea of the humanitarian imperative there also flows the notion of duty sharing so prominent in the code, the charter, and Sphere. If a person, government, or organization cannot or will not abide by a humanitarian duty, then that duty automatically falls to others. As a categorical imperative, humanitarian duty is boundless. We all ought to do it.

The explicit and categorical commitment to humanitarian values in these three professions of humanitarian faith is commendable in its frankness. These NGO documents certainly take a stand. This is in contrast to much recent academic and policy "scribbling" that has focused on critical analysis without presenting a truly alternative vision of humanitarian action. Nevertheless, such an imperative approach to humanitarian duty does raise some questions that require quite urgent answers if this duty-based position is not to be stereotyped and misrepresented. Three particular questions come to mind:

- First, is this imperative approach really some sort of blinkered humanitarian fundamentalism?
- Second, is this NGO approach likely to colonize humanitarian responsibility still further and institutionalize such duties within a select group of powerful humanitarian organizations?
- Third, does such an explicit emphasis on duty make it any likelier that governments and nonstate actors will actually do their humanitarian duty in armed conflict?

The rest of the chapter will try to give some satisfactory answers to these questions but does so fully realizing that they are not the only questions that can be leveled at the imperative position as it stands.

## Humanitarian Fundamentalism?

If fundamentalism is best understood as a very contemporary and innovative reaction to the challenges of modernism by making a radical appeal to an exaggerated tradition, religious texts, strict rules, and moral absolutes, are these three NGO documents the expression of a new humanitarian fundamentalism?[14] Has modern or postmodern humanitarian work just got so complicated and disorienting that some humanitarians feel that a simple radicalism is required?

It is possible to read the absolutist tone of the code's first article as positively extremist—nonnegotiable humanitarian fanaticism. It might also be possible to consider the detailed Sphere standards on excreta disposal and personal hygiene to be as religiously prescriptive as some of the bizarre codes of the Taliban. The constant insistence on personal responsibility and the endless citing of chapter and verse texts in the Humanitarian Charter might be reminiscent of a Christian televangelist. The exacting demands of Sphere's nutrition standards could read as something straight out of the food laws in Leviticus.

Perhaps the main charges of humanitarian fundamentalism could be leveled by humanitarian pragmatists and ethical consequentialists who see the humanitarian imperative and its specification of humanitarian duties as being deliberately blind to the variety and complexities of their operational context. The pragmatist criticism claims that these NGO documents have become simultaneously obsessed with universals and minutiae to claim an equivalent moral and technical response in every situation.[15] Instead, they would argue, humanitarian action must always be carefully judged within the very specific political, practical, and strategic choices available in every operation. This necessarily nuanced operational approach is unlikely to result in the idealized uniformity of the new documents. Alongside this pragmatic critique is that of the consequentialists—humanitarians and policymakers who judge it ridiculous to talk of a consistent humanitarian imperative that takes no account of how humanitarian work can be used instrumentally to play into the greater good or to increase the harm in a given situation.

These two main criticisms are important, but they are easily rebuffed. A careful reading of the documents makes it clear that the writers of these texts are very much alive to differences in operational contexts. The introduction to Sphere is explicit:

> [A]bility to achieve the minimum standards will depend on a range of factors, some of which are within their control, while others such as political and security factors, lie outside their control . . . availability of sufficient financial, human and material resources is also essential.[16]

This recognition is also repeated in the Humanitarian Charter[17] and is the basis of the differentiation of humanitarian responsibility in Section 2. So it would be wrong to present the idea of the humanitarian imperative and its specification of duties as absurdly idealistic and resistant to context. The charter is well aware of context and of the limits of what *can* be done. But it is equally well aware of what *ought* to be done and so what ought to be *willed*. In Kantian terms, actively striving to will what ought to be done is highly valued. Indeed, to Kant, there is no greater moral worth than genuinely willing the good even if it cannot be achieved:

> Even if, by some especially unfortunate fate or by the niggardly provision of stepmotherly nature [or, one might add, by the constant violations of warring parties], this will should be wholly lacking in the power to accomplish its purpose; if with the greatest of effort it should yet achieve nothing, and only the good will should remain (not, to be sure, as a mere wish but as the summoning of all the means in our power), yet would it, like a jewel, still shine by its own light as something which has its full value in itself. Its usefulness or fruitlessness can neither augment nor diminish this value.[18]

For Kantian humanitarians, the fact that their documents spell out what ought to be done and seek to activate humanitarian will in this direction is morally important. It does not mean that they are not realistic or pragmatic in a given context. It does not mean that they do not recognize that other Kantian reality of their "imperfect power."

Neither do these texts lay their signatory NGOs open to the consequentialists' charge that their humanitarian imperative implies that they think it right simply to dish out aid regardless of the consequences. The imperative position means that they have an unconditional humanitarian "ought," but it need not be a careless one. Indeed, what Des Gasper has described as "an ethics of virtue" and "an ethics of care" in humanitarian work is crucial to the three documents in question. Gasper describes this ethics of care as "a combination of general rules [acting as] prompts and guidelines that must be selected and used intelligently and with a good spirit."[19] Kant would tend to agree with this idea of complementing imperatives with the cultivation of practical virtues like courage and prudence. He sees virtues as the "moral strength" that enables a person (or an organization) to see through ethical imperatives and so implement duties.[20]

The three NGO texts are full of a demand for "an ethics of care" in humanitarian work. Articles 2–10 of the Code of Conduct are all concerned with careful (and not just caring) humanitarian action. The core humanitarian operating principles of Articles 2–4 (impartiality, the avoidance of political bias, and independence) are all practical ways of being careful in doing what one ought to do when responding to the humanitarian imperative. Judicious care in matters of culture, participation, mitigation, transparency, and the representation are all taken very seriously in Articles 5–10. Similarly, a duty of care is explicitly invoked around implementing the humanitarian imperative in the Humanitarian Charter and in Sphere. Section 2.4 of the charter notes how the failure of warring parties to respect humanitarian operations and so to abuse aid may

> potentially render civilians more vulnerable to attack, or may on occasion bring unintended advantage to one or more of the warring parties. We are committed to minimising any such adverse effects of our interventions in so far as this is consistent with the obligations outlined above.[21]

This do-no-harm clause of the charter shows the influence of the work of Mary Anderson and others exploring the political economy of aid in war.[22] It is repeated in the introduction to the Sphere standards. The notion of an ethic of care also runs throughout the standards themselves, especially the analysis standards that embody particular caretaking in implementing the humanitarian imperative. For example, the food aid analysis standards particularly emphasize an attention to "the impacts of food aid programmes . . . as critical" and specifically affirm that "agencies have a duty to monitor how food aid and programme funds are used."[23]

This all seems to suggest that any consequentialist critiques of the imperative approach are not really justified. With such an ethic of care complementing the imperative approach to humanitarian duty, it is not possible to characterize NGOs that take this approach as deontological fanatics giving out aid with their heads buried in the sand or with their eyes blinkered to the nature of their actions. Instead it shows that, although it is built on an ethical imperative, this view of humanitarian action is still careful in the best sense of the word.

Such carefulness does not make this form of humanitarianism de facto consequentialist. Operating carefully is very different from operating conditionally in the light of some other good. The kind of ethic that is prepared to make humanitarian action a hypothetical imperative that is conditional on a greater good of peace or political progress is of a very different order morally.[24] Mark Duffield has wisely warned against the rise of such consequentialist ethics in regard to humanitarian action, especially as operated by Western donor governments.[25] A morality that focuses on what it regards as greater political goods than humanitarian goods makes the humanitarian ethic conditional and instrumental rather than an end in itself. The good thing about the duty-based formulations of the code, the charter, and Sphere is that they reject both consequentialism and carelessness in humanitarian ethics.

## Colonizing Humanitarian Responsibility?

Several people have observed how these three documents may actually function to restrict future understanding and ownership of humanitarian responsibility.[26] They feel that by generating this kind of soft law around themselves so emphatically, NGOs may in fact overidentify themselves with the humanitarian imperative and its specific humanitarian duties so that, far from framing it as a duty for others, the NGOs will end up colonizing the humanitarian ethic as their duty alone. By spelling it out so precisely and writing it down by themselves, they might easily be maneuvered into taking sole responsibility for it. Rather than passing the buck of humanitarian duty, they will be left holding it. Fiona Terry has summed up this concern:

> From Sphere, through the Codes of Conduct and finally to the Ombudsman, the onus of responsibility for assisting vulnerable people shifts from states to humanitarian organizations, and finally to the victims themselves.[27]

Such a view cannot be argued from the texts themselves, which at every turn bend over backward to emphasize the primary humanitarian responsibility of others. Yet it may still be that the political effect of the texts is that they do indeed run the risk of focusing humanitarian responsibility on NGOs to the exclusion of states, nonstate actors, and individual citizens. If this is the result, then it will be not because NGOs have not shared their humanitarian responsibility with others but because they have not done so radically enough. The texts may be progressive, but they are still written by, and built around, an elite aristocracy of humanitarian agencies. This is reform rather than radical change.

But in an important sense, Sphere's critics are reactionary, too. Terry's concerns about the shift of humanitarian responsibility "to the victims themselves" is potentially patronizing. Her fears about where all this obligation might end up—with the people themselves—is in reality where the whole thing needs to *start*. As many of the NGO leaders of this process admit, the impetus that generated these three significant documents and their vital reaffirmation of the humanitarian ethic has been top-down and predominantly white. But for the important ethics and ideas in the documents to really gain momentum, this top-down process must be joined by a groundswell of popular support for the humanitarian ethic, its rights, and its duties.

The great challenge for the humanitarian ethic and its operating system in the twenty-first century is to decolonize. There is no doubt that humanitarian action functions in neocolonial ways. Still largely in the hands of the governments and NGOs of former or current imperial powers (Britain, France, and the United States), much humanitarian policy and practice must relinquish some of their power and hand it over to humanitarian movements in Africa, Asia, the Middle East, and Latin America. While these NGO texts certainly do not intend to colonize humanitarian responsibility and humanitarian action, the power structure behind the texts is largely neocolonial. It still tends to dangle the buck of humanitarian duty just beyond the reach of the people and their organizations. Real ownership of the ethic and resources of the humanitarian imperative needs to be shared more broadly throughout the societies that need it most.

## Cultivating Wider Humanitarian Will

This naturally brings us to the last question: Does such an explicit emphasis on duty make it any likelier that governments and nonstate actors will actually do their humanitarian duty in war? In other words, is this a form of ethics that just makes humanitarians feel better about the nature of their mission? Or is it a kind of ethics that effectively results in the improved protection of people who have experienced, or imminently face, extreme violations of their rights in armed conflicts? Do the new texts work any better than the old ones?

Not surprisingly, Kant has much to say about the doing of duty, and setting out four basic approaches to it.[28] The first is simply that you don't do it. The second is that you do your duty, though not because you really will yourself to do it but because you are impelled to do it for other self-interested reasons. For example, you might pay your tax, not because you want to, but because you do not want to be fined. The third is similar to the second but with a positive rather than negative motive. You do your duty not because you really want to but because you are inclined to do it anyway, since it is closely aligned with your interests as they stand at the moment. For example, you do not commit suicide, because you are happy being alive. Nor do you commit adultery if you currently have a gorgeous and loving spouse who makes you very happy. Kant concludes of the second and third approaches that people operate "in accordance with duty but not *from* duty."

Thus, it is the fourth approach to duty that is the only one of real moral worth, according to Kant. This is when you do your duty purely out of duty, on the basis of goodwill and in the face of many inclinations *not* to do it. Kant uses the example of suicide again, considering the imperative not to commit suicide as an absolute duty. A person who is in deep despair, overcome with hopeless sorrow and eagerly wishing for death, but who preserves his life without loving it, out of duty rather than fear, has a real "moral content" to his duty.

These four approaches to duty obviously have direct parallels when thinking about humanitarian duty. If, as their three documents suggest, many NGOs are keen to cultivate humanitarian duty in a wide array of people, governments, armed nonstate actors, social organizations, and business corporations, it is likely that they will be relating to all the above approaches. Basically, working from Kant, humanitarian NGOs have two types of approaches to the cultivation of humanitarian duty in others. First, they can work deeply and determinedly to foster a truly good humanitarian will in these groups and their individuals so that they obey the humanitarian imperative from the goodness of their will and in spite of their other inclinations or compulsions. Many theologians, not least among them St. Paul, might see this approach as the domain of God rather than of NGOs. Yet an interesting approach of this kind is currently being undertaken in a process to engage nonstate actors (NSAs) in a land-mine ban. This process seeks to use dialogue, persuasion, support, and monitoring to generate a "moral commitment" in NSA decision makers.[29] Second, NGOs can focus on identifying the particular self-interest that might "incline" or "impel" these groups to obey their humanitarian duty. This more tactical approach is perhaps the one most often pursued.

Using either strategy, the duty-based approach of the humanitarian imperative may have some advantages. Although it is framed in terms of rights, the emphasis on duty gives a clear moral commandment that might more easily resonate with human will as well as human interest. Expressed as a moral duty, the humanitarian ethic may travel farther across class and culture than more elaborate constructions of rights or principles. But being based in a framework of rights and law, the idea of humanitarian duty can draw equally on the normative power of law to try to incline or impel in certain situations. Therefore, it seems to be able to express humanitarian values both morally and legally with equal ease. Being bilingual in this way may be an enormous advantage when dealing with religious groups who are prepared to discuss ethics and morality but are not necessarily prepared to respect international law or are wary of the interests in which that law is deemed to function. Yet the legal framework of duties is appropriate for some groups. Recent experience in making big business more responsible for human rights has shown that the development of a corporation's goodwill is slow and not guaranteed. There is thus a need to work on approaches that go "beyond voluntarism" to make people do their duty.[30] Similarly, the recent international commission on humanitarian intervention and subsequent UN agreements have also emphasized the notion of state duty rather than human rights alone to point up the responsibility to protect.[31]

## Conclusion

So what can we make of this new imperative morality of humanitarian action in war? It is certainly an important part of the humanitarian writing of the past few years. It is certainly forthright and unambiguous. But how much has it been read and internalized by the very NGO community that espouses it? Is it, in fact, the product of a group of elite NGO scribblers operating between London, Oxford, Geneva, and Washington? Despite the Sphere project's wide-reaching training program, I am always surprised at how few NGO humanitarians have really studied and digested these texts. This is a pity because they are good texts. They are more sophisticated and more nuanced than their detractors proclaim. By and large, they probably do represent the moral view of most NGO humanitarians, and they are written in a manner that makes them relatively easy to read and own. Most important, perhaps, they are a testament to the fact that international NGOs did try to put their convictions on paper when faced with the fin de siècle challenges of the past century. Paper is not practice, but it can influence and shape it.

Realistically, then, how can this restatement of humanitarian morality as legal and political duty produce greater political will for the restraint of war? Kant has observed that any self-regulation is extremely problematic when "everywhere we come upon the dear self" or when we are always building moral projects with "the crooked timber of humanity." In the international arena, the power of law to enforce duty is still very problematic. It seems, therefore, that humanitarians will have to continue to work on stirring a mixture of humanitarian will and self-interest in the cultivation of humanitarian duties in state and nonstate polities. Ideally, the emphasis would be on making genuine humanitarian will a central ingredient of political will. The ability of NGOs to shape and organize public opinion on humanitarian values and to build globally networked social movements on the limits of war will be crucial to this effort. They have succeeded to some considerable degree on land mines and debt. Can they now do it for the Geneva Conventions, the Genocide Convention, and refugee law?

While NGOs can no doubt cultivate some humanitarian will and encourage the doing of some humanitarian duties, they will only ever be able to do a bit. Nevertheless, in these new documents they have firmly stated their particular moral project and sought to describe it in unprecedented detail. In a small but important way, they have described humanitarian duty in war for a new generation. The great advantage of the imperative approach is that it places moral responsibility for humanitarian values on everyone. As always, it remains to be seen what the combination of power, personality, and circumstance does with such responsibility in the wars to come.

## Notes

I am grateful to Professor Otto Hieronymi of Webster University in Geneva for inviting me to give the paper on humanitarian ethics, on which this chapter is based, at a conference on humanitarian values in Geneva in February 2002.

1. Michel de Montaigne, "On Vanity," *The Complete Essays,* trans. Michael Screech (London: Penguin, 1991), 1071.

2. See Hugo Slim, "The Humanitarian Ethic in the 1990s" (PhD diss., Oxford Brookes University, 2002).

3. See, for example, Hugo Slim, "Not Philanthropy but Rights: The Proper Politicisation of Humanitarian Philosophy," *International Journal of Human Rights* 6, no. 2 (2002).

4. Mark Duffield, *Global Governance and the New Wars* (London: Zed Books, 2001), chap. 4; Des Gasper, "Drawing a Line: Ethical and Political Strategies in Complex Emergency Assistance," *European Journal of Development Research* 11, no. 2 (1999); Hugo Slim, "Doing the Right Thing: Relief Agencies, Moral Dilemmas and Moral Responsibility in Political Emergencies and War," *Disasters* 21, no. 3 (1997).

5. Sphere Project, *Humanitarian Charter and Minimum Standards in Disaster Response* (Oxford: Oxfam, 2000).

6. Members include Caritas Internationalis, Catholic Relief Services, International Federation of Red Cross and Red Crescent Societies, International Save the Children Alliance, Lutheran World Federation, Oxfam, and the World Council of Churches. The International Committee of the Red Cross has observer status.

7. Code of Conduct, Article 1.

8. See, for example, Hugo Slim, "Relief Agencies and Moral Standing in War: Principles of Humanity, Impartiality, Neutrality and Solidarity," *Development in Practice* 7, no. 4 (1997); Thomas Weiss and Cindy Collins, *Humanitarian Challenges and Intervention* (Boulder, CO: Lynne Rienner, 2000), 99.

9. Sphere Project, *Humanitarian Charter.*

10. Ibid., 6–10.

**11.** Ibid., 6.

**12.** Immanuel Kant, *Grounding for the Metaphysics of Morals*, 1785, trans. James Ellington (Indianapolis, IN: Hackett, 1983), 13.

**13.** Ibid., 25.

**14.** For such an understanding of fundamentalism, see Youssef Choueiri, *Islamic Fundamentalism*, rev. ed. (London: Pinter, 1997).

**15.** For an excellent summary of the range of criticisms leveled against Sphere, see Koenraad Van Brabant, "Regaining Perspective: The Debate over Quality Assurance and Accountability," *Humanitarian Exchange*, October 2000.

**16.** Sphere Project, *Humanitarian Charter*, 2.

**17.** Ibid., 9.

**18.** Kant, *Grounding for the Metaphysics of Morals*, 8.

**19.** Gasper, "Drawing a Line."

**20.** Immanuel Kant, *Metaphysical Principles of Virtue*, 1797, trans. James Ellington (Indianapolis, IN: Hackett, 1983), 64.

**21.** Sphere Project, *Humanitarian Charter*, 8.

**22.** Mary Anderson, *Do No Harm: How Aid Can Support Peace or War* (Boulder, CO: Lynne Rienner, 1999); see also Philippe Le Billon, *The Political Economy of War: What Relief Agencies Need to Know*, HPN Paper 33 (London: ODI, 2000).

**23.** Sphere Project, *Humanitarian Charter*, 135, 142.

**24.** See Thomas Weiss, "Principles, Politics, and Humanitarian Action," *Ethics and International Relations* 13 (1999).

**25.** Duffield, *Global Governance and the New Wars*, 90–95.

**26.** See, for example, Fiona Terry, "The Limits and Risks of Regulation Mechanisms for Humanitarian Action," *Humanitarian Exchange* 17, October 2000; see also Hugo Slim, "Sharing a Universal Ethic: The Principle of Humanity in War," *International Journal of Human Rights* 2, no. 4 (1998).

**27.** Terry, "Limits and Risks," 21.

**28.** Kant, *Grounding for the Metaphysics of Morals*, 9–11.

**29.** "Engaging Non-State Actors in a Landmine Ban: A Pioneering Conference" in *Full Conference Proceedings* (Quezon City, Philippines: Swiss Campaign to Ban Landmines et al., 2001), 6–7.

**30.** International Council on Human Rights Policy, *Beyond Voluntarism: Human Rights and the Developing International Legal Obligations of Companies* (Geneva: ICHRP, 2002).

**31.** International Commission on Intervention and State Sovereignty, *The Responsibility to Protect: Report of the International Commission on Intervention and State Sovereignty* (Ottawa: IDRC, 2001).

# Claiming a Humanitarian Imperative
## Commentary

Jonathan Moore

In his chapter in this book, "Claiming a Humanitarian Imperative: NGOs and the Cultivation of Humanitarian Duty," Hugo Slim addresses the "humanitarian imperative" principally by examining three documents, produced by the NGO community, which he interprets to construct and support the concept of "humanitarian duty." This brief essay will focus on these two ideas by considering humanitarian duty in the context of its parent imperative, principally in terms of its practical application by various actors, including, but not limited to, NGOs.

The definition of the term "humanitarian" as used here, however, will not be confined to rights in armed conflicts or to efforts to constrain the impact of war on civilians, but encompasses activities to prevent and treat human suffering during and following war. Moreover, it will not be confined to efforts generally regarded as emergency humanitarian assistance, but addresses postconflict policies and programs of rehabilitation and development intended to confront the root causes of both war and poverty, thus protecting the investment of emergency relief measures.

This commentary accepts the invitation to carry the theoretical into the practical realm, inherent in the following passage by Hugo Slim: "writing about rights and detailing duties is no shortcut to realizing those rights and meeting those duties."[1] Indeed, in order for theory to "get a life," for instance, for a humanitarian imperative to be truly "claimed," it must be operationalized. There follows a limited effort to examine the theory in this light—still only writing, but writing about some contemporary

175

experience in testing the humanitarian imperative and realizing humanitarian duty.

■     ■     ■

The concept of humanitarian duty has no chance of being effectively activated without understanding the formidable realities involved. Many challenges must be recognized, and obstacles overcome, for duty to be carried out, whether by United Nations, bilateral, or NGO efforts. A few key hurdles here illustrate how problematic the concept of duty is when it attempts to be transformed from theory into practice.

For starters, those actors who are seized with the role of practicing humanitarian duty in crisis countries—herein meaning poor states that are contending with multiple problems, including the suffering and damages of war, along with the urgent need to develop—must accept the likelihood of continued failure by the international community to provide help, in sustained political and financial support, that is adequate to seriously meet the challenges involved. The so-called donor states, whether acting on their own or through multilateral organizations, wanting to respond to these crises out of a variety of motivations, nevertheless lower their depiction of the size and difficulty of the given crisis so that it matches the approximate level of their willingness to commit, thus attempting to do the job on the cheap and the quick. This doesn't work, and dashed expectations and recriminations follow. Most international emergency humanitarian assistance operations throughout the world today—concerned with refugees, food, health, shelter, protection—are seriously short-funded from pledge levels, and recovery and development programs intended to prevent slippage into future violence and destitution do not come close to being financed to meet requirements in the first place.[2] This is not to overlook that much aid that does flow in both respects is wasted or ineffectual, or that donor states have other pressing priorities to serve at home and abroad. But it is to say that humanitarian actors, in attempting to do their duty, should not act under the illusion that they will have the support needed to meet the conditions they face, should not pretend to be operating in an environment more rational and less chaotic than it is, and will have to figure out how to work within much more limited parameters than are appropriate.

The relationship between the external provider and the internal recipient, the international and the indigenous assets and actors, is a complex and delicate one, seldom achieved in the right balance and especially difficult in the transition from emergency to rehabilitation aid. This duality can be as treacherous as it is critical. It is fluid and has to be monitored and tended adaptively; there is no set formula or template that can be applied to it. A major factor in this relationship is the capacity of the government receiving the aid and working for self-sufficiency. Weak capacity can limit or cripple the ability of recipients to assume certain responsibilities and requires the humanitarian agents to assess, negotiate, and revise the types and phasing of their assistance accordingly. Such shortfalls can take the form of bureaucratic deficit, lack of technical proficiency, or the inability of the country's political actors to achieve enough consensus and cohesion to enable progress to take place. In Afghanistan, for example, the new transitional government resented that external aid was flowing through the United Nations and NGOs instead of directly to the government, whose ministerial talent was very thin but who argued that it couldn't develop capacity without money. A decision was made by the donors to take the risk of injecting more aid directly. In Haiti, the international community withheld funds earmarked for Haitian development while the government complained that it was the denial of funds that was responsible for the political impasse blocking the aid. The donors held firm. When the provision of international aid requires indigenous capacity that isn't there, what happens to the concept of humanitarian duty?

Accepting that development in several forms—that is, rehabilitation of physical infrastructure, restoration and strengthening of social services, institution building in governance at the national and local levels, reform of political processes, macrofinance and legal frameworks—is fundamentally humanitarian in nature, it is important not to ignore it when examining the exigencies of humanitarian duty. For those actors doing conflict-related recovery and rehabilitation work amid multifarious international activity, several phenomena need to be understood.

One is that when emergency assistance, political initiatives, military peacekeeping, and development are all involved, development invariably comes in a poor last. The reasons for this are not mysterious, including high demands in cost and difficulty, and short supply of talent and time. But the low priority invariably given development creates problems not only for humanitarian actors directly engaged but also for others whose success ultimately depends on the development process. This delinquency was evident in the crucial early stages of the UN-directed enterprises in both East Timor and Afghanistan. In the United Nations' Brahimi Report on overall peace operations reform, the development component had been given rhetorical recognition but was forsaken in the effect of its actual recommendations.[3]

Another aspect to be recognized is that the coordination demands among the various international interventions in humanitarian crises are greater than the ability to meet them. Apart from the disparate bilateral, multilateral, military, and NGO contingents, there is separation and competition even within the United Nations' own family of structures, agencies, and programs. Although the umbrella organization set up under the special representative of the secretary-general in the most intense situations is meant to provide coordination, it has limited influence over autonomous UN units and also inflicts bureaucratic divisions and inefficiencies of its own.

A third reality to be identified in this context is the difficult relationship between the emergency and the developmental humanitarian endeavors on the one hand and the security problems and programs trying to eliminate them on the other. Here is a symbiotic challenge of the nastiest type. Although sustained security cannot be accomplished without success in relief and development, efforts to assure immediate security are not just essential to but will dominate other undertakings until they prevail. Although this truth is perfectly logical, the complexity and tension in relationships that flow from it are extremely difficult to cope with, as experience in Kosovo, Somalia, and, again, Afghanistan and East Timor attests. The elemental and lasting nature of the security threat distorts other needs and efforts. The point here is that humanitarian duty cannot be performed solo. In addition to the pursuit of direct tasks, cooperation and respect need to be provided for various roles, and reciprocal understanding needs to be engendered about the impact of each set of actors on the others.

■   ■   ■

Looking at new or at least current actors, strategies, and ethical dilemmas not already mentioned above—which are found in countries trying to recover from and avoid conflict and get onto a development track—provides a further opportunity to elucidate the conditions and practice of "international humanitarian duty, obligation, and responsibility."[4]

Nonstate actors are prevalent in many situations of humanitarian urgency, sometimes overlapping with other groups of actors, such as NGOs. There can be international as well as indigenous nonstate actors. In Afghanistan, for instance, the warlords and freelancing commanders have considerable power, a large constituency, and a significant role in their country's efforts to wrestle with security and development, and their own national government as well as representatives of the international community must deal with them. This obviously becomes politically complicated, with the transitional government trying to incentivize, intimidate, and inveigle the regional paramilitary authorities into its legitimacy while the forces of the U.S.-led military coalition, including civic action teams, make side deals with those same players outside Kabul in the pursuit of military and political objectives that could have the opposite effect. The humanitarian agents needing security for relief and reconstruction work in the countryside are faced with a mottled and unpredictable complex of threats and former actors. They must deal with random banditry, as well as fighting between coalition troops and militias; the national police and army take a long time to be formed; and the UN International Security Force's presence outside the capital is sporadic. The UN Assistance Mission in Afghanistan (UNAMA), the UN umbrella staff led by the secretary-general's special representative for Afghanistan, could be considered another kind of nonstate actor; this type of entity, originally set up in places where peacekeeping operations were under way, continues to proliferate.

Political groups in some countries have some characteristics of nonstate actors, for example, the veterans' organizations in East Timor, which embody political activism, social and economic reintegration, and an incipient security threat. "Convergence," the coalition arrayed against the Aristide government in Haiti, was recognized by the Organization of American States in its efforts to mediate negotiations to end an electoral stalemate. In the northern and eastern parts of Sri Lanka, the Tamil Tigers are to some degree dealt with—by the Norwegian mediators, the government in Colombo, the United Nations, and bilateral and NGO humanitarians— as if they were a government. In Somalia, the self-declared independent state of Somaliland, though not recognized by the international community, nevertheless has had direct dealings with many international humanitarian programs.

Humanitarian actors must contend with several new strategies in the recovery/development realm that raise ethical dilemmas. One is "peacebuilding," frequently defined in vague or varying terms. This notion has the latent danger of subordinating humanitarian programs to political agendas, which can compromise the programs' neutrality. The problem can be handled—progress is unlikely if the various channels of effort remain hermetically sealed and immune to one another—but it needs to be guarded against. Peacebuilding can also be pursued in ways that tilt development agendas in the direction of more advanced institution building, macropolicy frameworks, and democratization promotion, with proportionally less emphasis on more fundamental recovery and poverty reduction efforts aimed at local populations and the grassroots of the society. This is a particularly relevant issue in countries still prone to political and security disruption problems, such as Somalia, Haiti, and East Timor, where programs to strengthen national institutions remain vulnerable and the more immediate and basic needs of the population remain unmet.

Strategies for demobilization, disarmament, and reintegration (DDR) and for resolving the plight of internally displaced persons (IDPs) are stubbornly problematic in many places. For instance, in Afghanistan and Rwanda, DDR efforts are hampered by reluctance to reduce military power; in Sri Lanka, resettling IDPs is blocked by security hang-ups over territory. Questions also arise over preferential treatment for certain groups and program integrity. Do soldiers get more help because they are more of a threat to future security than are ordinary villagers ravaged by conflict on top of poverty? What happens when the former combatants step down and surrender their arms, which might be accomplished with relatively straightforward processes, but find that roles and employment in civilian life are not forthcoming because they take much longer and, in any case, cannot be programmatically guaranteed? Do refugees get more help than the internally displaced because they are categorized as international and because aid programs for them are better organized and funded? One partial approach increasingly adopted to handle these dilemmas is to target humanitarian aid less on the individual returnees and more on the communities to which they come.

As the United Nations and supporting actors try out new combinations of policy, structure, process, and funding to assist nations in making the transition from war to peace, the old problem of trade-offs persists between emergency relief beyond a period of intense crisis and development assistance toward building self-sufficiency. This dynamic is sometimes characterized arbitrarily as saving lives versus building livelihoods, or as treating symptoms versus eliminating causes. Such tensions of course prevail in many transitional circumstances, Afghanistan and Sri Lanka being just two examples, where the needs for basic relief do not easily recede, yet where more ingenuity needs to be applied for a smoother merging into recovery aid. Both needs are humanitarian and endure indeterminately, and the best answers will no doubt be found in mix and timing. But because one need is more dramatic and proximate, better organized and funded, and easier to perform by the internationals without much involvement by national officials, while the other is more complex, long term, difficult, and poorly understood, an ethical distortion arises that must be better addressed.

Two more emerging strategies also define the topography of humanitarian duty at the grassroots level. The first, "building blocks," refers to development efforts focused on subregions of a country that appear ripe for progress because of a variety of factors, including political cohesiveness and stability, when the country as a whole has too many pockets of fragmentation and disorder, and may lack a central government strong enough, to be able to absorb a national development model. Somalia is an example of this phenomenon. Two problems with such investments, however, are that they will discriminate among equally needy groups and can be seen to act preemptively as a disincentive to national capacity. Similarly, efforts to promote pluralistic and inclusive decision making in local communities mobilizing to rehabilitate themselves from the ground up may be seen to threaten the central authority and may have difficulty connecting to the national rehabilitation plans promulgated from the capital. This issue is at play in Sri Lanka and Rwanda, where decentralization programs are struggling.

The various strategies cited above all provide examples of political problems with ethical dimensions, which can best be resolved by an approach that is humble and pragmatic: what actually works best to achieve the desired humanitarian results.

■    ■    ■

Neutrality and independence are two of the fundamental principles listed in the ICRC/ Red Cross and Red Crescent/NGO code of conduct for disaster relief that Slim cites in his chapter. A distinction can be made between the two when moving from theory to practice in complex, conflict-prone crises. Neutrality, when enforced as a rule, can actually frustrate various humanitarian undertakings, whereas independence, when pursued as an objective, can better accommodate competition among humanitarian needs while preserving the integrity of the given humanitarian agent. Independence is inherently more congenial with duty and can be applied more resourcefully and flexibly in implementing the humanitarian imperative.

Experience in Afghanistan shows that neutrality collides with war and politics and that in some situations it must give in order for humanitarian duty to proceed rather than be frustrated. Military forces in Afghanistan have infected, distorted, and even preempted the work of international humanitarian organizations. But aid workers, bent on doing their job in such a cauldron, can find that neutrality makes a shaky ally, and the delivery of humanitarian services itself becomes partisan. Unalloyed neutrality may be the first casualty of the translation of theory into practice, because duty may require it to be tempered tactically in order to preserve it over the long term. In the messy contexts being discussed here, it becomes a matter not of ordaining neutrality as a principle but of flexing without sacrificing it. Humanitarian organizations can't benefit from security help and then indignantly condemn it, and security forces can't simply override humanitarian action. Each needs the other, so a means of wary but practical coexistence must be found.

The challenge of sustaining neutrality while battling for human rights concerns, again in the midst of confused and volatile humanitarian crises, is particularly daunting and provides further insight into the tensions between aspiration and actuality. Broadly defined, human rights and humanitarianism converge—along with political and civil rights, we must consider economic, social, and cultural rights. Reality interweaves principles; almost everything interacts. It is obvious that human rights suffer in so-called peace operations, and it is true that protecting those rights may require some measure of departure from neutrality. When human rights protections are aggressively pursued, someone's ox is inevitably gored, and other initiatives with urgent humanitarian portent may be interrupted. In the fulfillment of humanitarian duty, the protection and advancement of human rights must be a constant devotion but not a mindless juggernaut.

In Afghanistan, some NGOs indicated that unless generally recognized human rights norms—particularly those affecting the treatment of women—were honored, their humanitarian services would be withheld. Later they yielded on this point, leaving the inference to be drawn that a results-based humanitarianism may top a rights-based humanitarianism. For its part, UNAMA took the calculated step to go easy on its human rights agenda in order not to upset the delicate political undertakings it believed necessary to build Afghan self-government that might then become capable of supporting various humanitarian principles, including human rights. The point here is not to argue whether such decisions were correct, and certainly not to suspend skepticism about easy rationalization. At the heart of the matter is the need to reject the illusion that compromises are not necessary, and to acknowledge that being serious about translating the humanitarian imperative into duty means we must make agonizing choices.

■    ■    ■

This effort to articulate some of the complexities, vagaries, and obstacles involved in the manifestation of humanitarian duty may seem discouraging. The intent, though, is first to illuminate just how formidable a challenge it is to project theory into action, principle into practice. Second, it is to assist the actual humanitarian actors by recognizing the environmental factors that define their duty. Third, the intent is to explain duty as inherently pragmatic, requiring flexibility in choice and judgment—doing the best job one can with one's ideals under the circumstances.

This brings us back to the humanitarian imperative found in the first article of the Red Cross code of conduct, which Slim started with. To me, an imperative means a principle, an ideal, that is dynamic in nature, that has an urgency, a force attached to it that cannot be ignored—that is fundamental to the strengthening of the human condition. It may be something less than an absolute in that it needs flexibility, adaptation, compromise; it needs to discover in what way it can be made relevant to reality in order to influence that reality positively. This requires knowledge of, respect for, and a willingness to work with the given environment. If the imperative is kept sacrosanct and inviolate—rigid—it is likely to remain an abstraction. "The moral imperatives cannot be given or give life unless they are applied relatively, with respect and allowance for other absolutes and for the requirements of bringing into being."[5] For this to happen, the humanitarian imperative needs a means to effect its own application. Here is where humanitarian duty comes in, and the really hard work begins.

## Notes

1. See the chapter by Slim in this volume, p. 161.

2. For example, for Sierra Leone, the United Nations requested $78 million in humanitarian relief for 2001 and received $60 million (80 percent); for 2002 the equivalent appeal requested $88 million and received $31 million (44 percent); for 2003, $83 million was requested and $660,000 (1 percent) received. For Afghanistan, the 2002 UN appeal for both relief and recovery requested $1.8 billion and received $1.2 billion (66 percent); the 2003 appeal requested $833 million and received $70 million (8 percent).

3. "Report of the Panel on United Nations Peace Operations," August 2000; Executive Summary, paragraphs 7, 8, 19, 24, 25, 26, 36; Summary of Recommendations, paragraphs 2, 18 (UN Document no. A/55/305–S/2000/809).

4. See the chapter by Slim in this volume, p. 161.

5. Jonathan Moore, ed. *Hard Choices: Moral Dilemmas in Humanitarian Intervention* (Lanham, MD: Rowman and Littlefield, 1998), 7.

# 7
# Humanitarian Intervention after Kosovo

Richard Falk

In the aftermath of the Cold War, conflicts internal to states have captured center stage in global politics. Numerous humanitarian catastrophes have occurred since 1989, partly as a result of weak structures of governance, producing the phenomenon of "failed states," especially in sub-Saharan Africa. Also, the emergence of human rights as a concern ranked rather highly, although selectively, on the global policy agenda has generated support for "humanitarian intervention."[1] This support also reflects the growing influence of TV and other global media in building public pressure to act in the face of severe humanitarian abuse.

Such a background has challenged the capacities of the United Nations to provide politically acceptable and logistically effective responses.[2] Although not paralyzed by the earlier ideological stalemates of the Cold War, and globally engaged through the intricacies of an enveloping world economy linked by the Internet, permanent members of the UN Security Council disagree intensely about the proper balance, in particular situations, between sovereign rights and humanitarian intervention. Moreover, geopolitical realities restrict an interventional option to circumstances in which the country involved is relatively weak or is disposed or induced to give consent. The whole pattern of response has also been affected in this period by the quality of global leadership provided by the United States, and the extent to which the nature of this leadership has been buffeted to and fro by domestic political tensions, particularly as exhibited by an inward-looking U.S. Congress, whose majority seems suspicious of, if not hostile to, an active and effective United Nations, especially concerning the agenda of global security.

Such a set of circumstances poses a series of difficult challenges directed at the relevant international institutions and international law norms. It is partly a matter of reconciling doctrine with practice. It is also partly a matter of evaluating the effect on world order of these various moves toward a new humanitarian diplomacy that is being shaped by contradictory pressures—the postcolonial revival of interventional diplomacy and the emergence of support for the international implementation of minimum human rights in the face of severe governmental abuses and criminality.

Many of these concerns are brought into focus by a consideration of the legal and world order controversy surrounding the NATO war in Kosovo, waged against the former Yugoslavia in 1999.

## A Point of Departure

Perhaps more fundamentally than any recent international occurrence, the NATO initiative on behalf of the Kosovars has provoked extremely divergent interpretations of what is truly at stake, about the prudence of what was undertaken, and about the bearing of law and morality on this course of events. This divergence of perspective can be suggestively framed by the positions adopted by two highly respected and morally engaged international figures: Vaclev Havel, acclaimed president of the Czech Republic, and Robert Fisk, renowned correspondent and feature writer for the British newspaper the *Independent*.

Acknowledging that the tactics adopted by NATO had given rise to controversy, Havel, in an address to the Canadian Senate and House of Commons on April 29, 1999, went on to affirm what was for him beyond controversy:

> But there is one thing no reasonable person can deny: this is probably the first war that has not been waged in the name of "national interests," but rather in the name of principles and values. If one can say of any war that it is ethical, or that it is being waged for ethical reasons, then it is true of this war. Kosovo has no oil fields to be coveted; no member nation in the alliance has any territorial demands on Kosovo; Milosevic does not threaten the territorial integrity of any member of the alliance. And yet the alliance is at war. It is fighting out of a concern for the fate of others. It is fighting because no decent person can stand by and watch the systematic, state-directed murder of other people. It cannot tolerate such a thing. It cannot fail to provide assistance if it is within its power to do so.[3]

Robert Fisk wrote with equal fervor in criticism of what NATO had done: "How much longer do we have to endure the folly of NATO's war in the Balkans? In its first fifty days, the Atlantic alliance failed in everything it set out to do. It failed to protect the Kosovo Albanians from Serbian war crimes. It failed to cow Slobodan Milosevic. It failed to force the withdrawal of Serb troops from Kosovo. It broke international law in attacking a sovereign state without seeking a UN mandate. It killed hundreds of innocent Serb civilians—in our name, of course—while being too cowardly to risk a single NATO life in defense of the poor and weak for whom it meretriciously claimed to be fighting. NATO's war cannot even be regarded as a mistake; it is a criminal act."[4] Although written in the midst of the war, the essential lines of Fisk's critical analysis remain untouched by subsequent events, except that Milosevic did eventually submit, although only in reaction to intensified and prolonged bombing and a diplomatic initiative, and after wresting several important political concessions from the Russian negotiators. This "diplomatic solution" has produced the withdrawal of Serbian military and police forces, the safeguarding of Kosovo though the presence of a strong NATO-led international peacekeeping force, and a central post-conflict administration and reconstruction role for the United Nations.

A difficulty of assessment arises because, in crucial respects, both these seemingly contradictory positions are persuasive. The Western mind, especially in its legal dimensions, tends toward an either-or resolution of adversary lines of interpretation, as modeled through judicial litigation. However arbitrary in a particular case, there is always a winner and a loser in a judicial setting. It is jurisprudentially problematic both to regard ethnic cleansing as intolerable by the international community and to condemn the form and substance of the NATO intervention designed to prevent it. And yet, just such a doctrinal tension seems to follow from the perspectives of international law and world order. My attempt here is to defend such a double condemnation as posing the essential normative challenge for the future: Genocidal behavior cannot be shielded by claims of sovereignty, but neither can these claims be overridden by unauthorized uses of force, delivered in an excessive and inappropriate manner.

The main line of argument can be anticipated. As long as a purely textual analysis of the relevant norms is relied on, no satisfactory way exists to reconcile the divergences between humanitarian imperatives and the prohibition on military intervention force not authorized by the United Nations. The only mode of assessment that can achieve a limited reconciliation depends on a contextual analysis along the lines of "configurative jurisprudence," or the closely related "incidents jurisprudence." Of course, contextual complexity creates ample opportunity for sharply divergent lines of factual and legal interpretation, as illustrated by the sharp controversies, among those who regarded themselves as adherents of a configurative approach, over the legality of the American intervention in Vietnam.[5] Nevertheless, what the configurative approach enables—indeed, entails—is a comprehensive assessment that includes an embrace of complementary norms as well as an appraisal of what has been done in the name of law, and an evaluation of whether preferable policy alternatives to the course taken were available to those with the authority to make decisions. For these reasons, the configurative orientation enhances the quality of legal debate even if it is generally unable to resolve the underlying legal controversy. Enhancing debate is particularly important for a democratic society, whose essence arguably lies in the core societal commitment to resolve controversy by nonviolent communicative discourse.

In the case of Kosovo, such a style of contextual assessment alone allows the double condemnation and yet helps to reveal a course of action that might have avoided both ethnic cleansing and recourse to warfare undertaken in a morally and legally dubious fashion. In this respect, the Kosovo precedent is critically examined to enable a more constructive line of response in the event of a comparable future challenge, or at minimum to encourage a more promising line of discussion and reflection. Admittedly, a retrospective contention that an alternative course of action might have produced a preferable outcome is an instance of counterfactual reasoning and, as such, necessarily highly speculative. Such uncertainty is unavoidable if the position taken, like Fisk's, is one that is critical of what occurred under NATO auspices but does not endorse the view that in this event nothing effective should or could have been done about meeting the challenge of ethnic cleansing. Attempting to find a preferable path of action for future responses to genocidal behavior and crimes against humanity inevitably involves an acceptance of hypothetical reasoning. This reasoning may itself be more or less convincing depending on the integrity and skill of its presentation of facts and legal considerations.

## Depicting the Fearful Policy Dilemma

There is no reasonable doubt that the Albanian majority population of Kosovo was being placed in severe jeopardy by actions taken under the authority of the Milosevic government in Belgrade during the 1990s. These policies involved fundamental denials of human rights, including the right to self-determination of "a people." The essence of these denials encouraged Serbian atrocities designed to intimidate Albanian Kosovars or to coerce their mass exodus, clearing the way for less-obstructed Serb dominance, which was the underlying goal of ethnic cleansing. Such factual

one-sidedness is itself not entirely accurate, since the formation of the
Kosovo Liberation Army (KLA), dedicated to waging an armed struggle to
achieve an independent Kosovo, involved a variety of violent provocations
that provided an ongoing pretext and rationale for harsh Serb security
measures.[6] Considering the nine-to-one Albanian majority in Kosovo, the
Serbian pressure to intimidate was undoubtedly intense, but the result was
one of unmistakable repression of the majority population, with a deliberate ethnic thrust that was genocidal in its overall effects.

It was also reasonable in light of earlier Serb tactics in Bosnia, as epitomized by severely abusive detention camps, numerous massacres and
crimes against humanity, and the brutal annihilation in 1995 of some 7,300
Bosnian Muslim men and boys sheltered at the UN safe haven of Srebenica,
that international action of significant magnitude was urgently needed if
full-scale ethnic cleansing in Kosovo was to be avoided. The Serb massacre
of forty persons in the Kosovo town of Racak, eighteen miles southwest of
Priština, in January 1999, was widely portrayed by Europe and Washington as the final warning bell and was so presented by the media.[7] Sources
sympathetic with Serb viewpoints continue to insist that the "civilians"
were actually KLA "fighters" killed in an encounter with Serb security
forces and then made to appear as massacre "victims" by local Albanians.
The dominant Euro-American perception was that something had to be
done, and quickly, or else the Bosnian ordeal would be catastrophically
reproduced in Kosovo, with damaging consequences for the future of Europe
and the credibility of the trans-Atlantic alliance with the United States.

Beyond this, it was evident to many influential leaders and advisers,
particularly in the United States, that the United Nations was ill suited for
this mission. It was seen as having failed in Bosnia, in part because of the
absence of political will by those who were committed to its peacekeeping
mission there, and partly because of friction within the Security Council
about the proper course of action to be adopted: whether one of neutrality
and impartiality, or on behalf of the ethnic group being victimized.[8] In the
context of Kosovo these problems seemed even more formidable than had
been the case in Bosnia. In the months before the war, China and Russia
appeared ready to veto any call for UN intervention, as well as any mandate that conferred such a right on NATO or any other entity. In this respect,
the only prospect for an effective humanitarian intervention *appeared* to
depend on actions outside the United Nations and in violation of the basic
letter and spirit of its charter. Such an appearance was reinforced, but also
undermined, by strong independent pressures to endow NATO with renewed credibility and meaningful security roles in the emergent post–Cold

War setting of a Europe unthreatened by an *external* adversary. Also of apparent significance was the post–Cold War opportunity to reassert the hegemonic role of the United States in European security policy. Without archival access, which will not be available for years, the impact of these pressures on shaping the response to ethnic cleansing and human rights abuse in Kosovo is impossible to evaluate, especially as long as their relevance is officially denied.

Also, the pro-intervention side maintained that diplomatic remedies had been exhausted. U.S. ambassador to the United Nations Richard Holbrooke (and Chris Hill) had visited Belgrade repeatedly in 1998 and early 1999 to induce Milosevic to accept a diplomatic solution. The elements of this solution consisted of the deployment of a NATO peacekeeping force in Kosovo, substantial interim autonomy for the province, and a commitment to hold a referendum on the future of Kosovo in three years. This diplomatic package was presented at Rambouillet to the former Yugoslavia as a nonnegotiable set of demands. It was summarily rejected by Belgrade and only reluctantly accepted by the KLA after considerable arm twisting by Washington, which insisted that KLA endorsement of Rambouillet was a precondition for military intervention. The diplomatic failure at Rambouillet, together with the KLA willingness to sign on, was treated as a sufficient political mandate for subsequent NATO military action, even without UN Security Council approval. In essence, recourse to military intervention arguably occurred after all reasonable opportunities for peaceful settlement had been sufficiently explored. Under these circumstances, NATO alleged that waiting any longer would expose the endangered Kosovar population to grave risks and irreversible harm and would make successful humanitarian intervention impossible.

The anti-intervention argument is comparably coherent.[9] It takes the fundamental view that NATO's recourse to war was legally unacceptable without explicit authorization by the UN Security Council, and that NATO could not validly act on its own in this setting.[10] It rejects as legalistic the textual claims that the NATO use of force was not directed at "the territorial integrity or political independence" of the former Yugoslavia and therefore was not prohibited by Article 2(4) of the UN Charter. The anti-interventionists also reject the parallel contention that NATO was not bound by Article 53 of the charter since, as an alliance, NATO was not formally a Chapter VIII "regional organization," and that its undertaking was not strictly "an enforcement action." In this reading of the charter, all uses of nondefensive force are strictly controlled by the UN Security Council, and to bypass the Security Council's authority on the basis of a self-serving evasion of prospective vetoes is unacceptably to take law into one's own hands. Indeed, one justification for the veto is precisely to prevent uses of force that are not responses to an armed attack, in the absence of a political consensus among the permanent members. And here, with the initiative being one of collective action by the Western powers within NATO, the bypassing of UN authority is seen as a devastating blow at the constitutional authority of the United Nations, and a violation of the most basic prohibition inscribed in international law, governing states' recourse to force outside the domain of self-defense. NATO's action is likely to be viewed with particular alarm by China and Russia, which understandably view their veto power as a protection against threats of "a tyranny of the majority" and as providing a measure of insulation from United States "hegemonic" claims. The NATO action concerning Kosovo also provides the Russian and Chinese governments with "a precedent" for their own contested claims to use force against dissident minority peoples and territorial units, as in Chechnya and Tibet.[11]

Beyond these considerations against intervention, the anti-interventionists do not accept the argument that diplomatic means were properly used or exhausted. They point to the limits placed on Russian diplomatic participation before NATO's recourse to war, the rigidity of the Holbrooke/Rambouillet formula, the absence of any evident diplomatic effort to induce China and Russia to accommodate the Security Council majority by shifting their vetoes to abstentions.[12] Critics of the NATO intervention compare this pattern of prewar negotiation with the success of the war-ending diplomacy based on a major Russian role and on face-saving gestures offered Belgrade, which included a willingness to "conceal" the dominant role of the NATO-led peacekeeping force beneath a UN cover story. It is notable in this regard that the war-ending diplomatic text, Security Council Resolution 1244, barely mentions NATO and, if "innocently" read, would suggest that Kosovo is fundamentally subject to UN peacekeeping authority.[13] The contention is that flexible diplomacy might have protected the Kosovars along the lines of Resolution 1244 while avoiding war, and that had a more credible diplomatic effort been made without yielding success, the subsequent recourse to force under NATO auspices would have seemed far more reasonable. Still, such reasonableness about recourse to war would not have met the objections relating to the modalities of force relied on by NATO, or altogether overcome the Article 2(4) prohibition on nondefensive force.

These objections fueled a parallel debate relating to the means chosen to conduct the war.[14] Those who defend NATO point to the outcome, which is viewed as submission by Belgrade and, substantively, the removal of Serb military and police from Kosovo, as resulting in an acceptance of the essential features of the Rambouillet framework reinforced by the elimination of the Serbian coercive presence. NATO's defenders also point to the political constraints that precluded other military options, such as reliance on ground troops or on a more focused bombing strategy, which would have subjected NATO aircraft to higher risks of damage from Yugoslav antiaircraft defenses. Public support in the NATO countries for intervention was supposedly conditioned on the prospect of minuscule casualties, making recourse to higher-risk options politically unavailable to the leaders of NATO countries, who felt themselves accountable to their respective electorates.[15]

Also, as President Clinton acknowledged shortly after the suspension of the Kosovo bombing, his expectation had been that Milosevic would either give in to threat diplomacy or, at worst, submit after a few days of bombing, which in this initial phase was in fact generally confined to military targets, reinforced by primary reliance on "smart" weaponry.[16] In light of expert military advice, it was arguable that such an expectation on the part of the NATO political leadership was reasonable, and that when this proved wrong, it was then necessary to carry on with the military effort, intensifying the attack until it reached its goals. To have abandoned the effort midway, it is maintained, would have wrecked NATO's credibility in relation to the future of European security and sent the wrong signals to future tyrants and oppressors. It would also have given a green light to the accelerated ethnic cleansing undertaken in Kosovo as soon as the war began—a response given guidance and direction by Belgrade. This latter assessment of complicity at the highest level of the Yugoslav government is reinforced by the May 1999 indictment of Milosevic and his closest aides on various criminal charges by the United Nations International Criminal Tribunal for the former Yugoslavia, which was the first time that a sitting head of state has been formally indicted.

Critics of the manner in which the NATO intervention was carried out see the situation very differently. They perceive alternative lines of action as having been available and far preferable on humanitarian grounds to a high-altitude bombing campaign. In this regard they favored either helping the KLA to secure an independent Kosovo or insisting on a NATO strategy that combined ground assault with lower-altitude air attacks. NATO's critics also rejected the extension of NATO bombing after its initial failure to induce submission by Milosevic, especially the decision to target key components of Serbia's civilian infrastructure. The expansion of the bombing campaign resulted in heavy damage to the water supply and electricity systems, caused severe pollution through the destruction of chemical factories and oil refineries, and introduced such unacceptable weaponry and tactics as B-52 attacks, cluster bombs, and depleted-uranium ordnance.[17]

Such critics also highlight the effects of the bombing: severe damage to Kosovo and its inhabitants, inducing a heavy flow of refugees (approaching one million), the destruction of many cities and towns, and hundreds, if not thousands, of civilian deaths in Kosovo. These critics are also inclined to regard the Serbs' massive resort to ethnic cleansing by the most brutal means as largely an *effect* of the bombing rather than as merely the acceleration of a plan that would otherwise have been carried out in a more gradual manner. A related criticism is that the severity of NATO's strategy, combined with the Serb responses to it, has produced a set of circumstances that is resulting in a second cycle of ethnic cleansing in Kosovo, which is being carried forth successfully by Kosovar Albanians against Serbs and Roma under the supposedly protective gaze of the UN/NATO peacekeeping operation.

Putting these two major lines of interpretation together leaves one with the disturbing impression that humanitarian intervention on behalf of Albanian Kosovars was *necessary* but, under the circumstances, *impossible*. It was necessary to prevent a humanitarian catastrophe in the form of ethnic cleansing. It was impossible because of the *political* unavailability of an appropriate means. The selection of such a means was blocked by deep divisions among leading European states and by the resolve to insist on a NATO solution. It also reflected the refusal by the citizenry of the NATO countries, especially Germany and the United States, to be prepared to bear the considerable and uncertain human costs that might have followed from the adoption of a legally and morally more acceptable type of intervention. As this phrasing suggests, the most helpful form of legal appraisal is one of *degree*, conceiving of legality and illegality by reference to a spectrum. The more "reasonable" a response, the closer to the legality end of the spectrum. Regarding Kosovo, the contention here is that plausible options were available to give the action taken a higher degree of legality (without compromising the humanitarian mission) and thereby improve its status as a precedent for the future.

## Rejecting Legalism

Although admittedly no jurisprudential approach to legal analysis leaves an entirely satisfying impression under the circumstances that existed in Kosovo, reliance on legalistic analysis is particularly unfortunate for the future of international law. It puts international lawyers in the uncomfortable role that Immanuel Kant accused them of playing in *Perpetual Peace*, namely, that of being "miserable consolers." There is no ultraliteralistic reading of the UN Charter provisions that does not strain credulity about the intentions of the founders of the United Nations. The basic undertaking of the charter was to assign exclusive control over nondefensive uses of force to the Security Council and to accept the limits on response that this entailed as a result of vesting the five permanent members with a right of veto. In the Gulf War setting, this charter framework was reaffirmed in the form of China's agreeing to "abstain"; an abstention, unlike a negative vote, is not treated as blocking a Security Council decision.[18]

Also, the idea that NATO can use force freely without the expected accountability of regional actors to the charter system, simply by refraining from denoting its undertaking as "an enforcement action," is to strain political and moral credulity to the breaking point. It would appear that a military alliance would be subject to greater constitutional constraints than would a regional organization as understood by Chapter VIII. Indeed, if NATO's actions do not qualify as "collective self-defense" under the charter, then the full weight of Article 2(4) would appear applicable. Such an analysis bears directly on NATO, which was set up in 1949 as a means to institutionalize the defense of Europe against the threat of a Soviet attack, with no indication of any claim to respond to intrastate strife even within the alliance area, much less beyond it.

Similarly, the legalistic contentions of those who point to the domestic jurisdiction and veto powers as precluding humanitarian intervention occupy untenable ground. It is correct that normal textual readings are on their side and that the charter system cannot be legally bypassed in the manner that NATO attempted. Yet it is equally true that to regard the textual barriers to humanitarian intervention as decisive in the face of genocidal behavior is politically and morally unacceptable, especially in view of the increasing qualifications imposed on unconditional claims of sovereignty by the growth of an international human rights tradition.[19] It is true that the United Nations was not constituted in a setting that addressed the challenges of intrastate conflict, and indeed the understanding among the founders was that such an agenda would be treated as falling within the "domestic jurisdiction" limitation on UN competence to act. But a series of normative developments throughout the years has eroded the clarity of this distinction: The Genocide Convention, an emphasis on crimes against humanity, the growing impact of human rights generally on global moral consciousness, the blurring of inside/outside distinctions (concerning the territorial state) under the various pressures of globalization, and the spread of democracy and of the media's capacity to report human tragedy in real time have generated a new global ethos of responsibility in relation to humanitarian emergencies.[20] Admittedly, this ethos is unevenly implemented on the level of political action, as the earlier experiences in Bosnia and Rwanda illustrate, but in the setting of Europe and given the perceived failures of the response to ethnic cleansing in Bosnia during the early 1990s, the pressure to act was legitimized in a manner that superseded legalistic restraints.

In essence, the textual level of analysis, upon which legalists rely, cannot give a satisfactory basis for NATO intervention, nor can it provide a suitable rationale for rejecting the humanitarian imperative to rescue the potential victims of genocidal policies in Kosovo. Nor does textualism help focus attention on whether the means chosen were legally acceptable in light of the goals being pursued. A more nuanced attention to context is required to reformulate the debate in a manner in keeping with the broad injunction to seek a global security system that contributes to the achievement of "humane governance" on a global scale. Otherwise, the self-marginalization of international law and international lawyers is assured in contemporary situations involving claims to use force, consigning their vocational fate to the demeaning role of "apologist" or "utopian." No less demeaning is to conflate law and policy by mechanically deferring to "practice" and "effective power" as vindicating extensions of the notions of legality in the use of force.

## The Geopolitical Prerogative

Another framework for assessment involves rationalizing special exemptions from the constraining impact of international law by reference to the special role of the United States as a self-anointed guardian of international order and thereby exempt from any inhibiting constraints of international law. That the United States chose to act within the collective framework of NATO is of mild relevance, suggesting some diminution of an essentially unilateral geopolitical prerogative. Yet not too much should be made of the U.S. recourse to NATO, because it is so overwhelmingly controlled by Washington. Revealingly, Richard Holbrooke reprints, in the text of his book on the Bosnian negotiations that produced the Dayton Agreement at the end of 1995, the text of a letter he later wrote to President Clinton, in which he unwittingly confirmed the prevailing view of NATO as a U.S. pawn: "Of the many organizations in the former Yugoslavia in the last five years, only NATO—that is, the United States—has been respected."[21]

Variations of this view have graced the pages of recent issues of *Foreign Affairs,* masquerading as a debate between two prominent American international law specialists, Michael Glennon and Thomas Franck (with some additional commentary from the respected former executive director of the United Nations Association of the United States, Edward C. Luck). Glennon grounds his argument on the premise that the charter was drafted to cope with interstate violence, whereas the contemporary world is beset with a series of intrastate challenges that can be met only by coercive forms of peacekeeping (that is, without the consent of the relevant government), or what he refers to as "the new interventionism."[22]

In rationalizing the Kosovo initiative, Glennon perceives the basic issue as one in which "justice (as it is now understood) and the UN Charter seemed to collide." He goes on immediately to contextualize the claim of justice by reference to what "enlightened states now believe . . . to be just" and then implicitly identifies this mandate with a validation of the NATO response to Kosovo.[23] It seems unavoidable to wonder whether Glennon's use of "enlightened" is not a late-twentieth-century updating of the now-unfashionable "civilized"—the normative pretension seems indistinguishable! Glennon does condition this affirmation with cautionary language about the risks of validation, given its ad hoc character and the vagueness of the guidelines, but concludes with the view that "the cost of abandoning the old anti-interventionist structure" is not as high as "[t]he failings of the old system were disastrous."[24] The essence of Glennon's careful argument is that the currently most powerful Western governments have an implicit authority to pursue lines of coercive diplomacy that accord with their sense of justice.[25] However, the viability of such diplomacy over time will depend on the capacity of such geopolitical actors to place "the new interventionism" within an appropriate principled framework of decision that comes to be widely accepted by the rest of the international community[26] and is thereby legitimized. In effect, Kosovo was an acceptable first step toward reformulating the relationship of power to justice, positing an alternative to the anachronistic charter conception, but this approach will be enduringly vindicated only by overcoming its appearance of being an ad hoc move.[27]

The response of Franck, also an evident supporter of the NATO initiative, is to contend that the charter framework is far more adaptive than Glennon lets on and that the charter can be used to address intrastate challenges whenever a Security Council consensus exists; in this sense, intrastate conflicts are essentially no different from the case presented by interstate violence, where the council can be paralyzed by a veto.[28] Franck points to a series of well-known instances of coercive peacekeeping that have achieved Security Council backing, such as in Bosnia, Somalia, Rhodesia, South Africa, Haiti, and Iraq.[29] He accepts the veto in this instance as but a trivial obstacle to NATO action—nothing more than a cautionary indication of serious opposition to a geopolitically preferred course of action. For Franck the veto does not operate as an unconditional bar to such action. In his view, "NATO's action in Kosovo is not the first time illegal steps have been taken to prevent something palpably worse."[30] The hegemonic power enjoys the privileged position of neglecting the restraints of international law for the sake of pursuing objectives that it deems of sufficient importance, as was the case in Kosovo. For Franck the basic charter framework continues to be a useful foundation for world order, although subject to a legitimized dynamic of geopolitical nullification.

The debate between Glennon and Franck, while interesting, misses the essential feature of the Kosovo challenge, which is what I have earlier referred to as "the fearful dilemma." By endorsing the Kosovo response as carried out by NATO, Glennon and Franck focus on finding an acceptable political rationale, and thus on what the United States should do in circumstances where its preferred line of policy is being blocked by a veto in the Security Council. Does one really want to encourage such a geopolitical prerogative, even if softened, as in Glennon's position, by an advisory that in the long term legality is important and can be achieved only through community acceptance of some new framework of principled action? Such a world order precedent seems dangerous and irresponsible and must be tested by reference to the acceptability of comparable conceivable claims that might be made in the future by a geopolitical adversary, such as Russia or China. As earlier suggested, the invocation of Kosovo by the highest Russian officials, to validate their brutality in Chechnya, is a reminder that geopolitical arguments for abandoning legal constraints can be turned in many directions.[31]

But even more centrally, both Glennon and Franck finesse the questionable modalities of the NATO response to Kosovo as casting considerable doubt on the central claim of an enactment of justice. They focus the argument on whether there was a fit occasion for an effective response to a credible challenge of ethnic cleansing, but without questioning the legally, morally, and politically dubious nature of the response itself.[32]

The main problem with presupposing the validity of NATO's response is that it focuses exclusively on the injustice of Milosevic's policies in Kosovo and does not consider the moral objections to the NATO response, including the decision to withhold reconstruction aid from Belgrade and to maintain sanctions despite the likelihood of widespread suffering by the

Serbian population. Unless this double injustice is placed in focus, no jurisprudential appraisal will be generally convincing, nor should it be. At most, such an appraisal will help those firmly within the NATO circle of support to find the most satisfying world order spin for their preferred course of action, and it will widen the gap between NATO's critics and supporters enough to render constructive dialogue impossible. And equally in error are those who one-sidedly condemn NATO for bypassing the United Nations, defying international law applicable to the use of force, and ignoring legal restraints on the initiation and conduct of war. They, too, unacceptably simplify the search for a conclusion, seemingly resigning themselves to a response of helplessness and regressive insensitivity to the humanitarian challenge posed by the ethnic cleansing and sustained, severe human rights abuse evident in Kosovo over a period of years and intensifying during 1998.

Against this background is the very real need to ground a legal appraisal and an appeal to justice on the contextual reality of Kosovo, which includes the inability and unwillingness of NATO to fashion a response that was commensurate to the challenge or to craft a humanitarian policy that included Serbia. Because of this fundamental circumstance, no clear line of legal inference can be persuasively drawn on what was done: In effect, it was justifiable to act, but not in the manner undertaken. Thus, the Kosovo precedent is flawed as a foundation for future action.[33]

## The Configurative Option

The argument being made is that an assessment of the NATO response to the humanitarian crisis in Kosovo cannot be usefully resolved by a reliance on positivist styles of legal appraisal, which, at most, can be subjectively bolstered by a combination of geopolitical and humanitarian claims. I regard the Glennon/Franck debate as an instance of positivist style. Both scholars view the legal controversy from the perspective of its rule-oriented character, Glennon arguing that the charter's legal regime be cast aside as obsolete, Franck responding that the charter is still useful but that in this instance it was acceptable to disregard its constraint; a more manifestly positivist style involves interpreting the charter's rules as either allowing or precluding the NATO initiative. In this setting, such lines of appraisal cannot illuminate the complexity of decisions arising from the apparent dilemma of either intervening without appropriate legal authorization or watching on the sidelines while ethnic cleansing of vulnerable ethnic, religious, and racial groups takes place. The best that such an appraisal can do is either to set international law aside or to mount legalistic arguments on one side or the other by strained reasoning that is insensitive to the main doctrinal contradiction embedded in this factual context. To some extent, every set of circumstances that gives rise to factual controversy exhibits these features, but to varying degrees. In some settings the hierarchy among legal considerations is clear enough to give decisive weight to textual factors and positivist lines of reasoning, such as when Indonesia attacked East Timor in 1975 or when Iraq attacked Kuwait in 1990.[34]

Jurisprudential options, then, are to be considered tools of illumination rather than as expressive of ontological truth and are to be evaluated primarily by whether they engender constructive debate about policy choices and past decisions. In this regard, the role of international law and lawyers is to clarify decisional contexts, recommend preferred options, and engender useful societal debate in the setting of controversial issues of great public significance.

With Kosovo, the analysis set forth here is based on respect for the charter framework relating to force, the acceptance of a humanitarian imperative, and criticism of the manner in which the response was fashioned. It is now necessary to explain the main lines of criticism.

## The Failure to Pursue Diplomatic Remedies

An authoritative assessment of whether a negotiated diplomatic solution for Kosovo was ever sought in good faith is not possible without unimpeded access to the minds and secret communications of the principal players on both sides. Nevertheless, certain preliminary conclusions can be reached on the basis of available information and circumstantial evidence. Without entering into the factual detail needed to support such assertions, the diplomatic stance of the U.S. secretary of state, Madeleine Albright, engenders a strong sense that the U.S. government was opposed to any sort of flexibility in dealing with Belgrade in the lead-up to the war and, further, was similarly opposed to entrusting the United Nations with any role relating to an agreed-on process of offering the people of Kosovo protection.[35] Such inflexibility was exhibited in a number of ways, including an insistence on the exclusive reliance on an American negotiator in discussions with Milosevic, the exclusion of Russia and China from the effort to find a diplomatic solution based on a political compromise, and the drafting of conditions for the NATO peacekeeping role in Kosovo in such an uncompromising fashion as to ensure that Belgrade could not possibly accept the final round of diplomatic proposals made in February 1999 to representatives of the Federal Republic of Yugoslavia and of Kosovar Albanians at the Rambouillet Castle, a French former royal hunting ground near Paris.

This impression of inflexibility revealingly contrasts with the approach accepted after the war strategy had failed to achieve either a prewar surrender or the expected quick collapse of resistance in Belgrade. At this point a prominent Russian negotiator, Vladimir Chernomyrdin, was given a central role, along with the Finnish president, Martti Ahtisaari. This diplomacy resulted in a return to a set of arrangements that were at least nominally under the auspices of the United Nations and in which the Russians (despite being nonmembers of NATO) were given an active role in the Kosovo peacekeeping process. Even the Kosovars have not yet *formally* benefited from the submission of Belgrade. At Rambouillet, Kosovo was promised immediate autonomy, with a referendum in three years allowing the population to decide its future status, including the option of secession and independence. Such a promise to apply the right of self-determination to Kosovo disappeared in the agreed-on Security Council Resolution 1244, although arguably the substantial attainment of de facto independence for Kosovo was a result of the war and could not have been otherwise achieved even if the Rambouillet terms had been accepted. Also helpful to the Albanian Kosovar side was the removal of all Serb military and paramilitary forces and the reconstruction of the Kosovo police.

There are several conjoined points here. First of all, flexible diplomacy was not pursued. Second, there are reasonable grounds for supposing that a more flexible approach might have averted ethnic cleansing without recourse to war. Third and most important, whether or not flexible diplomacy would have succeeded, which we cannot know at this point, the failure even to attempt flexible diplomacy raises serious doubts about the alleged necessity of the NATO initiative. This last point requires some clarification. We must recall that the basic undertaking of the UN Charter, as famously enunciated in its preamble, is "to save succeeding generations from the scourge of war." Arguably, the overriding ambition of international law in this century has been to take such a pledge seriously, although not absolutely, as the acceptance of a limited right of self-defense and of an international duty to prevent genocide and severe patterns of crimes against humanity concedes. The recourse to war by NATO in these circumstances seems to have cast aside the legal, moral, and political commitment to make recourse to war a *last resort,* that is, taken only after all reasonable attempts to achieve a peaceful settlement have failed. This is a serious allegation from the perspective of both international law and world order, as well as respect for the UN system. Its seriousness is magnified by the fact that three permanent members of the Security Council, including the main architect of the United Nations, established this precedent under the full glare of the global media.

Note that it is often argued that the failure of the United Nations itself to evolve a collective security system does justify greater latitude in interpreting the occasions on which it is *reasonable* for a state to use force.[36] This latitude allows for uses of force to uphold a state's vital security interests or to serve the cause of humane governance that the charter appears, on its face, to foreclose. In this regard, Articles 2(4) and 51, although important guidelines, are no longer dispositive regarding inquiries about legality. However, recourse to force should be clearly presented as the consequence of an energetic and credible good-faith attempt, via flexible diplomacy, to find a peaceful solution, and the failure to do this severely compromises the normative status of the NATO initiative. This is so regardless of the legal rationale selected to justify NATO's action. NATO's way of proceeding also weakens the argument for bypassing the United Nations and the restrictive constraints of international law. The United Nations was justifiably criticized along comparable lines for its apparent unwillingness to uphold war prevention goals by reliance on flexible diplomacy in the setting of the Gulf crisis, which followed in 1990 upon the Iraqi invasion and occupation of Kuwait.[37]

The situation is somewhat less clear concerning the modalities of force. The widespread reliance on strategic bombing by the Allies in World War II appeared to flaunt the prohibition on indiscriminate military tactics, but also established a pattern of practice that was repeated to a substantial degree in the Korean and Vietnam wars and again in the first Gulf War, as well as in a range of other war settings. At the same time, the NATO initiative was not a war in the conventional sense but was based on a claim of "humanitarian intervention." Thus, it would seem subject to stricter standards of constraint on the use of force, especially with regard to civilian harm, and particularly so considering the population that was being protected. NATO's style of high-altitude bombing after the first few days was to inflict heavy deliberate damage on civilian targets of a wide variety, relying on mastery of the air, "smart" weaponry, and a proclaimed intention to continue the bombing on an intensifying scale until Belgrade "submitted" to diplomatic demands without conditions. The magnitude and effects of such a bombing campaign are difficult to reconcile with the humanitarian claims made by NATO spokespersons. Such difficulty is compounded by NATO's reliance on tactics of warfare that minimized the risk of harm to the intervening forces, while shifting such risks to civilians in the former Yugoslavia, including Kosovo. And in that sense the absence of casualties among the military forces of NATO during the bombing campaign, when compared to the deaths of 2,000 or more civilians in Serbia and Kosovo, does seriously damage the humanitarian rationale for the action. It also makes skeptical observers wonder whether the primary motives for intervention were other than those publicly voiced—for example, keeping NATO alive and testing new weaponry and war-fighting doctrine. An additional subtext that seems to have been influential among American policymakers was to demonstrate that contrary to the teaching of "the Vietnam syndrome," internal wars can be fought and won at acceptable costs.[38]

## A Concluding Note

Several relatively clear conclusions emerge from a configurative assessment of the NATO initiative in Kosovo:

- There is a strong burden of persuasion associated with the rejection of the United Nations framework of legal restraint on the use of force as generally understood.[39]

- This burden can be initially met if there is a credible prospect of genocide or some distinct humanitarian catastrophe otherwise under way or imminent.

- Such a burden cannot be discharged fully if diplomatic alternatives to war have not been fully explored in a sincere and convincing manner.

- The humanitarian rationale is also sustained or undermined by the extent to which the tactics of warfare exhibit sensitivity to civilian harm and by the degree to which intervenors avoid unduly shifting the risks of war to the supposed beneficiaries of intervention in order to avoid harm to themselves.

- The humanitarian rationale is also weakened if there were less destructive alternative means to protect the threatened population than those relied upon.

- The humanitarian rationale is further weakened if punitive measures are imposed on the adversary after a termination of hostilities has been negotiated, especially if all civilians are not protected to the extent possible and indiscriminate sanctions are maintained.

The postwar Kosovo experience will also inform our sense of the precedent. It has been evident from the outset of its operations that the KFOR/UNMIK peacekeeping process has been unable to prevent a new phase of ethnic cleansing, that is, a lethal coercive process by which the Serbs and Roma are induced to leave Kosovo or endure the deadly consequences of remaining behind.[40] It is also evident that NATO has not been fulfilling its responsibility for economic and social reconstruction, including the reintegration of returning refugees, as well as its offers of stability to the South Balkans as a region.[41] It will also be important that KFOR remain a strong enough presence over a period of years, to ensure that Belgrade does not reimpose an oppressive structure of rule over Kosovo. And finally, it is important that NATO countries take responsibility for restoring the civilian infrastructure of Serbia, as UN secretary-general Kofi Annan proposed in a June 20, 1999, speech to a meeting of the Organization of Security and Cooperation in Europe (OSCE), and to do so for the neighboring Balkan countries as well. To have insisted, as Washington did, that as long as Milosevic remained in power, no assistance should be given to Serbia, was to dilute further and retrospectively the humanitarian claim of the overall operation by making the Serbian people continue to bear the burdens of war in a period of nominal "peace." An even more draconian approach has cast a dark backward shadow on the first Gulf War, exacting a severe toll on the Iraqi civilian population by imposing sanctions over a period of twelve years.[42] Of course, the events of late 2000 that resulted in the removal of Milosevic from power immediately transformed the relationship of the European Union and the United States to the former Yugoslavia. Aid and diplomatic support were extended and the sanctions terminated even before convincing reassurances were received from the new Kostunica leadership about the future of Kosovo.

In sum, unfortunately, the NATO initiative on behalf of Kosovo offers us a badly flawed precedent for evaluating future claims to undertake humanitarian intervention without proper UN authorization. Yet it must not be forgotten that the failure to act in Rwanda and Bosnia point in an opposite direction for the future of humanitarian intervention and form part of the background for reflection. Precisely because these flaws of the Kosovo war are the subject of widespread critical commentary, it is possible that "the lessons of Kosovo" will exert pressure to view war in the future as more of a last resort and will be relied on to achieve the humanitarian character of a humanitarian intervention. The overall experience of the 1990s may also build support for providing the United Nations with independent enforcement capabilities, for rethinking and restricting the veto, and for enabling a more timely and effective response to some humanitarian catastrophes with a minimum intrusion of geopolitical considerations. At this point such an approach may seem far-fetched, given the hostility to the

United Nations that persists in Washington, but over time the efficiency and legitimacy of global governance would seem to depend on establishing just such a capability.

Of course, even with such an enhanced UN capability, the capacities to engage in humanitarian intervention would be exceedingly limited and should not be exaggerated. A political consensus of permanent members of the Security Council would still normally be needed to provide the mandate. Such a consensus could be blocked for geopolitical reasons, as when the events are situated within a state aligned to a powerful country. Also relevant is the scale of the interventional operation required. To protect or emancipate the peoples of Chechnya, Kashmir, or Tibet, for instance would require military operations of such magnitude as to be impracticable, as well as to pose too serious a threat of major, unmanageable warfare.

The events in East Timor, following only months after Kosovo, also provide grounds for both concern and hope. The concern arises from the UN failure to provide the population with greater security at the time of a referendum on the future of East Timor, which had an expected outcome that should have been understood as quite likely to unleash an Indonesian backlash. The harshness of the Indonesian response to the overwhelming vote for independence by the East Timorese, while greater than reasonably expected, should not have come as a surprise, given the Indonesian record of abuse during a period of almost twenty-five years. But East Timor also offers grounds for hope. A political mandate was agreed on in the Security Council, effective pressure to back down was exerted on Jakarta, and an appropriate UN peacekeeping and postconflict operation was put into operation quickly, with strong regional participation. It remains too soon to pronounce the UN effort in East Timor a success, but the effort seems at the very least to have rescued the population from an extreme condition of abuse and danger and moved significantly along the process of respecting the declared will of the people to have an independent sovereign state of East Timor.

Each instance of humanitarian catastrophe presents the organized international community with a particular challenge based on an array of contextual features. There is no single overarching response that fits this variety of instances. The focus needs to be kept on the opportunities to mitigate human suffering and injustice while taking due account of constraints on effective action.[43] At this stage, the best that can be expected is a reluctance to engage in military intervention, combined with a maximum effort to build a consensus on response that enables the UN Security Council to determine whether humanitarian intervention is appropriate. In the event that such a consensus is not forthcoming despite best efforts, the burden of justification for an intervening state or coalition, with or without some sort of backing by a regional institution, is particularly heavy.

## Notes

1. For an excellent overview, see Sean D. Murphy, *Humanitarian Intervention* (Philadelphia: University of Pennsylvania Press, 1996).

2. Such a process was problematic from its turbulent inception. For a very balanced and illuminating analysis of the Congo operation, see Georges Abi-Saab, *The United Nations Operation in the Congo, 1960–1964* (Oxford: Oxford University Press, 1978).

3. Vaclev Havel, "Kosovo and the End of the Nation-State," *New York Review of Books*, June 10, 1999, 4–6.

4. Robert Fisk, "Who Needs NATO?" *Progressive*, July 22, 1999, 22–23.

5. For the full range of these controversies, see Richard Falk, ed., *The Vietnam War and International Law*, 4 vols. (Princeton, NJ: Princeton University Press, 1968–1976).

6. For a critical account of KLA and its role, see Chris Hedges, "Kosovo's Next Masters?" *Foreign Affairs* 78, no. 1 (1999): 24–42.

7. For the position of the U.S. government in the buildup to the NATO air campaign, see James B. Steinberg, "A Perfect Polemic: Blind to Reality in Kosovo," *Foreign Affairs* 78, no. 6 (1999): 128–33.

8. For a harsh assessment of the UN role, see David Rieff, *Slaughterhouse: Bosnia and the Failure of the West* (New York: Simon & Schuster, 1995); recently restated in Rieff, "The U.N. Remains a Bright, Shining Lie," *Wall Street Journal*, November 18, 1999. For a more balanced account, see Susan L. Woodward, *Balkan Tragedy: Chaos and Dissolution after the Cold War* (Washington, DC: Brookings Institution, 1995).

9. For a helpful legal assessment, see Bruno Simma, "NATO, the UN and the Use of Force: Legal Aspects," *European Journal of International Law* 10, no. 1 (1999). Professor Simma deftly clarifies the "illegality" of the NATO campaign while taking legal account of the humanitarian justifications for international action. For an overall legal assessment, see *Case Concerning Military and Paramilitary Activities in and against Nicaragua (Nicaragua v. United States of America), Meritz Judgment*, I.C.J. Reports 1986, 14.

10. The only independent basis for NATO action would be under the authority of Article 51 as an exercise of collective self-defense, which clearly did not fit the facts of Kosovo, however construed.

11. Russian diplomats and leaders at the time took account of this precedent to uphold their own claims to use force.

**12.** Such a prospect is not far-fetched, it would seem, because Russia and China endorsed earlier UN Security Council resolutions that declare the humanitarian crisis in Kosovo as falling within the domain of Chapter VII, being considered endangering international peace and security, and thereby not shielded by the domestic jurisdiction principle of Article 2(7). See Security Council Resolution 1199, September 23, 1998, S/RES/1199 (1998), and Resolution 1203, October 24, 1998, S/RES/1203 (1998). These resolutions were balanced in the sense of also calling on the KLA to comply with obligations to refrain from violence and imposing an arms embargo on both sides.

**13.** For text, see S/RES/1244 (1999), containing the extraordinary dispositive language as follows: "Decides on the deployment in Kosovo, under United Nations auspices, of international civil and security presences." Such terminology hardly accords with the insistence by Washington and Brussels that the United Nations merely ratified the NATO victory. This formulation should also be compared with the dictatorial language and tone of the Rambouillet agreement, with its explicit empowerment of NATO, especially in its famous Annex B, which gave NATO extensive powers throughout the whole of the former Yugoslavia. I share the view that it was "unreasonable" not to attempt to reach a "1244" solution *before* recourse to war.

**14.** For a well-formulated overall critique, see Michael Mandelbaum, "A Perfect Failure," *Foreign Affairs* 78, no. 5 (1999): 2–8.

**15.** Such a pragmatic argument for adopting legally dubious tactics is self-serving, undermining the central objectives of the law of war to set limits on the pursuit of belligerent objectives. The U.S. government relied on a variant of this argument to justify the use of atomic bombs against Hiroshima and Nagasaki at the end of World War II, contending that such weapons saved numerous American lives. Such an assertion has been contested as disguising the real motive for use, which was to gain the upper hand over the Soviet Union geopolitically in the Pacific.

**16.** See John M. Broder, "Clinton Underestimated Serbs, He Acknowledges," *New York Times*, June 26, 1999, A6.

**17.** For a summary overview of the environmental damage, including radioactive contamination resulting from widespread use of uranium-tipped antitank shells, see Joe Cook and Frances Williams, "Nato Uranium 'Polluting Yugoslavia,'" *Financial Times*, July 22, 1999, 3. The news story presents the preliminary conclusions of a fourteen-member UN team of scientists and other experts, known as the Balkans Task Force of the United Nations Environmental Program.

**18.** Although a textual reading of Article 27(3) of the UN Charter includes the requirement that a Security Council decision be supported "by an affirmative vote of nine members including the concurring votes of the permanent members," UN practice, going back to the Soviet boycott of the Security Council during the early stages of the Korean War, has treated absence or abstention as not preventing the Security Council from reaching valid decisions.

**19.** For a rationale in support of this trend toward limiting sovereignty, see Kofi Annan, "Two Concepts of Sovereignty," *Economist*, September 18, 1999, 49–50.

**20.** For an excellent theoretical exploration, see R. B. J. Walker, *Inside/ Outside: International Relations as Political Theory* (Cambridge: Cambridge University Press, 1993); for an overall assessment of globalization, see David Held and others, *Global Transformations: Politics, Economics and Culture* (Cambridge: Polity, 1999).

**21.** Richard Holbrooke, *To End a War* (New York: Random House, 1998), 339.

**22.** See Michael J. Glennon, "The New Interventionism: The Search for a Just International Law," *Foreign Affairs* 78, no. 3 (1999): 2–7.

**23.** Ibid., 2.

**24.** Ibid., 3.

**25.** Note the opposition by China and Russia to forcible modes of intervention by NATO. Two powerful but "unenlightened" states were opposed to this non-UN consensus.

**26.** For such an attempt, see Tom J. Farer, "A Paradigm of Legitimate Intervention," in *Enforcing Restraint: Collective Intervention in Internal Conflicts*, ed. Lori Fisler Damrosch (New York: Council on Foreign Relations, 1993), 316–47.

**27.** Glennon develops this position at the end of his essay, especially at 7.

**28.** Thomas M. Franck, "Break It, Don't Fake It," *Foreign Affairs* 78, no. 4 (1999): 116–18; see also Franck, "Lessons of Kosovo," *American Journal of International Law* 93 (1999): 864–67.

**29.** Ibid., 116.

**30.** Ibid., 118.

**31.** See note 11.

**32.** Several factors must be acknowledged as favorable to the NATO response: the attitude of the majority of Kosovo inhabitants, the return of the refugees, and the rescue of the Albanian Kosovars from the ordeal of Serb domination.

**33.** Such an analysis resembles in some respects the argument of Simma, note 9: that NATO's campaign was illegal, yet the humanitarian considerations meant that only "a thin red line" separated legality from the rescue operation. Compare here Antonio Cassese, "Ex iniuria ius oritur: Are We Moving towards International Legitimation of Forcible Countermeasures in the World Community?" *European Journal of International Law* 10, no. 1 (1999): 23.

**34.** In such circumstances, there are countervailing "legal" arguments, but of such an insubstantial character as to be generally ignored. For example, Indonesia argued in 1975 that its invasion was in response to an invitation from the pro-integrationist faction in East Timor; Baghdad contended in 1990 that Kuwait was an artificial creation of British colonialism that deprived Iraq of a valuable portion of its sovereign territory.

**35.** On the first point, it is possible that Albright shared the view that flexibility was unnecessary because the bluff of air strikes would induce surrender without the actuality of war.

**36.** See W. Michael Reisman, "Kosovo's Antinomies," *American Journal of International Law* 93 (1999): 867–69; for a fuller exposition, see Reisman, "Allocating Competencies to Use Coercion in the Post–Cold War World: Practices, Conditions, and Prospects," in *Law and Force in the New International Order,* ed. Lori Fisler Damrosch and David J. Scheffer (Boulder, CO: Westview Press, 1991), 26–48; for an earlier rationale along a similar line, see Julius Stone, *Aggression and World Order: A Critique of United Nations Theories of Aggression* (Berkeley: University of California Press, 1958).

**37.** Richard Falk, "Reflections on the Gulf War Experience: Force and War in the UN System," in *The Gulf War and the New World Order: International Relations of the Middle East,* ed. Tareq Y. Ismael and Jacqueline S. Ismael (Gainesville: University of Florida Press, 1994), 536–48.

**38.** The Gulf War allegedly established the same proposition for international wars.

**39.** That is, without various forms of strained interpretation. For example, see Steinberg, note 7. Also, for a presentation range of pro-NATO legal arguments, see Paul Williams and Michael P. Scharf, "NATO Intervention on Trial: The Legal Case That Was Never Made," *Human Rights Review,* forthcoming.

**40.** See Steven Erlanger, "Chaos and Intolerance Prevailing in Kosovo despite UN's Efforts," *New York Times,* Nov. 22, 1999, A1, A12.

**41.** See Ben Steil and Susan Woodward, "A European 'New Deal' for the Balkans," *Foreign Affairs* 78, no. 6 (1999): 95–105.

**42.** Cf. John Mueller and Karl Mueller, "Sanctions of Mass Destruction," *Foreign Affairs* 78, no. 5 (1999): 43–53.

**43.** Portions of this chapter have been drawn from Richard Falk, "Kosovo, World Order, and the Future of International Law," *American Journal of International Law* 93 (1999): 854–64.

# Humanitarian Intervention after Kosovo
## Commentary

Thomas G. Weiss

This commentary on the essay by Richard Falk, a former teacher and a colleague, brings to bear the conclusions of the International Commission on Intervention and State Sovereignty (ICISS). Its aptly titled report, *The Responsibility to Protect,*[1] was presented to UN secretary-general Kofi Annan in December 2001 and is pertinent in looking beyond the lessons in the Balkans. Falk and I share numerous philosophical views about Kosovo in particular and humanitarian intervention in general—for example, about the need for standards and principles, and the abysmal quality of leadership in Washington, where the current administration considers itself "exempt from any inhibiting constraints of international law" (p. 195).

Nonetheless, I concentrate here on crucial differences in our respective interpretations of the war in Kosovo. While Falk is concerned about the controversial precedents, I am frankly far more worried about another Rwanda—namely, in Darfur since early 2003. I emphasize *The Responsibility to Protect* because the efforts to refine principles governing humanitarian intervention have borne more fruit over the past decade than Falk's essay would lead us to believe—indeed, Pulitzer Prize–winning journalist Anthony Lewis described the ICISS report as capturing "the international state of mind."[2]

The ICISS was launched by Canada in late 2000. The intellectually and politically diverse twelve-person group met a forced-march pace and formulated its recommendations in less than a year after its establishment by Canadian foreign minister Lloyd Axworthy. Given the supposedly wide disparity of views across the north-south divide, it was cochaired by Gareth Evans (a former foreign minister of Australia, who is now president of the International Crisis Group) and Mohamed Sahnoun (a former Algerian diplomat and UN troubleshooter in Africa).[3] The new twist for independent commissions of this type was the behind-the-scenes role of a sympathetic government, Canada—a model replicated by Japan for the subsequent "human security" commission.[4] Moreover, Ottawa continues with follow-up efforts at several levels, so that the commission's findings are not relegated to coffee tables and bookshelves.[5]

Two sets of events motivated this undertaking. First, there were moral pleas in 1999 from future Nobel laureate UN secretary-general Annan. He argued in several speeches that human rights concerns transcend claims of sovereignty, a theme that he put forward more delicately a year later at the Millennium Summit.[6] The reaction was loud, bitter, and predictable, especially from China, Russia, and much of the developing world, where "intervention" remained taboo.[7]

Second, the ICISS was concerned about the divergent reactions or, rather, the nonreactions by the Security Council to dire humanitarian crises in Rwanda and Kosovo. In 1994 intervention was too little and too late to halt or even slow the murder of what may have been as many as 800,000 people in the Great Lakes region of Africa. In 1999 the formidable NATO finessed the council and waged war for the first time in Kosovo. But many observers saw the seventy-eight-day bombing effort as being too much and too early, perhaps creating as much human suffering as it relieved. In both cases, the UN Security Council was not in a position to act expeditiously and authorize the use of deadly force to protect vulnerable populations.

In taking issue with the central thrust of Falk's passionate essay, I must make my own point of departure clear: The lack of reaction in Rwanda represents a far more serious threat to international order and justice than did the Security Council's paralysis in Kosovo. At least in the latter case NATO finally acted, although, because of Washington's domestic politics, action was exclusively from an altitude of 15,000 feet, when ground troops would have prevented the mass exodus. Past or potential victims undoubtedly would agree with my judgment. For instance, the only survey to date of victims in war zones suggests that there is too little rather than too much humanitarian intervention. Fully two-thirds of civilians under siege in twelve war-torn societies who were interviewed by the International Committee of the Red Cross (ICRC) want more intervention, and only ten percent want none.[8]

The main reason for Falk's unease with NATO's efforts in Kosovo is that the UN Security Council was bypassed in order to avoid vetoes by China and Russia. To be fair, he weighs the pro-intervention position, epitomized by Vaclav Havel, and the equally (at least according to Falk) persuasive anti-intervention position, by Robert Fisk. The essential future normative challenge for Falk is to square the circle (his "configurative approach") so that "genocidal behavior cannot be shielded by claims of sovereignty, but neither can these claims be overridden by unauthorized uses of force, delivered in an excessive and inappropriate manner" (p. 187).

In fact, Falk is overly preoccupied with the possibility that major powers might intervene without just cause on humanitarian grounds and without Security Council approval (that is, using the precedent of Kosovo), and he is insufficiently concerned about a repetition of either a rapid, Rwanda-like genocide or the slow-motion variety in Darfur. He tries to distance himself from positivist international lawyers—he does not want to be in the uncomfortable role of apologist and cites Immanuel Kant's reference to legalistic interpreters as "miserable consolers." Yet Falk comes too close for comfort by denying the justifiability of NATO's decision to wage a humanitarian war in Kosovo. Indeed, he was part of the Kosovo Commission that subsequently ended up calling the intervention "illegal" (because it occurred without the Security Council's blessing) but "legitimate" (because it halted Serbia's inevitable march to subjugate or eliminate Albanian Kosovars).[9]

This space does not allow probing the intricacies and subtleties of Falk's argument, but his overriding concern is that the decision about humanitarian intervention in Kosovo was made without giving sufficient time and support for "flexible diplomacy" to work. Drawing on just war doctrine, he believes that NATO's overall approach casts doubt that "recourse to war [was] a last resort, that is, taken only after all reasonable attempts to achieve a peaceful settlement have failed." Moreover, he points to disproportionate civilian deaths.

Falk is more troubled than I by the magnitude of the civilian costs of the war, and less by what undoubtedly would have been higher ones without it. His estimate of 2,000 deaths is certainly not inconsequential, but, contrary to his view, it does not "seriously damage the humanitarian rationale for the action." This figure pales in comparison with what might have been the eventual costs of continued Serbian occupation of Kosovo. As Falk's argument relies on counterfactual reasoning, a different what-if seems more justifiable: What damage would Serbia have done in Kosovo without NATO's bombing? The Milosevic regime, which had been running a Gestapo-like administration in Kosovo since 1989, would undoubtedly have engaged in the same kind of massive ethnic cleansing there as in Croatia and Bosnia-Herzegovina earlier in the 1990s. How many times should one give benefit of the doubt to, and take seriously negotiations with, a regime headed by someone who is obviously willing to use murder and rape to achieve his ends? Indeed, regime change in Belgrade should also figure prominently in the positive column of any humanitarian balance sheet for the war in Kosovo.

In *The Responsibility to Protect*, the ICISS recommends six criteria for humanitarian intervention, which are relevant for this discussion. The most critical is a "just-cause threshold" whose conditions are "large-scale loss of life" or "large-scale 'ethnic cleansing'" that can be "actual or apprehended."[10] It does not take much historical memory to extrapolate from previous behavior and imagine that Serbia's continued control in Kosovo would undoubtedly have led to repression, death, and ethnic cleansing on a massive scale.

But if we permit military action without proper Security Council authorization, some readers, including Richard Falk, might ask, are we not sliding along a slippery slope that leads quite inevitably to justifying unjustifiable actions like the U.S. and UK decision to go to war against Iraq in March 2003? The answer is no if the wise counsel from the ICISS is followed.

Although the Bush administration eventually got around to playing the humanitarian card in an attempt to rationalize its actions, that was only after its initial justifications were exposed as empty—that is, no weapons of mass destruction or links to al Qaeda were found. Although the just-cause threshold proposed by the ICISS could arguably have been invoked, it was not invoked before the resort to force. After the fact, it has the hollow ring of rationalization.

But even if a humanitarian argument had been made, it is still more doubtful that the other five criteria could have been satisfied: right intention, last resort, proportional means, reasonable prospects, and right authority. The primary purpose of the war in Iraq was not to halt human suffering but rather to pursue geopolitical interests. There remains a question of whether reasonable nonmilitary options had been exhausted and whether the means were proportional (some 2,500 civilian and 10,000 military deaths between March and May 2003). Determining whether the consequences of the war are worse than inaction will require waiting to see how long the postwar misery will last and what the shape of a future Iraq will be.

And most important, even if the five previous criteria had been met—which clearly they were not—the ICISS emphasizes just authority, which essentially means an overwhelming show of support from the Security Council. Dissent within the Security Council about the war in Iraq, and indeed around the planet, was far more visible than it had been regarding Kosovo. When they withdrew the resolution to authorize military force against Iraq in March 2003, Washington and London were not assured even a simple majority and were confronting three vetoes. In Kosovo there were only three negative votes and two vetoes in the offing. Moreover, there was not unanimous approval for the Iraq campaign from a nineteen-member regional body—in fact, both NATO and the European Union were split. And all the regional organizations in the geographic area covered by the crisis were categorically against the war. In short, the "coalition" in Iraq was not truly multilateral in any meaningful way, and widespread international backing, not to mention right authority, was conspicuously absent.

In closing, I repeat that the greater danger for a more just world order —the guiding principle behind Falk's life work—comes from too little rather than too much humanitarian intervention. We should be less preoccupied that military action will be taken too often for insufficient humanitarian reasons, and more that it will be taken too rarely for the right ones. We need only look at the area contiguous to Rwanda, where since 1998 an estimated 4 million people have died in Congo, largely from the famine and disease accompanying armed conflict, according to the International Rescue Committee.[11] Or in western Sudan, where perhaps 300,000 people have died and 2.5 million have been displaced since early 2003.[12] The international efforts approved by the Security Council have been appallingly inadequate to these human tragedies.

Although the ICISS accords the primary role to the Security Council, this is not the only recourse for humanitarian intervention. Still, the council should remain the first port of call to authorize the use of military force. "The difficult question," as Gareth Evans has remarked, "is whether it should be the last."[13]

Richard Falk's answer comes close to a yes, whereas mine would be a definite no, and so would Kofi Annan's. In his General Assembly address in September 1999, the secretary-general regretted the Security Council's inability to approve intervention in Kosovo. At the same time, he also made clear that if the council should decline to act in a conscience-shocking case, such inaction was unacceptable. He asked his audience about their reactions had there been a state or a group of states willing to act in April 1994 without the Security Council's imprimatur. "Should such a coalition have stood aside," he asked rhetorically, "and allowed the horror to unfold?"[14]

The answer by any of the 800,000 slaughtered Rwandans would be obvious, even if among many UN legal and political commentators it often remains unclear.

## Postscript

The September 2005 World Summit—the largest-ever gathering of heads of state and government officials, who assembled in New York on the UN's 60th anniversary—provided the latest endorsement of R2P in what became General Assembly resolution 60/1. Consensus building can sometimes occur around controversial issues and with opposition from the strangest of bedfellows—in this case, John Bolton heading the U.S. delegation and the Non-Aligned Movement. The latter reiterated its rejection of the so-called right of humanitarian intervention—in spite of much support and even bullishness about intervention in Africa and the African Union's constitution —and the United States repeated its refusal to be committed to military action by others. But the proverbial bottom line is clear: when a state is incapable or unwilling to safeguard its own citizens and peaceful means fail, the resort to military force (preferably with Security Council approval) remains a possibility. The summit's final text reaffirms the primary roles of states in protecting their own citizens and encourages international assistance to weak states to exercise this responsibility. At the same time, it makes clear the need for international intervention when countries fail to shield their citizens from or, more likely, actively sponsor genocide or war crimes.

The historical normative pace captured by paragraphs 138–9 of the World Summit outcome is breathtaking. With the possible exception of the prevention of genocide after World War II, no idea has moved faster in the international normative arena than the responsibility to protect. At the same time, the Security Council's painful dithering over Darfur and the Democratic Republic of the Congo demonstrates the dramatic disconnect between multilateral rhetoric and reality.

## Notes

**1.** International Commission on Intervention and State Sovereignty, *The Responsibility to Protect: Report of the International Commission on Intervention and State Sovereignty* (Ottawa: IDRC, 2001). See also the accompanying volume by Thomas G. Weiss and Don Hubert, *The Responsibility to Protect: Research, Bibliography, and Background* (Ottawa: ICISS, 2001).

**2.** Anthony Lewis, "The Challenge of Global Justice Now," *Daedalus* 132, no. 1 (2003): 8. For reviews of the report, see Adam Roberts, "The Price of Protection," *Survival* 44, no. 4 (2002): 157–61; and Jennifer M. Welsh, Carolin Thielking, and S. Neil MacFarlane, "The Responsibility to Protect: Assessing the Report of the International Commission on Intervention and State Sovereignty," *International Journal* 57, no. 4 (2002): 489–512.

**3.** In addition to Evans, the northern side included Lee Hamilton, Michael Ignatieff, Klaus Naumann, Cornelio Somaruga, and Gisèle Côté-Harper. In addition to Sahnoun, the south's representatives included Ramesh Thakur, Cyril Ramaphonsa, Fidel Ramos, and Eduardo Stein. Russia's Vladimir Lukin completed the group.

**4.** Human Security Commission, *Human Security Now* (New York: Human Security Commission, 2003).

**5.** Additional information as well as translations of the report can be found at www.iciss-ciise.gc.ca. An updated bibliography with 3,000 key-worded entries can be found at http://web.gc.cuny.edu/ralphbuncheinstitute/iciss/iciss%20database/English/Biblio2.html.

**6.** Kofi A. Annan, *The Question of Intervention—Statements by the Secretary-General* (New York: United Nations, 1999); and Annan, *"We the Peoples": The United Nations in the 21st Century* (New York: United Nations, 2000). For a discussion of the controversy surrounding the speech in September 1999, see Thomas G. Weiss, "The Politics of Humanitarian Ideas," *Security Dialogue* 31, no. 1 (2000): 11–23.

**7.** For an overview, see Mohammed Ayoob, "Humanitarian Intervention and International Society," *Global Governance* 7, no. 3 (2001): 225–30; and Robert Jackson, *The Global Covenant: Human Conduct in a World of States* (Oxford: Oxford University Press, 2000).

**8.** Greenberg Research, *The People on War Report* (Geneva: ICRC, 1999), xvi.

**9.** Independent International Commission on Kosovo, *Kosovo Report: Conflict, International Response, Lessons Learned* (Oxford: Oxford University Press, 2000), 4.

**10.** ICISS, *The Responsibility to Protect*, xii.

**11.** See www.theirc.org/mortality/.

**12.** "Response to the Darfur Complex Humanitarian Emergency (2003-2005)," available at www.db.idpproject.org/Sites/IdpProjectDb/idpSurvey.nsf/wViewCounctires/ECD13A.

**13.** Gareth Evans, "The Responsibility to Protect and September 11" (speech, Ottawa, December 16, 2002), available at www.intl-crisi-group.org/projects/showreport.cfm?reportid=860.

**14.** Annan, *The Question of Intervention*, 39.

# 8

# Holding Military and Paramilitary Forces Accountable

John Cerone

## The Regulation of Armed Conflict under International Law

The traditional function of public international law is to regulate relations between and among states. This function continues even when these relations degenerate into armed conflict, for during such conflicts "the right of belligerents to adopt means of injuring the enemy is not unlimited."[1]

The law of armed conflict, known also as the law of war, the *jus in bello,* or international humanitarian law (IHL), is one of the oldest subject areas of international law. It refers to the corpus of international norms that regulates the conduct of hostilities and that provides protection for persons not taking part, or no longer taking part, in hostilities.

While IHL shares with international human rights law the purpose of protecting individuals, the two bodies of international law may be distinguished on several grounds. Most significantly, human rights law is primarily concerned with the way a state treats those under its jurisdiction, while "humanitarian law aims at placing restraints on the conduct of warfare so as to diminish its effects on the victims of the hostilities."[2] Humanitarian law must also be distinguished from arms control treaties. The latter are much narrower in scope, strictly limited to regulation of the development, possession, and use of certain types of weaponry. Another distinct body of international law is the *jus ad bellum,* which regulates the lawfulness of a state's initial recourse to the use of armed force. Once an armed conflict has begun, the *jus ad bellum* gives way to the *jus in bello.*

Humanitarian law applies only in times of armed conflict or occupation. One of the strengths of IHL is that it operates on the basis of facts and is unconcerned with political labels. Thus, a formal declaration of war is not necessary to trigger the application of IHL, as long as an armed conflict in fact exists.

## The Evolution of IHL

The corpus of IHL rests on a set of fundamental principles, which at the same time constitute the earliest antecedents of modern humanitarian law.[3] These include the complementary principles of necessity and humanity, and of distinction and proportionality.

While the principle of humanity is aimed at reducing human suffering, it is tempered by the principle of military necessity, which reflects the interests of the warring parties in avoiding conferral of a military advantage on the opposing party to the conflict. Thus, traditional weapons were prohibited only if they were calculated to cause *unnecessary* suffering.

A balance is similarly struck in the principle of distinction and the permissibility of civilian casualties in the form of proportionate collateral damage. The principle of distinction requires that "the Parties to the conflict shall at all times distinguish between the civilian population and combatants and between civilian objects and military objectives and accordingly shall direct their operations only against military objectives."[4] Civilian casualties may result, however, in the course of an attack against a military objective. The lawfulness of such an attack will be preserved as long as the expected loss of civilian life is not "excessive in relation to the concrete and direct military advantage anticipated."[5]

Further, many provisions of IHL are premised on a bargaining of sorts. For example, certain protected objects retain their protected status only as long as they are not used for purposes related to the hostilities. Thus, when Palestinian fighters took shelter in the Church of the Nativity in Bethlehem Square, the church became a lawful military objective, losing the protection otherwise afforded to it under humanitarian law.[6]

**Hague Law and Geneva Law.** The nineteenth century saw the conclusion of the first multilateral treaties codifying the law of armed conflict. The most comprehensive codifications were the Hague Conventions of 1899 and 1907. Following World War II, the international community, seeking to address the inadequacies of the Hague Conventions[7] and to further expand the scope of humanitarian law, elaborated the Geneva Conventions of 1949, to be later supplemented by the Additional Protocols of 1977. In general, these two sets of treaties track two different strands of humanitarian law, known simply as the Hague law and the Geneva law.

The Hague law consists primarily of restraints on the conduct of hostilities, including the outright prohibition of certain methods and means of warfare. The rules of the Hague law prohibit, for example, attacks against particular targets, such as undefended towns or religious institutions, and the employment of certain types of weapons, in particular those calculated to cause unnecessary suffering.

The Geneva law focuses on the protection of individuals who are not or are no longer taking part in hostilities. Each of the four 1949 Geneva Conventions protects a different category of such individuals. The First and Second Geneva Conventions protect sick and wounded soldiers in the field and at sea, respectively. The Third Convention regulates the treatment of prisoners of war. The protection of civilians is the focus of the Fourth Convention. The Additional Protocols to the Geneva Conventions simultaneously update and merge the Hague and Geneva law.

Among the most basic rules of IHL, in addition to the principles noted above, are the following. Persons *hors de combat* (i.e., who have been removed from combat, such as through sickness or detention) and those not taking direct part in hostilities must be protected and treated humanely, without adverse discrimination. It is forbidden to kill or injure an enemy who surrenders or is hors de combat. The wounded and sick must be collected and cared for by the party that has them in its power. The Red Cross emblem, which is used to protect humanitarian or medical establishments and personnel, must be respected. Captured combatants and civilians under the authority of an adverse party are entitled to have their basic rights respected; in particular, they must be protected against violence. All persons are entitled to basic judicial guarantees. Parties to the conflict cannot use weapons or methods of warfare causing unnecessary suffering. In addition, certain acts are specifically prohibited. These include torture, the taking of hostages, the use of human shields, rape, the imposition of collective penalties, pillage,[8] and reprisals[9] against protected[10] persons.

**The Continuing Relevance of Customary Law.** Notwithstanding the codification of humanitarian law, the general principles and customary law of war as developed through the centuries continue to apply in a residual manner, filling gaps between the express provisions of treaty law. As set forth in the famous Martens clause[11] of the Hague Conventions:

> Until a more complete code of the laws of war has been issued, the High Contracting Parties deem it expedient to declare that, in cases not included in the Regulations adopted by them, the inhabitants and the belligerents remain under the protection and the rule of the principles

of the law of nations, as they result from the usages established among civilized peoples, from the laws of humanity, and the dictates of the public conscience.[12]

In addition to this gap-filling function, customary law also has the advantage of binding all states. A number of states, including the United States, have failed to ratify the Additional Protocols to the 1949 Geneva Conventions and are thus not bound by them. However, these states are bound by the rules contained in those instruments to the extent that each particular rule has evolved into customary law. Thus, when the United States invaded Iraq in early 2003, it was bound by those norms of Protocol I that had attained customary status.

Among the more controversial provisions of Protocol I is the extension of prisoner-of-war status to guerrilla fighters in occupied territory. Thus, this provision is unlikely to be customary, and the United States may not be required to afford such status to captured guerrillas. At the same time, Article 75 of Protocol I, which provides basic protections for all persons within the power of a party to the conflict, has achieved customary status and thus binds the United States irrespective of the fact that the United States is not a party to Protocol I.

**The Law of Noninternational Armed Conflict.** A more fundamental distinction than that between the Hague law and the Geneva law is the distinction between the law of international armed conflict and the law of noninternational armed conflict.

Embedded in the classical system of international law, a system resting on the sovereign equality of states[13] and the related principle of nonintervention,[14] IHL is predominantly concerned with international (i.e., interstate) armed conflict. Among the four Geneva Conventions, only Common Article 3[15] expressly applies to noninternational armed conflict. Common Article 3 provides protection from only the most serious abuses.[16] While Protocol II also applies to noninternational armed conflict, it provides significantly less protection to individuals than does Protocol I, which is applicable only in international armed conflict or occupation and certain analogous situations. Application of the Hague Conventions is similarly limited to situations of international armed conflict.[17]

While neither the Hague Conventions nor the Geneva Conventions define the phrase "armed conflict," definitions for both international and noninternational armed conflict have been set forth in international jurisprudence. According to the jurisprudence of one international criminal court, an armed conflict exists "whenever there is a resort to armed force between States or protracted armed violence between governmental authorities and organized armed groups or between such groups within a State."[18]

A peculiar feature of the law of noninternational armed conflict is its application to nonstate groups. As noted above, the traditional subject of international law is the state. However, over the course of the past century, the principle that only states could be the subjects of international legal obligations yielded to the changing values and nature of the international community. By its terms, Common Article 3 of the Geneva Conventions binds both states and nonstate parties to noninternational conflicts. In addition, certain norms of IHL have evolved into norms of international criminal law, which directly binds individuals.

**Relationship between IHL and International Criminal Law.** The horrors of World War II spawned a host of developments in international law. Among the most significant was the crystallization of the principle that violation of certain norms of international law could give rise to individual criminal responsibility. According to this principle, certain serious violations of international law would engage not only the classical form of responsibility in international law, that is, the responsibility of the state, but also that of the individuals perpetrating the violation. Such perpetrators could be criminally prosecuted and punished directly under international law.

The emergence of this principle was driven by the need to develop effective means of enforcement. As reasoned by the International Military Tribunal at Nuremberg, "Crimes against international law are committed by men, not by abstract entities, and only by punishing individuals who commit such crimes can the provisions of international law be enforced."[19]

Indeed, it was the establishment of the International Military Tribunals[20] in the aftermath of World War II that spurred the development of international criminal law.[21] Thus, the overwhelming majority of international crimes that were given cognizance by the international community at that time were those relating to war, that is, violations of humanitarian law. In addition, international crimes, by their very nature and scale, will often coincide with times of massive upheaval, such as that which occurs during periods of armed conflict.

The Rome Statute of the International Criminal Court (ICC), adopted in 1998, provides the most comprehensive codification to date of international criminal law. Included within its subject matter jurisdiction are the crimes of aggression, genocide, war crimes, and crimes against humanity. War crimes are essentially criminal violations of IHL (i.e., violations of those norms of IHL that are deemed to give rise to individual criminal responsibility). Genocide and crimes against humanity are distinct from war crimes in that they need not be committed in times of armed conflict. However, war crimes comprise the richest array of norms within the Rome Statute.

## The Application of IHL in the Context of Peace Operations

The question of the applicability of IHL in the context of peace operations is not without controversy, and the United Nations and its member states have wrestled with this issue for decades. Although virtually all UN member states are states parties to the Geneva Conventions, the United Nations itself is not. The situation is further complicated by the notion that operations undertaken pursuant to the Chapter VII power of the Security Council[22] are somehow exempt from the ordinary application of international law, such that even the IHL obligations of member states participating in the operation are inapplicable.

Nonetheless, in recent years a consensus has emerged that IHL applies to any armed conflict or occupation, even those arising or occurring in the context of peace operations deployed under the auspices of the United Nations.[23] As noted above, one of the strengths of IHL is that it applies once the facts indicate that a state of armed conflict or occupation has arisen, irrespective of any political labels that are employed[24] and independently of the lawfulness of the initial resort to the use of force.[25]

Any remaining doubts were resolved in August 1999, when the UN secretary-general promulgated a code of "principles and rules of international humanitarian law applicable to United Nations forces conducting operations under United Nations command and control."[26] The code essentially sets forth, in summary fashion, the main provisions of IHL and holds that they are applicable "to United Nations forces when in situations of armed conflict they are actively engaged therein as combatants, to the extent and for the duration of their engagement."[27] It further provides that "they are accordingly applicable in enforcement actions, or in peacekeeping operations when the use of force is permitted in self-defence."[28]

This acknowledgment that UN peacekeepers may become combatants under the rules of IHL is also reflected in the Statute of the International Criminal Court. Attacks against peacekeepers constitute crimes under the ICC Statute only in situations where the peacekeepers "are entitled to the protection given to civilians or civilian objects under the international law of armed conflict,"[29] clearly implying that there would be times when they would not be so entitled.

**The Issue of Accountability.** The issue of whether IHL applies to peace operations must be distinguished from the question of who may be held accountable for IHL violations. The latter becomes particularly complex in the context of collective action.

Given the complex configuration of most peacekeeping missions, an IHL violation committed by a peacekeeper could possibly entail the responsibility of a number of different entities—the peacekeeper's sending or seconding state, the territorial state,[30] the United Nations, the regional intergovernmental organization (if any) deploying the mission or peacekeeping force, member states of the intergovernmental organizations under the auspices of which the peacekeeping mission was deployed, and, finally, the mission or peacekeeping force itself (to the extent it may be deemed to have limited international legal personality as a subsidiary body of an intergovernmental organization). In addition, as noted above, certain violations will entail the individual criminal responsibility of the perpetrator.

In order to ascertain which of these legal subjects may be held to account, it must be determined whether the particular subject is bound by IHL and whether that subject may be held responsible for the act committed by the individual peacekeeper. Each determination requires a complex analysis involving such considerations as the scope of each entity's international legal personality, whether such personality extends into the field of IHL,[31] and whether the conduct of the perpetrator may be attributed to the entity under the relevant rules of international law governing responsibility for the commission of internationally wrongful acts.[32] Quite apart from these considerations are the questions of whether any remedy is available, whether there is any forum with jurisdiction to examine an alleged violation, and whether international law affords immunity to the otherwise responsible entity.

**Immunities.** The United Nations, its organs, and its personnel are afforded broad immunity under international law. Under Section 2 of the Convention on the Privileges and Immunities of the United Nations,[33] the "United Nations, its property and assets wherever located and by whomsoever held, shall enjoy immunity from every form of legal process except insofar as in any particular case it has expressly waived its immunity." UN officials are granted similarly broad immunity.[34]

Experts (other than UN officials) performing missions for the United Nations are accorded "such privileges and immunities as are necessary for the independent exercise of their functions, [including] immunity from personal arrest or detention [and,] in respect of words spoken or written and acts done by them in the course of the performance of their mission, immunity from legal process of every kind."[35] In the context of territories under UN administration, this immunity may be entrenched in the form of UN mission regulations. In Kosovo, for example, UNMIK Regulation 2000/47 tracks the language of the Privileges and Immunities Convention, providing UNMIK personnel with functional immunity as well as complete immunity from arrest or detention. Personnel of KFOR, the NATO peacekeeping force, are accorded full immunity from legal process.

In addition, states sending troops abroad as contingents of peacekeeping operations, whether under the auspices of the UN or otherwise, frequently incorporate immunity provisions into their Status of Forces Agreements with host governments.

Peacekeepers may thus be, and typically are, granted immunities under several different sources of law. Fiercely maintaining their sovereign prerogatives, states are clearly quite careful to ensure that their troops will not be subject to foreign prosecution.[36]

## The Erosion of the Interstate Model

Notwithstanding the persistence of the classical interstate structure of the international legal system, over the course of the past century international law has evolved substantially in its relation to individual human beings. With the inception of the Westphalian system, the sovereign equality of states and the related principle of nonintervention were paramount. Only states were true subjects of international law, with individuals generally relegated to the status of mere objects, and international law's substantive norms consisted of a network of reciprocal obligations that focused almost exclusively on interstate relations.

However, one of the strengths of international law is its dynamism— its capacity to develop in response to the changing realities of international life and the evolving values of the international community. Two phenomena in particular have led to astonishingly rapid developments in the substance of international law and even in the very structure of the international legal system. The first is the universal recognition that the protection of human dignity is a proper concern of international law, and the second is the accumulation and exercise of power by nonstate actors.

These phenomena have led to the elaboration of rules governing state accountability for the conduct of nonstate actors, and, in a development that threatens to alter the structure of the system, the emergence of the individual as a subject of rights and duties under international law. These developments are seen most clearly in the great corpus of human rights law created since the conclusion of World War II. However, parallel developments may be discerned in the evolution of humanitarian law over the past century.

Indeed, the customary law of war was developed as much to promote efficiency and safeguard the interests of states as to provide protection to victims of war. Even the early codifications of humanitarian law retained the classical interstate structure. The Hague Conventions of 1899 and 1907, for example, applied only to interstate conflicts[37] and protected individuals only to the extent that they were objects of the adversary. The law was reciprocity based and applied exclusively to conflicts in which all states engaged in the conflict were also parties to the conventions.[38] Thus, the Hague Conventions could not apply during World War II, even as between states parties to the conventions, since several of the belligerents had not ratified those conventions.[39] Further, the language of those conventions was language of prohibition and obligation, as opposed to rights-based language. For example, rather than providing prisoners of war (POWs) with a "right" to humane treatment, the Fourth Hague Convention requires that POWs be "humanely treated."[40]

By 1949, humanitarian law had begun to recognize the increasing relevance of nonstate actors and to embrace the language of rights. Common Article 3 of the 1949 Geneva Conventions set forth standards expressly binding nonstate parties. This was the first time that a multilateral IHL treaty asserted that a nongovernmental party was bound by international law.

The Geneva Conventions also adopted an individual rights–based approach. This approach is exemplified in Article 8 of the Fourth Geneva Convention, which provides that "protected persons may in no circumstances renounce in part or in entirety the rights secured to them by the present Convention."[41] The Geneva Conventions also prohibit reprisals against protected persons, emphasizing a further deviation from the classical reciprocity-based system. Nonetheless, the conventions retained some of the baggage of the Westphalian system. The bulk of the protections of the Fourth Convention were afforded only to the nationals of the enemy state, preserving a degree of reciprocity.[42] By 1977, however, the drafters of Protocol I had recognized that human dignity demanded that all victims of conflict be provided with certain basic protections irrespective of nationality. Article 75 of Protocol I essentially encapsulates human rights law, providing basic rights to individuals even vis-à-vis their own government. Article 75 represents the complete abandonment of the nationality test, and the shedding of reciprocity at least with regard to protecting the fundamental rights of human beings.

Duties of the individual have evolved primarily through international criminal law. The International Military Tribunal at Nuremberg found individuals to be subjects of international law to the extent that they could bear individual criminal responsibility for certain serious violations of international law. In light of the dynamic relationship between IHL and international criminal law, as humanitarian law expanded to regulate the conduct of nonstate actors, so did international criminal law provide for their individual responsibility. International criminal law has also fed back into humanitarian law through, for example, expanding the scope of situations in which individual nonstate actors may be held to have breached IHL and even to elaborate on the standards for holding states responsible for the conduct of nonstate actors.[43]

**Regulating the Conduct of Nonstate Armed Groups.** Notwithstanding recent notable exceptions, the vast majority of today's conflicts are noninternational. Rather than being conflicts between two sovereign states, these conflicts pit the state against nonstate organized, armed groups operating within the state. Further complicating the situation, a growing number of such conflicts involve nonstate groups operating with the support of other states or launching attacks from outside the state's territory.[44]

As noted above, the erosion of the interstate model has enabled the direct regulation of nonstate actors. Unlike most other areas of public international law, IHL purports to apply directly to the conduct of nonstate groups. The law of noninternational armed conflict binds both the government and the nonstate armed groups who are parties to the conflict. Nonetheless, the prevalence of this type of conflict stands in stark contrast to the normative poverty of the law applicable to such conflicts.[45]

The 9/11 attacks against the World Trade Center and the Pentagon brought the issue of nonstate actors to the fore. In the aftermath of the attacks, jurists wrestled with the legal challenges posed by this novel form of conflict. Simply to determine the applicable law, it is necessary to consider which law applies to an armed conflict between a state and a nonstate armed group based within another state or states; the extent to which Protocol I to the Geneva Conventions of 1949 represents customary law; the extent to which human rights law continues to apply alongside humanitarian law; and whether the law of international armed conflict applies between a state and a de facto government that has not attracted international recognition, while the supposed de jure government has retained its seat at the United Nations. Even once the applicable law is determined, one must attempt to resolve a variety of issues arising from the application of that law, such as whether diversity of nationality is required for a combatant to be entitled to POW status; whether individuals detained in the United States by the Immigration and Naturalization Service could be deemed internees under the relevant provisions of humanitarian law; whether U.S. forces have occupied any part of Afghanistan for the purposes of the Fourth Geneva Convention; and whether Taliban fighters could be deemed "armed forces of a Party to the conflict" under the Third Geneva Convention.

The dearth of treaty rules applicable in noninternational armed conflict, and in particular those binding nonstate actors, is being addressed through the development of international criminal law, as exemplified in the context of crimes of sexual violence.

## Case Study 1: Rape as a War Crime

### Background

Until 1993, rape, even when carried out systematically as an instrument of war, was not clearly recognized as a war crime in international law. While the rape of civilians was prohibited by the Fourth Geneva Convention, it was not expressly enumerated among the so-called grave breaches, which states parties were obliged to criminalize and punish. Nor was rape expressly included in the charters of the Nuremberg and Tokyo tribunals.[46] Since then, there has been tremendous jurisprudential development, particularly in the realm of international criminal law, and rape is now widely recognized as a war crime in any armed conflict, international or noninternational.

On May 25, 1993, in response to the threat to international peace and security posed by the "widespread and flagrant violations of international humanitarian law occurring within the territory of the former Yugoslavia," the UN Security Council established the International Criminal Tribunal for the former Yugoslavia (ICTY) "for the sole purpose of prosecuting persons responsible" for these violations. For the first time, rape was expressly included within the subject matter jurisdiction of an international criminal tribunal.[47] Specifically, rape was enumerated as a crime against humanity under Article 5 of the ICTY Statute.

However, rape was not enumerated as a war crime under the relevant articles of the statute. This was problematic because rape could be prosecuted as a crime against humanity only when committed as part of a widespread or systematic attack directed against a civilian population.[48] Thus, a single or isolated act of rape that did not constitute part of such an attack could not be prosecuted under Article 5.

## Jurisprudential Developments at the ICTY — the "Foca" Case

The Trial and Appeals chambers of the ICTY addressed this lacuna head-on in a number of cases. The "Foca" case in particular is notable for its focus on crimes of sexual violence and its exhaustive treatment of the subject. The facts of that case, as summarized by the ICTY Appeals Chamber, outline a clear case of sexual violence employed as an instrument of warfare:

> From April 1992 until at least February 1993, there was an armed conflict between Bosnian Serbs and Bosnian Muslims in the area of Foca. Non-Serb civilians were killed, raped or otherwise abused as a direct result of the armed conflict. The Appellants, in their capacity as soldiers, took an active part in carrying out military tasks during the armed conflict, fighting on behalf of one of the parties to that conflict, namely, the Bosnian Serb side, whereas none of the victims of the crimes of which the Appellants were convicted took any part in the hostilities.

> The armed conflict involved a systematic attack by the Bosnian Serb Army and paramilitary groups on the non-Serb civilian population in the wider area of the municipality of Foca. The campaign was successful in its aim of "cleansing" the Foca area of non-Serbs. One specific target of the attack was Muslim women, who were detained in intolerably unhygienic conditions in places like the Kalinovik School, Foca High School and the Partizan Sports Hall, where they were mistreated in many ways, including being raped repeatedly.[49]

The Trial Chamber found all the accused criminally responsible for the rapes they had committed or facilitated. Although they were convicted of rape as a crime against humanity, they were also convicted of rape as a war crime. Even though rape was not expressly enumerated as a war crime under the statute, the Trial Chamber found the rapes to constitute both torture, which was expressly included in the statute as a war crime, and an "outrage upon personal dignity," a violation of Common Article 3.[50]

In finding rape to constitute a violation of Common Article 3, the Trial Chamber affirmed that rape was a war crime even when committed in non-international armed conflict. In doing so, it also affirmed that state action was not a required element and that the war crime of rape could thus be committed by nonstate actors.

International crimes of sexual violence are most comprehensively set forth in the Statute of the ICC. The Rome Statute includes among its war crimes provisions the proscription of rape, sexual slavery, enforced prostitution, forced pregnancy, forced sterilization, and other forms of sexual violence of comparable gravity.[51]

## Case Study 2: Afghanistan

As noted above, analyzing the application of humanitarian law to the September 11 attacks against the United States and the ensuing conflict in Afghanistan is a complex undertaking. In characterizing the conflict, there were those who asserted that the attacks against the World Trade Center and Pentagon did not rise to the level of armed conflict and thus were not governed by humanitarian law.[52] Others took the position that these acts were of sufficient intensity to constitute armed conflict, particularly when viewed in the context of earlier incidents, including the 2000 USS *Cole* bombing, the 1998 U.S. embassy bombings, and the 1993 World Trade Center bombing. Since the attack was launched by nonstate actors, those who held IHL to be applicable generally viewed the conflict as noninternational in nature, and thus governed only by Common Article 3 and other such rules of noninternational armed conflict as were customary in nature. However, it may also be argued that the conflict was international in nature, especially in light of the U.S. assertion that the Taliban, then de facto government of Afghanistan, could be held responsible for the attacks.

In any event, once the United States invaded Afghanistan, a state of armed conflict had clearly arisen, and it is universally acknowledged that IHL began to apply from that point forward. However, it was still unclear whether the applicable law was that of international or noninternational armed conflict. To view the conflict as international (i.e., interstate), one could point to the fact that the United States had crossed an international border and invaded another country and that is was not limiting its attacks to al Qaeda but was attacking the Taliban as well. On the other hand, it could also be argued that the conflict was noninternational in nature because the Taliban, which never attracted general international recognition as the government of Afghanistan, was itself a nonstate group and because the invasion was not opposed by the recognized government of Afghanistan.

Ultimately, the better view is that the conflict was international in nature, given that the Taliban controlled Afghanistan, that the United States relied on self-defense as its primary justification for the invasion (as opposed to invoking the consent of the recognized government), and that the Geneva Conventions apply once a factual situation has arisen, irrespective of the political labels attached to a state of affairs.

The invasion was followed by a military occupation. The Fourth Hague Convention and the Fourth Geneva Convention contain extensive provisions on the law of occupation.[53] However, another complex issue is the duration of the law of occupation. Certain provisions of the law of occupation apply for a period of one year. Other provisions continue to apply for the duration of the occupation. As for the application of those provisions, it is unclear whether the occupation terminated upon: the convening of the *loya jirga* and appointment of the interim administration in mid-2002; the adoption of the new constitution in January 2004; or the election of President Karzai in October 2004. Similarly, it may be argued that the law of occupation continued to apply beyond October 2004 until the direct election of the legislature. Another possible argument is that a state of occupation will continue until such time as the Afghan government is capable of withholding its consent to the presence of foreign troops.

Even once the state of occupation had terminated, IHL would still apply to the ongoing hostilities between insurgents on one side and Afghan and foreign armed forces on the other. While it is likely that such conflicts would be noninternational in nature, it remains possible to argue that such conflicts are international, at least where the insurgents are remnants of the former Afghan regime.

Another factor complicating the application of IHL in Afghanistan is the multiplicity of actors operating in the territory. In addition to U.S. forces, Coalition and ISAF (NATO) forces have undertaken security responsibilities in Afghanistan. The obligations of participating states will vary depending on which treaties have been ratified by the particular state. In addition, while the United States is clearly legally responsible for the forces under its command and control, it is unclear to what extent other participating states may be held responsible when their forces are acting through a supranational organization or have been subordinated to the command of a lead state.[54]

Recent allegations of detainee abuse by U.S. and Coalition forces in Afghanistan have led to calls for accountability. All states are under an obligation to take measures aimed at the repression of breaches of IHL by forces under their control. Crimes committed after July 1, 2002, the date on which the Rome Statute entered into force, may also come within the jurisdiction of the International Criminal Court.

As Afghanistan itself acceded to the treaty in February 2003, all international crimes[55] committed on its territory after that date would fall within the court's jurisdiction. However, the Karzai government has signed a number of bilateral treaties in which it has agreed not to surrender former military personnel to any international criminal tribunal. In any event, international crimes committed in Afghanistan will not be admissible before the ICC if the relevant states take responsibility for investigating and prosecuting these abuses.

## Case Study 3: Iraq

In contrast with the situation in Afghanistan, the application of IHL in Iraq is much clearer. The Iraq war was a traditional interstate conflict, followed by a clear case of military occupation.[56] Therefore, the Hague and Geneva Conventions apply in full.

The release of photos of inhumane acts committed by U.S. forces at Abu Ghraib prison in Iraq focused international attention sharply on the issue of accountability for abuses. As noted above, all states are obliged to prevent and respond to breaches of IHL by forces under their control. In the case of "grave breaches" of the Geneva Conventions, such as unlawful killing and torture,[57] all states have jurisdiction to prosecute perpetrators and are obliged to do so.[58] However, in order to constitute a "grave breach," the victim must qualify as a "protected person" under the conventions. Where the victim is a civilian, he or she will generally qualify as a protected person under the Fourth Convention unless he or she is a national of the perpetrating state or a cobelligerent state.

Where the victim is a combatant, the analysis is more complicated. If the individual is a lawful enemy combatant,[59] he or she will qualify as a POW and thus as a protected person under the Third Convention. However, the status of a combatant who does not qualify for lawful combatant status is less clear. The majority view (including that of the ICRC and ICTY) is that unlawful combatants are still eligible for protection under the Fourth Convention as civilians. Thus, they may qualify for "protected person" status under the Fourth Convention as long as the "diversity of nationality" test is met. However, others, including the U.S. government, take the position that unlawful combatants cannot be classified as civilians and are thus incapable of falling under the protection of the Fourth Convention. According to this view, such individuals cannot qualify for "protected person" status under any of the Geneva Conventions. A clear implication of this position is that crimes committed against them cannot qualify as grave breaches. In any event, the United States has ratified the Convention against Torture and is thus obliged to prosecute all acts of torture committed by its forces, irrespective of the status of the victim.[60]

Another issue arising in the Abu Ghraib context is the use of private contractors to conduct interrogations and perform other military and security functions. As noted above, the conduct of nonstate actors is not easily captured in the predominantly interstate grasp of international law. However, where such contractors are acting on behalf of a state—for example, where they are hired by a state to perform a public function or where they are otherwise acting under a state's instructions, direction, or control—that state bears responsibility for their conduct under international law.[61]

Individual nonstate perpetrators may be held directly responsible under international criminal law. While the ICC does not have jurisdiction over crimes committed in Iraq by nationals of states that are not parties to the Rome Statute,[62] the United States has a clear obligation to prosecute torture by nonstate actors. Even where the "grave breaches" regime is inapplicable —for example, where the victim does not qualify as a protected person— the Convention against Torture requires prosecution of all acts of torture.[63]

## Challenges for the Future

As noted above, one of the strengths of international law is its dynamism— its ability to respond to the evolving values of the international community and the changing daily realities faced, in particular, by victims of strife. This is particularly true of those bodies of international law, such as IHL, that have as their purpose the amelioration of suffering and the protection of individuals.

As armed intervention has increasingly taken place in the context of collective action, so has the international community recognized that such forces must be bound by the standards of IHL. As noninternational armed conflict has become the dominant form of conflict, so has the law applicable to noninternational conflicts been expanded through the practice of international criminal courts. Similarly, challenged by the increasing consolidation of power in the hands of nonstate actors, international criminal law has extended its reach to regulate their conduct.

Another major development has been the creation of supranational remedies with increasing authority to address violations. Existing human rights mechanisms have demonstrated an increasing willingness to address violations of international law occurring in times of armed conflict. The most significant development in this regard was the establishment, in July 2002, of the International Criminal Court, which has vast jurisdiction to prosecute war criminals.

Despite these extraordinary legal developments, significant challenges remain. The reach of international law remains limited by the law's primary focus on the state. Its power to regulate the conduct of human beings still relies primarily on the modality of domestic legislation and on the good faith of state authorities. Particularly in the suppression of international crimes, where the proscribed conduct generally requires a significant power base for its commission, reliance on domestic authorities has proven clearly inadequate. While the creation of the ICC represents a major step forward in remedying this inadequacy, the responsibility for ensuring its efficacy and preserving the integrity of its legal regime remains in the hands of individual states.

## Notes

1. Fourth Hague Convention Respecting the Law and Customs of War on Land, entered into force 1910, Annex, Article 22.

2. *Prosecutor v. Kunarac, Kovac, and Vukovic,* Judgment (ICTY Trial Chamber, 2001). Other distinctions between human rights and humanitarian law include the subjects of obligations, the institutions competent to determine violations, the period of application, the scope of beneficiaries, the locus of application, the range of rights protected, and the sources of obligations.

3. These principles are historically rooted in moral philosophy. The doctrine of collateral damage, for example, follows from the Thomist doctrine of "double effect."

4. Protocol Additional to the Geneva Conventions of August 12, 1949, and relating to the Protection of Victims of International Armed Conflicts ("Protocol I"), entered into force December 7, 1979, Article 48.

5. Protocol I, Article 57.

6. Note, however, that if there were civilians in the church as well, the principle of proportionality would still apply. If the number of civilians present in the church vastly outnumbered the number of combatants, it is likely that the principle of proportionality would bar attacking the church in a manner that would result in the deaths of those civilians.

7. One such inadequacy was the *si omnes* clause of the Hague Conventions, which required that all parties to a conflict be parties to the conventions in order for the conventions to be applicable. The fact that several states were not parties to the conventions rendered them inapplicable in World War II. See *infra* note 38 and accompanying text.

8. Pillage is essentially theft of civilian property. It must be distinguished from the lawful act of requisitioning supplies needed by an occupying army.

9. A reprisal is an otherwise unlawful act committed in response to an unlawful act by the opposing party. Reprisals are employed to induce compliance by the opposing party.

10. As noted above, the scope of protection afforded by the Geneva Conventions is limited to certain groups of individuals. The bulk of the protection afforded under the Fourth Convention, for example, is limited to a particular group of civilians—"those who, at a given moment and in any manner whatsoever, find themselves, in case of a conflict or occupation, in the hands of a Party to the conflict or Occupying Power of which they are not nationals." Geneva Convention

relative to the Protection of Civilian Persons in Time of War, entered into force October 21, 1950 ("Fourth Geneva Convention"), Article 4.

11. The "Martens clause," as it has come to be known, was included in the preamble of the Hague Conventions at the behest of F. F. de Martens, prominent jurist and Russian delegate to the 1899 Hague Peace Conference. The clause essentially invoked natural law to provide residual protection to victims of inhumane acts that were not expressly prohibited by the convention. This clause also provided the foundation for the evolution of "crimes against humanity" as they are understood today. See Theodor Meron, "The Martens Clause, Principles of Humanity, and Dictates of Public Conscience," *American Journal of International Law* 94 (2000): 78, 79. The International Court of Justice has found the clause itself to constitute a rule of customary international law. Advisory Opinion, Legality of the Threat or Use of Nuclear Weapons, 1996 I.C.J. 226, 257 (July 8).

12. Hague Conventions of 1907, preamble.

13. Charter of the United Nations ("UN Charter"), Article 2(1).

14. UN Charter, Article 2(7).

15. Article 3 is identical in each of the four Geneva Conventions and is thus referred to as Common Article 3.

16. Common Article 3 prohibits the following acts against persons taking no active part in the hostilities: "violence to life and person, in particular murder of all kinds, mutilation, cruel treatment and torture; [the] taking of hostages; outrages upon personal dignity, in particular, humiliating and degrading treatment; [and] the passing of sentences and the carrying out of executions without previous judgment pronounced by a regularly constituted court, affording all the judicial guarantees which are recognized as indispensable by civilized peoples."

17. Note, however, that the International Criminal Tribunal for the former Yugoslavia has greatly expanded the scope of norms applicable in noninternational armed conflict. In the *Tadic* case, the Appeals Chamber found that certain norms of international armed conflict have evolved through customary law and now apply during noninternational armed conflict as well. *Prosecutor v. Tadic*, Appeal Decision (ICTY, Appeals Chamber, 1995) ("*Tadic Appeal Decision*").

18. *Tadic Appeal Decision*, paragraph 70.

19. Judgment of the International Military Tribunal at Nuremberg.

20. At the close of World War II, the Allies established the International Military Tribunal at Nuremberg as well as the International Military Tribunal for the Far East.

21. Although "international criminal law" can refer to various distinct bodies of international law, ranging from extradition treaties to mutual assistance agreements, in this chapter it is used to refer to that body of international norms the breach of which gives rise to the criminal responsibility of the individual under international law.

**22.** Chapter VII of the UN Charter sets forth the enforcement power of the Security Council.

**23.** See J. Cerone, "Minding the Gap: Outlining KFOR Accountability under Human Rights and Humanitarian Law in Post Confllict Kosovo," *European Journal of International Law*, vol. 12, no. 3 (June 2001).

**24.** See, e.g., Fourth Geneva Convention, *supra* note 10, at Article 2 (the convention applies even if a state of war is not recognized by one of the parties). See also Jean Pictet, ed., *Commentary: IV, Geneva Convention Relative to the Protection of Civilian Persons in Time of War* (1958; 1994 reprint edition), 21 ("The Convention only provides for the case of one of the Parties denying the existence of a state of war. What would the position be, it may be wondered, if both the Parties to an armed conflict were to deny the existence of a state of war. Even in that event it would not appear that they could, by tacit agreement, prevent the Conventions from applying. It must not be forgotten that the Conventions have been drawn up first and foremost to protect individuals, and not to serve State interests").

**25.** It is a basic principle of IHL that its application is entirely independent of the *jus ad bellum*. Thus, all parties are bound by IHL, irrespective of which party (if any) initially resorted to the unlawful use of force.

**26.** "Observance by United Nations Forces of International Humanitarian Law," ST/SGB/1999/13, August 6, 1999. As the scope of the code is limited to regulating the conduct of UN forces "under UN command and control," it would be inapplicable to peacekeeping forces under the command and control of regional organizations, such as NATO, even in situations where such forces are deployed under UN auspices. For example, in Resolution 1244, the UN Security Council "authorize[d] Member States and relevant international organizations" to establish KFOR, the NATO-led peacekeeping force for Kosovo. Although KFOR was mandated to "coordinat[e] closely" with the work of the UN Interim Administration Mission in Kosovo, it remained under NATO command and control.

**27.** Ibid. at Section 1.1.

**28.** Ibid. See also Convention on the Safety of United Nations and Associated Personnel (1994), Article 2, which, while requiring states parties to criminalize attacks against peacekeepers, also stipulates that the convention "shall not apply to a United Nations operation authorized by the Security Council as an enforcement action under Chapter VII of the Charter of the United Nations in which any of the personnel are engaged as combatants against organized armed forces and to which the law of international armed conflict applies."

**29.** The Rome Statute of the International Criminal Court (1998) ("ICC Statute"), Article 8(2)(b)(iii).

**30.** I.e., the state within which the violation occurs.

**31.** For example, even following the promulgation of the IHL Code by the UN secretary-general, it remains unclear whether the UN itself is bound by IHL.

**32.** See, e.g., the International Law Commission's Articles on State Responsibility (2001), part I, chapter 2.

**33.** Convention on the Privileges and Immunities of the United Nations, 1 U.N.T.S. 15, February 13, 1946.

**34.** Ibid., Section 18.

**35.** Ibid., Section 22.

**36.** UNMIK Regulation 2000/47 provides that KFOR personnel are "subject to the exclusive jurisdiction of their respective sending States" and are "immune from any form of arrest or detention other than by persons acting on behalf of their respective sending States," and that "requests to waive jurisdiction over KFOR personnel shall be referred to the respective commander of the national element of such personnel for consideration."

**37.** However, the ICTY has held that the basic rules of these conventions have since evolved through customary law to apply to noninternational conflicts as well. *Tadic Appeal Decision.*

**38.** See, e.g., Fourth Hague Convention, Article 2. ("The provisions contained in the Regulations referred to in Article 1, as well as in the present Convention, do not apply except between Contracting Powers, and then only if all the belligerents are parties to the Convention.")

**39.** However, certain norms of Hague law had by that time acquired the status of customary law and were applicable as such.

**40.** Fourth Hague Convention, Annex, Article 4.

**41.** Parallel provisions are found in each of the other three 1949 Conventions.

**42.** See, e.g., Fourth Geneva Convention, Article 4.

**43.** *Prosecutor v. Tadic,* Appeal Judgment (ICTY Appeals Chamber, 1999).

**44.** It should also be noted that the law of noninternational armed conflict primarily contemplates internal armed conflict, i.e., conflict occurring within the territory of one state. The September 11 attacks exemplify a type of conflict that is neither interstate nor internal armed conflict, but a group or groups of nonstate actors who are based abroad, possibly in several countries, launching attacks against states. This phenomenon does not fit the typical model that international law provides. While there is some historical precedent, the law is not clear in such a situation. At a minimum, the law of noninternational armed conflict would apply.

**45.** As noted above, the law of international armed conflict constitutes a much larger proportion of IHL than that governing noninternational armed conflict.

**46.** It should be noted, however, that crimes of sexual violence were prosecuted at the Tokyo Tribunal under the rubric of "inhumane treatment."

**47.** While rape was included within the subject matter jurisdiction of the Control Council courts established in post–World War II Germany, those courts were more analogous to domestic courts than international courts.

**48.** ICTY Statute, Article 5. There is no such threshold requirement for war crimes.

**49.** *Prosecutor v. Kunarac, Kovac, and Vukovic,* Appeal Judgment (ICTY Appeals Chamber, 2002), paragraphs 2 and 3.

**50.** Although Common Article 3 of the Geneva Conventions was not expressly included in the ICTY Statute, it had been read into the statute by an earlier decision of the ICTY Appeals Chamber. See *Tadic Appeal Decision* (1995). In addition, the Trial Chamber appears to have found the accused guilty of the war crime of rape as such; however, no clear legal basis was referred to by the chamber.

**51.** The Rome Statute similarly expands the types of sexual violence that constitute crimes against humanity when committed as part of a widespread or systematic attack against a civilian population.

**52.** Recall that such acts could still constitute crimes against humanity, since this category of international crime may occur in peacetime.

**53.** There is no law of occupation in a noninternational context. This analysis proceeds on the assumption that the armed conflict and occupation were international in nature.

**54.** See J. Cerone, "Reasonable Measures in Unreasonable Circumstances: A Legal Responsibility Framework for Human Rights Violations in Post-conflict Territories under UN Administration," in *The UN, Human Rights and Post-conflict Situations,* ed. N. White and D. Klaasen (Manchester: Manchester University Press, 2004).

**55.** In this context, the term "international crimes" refers to the crimes enumerated in the Rome Statute.

**56.** Note, however, that similar ambiguities arise regarding the duration of the law of occupation in Iraq.

**57.** Recall that in order for the "grave breaches" regime to apply, the conflict must have been international in nature. The grave breaches provisions do not apply in noninternational conflicts. Nonetheless, torture is clearly prohibited in all conflicts. See Common Article 3 to the Geneva Conventions.

**58.** Alternatively, states parties to the Geneva Convention may extradite perpetrators to other states parties for prosecution.

**59.** See Article 4 of the Third Geneva Convention.

**60.** See Article 7 of the 1984 Convention against Torture and Other Cruel, Inhuman, or Degrading Treatment or Punishment.

**61.** See the ILC Articles on State Responsibility.

**62.** Unlike Afghanistan, Iraq has not acceded to the Rome Statute.

**63.** While the definition of torture in the Torture Convention requires at least some element of official involvement, this definition would clearly be met given the close relationship between the private contractors and the U.S. forces in Iraq.

# 9

# Human Rights, Terrorism, and Efforts to Combat Terrorism

Jordan J. Paust

There is an inescapable link between impermissible acts of terrorism[1] and violations of human rights. When human rights are protected, terrorism is necessarily set back and peace is necessarily promoted.

From one perspective, it is clear that strategies of impermissible terrorism necessarily involve violations of human rights law.[2] For this reason, one can recognize that all forms of impermissible terrorism involve conduct that is proscribed by international law, regardless of the excuse or whether such conduct is engaged in by state, private, or other actors. More generally, the United Nations General Assembly and Security Council have often condemned all acts of terrorism, in all its forms, wherever and by whomever committed.[3] The authoritative 1970 Declaration on Principles of International Law also confirms a responsibility of states "to refrain from organizing, instigating, assisting or participating in acts of civil strife or terrorist acts in another State or acquiescing in organized activities within its territory directed against the commission of such acts."[4] A similar proscription prohibits related attempts to "organize, assist, foment, finance, incite or tolerate . . . terrorist or armed activities."[5] From this perspective, we can see that the use of impermissible strategies or tactics of terrorism by governmental, private, and other actors occurs not because of a lack of relevant international legal proscriptions and obligations but rather from a lack of effective political, diplomatic, economic, juridical, and other sanctions against those either directly engaged or complicit in such acts.

From another perspective, we can see that effective assurance of human rights for all persons, and substantial civil and criminal sanctions against governmental and private perpetrators of human rights deprivations, will significantly reduce various forms of human rights abuse that often spawn acts of terrorism. This understanding is critical to formation of an adequate strategy for combating terrorism and promoting peace. It is thus also critical to the formation of an adequate strategy for dealing with alleged terrorists who are captured and others who are detained by a state as "security threats" during a so-called war on terrorism.

## An Objective Definition of Terrorism

Despite continued and sweeping UN condemnation of all acts of terrorism, the international community has been unable to agree on a definition of terrorism. Instead, general condemnations have occurred, newer treaties have been created for the suppression of terrorist bombings[6] and the financing of terrorism,[7] and several other international agreements have been created to proscribe various acts that can often involve impermissible acts of terrorism, such as aircraft hijacking[8] and sabotage,[9] boatjacking,[10] hostage taking,[11] attacks on internationally protected persons,[12] and disappearances of individuals involving governmental direction or complicity.[13] Tactics of "terrorism" against noncombatants and detained persons are also expressly proscribed under the laws of war.[14] However, terrorism by combatants against enemy combatants during an armed conflict and not otherwise violating international law (e.g., against persons detained) appears to be permissible.[15]

In earlier writings I have suggested the use of an objective definition that describes the process of terrorism most often identified by states and writers. A descriptive definition recognizes that terrorism involves the intentional use of violence, or the threat of violence, by a precipitator (the terrorist) against an instrumental target (e.g., a person or thing) in order to communicate to a primary target a threat of future violence, so as to coerce the primary target through intense fear or anxiety in connection with a demanded political outcome.[16] The instrumental and primary targets can be the same person or group of persons. This definitional orientation contains elements of (1) an intentional tactic or strategy, (2) the use of violence or the threat of violence, (3) a terror outcome (i.e., intense fear or anxiety), and (4) a political purpose. Overly broad and sometimes politically manipulated definitions of terrorism may leave out one or more of the first three elements. The fourth element differentiates politically motivated terrorism from that used by others for power or control (such as by members of organized crime against their own kind or others for nonpolitical purposes). As we will see, nearly all acts of impermissible terrorism covered by the descriptive definition will involve deprivations of the human rights of either an instrumental human target or a primary target, or both.

## Human Rights at Stake

### Types of Relevant Human Rights

Fundamental human rights that are often violated when strategies of impermissible terrorism are used include the right to human dignity and individual worth;[17] the right to life, including freedom from arbitrary deprivation of life;[18] the right to freedom from torture or cruel, inhuman, or degrading treatment or punishment;[19] the rights to liberty and security of person, including freedom from arbitrary detention or arrest and the right to have the lawfulness of detention determined by a court of law;[20] and the right to basic due process in case of arrest or prosecution.[21] Slavery or the slave trade[22] and other forms of human trafficking can involve impermissible acts of terrorism. Some assume that human rights are merely rights against the state and are not also rights against various nonstate actors, but such a limiting viewpoint is in error, since private actors can and do violate the human rights of other persons.[23]

It is not difficult to understand that aircraft hijacking can involve violations of passengers' and crew members' human rights to human dignity, liberty, security of person, and freedom from arbitrary detention.[24] Depending on the circumstances, other human rights might also be at stake. Aircraft sabotage leading to human death will usually involve violations of human rights to human dignity and individual worth, life, freedom from cruel or inhuman treatment, liberty, and security of person. Terroristic torture of individuals will involve violations of human rights to human dignity, liberty, security of person, and freedom from torture or cruel, inhuman treatment. Terroristic assassinations will violate human rights to life and security and, in the case of government-sponsored assassinations, the right to trial, freedom from summary execution, and basic due process during prosecution and appeal. Hostage taking as part of a strategy involving terrorism will violate human rights to human dignity, liberty, and security of person, including freedom from arbitrary detention. It may also involve cruel, inhuman, or degrading treatment. When terroristic tactics also constitute international crimes of genocide, other crimes against humanity, or war crimes, underlying human rights such as those noted above will often be violated as well. Each such deprivation or international crime involving violence constitutes a deprivation of the victim's security and that portion of peace most meaningful to the individual. Such violations of international law can also constitute a threat to regional or international peace and security. As the preamble to the International Covenant on Civil and Political Rights reminds us, "Recognition of the inherent dignity and of the equal and inalienable rights of all members of the human family is the foundation of freedom, justice and peace in the world."[25]

## Self-Determination and Human Rights

Terrorism used as a strategy to inhibit others from full and free participation in the political process of a given state or nation offends both human rights law and the related precept of self-determination of peoples enshrined in the United Nations Charter.[26] The International Covenant on Civil and Political Rights lists self-determination as a human right and recognizes that "by virtue of that right" all peoples have the right to "freely determine their political status and freely pursue their economic, social and cultural development."[27] To the extent that persons targeted by terrorist strategies or tactics are denied equal participation in the political process, they are denied the sharing of political power or shared participation in a process of political determination by an aggregate "self." A terroristic denial of self-determination by governmental or private actors operating in their own or in a foreign country can also infringe on human rights to freedom of expression, including the free exchange of ideas nationally and transnationally;[28] to freedom of assembly;[29] to take part in governmental processes directly or through freely chosen representatives;[30] and to equality, and can constitute impermissible discrimination on the basis of political or other opinion.[31]

The only legitimate or authoritative government, the Universal Declaration of Human Rights affirms, is one based on the will of the people: "The will of the people shall be the basis of the authority of government; this will shall be expressed in periodic and genuine elections which shall be by universal and equal suffrage and shall be held by secret vote or by equivalent free voting procedures."[32] Clearly, the human rights to participate freely in a domestic political process and to have a government based on the relatively free will of the people will be violated by terroristic strategies designed to deny the related right of a given people to political self-determination.

When a state engages in terroristic strategies or tactics to deny political participation of a majority, minority, or particular persons, it engages, however indirectly, in a process of political oppression and politicide (or the killing of an authoritative political process), which violates self-determination and related human rights. If the state uses armed force against a foreign people as part of such terroristic conduct, the state will also be violating Article 2(4) of the United Nations Charter, which proscribes the threat or use of force "against . . . the political independence" of another state "or in any other manner inconsistent with the Purposes of the United Nations," which include the need to respect and to observe human rights and to promote self-determination.[33] The latter proscription would also cover armed attacks by a government against its own population.[34] Such conduct is also clearly threatening to international peace and security, which are also listed among relevant purposes of the charter.[35] For these reasons, the 1970 Declaration on Principles of International Law affirms the charter's prohibition of "any forcible action" by a state that "deprives peoples . . . of their right to self-determination" or that supports "terrorist acts in another state."[36] Similarly, the 1974 Definition of Aggression adopted by the United Nations General Assembly reiterates "the duty of States not to use armed force to deprive peoples of their right to self-determination" and affirms that individual violations of such a duty constitute an international crime of aggression or offense against peace.[37] Ending terroristic governmental aggression against the government's own or a foreign people will not only obviate such forms of terrorism but also serve international peace and security.

## The Need for Effective Sanctions

States have a fundamental obligation to provide access to domestic courts for the victims of impermissible terrorism and to provide an effective remedy for the attendant human rights deprivations that inevitably occur.[38] Governmental assurance of the availability of civil sanctions against terrorists and complicitors in terrorism will not only serve human rights and fulfill governmental duties under international law but also provide a useful addition to governmental and international strategies in combating international terrorism. In certain circumstances, a state's denial of judicial remedies might also involve impermissible assistance to, acquiescence in, or encouragement or toleration of, underlying terrorist conduct, thereby implying state responsibility for failure to ensure human rights of access to courts and to an effective remedy.

Similarly, refusal by a state to prosecute or extradite an alleged terrorist can create state responsibility under international law, which in turn can subject the state to various political and public opinion, diplomatic, economic, and juridical sanctions. Several treaties proscribe particular forms of terrorism and set forth independent requirements that all persons within a state's territory or control who are reasonably accused of such pro-scribed conduct be taken into custody and, without exception whatsoever, be subjected either to prosecution or to extradition.[39] Under the principle *aut dedere aut judicare* (hand over or prosecute), customary international law implicates the same type of responsibility in crimes falling under customary international law, such as aircraft hijacking or sabotage, hostage taking, tor-ture, forced disappearance of persons, slavery or slave trade, war crimes, genocide, and other crimes against humanity—each of which can also involve impermissible acts of terrorism. As recognized also by the United Nations General Assembly, "a refusal by States to co-operate in the arrest, extradition, trial and punishment of persons guilty of war crimes and crimes against humanity is contrary to the purposes and principles of the United Nations Charter and to generally recognized norms of international law."[40] Indeed, nearly all forms of terrorism, regardless of the status of the perpetra-tor,[41] are crimes under customary international law, over which there is uni-versal jurisdiction[42] and a universal responsibility *aut dedere aut judicare*—either to prosecute or to extradite those reasonably accused of terrorism.[43]

A significant related responsibility exists to deny perpetrators of cus-tomary or treaty-based international crimes any form of immunity from criminal or civil sanctions. For example, there is absolutely no head of state, diplomatic, or public official immunity under customary international law or any international criminal law treaty or instrument.[44] As the International Military Tribunal at Nuremberg affirmed, acts in violation of international law are beyond the lawful authority of any state and are thus *ultra vires:*

> The principle of international law, which under certain circumstances protects the representatives of a state, cannot be applied to acts which are condemned as criminal by international law. The authors of those acts cannot shelter themselves behind their official position . . . [or] claim immunity while acting in pursuance of the authority of the State if the State in authorizing action moves outside its competence under international law.[45]

In a federal district court case involving a civil lawsuit against Iraq, the dis-trict court rejected the need for any contacts with the United States where universal jurisdiction pertained over alleged state-sponsored terrorism, since "states are on notice that state sponsorship of terrorism is condemned by the international community," and affirmed that "nations that operate in a manner inconsistent with international norms should not expect to be granted immunity from suit."[46]

The same lack of immunity applies to those following domestic laws or orders in violation of international law, and to those seemingly protected under domestic amnesties, pardons, statutes of limitation, or other limiting domestic laws, since such laws are not valid internationally.[47] As the Inter-American Court of Human Rights recognized in 2001, amnesty laws cannot eliminate responsibility "for serious human rights violations such as torture, extrajudicial, summary or arbitrary execution and forced disappearance."[48] Also in 2001, the Inter-American Commission on Human Rights ruled that Chile's amnesty law preventing criminal investigation and prosecution of those involved in disappearances, torture, and extrajudicial killing impermissibly interfered with the human right of claimants to obtain reparations through civil courts.[49] For local victims, such forms of domestic immunity created by political elites for present or former political elites are often merely one more form of oppression, one less measure of human dignity, and one more way to deny justice and accountability by violating international law concerning human rights of access to courts and to an effective remedy, and concerning the state's obligation *aut dedere aut judicare.* Far from serving peace, such forms of further oppression often exacerbate political tensions and can threaten long-term peace and security. Assuring nonimmunity in international crime can also serve more generally to sensitize elites and condition future human behavior in order to lessen international crime (including impermissible terrorism) and underlying human rights violations.

## Hostage Taking, Abductions, and Arbitrary Detention

Preventive and responsive measures ensuring human rights are also important during a so-called war on terrorism. Several treaties contain special obligations to prevent acts of terrorism, enact necessary legislation, promote cooperative investigation and prosecution efforts, and render other forms of assistance.[50] As part of an antiterrorism strategy, the United Nations Security Council has condemned all acts of hostage taking and abduction,[51] which are violations of basic human rights to liberty, security of person, and freedom from arbitrary detention.[52] Significantly, the Security Council has also affirmed an "obligation of all States in whose territory hostages or abducted persons are held urgently to take all appropriate measures to secure their safe release and to prevent the commission of acts of hostage-taking and abduction in the future."[53] The obligation identified by the Security Council is not unlike the customary prohibition of "denial of justice" by states in whose territory an offender is found or an offense is about to occur,[54] nor is it unlike the more general obligation of all states under the United Nations Charter to take action in order to ensure universal respect for and observance of human rights.[55] In its 1979 decision on the illegality of Iranian complicity in the continual holding of United States nationals hostage in Teheran, the International Court of Justice affirmed: "Wrongfully to deprive human beings of their freedom and to subject them to physical constraint in conditions of hardship is in itself manifestly incompatible with the principles of the Charter . . . as well as with the fundamental principles enunciated in the Universal Declaration of Human Rights."[56] In that case, the United States also rightly stated, "The existence of such fundamental rights for all human beings, nationals and aliens alike, and the existence of a corresponding duty on the part of every State to respect and observe them are now reflected, inter alia, in the Charter of the United Nations, the Universal Declaration of Human Rights and . . . other instruments defining basic human rights."[57]

Clearly, a state would be violating human rights law, the United Nations Charter, and the obligations identified by the Security Council and the International Court of Justice if it engaged in impermissible hostage taking or abduction in response to acts of terrorism. Significantly, states that engage in arbitrary detention of terrorists as part of a war against international terrorism will also be violating human rights law and the United Nations Charter, as well as engaging in conduct that may produce responsive acts of terrorism or other violence, perhaps leading to spiraling acts of violence and counterviolence, ultimately thwarting both peace and international law. Freedom from arbitrary detention is a relative right. Whether detention of an alleged terrorist or direct supporter of terrorism is arbitrary has to be considered in context and with reference to various interests at stake, such as the detainee's rights to liberty and security, the rights of others to liberty and security,[58] and the interests of the government in maintaining law and order. It is not necessary that detention be strictly required, and detention will not be deemed arbitrary if it is reasonably needed under the circumstances.

When a person is detained by a state, human rights law requires the availability of judicial review of the detention. As affirmed in the International Covenant on Civil and Political Rights, "Anyone who is deprived of his liberty by arrest or detention shall be entitled to take proceedings before a court, in order that the court may decide without delay on the lawfulness of his detention and order his release if the detention is not lawful."[59] Access to courts for determination of rights is also guaranteed under Article 14(1) of the International Covenant, as supplemented by general comments by the Human Rights Committee created by the covenant.[60] The standard concerning judicial review should involve contextual inquiry as to whether detention is reasonably needed and thus is not "arbitrary."

Under the International Covenant, however, the right to judicial review of detention is listed as a derogable right—that is, it could be taken away "in time of public emergency which threatens the life of the nation" when the existence of such an emergency is officially proclaimed and a denial of judicial review is "strictly required by the exigencies of the situation," provided also that such a denial is "not inconsistent with" the state's other obligations under international law (such as its obligations under the laws of war, and the customary prohibitions of "denial of justice" to aliens) and does "not involve discrimination solely on the ground of race, colour, sex, language, religion or social origin."[61] Thus, derogations are not permissible merely because they would be reasonable. Derogations must be "strictly required." Applying that standard, it is difficult to accept that denial of judicial review of the propriety of detention is ever "strictly required," perhaps especially given the fact that the state merely has to demonstrate to a court that a particular detention is reasonably needed under the circumstances. Moreover, the Human Rights Committee has recognized that freedom from arbitrary detention or arrest is a peremptory norm *jus cogens* and is thus a right of fundamental importance.[62] It would be difficult to accept a claim that enjoyment of such a peremptory and fundamental right should rest merely on the exercise of executive discretion to detain and that the executive decision should not be subject to judicial review. Indeed, the Human Rights Committee has declared that a state "may not depart from the requirement of effective judicial review of detention"[63] and has affirmed, "The right to take proceedings before a court to enable the court to decide without delay on the lawfulness of the detention must not be diminished by a State party's decision to derogate from the Convention."[64] Similarly, the Inter-American Court of Human Rights has recognized that judicial guarantees essential for the protection of nonderogable or peremptory human rights are also nonderogable in times of emergency,[65] and that the human right to be brought promptly before a judge must be subject to judicial control, and that judicial protection must include the right to habeas corpus or similar petitions and cannot be suspended during an emergency.[66] Similarly, the European Court of Human Rights has recognized that detention by the executive without judicial review of the propriety of detention is a violation of human rights law.[67] Unfortunately, as noted in another writing, the United States executive branch is violating such fundamental human rights of detainees held in the United States and at Guantanamo Bay,

Cuba, in response to the September 11 attacks and the war in Afghanistan.[68] Such is not a proper response to terrorism. It sets up the United States and all who participate as violators of international law, and it attempts to deny the judiciary its significant and necessary role in a democracy as a potential check on abuse of power. Retention of such forms of judicial power is especially important during war or other threats to national security.[69]

## Other Violations of International Law in Response to Terrorism

### Torture and Cruel and Inhumane Treatment

Other human rights violations by states responding to terrorism could also stimulate further terrorism and other forms of spiraling violence and counterviolence. Especially threatening to law, order, and long-term peace are violations of fundamental human rights—even of terrorist suspects—to freedom from "torture . . . or . . . cruel, inhuman, or degrading treatment or punishment."[70] Such rights are nonderogable—that is, even in time of national emergency threatening the life of a nation, when it may seem necessary to torture a terrorist suspect, torture or cruel, inhuman, or degrading treatment is impermissible.[71] During an armed conflict, the laws of war also proscribe torture and inhumane treatment of detained persons without exception, and a violation of the law of war is a war crime. For example, Common Article 3 of the 1949 Geneva Conventions provides a minimum set of rights for all persons detained, including those no longer taking an active part in hostilities, who, for example, may or may not be entitled to prisoner-of-war status, who may have been unprivileged or unlawful belligerents, or who may have been terrorists or war criminals. Article 3 prohibits, among other conduct, "violence to life and person, in particular . . . mutilation, cruel treatment and torture,"[72] as well as "outrages upon personal dignity, in particular humiliating and degrading treatment,"[73] and requires that all persons taking no active part in hostilities "shall in all circumstances be treated humanely."[74] The authoritative Commentary of the International Committee of the Red Cross (ICRC) notes that Articles 27–34 of the Geneva Civilian Convention apply during an armed conflict and "apply equally" in occupied territories.[75] These articles contain rights and prohibitions similar to those in Common Article 3, as well as more specific guarantees. For example, Article 27 expressly affirms, "Protected persons are entitled, in all circumstances, to respect. . . . They shall at all times be humanely treated, and shall be protected." Article 31 stipulates, "No physical or moral coercion shall be exercised against protected persons, in particular to obtain information from them or from third parties." Willful "torture or inhuman treatment" is also listed in Article 147 among "grave breaches" of the convention.

Thus, it is clear that prisoners or other detained persons may not be tortured or subjected to cruel, inhumane, or degrading treatment during interrogation. For example, the Israeli policy of using "moderate force" during interrogation of persons detained in or from the occupied territories is a clear violation of customary humanitarian law.[76] Further, a claim of "necessity" for violating Geneva prohibitions is legally unacceptable.[77]

## Collective Penalties

Customary international law concerning human rights and the laws of war also prohibits collective punishment, that is, punishment of persons not for what they have done and are individually liable for, but for the acts of others—for example, because they come from a group or family that contains an individual who can be subject to punishment under law or who is a suspected terrorist.[78] Article 50 of the Annex to the 1907 Hague Convention No. IV Respecting the Laws and Customs of War expressly affirms: "No general penalty, pecuniary or otherwise, shall be inflicted upon the population on account of acts of individuals for which they cannot be regarded as jointly and severally responsible."[79] Similarly, the 1919 List of War Crimes prepared by the Responsibilities Commission of the Paris Peace Conference expressly affirms the customary prohibition of "imposition of collective penalties."[80] Article 33 of the Geneva Civilian Convention affirms these customary prohibitions, stating, "Collective penalties and likewise all measures of intimidation . . . are prohibited," and adding: "Reprisals against protected persons and their property are prohibited." Collective punishments are also prohibited under Article 75(2)(d) of Protocol I to the Geneva Conventions and under human rights law.[81] As the ICRC notes, the prohibition "does not refer to punishments inflicted under penal law, . . . but penalties of any kind inflicted on persons or entire groups of persons, in defiance of the most elementary principles of humanity, for acts that these persons have not committed. . . . Responsibility is personal and it will no longer be possible to inflict penalties on persons who have themselves not committed the acts complained of."[82] The claim "One of them did the wrong; they must be punished" is tribalistic and potentially genocidal and serves the evil of impermissible discrimination. It is in fundamental opposition to the human rights of each person to individual worth and dignity, to recognition as a person before the law, to be presumed innocent, and to be free from "inhuman or degrading treatment or punishment."

Therefore, it is evident that the Israeli government's strategy during the past two decades or more of demolishing homes of Palestinian families merely because a member of the family was a terrorist or suspected of some other crime is a strategy using collective punishment violative of the laws of war and related human rights, and involving unlawful reprisals against protected persons. Moreover, the strategy has not lessened terrorism in the occupied territories or in Israel but instead seems to have stimulated more terroristic attacks and to have contributed to the destruction of opportunities for peace. A 1998 U.S. Department of State Country Report notes that Israeli security forces "demolish or seal the home (owned or rented) of a Palestinian suspected of terrorism without trial. . . . Residents of houses ordered demolished have forty-eight hours to appeal to the area commander; a final appeal may be made to the Israeli High Court. . . . After a house is demolished military authorities prohibit the owner from rebuilding the rubble. . . . Israeli authorities destroyed one Palestinian home for security reasons in 1998; in 1997 they destroyed eight. . . . In 1998, as in 1997, the Israeli Government did not allow any homes to be rebuilt or unsealed; it allowed one home to be unsealed in 1996."[83] Intentional demolishing of homes in response to Palestinian suicide bombings greatly increased in 2001 and 2002 and occurred without any form of appeal. Clearly also, such norms are violated by a Palestinian youth who is responsible for a terroristic bombing of civilians, as opposed to lawful military targets, on the streets of Tel Aviv. Moreover, such forms of violence are crimes against humanity.[84] Again, acts of collective punishment or reprisal by terrorists or those responding to terrorism are impermissible and, during an armed conflict or in occupied territory, are war crimes.

## Infusion of One's Own Population into Occupied Territory, and Annexation

Article 49 of the Geneva Civilian Convention also reflects the customary prohibition of the "transfer [by an occupying power of] parts of its own civilian population into the territory it occupies." As the ICRC notes, the relevant clause in Article 49 was "intended to prevent a practice adopted during the Second World War by certain Powers, which transferred portions of their own population to occupied territory for political and racial reasons or in order, as they claimed, to colonize those territories."[85] A similar customary prohibition of annexation of occupied territory is reflected in Articles 47 and 49. As the ICRC warns:

> Occupation as a result of war . . . cannot imply any right whatsoever to dispose of territory. As long as hostilities continue the Occupying Power

cannot therefore annex the occupied territory, even if it occupies the whole of the territory concerned. A decision on that point can only be reached in the peace treaty. That is a universally recognized rule which is endorsed by jurists and confirmed by numerous rulings of international and national courts.

Actions of this nature would have no effect on the rights of protected persons.

A fundamental principle emerges . . . an Occupying Power continues to be bound to apply the Convention as a whole even when, in disregard of the rules of international law, it claims during a conflict to have annexed all or part of an occupied territory.[86]

Similarly, Article 55 of the Annex to the 1907 Hague Convention recognizes that the occupying power "shall be regarded only as administrator and usufructuary of public buildings, real estate, forests, and agricultural estates," and Article 46 recognizes the customary prohibition of confiscation of private property.

In response to the Israeli government's practice of encouraging or creating settlements in the occupied territories, the United Nations General Assembly has specifically condemned these practices as violations of the 1949 Geneva Conventions.[87] As such, the practice creates criminal and civil liability for war crimes. The General Assembly has also affirmed that such unlawful activity will not have legal effects due to the passage of time.[88] Also, such violations of international law exacerbate tensions in the Middle East and make peace a far more difficult goal.

## Denials of Due Process

Needless violations of human rights law often occur with the use of military commissions to prosecute alleged terrorists, and the Bush administration's military commissions presently set forth on paper are no exception.[89] Military commissions are generally suspect under newer international criminal law–human rights treaties[90] and in human rights law. In a landmark case in 1999, the Inter-American Court of Human Rights denounced the use of military commissions in Peru, ruling that civilians should have been tried in civilian courts, that accused individuals were detained too long before being charged or tried, that the right to be brought promptly before a judge must be subject to judicial control, that the right to judicial protection must include the right to habeas corpus petitions (which cannot be suspended during an emergency), that defense attorneys lacked access to witnesses and evidence and did not have adequate time to prepare their cases, that the accused must be able to cross-examine all witnesses against them, that trials cannot be held in secret, and that there must exist a right of appeal to an independent and impartial tribunal.[91] Even earlier, in 1984, the Human Rights Committee created under the International Covenant on Civil and Political Rights declared that trial of civilians by military or special courts "should be very exceptional" and must "genuinely afford the full guarantees stipulated in article 14" of the treaty.[92] The 1999 U.S. Department of State Country Report on Human Rights Practices for Peru noted particular human rights violations, among them that "proceedings in these military courts—and those for terrorism in civilian courts—do not meet internationally accepted standards of openness, fairness and due process. Military courts hold treason trials in secret. . . . Defense attorneys in treason trials are not permitted adequate access to files containing the State's evidence against their clients."[93]

At a minimum, any court, military commission, or tribunal must now comply with Article 14 of the International Covenant on Civil and Political Rights, which sets forth a minimum set of customary and treaty-based human rights to due process guaranteed to all persons in all circumstances by customary international law,[94] by the International Covenant, and thus also by and through Articles 55(c) and 56 of the United Nations Charter.[95] These rights include the general right of all persons "in full equality" to "a fair and public hearing by a competent, independent and impartial tribunal established by law,"[96] although the press and public can be excluded for reasons, for example, of "public order (*ordre public*) or national security in a democratic society";[97] the right to be presumed innocent until proved guilty;[98] the right to be informed promptly and in detail, in a language the accused understands, of the nature and cause of the charge(s) against him or her; the right "to have adequate time and facilities for the preparation of his defence and to communicate with counsel of his own choosing"; the right "to be tried without undue delay"; the right "to be tried in his presence, and to defend himself in person or through legal assistance of his choosing";[99] the right "to examine, or have examined, the witnesses against him and to obtain the attendance and examination of witnesses on his behalf";[100] the right "to have the free assistance of an interpreter"; the right "not to be compelled to testify against himself or to confess guilt"; and the right "to have his conviction and sentence . . . reviewed by a higher tribunal according to law."[101]

Also, foreign states cannot lawfully extradite accused individuals to another state when there is a real risk that their human rights or protections under the Geneva Conventions will be violated.[102] Similarly, other states cannot lawfully tolerate violations of human rights and laws of war by military commissions operating within their territories.

After President Bush's November 13, 2001, military order created military commissions on paper for the prosecution of certain accused persons, the U.S. Department of Defense formally issued its first set of "Procedures for Trials by Military Commission of Certain Non–United States Citizens in the War against Terrorism."[103] President Bush's November 13 military order had set up several per se violations of international law.[104] Indeed, nearly every impropriety by the Peruvian military commissions that was addressed by the Inter-American Court of Human Rights has been built into the Bush military commissions.[105] Instead of attempting to avoid them, the U.S. Department of Defense (DOD) Order of March 21, 2002, continued the violations, set up additional violations of international law, and created various rules of procedure and evidence that, if not per se violations of international law, are highly problematic.[106] Clearly, such military commissions should not be used.

## Avoiding Other Overreactions

As we have seen, violations of international law in response to terrorism can exacerbate social and political tensions and be detrimental to peace. Overreactions to terrorism or terrorist threats can also be counterproductive by causing people to look more favorably on the terrorists. Impermissible excesses can actually enhance terrorist claims and rhetoric concerning the alleged propriety of their political preferences and the impropriety of opposing governments or governmental conduct. At times terrorist strategy pointedly seeks to stimulate governmental overreaction and a breakdown of relative peace. For these reasons, a rational, policy-serving response to acts of terrorism must not play into the hands of terrorist strategists and must be attentive to various legal policies at stake and to the probable short-term and long-term consequences.

In some countries, certain elites have manipulated circumstances involving sporadic antigovernmental terroristic acts for their own political gain; to stifle political opposition; to close down, terrorize, or otherwise control the media;[107] to eliminate threatening political and religious leaders through house arrests and more egregious forms of detention without trial, through political trials by military commissions lacking fair rules of procedure and judicial review, or through disappearances and assassinations; and to use so-called martial law. These tendencies are well known under certain present or past regimes, for example, in Argentina,[108] Chile,[109]

Ethiopia,[110] Guatemala,[111] Haiti,[112] Iraq,[113] Paraguay,[114] Peru,[115] and the Philippines.[116] The loss of civil liberties, and purposeful limitations of democracy, can sometimes be more threatening to human rights, self-determination, and peace than certain forms of nonstate terrorism are. Even in democracies, permissible detention can slip into arbitrary detention, interrogation can slip into cruelty or torture,[117] and permissible prosecution can slip into sham trials or procedures involving various violations of minimal due process guarantees under human rights law.

The best long-term weapon against terrorism is found in the duty set forth in the United Nations Charter to promote universal respect for, and observance of, human rights, because human rights, as Thomas Jefferson observed, are "what the people are entitled to against every government on earth."[118]

## Notes

1. Nearly all acts of terrorism are impermissible and will involve violations of human rights.

2. See, e.g., Jordan J. Paust, "Federal Jurisdiction over Extraterritorial Acts of Terrorism and Nonimmunity for Foreign Violators of International Law under the FSIA and the Act of State Doctrine," *Virginia Journal of International Law* 23, sect. III (1983): 191, 194–95, 214, 216, 231, 250.

3. See, e.g., UN Security Council (hereinafter S.C.) Res. 1373 (Sept. 28, 2001); UN S.C. Res. 579; UN SCOR, 40th sess., Res. and Decs., at 24; UN Doc. S/INF/41 (1985); UN General Assembly (hereinafter G.A.) Res. 49/60 (1994); UN G.A. Res. 46/51 (Dec. 9, 1991), 41 UN GAOR, at 4, UN Doc. A/46/654; UN G.A. Res. 40/61 (Dec. 9, 1985), 40 UN GAOR, Supp. No. 53, at 301, UN Doc. A/40/53; Jordan J. Paust, M. Cherif Bassiouni, et al., *International Criminal Law*, 2nd ed. (Durham, NC: Carolina Academic Press, 2000), 995, 1005, 1007.

4. UN G.A. Res. 2625, 25 UN GAOR, Supp. No. 28, at 121, UN Doc. A/8028 (1971); see also *Case Concerning Military and Paramilitary Activities in and against Nicaragua (Nicaragua v. United States)*, 1986 International Court of Justice (hereinafter I.C.J.) 14, at paras. 191–92, 202, 205 ("support for . . . terrorist armed activities within another State"), 209.

5. UN G.A. Res. 2625, *supra*.

6. See International Convention for the Suppression of Terrorist Bombings, adopted by UN G.A. Res. 52/164 (Jan. 9, 1998).

7. See International Convention for the Suppression of the Financing of Terrorism, adopted by UN G.A. Res. 54/109 (Dec. 9, 1999).

8. See, e.g., Hague Convention on the Suppression of Unlawful Seizure of Aircraft (Hijacking) (1970), 860 UNTS 105.

9. See Montreal Convention for the Suppression of Unlawful Acts against the Safety of Civil Aviation (1971), 974 UNTS 177.

10. See Convention for the Suppression of Unlawful Acts against the Safety of Maritime Navigation, done at Rome, March 10, 1988, International Maritime Organization Doc. SUA/CON/15/Rev.1.

11. See International Convention against the Taking of Hostages (1979), 1316 UNTS 205.

12. See Convention on the Prevention and Punishment of Crimes against Internationally Protected Persons, including Diplomatic Agents (1973), 28 UST 1975, TIAS No. 8532.

13. See Inter-American Convention on the Forced Disappearance of Individuals, done in Belém, Brazil, June 9, 1994, reprinted in Jordan J. Paust, Joan M. Fitzpatrick, and Jon M. Van Dyke, *2000 Documents Supplement to International Law and Litigation in the U.S.*, American Casebook Series (St. Paul, MN: West Group, 2000), 233 [hereinafter *Docs*].

14. See, e.g., Geneva Convention Relative to the Protection of Civilian Persons in Time of War of August 12, 1949, art. 33 ("all measures . . . of terrorism [against protected persons] are prohibited"), 75 UNTS 287 [hereinafter GC]; Protocol Additional to the Geneva Conventions of 12 August 1949, and relating to the protection of victims of international armed conflicts (Protocol I), art. 51(2) (prohibiting acts or threats of violence "the primary purpose of which is to spread terror among the civilian population"), 1125 UNTS 3; Protocol Additional to the Geneva Conventions of 12 August 1949, and relating to the protection of victims of noninternational armed conflicts (Protocol II), art. 4(2) ("acts of terrorism" against noncombatants and others "who do not take a direct part . . . in hostilities"), 1125 UNTS 609; 1919 List of War Crimes adopted by the Commission on the Responsibility of the Authors of the War and on Enforcement of Penalties, crime no. 1, March 29, 1919, reprinted in *Docs.*, *supra* 152.

15. See, e.g., Jordan J. Paust, "Terrorism and the International Law of War," *Military Law Review* 64 (1974): 1, 27–31; Jordan J. Paust, "An Introduction to and Commentary on Terrorism and the Law," *Connecticut Law Review* 19 (1987): 697, 705–10 [hereinafter, Paust, "An Introduction"].

16. See, e.g., Paust, "An Introduction," *supra* pp. 701–5.

17. See, e.g., International Covenant on Civil and Political Rights, preamble, art. 10(1), 999 UNTS 171 (Dec. 9, 1966).

18. Ibid. art. 6.

19. Ibid. art. 7.

20. Ibid. art. 9.

21. Ibid. arts. 14, 26.

22. See ibid. art. 8.

**23.** See, e.g., ibid. preamble, art. 5(1); Lung-chu Chen, *An Introduction to Contemporary International Law* (New Haven, CT: Yale University Press, 1989), 78, 205, 215–16; Jordan J. Paust, "Human Rights Responsibilities of Private Corporations," *Vanderbilt Journal of Transnational Law* 35 (2002): 801; Jordan J. Paust, "The Other Side of Right: Private Duties under Human Rights Law," *Harvard Human Rights Journal* 5 (1992): 51; *Ireland* v. *United Kingdom*, Eur. Ct. H.R., Ser. A, no. 25, para. 149 (Dec. 13, 1977) ("terrorist activities . . . of [private] individuals or groups . . . are in clear disregard of human rights").

**24.** See, e.g., Eleanor C. McDowell, *Digest of United States Practice in International Law 1975* (Washington, DC: U.S. Department of State), 168, 171 ("offense against the human rights of passengers and crew").

**25.** International Covenant on Civil and Political Rights, *supra* preamble.

**26.** UN Charter, art. 1(2); see also UN G.A. Res. 2625, *supra*.

**27.** International Covenant on Civil and Political Rights, *supra* art. 1(1).

**28.** Ibid. art. 19.

**29.** Ibid. art. 22.

**30.** Ibid. art. 25.

**31.** Ibid. arts. 2, 26.

**32.** Universal Declaration of Human Rights, art. 21(3), UN G.A. Res. 217A, 3 UN GAOR, UN Doc. A/810 (1948), 71.

**33.** See UN Charter, *supra* art. 1(2)–(3).

**34.** See, e.g., Jordan J. Paust, "Aggression against Authority: The Crime of Oppression, Politicide and Other Crimes against Human Rights," *Case Western Reserve Journal of International Law* 18 (1986): 283–96.

**35.** See ibid. art. 1(1).

**36.** See UN G.A. Res. 2625, *supra*.

**37.** See Definition of Aggression, G.A. Res. 3314, Annex, preamble, 29 UN GAOR, Supp. No. 31, at 142, UN Doc. A/9631 (1975).

**38.** See, e.g., Jordan J. Paust, *International Law as Law of the United States* (Durham, NC: Carolina Academic Press, 1996), 198–203, 212, 256–72nn468–527, 292nn617–23.

**39.** See, e.g., Paust, Bassiouni, et al., *supra* 1008–12, 1014–17; Paust, "Federal Jurisdiction," *supra* 195 and n15, 227–29.

**40.** UN G.A. Res. 2840, 26 UN GAOR, Supp. No. 29, at 2, UN Doc. A/8429 (1971), addressed in Paust, *International Law as Law of the United States, supra* 405–6.

**41.** See *supra* n3.

**42.** Concerning universal jurisdiction to provide criminal or civil sanctions with respect to any perpetrator of violations of customary international law, see, e.g., Paust, Bassiouni, et al., *supra* 132–34, 157–76; *United States* v. *Furlong*, 18

U.S. 184, 197 (1820) (piracy is "an offense within the criminal jurisdiction of all nations. It is against all, and punished by all . . . within this universal jurisdiction"); *Talbot* v. *Janson*, 3 U.S. 133, 159–61 (1795) ("all . . . trespasses committed against the general law of nations, are enquirable, and may be proceeded against, in any nation where no special exemption can be maintained, either by the general law of nations, or by some treaty which forbids or restrains it"); *United States* v. *Rezaq*, 134 F.3d 1121, 1131, 1133 (D.C. Cir. 1998), *cert. denied*, 525 U.S. 834 (1998); *Demjanjuk* v. *Petrovsky*, 776 F.2d 571, 581–83 (6th Cir. 1985), *cert. denied*, 475 U.S. 1016 (1986); *United States* v. *bin Laden, et al.*, 92 F. Supp.2d 189, 222 (S.D.N.Y. 2000); *Flatow* v. *Islamic Republic of Iran*, 999 F. Supp. 1, 14 (D.D.C. 1998) ("international terrorism is subject to universal jurisdiction"); *United States* v. *Yousef*, 927 F. Supp. 673, 681–82 (S.D.N.Y. 1996); *United States* v. *Yunis*, 681 F. Supp. 896, 900–901 (D.D.C. 1988), *aff'd*, 924 F.2d 1086 (D.C. Cir. 1991); *Restatement of the Foreign Relations Law of the United States*, 3rd ed. (St. Paul, MN: American Law Institute, 1987) §404 [hereinafter *Restatement*].

**43.** Concerning the universal responsibility of a state that has a person within its territory or power who is reasonably accused of a crime under customary international law to bring such person into custody and either initiate prosecution or extradite, see, e.g., Paust, Bassiouni, et al., *supra* 9, 132–36, 140–47, 170–71, 175; *The Prosecutor* v. *Dusko Tadic*, ICTY Appeals Chamber (Oct. 2, 1995), IT-94-1-AR72 ("concern of all States, and are to be opposed and punished" and "borders should not be considered as a shield against the reach of the law and as protection for those who trample underfoot the . . . rights of humanity"); *United States* v. *Arjona*, 120 U.S. 479 (1887); *United States* v. *Klintock*, 18 U.S. 144, 147–48, 152 (1820) (piracy "is punishable in the Courts of all . . . [and our courts] are authorized and bound to punish"); *Ex parte dos Santos*, 7 F. Cas. 949, 953 (C.C.D. Va. 1835) (No. 4,016) (quoting E. de Vattel: "duty to punish or surrender"); 1 Op. Att'y Gen. 68, 69 (1797) ("it is the interest as well as the duty of every government to punish"); see also 1 Op. Att'y Gen. 509, 513 (1821) (with respect to "crimes against mankind," the state "in which the guilty person lives ought not . . . obstruct" the right of an injured state to punish the perpetrator).

**44.** See, e.g., Paust, Bassiouni, et al., *supra* 27–34, 38, 132–34, 136, 170–71, 741–48; Paust, "Federal Jurisdiction," *supra* 220–47; but see *Case Concerning the Arrest Warrant of 11 April 2000 (Democratic Republic of the Congo v. Belgium)*, 2002 I.C.J. (tragically, unnecessarily, and, in my opinion, improperly applying diplomatic immunity).

**45.** Opinion and Judgment of the International Military Tribunal at Nuremberg (Oct. 1, 1946).

**46.** *Daliberti* v. *Republic of Iraq*, 97 F. Supp. 2d 38, 52–54 (D.D.C. 2000); also quoting *Flatow* v. *Islamic Republic of Iran*, 999 F. Supp. 1, 23 (D.D.C. 1998).

**47.** See, e.g., Paust, Bassiouni, et al., *supra* 133–36, 140, 170–71; Jordan J. Paust, Joan M. Fitzpatrick, Jon M. Van Dyke, *International Law and Litigation in the U.S.*, American Casebook Series (St. Paul, MN: West Group, 2000), 25, 303–4,

313–14, 574–75, 593–95, 651, 676, 709–11; *The Santissima Trinidad,* 20 U.S. (7 Wheat.) 283, 350–55 (1822); *La Jeune Eugenie,* 26 F. Cas. 832 (C.C.D. Mass. 1821); 9 Op. Att'y Gen. 356, 362–63 (1859).

**48.** *Chumbipuma Aguirre, et al.* v. *Peru* (Barrios Altos Case), Inter-American Court of Human Rights (March 14, 2001), para. 41.

**49.** See IACHR Report No. 61/01, Case No. 11.771 *(Catalán Lincoleo* v. *Chile),* Inter-American Commission on Human Rights (April 16, 2001).

**50.** See, e.g., Jordan J. Paust, "A Survey of Possible Legal Responses to International Terrorism: Prevention, Punishment, and Cooperative Action," *Georgia Journal of International and Comparative Law* 5 (1975): 445–52, 454–58.

**51.** UN S.C. Res. 579, UN Doc. S/RES/579 (1985).

**52.** See, e.g., International Covenant on Civil and Political Rights, *supra* art. 9.

**53.** Ibid.

**54.** Concerning "denial of justice," see, e.g., *Restatement, supra* §711; Paust, *International Law as Law of the United States, supra* 199, 259–61.

**55.** See, e.g., UN Charter, arts. 55(c), 56; International Covenant on Civil and Political Rights, *supra* preamble; UN G.A. Res. 2625, *supra.*

**56.** *Case Concerning United States Diplomatic and Consular Staff in Tehran (United States* v. *Iran),* 1980 I.C.J. 1, 42.

**57.** Memorial of the United States before the International Court of Justice (1980), 17.

**58.** The need to accommodate interests of others is also reflected indirectly in Article 5(1) of the International Covenant on Civil and Political Rights, which states that nothing in the covenant "may be interpreted as implying for any . . . group or person any right to engage in any activity or perform any act aimed at the destruction of any of the rights and freedoms recognized herein or at their limitation."

**59.** See International Covenant on Civil and Political Rights, *supra* art. 9(4); Jordan J. Paust, "Antiterrorism Military Commissions: The Ad Hoc DOD Rules of Procedure," *Michigan Journal of International Law* 23 (2002): 679–81. Similar provisions exist in other human rights instruments. See, e.g., American Convention on Human Rights, art. 7(5)–(6), 1144 UNTS 171 (1966); African Charter on Human and Peoples' Rights, art. 7(1), OAU Doc. CAB/LEG/67/3 Rev. 5 (1981); European Convention for the Protection of Human Rights and Fundamental Freedoms, art. 5(3)–(4), 213 UNTS 221, Eur. T.S. No. 5 (1950); Universal Declaration of Human Rights, *supra* arts. 8, 10; American Declaration of the Rights and Duties of Man, arts. XVIII, XXV, XXVI, O.A.S. Res. XXX (1948), O.A.S. Off. Rec. OEA/ser.L./V./I.4, rev. (1965); *Boudellaa, et al.* v. *Bosnia and Herzegovina,* Human Rights Chamber for Bosnia and Herzegovina, merits (Oct. 11, 2002) paras. 297, 299; *Velasquez Rodriguez Case,* Judgment, Inter-Am. Ct. Hum. Rts., Ser. C, at para. 186 (July 29, 1988). If a detainee is also "arrested," the detainee has additional rights.

**60.** See International Covenant on Civil and Political Rights, *supra* art. 14(1); H.R. Comm., General Comment No. 13, paras. 1–4, 39 UN GAOR, Supp. No. 40, at 143, UN Doc. A/39/40 (21st sess. 1984); H.R. Comm., General Comment no. 15, paras. 1–2, 7, 41 UN GAOR, Supp. No. 40, Annex VI, at 117, UN Doc. A/41/40 (Twenty-third sess. July 22, 1986); H.R. Comm., General Comment no. 20, at para. 15, UN Doc. CCPR/C/21/Rev.1/Add.3 (April 7, 1992); H.R. Comm., General Comment No. 24, paras. 8, 11–12, UN Doc. CCPR/C/21/Rev.1/Add.6 (1994); Paust, *International Law as Law of the United States, supra* 75n97, 198–203, 262 n483, 256–72nn468–527, 362, 375–76, passim, and numerous cases cited; *Dubai Petroleum Co., et al. v. Kazi,* 12 S.W.3d 71, 82 (Tex. 2000) ("The Covenant not only guarantees foreign citizens equal treatment in the signatories' courts, but also guarantees them equal access to these courts").

**61.** See International Covenant on Civil and Political Rights, *supra* art. 4(1). Similar provisions exist in other human rights instruments. See, e.g., American Convention on Human Rights, *supra* art. 27(1); European Convention for the Protection of Human Rights and Fundamental Freedoms, *supra* art. 15(1).

**62.** See H.R. Comm., General Comment on Issues Relating to Reservations Made upon Ratification or Accession to the Covenant and Optional Protocols, General Comment no. 24, UN Doc. CCPR/C21/Rev.1/Add.6, para. 8 (Nov. 2, 1994).

**63.** See H.R. Comm., 63rd sess., 1694th mtg., para. 21, UN Doc. CCPR/C/ 79/Add.93 (1998).

**64.** H.R. Comm., General Comment no. 29, at para. 16, UN Doc. CCPR/ C.21/Rev.1/Add.11 (2001); Amnesty International, *Memorandum to the US Government on the rights of people in US custody in Afghanistan and Guantanamo Bay* (2002), 4 and n16, 22 and n167 (quoting Hum. Rts. Comm., UN Doc. CCPR/ C/79/Add.93 (Aug. 18, 1998) (a state "may not depart from the requirement of effective judicial review of detention") [hereinafter Amnesty International, *Memorandum*], available at http://web.amnesty.org/ai.nsf/Index/AMR510532002? OpenDocument&of=COUNTRIES\USA.

**65.** See Judicial Guarantees in States of Emergency (arts. 27(2), 25, and 8 of the American Convention on Human Rights), Advisory Opinion OC-9/97, Inter-Am. Ct. H.R., Ser. A, No. 9 (Oct. 6, 1987); ibid. Advisory Opinion OC-8/97, at paras. 35, 38, 41–42, 48, Inter-Am. Ct. H.R., Ser. A, No. 8 (Jan. 30, 1987) ("habeas corpus and . . . 'amparo' are among those judicial remedies that are essential for the protection of various rights," "essential judicial guarantees necessary to guarantee" various rights).

**66.** See *Castillo Petruzzi,* Merits, Judgment, Inter-Am. Ct. H.R., Ser. C, No. 52 (May 30, 1999).

**67.** See *Aksoy v. Turkey,* 23 E.H.R.R. 553, 588–90 (1997).

**68.** See Paust, "Antiterrorism Military Commissions: The Ad Hoc DOD Rules of Procedure," *supra* 677, 679–85.

**69.** See, e.g., Paust, *International Law as Law of the United States, supra* 469–78.

**70.** See, e.g., International Covenant on Civil and Political Rights, *supra* art. 7; Jordan J. Paust, "Executive Plans and Authorizations to Violate International Law Concerning Treatment and Interrogation of Detainees," *Columbia Journal of Transnational Law* 43 (2005): 811, 820-23, available at www.columbia.edu/cu/jtl/vol_43_3_files/Paust.pdf.

**71.** See, e.g., ibid. art. 4(1)–(2).

**72.** See, e.g., GC, *supra* art. 3(1)(a).

**73.** Ibid. art. 3(1)(c).

**74.** Ibid. art. 3(1).

**75.** See Jean S. Pictet, ed., *Commentary, Geneva Convention Relative to the Protection of Civilian Persons in Time of War* 4 (Geneva: International Committee of the Red Cross, 1958), 272 [hereinafter 4 Pictet].

**76.** See also *Country Reports on Human Rights Practices for 1998, The Occupied Territories* (Washington, DC: U.S. Department of State, 1998), 3 ("Israeli security forces abused, and in some cases tortured, Palestinians suspected of security offenses. Human rights groups and lawyers say that abuse and torture is widespread and that Israeli security officials use a variety of methods designed to coerce confessions that threaten prisoners' health and inflict extreme pain, including the use of violent shaking"), 6–7 (same, adding: "Interrogation sessions are long and severe, and solitary confinement is used frequently for long periods. . . . Common interrogation practices include hooding; forced standing or squatting for long periods of time; prolonged exposure to extreme temperatures; tying or chaining the detainee in contorted and painful positions; blows and beatings with fists, sticks, and other instruments; confinement in small and often filthy spaces; sleep and food deprivation; and threats against the detainee's life or family. . . . The International Committee of the Red Cross (ICRC) declared in 1992 that such practices violate the Geneva Convention. Human rights groups and attorneys challenged the use of 'special measures,' especially shaking, before the Israeli High Court a number of times during the year. In each case, the court either rejected the petition or ruled in favor of the GSS.") [hereinafter 1998 *Country Report*].

**77.** See, e.g., 4 Pictet, *supra* 34, 37, 39, 47, 200-202, 204–5, 207; Paust, Bassiouni, et al., *supra* 130–31, 833, 846–47; GC, *supra* art. 1.

**78.** Concerning violations of human rights relevant to collective punishment, see, e.g., Jordan J. Paust, "Human Dignity as a Constitutional Right: A Jurisprudentially Based Inquiry into Criteria and Content," *Howard Law Journal* 27 (1984): 145, 192–93 and n206.

**79.** Hague Convention no. IV Respecting the Laws and Customs of War on Land, Annex, art. 50 (Oct. 18, 1907), 36 Stat. 2277, Treaty Series no. 539.

**80.** Crime number 17, reprinted in Paust, Bassiouni, et al., *supra* 33; on collective penalties, see also ibid. 43, 45–46, 131.

**81.** See, e.g., Paust, Bassiouni, et al., *supra* 45–46.

**82.** 4 Pictet, *supra* 225; see also ibid. 228 (regarding reprisals and collective penalties).

**83.** 1998 *Country Report, supra* 13–14; see also *Annual Report* (Geneva: International Committee of the Red Cross, 1996), 233–34 ("the IDF, citing security reasons, destroyed nine houses belonging mainly to families of suicide bombers. This was in contravention of the Convention, which prohibits destruction of real or personal property, except where such destruction is rendered absolutely necessary by military operations"); *Country Reports on Human Rights Practices for 1997, The Occupied Territories,* 13 (Washington, DC: U.S. Department of State, Jan. 1998), 13 ("Israeli authorities destroyed eight Palestinian homes in 1997, compared with eight in 1996, and one in 1995. In Surif four homes were demolished. In Assira Shamaliyya, two homes were demolished and two filled with concrete").

**84.** Concerning the nature of crimes against humanity, see, e.g., Paust, Bassiouni, et al., *supra* 855–916.

**85.** 4 Pictet, *supra* 283.

**86.** Ibid. 275–76.

**87.** See, e.g., UN G.A. Res. ES-10/6 (Feb. 9, 1999); UN S.C. Res. 607 (Jan. 5, 1988) (which affirmed that the Geneva Civilian Convention was applicable to Palestinian and other Arab territories occupied by Israel since 1967, including East Jerusalem); UN G.A. Res. ES-10/5 (March 17, 1998); UN G.A. Res. ES-10/4 (Nov. 13, 1997); UN G.A. Res. ES-10/3 (July 15, 1997); UN G.A. Res. ES-10/2 (April 25, 1997).

**88.** See, e.g., ibid.

**89.** See, e.g., Jordan J. Paust, "Antiterrorism Military Commissions: Courting Illegality," *Michigan Journal of International Law* 23 (2001): 1, 10–18. Much of the material that follows in this subsection is borrowed from that publication.

**90.** See ibid., 10; the Inter-American Convention on the Forced Disappearance of Persons, art. IX ("Persons alleged to be responsible . . . may be tried only in the competent jurisdictions of ordinary law in each state, to the exclusion of all other special jurisdictions, particularly military jurisdictions"), done in Belém, Brazil (June 9, 1994), reprinted in Paust, Bassiouni, et al., *supra, Documents Supplement,* 281.

**91.** See *Castillo Petruzzi,* Merits, Judgment, Inter-Am. Ct. H.R., *supra.*

**92.** H.R. Comm., General Comment no. 13, on Article 14, at para. 4, (21st sess. April 12, 1984), reproduced at www1.umn.edu/humanrts/gencomm/hrcom13.htm.

**93.** U.S. Department of State Report on Peru, at 14, available at www.state.gov/www/global/human_rights/1999_hrp_report/peru.html; concerning reports for Egypt, Nigeria, and Thailand, see Paust, "Antiterrorism Military Commissions: Courting Illegality," *supra* 11.

**94.** See, e.g., *The Prosecutor* v. *Dusko Tadic*, Appeals Chamber, *supra* at paras. 45–48; Advisory Opinion on the Right to Information on Consular Assistance in the Framework of the Guarantees of the Due Process of Law, Inter-Am. Ct. H.R. (Oct. 1, 1999), reviewed in William J. Aceves, "International Decisions," *American Journal of International Law* 94 (2000): 555, 559; Report of the Secretary-General Pursuant to Paragraph 2 of Security Council Resolution 808, at para. 106 and Annex, arts. 20–22, 25 (1993), UN Doc. S/25704 (May 3, 1993), also noting that "the right of appeal . . . is a fundamental element of individual civil and political rights," ibid. at para. 116; Report of the Mission of the International Commission of Jurists, Inquiry into the Israeli Military Court System in the Occupied West Bank and Gaza, reprinted in *Hastings International and Comparative Law Review* 14 (1990), 1, 10, passim; Gabrielle Kirk McDonald and Olivia Swaak-Goldman, ed., *Substantive and Procedural Aspects of International Criminal Law* 1 (The Hague: Kluwer Law International, 2000), 420, 430–31. See also Human Rights Committee, General Comment no. 29 (Aug. 31, 2001), UN Doc. CCPR/C/21/Rev.1/Add.11 ("As certain elements of the right to fair trial are explicitly guaranteed under international humanitarian law during armed conflict, the Committee finds no justification for derogation from these guarantees during other emergency situations. The Committee is of the opinion that the principles of legality and the rule of law require that fundamental requirements of fair trial must be respected during a state of emergency. Only a court of law may try and convict a person for a criminal offence."), available through www.unhchr.ch. In its General Comment no. 24, the Human Rights Committee also noted that "a general reservation to the right to a fair trial would not be" permissible because of the customary, nonderogable, and peremptory character *jus cogens* of the human right to a fair trial. UN Doc. CCPR/C/21/Rev.1/Add.6, at para. 8 (Nov. 2, 1994). Customary international law also requires that there be no "denial of justice" to aliens, such as "denial of access to courts, or denial of procedural fairness and due process in relation to judicial proceedings." *Restatement, supra* §711, cmnt. a, also listing among customary violations: denials of due process in criminal proceedings, an unfair trial, a tribunal manipulated by the executive, denial of the right to defend oneself and to confront witnesses, conviction without diligent and competent counsel, and denial of an interpreter. Ibid. §711, reporters' note 2. Common Article 3 of the Geneva Conventions incorporates such customary guarantees by reference, and they are nonderogable under Geneva law.

**95.** Concerning the guarantee of customary human rights to all persons by and through the UN Charter, see, e.g., *Filartiga* v. *Pena-Irala*, 630 F.2d 876, 882 (2d Cir. 1980). The legal duty of states under the charter to promote respect for and to observe human rights, like customary international law, is "universal" in its reach. See, e.g., UN Charter, arts. 55(c), 56; International Covenant on Civil and Political Rights, *supra* preamble.

**96.** Also see Paust, "Antiterrorism Military Commissions: The Ad Hoc DOD Rules of Procedure," *supra* 687–88; *Boudellaa* v. *Bosnia and Herzegovina, supra* paras. 287, 291–92, 299; Amnesty International, *Memorandum, supra* 25–26 and n198, quoting Human Rights Commission, *Gonzalez del Rio* v. *Peru* (263/ 1987) (Oct. 28, 1992), 2 Report A/48/1993, p. 20 ("an absolute right that may suffer no exception").

**97.** Cf. Geneva Convention Relative to the Treatment of Prisoners of War, art. 105 ("exceptionally . . . held in camera in the interest of State security"), 75 UNTS 135 [hereinafter GPW]; GC, *supra* art. 74 ("as an exceptional measure, to be held *in camera*"); but see *Castillo Petruzzi*, Merits, Judgement, *supra; United States ex rel. Knauff* v. *Shaughnessy*, 338 U.S. 537, 551 (1950) (Jackson, J., dissenting) ("In the name of security the police state justifies its arbitrary oppression on evidence that is secret."); *Rafeedie* v. *INS*, 880 F.2d 506, 516 (D.C. Cir. 1989). It is in the dark of secrecy that evil often lurks.

**98.** Human rights and law-of-war treaties typically do not mention the standard of proof, but the trend evident in rules of procedure and the newer international criminal tribunals, reflecting current and widespread *opinio juris* concerning human rights to due process, is to require proof beyond a reasonable doubt. See, e.g., Statute of the International Criminal Court, art. 66(3) ("the Court must be convinced of the guilt of the accused beyond reasonable doubt"), reprinted in Paust, Bassiouni, et al., *Documents Supplement, supra* 238; Rules of Procedure and Evidence of the International Criminal Tribunal for the Former Yugoslavia, Rule 87(A) ("A finding of guilt may be reached only when a majority of the Trial Chamber is satisfied that guilt has been proved beyond a reasonable doubt."), reprinted in Paust, Bassiouni, et al., *Documents Supplement, supra* 189.

**99.** Concerning access to counsel and adequate time and facilities for preparation, see also Paust, "Antiterrorism Military Commissions: The Ad Hoc DOD Rules of Procedure," *supra* 690; Report of the Mission, *supra* 37–42; GPW, *supra* arts. 104–5; GC, *supra* art. 72; see also GC, *supra* arts. 3(1)(d), 5 (para. 3 therein), 71 (three weeks' notice before trial), 76 ("right to be visited"), 146 ("In all circumstances, the accused persons shall benefit by safeguards of proper trial and defence, which shall not be less favourable than those provided by Articles 105 and those following of" GPW); GPW, *supra* arts. 3(1)(d), 102, 129; Geneva Protocol I, *supra* art. 75(4)(a); 4 Pictet, *supra* 356–57, 595–96 (GC art. 146 guarantees are too numerous to list but include those mirrored in GPW arts. 87, 99, 101, 103, 105–6); McDonald and Swaak-Goldman, *supra* 439–41, 531; *Restatement, supra* §711, reporters' note 2; *Boudellaa* v. *Bosnia and Herzegovina, supra* paras. 296, 299. Once a detainee is reasonably accused of a crime, the detainee should be provided notice of the right to counsel, and foreign accused should be notified of the right to communicate with their government under Article 36 of the Vienna Convention on Consular Relations, 596 UNTS 261 (1963).

**100.** Also see Paust, "Antiterrorism Military Commissions: The Ad Hoc DOD Rules of Procedure," *supra* 688–89; GPW, *supra* art. 105; GC, *supra* arts. 3(1)(d),

72; Geneva Protocol I, *supra* art. 75(4)(g); *Boudellaa* v. *Bosnia and Herzegovina,* *supra* paras. 295, 299. Unlike U.S. practice, this does not include full cross-examination and does not seem to preclude every use of hearsay evidence. See, e.g., McDonald and Swaak-Goldman, *supra* 448–49, 460–62, 473–74, 532–35, 556–57, 569–70, 580; Paust, Bassiouni, et al., *supra* 649, 669–71, 712; Statute of the International Criminal Court, *supra* arts. 63, 67–69, 72–73; Marsha V. Mills, "War Crimes in the 21st Century," *Hofstra Law and Policy Symposium* 3 (1999): 1, 55–56 (also addressing ICTY and ICTR decisions regarding: permissible hearsay evidence); *Restatement, supra* §711, reporters' note 2. Additionally, prisoners of war must have at least the same due process rights that military personnel in the prosecuting state would have. See GPW, *supra* art. 102; Jean S. Pictet, ed., *Commentary, Geneva Convention Relative to the Treatment of Prisoners of War* 3 (Geneva: International Committee of the Red Cross, 1960), 623; see also GC, *supra* art. 146; 4 Pictet, *supra* 595–96 ("the same system" is required for civilians and others protected by the convention who are prosecuted for war crimes); Geneva Protocol I, *supra* art. 75(1). Further, human rights law requires equal protection for all accused. Prisoners of war are also specifically entitled to "the documents which are generally communicated to the accused by virtue of the laws in force in the armed forces of the" prosecuting state. See GPW, *supra* art. 105.

**101.** Also see Paust, "Antiterrorism Military Commissions: The Ad Hoc DOD Rules of Procedure," *supra* 685–86; Paust, "Antiterrorism Military Commissions: Courting Illegality," *supra* 12 n26, 15, 25–26.

**102.** See, e.g., *Chahal* v. *United Kingdom,* Eur. Ct. H.R., No. 70/1995/576/662 (Nov. 15, 1996); the *Soering Case,* 161 Eur. Ct. H.R., Ser. A (1989), 11 Eur. Hum. Rts. Rep. 439 (1989); see also UN Charter, arts. 55(c), 56 (duty to take action to achieve universal respect for and observance of human rights); GPW, *supra* art. 12 (transferee must be willing and able to comply with the convention); GC, *supra* art. 1 (it is the duty of all signatories "to respect and to ensure respect for the present Convention in all circumstances"); Geneva Protocol I, *supra* art. 88(2)–(3); 4 Pictet, *supra* 16. Spain has already indicated that it will not extradite eight persons suspected of complicity in the September 11 attacks unless the United States agrees that they will not be tried in a military commission. See, e.g., S. Dillon and D. G. McNeil Jr., "A Nation Challenged: The Legal Front; Spain Sets Hurdle for Extradition," *New York Times,* Nov. 24, 2001, A1 (adding: "a senior European Union official . . . doubted that any of the 15 [EU] nations . . . would agree to extradition that involved the possibility of a military trial."); T. Shanker and K. Q. Seelye, "Behind the Scenes Clash Led Bush to Reverse Himself on Applying the Geneva Conventions," *New York Times,* Feb. 22, 2002, A12 ("Britain and France warned they might not turn over Taliban and Al Qaeda fighters captured by their troops in Afghanistan unless Mr. Bush" pledges to honor the Geneva Conventions). Further, an occupying power cannot transfer a person protected under the Geneva Civilian Convention out of occupied territory. See, e.g., GC, *supra* arts. 49, 66, 76, 147; Geneva Protocol I, *supra* art. 85(4)(a); Statute of the International Criminal Court, *supra* art. 8(2)(a)(vii) and (b)(viii).

**103.** U.S. Department of Defense Military Commission Order No. 1 (March 21, 2002) [hereinafter DOD Order], available at www.defenselink.mil/news/Mar2002/d20020321dact.pdf.

**104.** See, e.g., Paust, "Antiterrorism Military Commissions: Courting Illegality," *supra* 10–17, 25–26.

**105.** Compare ibid. 10 and n20.

**106.** See, e.g., Paust, "Antiterrorism Military Commissions: The Ad Hoc DOD Rules of Procedure," *supra* 678–81, 685–90.

**107.** See, e.g., Jordan J. Paust, "International Law and Control of the Media: Terror, Repression and the Alternatives," *Indiana Law Journal* 53 (1978): 621–62 (also identifying earlier forms of media repression in many countries).

**108.** See, e.g., *Siderman de Blake* v. *Republic of Argentina*, 965 F.2d 699 (9th Cir. 1992); *Forti* v. *Suarez-Mason*, 694 F. Supp. 707 (N.D. Cal. 1988).

**109.** See, e.g., *Barrueto, et al.* v. *Larios*, 205 F. Supp.2d 1325 (S.D. Fla. 2002); *Estate of Cabello, et al.* v. *Fernandez-Larios*, 157 F. Supp.2d 1345 (S.D. Fla. 2001); *Letelier* v. *Republic of Chile*, 488 F. Supp. 665 (D.D.C. 1980).

**110.** See, e.g., *Abebe-Jira* v. *Negewo*, 72 F.3d 844 (11th Cir. 1996).

**111.** See, e.g., *Xuncax* v. *Gramajo*, 886 F. Supp. 162 (D. Mass. 1995).

**112.** See, e.g., *Paul* v. *Avril*, 812 F. Supp. 207 (S.D. Fla. 1993).

**113.** See, e.g., *Daliberti* v. *Republic of Iraq*, 97 F. Supp.2d 38 (D.D.C. 2000).

**114.** See, e.g., *Filartiga* v. *Pena-Irala*, 630 F.2d 876 (2d Cir. 1980).

**115.** See, e.g., *Chumbipuma Aguirre, et al.* v. *Peru* (Barrios Altos Case), Inter-American Court of Human Rights, *supra;* U.S. Department of State Report on Peru, *supra.*

**116.** See, e.g., *Hilao* v. *Estate of Ferdinand Marcos*, 103 F.3d 767 (9th Cir. 1996).

**117.** See, e.g., *Ireland* v. *United Kingdom*, Eur. Ct. H.R., Ser. A, No. 25 (Dec. 13, 1977); *supra* n70.

**118.** See Ford, Paul, ed., *The Writings of Thomas Jefferson* 4 (New York: GP Putnam and Sons, 1894), 477.

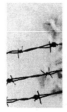

# Human Rights, Terrorism, and Efforts to Combat Terrorism
## Commentary

David P. Stewart

The conceptual origins of international human rights law, like those of refugee law, lie in a different era from today. Formulated in the years following World War II and during the beginning of the Cold War, the basic documents of human rights law—in particular, the ones making up the so-called International Bill of Rights[1]—focus on the need to protect individuals from abuse by governmental authority. This orientation, of course, reflected recent experience. Nazism, communism, totalitarianism, and other forms of official violence, repression, and deprivation were the principal evils on the minds of those who drafted and negotiated those documents. Indeed, what was so very revolutionary about the idea of human rights was exactly that the international community would dare to articulate limitations on the ability of governments and governmental officials to deal with their own citizens and others within their own jurisdictions.

While states and "state actors" have by no means ceased committing gross human rights violations, there has been over time an increasing realization that nonstate actors, groups, and organizations—especially terrorists—can also be responsible for many atrocities. In due course, a government's failure to protect its people from such acts has come to be considered a human rights violation itself. But when powerful nongovernmental forces overwhelm governmental authorities and institutions, when the criminal process no longer suffices to bring to justice the perpetrators of crime, violence, and privation, how, under international law, can such perpetrators be held liable for the harms and injustices they visit intentionally on individuals? Limiting the idea of human rights violations to governmental action (or inaction) thus appears to leave a lacuna in the law.

This has posed a dilemma for human rights proponents: whether, and to what extent it makes sense, to deal with nonstate actors in the same way and with the same expectations as states and "state actors" in terms of human rights duties and remedies. In the preceding chapter, Professor Jordan Paust asks us to consider the links between terrorism and human rights in this context. Clearly, acts of terrorism by a state or its agents, and state sponsorship of terrorism, violate human rights and implicate state responsibility. But how can or should the governments of orderly societies, those committed to the rule of law and the protection of fundamental human rights, respond to acts of terrorism, particularly by individuals or other nonstate actors? Is the human rights construct relevant? Does it constrain? And if so, how? Is it time for a new model?

Paust's premise is indisputable: that there is an inverse relationship between terrorism and human rights. Terrorism is fundamentally antithetical to human rights. Indeed, at its base terrorism is aimed precisely at the disruption and denial of human rights. Protecting and promoting human rights, and effectively deterring violations of those rights, will unquestionably reduce the various deprivations, real or perceived, that often spawn terrorists and terrorism.[2] At the same time, it is impermissible, as well as counterproductive, to fight terrorism with terrorism. A government cannot justify subjecting its own people to severe repression, or denying them the right to political participation, or torturing the suspects it captures, on the grounds of combating terrorism (although in many cases that is exactly what the terrorists want). Severe human rights violations, regardless of motivation, are likely to provoke violence and counterviolence.[3] While one cannot say that acts of terrorism never take place in societies where human rights are in fact protected and promoted, who would argue against Paust's assertion that "[e]nding terroristic governmental aggression against the government's own or a foreign people will not only obviate such forms of terrorism but also serve international peace and security"?[4]

In its "Report on Terrorism and Human Rights," the Inter-American Commission on Human Rights has put it even more powerfully: "The very purpose of anti-terrorist initiatives is to preserve the fundamental rights and democratic initiatives that terrorism seeks to undermine and destroy."[5] The newest international legal instrument in the war against terrorism—the Inter-American Convention against Terrorism, opened for signature in June 2002[6]—explicitly recognizes that antiterrorist measures must be implemented "with full respect for the rule of law, human rights, and fundamental freedoms."[7]

But it is a different proposition to say that terrorists themselves commit human rights violations, or that all forms or acts of terrorism violate human rights,[8] or that "strategies of impermissible terrorism necessarily involve violations of human rights law."[9] As noted above, the concept of human rights in its classic formulation delineates claims of individuals against governments and describes limitations and restraints on the actions of governments.[10] In this view, an individual terrorist or nongovernmental group may commit crimes but cannot violate human rights. Treating terrorism as a crime has been the consistent approach of the international community, and most "antiterrorism" conventions are in fact law enforcement treaties.[11] The 2002 Inter-American Convention on Terrorism is solidly in that tradition, declaring that "terrorism is a serious criminal phenomenon," defining terrorist acts as "offenses" and requiring states parties to "punish" the offenders.[12]

Does the distinction matter? From the nontechnical point of view, the victim of an aircraft hijacking, a car bombing, a "forced disappearance," or an attack with biological agents may justly consider that his or her human rights have been violated no matter who the perpetrator may have been and no matter what purpose motivated the act. Paust evidently shares this view, saying explicitly that "private actors can and do violate the human rights of other persons."[13] And obviously a given act may be at one and the same time a crime and a human rights violation. Still, not all crimes involve human rights violations, and the converse is even clearer.[14] It has been a fairly consistent approach to keep the two separate and, at least in the context of terrorism, to maintain a focus on criminality. Crimes can be punished.

Does it diminish or enhance the severity of our condemnation to call a particular atrocity a human rights violation rather than an act of terrorism? When a government infringes on freedom of expression or belief, discriminates on the basis of national origin or some other impermissible basis, or denies a defendant a fair trial, it clearly violates internationally recognized human rights. But even on a massive scale, such violations simply are not comparable to suicide bombings or holding hostage a theater full of civilians—which are all-too-typical acts of terrorism. But what are the implications? It cannot be that calling an act of terrorism a human rights violation makes the perpetrator less culpable, or more so. Does it somehow shift the onus of prevention and response to the state? Are states required to do more to protect their populations from human rights violations by nonstate actors than they are to prevent crimes? That seems an inherently doubtful proposition, even though it is more and more popular to look to the state to shield people from human rights abuses (an interesting *renversement* of roles from the time when the state was considered the main, if not only, transgressor of human rights).

And how does one distinguish between terrorists and other nonstate actors who intrude on the fundamental rights of everyone? Does the murderer, the thief, the embezzler also violate the human rights of her victims?[15] The defamer, the usurer, the manufacturer of a defective consumer product? Does everyone owe everyone "human rights"? Is everything a human right? Definitional issues abound.

One need not resolve all these questions in order to agree entirely with Paust's other main conclusion, that the principal problem is the "lack of effective political, diplomatic, economic, juridical, and other sanctions against those either directly engaged or complicit in such acts."[16] The main task is to identify effective strategies for dealing with terrorism which are themselves compliant with human rights principles.

Adopting more criminal treaties is not the answer any more than adopting more human rights treaties will improve human rights adherence. While some would quibble with Paust's proposition that *all* acts of terrorism (regardless of the status of the perpetrator) are already crimes under customary international law, over which there is universal jurisdiction, there really can be no serious argument that lack of a treaty prevents prosecution or punishment of perpetrators of terrorist violence. Nor can it be cogently argued that, however desirable an "objective definition" of terrorism may well be, its absence impedes effective strategies of prevention and response.[17]

If the law itself is not deficient, what about stiffer punishments? The typical reaction of a domestic legislature to an increase in specific types of criminal activity is to increase the penalties. There seems to be little reason, however, to expect the prospect of tougher sentences to deter most terrorists. In any event, as Paust amply demonstrates, terrorists themselves have human rights and it is not justifiable to commit human rights violations in pursuit of counterterrorism.

In the aftermath of the horrific tragedies of September 11, 2001, the current administration adopted a very different perspective, proposing to treat terrorism as an act of war, and captured terrorists as unlawful combatants under the law of war. While there is ample basis for such an approach,[18] it requires some "recalibration" on the part of international lawyers. The simple reason is that international law distinguishes, at least in principle, between the regimes that govern in three different circumstances: ordinary peacetime (when human rights law applies), times of civil emergency threatening the life of the nation (when some exceptions to or "derogations" from human rights protections are permissible), and times of armed conflict (when international humanitarian law governs). Increasingly, the line between human rights and humanitarian law has become blurred, and today some maintain that both human rights law and humanitarian law apply during times of armed conflict.[19] Still, many commentators have criticized this new departure as risking serious infringements on the rights of those accused of terrorism.

Under either legal system, it is entirely possible to afford fair treatment and fair trials to those accused of terrorist or other unlawful acts, and to protect their basic human rights. In fact, this fundamental point underlies the approach taken by the Inter-American Commission on Human Rights in its "Report on Terrorism and Human Rights."[20] The report offers a detailed analysis of the protections that must be afforded to accused terrorists under international human rights as well as international humanitarian law. The report states, for example,

> Fundamental protections of due process and a fair trial applicable at all times also entail the right to be tried by a competent, independent and impartial tribunal as defined under applicable international human rights law or humanitarian law.[21]

Thus, the basic principles of legality, such as *non bis in idem, nullum crimen sine lege,* and *nulla poena sine lege,* apply regardless of the governing regime.[22] In addition to humane treatment, protection against torture, and the protection of "human dignity," the report clearly and persuasively articulates the fundamental entitlement of detainees to fair trial procedures, including prior notification of charges, access to counsel, the right to present an adequate defense, the privilege against self-incrimination, and so on.

To be sure, some limitations may be available under humanitarian law that would not be acceptable in ordinary courts, depending on the specific legal system. Among others, the IACHR report notes that the right to a public trial and the right of confrontation (the right to question one's accusers) may be limited where necessary to ensure safety of participants in the trial.[23] These possibilities may make prosecutions more attractive under this construct, but the exceptions need to be narrowly drawn and amply justified. In this connection, Paust is not alone in voicing concerns about the possibility of abuse in the practice of prolonged "preventive" or "administrative" detention.[24]

The antidote, of course, is to guarantee the availability of some measure of judicial or equivalent recourse so that the detainee can obtain an independent, reasoned review of the legality of his or her continued detention. The right of habeas corpus is clearly fundamental whenever a person's liberty has been curtailed by governmental authority, regardless of the prevailing legal "system." Paust questions why the right to judicial review of detention is properly considered a "derogable" right.[25] A form of review is, of course, guaranteed even by humanitarian law. As noted in the Inter-American Commission's report, "when individuals have committed belligerent acts and have fallen into the hands of the enemy in the context of an international armed conflict and a doubt arises as to their entitlements to prisoner of war status, a competent tribunal should determine the status of the detainees."[26]

The principal concern of some commentators has been that the supervisory mechanisms available under international humanitarian law are weaker than those under human rights regimes, and in both cases those mandated by international law are not as vigorous as those required under domestic U.S. law.[27] Is it warranted, then, for human rights institutions to assume the role, as the IACHR suggests?[28]

The right to adequate judicial (or comparable) review is different from the question of whether military commissions are *ever* permissible to prosecute alleged terrorists. It is clear that a strong presumption exists in human rights law that military tribunals should be limited to offenses under military law by military personnel and may not be used either to prosecute civilians for offenses against the military or in lieu of civilian courts.[29] Far from justifying an absolute rule against any reference to military commissions, the President's Military Order of November 13, 2001, and the subsequently issued set of procedures[30] reflected different regimes of international law. Thus, there may be a dividing line between the mechanisms for treating acts of terrorism as crimes, on the one hand, and those for treating them as hostile acts of war, on the other. As the 2002 IACHR report stated,

> Where individuals fall under the authority and control of the state in situations outside of armed conflict, their treatment is governed exclusively by international human rights law. Where an armed conflict is underway, however, the treatment of detainees and others is also subject to international humanitarian law.[31]

The report demonstrates and documents that in most important respects there is little enough practical difference between the regimes of international human rights law and international humanitarian law in terms of requiring fundamental fairness and protections.

At bottom, Paust leaves us to consider this fundamental proposition: given the "inescapable link" between terrorism and human rights, isn't protecting and respecting human rights (including of accused terrorists themselves) one of the most effective counterterrorist strategies a government can pursue?

## Notes

The views expressed here are those of the author and do not necessarily reflect the position of the Department of State or the U.S. government.

**1.** In common parlance, the International Bill of Rights consists of the Universal Declaration of Human Rights, UN General Assembly Res. 217A (III), UN Doc. A/811, at 71 (1948), and the two main human rights treaties: the International Covenant on Civil and Political Rights, Dec. 16, 1966, 999 UNTS 171; and the International Covenant on Economic, Social and Cultural Rights, Dec. 16, 1966, 993 UNTS 3.

**2.** *Supra*, p. 240: "effective assurance of human rights for all persons, and substantial civil and criminal sanctions against governmental and private perpetrators of human rights deprivations, will significantly reduce various forms of human rights abuse that often spawn acts of terrorism."

**3.** As Paust notes, *supra* at p. 253, "Impermissible excesses can actually enhance terrorist claims and rhetoric." The point would be valid even if, as a matter of law, the "excesses" in question were technically "permissible."

**4.** *Supra*, p. 243. Exactly what might be encompassed by the phrase "terroristic governmental aggression" is unclear, and international lawyers might dispute whether governments can commit "aggression" against their own people.

**5.** See Preface, "Report on Terrorism and Human Rights," Inter-American Commission on Human Rights, OAS doc. OEA/Ser.L./V/II.116 Doc. 5, rev. 1 corr. (October 22, 2002).

**6.** Inter-American Convention against Terrorism, adopted by the OAS General Assembly on June 2, 2002; see AG/RES 1840 (XXXVII—O/02). This instrument supplements the 1971 OAS Convention to Prevent and Punish the Acts of Terrorism Taking the Form of Crimes against Persons and Related Extortion That Are of International Significance, OAS Treaty Series, no. 37.

**7.** Ibid., art. 15(1).

**8.** Paust's statement that "all forms of impermissible terrorism involve conduct that is proscribed by international law," *supra* p. 239, is also debatable. Unless it is merely tautological, that position overstates contemporary international law.

**9.** *Supra*, p. 239. Some may find the phrase "impermissible acts of terrorism" to be objectionable, or at least internally redundant, arguing that by definition *no* act of terrorism can ever be permissible or justified. Paust does not make clear his meaning but suggests in note 15 that his intent is to exclude acts of terrorism engaged in by combatants during armed conflict that do not otherwise violate international law. He notes that a "terroristic denial of self-determination" (supra, p242) can violate fundamental rights but appears not to mean that acts of terrorism may be justifiable if committed in pursuit of legitimate ends, such as in the exercise of the right of self-determination, to bring an end to brutal governmental repression, or to establish political freedom or a democratic system of governance.

10. "International human rights law governs directly the conduct of the state and its agents. Accordingly, certain violations of such norms may imply state responsibility." IACHR report, para. 72.

11. See, e.g., the 1970 Convention for the Suppression of Unlawful Seizure of Aircraft, 860 UNTS 105; the 1979 International Convention against the Taking of Hostages, 1316 UNTS 205; the 1971 Convention for the Suppression of Unlawful Acts against the Safety of Civil Aviation, 974 UNTS 177; the 1973 Convention on the Prevention and Punishment of Crimes against Internationally Protected Persons, including Diplomatic Agents, 1035 UNTS 167; 1999 UN Convention for the Suppression of the Financing of Terrorism, UNGA Res. 54/109, 39 ILM 270 (2000).

12. Convention, preamble, para. 6; arts. 1 and 2.

13. *Supra*, p. 241.

14. In fact, with few exceptions, such as torture, international human rights law does not address violations as crimes.

15. Some may question the term "terroristic assassination" (*supra*, p. 241) and wonder how it can be distinguished from an "ordinary" or "nonterrorist" one.

16. See *supra*, p. 239.

17. Paust's proposals concerning such a definition deserve careful consideration, but more effective steps to confront terrorism and eliminate its causes clearly cannot be deferred until there is agreement on the term.

18. See, for example, para. 3 of the IACHR's report, which recognizes that "the nature of the terrorist threat faced by the global community has expanded both quantitatively and qualitatively, to encompass private groups having a multinational presence and the capacity to inflict armed attacks against states." The report also acknowledges the possibility of "future developments in international law that will address recent manifestations of terrorism as a new form of international warfare between private individuals or groups and states."

19. See, e.g., para. 61 of the IACHR report, which suggests that "in situations of armed conflict, international humanitarian law may serve as *lex specialis* in interpreting and applying international human rights instruments."

20. IACHR report, *supra* n5.

21. IACHR report at para. 18.

22. Cf. IACHR report, para. 261.

23. See IACHR report, paras. 250–53.

**24.** It is not altogether clear what Paust means in saying, *supra* p. 246, that freedom from arbitrary detention is a "relative" right that has to be considered "in context and with reference to various interests at stake, such as the detainee's rights to liberty and security, the rights of others to liberty and security, and the interests of the government in maintaining law and order."

**25.** See *Castillo Petruzzi,* Merits, Judgment, Inter-Am. Ct. H.R. Ser. C., no. 52 (May 30, 1999); *Aksoy* v. *Turkey,* 23 EHRR 553 (1997).

**26.** IACHR report, para. 203, citing art. 5 of the 1949 Geneva Convention relative to the Treatment of Prisoners of War, 75 UNTS 135 (the "Third" Geneva Convention).

**27.** Thus, for example, in discussing the relationship between human rights and humanitarian law, the Inter-American Commission notes that "the right to personal liberty and security, to the extent that it is addressed by these two regimes of international law, may give rise to varying requirements as to when a person may be detained, for what duration, and subject to what supervisory mechanisms; in all circumstances, however, such requirements must conform to and be continuously evaluated in accordance with the fundamental principles of necessity, proportionality, humanity and non-discrimination." IACHR report, at para. 137.

**28.** See report, Conclusion C, para. 9(c): "Where these mechanisms [i.e., the Protecting Powers regimes and access by the International Committee of the Red Cross] are not available or prove ineffective in ensuring the proper treatment of detainees, . . . international human rights law and domestic law standards and procedures may supersede international humanitarian law in order to guarantee the effective protection of detainees in all circumstances."

**29.** General Comment no. 13 of the Human Rights Committee under the International Covenant on Civil and Political Rights. The Inter-American Human Rights Commission states that states "must refrain from the use of ad hoc, special, or military tribunals or commissions to try civilians" and "ensure that trials of members of the military or combatants by military courts offer the essential guarantees of independence and impartiality as generally recognized in international humanitarian law instruments." Report, *supra*, Recommendations, E, paras. 10(c) (d). In contrast, the use of military tribunals in the trial of prisoners of war is not prohibited.

**30.** U.S. Department of Defense Military Commission Order No. 1 (March 21, 2002).

**31.** IACHR report, para. 202.

# 10

# Bridging Conflict Transformation and Human Rights
## Lessons from the Israeli-Palestinian Peace Process

Mohammed Abu-Nimer
and Edward (Edy) Kaufman

I n this joint article, drawing from the authors' own work in nongovernmental organizations (NGOs) in Israel and Palestine, we examine how conflict resolution practitioners can benefit from introducing a human rights framework within their overall strategies, and the types of obstacles that face them in such efforts. As used by academics, the terms "human rights," interpreted as the current international standard of "justice," and "conflict resolution," interpreted as the agent of "peace," have been mainly associated with the legal and social sciences paradigms respectively. In prevailing asymmetric conflicts, the stronger parties generally advocate the maintenance of "peace and security" in terms as close as possible to the status quo (in Hebrew, *shalom emet,* a "true peace"), while the weaker side advocates change justified in terms of justice, that is, recognition of its "legitimate rights" (in Arabic, *hoquq shara'ia*) before moving into a true reconciliation (or *sulh*). The gap between the two interpretations was captured in the wording "just and lasting peace" by United Nations Security Council Resolution 242, which followed the Six-Day War of June 1967. The Oslo peace process, initiated in 1993 after the two sides reached what was perceived by many on both sides to be a promising agreement, suffered a severe backlash in September 2000 with the failure of the Camp David negotiations and the subsequent cycle of violence. Frustration prevails among those of us who share across the divide the values of human rights, democracy, and peace. Hence, the importance of finding avenues to channel the intersection of such values becomes more relevant than ever.

We start by showing how the human rights dimension was mostly absent from the failed Oslo experiment and from the potential benefit of introducing it into a renewed peace process. Civil society organizations (CSOs) face many difficulties, and not only with policymakers, in highlighting the advantages of including human rights principles in the peace process. Even within the CSO community within and across the national divide, it has been difficult to get the human rights and peace/conflict resolution NGOs to act together in the pursuit of their shared goals. Additionally, we often find reluctance on the part of the underdog to share with the "Other" its exclusive victim status. Given the unremitting level of violence against civilians in recent years, and the societal support on both sides for a "stronger hand" policy, special emphasis is given to NGO work in defense of the right to "life, liberty and security of person" (Art. 3, Universal Declaration of Human Rights, hereinafter UDHR)—a precondition for preventing massacres of large groups and the further development into genocidal situations. Over the long years of the conflict, and particularly since the Oslo agreements of 1993, CSOs have undertaken myriad projects, from which lessons, learned by trial and error can be drawn. The article concludes with brief recommendations for advancing coordination and integration between human rights and conflict resolution in Israel/Palestine. It also follows the authors' project of bringing together human rights and peace organizations from both sides of the conflict to search for common ground and endorses an action plan based on their joint work. To provide the reader with a touch of reality, we have documented our thoughts and findings with concrete illustrations and testimonial evidence. We trust that our own reflection and experience can be relevant for the many other protracted communal conflicts worldwide and perhaps also generate feedback from other experts and practitioners in this field, thus enriching what is for us still a work in progress.

A word of caution about what we are *not* going to discuss here. First, we do not pass judgment on the claim of a "right to peace,"[1] since such a shortcut in the connection of the two issues has not yet received any formal recognition by the international community. Collective rights such as "self-determination" and "peace" have not passed the declaratory stage in the international human rights regime.[2] We also exclude any discussion on adherence to nonviolence versus "just wars," as explored in studies by Walzer,[3] since here, too, it has been difficult to find a broad consensus. Nor do we cover the prospects for nonviolence, which is in itself a strategy respectful of human rights. But human rights do not preclude the rebellion against tyranny. Our analysis will focus heavily on the connection between the struggle for peace and internationally recognized human rights. The universal protection of *individual* human rights has been widely endorsed and ratified, including by our related partners to the conflict. The covenants embodying *group* rights have been more limited (to women, children), but notably there has been no significant progress toward a consensus on minority rights except when abuses reach genocidal dimensions.

In the concluding section, we will dwell only briefly on the proposition that introduces "democracy" as an intervening variable, covered in UDHR Article 21 as the right to elect and be elected. The hypothesis that the international action against gross violations of human rights has made processes of democratization possible has been widely studied. The connection can be further made with the widely accepted proposition that democracies tend not to fight wars with each other, although there is no agreement about the causes of such a phenomenon.[4] This argument has also been applied to the analysis of the Israeli-Palestinian case.[5] The combination of the two assumptions has led to the proposition that the defense of fundamental human rights has contributed to a process of democratization that, in its consolidation, strengthens the prospects of peace.[6] Unfortunately, the inverse process is also occurring, in which retreat in the peace process has caused a decline in the standard of democracy in Israel and paralyzed the process of democratization in the Palestinian territories.

## Human Rights: Missing in Israeli-Palestinian Track I Diplomacy

By referring generically to the Israeli-Arab conflict, we risk missing a clear-cut differentiation between the protracted *intrastate Israeli-Palestinian* communal conflict and an *interstate border dispute* with an established neighboring country—such as the past and present disputes between Israel and Egypt, Lebanon, and Syria. The Palestinian-Israeli conflict has a large human dimension and as such is different from that over the Golan Heights, which was sparsely populated before 1967, when it was a Syrian militarized zone, and which today, under Israeli occupation, is home to only about 35,000 people, half of them Jewish and the other half Druze. As an intrastate conflict, the Palestinian-Israeli conflict should be seen above all as a major human problem involving approximately three million people who have been systematically deprived of their individual freedoms and the right of self-determination through nearly three decades of military occupation—no doubt one of the longest in modern postcolonial history. The Jewish settlements in the Occupied Territories of the West Bank and Gaza are seen by

Palestinians as a ploy to regain control over the entire promised "Land of Israel." On the other hand, most of the five million Israeli Jews fear that the Palestinian maximal goals are not only to take back the Occupied Territories of the West Bank and Gaza but to regain control over "historic Palestine"— in other words, the eradication of the Jewish state. If a territorial split of the Holy Land into two separate states does not happen, the human rights perspective provides the alternative of a binational state, that is, a state for all its citizens. But this is not expected in the foreseeable future.

In the Israeli-Palestinian conflict, in contrast to the wars fought between Israel and its Arab neighbors, the majority of victims on both sides have been civilians. Therefore, it may be more important in this case than in the border disputes (with Egypt, Syria, and Jordan) to secure the acceptance of peace not only by the leaders but also through the active endorsement of the citizenry. From this perspective, the Israeli-Palestinian case shares with the examples of South Africa, Sri Lanka, Yugoslavia, Cyprus, and Northern Ireland the attributes of "identity-driven conflicts," which are often referred to as intractable or protracted.

There are many explanations for the decline of the Israeli-Palestinian Oslo peace process, officially launched at the White House in 1993. Appendix 1 shows the results of systematically revisiting the extent to which the decisions and implementations related to human rights principles are absent or present in the Oslo agreement. While compromises with such norms will often need to be made, these criteria should remain a universal yardstick by which an agreement is measured, even if adjustments are required in order to progress. And yet, often the rights of one group conflict with those of the other (such as the right to security and the right to life versus the right to return and the right to freedom of movement). This is precisely where facilitation of the process by a third party can play a key role, transforming the rigid zero-sum equation into an innovative win-win. Some of the intangible principles, such as respect, acknowledgment, and punishment, do not carry a material gain per se, but even disputes over such finite resources as land and water can be resolved by incentives such as "expanding the pie," no-same-kind compensation, and so on. However, in the Israeli-Palestinian conflict we find negotiations to be more of a Middle Eastern bazaar than a logical dialogue using recognition of entitlements and equal rights as the departing point. Without concrete improvement of basic human rights as confidence-building measures in real time, and integration of those rights in the delineation of the agreements in the final/permanent-status issues (involving refugees, sovereignty in Jerusalem, borders, settlements, security), such signed documents have so far been worthless and cannot be sustained.

A decade after the first Oslo agreements, the economic and political rights of Palestinians have deteriorated to a situation far worse than the starting point. Basic rights are being violated on a daily basis for all Palestinians in the Occupied Territories. On the other hand, despite the asymmetric power realities of the occupation and all the security arrangements, the Israeli public is terrified of the suicide bombings that have violated the basic rights of personal and collective security of all Israelis. Based on this experience, it is clear for many Israeli and Palestinian analysts and peace workers that the next political agreement has to tackle the respect of fundamental freedoms, the granting of civil-political rights, and the provision of a minimal level of socioeconomic rights in a more effective way than the various Oslo accords have done.

For those who support its full integration, a human rights framework can provide a road map for designing these processes,[7] particularly if merged with the "Dual Concern Model," a cornerstone in the field of conflict resolution.[8] While there has been a growing consensus that introducing human rights issues at a later stage may consolidate the tenuous and often minimalist peace accords, we the authors have been investigating the potential advantage of addressing the two agendas simultaneously from the early stages of the process on. The advocacy for human rights is often perceived by those involved in conflict resolution to be part of the problem, but it may instead be an important ingredient toward the conflict's solution. While I can be respected for demanding my rights, according to the UDHR preamble's "common standards of all nations," I will fare better if I also attend the needs of the "Other." Addressing the psychological dimension of protracted social conflict is a key to its resolution, for sometimes the mere recognition of my *rights* as a matter of principle is more important than their immediate implementation. When I know that being attentive to the needs of the "Other" can bring the solution closer, I may be ready to sacrifice my inalienable rights for the common good, and it is my prerogative to do so. The necessity for addressing basic needs (and identities) of the contending parties is self-evident. Human needs of identity, security, and access to political power are at the core of protracted communal conflicts.[9] Let us illustrate the amalgamation of rights-based and needs-based approaches, using several examples from the Israeli-Palestinian conflict.

## Conflict of Rights

The Palestinian right of return and the Israeli Law of Return have generated conflicting demands over the same territory, making it very difficult to pass judgment sensibly. Jewish refugees have already found their safe haven. When we look into the Palestinian right of return, there is no question that they are entitled to do so according to human rights covenants. How could Jews deny the Palestinians' right of return to the land of their ancestors after five decades while at the same time legitimately asking the Arab world to recognize the Jews' own right of return to the land of Israel after two thousand years? Who is to say which people has the greater right: the group that was expelled from the Holy Land earlier or the group that was expelled later? Rather than deciding who has *more* rights, both Arabs and Jews, who have fought stubbornly for preserving their presence, must have *enough* rights, and the issue at stake is how to satisfy the core needs of the members of both communities. It can also help the healing process to share the concern for all the suffering by the Palestinian refugees; however, from the human rights point of view, neither the plight of the population, expulsion, nor any other reason makes more or less valid that people's right to return. Once legitimate rights are recognized, we can put aside the statement of principle, and Israelis can communicate their core need to maintain the Jewish majority in Israel—hence their request to all Palestinians to implement their right by coming back not to their *homes* in Israel but to their *homeland* in the new Palestinian state. While the original claim of both sides was the right to live and settle in the entire Holy Land, restricting settlement to their respective states may be a pragmatic mutual compromise to restrict the number of Palestinian refugees returning to Israel, as well as the number of Jewish settlers in the Palestinian Territories. A generous compensation is to be offered, and priority should be given to those who are deprived of their socioeconomic (and often civil and political) rights: the Palestinians still in refugee camps.

## Unilaterally Granting Rights

Social Security (SS) for Palestinians in East Jerusalem has been part of their rights as residents of the city, which was officially annexed by Israel. The solution discussed for Jerusalem is that it serve as capital for two states. But meanwhile, Palestinians in East Jerusalem have been paying SS and enjoying the privileges after retirement. Israel's transfer of control of the city to the Palestinian government, would not automatically ensure the Palestinian government's readiness to assume responsibility for such social security services. The elderly population in particular would be deprived of an important part of their livelihood. This is an important *need* for them; could the Israeli government accept unilaterally to take responsibility for such care?"

## Subordinate Rights

Not all just claims guaranteed by human rights need to be addressed with the same sense of urgency; some setting of priorities may be in order. For one thing, the punishment of perpetrators of gross human rights violations may need to be postponed, perhaps indefinitely.[10] Both Israeli and Palestinian political leaders could possibly be held responsible by the opposing community for acts of omission or commission that amount to crimes against humanity. But even though such charges are legally feasible, the international community as well as the civil societies of both nations may decide to refrain from pursuing them, given that the main goal is to encourage the two leaderships to move toward peace and reconciliation. Other elements that are important for exemplary justice, however, can be kept and even emphasized, such as truth mechanisms to prevent such gross violations from occurring again.

## Generating Rights

It is important to remember that even during atrocious situations all human beings, including terrorists, "collaborators," and oppressors, have inalienable rights. The release of Palestinian prisoners who have "blood on their hands"—an expression used commonly in Israel to refer to those who have planned, assisted in, or carried out acts of violence against noncombatants—is a thorny issue. While there is no clear obligation for a state to release those who carry one or more sentences of life imprisonment, there has been a tradition of granting amnesties during peace processes, and even including this provision as a part of the accords, as was done in the Good Friday Agreement in Northern Ireland. The underlying need of the Palestinians as a whole, and the families of the prisoners in particular, to see those who are behind bars released is obvious. So how can Israel be sensitive to these needs and, through confidence-building measures (CBMs), find ways to move toward such an accord? Human rights principles can help; according to these, the policy to be implemented should be applied equally to both Arab and Jewish prisoners with "blood on their hands." Given that several amnesties were granted in the past to Jews accused of such acts, it would not be a good idea to hold the Palestinians to be released to the same standards as Jewish members of the terrorist underground (individual petition, expressions of remorse, and a promise of no future acts of violence). This last issue is of crucial importance and, in the release process mechanisms, should be jointly worked out to minimize recidivism.[11]

In all cases, the dry letter of the human rights wording is important. But what is more important is to find a formula that, while accepting the validity of claims as just, at the same time shows humanity and understanding toward the needs of the "Other." Not all such needs are guaranteed by international human rights law, which is but a work in progress by the world community.

Having clarified the crossroads between needs and rights, we return to a more systematic analysis of the human rights dimension. A thorough review (see appendix 1) of the many documents signed reveals that only a handful actually mention "human rights" or specific "rights" as listed in the Universal Declaration of Human Rights in Geneva. Kaufman and Bisharat present a detailed illustration of possible integration of human rights in peacemaking.[12] Briefly summarizing their study, we show that human rights can be an integral part of the three stages of the process.

**The Prenegotiation Phase.** It may well be that in Oslo both the Israeli Labor Party and the Palestine Liberation Organization, with their emphasis on pragmatism, considered human rights language merely rhetorical burden, or perhaps its omission results from the two sides' leadership's lack of socialization in the use of such language.[13] No doubt, the negotiators took upon themselves a formidable task in devising solutions to a large number of pressing concrete issues. The title, "Put an End to Decades of Confrontation and Conflict," and the short preamble to the text inspire us to move in the direction of rights;[14] however, there is little specific commitment to the improvement of human rights as a stimulus for progress in the process itself or whenever reference is made to "final-status issues."[15] Such has also been the case in Northern Ireland with the incorporation of the European Convention on Human Rights into the 1998 Good Friday Agreement.[16]

Human rights clauses can reduce the perceived asymmetries between groups. Language of dignity and respect is important for persecuted people, who are often reluctant to confront the cost of compromise, for on the losing side, rejection, negatives, and boycotts are often perceived as the only remaining source of strength. The use of a language of "entitlements" by the strong is expedient, since it may elicit from the underdog a more constructive attitude. Rather than conceding to "give up" territories in "Judea and Samaria," let the Israeli authorities stress that Palestinians have an inherent right to a state in part of historic Israel or Palestine. Granted, inclusion of a human rights provision may not guarantee its implementation, but without its inclusion there will be no chance for implementation at all.

**The Negotiation Phase.** Peacemaking in protracted communal conflicts is normally a rather lengthy process that requires public acceptance during the interim stages. The transition from one stage to another can be facilitated by CBMs, often delineated in human rights principles. Palestinians do not regard "peace dividends" in terms of the above-mentioned rights. Equally, Israelis do not consider the peace negotiation process as providing personal or collective security. In a comprehensive sense, including socioeconomic and cultural rights, the concept of "human security" as developed by the United Nations[17] stresses the importance of the satisfaction of fundamental needs to prevent violent conflict. Socioeconomic deprivation fosters violence, adding to the ethnopolitical nature of the conflict. More concretely, some of these measures include that Israel desist from holding prisoners in administrative detention without trial, respect the freedom of movement within the Occupied Territories, refrain from housing demolitions, halt confiscation of property, stop using collective punishment against Palestinian civilians in response to individual suicide bombings, and bring to an end the excessive use of force in dealing with Palestinian demonstrators. The interim period includes an improved but so far unequal distribution of water. Both the Israeli and Palestinian authorities should offer financial compensation for innocent victims of violence, adhere to their own commitment to prohibit the use of torture or "moderate physical pressure" in interrogations (even when the "bomb is ticking"), and above all denounce and effectively act upon the violation of the right to life by suicide bombers and extrajudicial, targeted assassinations.

The inclusion of a human rights element is relevant as a CBM during the process's interim phases. Human rights principles, while opening new dimensions for the duration of the negotiation, also propose to resolve permanent-status issues. What might such an approach offer? In addition to the already mentioned conflict of rights concerning refugees, let us briefly illustrate two other important issues:

- *Jerusalem.* The future status of the city, considered the major stumbling block to the resolution of our conflict, can be viewed at three different levels in terms of rights. The expectation of interested members of the international community (mostly Jews, Muslims, and Christians) is that freedom of religion (UDHR, Art. 18) will be upheld, although no additional rights of citizenship will be provided to nonresidents. Second, while Israelis and Palestinians alike desire "Yerushalaim" or "al-Quds" as their capital—and their aspirations are understandable and should be supported—no such right can be determined based on international human rights law. Finally, the right of both major groups in Jerusalem to enjoy fully their individual rights in the city (see UDHR, most articles) may result in the overwhelming majority of the city's Muslim and Jewish populations living in the city under the authority of their own respective sovereign states. Emphasis on individual rights would mean that those who are affected more directly should have greater priority in determining the quality of life and the future of their own city. This could potentially generate a shared Jerusalemite identity based on rights and privileges for its residents. This important dimension has been neglected in the negotiations so far (as in the mentioned example of social security services to Palestinians in East Jerusalem).

■ *Water Rights.* Water need no longer be seen as a finite, zero-sum resource. Though water resources are scarce, it may be possible not only to come to an agreement on joint management of the shared aquifers but also to determine general principles for water rights.[18] Such principles could be based on equal rights to the basic water supply for all, with scaled greater payments for excess consumption. The incremental pricing policy for increased consumption will allow the biggest users to finance the cost of desalinization.

**The Postnegotiation Phase.** Often called the "postconflict" stage, this is the time for implementation of the agreements and for reconciliation. Given the current depressive status of the Israeli-Palestinian peace process, dealing in detail with the postconflict stage may seem impractical and idealistic. But of the three phases, this last has received perhaps the largest consensus for integrating human rights concerns. Examples include Latin America's special commissions, such as Argentina's National Commission on the Disappeared (CONADEP), the Chilean Truth and Reconciliation Commission or Rettig Commission, the UN Verification Mission in Guatemala (MINUGUA), and the UN Observer Mission for El Salvador (ONUSAL),[19] as well as the South African Truth and Reconciliation Commission, which stressed the justice, truth, and healing aspects.[20]

Addressing past human rights violations is a strategy widely accepted by the international community in the effort to end the cycle of violence, and indeed these steps can enable the beginning of a new chapter in a collective and cooperative history. It seems, however, that the parameters for the transition from the postnegotiation period to the envisaged consolidation into a "warm" peace need to be reexamined. Granted, nearly all cases of transitional justice relate to intrastate, domestic strife, and the review being undertaken by a new regime must critically investigate the past violations of its predecessor.[21] In our context, the impunity of individuals involved in acts of violence is likely to remain unquestioned, since those who continue to share power have, more often than not, officially sanctioned their actions. With the formal establishment of the Palestinian state there will be two sovereign governments, each representing more continuity than change. Both entities have already been perpetrators and victims of individual, group, and state terror. Given the asymmetry of power and the level of violence sanctioned by the authorities of both nations in the past, it appears unlikely that either side will unilaterally undertake an initiative to investigate past crimes.

It is not surprising that a gap exists between the ideals and the feasibility of using the "Truth and Reconciliation" mechanisms used in South Africa. This has been discussed by a Palestinian (Fatah Azzam) and an Israeli (Yuli Tamir). According to Azzam, "We must develop a sense of justice to make reconstruction possible . . . being tired of war is not enough . . . if people believe that justice has been served, even though it may be incomplete—moral reconstruction will occur." Then Tamir states: "I think it is dangerous to build reconciliation on victimization and suffering . . . people tried to determine who was victimized more than the others. This kind of inquiry only increases the tensions created by past actions. Nobody wants to forget anything, because the basis of rights is grounded in the degree of suffering."[22]

The mentioned convergence of the human rights paradigm with the "basic needs" approach can result in a real advantage at the postconflict stage. Human rights should be used not only as an important criterion to remind the parties that there are international standards but also to stress that the expected concessions are not unwarranted—that is, that these guidelines follow established principles and customs agreed upon by the international community. Yet human rights, though a necessary condition, are not enough by themselves to be effective in conflict transformation. Justice, too, can now emerge as a leading consideration. We can now move minimalist pragmatic treaty arrangements into declaratory and real policies that acknowledge accumulated suffering. For a durable and lasting peace, both sides will need to see the justice of individual, minimalist, restorative (rather than punitive) measures acknowledged and, to a certain extent, will also need to assist in practical ways to redress suffering.[23] If experience in peacemaking with Egypt and Jordan is any indicator, reconciliation in the Israeli-Palestinian context will probably be easier to obtain by "carrots" (financial compensation) than "sticks" (the punishment of the perpetrators). The collective memory can be improved by reports on "peace and reconciliation" that document human rights violations of the past, where intangible "carrots," without necessarily a price tag, can also become cathartic for healing the wounds. Acknowledgment of morally problematic actions in the past, the prospects of a brighter future without discriminatory acts, sincere efforts to seek equality before the law, and the satisfaction of basic needs could be jointly understood as pragmatic choices that are worth the effort.

In moving toward a progressive and shared vision, we can engage in brainstorming scenarios for a future in which the rights of Palestinian and Israeli individuals will be dramatically improved once formal peace is agreed to. Although sovereignty rests in two separate political entities, interdependence can provide the long-expected peace dividends needed to begin improvement in social and economic conditions, while full civil-political rights of all citizens are ensured.

The implementation of agreements, based on equal rights, will require monitoring and regulation. In cases of disagreements, there is a need for mediating mechanisms and procedures that can effectively acknowledge the complexities of emerging problems. This effort should incorporate clearly designed early-warning indicators and provide training in preventive action. There must also be a procedure for dealing with unresolved issues from the past, when the abrogation of rights (violence, economic deprivation) was not given due attention. Clearly, the more the process can, over time, address and eradicate causes of "structural violence,"[24] the more durable peace will be.

## Conflict Resolution and Human Rights at the Governmental Level: The "Top Dog"

Although the more powerful actor can attempt to maximize security for the ruling group—often at a high human cost—it has no effective way of silencing long-term ethnopolitical opposition by sheer intimidation or limited repression. To win a war so comprehensively as to be able to dictate the nature of the postconflict settlement, the victor must usually act ruthlessly (e.g., conducting ethnic cleansing or massacring large numbers of civilians) —more ruthlessly than legal and public opinion in most democracies can tolerate. And when a majority imposes its rule over a disenfranchised, rebellious minority, it cannot expect its "solution" to endure indefinitely; hopes for a lasting outcome require a genuine endorsement by both sides.

This principle is vitally relevant to the Israeli-Palestinian peace process, in which military victories have not resulted in compliance.[25]

For the Jewish state, reaching a historic, mutually internalized reconciliation will lead the way to the eventual closure of the cycle of violence. The declared finality of the conflict can be included in a treaty, and the public can better understand that isolated acts of terror—rejected by the leadership and civil societies of both sides—are a serious but unavoidable price to pay. Moreover, the application of human rights standards can also be invoked for the sake of the citizens of the stronger party. Although they often enjoy more rights than the oppressed minority, their right to life is often challenged by the armed opposition, which can also be made accountable for the respect of human rights standards.

In the case of Israel, as in other Western cultures, there is a fear of commitment to principles that can bring about demands that the declaratory policy be meticulously implemented. However, it has often been argued that in high-context cultures—where individual behavior is highly controlled by traditional collective rules—the minority or the weaker side is expecting a symbolic recognition of rights that does not necessarily mean full implementation. The extraordinary value of the acknowledgment of injustices has been increasingly recognized in the apologies of distinguished political leaders around the world. Nations that have been oppressed throughout decades or centuries may find healing in the expression of such statements and in what often amounts to symbolic and very partial redress of past violations. Many of the issues accumulated in protracted conflicts are related to human suffering and not necessarily to tangible goods that may have been lost forever. When revisiting the Palestinian refugee issue, it is clear that Israel is afraid that recognition of shared responsibility carries the acceptance of the principle of implementation. This fear reflects a flawed understanding; there needs to be reassurance that once the wording of the recognition is agreed on, one can put the magnanimous declaration aside and work out the practical implications.

A "realpolitik" critique often reminds us that demands to include human rights clauses in the formulation of an accord may well be a delaying factor at a time when the window of opportunity is relatively short. Moreover, there have been more than a few cases in which aspects of the text of the agreement seem to violate, explicitly or implicitly, universal standards. The plausible political counterargument is that appealing to human rights as a paradigm does not necessarily mean that all measures must be congruent with such lofty principles. Rather, the purpose of the human rights language in the agreement is mostly to communicate an expectation of achieving the highest standards possible. On the other hand, the total avoidance of human rights considerations may in fact prolong the peace process. Adherence to universal standard setting by Israel, the stronger side, can be beneficial for its image and its diaspora and, in the long run, help ensure the cherished "lasting" peace.

## Conflict Resolution and Human Rights at the Governmental Level: The "Underdog"

Reconciliation builds on overcoming the scars of past injustices and victimhood. When members of the "victimizing" community express acknowledgment of the victims' suffering, the process can move forward. However, in the Israeli-Palestinian conflict, each side subjectively considers itself the major or even sole victim; thus, acknowledgment is often difficult to elicit, as it is associated with "weakness." Until we find ways to share victimhood status and express empathy toward the suffering of the "Other," legal sanctions and punishment will not bring the conflict closer to resolution. Going beyond rights into "gestures of reconciliation"[26] is necessary for moving the negotiation process forward, as well as being part and parcel to healing. While most Jews with a collective memory of suffering through history, and of the Holocaust in particular, would expect some understanding of their plight, most Palestinians do not seem to be able to empathize openly, at this stage, with Jewish suffering. What with fears of intimidation by extremists, and of being misunderstood by one's own society in the high-context Palestinian culture, individual initiatives, though remarkable when they occur, have been very few.[27]

Such recognition of a shared victimhood becomes almost impossible for the large segment of Palestinians who currently live under an occupation reality based on "ghettoization policy" as a result of the "separating wall." Hundreds of thousands of Palestinians are deprived of their daily basic right to move or even leave their town, village, or house. The construction of the separating wall brought a new level of collective imprisonment and punishment to the Palestinian population. Such sense of collective victimization needs to be recognized by the "Other" in order to restore a basic degree of dignity that allows a person or group to recognize or even look outside its humiliating reality.

Within this context, the horrendous suicidal homicides, by individuals or extremist groups targeting innocent Israeli civilians, have had a disastrous impact on the peace process. Many moderates tend to be paralyzed when tragic events such as terror attacks or structural violence occur. This paralysis is caused by shame, awkwardness, or ignorance of the "legitimate" responses. As a result, opportunities for expression of empathy through public or private grieving are lost. In an even more insidious way, chances for manifesting solidarity are missed whenever we fail to comfort the victims of structural violence, which, although bloodless, is no less damaging psychologically.

Basic principles of human dignity, highlighted already in the UDHR, are essential in pursuing a partnership for peace. Just to illustrate, Mohammed Abu-Nimer, one of this essay's authors, was a member of an international team working to facilitate a Palestinian-Israeli meeting to discuss Palestinian elections. Because of recent suicide bombings, the Palestinian delegates were not allowed to leave their cities and participate in joint meetings in Jerusalem. A member of the Palestinian Legislative Council described our efforts to get the author to ask permission to leave his town in Ramallah as legitimizing the violation of his basic human right to vote and elect. The author decided not to ask the Israelis for clearance, in order not to negotiate his basic right.

This restriction not only is a violation of "freedom of movement" but also has generated a situation of structural violence, causing loss of lives and permanent damage to a large number of innocent people. By preventing movement at all levels, the policy has also limited the possibility of medical treatment for chronically sick people and made birth delivery more difficult; it has jeopardized the possibility of employment and hence caused increased poverty and often malnutrition; it has prevented educational institutions, from kindergartens to universities, from functioning normally, causing the loss of countless days and hours of classes; it has also prevented the reconstruction of demolished houses resulting from yet another illegal policy of collective punishment. With such levels of deprivation, it takes an incredible inner strength to empathize with the pain caused to the "Other."

## Conflict Resolution and Human Rights at the NGO Level: Challenges and Potential

Nongovernmental organizations and civil society are the type of setting in which necessary linkages between human rights and conflict resolution groups should take place. However, as is typically the case in protracted communal conflicts, unilateral claims are not confined to the political leaders in power but are widely shared within their respective nations.[28] It should not be surprising that many of the Israelis searching for a compromise have been involved in what has been called the "peace movement" or "peace camp," while the human rights groups have been mostly small, staff-driven organizations. In its largest demonstration, Peace Now was able to gather some 400,000 people in Tel Aviv to protest the massacre of Palestinians by Maronite Lebanese in the Sabra and Shatila refugee camps in 1982—an action tacitly facilitated by the Israeli military. The group has also held large yearly masses to commemorate Prime Minister Yitzhak Rabin's assassination. On the other hand, identifying with the rights of the "Other," particularly when Palestinians are involved in brutal violence against Israelis, is not an easy proposition. Hence, only a few Israelis come to protest house demolition as a form of inhuman collective punishment. There is a certain tension between those who call for an "end of occupation" and those who are concerned with the daily violation of Palestinian rights, whose efforts are perceived to be a useless effort to "humanize occupation." As a result, and compared with Palestinians NGOs, very few Israeli organizations have monitored or paid systematic attention to the human rights violations caused by the Israeli occupation since 1967. (B'tselem is one well-recognized Israeli organization that has led campaigns of public awareness and advocacy since the late 1980s.) Conversely, on the Palestinian side, there has not been an organized massive "peace movement." Only a few small NGOs espousing nonviolence have been in existence for more than a decade, although lately a few staff-driven conflict resolution NGOs have been a welcome addition. Only one small university-based peace center continues to operate. Often, like their Israeli counterparts, Palestinian peace and nonviolence advocates have been ostracized and criticized by their fellow citizens, although a sizeable group continues to persevere in the face of daunting adverse circumstances. On the other hand, there has been a mushrooming of human rights organizations, mobilizing around issues such as deportation, imprisonment, house demolition, and land confiscation. A debate emerged about the duty of Palestinian human rights organizations to monitor not only the violations of the Israeli government but also those committed by the Palestinian National Authority.

In the pre-Oslo era, most of the Palestinian and Israeli groups worked on monitoring human rights violations separately along their ethnic divides —to some extent similar to the Sri Lankan peace and human rights groups.[29] And even now, although Palestinian and Israeli human rights organizations cooperate in gathering and distributing data, they run mostly separate and independent operations. The Palestinian human rights organizations often refuse to engage in formal dialogue with Israelis. However, this started to change after the Oslo peace processes started to decline, at which point many Palestinian and Israeli organizations initiated joint peace and conflict resolution projects. Still, many Arab activists continue to criticize the Oslo peace process for lack of protection of human rights, a situation that has worsened during the al Aqsa intifada.[30]

The asymmetry of power in the situation between Israel and Palestine not only makes it materially difficult for the Palestinians to attend meetings but also has psychological implications.[31] Most Palestinians have claimed, when asked to attend joint peace meetings with Israelis, that attaining basic rights for free movement and freedom of expression is far more important than engaging in joint peace work. Thus, advocacy to gain and ensure such rights becomes more central to those who live under occupation, especially in view of the targeted assassinations; torture; administrative detention; mass, forced migration; massive curfews; closure of schools; and so on, that are an integral part of their daily lives. Palestinians also argue that in order to be able to engage in and learn tactics of peace-building and dialogue, a minimal number of basic socioeconomic needs must be met so that they can exist with dignity.

Several projects based on both universality and reciprocity aptly illustrate the search for common ground in defending the right to life as well as addressing the need for apology, joint sorrow, and truth. A dialogue was begun, which later led to the establishment of Healing Early Action Link (HEAL).[32] During its first year, HEAL realized that condolence and comfort visits to victims require a significantly higher level of preparation than originally anticipated. To give a deeper understanding of the meaning of political violence, Palestinian participants revealed to the Israelis the flagrant issue of structural violence. This altered the objectives of the project and restored symmetry to the work of HEAL in its second year. Sensitivity-enhancing dialogue is just as legitimate and effective in alleviating human suffering as the more visible and concrete interventions, such as condolence visits; practical, logistical help for the sick and wounded (in cases of closures of Palestinian towns); contacting victims of (impending) house demolitions; mediating in legal aid; and articles published through various media venues.

Another, albeit short-lived, project responded to the large number of children killed during the first stages of the al Aqsa intifada, as published in the mainstream Israeli and Palestinian newspapers (see appendix 2). Many from both sides who were concerned with the right to life signed, but a few had reservations about the inclusion of children of Jewish settlers.

Another project brought together sixteen Israeli and Palestinian human rights and peace workers in a joint research and conceptualization initiative on how best to "humanize" the new peace process, including a state-of-the-art training course for trainers, on peacebuilding and on further developing a campaign to reach out to a wide audience.[33] Currently, in the project's third phase, the focus on "freedom of movement" works primarily on the draconian restrictions in the Palestinian Territories, though it is also concerned about the fear of Israeli Jews and Arabs alike of riding buses.

In most of these joint meetings, Palestinians have chosen the empowering language of basic human rights to stress their victimhood, calling for universal justice. A sense of moral superiority emerges when advocacy details the violation of human rights under occupation. Many Israelis in such encounters experience a sense of shame and the need to be defensive.[34] In this context, Palestinians often criticize the conflict resolution and peace workers who insist on creating balance between Palestinian just claims and suffering and the Israeli sense of victimhood,[35] particularly when the state violence carried out by Israel is recognized as a legitimate defense policy, whereas Palestinian reactions to the occupation are termed "terrorism."[36]

The difficulties usually appear in the relative ability to relate to peace in the future while insisting on the principles of justice and accountability in the present tense. On the other hand, such a sense of equality is not reflected in negotiation and dialogue, and in some cases the dialogue itself can perpetuate the sense of asymmetric power relations and inequality.[37] Peace work promoted by Israelis often addresses the psychological and perceptional aspects of the conflict, focusing on reduction of stereotypes through dialogue, teaching communication skills, and exploring cultural differences and similarities. While such peace encounters are helpful in relieving the individual fears and stereotypes of the Israeli participants, they often fall short in addressing the basic human rights violations that the Palestinians experience at all times, including while on their way to the dialogue or peace worker meeting and as they return home afterward. Conversely, the Palestinian participants' exclusivist human rights point of view often fails to empathize with the needs of the Israelis and sometimes even with those Israelis who have a basic willingness to compromise.

## Conclusions

Ultimately, the political elites of both nations have not been socialized, on the whole, into the language and use of human rights as universal principles. In general, due to the short-term electoral objectives of political gain, politicians have rarely engaged in peace and justice initiatives. In Israel, rather than confronting the settlers and the political forces behind them, many political leaders have deferred any decisive policy of withdrawal from the Occupied Territories, ignoring the long-term consequences for the transformation of their country into a binational state. On the Palestinian side, survival in their positions seems to be the prevailing preoccupation of the leadership.

At this stage it seems impossible that the recognition of the intrinsic relationship between peace and justice for both sides will come from a top-down initiative. Still, we should continue, jointly and separately, to point out that while the relative strength of forces provides one side with the ability to win wars, it will never provide the ability to impose a stable peace. We must also continue to condemn strongly the use of violence against civilian targets, be it suicide bombing or targeted assassination, as the equivalent of a crime against humanity and a major obstacle to the peace process. By formulating claims in accepted universal principles, we can strengthen the possibility of achieving a higher level of legitimacy internationally and, hopefully, within our own societies as well. The acceptance of the humanity of the "Other" and the inherent human dignity of the person, even at the declaratory level, can set up a better atmosphere conducive to more successful negotiations.

And yet, the asymmetry of power is clear, and there may not be a strong immediate incentive for the more powerful side (Israelis) to recognize the grievances of the weaker one (Palestinians) without the direct involvement of the international community, as was the case in Rwanda and the former Yugoslavia. But the strong international alliance of Israel with the United States, the still comparatively "low-intensity" level of casualties, and the shared responsibility of both sides make any external military intervention to take control of the West Bank and Gaza unlikely. Moreover, such intervention could meet with much resistance by the Israeli public at large, which is understandably fearful of existential threats as recorded in its traumatic historical memory.

Hence, the challenge is to develop a shared understanding on how to move "from here to there." While there seems to be a growing understanding that an Israeli-Palestinian agreement on final-status issues should be close to the agreements reached at the 2000 Taba meeting or the "Geneva Accord" launched by Yossi Beilin and Abed Rabbo,[38] we must not forget to include a dimension that can strengthen people-to-people relations and provide a renewed hope in political peace negotiations. Since, in general terms, large majorities in both nations profess to ascribe to universal human rights values and to democracy, and the leadership of both nations has also uttered such declaratory adherence, we need to work hard to make all concerned understand the implications of such a stand. If the universal jurisdiction of such principles is accepted, both Palestinians and Israelis should be guaranteed at least the fundamental freedoms and fulfillment of basic needs that each individual deserves as a human being.

Human rights principles can provide the Palestinians with new ideas for unilateral initiatives, such as struggling for the right of freedom of movement now; calling for elections and struggling nonviolently for the right to conduct them under the scrutiny of the international community; and demanding that Israel not forestall any longer the exercise of their citizen rights, by allowing them to become citizens of the occupying state and, eventually, decide by referendum whether to secede or to become part of a multinational secular state.

Approximately half the peace treaties since World War II have not been fully implemented, and the overall ratio for Israeli-Arab agreements does not seem to be better. Given the protracted and bloody nature of our conflict and the numerous problems already faced in the implementation of the Oslo agreement, unless we consolidate any new accords into a stronger bottom-up bond, we will slip back time and again into a cycle of violence.

Facing such realities places a heavy burden on the human rights and peace groups of both sides to take a leadership role in the process. Awareness of the intrinsic connection of the two principles has been confined to the minds and deeds of only a few academics and activists, but the potential to expand the ranks is there. Even if it is difficult to conceive at this time that the leaders of both nations will find common ground, building a "sectorial peace" involving understanding between important social movements of the two societies can provide a strong basis for a concerted international and domestic action. We have seen human rights and peace/conflict resolution NGOs on both sides working separately on a variety of causes, and the mixed composition of the mentioned core groups already shows the potential of this initiative. Lisa Schirch[39] makes several recommendations to theoretically link the two fields of human rights and peacebuilding. We can easily adapt and expand some of those recommendations to the Israeli-Palestinian context, as follows:

- Stimulate consensus building around the convergence of human rights and peace work as represented by the term of "just peace"— the unifying concept toward a sustained process of reconciliation.
- Focus the attention of Israeli and Palestinian peacebuilding groups and organizations on the human needs and rights both of themselves and of the "Other" as an analytical framework for action

and evaluation of impact. Doing this will also allay the skepticism among participants that peacebuilding work tends to neglect the concrete and tangible needs of individual participants.

- Make sure that peacebuilding work is guided by the fulfillment of human needs and rights of Palestinians as well as Israelis, making the issue of impartiality and neutrality of the third party less relevant. It will also address, even though only partially, the concern about asymmetric relations between the Israelis and Palestinians who participate in peacebuilding projects.

- Create a broad-based effort to institutionalize coordination networks among human rights and peacebuilding groups.[40] When such networks are actively planning, implementing, and evaluating their various projects and initiatives, they become a source of strength and complementarities rather than weakness and competition.

- Encourage the use of nonviolent sanctions in the struggle for a just peace, since doing so translates the concept from mere goals to means. Regardless of the individual or group endorsement of pacifism or "just war" as a last resort, searching for common ground can result in the preference for nonviolence as a first choice of action.

- See that the joint actions of both Palestinian and Israeli human rights and peace/conflict resolution civil society organizations focus on agendas with issues of current relevance, such as defending the right to life (UDHR, art. 3) of innocent civilian victims of suicide bombers and targeted assassinations, and easing the restrictions on freedom of movement because of checkpoints or the erection of a separating fence/wall (UDHR, art. 13). Such blatant violations are also an impediment to peace (e.g., the illegitimacy of the killings increases the reciprocal level of hatred; the building of the wall changes unilaterally the future borders of the two states).

Facing this challenge, we must also acknowledge the obstacles from within our own civil societies and seek out a better understanding of our mutual values and expectations. Generating "epistemic communities"[41] of those who have developed a shared understanding across the divide and ways to implement this shared understanding is an important prerequisite for progress. Facing the current adverse circumstances, we the authors find some source of encouragement in the ability to have expressed together this analysis of the problem. Still, the hard work has only begun.

■　　■　　■

# Appendix 1

## Human Rights References in the Israeli-Palestinian Peace Agreements

In determining whether the concept of "human rights" has been used in the negotiations, we have analyzed hundreds of pages of the official documents from the Israeli-Palestinian peace process, beginning with the Letters of Israel-PLO Recognition that were exchanged after the Oslo negotiations, from September 9, 1993, until the Wye River Memorandum (1998).[42]

The following documents were analyzed:

- Israel-PLO Recognition, September 9–10, 1993
- Israel-Palestinian Declaration of Principles, September 13, 1993
- Agreement on the Gaza Strip and the Jericho Area, May 4, 1994: Preamble and Articles

  Annex I: Security Arrangements

  Annex II: Civil Affairs

  Annex III: Legal Matters

  Annex IV: Protocol on Economic Relations, April 29, 1994

  Maps
- Rabin-Arafat: Exchange of Letters
- Agreement on the Preparatory Transfer of Powers and Responsibilities (Israel-PLO), August 29, 1994

  Annex I: Protocol Concerning Preparatory Transfer of Powers and Responsibilities in the Sphere of Education and Culture

  Annex II: Protocol Concerning Preparatory Transfer of Powers and Responsibilities in the Sphere of Health

  Annex III: Protocol Concerning Preparatory Transfer of Powers and Responsibilities in the Sphere of Social Welfare

  Annex IV: Protocol Concerning Preparatory Transfer of Powers and Responsibilities in the Sphere of Tourism

  Annex V: Protocol Concerning Preparatory Transfer of Powers and Responsibilities in the Sphere of Direct Taxation

  Annex VI: Protocol Concerning Preparatory Transfer of Powers and Responsibilities in the Sphere of VAT on Local Production

- Interim Agreement between Israel and the Palestinians, September 28, 1995

  Annex 1: Redeployment and Security Arrangements

  Annex 2: Elections Protocol

  Annex 3: Civil Affairs

  Annex 4: Legal Matters

  Annex 5: Economic Relations

  Annex 6: Israeli-Palestinian Cooperation

  Annex 7: Release of Palestinian Prisoners

  Maps

- Summit of Peacemakers: Final Statement (Sharm el-Sheikh), March 13, 1996

- Agreement on Temporary International Presence in Hebron, May 9, 1996

- Protocol Concerning the Redeployment in Hebron, January 17, 1997

## Results

In the main documents the term "human rights" is not used. It is used only in secondary items and annexes, as follows:

A. In the exchange of letters between Prime Minister Rabin and Chairman Arafat the term "human rights" was never mentioned.

B. In the "Declaration of Principles" (an eleven-page document), the concept was never mentioned. In the introductory paragraph, there is only an allusion to the recognition of the two sides' mutual legitimate and political rights.

C. In the "Agreement on the Gaza Strip and the Jericho Area" (a twelve-page document), the concept is mentioned only once, in one small article (Article XIV: Human Rights and the Rule of Law).

> Israel and the Council [of the Palestinian Authority] shall exercise their powers and responsibilities pursuant to this Agreement with due regard to internationally accepted norms and principles of human rights and the rule of law.

In the various annexes, human rights are mentioned as follows:

> Article VIII: Rules of Conduct in Security Matters [same Gaza agreement, in an annex]

> Subject to the provisions of this Agreement, the security and public order personnel of both sides shall exercise their powers and

responsibilities pursuant to this Agreement with due regard to internationally-accepted norms of human rights and the rule of law and shall be guided by the need to protect the public, respect human dignity and avoid harassment.

2. Both sides shall take all necessary measures to ensure that the treatment of individuals transferred under this Article complies with the applicable legal arrangements in Israel and in the Territory and with internationally accepted norms of human rights regarding criminal investigations.

D. In the "Interim Agreement between Israel and the Palestinians on the West Bank and the Gaza Strip" (twenty-one pages), the concept appears once in Article XIX: Human Rights and the Rule of Law.

Israel and the Council shall exercise their powers and responsibilities pursuant to this Agreement with due regard to internationally accepted norms and principles of human rights and the rule of law.

E. In Annex 1, "Protocol Concerning Redeployment and Security Arrangements" (sixty-nine pages), it also appears once, in Article XI: "Rules of Conduct in Mutual Security Matters."

1. Human Rights and the Rule of Law:
Subject to the provisions of this Agreement, the Palestinian Police and the Israeli military forces shall exercise their powers and responsibilities pursuant to this Agreement with due regard to internationally-accepted norms of human rights and the rule of law, and shall be guided by the need to protect the public, respect human dignity and avoid harassment.

And once, in Article IX, "Movement Into, Within and Outside the West Bank and the Gaza Strip," it mentions Israel's right to consider its security and safety.

d. The provisions of this Agreement shall not prejudice Israel's right, for security and safety considerations, to close the crossing points to Israel and to prohibit or limit the entry into Israel of persons and of vehicles from the West Bank and the Gaza Strip. In addition, the provisions of this Agreement shall not prejudice the use of safe passage.

In Annex 3, "Protocol Concerning Civil Affairs" (sixty-six pages), the term is not used. However, there are some references to academic rights under Article 2, concerning archaeology; Article 11, concerning the right of employment; Article 21, concerning the rights of the workers; Article 23, concerning intellectual property rights; and Article 32, concerning religious rights.

In Annex 4, "Protocol Concerning Legal Affairs" (eight pages), the term is mentioned once, under Article II, "Legal Assistance in Criminal Matters":

> h. (l) Both sides shall take all necessary measures to ensure that the treatment of the individuals transferred under this article complies with the applicable legal arrangements in Israel and in the Territory and with internationally-accepted norms of human rights regarding criminal investigations.

Under Article IV, concerning scientific and technological cooperation, intellectual property rights are mentioned.

F. In the Final Statement—Summit of Peacemakers: Sharm el-Sheikh (two pages), the term is not used.

G. In the Wye River Memorandum, 1998 (eight pages), the concept appears only once, in reference to the Palestinian police, Article II, under section C, numeral 4.

> Pursuant to Article XI (1) of Annex I of the Interim Agreement, and without derogating from the above, the Palestinian Police will exercise powers and responsibilities to implement this Memorandum with due regard to internationally accepted norms of human rights and the rule of law and will be guided by the need to protect the public, respect human dignity, and avoid harassment.

# Appendix 2

## "Stop Killing Our Children" Campaign

The following text was part of advertisements published in Hebrew (in *Ha'aretz*) and Arabic (in *Al Quds*) in March and April 2001.

> We should make our voices heard loud and clear: PLEASE DO NOT MAKE OUR CHILDREN AND YOUNG THE TARGETS OF THE FIGHT AMONG OUR ADULTS. KEEP THEM OUT. . . . We do not want to go into a futile discussion about who is killing more children, who are the killers, and whether or not they were officially sanctioned and instigated. The crux of the issue is undisputed—children and infants are dying. . . . Children under the age of 16 are normally protected by society. We do not allow them to drive nor to vote or drink. Many of us question the morality and expedience of using violence against each other. Indeed, there are different opinions, but it seems to me that there is a universal consensus—amongst Arabs and Jews—as part of the world at large, that

the human rights of minors must be protected. Most certainly, unarmed, innocent children should not be killed and wounded. We must take responsibility and prevent their deaths, both by commission and omission. By not using lethal weapons against them, as well as preventing them from venturing into life-threatening situations, and unsafe environments. Not only are our own brothers cutting short the precious lives of our innocent children, but the family, at large, is deeply suffering . . . the community is crying. . . .

(1) We should ask our leaders, both Arafat and Sharon, to record, in their own voices, a general statement deploring the death of children and young, and calling our nations and armed forces to refrain from such acts. We should ask the official media to broadcast these statements daily until violence stops and start again if there is another minor killed.

(2) The Israeli Government and the Palestinian National Authority should at least officially undertake to investigate the death of each minor and publish the findings. Furthermore, if they could agree to have joint teams including a representative of an international organization protecting the rights of children (e.g. UNICEF, Save The Children, Defense for Children International) that would be a great step forward.

(3) Regardless of what the governments are going to do or not do, we must agree to act ourselves: it could be as simple as sending joint letters of condolences to the families of victims, or newspapers; that we ask our own Jewish and Arab children or pupils to find ways to communicate to children of the other nation that are wounded by our own people (Send books and/or pictures to one another, establish pen-pals etc).

## Notes

1. See Philip Alston, "Peace as a Human Right," in *Human Rights in the World Community*, ed. R. P. Claude and B. H. Weston (Philadelphia: University of Pennsylvania Press, 1992), 198–209.

2. David P. Forsythe, *Human Rights and Peace: International and National Dimensions* (Lincoln: University of Nebraska Press, 1993).

3. Michael Walzer, *Just Wars and Unjust Wars* (New York: Basic Books, 1977).

4. Bruce Russet, *Grasping the Democratic Peace: Principles for a Post–Cold War World* (Princeton, NJ: Princeton University Press, 2003); James Lee Ray, *Democracy and International Conflict: An Evaluation of the Democratic Peace Proposition* (Columbia: University of South Carolina Press, 1995).

5. Edy Kaufman, Shukri B. Abed, and Robert L. Rothstein, eds., *Democracy, Peace, and the Israeli-Palestinian Conflict* (Boulder, CO: Lynne Rienner, 1993).

**6.** Edy Kaufman, "The Relevance of the International Protection of Human Rights to Democratization and Peace," Occasional Paper Series, Kroc Institute for International Peace Studies, University of Notre Dame (July 1994).

**7.** Lisa Schirch, "Human Rights and Peacebuilding: Toward Just Peace" (unpublished paper, delivered at annual meeting of International Studies Association, April 2002); Schirch, *A Peacebuilding Framework to Link Human Rights and Conflict Transformation* (Harrisonburg, VA: Eastern Mennonite University, forthcoming.

**8.** See section on the Dual-Concern Model, in John Davies, "Power, Rights, Interest, and Identity: Conflict Management Strategies for Building a Democratic Peace," in *Track II /Citizens Diplomacy: Applied Techniques of Conflict Transformation,* ed. John Davies and Edy Kaufman (Lanham, MD: Rowman and Littlefield, 2002), 115–16.

**9.** Edward Azar, "Protracted Social Conflicts and Second Track Diplomacy," ibid. 15–30.

**10.** Schirch coined the expression BATARJ (best alternative to truth and reconciliation), adapting from R. Fisher and W. Ury's BATNA the realistic concept that the options need to be seen in the relative sense and not as absolute demands. Schirch, *A Peacebuilding Framework,* 28.

**11.** Mubarak Awad and Edy Kaufman, "Prisoner Release as a Fork in the Road Map: Switching from the Past toward the Future to Bring Palestinians and Israelis Together," *Al Quds* (daily), August 11, 2003 (in Arabic).

**12.** Edy Kaufman and Ibrahim Bisharat, "Humanizing the Israeli/Palestinian Peace Process, *Israel-Palestine Journal* 6, no. 1 (1999): 8–13.

**13.** A later content analysis of the speeches made by Prime Minister Ariel Sharon and President Yasser Arafat during 2000–2003 shows a nearly total absence of the term "human rights" by the first, and the use of "rights" by the second only as attributed to the Palestinian people.

**14.** Article XIV of the Gaza-Jericho Agreement stipulates, "Israel and the Council [of the Palestinian Authority] shall exercise their powers and responsibilities pursuant to this Agreement with due regard to internationally accepted norms and principles of human rights and the rule of law," and in Annex III, Article 2 discusses the issue of treatment of individuals of either group when transferred to the judicial authorities of the other.

**15.** For an overall detailed analysis see appendix 1. One of the few one-sided examples was the Wye River Memorandum, which has a reference only to the Palestinian police, admonishing them to behave according to "internationally accepted norms of human rights and the rule of law," but the Israeli delegation, led by Prime Minister Netanyahu, was allegedly adamant in refusing to accept any commitment to human rights standards.

**16.** Committee on the Administration of Justice, "Human Rights: The Agenda for Change" (Belfast, December 1995), 3. In an analysis of the 1998 Northern Ireland Peace Agreement, Human Rights Watch expressed that the organization "is particularly pleased to note that the new agreement reflects an understanding of the relationship between the protection and promotion of universal human rights and the probabilities for a lasting just and durable peace." Human Rights Watch, *Justice for All?* 10, no. 3 (April 1998), www.hrw.org/reports98/nireland.

**17.** United Nations, "Human Development Report, 1994," *UN Documents* (New York: United Nations Publications, 1994).

**18.** Eran Feitelson, Marwan Haddad, Shaul Arlosoroff, and Taher Nassereddin, "A Proposed Agenda for the Joint Management of the Shared Groundwater," in *The Management of Shared Groundwater Resources: The Israeli-Palestinian Case within an International Perspective,* ed. E. Feitelson and M. Haddad (Boston: Kluwer Academic Publishers, 2000).

**19.** For an analysis of the human rights dimension in several postnegotiation contexts in the Western Hemisphere, see Cynthia J. Arnson, ed., *Comparative Peace Processes in Latin America* (Palo Alto, CA: Stanford University Press, 1999).

**20.** Eileen R. Borris, "Reconciliation in Postconflict Peacebuilding: Lessons Learned from South Africa," in *Track II/Citizens Diplomacy,* ed. Davies and Kaufman, 161–82.

**21.** See Neil J. Kritz, ed., *Transitional Justice: How Emerging Democracies Reckon with Former Regimes,* 3 vols. (Washington, DC: United States Institute of Peace Press, 1995).

**22.** Henry Steiner, ed., *Truth Commissions: A Comparative Assessment* (Cambridge, MA: Harvard Law School, Human Rights Program, 1996).

**23.** Daan Bronkhorst, *Truth and Reconciliation: Obstacles and Opportunities for Human Rights* (Amsterdam: Amnesty International Dutch Section, 1995).

**24.** On the concept of "structural violence," see Joan Galtung, "Violence, Peace, and Peace Research," *Journal of Peace Research* 6, no. 3 (1969): 167–91.

**25.** Edy Kaufman and Ibrahim Bisharat, "Are Human Rights Good for the Top Dog as Well? Rescuing the Missing Dimension of the Israeli-Palestinian Peace Process," *Palestine-Israel Journal* (September 2003): 81–88.

**26.** Christopher Mitchell, *Gestures of Reconciliation: Factors Contributing to Successful Olive-Branches* (New York: Macmillan, 2000).

**27.** One overall expression of such reluctance is to avoid visiting the Holocaust Museum; only lately a group of Israeli Palestinians challenged this attitude by visiting the sites of former Nazi concentration camps in Europe.

**28.** As on the more global level, the difference between human rights and peace NGOs has been that "whilst the former campaigns publicly on the consequences of conflicts, namely human rights abuses, the latter has eschewed the public approach in favor of quietly building trust and understanding amongst the various parties to a conflict. In the past, this has led to a certain amount of tension with both sides concerned that their work is being hampered or even undermined by the other's distinct approach and different sets of priorities." International Alert, *Code of Conduct—Conflict Transformation Work* (London: International Alert, 1998), 20.

**29.** Jehan Perera, "Building Legitimacy and Trust," *Human Rights Dialogue* (Winter 2002): 9–10.

**30.** Quoting a Palestinian in the HEAL network (see note 32): "In speaking about the challenges that we face, these days many Palestinians ask, why do you do joint projects with Israelis? The Israelis have everything and we don't have anything. This project is part of normalization, part of perpetuating the status quo, and part of creating facts on the ground. . . . The asymmetry will continue, and I feel it is time for Palestinians and Israelis to shift from victim and guilty to social responsibility."

**31.** As Abu-Nimer has observed: "We cannot work on dialogue and peace when we are deprived of our basic rights of freedom, mobility, and expression. The emphasis of the Palestinian civil society should be on the advocacy for protection of human rights and not wasted on psychological manifestation of the conflict. When Israelis call for dialogue during these times when there is a total closure on all Palestinian civilians, it is clear that the dialoguer does not recognize the harsh reality of occupation that Palestinians experience" (taken from conversations with Palestinian political and civil society leaders who were invited to participate in a joint meeting with Israeli leaders, to discuss Palestinian elections in Jerusalem, January 2003).

**32.** "Healing Early Action Link," a network of Israelis and Palestinians working (a) to alleviate suffering inflicted by political and structural violence in the conflict, inter alia; (b) to transform cumulative hatred into a tool for reconciliation; (c) to prepare proactive strategies and tools for coping; (d) to study how to improve the quality of solidarity and grief-sharing activities in the Israeli-Palestinian conflict; (e) to reflect on novel ways of symbolically and jointly coping with pain and injustice; (f) to develop alternative ways of releasing stifled and suppressed emotions." Over fifty Israeli and Palestinian psychologists, social workers, conflict resolution practitioners, educators, and writers were involved in HEAL. The participants were committed to effecting change through their personal intervention and to limiting the effects of political and structural violence. HEAL activities consisted of interactive brainstorming and problem-solving workshops, intervention activities by small groups, training in sharing and coping with emotions, and formal dialogues. Over a period of two years (1997–99) HEAL participants worked to gain indispensable skills for dealing with culturally and religiously accepted codes of grieving among Jews, Muslims, and Christians. In addition, critical insights were gained through researching ways of releasing fury, anguish, and dejection in post-traumatic stress situations. Sensitivity training focused on learning how to express contextually appropriate messages of support.

**33.** Panorama—the Palestinian Center for the Dissemination of Democracy and Community Development (Jerusalem), a Palestinian NGO, and the Truman Institute (at the Hebrew University of Jerusalem), in cooperation with American University, coordinated this initiative. Because of political events, participants from the various NGOs mostly met separately, and only a few Palestinians from Jerusalem managed to attend the joint meetings.

**34.** Members of the Israeli team were divided between those from several human rights organizations who agreed with the Palestinian arguments and those who counterattacked, defending their national stance, detailing the abuses carried out by the Palestinian Authority against Palestinians and the impact of suicide bombings on Israeli society.

**35.** When facilitating one of the group's activities, Abu-Nimer observed, "Divides and stereotypes between human rights and peace workers are also reflected in the Palestinian/Israeli context, too. Several concrete arguments were made by group members who pointed out the different perspectives held by various members of the group. Palestinian members of the group emphasized the constant violation of human rights committed by the Israeli occupation, and insisted on a vivid description of the violations, with occasional reference to the international laws and the 1949 Geneva Convention on Human Rights that have to be respected even under armed conflict. Members of the Israeli delegation were divided between those who agreed with the Palestinian arguments (especially those who were in the human rights organization) and those who felt the need to defend their national side. Thus, they launched a counterattack detailing the violation of human rights carried out by the Palestinian Authority against Palestinians, and the impact of suicide bombings on the Israeli society. The Palestinian participants' exclusive human rights point of view often would fail to engage the needs, fears, and interests that caused the reluctance of Israeli public opinion and sometimes even of those Israelis who have a basic willingness to compromise. When meeting with Israelis, Palestinians who insist on moral absolutism and absolute justice become more frustrated and angry at their Israeli counterparts. Similarly, the Israeli participants express their disappointment that the Palestinians cannot understand their collective concerns, even when they acknowledge the destructiveness and evil of the occupation."

**36.** Richard Falk has captured such asymmetry: "The impression is that Israeli violence against Palestinian refugees and neighboring states constitute generally acceptable acts of war and expression of security policy, while Palestinian violence is treated as "terrorism." Richard Falk, *Human Rights Horizons: The Pursuit of Justice in a Globalizing World* (New York: Routledge, 2000), 158.

**37.** Mohammed Abu-Nimer, ed., *Reconciliation, Coexistence, and Justice: Theory and Practice* (New York: Rowman and Littlefield, 2001).

**38.** See the Geneva Accord Web site, www.heskem.org.il/Heskem.

**39.** Schirch, "Human Rights and Peacebuilding."

**40.** According to a representative of the International Donors Forum (interview with author, Jerusalem, January 7, 2003), the international donors in Palestine have an informal network for coordination, headed by a representative from Norway. (Members of this network include USAID, Norway, UNDP, Sweden, Japan, Germany, and others.) Also, there are several networks among Palestinian and Israeli NGOs, although there is no overall systematic coordination among these separate yet interdependent entities.

**41.** Emanuel Adler, "Cognitive Evolution: A Dynamic Approach for the Study of International Relations and Their Progress," in *Progress in Postwar International Relations,* ed. E. Adler and B. Crawford (New York: Columbia University Press, 1991), 43–88.

**42.** We would like to express our gratitude to our research assistant, Sonia Martinez.

# 11

# The Human Rights Dimensions of War in Iraq
## A Framework for Peace Studies

Julie A. Mertus and Maia Carter Hallward

S cholars and practitioners of peace and conflict resolution have written persuasively against the U.S. intervention in Iraq and continue to criticize the U.S. role in "post-Saddam Iraq." However, one powerful framework is largely missing from their analysis: human rights. The invocation of a human rights framework provides a vocabulary and space within which alternatives may be considered and evaluated. By failing to integrate the human rights dimensions of the problem into their analysis, peace studies scholars may be overlooking key support for their general argument and may thus miss an integral component of any long-term solution.

This chapter illustrates how the adoption of a human rights framework may prove useful for analyzing issues of pressing concern to peace studies, such as the use of force, the imposition of sanctions, and general neglect of nonviolent alternative responses to state violence. Although the focus of this paper is Iraq, the human rights framework introduced here has broad applications. Our discussion is divided into three parts. We begin first by defining what is meant by the "human rights framework," pointing especially to its intended goals and emerging utility in policy analysis. With this framework in mind, we then turn to the case study and analyze two human rights records: Iraq's human rights record under Saddam Hussein,[1] and the human rights impact of the international sanctions regime during the same time period. We consider diplomatic options and other avenues for addressing both of these regimes, which, according to human rights principles, should have been more fully considered before the United States resorted to force in Iraq. In conclusion, we underscore the importance of applying a human rights framework to the treatment of prisoners under U.S. control.

## The Human Rights Framework

To the extent that scholars and practitioners can find agreement on the content of human rights, they do so on three fundamental precepts: First, adherence to human rights requires acknowledgment of the dignity of individuals. That this principle focuses on the individual does not negate the importance of community. Individuals are not free-floating entities; they exist and derive meaning through social relationships and communal responsibilities and duties.[2] The identification and enforcement of human rights thus depends greatly on community. As Jean Bethke Elshtain notes, "[rights] are woven into a concept of community . . . [and] . . . are intelligible only in terms of the obligations of individuals to other persons."[3] The idea of human rights, however, necessitates recognition of the agency and identity of the individual that may exist apart from the community. It insists that "essential to [each individual's] dignity, and to a life worthy of a human being, is the simple fact that they are human beings."[4]

The notion that each human being should be treated with dignity solely because he or she is human[5] requires acceptance of a second principle: the moral equality of human beings. "Since all human beings have dignity and need common conditions of growth," Bhikhu Paarekh observes, "their claims to them deserve equal consideration and weight."[6] Equality is inherent to the very premise of human rights, and it informs day-to-day application of human rights norms. This equality does not equate with uniformity, nor should it be confused with homogeneity. Equality and pluralism are not mutually conflicting values but often prove challenging to hold simultaneously to the same degree.

The third integrally related principle pertains to the notion of moral worth. This is the idea that all humans have value and therefore all can make a contribution to society. This notion of worth, like the related concept of equality, does not mean that all people are treated the same or that all benefits and burdens in society must be distributed in identical fashion. Differences in treatment may still exist, but any differential treatment must respect the moral worth and dignity of individuals.[7]

The central task of the human rights framework is to organize these three fundamental principles—the equality principle, the human dignity principle, and the moral worth principle—and more specific widely held values into a structure of legally enforceable rights. The foundational international instruments of the international human rights framework—the Universal Declaration of Human Rights,[8] the International Covenant on Civil and Political Rights,[9] and the International Covenant on Economic, Social, and Cultural Rights[10]—focus on the need to protect individuals from abuse by governmental authority. Moreover, although these documents put all civil and political rights (such as the right to free speech and religion) on an equal footing with economic, social, and cultural rights (such as the right to education or health care), greater attention has been paid by most Western governments and NGOs to civil and political rights. "Politicized by the Cold War-era ideological debates, the human rights system was bifurcated and economic and social rights historically relegated to a secondary and at best 'aspirational' status."[11] This orientation has been reconsidered in recent years with an increasing realization that nonstate actors, groups, and organizations can also be responsible for many atrocities and that economic wrongs may be as grave and in need of redress as any civil and political abuses committed by state actors.[12]

Thus, in recent years NGOs have increasingly argued that human rights standards should be applied to the United Nations as a collective body. The United Nations is not a party to any human rights instruments, and indeed many treaties specify that they will entertain only states as parties, thereby foreclosing participation by nonstates in these regimes. Nonetheless, several grounds have emerged for holding the United Nations accountable to human rights standards whenever it intervenes in a state, for example, when it imposes economic sanctions.[13] One argument for this development is that "the United Nations is bound by international human rights standards as a result of being tasked to promote them by its own internal and constitutional order."[14] In other words, the United Nations is "obliged to pursue and try to realize its own purpose."[15] Alternatively, the United Nations may be said to be bound by international human rights norms when it is acting as a state. The reasoning here is that "states should not be allowed to escape their human rights obligations by forming an international organization to do their dirty work."[16] At a minimum, the argument can be made that because the United Nations is bound by customary international law, it must follow those international human rights standards that have reached customary international law status.[17]

Enforcement of human rights depends on their recognition, not only at the international level but at the regional and domestic (state) level as well. The achievement of any human rights at any level is political in the sense that human rights claims are assertions for power. As Ram Manikkalingam observes, the key to political change is linking "human rights as a strategy to improve the lives of the vulnerable [with] human rights as a universal philosophy that applies to everyone." He explains that "[w]hen the powerless or the dispossessed realize they have human rights because these rights are for everyone, they will be empowered to resist their oppressors and struggle for better conditions and improve their lives. And when the powerful realize that human rights apply to everyone, they will be shamed by a human rights report naming them as abusers of others' human rights."[18]

To some extent, however, the addition of the human rights framework to political discourse only perpetuates conflict. To say that an individual has rights against a state is to create a conflict between the "rights holder" and the "rights withholder." Those who assert their own and others' human rights necessarily conflict with the violators and, in a different way, with bystanders to the abuse. Nonetheless, human rights do provide a common framework and language for hearing disputes, and conflicts over the meaning and application of human rights standards need not turn violent. Human rights may increase citizen participation in problem solving and provide a civil mechanism for translating, reflecting on, and challenging claims to power.[19]

The application of a human rights framework may play a *transformative role* in changing malfunctioning relationships and structural problems that lie at the root of conflict. So instead of just helping to manage conflict, human rights actually wield transformative potential.[20] Certainly human rights institution-building projects can happen in a manner that legitimizes regressive structures, but they can also support new structures and alternative modes of understanding and reacting to conflict. A human rights approach helps unravel the connection between social wrongs and structural and cultural divisions and inequities.[21] At the same time, attention to human rights issues promotes social justice and civic participation and supports the establishment of institutions consonant with these norms.[22]

How does the human rights framework assist in identifying problems lying at the root of violent conflict in Iraq? And to what extent were policy options with respect to U.S. actions in Iraq informed by the human rights framework? Human rights issues appear at each stage of the responses to Iraq. Some critics would point to the failure of the United States to respond effectively to the abusive record of the Saddam Hussein regime. Others would point to the human cost of U.S.-supported United Nations sanctions on Iraq. And yet others would focus on the U.S. decision to intervene in Iraq, or the behavior of U.S. troops and other U.S. actors during and after the intervention (including the mistreatment of detainees and prisoners of war, and the abuse of civilian noncombatants). This chapter examines the application of the human rights framework at all the stages leading up to and including the decision to intervene; it leaves discussion of the human rights abuses during and after intervention to a later date, although the conclusion sketches the contours of how the human rights framework might be applied to examine behavior during and after conflict. One of the premises of this paper is that human rights provides a useful lens for analyzing and interpreting international relations, and that using a human rights framework will affect the problems one sees and the policy options one recommends as a result. While the data may be the same used by mainstream political analysts, human rights provides an added dimension to assessing tyranny and abuse. Applying the human rights framework reveals a different human rights problem in Iraq than was commonly voiced in the political debates.

## Application of Framework, Part 1: Identification of Problem

Not one but two regimes adversely impacted the human rights of the Iraqi people: the regime of Saddam Hussein and the international sanctions regime. While the Bush administration was interested in deploying the language of human rights in order to change the former—through military-induced regime change—it was consistently opposed to any changes in the latter. In this essay we assert that if international human rights and humanitarian norms are to have any credibility, the effects of both regimes must be acknowledged and addressed. In turn, recognizing human rights concerns will contribute toward improving the human rights situation in Iraq and may also help to stabilize the country, with a minimum of violence.

### Human Rights Violations within Iraq

The Iraqi people suffered a consistent pattern of gross violations of internationally recognized human rights under Saddam Hussein, including political imprisonment, torture, and summary and arbitrary executions. This section outlines these violations because, while they are often cited by the Bush administration as justification for invading Iraq and removing Saddam Hussein, the timing and nature of the abuses shed light on whether this case justified humanitarian intervention according to generally agreed-upon criteria.

Iraq used a variety of mechanisms to squelch political dissent, including house-to-house searches; arbitrary arrests, often in large numbers; surveillance; harassment and questioning of family members; detention of targeted individuals, such as those returning to Iraq pursuant to amnesties, at unknown locations; and the use of torture before and during interrogation.[23] Any form of street protest was put down by force. During the demonstrations in March 1991, for example, armed security forces and party loyalists opened fire on the crowd without warning, killing approximately thirty people and wounding many more.[24]

The U.S. Department of State reported that the Iraqi government's security apparatus included militias attached to the president, the Ba'ath party, and the Interior Ministry. The security forces played a central role in maintaining an environment of intimidation and fear.[25] Former detainees reported being picked up by police without a warrant or even an explanation. The vast majority of political detainees were held incommunicado and were routinely physically and psychologically tortured during interrogation.[26]

With respect to detentions, Iraqi authorities did not follow international standards of due process. Prisoners were routinely held in detention arbitrarily, perhaps up to six months before being brought before a court.[27] Judicial review was not provided. The Revolutionary Command Council was both the legislative and executive body under the provisional constitution of 1968, and Saddam Hussein served as its chairman, in addition to serving as the president and the prime minister.[28]

The difference between extrajudicial killings and judicial punishment was blurred in Iraq. "The government rarely announce[d] executions or [made] public any official statistics in relation to the death penalty," Amnesty International explained, adding, "Given the secrecy surrounding them in many cases it is impossible to determine whether the reported executions [were] judicial punishments or carried out extrajudicially."[29] The death penalty in Iraq could be applied to those convicted of committing robbery with a weapon, members of the civil service or armed forces who committed theft or robbery, those convicted three times of desertion or assisting deserters, smugglers of Iraqi cultural artifacts, and those convicted of organizing prostitution. The death penalty was also applied for smuggling vehicles and machinery out of Iraq.[30] Many of those judicially executed were charged with offenses punishable by death according to the Iraqi penal code, including Article 156, relating to membership in a party or organization whose aim is to change the system of government, and Article 175, relating to plotting against the state, both of which were used in the past to execute prisoners of conscience. In some cases those executed were buried in mass graves in the vicinity of the prison. Families of those executed were often not allowed to hold public mourning.[31]

In addition, substantial forced expulsions of peoples from their land raised serious human rights implications. In one prominent case, thousands of Kurdish and other non-Arab families were forcibly expelled by the security forces from their homes in the north to areas controlled by the two Kurdish political parties in Iraqi Kurdistan on the basis of their ethnic origin. The authorities gave targeted Kurdish families the choice of going either to southern Iraq or to the Kurdish provinces. These forcibly displaced families faced harsher consequences if they chose to go to the northern Kurdish areas. They were not permitted to take their possessions and Iraqi authorities confiscated many of their belongings, including such items as their food rationing cards.[32] Amnesty International researchers found that "[t]hese mass human rights violations and the climate of terror inside the country have forced thousands of Iraqi nationals to flee the country illegally and seek asylum in neighboring countries, but also in many other countries worldwide."[33]

While all citizens in Iraq experienced denial of their human rights, Iraqi Kurds and Shi'a Muslims were among those singled out for forced displacement, mass arrests, and summary executions. The 1987–89 Anfal campaign against the Kurds was among the worst of many anti-Kurd campaigns.[34] Researchers documented the following gross violations of human rights during this time: mass summary executions and mass disappearances of many tens of thousands of noncombatants; widespread use of chemical weapons, including mustard gas and the nerve agent GB, or sarin;[35] and the wholesale destruction of some 2,000 villages, which are described in government documents as having been "burned," "destroyed," "demolished," or "purified."[36] The UN High Commissioner for Human Rights raised concerns regarding "the fact that chemical weapons have been used on the Kurdish civilian population, by the forced displacement of hundreds of thousands of Kurds and the destruction of Kurdish towns and villages, as well as . . . tens of thousands of displaced Kurds living in camps in the north of Iraq, and . . . the deportation of thousands of Kurdish families."[37]

In the aftermath of the chemical attacks, the government set out to destroy 700 villages, burning and bulldozing them. The clearance of these villages created a buffer zone between government and rebel zones. Thereafter, the government ordered all those remaining in prohibited areas to relocate to camps or be stripped of their citizenship, on grounds equivalent to military desertion. Following this decree, a nationwide census was conducted, according to which individuals were forced to define themselves as either Arab or Kurdish, which had consequences for other minority groups who continued to live in Kurdish areas.[38]

Shi'a Muslims in Iraq were another group subject to arbitrary arrest and torture. Thousands of Shi'a Muslims were arrested during the Iran-Iraq war and charged with supporting the 1979 Iranian revolution, whereupon many "disappeared" and others died under torture or were executed. Following this campaign, during the 1980s over half a million Shi'a were forcibly expelled to Iran. Before the expulsion of their families, however, approximately 50,000–70,000 men and boys were arrested and imprisoned indefinitely without charge. Shi'a Muslim clerics continued to "disappear" after the Gulf War at an accelerated rate.[39]

In sum, the human rights climate in Iraq was long deplorable. The list of human rights abuses committed by the government included what has been called "a supreme right from which no derogation is permitted even in time of public emergency": the right to life.[40] Nonetheless, unlike other cases in which human rights factors were part of the articulated justification for armed intervention, there was no particular immediate and extreme human rights crisis at the time of the U.S.-led intervention.[41] The conventional test for humanitarian intervention is a "shock the conscience" standard, which "requires proof of human rights abuses likely to lead to the physical harm or death of a large group of people before force can be used as a response."[42] In this case, the most egregious abuses had been committed in the past, and the kinds of violations continuing before intervention—such as denial of due process and abuse of political prisoners—are addressed by human rights mechanisms and international diplomacy and therefore did not justify armed intervention. Moreover, unlike other cases where "humanitarian intervention" was invoked to justify the use of force, in this case the population subjected to grievous human rights violations did not request the intervention. On the contrary, the vast majority of citizens in Iraq—including those critical of Saddam Hussein—expressed a desire to *not* be "liberated" by the United States.[43] Under such conditions, armed intervention pushed the doctrine of "humanitarian intervention" beyond its legal and moral bounds.[44]

## The Human Rights Records of the Sanctions Regime

The United Nations Security Council voted in May 2003 to adopt a U.S.-sponsored resolution supporting the formal lifting of UN economic sanctions against Iraq.[45] The UN sanctions regime against Iraq had been instituted, also under U.S. sponsorship, after Iraq invaded Kuwait in August 1990.[46] The thirteen-year-old sanctions regime was, as Christopher Joyner has noted, "the most extensive and prolonged ever applied by the United Nations . . . the most economically devastating on their targeted citizenry as well as the most politically controversial among human rights advocates."[47]

The articulated legal basis for the economic sanctions was said to rest in Chapter VII of the UN Charter, which grants the Security Council the authority to determine the existence of any threat to international peace and to respond appropriately.[48] Specifically, Chapter VI provides that the Security Council "may decide what measures not involving the use of armed force are to be employed to give effect to its decisions, and . . . call upon the Members of the United Nations to apply such measures."[49] The Security Council's discretion is not unlimited. Article 24 of the charter directs the council "to act in accordance with the Purposes and Principles of the United Nations." Article 1 of the UN Charter makes clear that the promotion of human rights is a fundamental purpose and principle of the organization. Thus, in issuing sanctions against Iraq, the Security Council was tasked with consideration of the human rights of the Iraqi people.

Security Council Resolution 661, which initially applied to both Iraq and Kuwait, called for all nations to end all trade with Iraq. Specifically, countries were instructed to end the "import into their territories of all commodities and products originating in Iraq or Kuwait exported there from after the date of the present resolution." Supplies used for "strictly medical purposes" and "in humanitarian circumstances," specifically foodstuffs, were exempt from the ban.[50] The Security Council established a committee to make judgments regarding the applicability of the exceptions.[51] In practice, the list of humanitarian articles deemed to be "nonessential" or "dual-use" objects, serving both military and civilian purposes, was extensive. As one commentator observed, "Textbooks, spare parts for ambulances, nails, a variety of textiles, light bulbs and other commodities that were once readily available, are now unavailable to Iraqi persons."[52] Iraqis thereby lacked the supplies needed to maintain and improve a civilian infrastructure. This negatively affected their economic and social rights by limiting their opportunities for and access to jobs, education, and health care, which in turn detracted from their ability to engage with the regime and advocate for their political and civil rights.[53]

The human costs of the sanctions were particularly great because they had been levied against a country already devastated by six weeks of intensive bombing. As noted by the World Health Organization (WHO), many public facilities, such as water purification and sewage treatment systems and electric generators, were destroyed, thereby hindering provision of health care. Sanctions often prevented the repair of such facilities, and the restrictions on imports, coupled with lack of foreign exchange, meant that families had little money for food or medicine.[54] Undersecretary Martti Ahtisaari provided the first early warning on the humanitarian impact of the Gulf War, emphasizing the need for immediate repair of energy, communications, and other infrastructure projects in addition to emergency food and medicine, in March 1991. In July 1991, the secretary-general's executive delegate, Sadruddin Aga Khan, reported the need for a $22 billion investment in Iraq's reconstruction and humanitarian assistance, with the mere necessities for the first year totaling $6.8 billion. However, Security Council Resolutions 706 and 712 established a cap on oil sales that fell far below these needs.[55] This lack of materials and revenue had a major impact on the economic and social well-being of the Iraqi people and severely impinged on their rights to make a living, receive health care, and obtain a decent education.

The WHO presented data on health, morbidity, and mortality in 1996, and other agencies, such as UNICEF and numerous faith-based NGOs, also prepared reports on the dire economic situation that threatened the human rights of those already most at risk in Iraq.[56] Pressure to modify sanctions grew. A UN mission sent to Iraq at the conclusion of the Gulf War reported "an imminent catastrophe . . . if minimum life supporting needs are not met rapidly."[57] The UN Security Council responded with Resolutions 706[58] and 712,[59] authorizing the sale of up to $1.6 billion of oil, the proceeds of which would be deposited into a UN-controlled escrow account and then divided between humanitarian use, UN operating expenses in Iraq, and compensation to Kuwait. Iraq initially resisted implementation of these two resolutions, arguing that they violated Iraqi sovereignty. Four years later, however, Iraq accepted a modified version of the plan.

On April 14, 1995, Resolution 986[60] created the United Nations Oil-for-Food Program.[61] The agreement allowed for the sale of oil to pay for humanitarian and other vital imports.[62] Even with the creation of the Oil-for-Food Program, little of the money—only $172 per person per year—reached the Iraqi people.[63] And of the items ordered from oil sales after 1996, only 60 percent arrived in Iraq.[64] Without the free monthly food basket provided through distribution centers, 90 percent of the Iraqi people were beneath the poverty line, and even with the service, 55 percent lived in conditions of poverty.[65]

The Oil-for-Food Program did little to change the humanitarian crisis in Iraq, because importation of supplies for repairing water purification and sewage treatment systems and communications and transportation networks damaged during the Gulf War remained prohibited by the sanctions.[66] Only about half the people living in Iraqi cities had potable water. This number dropped to 33 percent in the rural areas.[67] Seventy percent of childhood deaths (which annually totaled about 90,000 more than before the first Gulf War)[68] were from preventable illnesses such as diarrhea, stemming from inadequate water treatment facilities and the dumping of raw sewage into the water supply.[69] Women and children were disproportionately affected by the sanctions,[70] with UNICEF officials estimating that as many as five thousand to six thousand Iraqi children were dying each month primarily because of sanctions.[71] The poor economic conditions in Iraq also led to a severe drop in literacy, particularly among females, owing to the lack of funds for school supplies, rebuilding damaged schools, and paying teachers. Female literacy dropped to 45 percent in 1995 from a prewar rate of 80 percent,[72] and 23.7 percent of children were not attending primary school.[73]

The Oil-for-Food Program's failure to address humanitarian needs is underscored by successive high-level resignations of UN staff charged with implementation of the program. In 1998, Denis Halliday, the UN humanitarian coordinator in Baghdad and overseer of the Oil-for-Food Program, quit his post when it was clear that the Iraqi population was not receiving its daily minimum dietary requirements.[74] Halliday later became a lobbyist against economic sanctions.[75] Halliday's replacement, Hans von Sponeck, lasted only fifteen months in the position before moral concerns about the politicization of humanitarian aid convinced him to step down.[76] Almost simultaneously, Jutta Burghart, chief of the United Nations' World Food Program in Iraq, also resigned in protest over the failure of the United Nations to address the negative impact of sanctions on the civilian population.[77]

Despite the attention generated by these high-level resignations, the human rights dimensions of the Iraqi sanctions went largely unrecognized by a U.S. government that regarded economic, social, and cultural rights as foreign to U.S. legal traditions and thus an inappropriate focus of U.S. human rights policy. However, in the new policy environment that emerged in the late 1980s and early 1990s, nongovernmental advocacy groups widened the scope of their human rights work. The Geneva-based International Council on Human Rights explains:

> They continued to press governments to respect civil and political rights, but in addition called on them to implement the full range of human rights contained in the Universal Declaration. Much more attention began to be given to economic, social and cultural rights.[78]

This new focus brought the human rights impact of the sanctions squarely to the attention of many advocacy groups that had previously spent little or no time on any issue involving economic, social, or cultural rights.

Several strong human rights arguments were levied against the sanctions. As mentioned previously, sanctions ran against Article 1 of the UN Charter, which specifies that a central purpose of the United Nations is promoting and encouraging respect for human rights. Specific rights implicated include the right to life (Article 6, the International Covenant on Civil and Political Rights, or ICCPR); health (Article 12, the Convention on Economic, Social, and Cultural Rights, or ICESCR); education (Article 13, ICESCR); and an adequate standard of living (Article 11, ICESCR).[79] Also applicable were the specific thematic human rights instruments, such as the Convention on the Rights of the Child. Sanctions ran afoul of this convention's requirement that all states "ensure to the maximum extent possible the survival and development of the child" and "take appropriate measures to diminish infant and child mortality."

At the time sanctions were initially imposed on Iraq, some policymakers may have viewed them as an acceptable nonviolent response to the human rights abuses in Iraq and to the threat to international peace and security posed by Iraq.[80] The sanctions may have held inherent political appeal in that they appeared to be a measured response to aggression, falling short of military force.[81] Over time, however, it became clear that the sanctions themselves were a form of violence that led to even greater violence.[82] A growing body of literature now questions the ethical and legal grounds of sanctions.[83] Former UN secretary-general Boutros Boutros-Ghali pinpointed one of the main issues: "Sanctions, as is generally recognized, are a blunt instrument. They raise the ethical question of whether suffering inflicted on vulnerable groups in the target country is a legitimate means of exerting pressure on political leaders whose behavior is unlikely to be affected by the plight of their subjects."[84] In the case of Iraq, a strong argument can be made that the sanctions regime not only failed to address the anti–human rights tendencies of Iraq but opened the door to new abuses.[85]

That the Iraqi government contributed to the negative impact of sanctions and worsened it through its own behavior does not absolve the Security Council and individual sanctioning states of their legal and moral responsibility in the matter. When, for a decade, dozens of studies documented in great detail the suffering caused by sanctions in Iraq,[86] the antihumanitarian impact of the sanctions was a foreseeable one that carried legal responsibility. Moreover, even if the humanitarian impact can be deemed unforeseeable at the time, after the human cost of the measures became known they should have been discontinued, and other options pursued. Alternatively, at the very least, continuation of the sanctions should have been conditioned on a new Security Council resolution calling for such measures.[87]

The application of a human rights framework would have led to a change in course in the sanctions regimes. Would application of the framework also have led to a significant change in the U.S. response to the human rights abuses committed by Saddam Hussein? The next section considers this question by exploring alternative means of addressing the human rights abuses of the two regimes (that of Saddam Hussein and that of the sanctions) while also upholding the human rights of the Iraqi people. Skeptics who may see the following suggestions as "time-consuming" or "idealistic" should remember that war also requires advance planning and a certain set of ideals, as the Bush administration continually reminds us.[88] Indeed, the United States planned the war in Iraq for months—or even years, if one goes back to the first Gulf War—while devoting only twenty-eight days to planning for peace.[89] Further, as time generally reveals, military responses do not necessarily bring about a quick solution, especially in terms of human rights, which require some semblance of stability, law, and order to be upheld. That said, what other responses existed that might have addressed the human rights problem in Iraq?

## Application of Framework, Part 2: Identification of Responses

The United States judged traditional diplomatic channels insufficient for dealing with a "threat" such as Saddam Hussein and devoted very little energy to pursuing negotiations with the Iraqi regime itself. Legal principles governing the pursuit of war were stretched beyond their traditional application, and U.S. conceptions of "sovereignty" and "self-defense" varied significantly from those set forth in the UN Charter. Although the Bush administration eventually did approach the United Nations in pursuit of a mandate, its original policy was strictly unilateral, and as Richard Falk has noted, Bush has publicly claimed "the personal authority to make war any time and any place he alone chooses."[90] Secretary of State Colin Powell's visit to the United Nations was largely a last-minute affair that gave little time to deliberative process, and the United States rejected other proposals, such as that of Canada,[91] as generally inadequate. Indeed, the United States practically gave the United Nations an ultimatum for action and provided monetary incentives for countries to join the "coalition of the willing."[92] When the Security Council did not approve the resolution sponsored by the United States, the UK, and Spain, Bush delivered an ultimatum to Saddam Hussein.[93] Further, as Bob Woodward's recent book reveals, the George W. Bush administration chose war even before all diplomatic channels had been tried.[94] At present, the international community is beginning to see the repercussions of the U.S.-led invasion, including the worsening situation of Iraqi social, health, and security services. But before the decision to go into Iraq—as is the case whenever armed intervention is considered—all results were hypothetical and all strategies were possible options. As a result, when applying our human rights framework, we rely primarily on pre-invasion predictions for war's repercussions and use actual current statistics for mortality, disease, education, and access to foodstuffs only to emphasize the accuracy or inaccuracy of predictions and their relevance to human rights. The goal of this chapter is to provide a more general human rights framework for assessing policy options *before* armed intervention rather than assessing the specifics of the Iraqi case. As a result, following the human rights framework articulated above, we begin by evaluating the impact of alternative intervention strategies on civilians.

## Humanitarian Costs of Armed Intervention

When evaluating the pros and cons of humanitarian intervention, policymakers and activists must consider the costs of the planned intervention in human rights terms and weigh these against the benefits. The war strategy announced by the Bush administration involved attacking Baghdad, a crowded city of five to six million civilians, all of whom would be drastically affected by this incursion.[95] Military planners suggested using "shock and awe" tactics to "deter and overpower an adversary through the adversary's perception and fear of his vulnerability and our own invincibility."[96] Harlan Ullman's ideas, which formed the basis of Pentagon war plans, included "destroy[ing] everything that makes life in Baghdad livable" with 800 cruise missiles in the first two days of war, in order to create an effect reminiscent of Hiroshima.[97]

Military plans to attack Baghdad could not avoid civilian casualties in a city of five to six million.[98] Forecasts of the potential impact of a U.S.-led war in Iraq vary greatly, but all envisioned a substantial loss of civilian lives. MedAct reported that up to four million could die if the war involved nuclear weapons, and 48,000–260,000 could die in a more contained war, with postwar deaths adding another 200,000.[99] Friends Committee on National Legislation (FCNL) estimated 50,000–500,000 Iraqi casualties during bombing.[100] These estimates did not address the military deaths—Iraqi and U.S.—that could result from the war, especially if nuclear, chemical, or biological attacks where used, as was believed to be a possibility. Reports also indicated that the United States would continue to use the depleted uranium weapons used in 1991, which are believed to be responsible for the dramatic rise in cancer deaths in parts of Iraq and among Gulf War veterans.[101]

The impact of war on social and economic rights was forecast to be, and has proved to be, substantial. Various agencies believed that the war's aftermath could include civil war, famine, epidemics, and total collapse of agriculture, manufacturing, and health services.[102] UN humanitarian planners predicted that as many as 4.5 to 9.5 million people would need outside food to survive once any war began,[103] and Refugees International forecast up to two million internally displaced persons within Iraq, and one to two million refugees.[104] In 1994, after the first Gulf War, malaria cases rose from 95 cases per 100,000 to 2,600 per 100,000. With the low vaccination rate, resulting from sanction-impacted health programs, for diseases such as measles and meningitis, officials estimated that the spread of disease would likely be worse than before.[105] And indeed, while we have yet to witness the lasting effects of the recent war, maternal anemia has increased, threatening the lives of pregnant women, children's deaths from diarrhea have increased, and the incidence of uncommunicable diseases such as diabetes has risen from 20–25 percent to 30–35 percent in some areas. Further, after the destruction of the communications network, the centralized health system has been severely weakened, and many hospitals have neither medicine nor funds for staffing.[106]

Armed intervention often exacerbates existing human rights violations or creates the opportunity for new forms of abuse.[107] This case is likely to be no exception. Middle East experts predicted that war in Iraq would usher in a new round of communal violence. With no clear emergent Iraqi opposition before the war, forecasters believed Iraq would face a battle for succession, which could include bloody civil war and ethnic conflict, with various groups—including Sunni Arabs, Kurds, and Shi'a—wanting to separate from Baghdad.[108] Not only would conflict among these groups put civilian lives in danger, but civilian groups would likely be targeted intentionally as members of the "enemy" community. Further, sectarian violence decreases the chances for a viable government that upholds the political, civil, economic, and social rights of all its citizens. Rather, sectarian-based governments, such as Saddam Hussein's Ba'athist regime, tend to favor one subgroup of society over others, thereby reducing others' access to public goods and impinging on their human rights, which in turn breeds tension and conflict.

War with Iraq should also be evaluated in terms of the impact on U.S. civilians, since many predicted that the war would contribute to rising anti-American sentiment and the increased targeting of Americans around the world, extending beyond the Arab world to the large Asian Muslim population, who saw U.S. actions in Iraq as anti-Muslim. Past military interventions have often proved counterproductive, generating what the CIA calls "blowback." As Glen Gersmehl, national coordinator of the Lutheran Peace Fellowship, noted, "Even wars considered 'successful' have often caused serious future problems."[109] U.S. training of Osama bin Laden is a case in point, as is Saddam Hussein, who was supported by leaders (including Secretary of Defense Donald Rumsfeld) as a U.S. ally. As one politician has noted, "The long-term consequences of power used arrogantly are hard to measure" but carry severe consequences.[110] In addition, military spending has drastically reduced money for schools, health care, social security, urban infrastructure, and other domestic programs and fails to address current economic difficulties. Estimates of the war's cost ranged from $100 to $200 billion, with another $600 billion to $1.6 trillion for nonmilitary peacekeeping and reconstruction costs.[111] Senator Richard Byrd highlighted the squandering of a projected $5.6 trillion budget surplus, and the enormous projected deficit incurred, by the Bush administration. Safety deficits have increased as well, since such important services as fire and police protection are short staffed due to deployment of reserve and National Guard troops.[112]

Regardless of motive, and even with the most careful of methods, war has a negative impact on the humanitarian and human rights climate of any country, and in the case of Iraq that impact was forecast as particularly severe.[113] The kind of war planned for Iraq was "expected to cause incidental loss of civilian life, injury to civilians, [and] damage to civilian objects . . . which would be excessive in relation to the concrete and direct military advantage anticipated."[114] At the same time, the war violated the principle of necessity, since nonviolent alternatives existed that would respect human rights and humanitarian norms while better promoting long-term U.S. and international interests in peace and justice.

## Diplomatic Options

Several diplomatic options existed in the case of Iraq—options not given adequate time, resources, or political will. One notable case in point is weapons inspections, which, had they been given adequate support, might have succeeded not only in demonstrating the refusal of the international community to tolerate weapons of mass destruction but also in strengthening a nonviolent political mechanism for finding and removing such weapons. While the UN inspection process was much criticized as inadequate at the time, independent surveillance by the U.S. State Department also advised that it was premature to conclude that mysterious Iraqi trailers were used in making biological weapons. Indeed, the U.S. military invasion has failed to uncover any stockpiles of weapons, and many doubted the existence of weapons of mass destruction before the invasion. As UN chief weapons inspector Hans Blix noted, the United States conflated "unaccounted-for" weapons with "existing" weapons, which have yet to materialize.[115]

Even if the weapons had existed, removing the threat of chemical, nuclear, and biological weapons would reduce only one potential human rights abuse in Saddam Hussein's repertoire. However, disarmament (in the case of his possession of such weapons) would reduce his capacity to inflict harm on his own people and on surrounding countries. The presence of weapons inspectors would also have kept an international eye on Saddam's regime, thereby likely reducing the scale of public abuses of the Iraqi people. Documentation of the abuses, if seen by high-level authorities and if broadcast on international media, could also have led to international pressure for political reform, and UN support for that process. The lack of international access to Iraq, and the lack of political will to force Saddam Hussein to change or step down (as seen in the failure of the U.S. political and military leadership to depose him in the first Gulf War or its aftermath), legitimized and perpetuated Saddam's tyrannical control over his own people.

The failure of the United States to remove Saddam Hussein from power when it had the opportunity, combined with the ongoing support of the United States for other repressive regimes, further detracted from diplomatic efforts to address the crisis. As a result, the United States could have increased its power and supported the Iraqi people (as well as others facing human rights abuses around the world) by ending its support for similarly abusive regimes elsewhere and by maintaining a consistent stance on human rights. Given the U.S. record toward Iraq in the past, as well as its continued support for Israel's occupation of the West Bank and Gaza and for the Egyptian and Saudi Arabian restrictions on their own populations— not to mention the long history of U.S. involvement in Latin America—the United States was not guiltless. By supporting UN mechanisms such as weapons inspections, removing the harmful sanctions, and supporting democratic civil society movements rather than oppressive governments, the United States could advance the cause of human rights and peace. Instead, as senior UN officials and constitutional experts insisted, going to war in Iraq without a UN resolution would place the United States in violation of international law and the UN Charter, and in disregard of the "overwhelming opposition by most of the 191 member states."[116]

Another alternative to war—while not strictly diplomatic in the classical sense—involves regional partnerships and leadership training. Michael Isherwood, a lieutenant colonel in the U.S. Air Force, suggested fostering "cooperative security alliances with conservative Persian Gulf nations" and framing the administration's policy within an inclusive Middle East strategy that includes Israel and the Palestinian territories as well as Iran.[117] Without the long-term cooperation of Iraq's neighbors and European allies, any

U.S. initiative—even if "successful" in the short term—will not provide a clear solution. Regional partnerships would provide an opportunity for interaction among civil society representatives from a variety of Middle Eastern countries and thereby strengthen the ties among people sharing a common goal of peace with justice. The regional approach would also expose members of individual countries to different social and political systems and could serve as an opportunity for encouraging pluralism, democracy, and human rights in a new cadre of leaders. The United States failed to develop alternative leaders in Iraq after the first Gulf War and ignored those Iraqis who rose up to resist Saddam Hussein, leaving them to be crushed after the United States withdrew.

Isherwood's plan for preparing this new cadre of leaders involves a long-term civic development program aimed at Iraq's youth and would involve sending hundreds of Iraqis to other countries "to gain theoretical and hands-on experience in how a modern civil society provides for its citizenry, administers municipal governments, and manages key industries and public utilities."[118] The plan would include university study and a lengthy on-the-job internship and would be continued and repeated for over a decade, thereby providing social and intellectual resources for the new regime.[119] Isherwood also suggested infusing extensive development funds for rebuilding Iraq's shattered economy and infrastructure, as well as revitalizing agriculture, water purification, and manufacturing and providing much-needed income-generating jobs. Such efforts could have begun in UN- or U.S.-protected safe havens governed by an alternative leadership in the regions of the no-fly zones and could have included social services such as schools, hospitals, and a legal system.[120]

Ending the economic sanctions would have had a similar effect on society, since it would have lessened the Iraqis' dependence on Saddam Hussein and would thereby have removed one of the key tools with which he manipulated public support. The sanctions improved Saddam's standing as an Arab leader, marking his symbolic protest of the West. Moreover, by encouraging black marketers and cronies of the government, sanctions weakened the resources available to civil society. Further, because Saddam Hussein controlled access to critical food and material supplies, the sanctions reduced the likelihood of political opposition to his regime, since this would have entailed tremendous risk. Recent nonviolent depositions of authoritarian regimes have often been led by elements of civil society, notably the middle class. The potential for Iraqi civilians to rise up and politically oust Saddam Hussein's government was unlikely until the civilian economy resumed and brought with it normal flows of goods, services, and information into the country.[121] Despite such restrictions, however, Iraqis genuinely wanted to overthrow their oppressive government, and there were nonviolent ways in which this could have been supported and encouraged.

## Supporting Nonviolent Change from Within

The theory of nonviolence includes those who use nonviolence *strategically*, in the pursuit of a concrete aim, and those for whom nonviolence is a *way of life*, "an attitude of mind, an emotional orientation towards loving care and concern."[122] Nonviolence theory reformulates power in terms of human willpower and the moral power of truth and love. Its strength comes from its pure energy, which is not "being drained by negative emotions such as worry, self-pity or dislike" and therefore can be applied in its entirety to the problem at hand.[123] The basis of nonviolent power stems from a belief that power depends on the consent of the governed and hence can be removed, thereby denying the ruler authoritative power. Strategically, this translates into "a technique used to control, combat and destroy the opponent's power by nonviolent means of wielding power."[124] For nonviolent theorists, power is pluralistic, and political power is fragile because it depends on many groups within society for reinforcement. This contradicts the traditional view of political power, which assumes that governments have monolithic control over their citizens.[125]

One-third of the world experienced (and participated in) successful nonviolent regime change during the past twenty years, including citizens of the Philippines, South Africa, and Romania. In the past fifty years, two-thirds of the world's population has been affected by nonviolent social change, through the actions, for example, of Mahatma Gandhi in India, Martin Luther King Jr. in the United States, and anti-Nazi resisters in Denmark and Norway.[126] The authors of *A Force More Powerful* explain, "[Nonviolent strategic action] involves the use of a panoply of forceful sanctions—strikes, boycotts, civil disobedience, disrupting the functions of government, even nonviolent sabotage—in accordance with a strategy for undermining an oppressor's pillars of support. It is not about making a point, it's about taking power."[127] In dire socioeconomic situations such as Saddam's Iraq, in which there was little functioning economy to boycott and a wide dispersal of government informants throughout society—which led to a lack of trust and fear of speaking openly against the regime—such a strategy poses a challenge. We now explore how this could possibly have worked in the case of Iraq by the use of some nonviolent alternatives to war—alternatives that may have proven more positive in regard to human rights.

Before the war, many policy analysts delivered a post mortem on Iraqi civil society. This was tremendously premature, however.[128] Civil society groups existed, albeit largely underground and facing enormous obstacles. Between Saddam's use of "terror and fear to wipe out civil society in Iraq"[129] and the economic and social destruction resulting from the first Gulf War and twelve years of sanctions, such groups had limited physical, spiritual, emotional, and psychological resources for open dissent. The sanctions also produced a generation of youth hardened to a life of suffering, weakened physically, and denied access to the educational and social resources necessary for informed, active democratic citizenship. Decades of authoritarian rule diminished the willingness of those whose lives were already insecure to engage politically, and with no democratic alternatives, people opted for stability rather than political freedoms. However, educated Iraqis had—and still have—the capabilities and the desire to create a new society. Such groups as FCNL and a host of religious leaders have long criticized the plans for a U.S. military occupation of post-Saddam Iraq, suggesting instead that a true democratic opposition should be fostered and the United Nations should plan for any postwar administration. U.S. support of local democracy, in the form of supporting an active civil society, is especially important given Iraqi distrust of U.S. motives in Iraq. Iraqis have ample reason for distrusting the U.S. intention to create a "free and democratic Iraq": Not only did George H. W. Bush refuse to provide U.S. help for the Iraqi uprisings against Saddam Hussein in 1991, but the current President Bush ignored emissaries from the Iraqi government before the 2003 invasion, and his promises of a Palestinian democratic state have been followed by continued support for Israeli prime minister Ariel Sharon's violent tactics.[130]

Social spending in Iraq was considerable before the first Gulf War, creating a society that was well educated and thriving because of the billions of dollars Saddam's party spent on health, education, housing, transportation, industry, and other aspects of infrastructure. Like many other parts of the world, Arab societies today have a critical mass of highly educated people with considerable experience in advocacy and organizing. While oil revenues and resource wealth may indeed contribute to authoritarianism and large internal security forces, there are pockets of civil society waiting to be tapped, which, if given the freedom to express dissent, will work to change the system.

Numerous international delegations visited civil society groups and social institutions within Iraq, including Voices in the Wilderness, Christian Peacemaker Teams, and American Friends Service Committee, and academic groups of all political orientations sought to witness human rights violations and to report on their own experiences. Iraqi groups were ready to speak out and actively pursue a new society, but they needed the assurance that they would be protected from repression. Iraqi political exile Kamil Mahdi expounded on Iraqis' vibrant political tradition, which includes "the determination of people to challenge tyranny and bring about political change."[131] Despite Saddam Hussein's attacks on opposition, waves of resistance continued over the decades. One major reason none succeeded was that regional and international leaders consistently supported Saddam rather than the Iraqi people.[132] As one nonviolent Iraqi opposition leader noted, the 22 million Iraqis who despised Saddam Hussein's dictatorship represented an enormous force for political change.[133] Millions of people around the world voiced their opposition to war and their support for Iraqi citizens. Given such numbers, the results of popular resistance, matched by the support of international institutions, would have been remarkable.

Nonviolent peace researchers Peter Ackerman and Jack DuVall suggested the transformative potential of scattered protests all over Iraq by a wide spectrum of Iraqi society. As resisters made their presence felt, even if it was only as a nuisance, the very knowledge that Saddam Hussein was being openly opposed would have lessened others' fear of engaging in further resistance. Especially if the resistance had gained the support of police and soldiers, Saddam's regime would not have been able to counter such widespread dissent. Widespread civilian-based protest would not have provided convenient targets, and Saddam would have had to rely on the outermost security forces—those who were also the least skilled. Further, as opposition increased, dissenting elements within the government might have felt free to defect, thereby making it even more difficult to conduct business as usual.[134]

Recently, civil society groups throughout the Arab world have become more vocal and public, demanding rights and representation. Although many governments restrict the activities of NGOs and make it difficult to obtain permits, such groups do form, even around controversial issues such as honor killings.[135] Throughout the region, people took to the streets—nonviolently—to protest the U.S. invasion in Iraq. Peaceful marches in Bahrain included members of NGOs and parliament and human rights activists, and elsewhere the Arab world is voicing its displeasure with the course of events.[136] Many noted the ethnic divisions within Iraqi society—exploited by Saddam over the years—and predicted the likelihood of conflict if Saddam was removed.[137] However, if civil society had been constructively engaged, as it was in Northern Ireland's concord organizations, groups could have begun to transcend their differences and learned to work together, especially since they had the shared goal of removing an authoritarian leader.[138] George W. Bush argued that removing Saddam Hussein would give the Iraqis "freedom," but without engaging and addressing communal divisions within Iraq, Iraqis will not "achieve the civil peace that is the precondition for democracy, freedom, and life itself."[139]

Middle East experts suggested that the United States support civil society groups around the Arab world and encourage them to advocate and work for regime change in Iraq.[140] Following lessons learned from similar programs in the Balkans, the United States could have provided skills training and resources—educational, organizational, technical, and media—to create leaders and organizers within Iraqi society.[141] As it did with the student demonstrations in Serbia, the United States could have promoted the visibility of such groups, giving them media coverage and providing emotional and financial support.[142] Fostering civil society exchanges between U.S. and Iraqi groups could have provided training in democratic practice and would have encouraged collaboration and sharing in areas including education, culture, science, and health.[143] By creating positive relationships, Iraqi citizens would have felt connected to the world and gained a picture of U.S. citizens different from that posed by Saddam Hussein. Similarly, U.S. citizens would have gained a wider awareness of the world beyond U.S. borders. Additionally, building bridges and creating opportunities for positive interaction internally, among Iraqi groups, and externally, with groups from the United States, could have helped reduce the resentment and distrust that increases tensions between parties and can lead to future conflicts and abuse of human rights.[144]

The existence of nonviolent alternatives to war is a key factor in crafting a human rights argument against war. The principles of nonviolence support basic human rights and seek the prevention of armed conflict (which inevitably results in loss of life) while upholding a commitment to freedom, justice, and equality. Nonviolence is a powerful means of addressing human rights abuses in a manner that does not of necessity create more abuses in the process. In the case of Iraq, nonviolent options did exist, and because these measures would better respect the humanity of the Iraqi people, the United States and other world powers were obligated to explore them—and still are as they consider the future of Iraq.

## Conclusion

Recent events have demonstrated just how important human rights concepts are to foreign policy and democratic practices. Human rights principles and issues must guide foreign policy in the conduct of conflict and its after-math, in addition to guiding any decision to intervene and seeing that the course of any intervention remains respectful of the human dignity of civil-ians and combatants. As of this writing, recent reports raise disturbing ques-tions about U.S. soldiers' abuse of Iraqi prisoners. The abuse has also led to an extensive army report that suggests that illegal tactics were used and sanctioned by the Pentagon to interrogate prisoners.[145] Whether the Penta-gon explicitly ordered such human rights–violating practices is largely ir-relevant (although it appears that high-level officials were involved in ordering the interrogation regimen), because the abuses took place under the rubric of the U.S. occupying authority and its claim to be replacing Sad-dam Hussein's abusive regime with a better, more just and more democratic alternative. Moreover, U.S. officials knew about the abuses for months before commissioning an investigation.[146] Knowledge of the U.S. military's human rights abuses becomes public at the same time that escalating vio-lence and disorder are taking control of the Iraqi streets. The United States and allied forces have been unable to create a secure environment, and the instability is unlikely to disappear in the weeks remaining until the June 30 transfer of power.

Although President Bush long ago declared the Iraq war over, and Saddam Hussein was captured months ago, the struggle to secure the human rights of the Iraqi people remains critical. If human rights concerns are invoked as a justification for military intervention, the human rights framework should remain at the forefront of political and social planning throughout the reconstruction process and should be used as a compass when formulating decisions and taking actions on a range of issues, from the formation of a representative democratic government to empowering local educational institutions and creating a social and economic infrastructure that meets the needs of local people. The United States must be held account-able for its human rights violations, yet the congressional investigations of Defense Secretary Rumsfeld are only the first phase of that process. Fur-ther, the occupying authority has a responsibility to ensure that the political and civil rights of the Iraqi people are safeguarded. Raids on Iraqi National Congress officials—once the source of information and guidance for the Bush administration—seem linked to leaders' outspoken criticism of U.S. postwar policies in Iraq[147] and raise new questions about U.S. observance of human rights there.

As we write, the violence in Iraq is on the rise. Many claim that the new attacks are aimed at driving a wedge between the U.S. occupation forces and the Iraqis who support them. The killing of prominent Iraqi lead-ers working with the United States, such as the leader of the Iraqi council,

Izzedine Salim, negatively affects the human rights of the Iraqi people as well as those of foreign nationals in Iraq.[148] Economic reconstruction projects are at a standstill because of the threat of car bombs and other armed attacks. The power vacuum left in the wake of Saddam's removal is largely due to the lack of a well-developed, politically active civil society, because Saddam Hussein removed potential threats to his power and because the United States failed to engage with any Iraqi civil society except for elites in exile. However, political parties have developed, and new political and professional syndicates have emerged, that demonstrate Iraq's potential for a pluralist democracy, provided that the prodemocratic sentiments are not reversed in light of extensive frustration with unemployment, lawlessness, and lack of public services.[149]

Establishing a strong civil society to support a flourishing democracy in Iraq is crucial to upholding and implementing a human rights framework.[150] Recently, however, news reporters and human rights workers in Iraq have been kidnapped, which affects the work of their remaining colleagues and lessens the degree of transparency of both the occupation forces and the Iraqi insurgents because there is no one to broadcast their misdeeds. Without media and NGO updates, many human rights abuses remain concealed, but even if human rights abuses were widely known in the international community, the lack of stability in Iraq would prevent any system of law and order from developing. Such a system is necessary in order to enforce and uphold human rights practices—officially through the courts of law, and unofficially through the respect and enforcement of human rights practices by Iraqi civil society in its daily interactions. Human rights is a lived practice, ultimately a guide for human relations. Ignoring human rights issues only serves to build up resentment, fear, and hatred and thereby fuels cycles of violence. The United States, therefore, as an occupying power has a responsibility to live up to the standards set by human rights and humanitarian law and to lay the groundwork for a truly democratic Iraq, one in which Iraqis are free to openly debate issues of importance and choose a system of governance—and political leaders—based on the will of the majority of Iraqis, not of the U.S. authorities.

## Notes

1. We gathered information for assessing these regimes from advocacy organizations such as Human Rights Watch and Amnesty International, as well as from a recent independent documentary film, *About Baghdad*, and from UN and U.S. briefing documents.

**2.** Chris Brown, "Universal Human Rights: A Critique," in *Human Rights in Global Politics,* ed. Tim Dunne and Nicholas J. Wheeler (Cambridge: Cambridge University Press, 1999), 103–27.

**3.** Jean Bethke Elshtain, "The Dignity of the Human Person and the Idea of Human Rights" (book review), *Journal of Law and Religion* 14 (1999–2000): 53, 57; see also Lisa Sowle Cahill, "Toward a Christian Theory of Human Rights," *Journal of Religious Ethics* 9 (1980): 278.

**4.** Jack Donnelly, *Universal Human Rights in Theory and Practice* (Ithaca, NY: Cornell University Press), 81.

**5.** David P. Forsythe, *Human Rights in International Relations* (New York: Cambridge University Press, 2000), 3.

**6.** Bhikhu Paarekh, "Non-Ethnocentric Universalism," in *Human Rights in Global Politics,* ed. Dunne and Wheeler, 149.

**7.** This notion of dignity allowing for differential treatment in certain cases informs good parenting. We love each of our children equally but treat them differently at times because they *are* different. Moreover, in some cases identical treatment could cause great harm (e.g., giving all children medicine if one child is ill).

**8.** UN General Assembly Res. 217A (III), UN Doc. A/810, at 71 (1948).

**9.** UN General Assembly Res. 2200A (XXI), 21 UN GAOR (Supp. No. 16) at 52, UN Doc. A/6316 (1966), 999 UNTS 171.

**10.** UN General Assembly Res. 2200A (XXI), 21 UN GAOR (Supp. No. 16) at 49, UN Doc. A/6316 (1966), 993 UNTS 3.

**11.** Ellen Dorsey and Paul Nelson, "New Rights Advocacy: Origins and Significance of a Partial Human Rights–Development Convergence" (paper presented at the annual meeting of the International Studies Association, Montreal, March 17, 2004), 6.

**12.** See International Council on Human Rights, *Demanding Trust: Issues of Accountability for Human Rights Actors* (occasional paper, Versoix, Switzerland, 2003).

**13.** Frederic Megret and Florian Hoffman, "The UN as a Human Rights Violator? Some Reflections on the United Nations' Changing Human Rights Responsibilities," *Human Rights Quarterly* 25, no. 2 (2002): 314–42.

**14.** Ibid., 317.

**15.** Zenon Stavrinides, "Human Rights Obligations under the UN Charter," *International Journal of Human Rights* 3 (1999): 40.

**16.** August Reinisch, "Securing the Accountability of International Organizations," *Global Governance* 7 (2001): 137–38.

**17.** Megret and Hoffman, "The UN as a Human Rights Violator?" 317.

**18.** This is the "naming and shaming" that the success of most international human rights activism tends to depend on.

**19.** Upendra Baxi, "Voices of the Suffering, Fragmented Universality and the Future of Human Rights," in *The Future of International Human Rights,* ed. B. H. Weston and S. P. Marks (Ardsley, NY: Transaction, 1999), 101–56.

**20.** See John Paul Lederach, "Civil Society and Reconstruction," in *Turbulent Peace: The Challenges of Managing International Conflict,* ed. Chester A. Crocker, Fen Osler Hampson, and Pamela Aall (Washington, DC: United States Institute of Peace Press, 2001).

**21.** Lederach, "Civil Society and Reconstruction," 841–54.

**22.** Michelle Parlevliet, "Bridging the Divide: Exploring the Relationship between Human Rights and Conflict Management," *Track Two* 11, no. 1 (March 2002): 28.

**23.** Human Rights Watch, "Iraq: Background on Human Rights Conditions, 1984–1992," August 1993, www.hrw.org/reports/1993/iraq/ (accessed February 15, 2003).

**24.** Human Rights Watch, "Iraq: Background on Human Rights Conditions."

**25.** United States Department of State, "Iraq: Country Reports on Human Rights Practices, 1999, Introduction," February 23, 2000, www.state.gov/g/drl/rls/hrrpt/1999/410.htm (accessed February 15, 2003).

**26.** United States Department of State, "Iraq: Country Reports on Human Rights Practices, 2001," March 4, 2002, section 1c, www.state.gov/g/drl/rls/hrrpt/2001/nea/8257.htm (accessed February 15, 2003).

**27.** Human Rights Watch, "Iraq: Background on Human Rights Conditions, 1984–1992."

**28.** United States Department of State, "Iraq: Country Reports on Human Rights Practices, 2001."

**29.** Amnesty International, "Iraq: Victims of Systematic Repression," November 24, 1999, http://web.amnesty.org/ai.nsf/Index/MDE140101999?OpenDocument&of=COUNTRIES\IRAQ (accessed February 15, 2003).

**30.** Human Rights Watch, "Human Rights Watch Criticizes Iraq's Execution of Four Jordanians," www.hrw.org/press97/dec/saddam1.htm (accessed February 15, 2003).

**31.** Amnesty International, "Iraq: Victims of Systematic Repression"; see also Amnesty International, "Iraq: State Cruelty."

**32.** Amnesty International, "Iraq: Victims of Systematic Repression."

**33.** Ibid.

**34.** See generally Dilip Hiro, *The Longest War: The Iran-Iraq Military Conflict* (New York: Routledge, 1991); Human Rights Watch, *Iraq's Crime of Genocide: The Anfal Campaign against the Kurds* (New York: Human Rights Watch, 1995); Middle East Watch, *The Anfal Campaign in Iraqi Kurdistan: The Destruction of Koreme* (New York: Human Rights Watch, 1993), 31–44.

**35.** See S.C. Res. 687, UN SCOR, 2981st mtg., UN Doc. S/RES/687 (1991).

**36.** Human Rights Watch, "Genocide in Iraq: The Anfal Campaign against the Kurds," July 1993, http://www.hrw.org/reports/1993/iraqanfal/ (accessed February 15, 2003).

**37.** UN Commission on Human Rights Resolution on "The Situation of Human Rights in Iraq," E/CN.4/RES/1991/74 (1991).

**38.** Human Rights Watch, "Genocide in Iraq."

**39.** Amnesty International, "Iraq: Victims of Systematic Repression."

**40.** UN Human Rights Committee, General Comment 6/16 (July 27, 1982) (on file with authors).

**41.** See Julie Mertus, "Examining the Legality of the NATO Bombing of Yugoslavia," *William and Mary Law Review* 41: 1743; see generally W. Michael Reisman, "Criteria for the Lawful Use of Force in International Law," *Yale Journal of International Law* 10 (1984): 279–80.

**42.** John J. Merriam, "Kosovo and the Law of Humanitarian Intervention," *Case Western Reserve Journal of International Law* 33 (Winter 2001): 111.

**43.** Richard Couto, "US Calls on Iraqi Nationals to Oust Saddam," *Times of India,* February 24, 2003, http://timesofindia.indiatimes.com/cms.dll/html/uncomp/articleshow?artid = 38447848.

**44.** The many interviews in *About Baghdad,* for example, document the Iraqi people's gratitude for being rid of Saddam Hussein, but their frustration at the U.S. military occupation.

**45.** The removal of sanctions permitted Iraqi oil to be sold on the world market. Legal control over Iraq's oil industry had been transferred to the United States and its allies. S.C. Res. 1483, UN Doc. No. S/RES/1483(2003).

**46.** S.C. Res. 661, U.N. SCOR, 2932 meeting (1990), 19, http://www.un.org/Depts/oip/scrs/scr661onu.html (accessed March 21, 2002).

**47.** Christopher C. Joyner, "United Nations Sanctions after Iraq: Looking Back to See Ahead," *Chicago Journal of International Law,* 4, no. 2 (Fall 2003): 229–353, 330.

**48.** For a general overview of the debate on the legality of economic sanctions, see Mary Ellen O'Connell, "Debating the Law of Sanctions," *European Journal of International Law* 13, no. 1 (2002): 63–79; George Lopez and David Cortrights, "Economic Sanctions and Human Rights: Part of the Problem or Part of the Solution," *International Journal of Human Rights,* 1 (1997): 1.

**49.** UN Charter art. 41.

**50.** S.C. Res. 661, supra note 82, para. 3(c).

**51.** Authority to determine "humanitarian circumstances" was vested in the committee a short time later. S.C. Res. 666, UN SCOR, 2939th mtg., UN Doc. S/RES/666 (1990).

**52.** Peggy Kozal, "Is the Continued Use of Sanctions as Implemented against Iraq a Violation of International Human Rights?" *Denver Journal of International Law and Policy* (Fall 2000).

**53.** Andrew K. Fishman, "Between Iraq and a Hard Place: The Use of Economic Sanctions and Threats to International Peace and Security," *Emory International Law Review* 13 (1999): 687, 719; Adam Winkler, "Just Sanctions," *Human Rights Quarterly* 21, no. 1 (1999); Arne Tostensen and Beate Bull, "Are Smart Sanctions Feasible?" *World Politics* 54, no. 3 (2002); see also American Friends' Service Committee, "Campaign of Conscience," www.afsc.org (accessed February 15, 2003).

**54.** World Health Organization (WHO), "The Health Conditions of the Population in Iraq since the Gulf Crisis," March 1996, WHO/EHA/96.1, www.who .int/disasters/repo/5249.html.

**55.** Save the Children UK et al., "Iraq Sanctions: Humanitarian Implications and Options for the Future," Global Policy Forum, August 6, 2002, www.globalpolicy.org/security/sanction/iraq1/2002/paper.htm (accessed February 15, 2003) (unpaginated).

**56.** Ibid., section 3.2.

**57.** United Nations Office of Iraq Programme, "Oil-for-Food Background Information," www.un.org/Depts/oip/backgroundindex.html (accessed February 15, 2003).

**58.** S.C. Res. 706, UN SCOR, 3004th mtg., UN Doc. S/RES/706 (1991), www.fas.org/news/un/iraq/sres/sres0706.htm (accessed February 15, 2003).

**59.** S.C. Res. 712, UN SCOR, 3008th mtg., UN Doc. S/RES/712 (1991), www.fas.org/news/un/iraq/sres/sres0712.htm (accessed February 15, 2003).

**60.** S.C. Res. 986, UN SCOR, 3519th mtg. (1995), www.un.org/Depts/oip/ scrs/scr986.html (accessed February 15, 2003).

**61.** See United Nations Office of Iraq Programme, "Oil for Food," www.un.org/Depts/oip/chron.html (accessed February 15, 2003).

**62.** United Nations Office of Iraq Programme, "Oil-for-Food Background Information."

**63.** Hans von Sponek, "Four Questions, Four Answers" (lecture at the European Colloqium, Brussels, September 25, 2002), www.afsc.org/iraq/guide/ 4questions.shtm (accessed February 15, 2003).

**64.** Save the Children UK et al., "Iraq Sanctions" (unpaginated).

**65.** Hans von Sponek, "Iraq: Are There Alternatives to a Military Option?" December 9, 2001, www.afsc.org/iraq/guide/alternatives.shtm (accessed February 15, 2003).

**66.** WHO, "The Health Conditions of the Population in Iraq since the Gulf Crisis," March 1996, WHO/EHA/96.1, 17.

**67.** United Nations, "Report of the Second Panel Established Pursuant to the Note by the President of the Security Council Concerning the Current Humanitarian Situation in Iraq," S/1999/100 (1999), www.un.org/Depts/oip/panelrep.html (accessed February 15, 2003).

**68.** UNICEF, "Situation Analysis of Women and Children in Iraq," April 30, 1998, www.childinfo.org/Other/Iraq_sa.pdf (accessed February 15, 2003); UNICEF, "Donor Update," January 14, 2003, 3 (on file with author).

**69.** Quaker/AFSC Delegation to Iraq, "Baghdad Epistle," June 18, 2002, www.afsc.org (accessed February 15, 2003); WHO, "The Health Conditions," 8.

**70.** UNICEF Report, "Situation Analysis of Children and Women in Iraq," 42–44, www.childinfo.org/Other/Iraq_sa.pdf (accessed February 15, 2003).

**71.** UNICEF, "Iraq Child and Maternal Mortality Surveys," July 23, 2000, www.unicef.org.uk/news/Iraq1.htm.

**72.** Von Sponek, "Four Questions, Four Answers."

**73.** UNICEF, "Situation Analysis: Executive Summary," www.childinfo.org/Other/Iraq_sa.pdf (accessed February 15, 2003).

**74.** Carol Christian, "Sanctions against Iraq Killing Thousands, Ex-U.N. Official Says," *Houston Chronicle,* February 24, 1999, 25.

**75.** Denis Halliday, "End the Public-Health Catastrophe of Sanctions against Iraq," *Austin American-Statesman,* February 24, 1999, A15.

**76.** Roula Khalaf, "US, Britain Urge U.N. Official in Iraq to Quit," *Financial Times,* November 2, 1999, 1.

**77.** Carola Hoyos, "U.N. Food Chief for Iraq Resigns," *Financial Times,* February 16, 2000, 12.

**78.** See International Council on Human Rights, *Demanding Trust: Issues of Accountability for Human Rights Actors* (occasional paper, Versoix, Switzerland, 2003).

**79.** Save the Children UK et al., "Iraq Sanctions," chap. 7.2.

**80.** See Thomas G. Weiss et al., eds., *Political Gain and Civilian Pain* (Oxford: Oxford University Press, 1997).

**81.** James A. Paul, "Sanctions: An Analysis," Global Policy Forum, www.globalpolicy.org/security/sanction/analysis.htm (accessed February 15, 2003).

**82.** See Bossuyt Report: "The Adverse Consequences of Economic Sanctions on the Enjoyment of Human Rights," E/CN.4/Sub.2/2000/33; Vera Gowlland-Debbas, *United Nations Sanctions and International Law* (The Hague, 2001).

**83.** See, e.g., Hans Köchler, "Ethical Aspects of Sanctions in International Law," International Progress Organization, http://i-p-o.org/sanctp.htm (accessed April 7, 2002); Weiss et al., eds., *Political Gain and Civilian Pain;* Marc Bossuyt, "The Adverse Consequences of Economic Sanctions on the Enjoyment of Human

Rights," Global Policy Forum, www.globalpolicy.org/security/sanction/ unreports/bossuyt.htm (accessed April 8, 2002).

**84.** Supplement to an Agenda for Peace, Position Paper of the Secretary-General on the Occasion of the Fiftieth Anniversary of the United Nations, UN GAOR/SCOR, 50th sess., UN Doc. A/50/60-S/1995/1 (1995), www.un.org/Docs/SG/agsupp.html#SANCTION (accessed February 15, 2003).

**85.** Emmanuel Sivan, "Constraints and Opportunities in the Arab World," *Journal of Democracy* 8, no. 2 (1997): 111; see also Mehran Kamrava and Frank O'Mora, "Civil Society and Democratization in Comparative Perspective: Latin America and Middle East," *Third World Quarterly* 19, no. 5 (1998).

**86.** Save the Children UK et al., "Iraq Sanctions" (unpaginated).

**87.** The argument has been made that sanctions should always be subject to time limits. Under such an approach, after the expiration of a set period of time (for example, one year), the sanctions would discontinue automatically. Lutz Oette, "A Decade of Sanctions against Iraq: Never Again! The End of Unlimited Sanctions in the Recent Practice of the Security Council," *European Journal of International Law* 13, no. 1 (2002): 93–103.

**88.** The news conferences led by Bush administration representatives and military officials often discuss the war in Iraq in terms of U.S. ideals, notably "freedom" and "democracy."

**89.** Dawn Brancati, "Can Federalism Stabilize Iraq?" *Washington Quarterly* 27, no. 2 (2004): 7.

**90.** Richard Falk, "Why International Law Matters," *Nation* 276, no. 9 (2003): 19–22; Paul Findley, "A Republican's Case against George W. Bush," *Washington Report on Middle East Affairs* 23, no. 3 (2004): 20–21.

**91.** Arthur Kent, "War—at Any Cost? Washington Doesn't Really Want to Give Diplomacy a Second Chance," *MacLeans* 116, no. 11 (2003): 18.

**92.** Thalif Deen, "Politics: U.S. Uses Economic Muscle to Win U.N. Votes," *Global Information Network* 24 (February 2003).

**93.** "The Final Ultimatum," Economist.com/Global Agenda, March 17, 2003, www.economist.com.

**94.** Bob Woodward, *Plan of Attack* (New York: Simon and Schuster, 2004).

**95.** Phyllis Bennis, "Understanding the U.S.-Iraq Crisis: A Primer" (printed report, Institute for Policy Studies, January 2003), 2, 11.

**96.** Harlan Ullman, quoted in Ira Chernus, "Shock and Awe: Is Baghdad the Next Hiroshima?" January 27, 2003, www.commondreams.org (accessed February 15, 2003).

**97.** Ibid.

**98.** Bennis, "Understanding the U.S.-Iraq Crisis," 11.

**99.** MedAct, "Collateral Damage: The Health and Environmental Costs of War," November 11, 2002, on Relief Web, www.reliefweb.int.

**100.** FCNL, "Costs of War," February 20, 2003, www.fcnl.org/issues/int/sup/iraq_war_costs.htm (accessed March 10, 2003).

**101.** Quaker/AFSC Delegation to Iraq, "Baghdad Epistle."

**102.** MedAct, "Collateral Damage."

**103.** Irwin Arieff, "UN Sees 500,000 Iraqi Casualties at Start of War," Reuters, January 7, 2003.

**104.** FCNL, "Costs of War."

**105.** WHO, "Health Conditions in Iraq 'Serious,' WHO Study Finds" (press release WHO/23), March 25, 1996, www.who.int/archives/inf-pr-1996/pr96-23.html (accessed February 15,2003).

**106.** Mary Trotochaud, "Resourceful People in a Fractured Nation," AFSC Iraq Aftermath Relief Updates, www.afsc.org/human-face/relief_updates/entries/061303.htm#top (accessed June 13, 2003).

**107.** Bertil Duner, "Violence for Human Rights," *International Journal of Human Rights* 5, no. 2 (Summer 2001): 52.

**108.** Stephen Zunes, "Six Arguments for Everybody against the Invasion of Iraq," *Fellowship of Reconciliation,* November/December 2002.

**109.** Glen Gersmehl, "Why Is Our Best Option Invisible? Nonviolence and the Iraq Crisis," Lutheran Peace Fellowship, www.lutheranpeace.org (accessed March 10, 2003).

**110.** Kent, "War—at Any Cost?" 18.

**111.** "Letter No. 62," *The Quaker Economist* (St. Lawrence Valley, NY: Russ Nelson, 2003), quotes Michael Ignatieff (*New York Times* magazine, Jan. 5, 2003) and William Nordhaus (*Economist,* Dec. 7, 2002).

**112.** Sen. Richard Byrd, "Reckless Administration May Reap Disastrous Consequences," speech on the Senate floor, February 12, 2003.

**113.** Vojin Dimitrijevic, "Human Rights and Peace," in *Human Rights: New Dimensions and Challenges,* ed. Janusz Symonides (Dartmouth: Ashgate, 1998), 58; Gareth Evans and Mohamed Sahnoun, "The Responsibility to Protect," *Foreign Affairs* 81, no. 6 (2002): 100; David Rieff, "Humanitarianism in Crisis," *Foreign Affairs* 81, no. 6 (2002): 119.

**114.** Protocol Additional to the Geneva Conventions of 12 August 1949 (Protocol I), June 8, 1977, art. 51, para. 5, 1125 UNTS 3.

**115.** Joe Fiorill, "Blix: Iraq War Was Not Justified," *National Journal* 36, no. 13 (2004): 978; Andrew Killgore, "The Mystery of Iraq's 'Weapons of Mass Destruction,'" *Washington Report on Middle East Affairs* 23, no. 3 (2004): 19.

**116.** "Iraq: War Would Be Fault of U.S., Not UN, Diplomats Say," *Global Information Network,* March 18, 2003.

**117.** Michael W. Isherwood, "U.S. Strategic Options for Iraq: Easier Said Than Done," *Washington Quarterly* 25, no. 2 (2002): 145.

**118.** Ibid., 150.

**119.** Ibid., 150.

**120.** Ibid., 152.

**121.** FCNL, "Alternatives to War," 4.

**122.** Adam Curle, *Another Way: Positive Response to Contemporary Violence* (Oxford: Jon Carpenter, 1995), 71.

**123.** Ibid., 71.

**124.** Gene Sharp, *The Politics of Nonviolent Action, Part One* (Boston: Extending Horizons Books, 1973), 4.

**125.** Ibid., 8.

**126.** Gersmehl, "Why Is Our Best Option Invisible?" (unpaginated).

**127.** Peter Ackerman and Jack DuVall, "With Weapons of the Will: How to Topple Saddam Hussein—Nonviolently," *Sojourners,* Sept.–Oct. 2002, www.sojo.net/index.cfm?action=magazine.article&issue=soj0209&article=020910) (accessed March 10, 2003).

**128.** Kamrava and O'Mora, "Civil Society and Democratization," 893; Emmanuel Sivan, "Constraints and Opportunities in the Arab World," *Journal of Democracy* 8, no. 2 (1997): 105; Aymen M. Khalifa, "Reviving Civil Society in Egypt," *Journal of Democracy* 6, no. 3 (1995): 155.

**129.** Tareq Y. Ismael and Jacqueline S. Ismael, "Civil Society and Democratic Transformation in the Arab World," *Middle East Journal* 52, no. 3 (Summer 1998): 444.

**130.** Paul Findley, "A Republican's Case," 20–21.

**131.** Kamil Mahdi, "Iraqis Will Not Be Pawns," *Guardian,* February 20, 2003, www.zmag.org/content/showarticle.cfm?SectionID=15&ItemID=3092 (accessed March 10, 2003).

**132.** Ibid. (unpaginated).

**133.** Ackerman and DuVall, "With Weapons of the Will" (unpaginated).

**134.** Ibid.

**135.** See Stephanie Eileen Nanes, "Fighting Honor Crimes: Evidence of Civil Society in Jordan," *Middle East Journal* 57, no. 1 (Winter 2003): 112–29.

**136.** George Baghdadi, "Anti-war Protests across Arab World," Inter Press Service Agency, January 20, 2003.

**137.** See, for example, Barham Salih, "A Kurdish Model for Iraq," *Washington Post,* December 9, 2002, A23.

**138.** Barbara J. Nelson and Linda Kaboolian, "A More Civil Society," *American Prospect* 13, no. 3 (February 11, 2002).

**139.** Ibid. (unpaginated).

**140.** FCNL, "Alternatives to War," 4.

141. Ibid.

142. Albert Cevallos, *Whither the Bulldozer: Nonviolent Revolution and the Transition to Democracy in Serbia,* United States Institute of Peace Special Report no. 72 (Washington, DC: United States Institute of Peace, August 2001), www.usip.org/pubs/specialreports/sr72.html (accessed February 15, 2003).

143. FCNL, "Alternatives to War," 4.

144. David Lorey, David Beezley, and William Beezley, eds., *Genocide, Collective Violence, and Popular Memory* (Wilmington, DE: Scholarly Resources, 2002), xv.

145. "Article 15-6: Investigation of the 800th Military Police Brigade," www.globalsecurity.org/intell/library/reports/2004/800-mp-bde.htm (accessed May 20, 2004).

146. Peter Slevin, "Systems Failures Cited for Delayed Action on Abuses," *Washington Post,* May 20, 2004, A19.

147. Scott Wilson and Ariana Cha, "Chalabi's House Raided by U.S. Troops," *Washington Post*, May 20, 2004, www.washingtonpost.com/wp-dyn/articles/A41871-2004May20.html.

148. Daniel Williams, "As Violence Deepens, So Does Pessimism," *Washington Post*, May 18, 2004, A01.

149. Adeed Dawisha, "Iraq: Setbacks, Advances, Prospects," *Journal of Democracy* 15, no. 1 (2004): 5–20.

150. Daniel Byman and Kenneth Pollack, "Democracy in Iraq?" *Washington Quarterly* 26, no. 3 (2003): 119–36.

**PART III**

# The Contributions of Human Rights in Post–Armed Conflict and Postcrisis Situations

# 12

# Human Rights, Peace Agreements, and Conflict Resolution

## Negotiating Justice in Northern Ireland

Christine Bell

This chapter explores the relationship between human rights, negotiated peace agreements, and conflict resolution.[1] It uses Northern Ireland and the Belfast Agreement as a case study to argue that human rights can and should be an integral part of conflict resolution. Addressing human rights is important to addressing root causes of violence, and if undertaken with awareness of the complicated relationship to conflict resolution, it can also facilitate agreement on issues other than human rights (such as political accommodation). The relationship between human rights abuses and conflict is important, not just at the point of agreement, but in the prevention of conflict escalation in the first place.

The assertion that human rights protections are a vital part of a peaceful society is not new. It was the very experience of World War II that led to the birth of international human rights law and grounded that birth in the assumption that there was a link between human rights abuses occurring within established state borders and international conflict. The UN Charter, while not containing substantive human rights provisions, opens with the objective of avoiding war and immediately references the concept of human rights.[2] The Universal Declaration of Human Rights makes a "just peace" thesis more explicit, claiming, "It is essential, if man is not to be compelled to have recourse, as a last resort to rebellion against tyranny and oppression, that human rights should be protected by the rule of law."[3] More recently the Council of Europe's Framework Convention notes that "the upheavals of European history have shown that the protection of national minorities is essential to stability, democratic security and peace in this continent."[4]

However, the assumption that human rights protections are vital to peace has come to be challenged. At the center of this challenge is the idea that the clear normative demands of international human rights law at times run counter to the practical imperatives of peacemaking. For human rights lawyers the gauntlet was set down in 1996 in the *Human Rights Quarterly*.[5] The anonymous writer castigated the international human rights community for prolonging the war in the former Yugoslavia by insisting that proposed settlements include requirements for justice. In judging every peace blueprint in terms of whether it rewarded aggression and ethnic cleansing, human rights "pundits" and negotiators were accused of rejecting pragmatic deals that, in hindsight, were as good as or better than the eventual settlement. The anonymous writer argued that as a result "thousands of people are dead who should have been alive—because moralists were in the quest of the perfect peace."[6]

A number of other writers have suggested that there is an inherent tension between conflict resolution and human rights actors, in a debate that is gathering momentum. Kent Arnold, for example, in questioning why the fields of conflict resolution and human rights are not better integrated, notes four principal reasons.[7] First, he notes a difference between adversarial and cooperative approaches—human rights advocates use primarily legal approaches and conflict resolution practitioners use primarily cooperative approaches. Second, Arnold notes a difference between human rights and conflict resolution actors on whether justice or reconciliation is the primary need. Third, he notes different approaches on whether to label parties to the conflict "human rights violators." Conflict resolution practitioners tend to avoid these labels as ones that can escalate conflict, while human rights advocates may find labeling necessary. Fourth, he suggests that human rights actors are guided by human rights principles and advocate adherence to the highest possible human rights standards, while conflict resolution actors are guided by principles that help them maintain their impartiality and acceptability to all parties. Both sets of actors view their approach as integral to their legitimacy. Pauline Baker conceives of the clash as between "conflict managers" and "democratizers."[8] See table 1 for the differences between these two approaches.

In summary, she suggests:

> [C]onflict managers tend to concentrate on short-term solutions that address the precipitous events that sparked the conflict; above all, they

**Table 1.** Peacemaker Profiles

| Conflict Managers | Democratizers |
|---|---|
| Inclusive approach | Exclusive approach |
| Goal is reconciliation | Goal is justice |
| Pragmatic focus | Principled focus |
| Emphasis on the process | Emphasis on outcome |
| Particular norms and cultures of the societies in conflict | Universal norms endorsed by the international community |
| Assume moral equivalence | Insist on moral accountability |
| Conflict resolution is negotiable | Justice is not negotiable |
| Outside actors should be politically neutral | Outside actors cannot be morally neutral |

*Source:* Pauline Baker, "Conflict Resolution versus Democratic Governance: Divergent Paths to Peace?" in *Turbulent Peace, The Challenges of Mananging International Conflict,* ed. Chester A. Crocker, Fen Osler Hampson, and Pamela Aall (Washington, DC: United States Institute of Peace Press, 2001), 759.

seek a swift and expedient end to the violence. Democratizers tend to concentrate on the longer-term solutions that address the root causes of the conflict; they search for enduring democratic stability. The former see peace as a precondition for democracy, the latter see democracy as a precondition for peace.[9]

Both Arnold and Baker have acknowledged that there are reasons for human rights and conflict resolution approaches to remain distinct, but both argue for greater synthesis between the two fields. This argument is taken up in an excellent review of the subject by Michelle Parlevliet.[10] She points to similar tensions between the approaches but sets out six analytical propositions that highlight the inherent complementarity between the fields of conflict resolution and human rights:

- Human rights abuses are both symptoms and causes of violent conflict.
- A sustained denial of human rights is a structural cause of high-intensity conflict.
- Institutionalized respect for rights and structural accommodation of diversity are a primary form of conflict prevention.

- For the effective and sustainable resolution of intrastate conflict, the prescriptive approach of human rights actors must be combined with the facilitative approach of conflict resolution practitioners.

- Whereas human rights and justice per se are nonnegotiable, the application and interpretation of rights and justice are negotiable in the context of a negotiated settlement.

- Conflict management can function as an alternative to litigation in dealing with rights-related conflicts.

Parlevliet uses these connections to argue primarily for greater understanding between the actors in the two fields, and for exploring how activities in each field can be strengthened with insights and approaches from the other field.

Edy Kaufman and Ibrahim Bisharat present similar arguments in the form of a strong plea that human rights issues be integrated into peace processes.[11] They are driven by the Middle East peace process, which marginalized human rights. Kaufman and Bisharat attempt an intellectual merging of human rights (justice) and conflict resolution (peace). They argue that human rights standards and approaches can provide an impartial content to vague notions of "justice," which is useful to conflict resolution because it provides a framework for addressing concerns and limiting conflict, which also encourages respect for the rights of the "other side." However, they remain uncertain whether they can be convincing either to "decision-makers in the core" or "even to those participants in second track diplomacy in the periphery of the political process."[12]

One initial difficulty with discussion thus far has been its failure to distinguish between the different contexts in which the debate over human rights and conflict resolution takes place. The abstract nature of the discussion makes no distinction between two very different contexts for the relationship between human rights and conflict resolution: the context of discrete subconflicts (such as specific triggers of intercommunal violence) and the context of attempts to draft peace agreements aimed at providing a "big fix" to the conflict as a whole. While the two types of negotiations are clearly linked, there are also differences between them that deserve more attention. This chapter focuses attention on the former—peace process negotiations, wherein it is suggested that rights discourse can have a broad facilitative role. A related observation is that at this level abstract distinctions between "conflict resolvers" and "human rights actors" often do not reflect the key distinction, which is between track one (official, political) and track two (civil society, informal) approaches. It is unclear that the political elites involved in track one (either as parties or as mediators) are either "human rights" or "conflict resolution" actors in the self-conscious way that civil society uses the labels. A complex "deal-making" dynamic will often involve both local and international political elites, using the peace negotiations and arguments about conflict resolution and human rights to satisfy their own various agendas.

This chapter aims to build on the work of Parlevliet and of Kaufman and Bisharat in reinforcing the need to consider human rights as complementary to conflict resolution, challenging the notion of a clash between the two fields. I examine the current context in which this debate is taking place, noting the prevalent recourse to human rights standards and mechanisms in a range of peace agreements. I also look at why and how human rights provisions make it into peace agreements and the difficulties with implementation that this causes. While dilemmas about the relationship between justice and pragmatic peacemaking are often presented as clashes between principle and pragmatism, this chapter suggests that they can be better understood as dilemmas of how to move from short-term peacemaking requirements to longer-term peace-building requirements. In conclusion, I turn to Northern Ireland, using experiences there to illustrate some strategies for human rights actors who wish to shape or influence peace agreements and their implementation.

## Principle and Pragmatism: A Misunderstood Relationship

Behind abstract depictions of human rights activists shouting slogans at negotiators, and conflict resolution actors forsaking all principled argument in the need for an immediate fix, lies a complicated context. The debate at issue has been spawned by a particular post–Cold War environment characterized by three dimensions.[13] First, internal conflict has come to rival interstate conflict in terms of number of deaths caused and as a focus for concern, international intervention, and study. Second, the prevalent way of addressing such conflicts now is to attempt to negotiate their end by engaging with the political and military actors in them and to document agreement in a formal peace agreement. Since 1990 more than three hundred peace agreements have been signed between adversaries in more than forty jurisdictions.[14] These conflicts were internal in nature and can be placed in three overlapping categories: centralist/revolutionary, regional/identity, and economic/criminal.[15] Negotiated settlements necessarily involve some compromise between the different parties waging war, and this compromise is translated into the design of legal and political institutions, giving rise to ongoing political, legal, and moral dilemmas about how best to achieve transition from violence. This is most obviously seen in the dilemma of whether to hold past human rights abusers to account, given that these same actors are integral to sustaining "the deal." The third dimension to the context is the increasing scope of human rights law, which not only provides a basis for international involvement in internal matters but also offers possibilities for mitigating the worst excesses of conflict, as well as providing a variety of tools, such as blueprints for institutions capable of assisting negotiators. The current interest in the relationship between conflict resolution and human rights, and the tension surrounding how to reconcile the requirements of justice and the practicalities of negotiating an end to conflict, emerges from the particularities of this context.

## Why Do Human Rights Get into Peace Agreements?

The common dynamics above have given rise to some similar "design features" in many of the agreements. Peace processes across all types of internal conflict typically aim toward a peace agreement that documents a new political compromise addressed at eliminating violence. Thus, peace processes often move toward agreements that set out a constitutional framework defining access of different groups to power, coupled with protection of human rights through bills of rights, human rights commissions, and new or reformed judiciary, police (and other military forces), and criminal justice systems. The new arrangements for holding power are in some cases aimed at moving from a failed state or an undemocratic state to coherent, accountable, and legitimate political structures. In other cases they are aimed at including previously excluded minority groups in government in an attempt to address self-determination claims, through mechanisms such as territorial divisions of power, and consociational forms of government. In each case, human rights institutions are included, if at all, as part of a broadly liberal democratic package, fine-tuned by a group rights dimension in cases of ethnic conflict. There are, of course, exceptions to this: Some framework peace agreements, most notably in the Israeli/Palestinian conflict, have sidelined human rights issues, often for geopolitical reasons.

While there is a similarity between the political and human rights institutions in peace agreements, they emerge in different ways and for different reasons in different peace processes, which crucially affect whether human rights measures are implemented and made effective or remain mere "paper" commitments. The negotiation dynamics surrounding human rights issues point up a dialectical relationship between principle and pragmatism, which frustrates attempts to present a straightforward clash between disconnected concepts of human rights and conflict resolution.

Where agreement is reached under international pressure, the international community, in the form of international mediators, mediating Western states, or international organizations, often requires that negotiated solutions move in a liberal, democratic direction as typified by elected legislatures and a bill of rights. National institutions for protecting rights, reform of the justice apparatus, and incorporation of international standards flag a move toward democratic legitimacy. However, several problems affect the extent to which these provisions translate into changed human rights conditions. First, institutional provision in peace agreements varies vastly in its coherence and, as a consequence, varies in the capacity of those institutions to deliver effective human rights protection. A learning curve is evident, for example, in institutional provision for human rights in the Dayton Peace Agreement in Bosnia and Herzegovina, in the Rambouillet Accord in Kosovo, and in the Macedonian peace agreement.[16] In Dayton, the 1995 agreement listed nineteen human rights and humanitarian law conventions and their protocols as apparently incorporated and "to be applied in Bosnia and Herzegovina," with no attention given to the mechanisms for translating these instruments into local practices, for example, through training of police or judiciary or through more specific rights protections tailored to local problems.[17] In contrast, the 2001 Macedonian Peace Agreement provided detailed constitutional amendments and a set of time-tabled legislative changes, aimed at ensuring the implementation of principles relating to nondiscrimination and equitable representation in public administration, business, and education. The role and perspective of the mediator on rights may be crucial in a peace agreement's design (implementation issues aside); for example, the "rights"-oriented agreement in Burundi, particularly striking in its provision for women, is in part explained by the fact that Nelson Mandela was the mediator.[18]

Second, there is a question of whether one-size-fits-all liberal democracy offers a long-term solution to the problems of failed states or ethnic conflict.[19] The experience of trying to impose liberal democratic institutions and ideals has not been particularly successful.[20] Institutions designed to implement change where there are no indigenous processes of change have often proved ineffective. Indeed, imposing the language and institutions of change without delivering real change is often a recipe for long-term cynicism regarding both language and institutions, in a way that is almost impossible to repair.

Third, the international community may be engaged in several different transitions at once. J. 'Bayo Adekanye has noted "the problem of three transitions in one."[21] The first is a transition to democracy proper, under which political tasks such as the conduct of elections, formation of power-sharing government, and judicial and police reform take place. The second transition relates to the change from state-centered, or "command," economy to a more liberal one, marked by the rule of market forces and the introduction of adjustment-style reform and presided over by the IMF and World Bank. The third transition is the transition from war to peace proper, from violence to politics, from conflict to postconflict. These transitions happen simultaneously but often undercut one another. To use an example from Adekanye, the move of financial institutions to reduction in public spending at a time when increased public spending is required for reconstruction and delivery of socioeconomic rights puts the economic transition at odds with the broader democratization transition. The short-term "stop the violence" peace-building objectives may also run contrary to longer-term "address root causes of violence" projects, as Fen Olser Hampson also suggests.[22] This clash revolves particularly around the application of human rights norms. In the short term, parties will move from violent conflict only if they believe that they can pursue their agendas around the negotiating table better than on the battlefield. Thus, the pressure to concede moral issues on the path to agreement will be almost overwhelming. However, in the longer term, a "positive" peace can be given substance only by providing political and legal mechanisms through which disputes can be continuously channeled. In the short term, parties may not be able to reach agreement on questions of accountability for the past, reform of legal institutions, or return of refugees; however, over the long term, addressing such issues is a necessity. Accountability for past abuses may prove impossible to address in the text of any agreement, but over time it may become less difficult as a political consensus around the past emerges from the peace process (or not, if such consensus does not emerge). The difficult question is less a problem of principle versus pragmatism and more one of how transition can best be moved from short-term to long-term peacemaking requirements. International peace agreement brokers often view deal making as the endpoint in a process, when it is actually the beginning. Thus, reconciling justice and peace might well be reconceived less as a clash and more as a management challenge of how to move pragmatically from violent conflict while keeping open future possibilities for justice.[23]

Where the internal dynamics of the conflict are driving the peace process, as in South Africa or Northern Ireland, human rights protections come to be written into an agreement as responsive to substantive issues in the conflict. Human rights abuses are often asserted by at least one of the parties to a conflict as a key concern. At the start of a process, human rights are typically asserted by the less powerful in an attempt to redress a military and political status quo and are resisted accordingly by those in power. However, human rights provisions only make it into framework agreements if the main parties involved in negotiations agree to their inclusion. This leads to the question of why and how those in power come to accede to human rights demands. Again, the answer lies in a mix of principled, unprincipled, and pragmatic reasons, the precise dynamics of which are different in different conflicts.

The dynamics of the process may create mutually reinforcing self-interests that drive the inclusion of human rights institutions. Thus, a move toward new territorial boundaries and political structures may be accompanied by a move toward designing human rights institutions aimed at providing safeguards against the abuse of any power reallocated, drawing the constitutional "sting." Those who were once a majority, or in power as such, and resisted human rights protections may come to push for them in a process that destines them to become a minority. This was the case in South Africa, where the move toward a bill of rights was driven by African National Congress (ANC) interests in establishing a multiracial democracy, which was distinguished from past governments by its commitment to human rights, and by the then (National Party) South African government (SAG/NP) interests in protecting its forthcoming position as a political minority. Alternatively, those who resist human rights protections for minorities during the conflict may, in negotiations, come to view these protections as a price worth conceding to legitimize the borders and sovereignty that ensure their majority status. This was the case in Northern Ireland, where Unionists could concede human rights and equality issues more easily than they could issues involving sovereignty, such as cross-border bodies with British/Irish executive powers. These bigger issues could even be secured by human rights concessions. In Bosnia, human rights protections operating at an interentity state level and focusing on minority protection and a "right to return" were the international community's price for devolving power to ethnically defined entities.

Human rights therefore can provide a way of enabling parties to a conflict to move from irreconcilable positions to addressing the much more reconcilable interests underlying these positions, such as mutual fears of discrimination and domination. They can also offer standards objective to the parties involved in the dispute, which have a claim to legitimacy.

However, political elites are often not good at moving beyond their positions as traditionally conceived. Human rights actors can play a key enabling role in providing suggestions and encouraging debate on how new institutions can best ensure protection of human rights or basic fair treatment for all individuals and groups. Both the processes and the fruits of such debate can contribute to reframing positions. Vital to this is an openness to the negotiation process, with good opportunities for interchange between the formal negotiation process and civil society. Indeed, the absence of such exchange in many internationally driven processes—where politicians are rushed off to secret locations and a hothouse environment—may further explain why there is often an inverse correlation between international involvement in a peace process and the coherence and effectiveness of human rights provision.

There can also, of course, be more cynical reasons for resistant parties to adopt increased human rights provisions in a peace agreement. The most internal of peace processes has a measure of international involvement, and domestic parties are well aware that human rights measures and provisions constitute the badge of democracy and, thus, entry into the club of legitimate players. This makes human rights provisions difficult to resist. Human rights measures can often be conceded in abstract language, meaning that disagreement about what implementation will entail in practice can be postponed until the postagreement stage. In Northern Ireland, for example, agreement was reached on rights-based terms of reference for a commission to examine the way forward for policing.[24] However, while (Catholic) Irish Nationalists asserted that this required radical change to the then Royal Ulster Constabulary (RUC), British Unionists asserted that the RUC already complied fully with the terms of reference. Agreement on terms of reference papered over fundamental disagreements about the relationship of the police to past conflict and about the relationship between police reform and transition to peace. This disagreement was postponed, resulting in disagreement about the implementation of reforms later put forward by the Independent Commission on Policing in Northern Ireland.[25]

Human rights institutions may also have functions that go beyond the direct protection of rights and make them attractive to mediators. A broad human rights agenda may provide the staging for a peace process. At a prenegotiation stage, human rights standards may provide a basis for beginning to set limits on the conflict—limits that can later be extended. In El Salvador, a human rights agreement implemented before a cease-fire and monitored by the United Nations helped create a dynamic that enabled a full cease-fire.[26] At the agreement stage, human rights mechanisms may provide for staged reform or transformation of key institutions. Difficult issues such as restructuring of policing can be postponed to a postagreement implementation phase by the parties' agreeing on general principles and on an independent process to take these forward.

International mediators may also turn to international standards in an attempt to provide some shared principles for divided societies. Where political arrangements focus on territorial divisions or consociational arrangements defined around acknowledging and working with ethnic divisions, human rights institutions may appear to offer an opportunity to design "cross-community" forums, capable of operating across entity divisions and building an intercommunally shared space. The institutions may be the only official forums in which good-faith cooperation between divided groups is expected. Thus, human rights provision may be portrayed as having both "integrative" and "legitimizing" roles.[27] In providing values capable of applying to all groups, human rights standards may be held out as a potentially shared value system able to give political cohesion to deeply divided societies, in the way that the U.S. Constitution is sometimes invoked to provide a unifying force in American society. However, human rights standards also provide a key legitimizing role, legitimizing new political structures by promising accountability and fair treatment where it was missing before. At the point of implementation, integrative and legitimizing ambitions may pull in different directions and appear to evidence a clash between rights-based and conflict resolution approaches. Integration may require an approach focused on intercommunal or political "balance" and on an ongoing attempt to move opposing parties to a place where internalized human rights standards can form a common societal value. In contrast, legitimation may require a normative approach to rights enforcement that is in some instances seen as deeply partisan, and widening communal divisions over human rights. Again, this suggests the need for new thinking about the relationship between human rights and conflict resolution, focused on reconciling the legitimation and integration roles of human rights mechanisms.

Finally, human rights institutions may provide a basis for international organizations to remain involved in the day-to-day implementation of a peace agreement. This enables international organizations to undertake an ongoing mediating role. In Bosnia, domestic human rights and justice mechanisms all had international members, along with ethnically balanced representation. Such a situation typically raises questions about the accountability of international actors and their relationship to the emergence of an indigenous democratic or peaceful culture.

## Understanding Transition

All these factors point to a range of principled and pragmatic reasons why human rights provisions and institutions come to be included in peace agreements. They also point to a distinctive relationship between rights and politics in transitional periods. The very inclusion of human rights provisions in a peace agreement places human rights issues at the center of ongoing debate and controversy over what implementation of an agreement means and requires. Human rights provision is rarely included in a peace agreement for purely principled reasons and typically works in broad brush strokes by providing for rights frameworks and blueprints for institutional reform, whose effectiveness will depend on how they are interpreted and implemented after the agreement. Paradoxically, the facilitative role that human rights may have in reaching agreement, by forming a common language through which parties can address their basic needs, subjects human rights provisions to the ongoing process of negotiation. This reinforces the view that conflict resolution and human rights need to continue to be addressed together. Human rights provisions and mechanisms will continue to be negotiated as they are implemented, requiring ongoing conflict resolution practices attuned to normative constraints and international best practice.

However, the transitional justice landscape is also relevant to understanding why a clash between human rights and conflict resolution actors is often perceived. Neither conflict resolution nor human rights actors stand outside the conflict that they aim to address. In debating the causes of ethnic conflict, political scientists have pointed out that such conflicts are often characterized by the existence of a "meta-conflict," that is, a "conflict about what the conflict is about."[28] This observation can be extended to most forms of conflict. Debates about the causes of conflict are closely related to debates about their solutions: If a conflict is about interethnic hatred, this suggests that measures aimed at reducing that hatred are required; if a conflict is about lack of democracy, its solution may involve democratization.

Debates about the relative priorities of conflict resolvers and human rights promoters can be viewed as merely another example of the meta-conflict in practice. The bitterness and recriminations that sometimes accompany local debates between the two approaches bear this out. The clash is a question not merely of different priorities but of different analyses of the causes of the conflict. One actor's analysis negates another's. Mutual training in each other's tactics, or awareness of each other's approaches and goals, may be futile in addressing what are in essence different analyses of the conflict. In fundamentally disagreeing about the analysis that drives the other's interventions, each set of actors can view the other as working in opposition. Human rights activists may be fully trained in conflict resolution skills, and this may change how they present arguments and approach strategies, but it will not change their analysis of human rights protections as important to addressing the conflict. Conflict resolvers may be trained in human rights standards but still feel that addressing human rights violations is unnecessary, divisive, and disruptive to attempts to foster peace or reconciliation. The hard end of the debate occupies the same space as the violent conflict itself, even though articulated by different actors using different tools.

This indicates another way that some supposed clashes between conflict resolution and justice can be understood: as a debate about what implementation of an agreement entails. Where political institutions collapse or become stalemated through vetoes, human rights institutions may become the primary site of postagreement tension around the meaning and direction of transition. Moreover, human rights institutions may be the inevitable site of such tensions in any case.[29] The politics of human rights provision in peace agreements means that implementation of that provision is not "neutral" concerning the parties to an agreement. Some parties will attempt to use human rights provisions to effect change, while others will resist both human rights and change.

## Case Study: Northern Ireland

Northern Ireland offers an interesting example of the dynamics and dilemmas sketched out thus far. This short case study illustrates how human rights actors attempted to insert human rights concerns into a peace process primarily concerned with "splitting the difference" between claims to Irish and British sovereignty. It can be argued that the insertion of human rights concerns reframed the clash of sovereignties so as to enable agreement between parties who had irreconcilable positions, marking an important step forward in conflict resolution. The difficulties of implementation have revolved less around clashes of rights and conflict resolution and more around the difficulties of getting the different parties to implement their agreement commitments, including human rights commitments.

The Northern Ireland conflict illustrates the dynamic mutating relationship between human rights abuses and conflict, and the controversy over designating human rights abuses as a cause or a consequence of conflict.[30] The conflict in Northern Ireland began its most recent phase in the late 1960s with the demand by the Catholic/Nationalist community for civil rights—in particular equality in jobs, voting, and housing. The state's response to what were essentially demands for more human rights was both political and military. Politically, reform was undertaken to address inequalities, but at the same time increasingly repressive security measures, including internment without trial and the use of lethal force, served not to limit the conflict but to escalate it. The military response fell disproportionately on the Catholic/Nationalist community and undercut the delivery of reforms aimed at providing equality to that same community.[31] Soon violence replaced more peaceful forms of protest, with the consolidation of the Provisional Irish Republican Army (PIRA) and with a plethora of Loyalist paramilitary groups. Claims for internal reform of Northern Ireland's political structures were replaced by claims (which had always existed) for Irish unity. A war of attrition dragged on until, with little prior indication, the IRA declared a cease-fire in August 1994, marking the public beginning of a peace process that was to culminate in the signing of the Belfast Agreement on April 10, 1998.

A short description of the work of human rights actors, and in particular a Belfast-based human rights nongovernmental organization, the Committee on the Administration of Justice (CAJ), indicates some of the possibilities for and difficulties with inserting human rights into a peace process. A full review and critique of CAJ's work is not possible here, nor is there any intention to overplay the organization's role. Rather, the discussion is offered as an illustration of an interesting attempt by human rights activists to affect the "conflict resolution" attempts of the peace process.

CAJ was formed in 1981 as an attempt to coordinate the work of several peace and civil liberties groups in Northern Ireland.[32] Its founding objective was "to secure the highest standards in the administration of justice in Northern Ireland by examining the operation of the current system and promoting discussion of alternatives."[33] During the late 1980s, as the organization developed, it increasingly turned to the use of international human rights mechanisms, such as European Court of Human Rights cases, submissions to international bodies, and the involvement of UN special rapporteurs.[34] This was a response both to the lack of domestic remedies and to a democratic deficit that reduced the impact of local lobbying but also reflected a general international "coming of age" of international human rights law. The organization's work progressed through subgroups working on eight areas: prisoners' rights, policing, emergency law, bill of rights, fair employment, lethal force, racism, and juvenile justice. CAJ developed three core positions, which, while aimed at ensuring a kind of "political impartiality," also indicated a particular interface with the politics of the conflict. First, CAJ took no position on the "constitutional question" of whether Ireland or Britain should have sovereignty over Northern Ireland but argued that however this was resolved, human rights would have to be protected without fear or favor. Second, CAJ used international human rights standards as its basis for critiquing local law, policy, and practice concerning human rights. Third, CAJ opposed the use of violence for political ends in Northern Ireland. Although not articulated, these organizing principles were aimed at keeping the organization open to both Protestant/Unionist and Catholic/Nationalist participation while ensuring a form of independence from Unionist or Nationalist politics and the politics of violence.[35]

The IRA and, later, Loyalist cease-fires of 1994 prompted a reevaluation by CAJ of its approach to its work in light of the emerging peace process. In early 1995 CAJ held a public conference attended mainly by human rights activists, titled "Agenda for Change." This conference focused on five key areas where it was felt that change was more likely, given a peace process: policing, criminal/emergency law, bill of rights, equality, and a "right to truth" concerning past abuses. CAJ had always coupled its condemnation of defects in the administration of justice with policy suggestions for how these defects could be remedied, as indicated in its founding objective. However, the possibilities of the peace process opened up the possibility of more wholesale institutional reform in each area. Accordingly, in each area, CAJ began to think through in more detail just what the ideal institutional reforms would look like from a human rights point of view. This required leaps of faith from the organization and from funders. As Maggie Beirne noted on policing:

> After the republican and loyalist cease-fires were announced debates took place around the need to reform policing. These debates focused around polarities of "disband the Royal Ulster Constabulary (RUC)" to "do nothing" it is fine already. CAJ decided at the end of 1994, beginning of 1995, that we should commission a piece of international comparative research to focus on how best to design police forces which conform to human rights standards, as a useful contribution to the debate. However it took some time to get funding, ages to get researchers appointed, and a lot longer than we thought to do the work. In the meantime the peace process collapsed and no-one was talking about policing. We worried about bringing out the report and it being a dead letter, but we carried on regardless saying it is a useful piece of research and perhaps people will return to it. Eventually the report "Human Rights

on Duty" was issued at the end of 1997, which turned out to be just four months before the Good Friday Agreement was signed and reform of policing was included. We were then in the position of being really clear about what we wanted, and impacting on debates. But in ways this was planned and in ways the timing was accidental.[36]

The resulting report, "Human Rights on Duty," in focusing on human rights concerns, touched on issues key to broader debates: of composition, training, legal and democratic accountability, police structures, and policing in transition. In providing models of how change had been achieved in other situations, it played an important role in shaping the commission's recommendations, but more than that, it has since been widely used in many processes beyond that of Northern Ireland.

With work ongoing on how to advance human rights issues, one clear problem remained of how to convince political elites that human rights issues were centrally important. Peace attempts had focused on devolving power to consociational power-sharing governments and a north/south dimension as the key strategy for conflict resolution.[37] It was always clear that this would be the central emphasis of the new negotiations. In contrast, CAJ constantly asserted that "human rights were *part* of the problem and therefore had to be *part* of the solution." The organization now attempted to think through this phrase more fully and construct arguments on why negotiators should address human rights issues as an integral part of the negotiations. The organization formed two arguments. First, human rights provided a package of issues that went to the heart of the relationships in Northern Ireland and that, if addressed, would begin to provide fairness and equality between communities, which could provide a firm basis from which to address the sovereignty question. Second, CAJ argued that when negotiations became blocked, continued progress on addressing human rights abuses could assist in unblocking negotiations.

The organization argued that human rights issues existed that encapsulated shared interests between Protestant and Catholic communities, and that these could be usefully focused on. These included a bill of rights, economic regeneration and targeting of social need, miscarriages of justice, and speedy transfer of prisoners to locations near their families. Here both Protestants and Catholics would benefit and understand themselves to be benefiting from reform, in similar ways. CAJ also identified "harder" issues, where there were clearer divisions between Catholic/Nationalist and Protestant/Unionist positions on human rights. These included policing and emergency law, where views on whether there were human rights issues, and what should be done about them, was more polarized. CAJ did not avoid these issues. Here CAJ argued that certain interim steps could easily be taken, such as banning the use of plastic bullets, and that the broader issues would have to be addressed as part of any long-term solution. There was unease within the organization about how far to go in "marketing" human rights concerns in this way; however, CAJ took its central analysis and attempted to insert it into every level of the peace process: with local political groups of all leanings, with the Irish, U.S., and British governments, with international bodies, and with the various forums that the peace process spawned. However, even with human rights progress marketed in this way, a clear line was drawn between presenting such progress as key to the peace process (which was vital) and encouraging "horse trading" between human rights and other issues. Thus, CAJ did make many efforts to reframe human rights issues and illustrate their relationship to other aspects of the process, and even accepted that there might be possible staging of human rights implementation. However, CAJ did not seek to link progress on human rights issues to progress in other areas. This was because all the changes advocated by CAJ during the peace process had been asserted by CAJ to be requisite even before that, in order to bring the government into line with international best practice and international human rights standards. Given that those international standards provide for permissible exceptions to human rights in cases of emergency, CAJ did not seek to create further exceptions (such as paramilitary decommissioning as a prerequisite for state human rights enforcement). This would, in essence, have amounted to an argument for human rights positions that were weaker than those already committed to on paper by the government.

Another approach also argued for integration of human rights and political conflict resolution initiatives, in a way that explicitly linked political accommodation with human rights. In 1996, Asbjørn Eide, a Norwegian, wrote a paper commissioned by the Forum for Peace and Reconciliation, which had been established by the Irish government as an immediate response to the cease-fires and to the lack of progress of political talks.[38] This paper began to conceptually reframe the link between conflict resolution and human rights by, in effect, arguing that the question of political accommodation was a "minority rights" issue and, conversely, that "individual rights" protections were vital to enabling political accommodation. Eide's paper effectively created a blueprint for settlement by sketching out how human rights measures could and should be part of the type of power-sharing package that the governments were contemplating.

The approach he suggested contained four elements. First, robust protection of human rights was needed to ensure that no negative consequences would flow from ethnicity/national identification, involving initiatives such as domestic incorporation of the European Convention on Human Rights or the International Covenant on Civil and Political Rights. Eide also suggested the explicit recognition of separate groups or identities, with a requirement of equality of treatment. Second, Eide suggested power sharing and equal representation in institutions. Given that Northern Ireland is a divided society, Eide suggested that power-sharing mechanisms, such as proportional representation and weighted voting, could be used to reward compromise over exclusively ethnic voting. Interestingly for the current debate, he argued that these mechanisms should not be implemented, and power not devolved, until adequate arrangements were in place to ensure "equality in the common domain," that is, stringent and positive equality measures and the "organization of the administration of justice, security forces and others, on a basis of impartiality."[39] Third, Eide suggested equality in the common domain and special measures to ensure "pluralism in togetherness"; that is, political arrangements should include not just the mere provision of equality but also "equal respect for the traditions and identities of each group, within the framework of universally recognized human rights."[40] He identified two layers: at one level, a common identity for everyone living within the territory, based on equality ("equality in the common domain"); and at the other, acceptance of the existence of separate ethnically or culturally based national identities, with mutual respect for the two identities and the provision of a separate domain in certain areas. The first level would be established by the existence of a functioning democracy where basic civil, political, and economic rights were guaranteed without discrimination. Special attention should be given to the "prevention of discrimination in the administration of justice, including the role and performance of the security forces, police, and agents of prosecution, as well as the judiciary."[41] At the second level, Eide identified further special measures and collective rights that could provide for autonomy in certain areas, notably that of identity, with provision for language, culture, and education. In this, he drew on the UN Declaration on the Rights of Persons Belonging to National or Ethnic, Religious, and Linguistic Minorities (1992) and the Council of Europe's Framework Convention on National Minorities (1995). Fourth, Eide recommended methods of securing group accommodation, considering the possible roles of the international community in enforcing any legal mechanisms for group accommodation, through bilateral treaties or through the assistance of the institutions of the Council of Europe and the Organization for Security and Cooperation in Europe.

It is impossible to measure the extent to which interventions such as these affected the process. The first clear evidence of these arguments being acknowledged at the level of the formal negotiations can be traced to an unlikely mechanism and stands as testimony to the advantages of raising the importance of human rights issues at every possible point in a process. In February 1995 the British and Irish governments produced a Frameworks for the Future document, the centerpiece of which was a form of power-sharing government with cross-border cooperation.[42] However, the process became stalled, in particular over opposing positions of Sinn Féin and the Irish government on one hand and the British government and Unionists on the other, over whether the IRA was required to decommission weapons before all-party talks or whether all-party talks could take place before decommissioning. United States senator George Mitchell was invited to chair an International Body on Arms Decommissioning to address the impasse, in what was to prove the start of an ongoing personal commitment to the process. This body took submissions from political parties, civil society, and interested individuals. Human rights actors did not have a clear position on the human rights implications of paramilitary decommissioning and whether it should happen before or after talks. Nor did they seek to develop one, viewing this as a political rather than a human rights matter. Nevertheless, groups like CAJ took the opportunity to argue the human rights dimension of conflict resolution. CAJ met with the International Body, arguing the need to appreciate the human rights context in which all the political debates were taking place. CAJ contended that while fears of paramilitary violence were a part of that context, so also were state human rights abuses.[43] Thus, accountable policing, reduction of emergency law, and movement on human rights issues were not only matters of principle but measures whose implementation would build confidence and positively influence the decommissioning debate.

In its resulting report, the International Body suggested the compromise of a parallel process for talks and for decommissioning. Although not taken up at the time, in 1997 after the breakdown and reinstatement of the IRA cease-fire and the election of the new Blair government in Britain, it was to provide the way forward.[44] Significantly, however, Mitchell's document began to create space for the human rights agenda by stating the importance of matters such as reform of policing as relevant to "further confidence building." This later resulted in the establishment of two "liaison sub-committees" as part of the talks process—one on decommissioning and one on confidence-building measures, with both dimensions culminating in Strand Three of the Belfast Agreement: "Rights, Safeguards and Equality of Opportunity."[45]

Mitchell's acceptance of the need for human rights and equality measures to build confidence was a testimony to the efforts of nongovernmental groups to reframe the decommissioning debate away from zero-sum positions by addressing the underlying reasons for the positions. These types of approaches were continue to prove successful, not just for the inclusion of human rights measures but for the very effort to reach agreement.

In addition to making human rights arguments attuned to their conflict resolution implications, CAJ also began to work on using processes that reframed debates away from a Protestant/Catholic dynamic and demonstrated conflict resolution in action. Its work on equality provides a good example. Although the government had provided legislative responses aimed at antidiscrimination from 1976 onward, these had not proved effective in addressing structural inequalities between Nationalists/Catholics and Unionists/Protestants, with the government acknowledging that "on all socio-economic indicators Catholics remained worse off."[46]

Accordingly, human rights activists, including CAJ, began trying to find measures that would establish equality as a practical reality rather than just a legality. To this end, CAJ looked not just at standards for equality but at how marginalized groups might assert equality in practice, and what mechanisms would be needed to do this effectively. In so doing, it contributed not just to a notion of equality but to building processes for participatory democracy. Enabled by CAJ and the progressive trade union UNISON (representing, among others, large numbers of women in low-paid manual labor), a coalition of marginalized groups, cutting across Protestants; Catholics; disabled persons; gay, lesbian, and bisexual persons; women; ethnic minorities; and others, was forged.[47] This coalition lobbied for mainstreaming of equality, with a focus on achieving legislation that would ensure "policy appraisal" of public decision making in terms of its implications for equality.[48] The legislation, modeled to some extent on environmental impact assessment schemes, aimed to force public bodies to appraise their decisions with regard to the equality implications for marginalized groups, and to consult with those groups as part of this process. Thus, the scheme not only aimed to deliver "equality-proofed" decisions but, in its mechanism, opened up decision making to public scrutiny and intervention, with a particular focus on the marginalized. In covering public decision making it reached beyond the usual limits of constitutionalism—"big government"—to the more diffuse elements of modern governance found in a range of miscellaneous public bodies.[49] The initiative had three important attributes: It created a common platform around which a rainbow coalition across all possible communal divides was formed, operating as a living example of justice and conflict resolution in action; it aimed to address structural inequalities that lay at the heart of the conflict; and it opened up official decision-making processes to public participation and challenge, redefining what it meant to "do politics."

Many of the human rights measures argued for by CAJ found their way into the Belfast Agreement, which had substantial provision for human rights protections.[50] The agreement provided for a Human Rights Commission and an Equality Commission; equality appraisal of public decisions, as pushed for by CAJ; and reform of policing along agreed-on terms of reference that addressed rights concerns. These terms of reference included that "the police service is representative of the society it polices," with potential future benefits for marginalized communities as well as for the Catholic minority. The agreement also provided for reform of criminal justice with four shared aims: to deliver a fair and impartial system of justice to the community; to be responsive to community concerns and to encourage community involvement where appropriate; to have the confidence of all parts of the community; and to deliver justice efficiently and effectively. The Belfast Agreement further provided that the Northern Ireland Human Rights Commission would consult and advise on a bill of rights for Northern Ireland and for a joint Charter of Rights between the north and south of Ireland; propping the door firmly open for future human rights protections.

CAJ had no special leverage on the peace process, apart from the power of its analysis and its skills at disseminating it. Neither was it in any way represented in the talks process. It is therefore worth casting around a little to find why and how the human rights dimension came to be included in the peace process and peace agreement. Christopher McCrudden has suggested that the answer lies in a combination of three factors, illustrating an interesting human rights/conflict resolution dynamic. The first factor was the increasing emphasis of the British and Irish governments on human rights and equality issues as an important part of "confidence building" in the Catholic/Nationalist community. The second factor was the lobbying of those working outside the formal negotiating process, as evidenced by the work of human rights activists and coalitions. Referring to the low level of Catholic unemployment compared to Protestant unemployment, Mary Holland, in March 1998, described how "a parallel peace process" had started to take place beyond the doors of the talks:

Many people in Northern Ireland who are deeply committed to securing a lasting settlement know that these and other indices of inequality and social exclusion must be tackled. They are drawn from the trade unions, community groups, the churches, and others who represent what Bea Campbell memorably described as "the constituency of the rejected."

Together they make up what might almost be described as a parallel peace process—and one which is in many ways as important as the talks at Stormont. It is no coincidence that the same names and organisations crop up again and again when the issues of discrimination and social exclusion are discussed—the Commission [sic] for the Administration of Justice, the public service union UNISON, the Women's Support Network and many others.

These groups know that the people for whom they speak care far more about their prospects of getting a job and a fair deal for their children than about the exact words used to define nationality in the Irish Constitution. If they can see that this time around a period of peace will be accompanied by concrete social and economic change, then the likelihood of their supporting a return to violence will be enormously reduced.[51]

Finally, a shift by Sinn Féin and the various Loyalist parties, especially the Progressive Unionist Party (PUP), in setting priorities for human rights and equality issues also played a part. Upon reentry into talks, Sinn Féin realized that it would not achieve what it wanted in terms of sovereignty and self-determination and turned to the "human rights and equality agenda" as a way of addressing day-to-day concerns of exclusion, domination, and discrimination. The PUP also viewed issues of social exclusion as vital to its community. As McCrudden writes, this was significant to the agenda's inclusion in the talks process:

> [A] failure to address human rights and equality issues of importance to their communities would make it much more difficult to "sell" any agreement. Once human rights was identified as an area that was important, particularly to Sinn Féin, it then became important for those who wanted to keep Sinn Féin "on board" to include it for reasons of strategy as well as for reasons of principle in the final Agreement.[52]

This shift was reinforced by the continued fruits of the coalition-building work outside the formal process, and the agenda began to form an area of common ground between the Women's Coalition, Sinn Féin, the Social Democratic and Labour Party (SDLP), and the two Loyalist parties, the PUP and the Ulster Democratic Party (UDP).

The insider/outsider dynamics of the peace process and the bridge between the two provide an interesting example of how human rights can move linear definitions of the problem, which lead to linear solutions focused on divisions of power and territory, toward a broader set of concerns. In Northern Ireland, the human rights and equality agenda provided an opportunity to reframe positional clashes of sovereignty toward underlying interests of fair treatment, which were easier to reconcile, taking the "sting" out of whatever sovereignty outcome would prevail. While the human rights and equality agenda was often assumed by politicians and mediators to respond to Catholic/Protestant inequalities, the language and mechanisms put forward by human rights actors stood to deliver equality and rights for a much broader range of marginalized constituencies, such as disabled people; children; elderly persons; and gay, lesbian, and bisexual communities. Each reinforced the other. Inclusion of constituencies beyond the Catholic/Protestant divide helped to negate arguments that human rights were "concessions" made by one community to another, demonstrating their international and "best practice" legitimacy. In turn, the emphasis on the Catholic/Protestant reconciliation brought governmental concessions toward stronger and more empowered institutions than would otherwise have been considered, upon which women and others could "piggyback" by asserting a broad-based equality.

## Conclusions

This discussion illustrates how human rights measures can be useful to a peace process, not just because they address root causes of violence but because they can assist parties in finding agreement on issues such as political accommodation by reducing the zero-sum dimension to intercommunal power tussles. It is possible to assert that, despite difficulties in implementing the peace agreement and despite continuing violence, conflict in Northern Ireland has greatly diminished in the short term. However, implementation difficulties have affected all the agreement's institutions. These problems bear witness to the limits of even a "good" peace agreement: During implementation both improved human rights protections and movement toward resolving or transforming the conflict will have to continue to be won. In Northern Ireland the assembly has been suspended four times, including the current indefinite suspension of both the assembly and elections to it. Policing reform, reform of criminal justice, and implementation of the equality agenda have taken place but are still the subject of contentious debate, with implementation being incomplete and in many respects problematic. National bodies for enforcing human rights, such as the Northern Ireland Human Rights Commission, have been beset by problems, raising serious questions about their effectiveness. The issue of paramilitary decommissioning addressed in the agreement, has also not been resolved. Against the political stalemate, intercommunal violence has continued and arguably increased along "interface" areas on either side of the "peace walls" that divide largely homogenous working-class Protestant and Catholic communities.

It is difficult at this stage to assess either the long-term success or failure of the agreement or the relationship of human rights issues to such success or failure in any straightforward way. This is in part because it is all a work in progress, and it is often difficult to see when and how implementation will continue. However, interestingly, the most obvious difficulty for the agreement has been that of sustaining the political institution at its heart—the assembly. This difficulty has had little to do with human rights and more to do with a more general crisis within Unionism about whether to support the agreement—a crisis that at the time of writing has become focused on the issue of when and whether the IRA will decommission its weapons and disband.

Despite these implementation difficulties, it can be argued that the case study's illustration of the relationship between human rights and conflict resolution attempts to find a framework agreement is a constructive one. It could be said that the Northern Ireland experience is unique; Northern Ireland is a transitional society often compared to countries such as South Africa but is one of the few such societies (if not the only one) where the jurisdiction is recognized to be part of a major Western liberal democracy, which throughout the conflict has signed on to, and purported to comply with, the main international and regional human rights institutions. Northern Ireland human rights attempts therefore stand at an interface between "transitional justice" and "democratic renewal." As a result, human rights reform has generated creative attempts to move beyond merely instituting the liberal democratic legal "package," toward providing for social relegitimation of that democracy by providing institutions that are, in practice, capable of responding to challenges of exclusion from a range of constituencies. Northern Ireland may therefore hold conflict resolution lessons for other deeply conflicted societies and also for the less destabilizing (but not less individually damaging) communal conflicts of liberal democracies.

Concerning "transitional societies," it is in the broad concept of using human rights to reframe absolutist clashes over power and sovereignty that some more straightforward lessons lie. The experience of Northern

Ireland, and in particular of CAJ, indicates practical strategies that could be more broadly applicable, aimed at moving toward an approach that sees human rights as integral to conflict resolution.

First, there is a need for human rights actors to create the space for reflection and strategizing on the politics of the peace process. Organizations need to be able to identify on an ongoing basis which issues will be difficult and which will be easier and to remain alert to what ideas and processes may work to argue for addressing human rights. Related to this, human rights groups will often find their greatest power to be the "leverage of a good idea." As Parlevliet argues, while human rights and justice per se are not negotiable, the interpretation and application of rights and justice are negotiable in the context of political settlement.[53] Human rights actors will need to identify what research, information, or training will be needed to make constructive suggestions on human rights and the future, and how coalitions can be forged that open up the debate in helpful ways. This will often be difficult to do in a peace process, where changing patterns of violence mean that ongoing tasks such as monitoring violations may also be more difficult. Funders need to recognize the difficulties a peace process poses for human rights NGOs and take risks with them.

Second, the differences in approaches between political elites and civil society mean that it is important that civil society have access to the politicians and the political debate during any negotiation process. This access does not need to be formal. Peace processes reveal a particular problem in negotiations undertaken by the international community, and steps need to be taken to ensure such access in all negotiations. Indeed, some soft law standards to this effect might be useful.[54]

Third, coalition building across communities with different experiences of exclusion can prove a vital tool in moving political elites toward accepting the importance of human rights provisions. Enabling this sort of coalition can contribute to designing institutions that will address real needs while reframing human rights issues as "owned" by narrow sectional groups.

Fourth, there may be difficult issues to which the approaches of human rights actors and conflict resolution actors are different, and it is important that each group assert its primary focus. Tensions are not always a problem, but they can signify real dilemmas that must be managed. In such cases, both principled and pragmatic approaches must be aired, contrasted, and debated.

Fifth, the real work often begins at the point of an agreement's implementation. The inclusion of human rights in an agreement does not mean that they will be implemented. The battle for implementation must take place in an ongoing way, representing a new type of challenge for human rights actors. The very mainstreaming of human rights may open up stronger political challenges to the discourse, which have to be addressed, with dilemmas for human rights actors about how best to respond effectively. One of those challenges is how to renegotiate the relationship between human rights, the new political order, and the conflict (whether minimally changed or transformed). Ongoing examination of the relationship between human rights and conflict resolution—what it is and what it should be—has emerged as a clear part of this constantly mutating interface.

## Notes

The author would like to thank Maggie Beirne and Michelle Parlevliet for comments on an earlier draft. Mistakes which remain are my own.

**1.** The chapter draws on and applies the author's earlier work, *Peace Agreements and Human Rights* (Oxford: Oxford University Press, 2000), and *Negotiating Justice? Human Rights and Peace Agreements* (International Council on Human Rights Policy: Geneva, 2006).

**2.** Preamble, United Nations Charter, 1945.

**3.** Preamble, Universal Declaration of Human Rights, 1948.

**4.** Preamble, Framework Convention on the Rights of National Minorities, 1995.

**5.** Anonymous, "Human Rights in Peace Negotiations," *Human Rights Quarterly* 18, no. 2 (1996): 249–58.

**6.** Anonymous, "Human Rights in Peace Negotiations," 258.

**7.** Kent Arnold, "Exploring the Relationship between Human Rights and Conflict Resolution," *National Institute for Dispute Resolution FORUM* (December 1998): 1–5.

**8.** Pauline H. Baker, "Conflict Resolution versus Democratic Governance: Divergent Paths to Peace?" in *Turbulent Peace: The Challenges of Managing International Conflict*, ed. Chester A. Crocker, Fen Osler Hampson, and Pamela Aall (Washington, DC: United States Institute of Peace Press, 2001), 753–64; see also Pauline H. Baker, "Conflict Resolution versus Democratic Governance: Divergent Paths to Peace?" in *Managing Global Chaos: Sources of and Responses to International Conflict*, ed. Chester A. Crocker and Fen Osler Hampson, with Pamela Aall eds., (Washington DC: United States Institute of Peace Press, 1996), 563–72.

**9.** Ibid., 760.

**10.** Michelle Parlevliet, "Bridging the Divide: Exploring the Relationship between Human Rights and Conflict Management," *Track Two* 11, no. 1 (March 2002): 6–43.

**11.** Edy Kaufman and Ibrahim Bisharat, "Human Rights and Conflict Resolution: Searching for Common Ground between Justice and Peace in the Israeli/Palestinian Conflict," *National Institute for Dispute Resolution FORUM* (December 1998): 16–23; see also Edy Kaufman and Ibrahim Bisharat, "Bringing Human Rights into the Israeli-Palestinian Peace Process," *Palestine-Israel Journal* 6 (1998): 8–13.

**12.** Kaufman and Bisharat, "Human Rights and Conflict Resolution," 21.

**13.** Cf. Colm Campbell, "Peace and the Law of War: The Role of International Humanitarian Law in the Post-conflict Environment," *International Review of the Red Cross* (2000): 627–52.

**14.** Christine Bell, *Peace Agreements and Human Rights* (Oxford: Oxford University Press, 2000).

**15.** See Mary E. Mulvihill and George A. Lopez, "The Human Rights Dimensions of Peace Accords in Internal Conflicts: Insights for a Research Design" (paper prepared for the panel of Do Good Things Go Together? Rights and Resolution, 43rd annual meeting of the International Studies Association, New Orleans, LA, March 24–27, 2002) (copy on file with author); cf. Integrated Network for Societal Conflict Research, *State Failure Project: Internal Wars and Failures of Governance 1954–1996*, Centre for International Development and Conflict Management (2003), available online at www.cidcm.umd.edu/inscr/stfail/sfdata.htm (categorizing revolutionary wars and ethnic wars); and William Zartman, *Elusive Peace: Negotiating an End to Civil Wars* (Washington DC: Brookings Institution, 1995) (categorizing centralist and regionalist types of internal conflict).

**16.** See, respectively, General Framework Agreement for Peace in Bosnia and Herzegovina, December 4, 1995 (hereinafter DPA); Interim Agreement for Peace and Self-Government (Rambouillet Agreement), February 23, 1999 (not agreed to); The Framework Agreement, August 13, 2001 (Macedonia). All available at www.usip.org/library/pa.html.

**17.** Article II(4), Annex 4, DPA. The Agreement on Human Rights provided in Annex 6 of the DPA reiterates the commitment to the ECHR and its protocols, the enumerated rights, and the list of international human rights and humanitarian law instruments. Some of these matters were dealt with subsequently through the International Police Task Force mandate of the United Nations.

**18.** See Arusha Peace and Reconciliation Agreement for Burundi, August 28, 2000; available at www.usip.org/library/pa.html.

**19.** Cf. Anne-Marie Slaughter, "Pushing the Limits of Liberal Peace: Ethnic Conflict and the 'Ideal Polity,'" in *International Law and Ethnic Conflict*, ed. David Wippman (Ithaca, NY: Cornell University Press, 1998), 128–44.

**20.** See Ivan Pogeny, "Constitution Making or Constitutional Transformation in Post-communist Societies?" in *Constitutionalism in Transformation: European and Theoretical Perspectives,* ed. Richard Bellamy and Dario Castiglione (Oxford: Blackwell, 1996), 157–79; see also Julie Mertus, "From Legal Transplants to Transformative Justice: Human Rights and the Promise of Transnational Civil Society," *American University International Law Review* 14 (1999): 1335–89.

**21.** J. 'Bayo Adekanye, "From Violence to Politics: Key Issues Internationally" (keynote presentation delivered at Ethnic Studies Network conference From Violence to Politics, hosted by INCORE, University of Ulster at Magee College, Derry/Londonderry, Northern Ireland, June 27–30, 2001) (copy on file with the author), 10.

**22.** Fen Olser Hampson, "Making Peace Agreements Work: The Implementation and Enforcement of Peace Agreements between Sovereigns and Intermediate Sovereigns," *Cornell International Law Journal* 30 (1997): 701.

**23.** Contrast the human rights agreement in Guatemala, providing for no impunity (Comprehensive Agreement on Human Rights, March 29, 1994) with the El Salvador human rights agreement, which had no such provision and where an amnesty was passed much later in the process (Agreement on Human Rights, July 26, 1990); all available at www.usip.org/library/pa.html.

**24.** Agreement Reached in Multiparty Negotiations, April 19, 1998 (hereinafter Belfast Agreement), Rights, Safeguards, and Equality of Opportunity, Policing and Justice, para. 6 and Annex A; available at www.cain.ulster.ac.uk/events/peace/docs/agreement.htm.

**25.** For eventual recommendations see Independent Commission on Policing for Northern Ireland, *A New Beginning: Policing in Northern Ireland* (Belfast: Independent Commission on Policing in Northern Ireland, September 1999). Available at www.belfast.org.uk/report/fullreport.pdf.

**26.** See Agreement on Human Rights, July 26, 1990 (El Salvador).

**27.** Cf. Grainne De Burca, "The Language of Rights and European Integration," in *New Legal Dynamics of European Union,* ed. Joe Shaw and Gillian More, (Oxford: Clarendon Press, 1995), 29–54.

**28.** See John McGarry and Brendan O'Leary, *Explaining Northern Ireland: Broken Images* (Oxford: Blackwell, 1995), 1.

**29.** Cf. Ruti Teitel, *Transitional Justice* (New York: Oxford University Press, 2000).

**30.** For various explanations of causes of conflict, see McGarry and O'Leary, *Explaining Northern Ireland.*

**31.** Stephen Livingstone, "Using Law to Change a Society: The Case of Northern Ireland," in *Law, Society and Change,* ed. Stephen Livingstone and John Morison (Aldershot, UK, and Brookfield, VT: Dartmouth, 1990), 51–70; cf. Stephen Livingstone and Colin Harvey, "Human Rights and the Northern Ireland Peace Process," *European Human Rights Law Review* 2 (1998): 162–77.

**32.** For a thorough overview of the context, background, and work of CAJ during the 1980s, see Leo Whelan, "The Challenge of Lobbying for Civil Rights in Northern Ireland: The Committee on the Administration of Justice," *Human Rights Quarterly* 14 (1992): 149–70.

**33.** Dermot P. J. Walsh, "Application for Finance for the Committee on the Administration of Justice" (CAJ office document, Oct. 14, 1981), cited in Whelan, "The Challenge of Lobbying," 57.

**34.** For a review see Martin O'Brien, "Nongovernmental Organizations and the United Nations," in *Human Rights: An Agenda for the Twenty-first Century*, ed. Angela Hegarty and Siobhan Leonard, (London: Cavendish, 1999), 247–65.

**35.** The opposition to the use of force was intended to draw a line between the organization and supporters of violence who sometimes made selective human rights arguments. The organization was to be criticized particularly during the peace process for failing to hold paramilitary groups accountable. However, whether humanitarian law applied was very much open to debate, with its application strenuously resisted by the British government as giving paramilitary groups legitimacy. A decision to apply it would have been viewed as political rather than legal. Moreover, it can be argued that the organization's blanket statement went beyond the scope of humanitarian law's distinctions between military and non-military targets.

**36.** Interview with Maggie Beirne, Committee on the Administration of Justice, May 2002.

**37.** See Sunningdale Agreement, 1973; available at www.cain.ulster.ac.uk/ events/sunningdale/agreement.htm. Anglo-Irish Agreement, 24 I.L.M. 1579 (1985), available at www.cain.ulster.ac.uk/events/aia/aiadoc.htm; Anglo-Irish Agreement, 1995; Frameworks for the Future, 1995 (consisting of "A New Framework for Agreement," 34 I.L.M. 946 [1995], agreed to by the British and Irish governments, and "A Framework for Accountable Government in Northern Ireland," by the British government); available at www.cain.ulster.ac.uk/events/ peace/docs/ fd22295.htm).

**38.** Asbjørn Eide, *A Review and Analysis of Constructive Approaches to Group Accommodation and Minority Protection in Divided or Multicultural Societies*, Consultancy Studies No. 3, Forum for Peace and Reconciliation, July 1996, Dublin Castle (Dublin: Forum for Peace and Reconciliation, 1996).

**39.** Ibid., 12, para. 41.

**40.** Ibid., 14, para. 1.

**41.** Ibid.

**42.** Frameworks for the Future (1995).

**43.** Committee on the Administration of Justice, *Submission to the International Body*, December 1995. Submission to the International Body, chaired by George Mitchell. Ref. S. 33; Belfast: Committee on the Administration of Justice.

**44.** Report of the International Body on Arms Decommissioning, January 22, 1996, available at www.cain.ulst.ac.uk/events/peace/soc.htm.

**45.** Procedural Motion, September 24, 1997, available at www.cain.ulst .ac.uk/events/peace/soc.htm.

**46.** *Aspects of Britain: Northern Ireland,* 2nd ed. (London: HMSO, 1992), 29.

**47.** See Paul Mageean and Martin O'Brien, "From the Margins to the Mainstream: Human Rights and the Good Friday Agreement," *Fordham International Law Journal* 22 (1999): 1499–1538.

**48.** See Christopher McCrudden, *Mainstreaming Fairness? A Discussion Paper on Policy, Appraisal and Fair Treatment* (Belfast: Committee on the Administration of Justice, 1996).

**49.** For a description of the shift away from "big government," see Stephen Livingstone and John Morison, *Reshaping Public Power: Northern Ireland and the British Constitutional Crises* (London: Sweet and Maxwell, 1995).

**50.** Belfast Agreement, Strand 3: "Rights, Safeguards and Equality of Opportunity"; available at www.cain.ulster.ac.uk/events/peace/docs/agreement.htm.

**51.** Mary Holland, "Latest Plan to Tackle Inequality Crucial to North Peace," *Irish Times,* March 12, 1998, 16, as cited in McCrudden, *Mainstreaming Fairness?* 1725.

**52.** Christopher McCrudden, "Mainstreaming Equality in the Governance of Northern Ireland," *Fordham International Law Journal* 22 (1999): 1696–1775, 1724–25.

**53.** Parlevliet, "Bridging the Divide," 24–26.

**54.** See United Nations Security Resolution 1325 of October 31, 2000, dealing with the need for inclusion of women in peace negotiations; available at www.un.org/Docs/sc/unsc_resolutions.html.

# 13
# Truth vs. Justice?
## Commissions and Courts

Vasuki Nesiah

## Transitional Justice: Current Debates

From Peru to South Africa, the former Yugoslavia to East Timor, countries have developed diverse mechanisms to address accountability for past atrocities and collectively grapple with the fault lines of historical memory. In the context of large-scale transitions in these countries' political landscapes, the past decade has seen the evolution of the field of transitional justice—a field directed at developing, and engaging with, the plural paths to addressing accountability and acknowledgment of past human rights abuse in ways that shape the political landscapes of the future.[1]

The field remains divided between more teleological[2] understandings of transitional justice as an end stage that societies move toward after a context of mass repression or civil war and a more open-ended understanding of transitional justice as a path to address a range of transitional contexts—from the legacy of racism and slavery in the United States[3] to the legacy of human rights abuse by Fujimori and by the Shining Path in Peru.[4] In keeping with this latter notion of transitional justice as the journey rather than the destination, we argue for a conception of "justice" in such political transitions as the always-unfinished project of democratic change, whose task at any given point is precisely to create the democratic possibility to reimagine the specific paths and goals of democratization. On one hand, this thinking may render justice as inevitably partial and incomplete; on the other, it is also more ambitious about the relevance of transitional justice, as partial and incomplete as it may be. For instance, it would mean that transitional justice is potentially as relevant in Arkansas as in Accra, although transitional justice may involve a completely different set of initiatives and address very different social divisions in those two places.[5] In contrast, the notion of stages that informs the teleological vision suggests not only a simplistic attempt to box the complexity of historical change into linear chronological dominoes but also implicit ideological closure regarding the possibilities of democracy. In thinking of transitional justice as an endgame that can be achieved and consolidated, the stage theory approach is more likely to lead toward a narrower understanding of the scope and relevance of the field—and accordingly of our understanding of justice.

Against that broader backdrop of the plural and contested ways in which the notion of transitional justice is mobilized, this chapter focuses narrowly on one of the central debates animating the field as a whole, namely, the relationship between truth-seeking mechanisms and criminal justice mechanisms, the tensions and complementarities that characterize each, and their interrelationship. In particular, the author was asked to offer a synopsis and analysis of the debate about official truth commissions versus courts of law[6]—often taken to represent the relative priority of truth versus justice. This paper problematizes this representation and shows the complexity of each of these mechanisms and the standard sets of characteristics attributed to each by those who stress the contrast between them. In addressing the relationship between truth commissions and courts, however, I would first like to situate it in two other constitutive debates in the field that pertain to the notion of transitional justice that informs the truth-versus-justice debate. The first debate goes to notions of justice; the second, to notions of truth.

First, whether justice is a reference to an a priori normative signpost or a field of inquiry into what constitutes fairness, we begin with the appreciation of the rich diversity of understandings of justice. Rather than adjudicating between those different understandings, this paper uses the term "justice" in an operational or pragmatic sense, keeping in play those diverse understandings by focusing on how "justice" takes different meanings in different contexts. Thus, rather than seeking to establish justice as an overarching philosophical concept, this paper focuses on how the term is used.[7] In some cases "justice" is equated with criminal justice; in others it is invoked in a variety of ways that go far beyond establishing the criminal culpability of wrongdoers in a court of law, to include goals often identified with restorative justice.[8] In many cases invocations of transitional "justice" are likely to include at least notions of acknowledgment of wrongdoing and reparations for victims, measures to document the "truths" of the past, and measures to prevent further violations in the future—including efforts to address the background conditions that enabled mass human rights violations.

Mechanisms (courts, commissions, and so on) directed at furthering justice in any particular situation operate in a complex and context-specific set of constraints and opportunities—not just the intricacies of power, hierarchy, and difference that mark most communities, but also myriad other dimensions of local and global background conditions. Thus, although a loosely defined family of political principles and institutional mechanisms may be invoked by the term "transitional justice," what the term actually means in any given situation is open and contested.

Alongside the debate on justice, we also note ongoing debate concerning the appropriate compass of "truth" in transitional justice mechanisms.[9] In one view, the focus of truth-seeking mechanisms should be to marshal a forensic analysis of a narrow range of human rights violations recognized by international law and should be the subject of an evolving global consensus regarding core rights. Alternatively, it could be argued that to abstract such crimes from their context is to miss the larger truth, to ignore the fundamental material and ideological structures that were the enabling conditions of those crimes.[10] For instance, it has been argued that to the extent that truth-seeking mechanisms in South Africa identify the crimes of apartheid as disappearances or torture but do not pass laws and forced removals, they may be missing what was most distinctive about apartheid.[11] Invariably this focus on a narrow set of human rights violations is also a move in the direction of a particularly positivist notion of "truth" that takes international human rights and humanitarian law as the central focus of transitional justice. On the other hand, the alternative, broader notion of truth also situates truth in the contested, pluralized terrain of social struggle and public debate.

The references in the preceding paragraphs to the debates regarding "justice" and "truth" barely touch the surface of the complexity and reach of the discussions surrounding these terms. By invoking these discussions, I merely seek to foreground the fact that notions of justice and truth are themselves fundamentally contested; thus, while this paper's modest agenda does not allow it to delve into these debates, these debates should be seen as a central fault line beneath the truth-versus-justice debate being carried out in the discussion of courts and commissions. Thus, although this paper focuses on how "justice" and "truth" are deployed against each other, we also need to flag the fault lines within these categories. That said, we now turn to the central task of this chapter: the truth-versus-justice debate as it manifests in the contrast between truth commissions and courts. The next section offers a quick survey of arguments premised on this contrast. The following section seeks to problematize this contrast, with attention to the diversity within each of these institutions. In closing, the paper also addresses the complexity of the relationship between courts and commissions.

## Arguments Premised on the Contrast between Truth Commissions and Courts

The relationship between truth commissions and courts is sometimes misunderstood as one of contradictory or contrasting approaches—somehow fundamentally opposed mechanisms, reflecting alternative visions of transitional justice and invariably operating in a zero-sum framework of transitional justice mechanisms. Some scholars and practitioners argue for one or the other of these approaches, presenting a repertoire of arguments in defense of either "truth" or "justice" as the priority of the moment, and thus of either truth commissions or courts as the ideal transitional mechanism.

We begin with arguments advanced by those concerned with the apparent popularity of truth commissions in recent years. Some of these commentators have described truth commissions as substituting for, or coming at the expense of, prosecutions for human rights abuses.[12] From Chile to South Africa to Ghana, truth commissions have sometimes been described as a soft option, born of political necessity and avoiding an unequivocal attack on impunity. Rather than holding perpetrators responsible for their crimes, truth commissions are said to cobble together a constituency of compromise and a program of appeasement.

Others criticize truth commissions not because they are weak but because they are said to be too strong, that is, that they pursue a pernicious Orwellian project of producing a new official "truth."[13] In countries such as Sri Lanka it is often said that truth commissions are regularly convened as political footballs for partisan politics.[14] In South Africa the truth commission has been accused of exploiting the injury of some victims and neglecting the injury of others, its success lying not in telling the truth about human rights abuse under apartheid but in legitimizing the current elite and the transitional arrangements that brought it to power[15] and, moreover, the injustices that persist even in the "new" South Africa.[16] From the perspectives of these critics, prosecutions hold the past accountable while truth commissions commandeer the past to engineer legitimacy for the new order.[17] Truth commissions have been accused of canonizing an official history and laying the foundation for a new orthodoxy.[18]

Many of those who have remained skeptical of truth commissions' ability to deliver on accountability have often held on to prosecutions as the most effective weapon against impunity.[19] The judicial system is geared toward establishing guilt and innocence under due process of law and established standards of proof.[20] It is frequently argued that, at least since Nuremberg, judicial findings of guilt for mass atrocity unequivocally testify to the fact that identifiable individuals, not anonymous entities, commit violations.[21] Judicial systems impose sanctions on the perpetrators and order reparations for victims—crucial elements, it is argued, in ensuring that justice is delivered.

The arguments raised in the preceding paragraphs are advanced primarily by those who argue for courts and criminal justice processes as the paradigmatic institutional avenue to address the challenges of transitional justice. Again, I present these arguments but do not necessarily endorse them; in fact, in the next section I subject arguments based on a contrast between commissions and courts to an extended critique. For now, the ironic aspect of the purchase that commentators draw from this contrast is that others rely on the same mapping of a truth-versus-justice polarity to argue the opposite case—namely, that it is truth commissions that offer resources for a nuanced and holistic response to the complexities of transitional societies.[22] For instance, those who have been more critical of the criminal justice end of the truth-versus-justice dichotomy have argued that criminal justice processes are focused on perpetrators, not on the dignity of victims or their priorities for justice. Thus, it is argued that judicial processes such as the International Criminal Tribunal for Rwanda (ICTR)[23] not only neglect the complexity of victims' needs but may even disempower them. For instance, hostile cross-examination can further exacerbate the injury suffered by victims even in the process of providing accountability.[24] This is perhaps a symptom of a broader problem regarding how judicial systems are often alienated from victims, attuned as they are to law and legal victory rather than to victims. In many common-law jurisdictions, the decision as to whether to issue an indictment is at the sole discretion of the prosecutorial authority, with little input from victims. In some cases, judicial mechanisms may also function primarily in closed sessions that deny victims the right to public accountability. Tailored as they are to the facts regarding the culpability of individual defendants, often the case records offer little information on the historical context of the violation, or even relevant demographic or regional patterns of violations. Thus, on many fronts criminal accountability processes are said to be held hostage to the needs of the legal system rather than answering broader social needs relating to victim empowerment, civic dialogue, historical memory, public acknowledgment, and so on.

Moreover, it is often argued that judicial mechanisms are adversarial efforts that are less than constructive in postconflict societies. At worst, they may endanger a fragile peace; at best, they may fail to take advantage of an opportunity to forge reconciliation and move a community to a new future. Seen as retributive and backward looking, the blunt instrument of criminal justice is thought inadequate to the complex and forward-looking needs of a transitional society. Thus, even in such a celebrated case as the one brought against Pinochet in Spain and the UK,[25] victims' groups were themselves openly divided about the wisdom of raking up Chile's past and opening old wounds in Spanish and British courtrooms. It was feared that the Pinochet case was feeding the needs of the international legal community's infatuation with universal jurisdiction, rather than the current priorities of victims in Chile. Thus, some victims argued that his arrest violated Chilean sovereignty and that the retired general's alleged complicity in human rights abuses during his seventeen-year rule is Chile's problem to solve. Their position underscores an extraordinary dilemma for dissidents who have returned to the Chilean political scene since 1990, when Pinochet's reign as head of state came to a close. In a bizarre twist of fate, some of Pinochet's victims felt that prosecutorial zeal in Europe forced them into the role of protecting him from international trial.[26]

In contrast, truth commissions are heralded for being victim-centered and community-oriented efforts at restorative justice. In countries as diverse as South Africa and Guatemala, truth commissions are said to take a more holistic view of a society's needs. Given their potential for a broader mandate than is practicable with trials, they are said to be better able to go beyond individual culpability, to address the complexity of systemic violence and even catalyze a national debate on past accountability and the factors underlying mass atrocity, and yet do so in ways that repair the fabric of a torn nation.[27] Truth commissions have the potential to bring a divided community into a common conversation about the most painful events that divided them in the first place. To this extent they are said to address the past in ways that are honest but also constructive, offering acknowledgment but also reconciliation.[28]

## Unmooring the Contrast between Truth Commissions and Courts

As we have seen, there are standard sets of characteristics and tendencies attributed to truth commissions or courts by both advocates and critics of one or the other mechanism. However, the standard generalizations contrasting these two mechanisms are a less than compelling guide to how each operates in specific contexts. In fact, what is most interesting about the truth-versus-justice debates is that the very same criticisms directed against truth commissions—and the very same virtues attributed to it—in one context turn out to be equally valid statements about criminal justice processes in another context. This means not that truth commissions and courts do not vary in important and interesting ways, but that the significance of each family of mechanisms is not best captured in the generalized contrast between them.

We can begin by scrutinizing the claim that we need to privilege the prosecutorial path because truth commissions compromise on accountability —in fact, let us do this by examining contexts where prosecutions have been the primary route to transitional justice. Rwanda and the Balkans may provide the most paradigmatic contemporary examples of this—and unfortunately, both of these cases suggest that the promise of judicial accountability has proved to be equally elusive and illusory. In Rwanda, after a genocide that killed some 800,000 people, the ICTR has issued indictments against only sixty-three people, with only eight convictions to date.[29] If the war crimes tribunal is the centerpiece of accountability, then courts can be said to be at the center of an accountability crisis in Rwanda.[30] Similarly, the International Criminal Tribunal for the Former Yugoslavia (ICTY)[31] has indicted seventy-nine people.[32] Moreover, the sentences that convicted war criminals have received themselves offer a weak testament to the judicial route's power against impunity—thus, Dragoljub Prcac, one of the two deputy commanders of Omarska, one of the most infamous prison camps of the war, received a sentence of five years after being found guilty of one count of crimes against humanity and two counts of violations of the laws or customs of war by Trial Chamber I of the ICTY on November 2, 2001.[33] Undoubtedly, sentencing is not the only register of accountability, not only because there may be mitigating circumstances that argue for leniency, but also, and more importantly, because a crime against humanity suggests that there may be no punishment that is adequate to the crime. However, the legitimation discourse of war crimes tribunals is precisely to argue that the identification of a harm as a crime against humanity is an important advance for justice. From this standpoint, the argument that we should choose war crimes tribunals because they travel the distance in holding perpetrators accountable appears less than convincing if a crime against humanity results in a five-year sentence.

Similarly, the claim that truth commissions condense a new, manipulated truth while prosecutions offer a more impartial path has also proved less than convincing. Not only have we seen efforts, such as the newly inaugurated Greensboro commission, that are directed at contesting official truths and going beyond the jurisprudence of the crime to pluralize historical memory, but many criminal justice processes have themselves been directed at entrenching a canonical and, arguably, partisan truth.[34] Many have condemned the "justice" advanced at Nuremberg as "victor's justice"—doing more to consolidate the Allies' victory off the battlefield than to provide accountability for the Holocaust. Nuremberg not only failed to offer an account of wider structural responsibility by many sectors of the German citizenry as "willing executioners" implementing the Holocaust;[35] it also failed to address the responsibilities of the Allies themselves in sustaining Hitler and anti-Semitism in the 1930s, of failing to act sooner to contest the agenda of the Third Reich—and, of course, of the Allies' own crimes against civilians in the course of the war. Thus, while truth commissions have been condemned as legitimation exercises manipulated by successor elites, even celebrated trials may sometimes do more to advance the interests of those who won the transitional battles, than to set in motion accountability processes that address the society that underwent the transition or offer a more complex account of all actors responsible for atrocities.

Yet if the criticisms of truth commissions in the truth-versus-justice debates extend to courts, the central claims made for the merits of truth commissions may also have applicability for judicial processes. For instance, since truth commission mandates are guided by a national vision, it is argued that they are better suited to move beyond individual cases in order to have a social impact. While the governing questions of specific cases may restrict courts to an individualized focus cabined by a "limited charge sheet,"[36] it is argued that truth commissions have a broader mandate that directs and enables them to track patterns of violations, identify victim groups, and catalyze public debate on issues of historical memory and other important touchstones of deep social division.[37] Yet interestingly, the development of jurisprudence regarding mass atrocity in recent years has led prosecutorial efforts to go beyond narrowly justiciable claims by developing more complex notions of accountability. Thus, even when triggered by individual allegations of guilt, criminal justice processes have uncovered information that extends far beyond the individual in question to offer us a portrait of the social structures and institutional arrangements that provided enabling conditions for such atrocities. It is widely recognized that one of the most remarkable advances in this regard is the development in the ICTY of jurisprudence around the notion of command responsibility. In arguing that defendants had command responsibility for the war crimes at trial, prosecutors conducted in-depth research into how state structures were organized, and ethnic-chauvinist ideologies mobilized, to present the court with a comprehensive and multifaceted view of the lines of authority that brought about those abuses.[38] At present, the alienation of the Hague proceedings from civil society and the war's enduring fissures in the Balkans ensure that the social impact of these findings remains an open question. However, it certainly does suggest that courts could move beyond the lens of individual fact patterns to make the same kind of broader investigative findings that truth commissions do in uncovering how an abusive system functioned.

Irrespective of whether such research is conducted by courts or commissions, the extent to which these processes set the priorities for public engagement and make proactive efforts to involve victim communities will often determine whether such findings have a social impact or merely collect dust in an archive.[39] Some have argued that courts, unlike truth commissions, by the very nature of their function are driven by the imperatives of the case at hand and are unable to address and engage with a broader vision of accountability processes. Yet in recent years we have found that judicial mechanisms can also have a deeper grounding in victim communities when court proceedings take into consideration victims' justice priorities rather than following a prior agenda or one that is independent of victim communities. For instance, in Guatemala, the work of the Centro Para Acción Legal en Derechos Humanos (the Center for Human Rights Legal Action, or CALDH) has been shaped by an ethos of victim-centered accountability processes that is grounded in ongoing consultation with victim communities.[40] Thus, court processes can vary in the extent to which they are victim centered, making them no different in this respect from the different truth commissions; the truth commissions in El Salvador and Nigeria could be held up as particularly poor examples of victim-centered processes, while the commissions in South Africa and East Timor may offer more promising examples. Similarly, although ICTY may be exceptionally alienated from victim communities in the former Yugoslavia, we cannot paint all court processes with the same brush—CALDH's approach to prosecutions premised on consultations with victim groups may offer instructive insights to commissions and courts.

Yet just as criminal justice processes may succeed in reaching out to victim communities, truth commissions can also make advances in regard to the central goal of prosecutions: accountability for crimes. Truth commissions and other nonjudicial accountability mechanisms have elicited accountability through naming,[41] shaming, and using a range of noncriminal sanctions such as community service.[42] Truth commissions serve as a particularly valuable avenue for accountability in cases such as Sierra Leone, where the sheer scale of violations makes prosecution of all perpetrators impossible; in East Timor, where prosecutorial capacity is limited because of human and financial resource constraints; in Ghana, where an amnesty prohibits criminal prosecutions; in South Africa, where the imperatives of a negotiated peace rendered prosecutions too politically volatile, and hence the compromises of a conditional amnesty difficult to avoid; and in the United States, where in some contexts of racist violence the judicial route was traveled but emerged as blind to (and perhaps even complicit with) the repression and institutionalized prejudice that engendered the violence and therefore carried little legitimacy with victims.[43] In all these varied contexts a truth commission could be the only avenue to ensuring that victims have access to some measure of accountability that addresses their goals. Moreover, the work of truth commissions could be particularly valuable in advancing criminal accountability in the long term. Chile may offer the paradigmatic example of a transformed political environment making it possible to revisit prosecution options; in that context, the work of an earlier truth commission provides an invaluable archive of evidentiary resources gathered at a time closer to that of the original crime. Finally, truth commissions have the capacity to address accountability on multiple registers: at the individual level and the structural level, with a focus on the immediate perpetrator and on those with command responsibility.

In sum, the discussion above has suggested that the contrast between truth commission and courts is misguided—we have found that few generalizations could be made about either end of that polarity. There is great internal diversity within both truth commissions and courts, which diminishes the contrast between them. Invariably we are much better off thinking of these mechanisms not as singular models but as two complex traditions of accountability and acknowledgment, each representing a family of mechanisms characterized by internal variation.

## Complementarities and Contradictions

The principal focus of this chapter has been on conveying the complexity and internal diversity within the family of courts and commissions respectively in problematizing the polarized viewpoint through which each of these mechanisms is often represented. As a final note we should address how truth commissions and courts relate to each other. Although the contrast attributed to commissions and courts may not obtain, judicial processes and truth commissions should not necessarily be viewed as always operating in completely complementary ways. While some argue that these approaches are fundamentally at odds, others argue that they are distinct but fundamentally compatible. Some see this complementarity, at a philosophical level, as the affirmation that retributive and restorative approaches are two equally important dimensions of transitional justice. Others see this complementarity in terms of policy rationality, where truth commissions have jurisdiction over a different set of crimes than do courts, or, in more operational terms, where truth commissions prepare the way for courts by procuring evidence in broad investigative sweeps. The truth commissions' actions then provide a basis for strategizing more narrowly forensic approaches to legal investigation. In pragmatic terms, in this way both mechanisms can be staggered to phase in accountability processes to reflect the fact that a society may have different fruition times for different degrees of accountability.

Some or all of these dimensions of complementarity may indeed obtain in many cases. Yet any generalization that these mechanisms are *always* complementary fundamentally understates the complexity not only of their interrelationship but also of the internal diversity of both commissions and courts. As the preceding pages have suggested, analysis of these institutions requires attention to how each mechanism varies from context to context; equally, then, how these diverse mechanisms interrelate also varies from context to context. Moreover, given that courts and commissions are *internally* complex and multidimensional, different aspects and institutional arms of courts and commissions may operate in different ways and are constantly working out the internal tensions and the multiple objectives they pursue.[44] Thus, in certain instances commissions and courts may travel colliding paths in regard to the different ways in which they define their objectives (and the priorities they may accord to those different objectives).[45] For instance, when commissions and court processes operate simultaneously (as is currently the case in Sierra Leone, East Timor, and Peru),[46] the question of information sharing between these institutions raises a whole range of tensions between the requirements of criminal justice and the goals of accessing the greatest amount of information from as many victims, perpetrators, and witnesses as possible.

There has been extensive speculation and debate among scholars and practitioners in the transitional justice field about how this very issue should be worked out in the relationship between the court and the truth commission in Sierra Leone. The issue remains an open question because, unlike in East Timor,[47] the implementing legislation in Sierra Leone offered no clear rules about information sharing between these institutions or balancing their different mandates. There have been proposals that the two institutions develop a memorandum of understanding (MOU) that establishes protocols for information sharing.[48] Such an MOU cannot escape the fact that the institutions have conflicting priorities and modi operandi and that one or both of the institutions will have to compromise on their distinct mandates to establish conditions for them to work together constructively; however, the MOU could offer a rationalized and constructive process for the terms of such compromise. In other words, it will not transform the conflict into complementarity, but it creates a constructive process for cramping an institution's unhindered pursuit of its mandate, in ways that accommodate competing priorities and balance the different goals of transitional justice in Sierra Leone. Such balancing is possible because, although the tensions between the distinct institutional mandates and modi operandi are significant, these tensions do not overdetermine the interrelationship question. On the contrary, by and large there is considerable overlap in the objectives of the two institutions, and they may even assist with each other's work. However, appreciating this measure of complementarity is precisely the reason also to recognize areas of deep tension and squarely confront the inescapable policy choices we have to make in shaping rules of information sharing.

South Africa offers another instance where the relationship between court processes and a truth commission could be studied. Clearly the truth commission and courts were not traveling alternative and colliding paths, but these were not paths that could be simply harnessed into symbiotic harmony, either. According to the terms of the amnesty-for-truth bargain, those who applied for amnesty and offered the full truth about politically motivated crimes were to be processed according to the amnesty provisions of the TRC Act, while those who failed to do so would be vulnerable to prosecution. The creation of this conditionality provided some degree of accountability for apartheid-era crimes, without giving a blanket amnesty that would have made courts entirely irrelevant to postapartheid justice. In fact, prosecutions and amnesties were said to operate in terms of what Alex Boraine has described as a "carrots and sticks" approach to accountability[49]—that is, the terms of the carrot-and-stick formula were then the de facto framework of complementarity between courts and the commission in the South African transition. Thus, when the Eugene De Kock trial resulted in a conviction and information regarding several other perpetrators, it prompted a slew of amnesty applications and, presumably, more information for the commission's truth-seeking efforts.[50] On the other hand, as strong efforts by the prosecutorial authority repeatedly generated amnesty applications, it discouraged the judicial system from pursuing more indictments and criminal investigations.[51] To some extent this represents a dynamic that wasn't anticipated by the "framework of complementarity," and to that extent it was also a dynamic that had some corrosive effect on the moral legitimacy of that framework, because the stick in the carrot-and-stick formula was no longer a credible and ongoing threat. This may be seen partly as the unfolding of a tension between the different constituencies that had a stake in prosecutorial success versus greater information, and the competing incentive structures that informed each. Thus, in the South African case (as is likely in most cases) it would be too simplistic to describe the relationship between the commission and courts as either contradictory or complementary—we need to go beyond that polarity to work out a more nuanced understanding of the complex dynamics of these institutions.

## Concluding Thoughts

The study of commissions and courts requires a case-by-case analysis that pays attention to how different notions of justice, truth, and law are contested in different moments of the life of transitional justice mechanisms. Easy generalizations about the relationship between commissions and courts not only understate the significant variation that characterizes each of these mechanisms but also understate the complexity of their interrelationship. This does not mean that we look to the past only to track the diversity of courts and commissions in different contexts. There may be equal value in also tracing some shared vocabularies and traditions that have characterized the evolution of these two mechanisms up to this point. However, we should be hesitant about slipping from that historical narrative into a normative argument that translates those particular traditions as "core" characteristics of the two mechanisms. To do the latter too hastily would be to entrench a contingent development into a universal model and, in effect, curb the future development of both commissions and courts. This is a time of great innovation and creativity for both these families of mechanisms: commissions and courts. Thus, our account of their development thus far must convey the internal diversity that has characterized their past, just as it must open the door to further innovation and transformation that may expand and enrich the potential of both these types of institutions and their interrelationships.

## Notes

This chapter owes a great debt to the knowledge I have gained at the International Center for Transitional Justice (ICTJ) about the varied and rich experiments in transitional justice taking place all over the world—the chapter bears the footprints of the work of all my colleagues. I have benefited enormously from Elizabeth Webber's extremely thorough and insightful research assistance. Priscilla Hayner's detailed comments through the various drafts have been invaluable. Paul Seils's close scrutiny and engaged critique—and his numerous points of contention regarding various arguments advanced in this chapter—improved the final text considerably, even if they didn't always settle the arguments! The views expressed here are the author's alone.

**1.** In most cases, the human rights record referred to in transitional justice efforts covers only a modest slice of justice issues, namely, conventionally justiciable claims. This means that our working definition of human rights claims is often both excessively legalistic and (and this is not unrelated) conforming to a fairly orthodox centrist liberal tradition. There are increasing efforts to change what is a justiciable human rights claim (for instance, note the jurisprudence on rape as a war crime in the ICTR), as well as what constitutes a human rights claim. (Efforts to address systemic violations of socioeconomic rights are among the most long-standing efforts in this regard.)

**2.** By teleological visions of transitional justice we want to describe an approach that sees the transition as directed toward a specific political arrangement as the "telos," or end goal, of the transition. For some in the field this telos is defined broadly (as, for example, liberal democracy); for others it is defined more narrowly (as, for instance, the specific approach to democracy and markets advanced by institutions such as USAID).

**3.** The Greensboro Truth and Community Reconciliation Project (GTCRP), a coalition of the Greensboro Justice Fund and the Beloved Community Center, with support from the University of Massachusetts Labor Relations and Research Center and a national advisory board, is establishing the first truth commission in the United States, in response to unresolved questions surrounding the events of November 3, 1979, when five people were killed and ten wounded as Ku Klux Klan and Nazi party members opened fire on a crowd of people gathered for a legally scheduled parade in Greensboro, North Carolina. It will address what, according to project organizers, remains the unspoken subtext to labor, race, and community relations issues in the city today.

**4.** Peru's Truth and Reconciliation Commission was established in June 2001 by order of Peru's interim president, Valentín Paniagua. The commission's mandate is to investigate the causes of the violence and to determine individual responsibility for crimes carried out from May 1980 to November 2000. The commission is to consider the effect of violence on indigenous communities, make proposals for reparations, and propose a way for the country to deal with the past and move forward. To date the commission has collected fifteen thousand testimonies, representing forty thousand individual victims.

**5.** Many in the field may argue for treating those abuses conventionally labeled "gross human rights violations" as being of a fundamentally different order of significance and warranting a fundamentally different level of scrutiny and critique; unless we hold on to that fundamental difference, it is argued, we risk diluting transitional justice into a vague "wish list" that is "endless" and "unhelpful" (written comments to the author on a draft of this paper, by Paul Seils, January 29, 2003). However, expanding our conception of transitional justice to critically scrutinize "normalized" injustices, to have the potential to include contexts such as Arkansas, makes transitional justice not more vague but more relevant—it is an effort to give further specificity to what transitional justice would mean in any particular context, by situating the agendas and priorities of transitional justice in social and historical analysis, and the specific struggles that animate the political fault lines of that context. Entrenched orthodoxies about which finite set of abusive situations should be identified as "gross human rights violations" predetermines the agendas and priorities of transitional justice in ways that are problematic; it settles transitional justice into naturalized distinctions regarding ordinary and extraordinary violence, and sweeping taxonomies that advance, a priori, universalized indices ranking what counts as serious human rights abuse.

**6.** While a discussion of alternative processes is beyond the mandate of this paper, it should be noted that truth-seeking and accountability efforts extend far beyond official truth commissions and formal criminal justice processes. The *gacaca* process in Rwanda and the people's tribunals in India are but two of the many examples showing the range and scope of mechanisms, official and unofficial, that advance transitional justice objectives in truth seeking and accountability.

**7.** Different usages seek to produce legitimacy in different ways for different ends; discursive analysis of struggles over the production of legitimacy requires a close reading of how "justice" is used in a specific context. The goal of this chapter is to offer a broad survey of many cases, and thus it cannot offer a more detailed reading of the pragmatics of justice in particular sociohistorical and institutional contexts, although the beginnings of a tentative interrogation about "justice" and "truth" in the field of transitional justice as a whole are scattered throughout.

**8.** See Ruti Teitel, *Transitional Justice* (New York: Oxford University Press, 2000).

**9.** The South African TRC itself spoke of being directed toward four kinds of truths, defined in its *Final Report*, vol. 1, 110–14:

1. *Factual or forensic truth*, defined as the legal or scientific notion of factual, corroborated evidence, of obtaining accurate information
2. *Personal or narrative truth*, referring to individual truths of victims and perpetrators and established through telling "their own" stories, based on the value of oral tradition

3. *Social or "dialogue" truth,* which "is established through interaction, discussion and debate"

4. *Healing and restorative truth,* "the kind of truth that places facts and what they mean within the context of human relationships—both amongst citizens and between the state and its citizens"

**10.** Of course, truth commissions have also been charged with focusing on a global truth in ways that distort or ignore local truth. See Lars Buur, "Monumental Historical Memory: Managing Truth in the Everyday Work of the South African Truth and Reconciliation Commission," in *Commissioning the Past: Understanding South Africa's Truth and Reconciliation Commission,* ed. Deborah Posel and Graeme Simpson (Johannesburg: Witwatersrand University Press, 2002).

**11.** The South African Truth and Reconciliation Commission (TRC) was established by Parliament through the Promotion of National Unity and Reconciliation Act 34 of 1995 (the Act). The Act defined the focus of the TRC as the causes, nature, and extent of gross violations of human rights that occurred between March 1, 1960, and May 10, 1994. Mamdani argues, in "Reconciliation without Justice," *Southern African Review of Books,* November–December 1996, 3–5, that the TRC defined victims too narrowly. He writes that the focus on victims and perpetrators of gross violations ignored the unique structural issues related to victimization produced by apartheid in South Africa. Mamdani criticizes the TRC for paying insufficient attention to those who benefited from apartheid but may not have been direct perpetrators of human rights violations, saying that the TRC thereby lost a wider, more contextual truth. Further, in "The Truth According to the TRC," in *The Politics of Memory: Truth, Healing and Social Justice,* ed. Ifi Amadiume and Abdullahi An-Na'im (London: Zed Books, 2000), Mamdani claims that in this process of institutionalizing truth, the TRC has compounded the political compromise struck in the handover of power with a moral compromise, obscuring the wider truth to serve the purposes of the new regime.

**12.** See, for example, Reed Brody, "Justice: The First Casualty of Truth?" *Nation,* April 30, 2001, also available at www.hrw.org/editorials/2001/justice0430.htm.

**13.** As Colin Bundy describes the South African TRC, following Brent Harris, it was engaged in an effort "to establish a version of the past that transcends subjective and contested views." Colin Bundy, "The Beast of the Past: History and the TRC," in *After the TRC: Reflections on Truth and Reconciliation in South Africa,* ed. Wilmot James and Linda Van de Vijver (Athens: Ohio University Press, 2001), 15.

**14.** See, for example, the quotation from Neelakandan Jandasamy: "This is just a witch hunt to blame the opposition UNP," in Feizal Samath, "Politics—Sri Lanka: Probe of Ethnic Violence Branded as 'Witch Hunt,'" Inter Press Service, September 5, 2001.

**15.** Mamdani defines the great achievement of the South African TRC as discrediting the former apartheid regime in the eyes of its beneficiaries, in Mamdani, "Reconciliation without Justice," 183. However, he says that in its eagerness to reinforce the new order, the TRC wrote the majority of victims out of its version of history.

**16.** "Parented by compromise there is a final ironic risk . . . will the (TRC) Report help to build a nation in the longer term, or will it legitimize a lopsided structure—two nations disguised as one, a hybrid social formation consisting of increasingly deracialised insiders and persistently black outsiders?" Bundy, "The Beast of the Past," 20.

**17.** As Charles Villa-Vicencio suggests, "A state-sanctioned program on national reconciliation can, of course, favor a new brand of nationalism while playing down an overt concern or the basic rights of victims," in Charles Villa-Vicencio, "Why Perpetrators Should Not Always Be Prosecuted: Where the International Criminal Court and Truth Commissions Meet," *Emory Law Journal* 49 (2000): 9.

**18.** Referring again to the South African TRC report, Posel and Simpson write, "The TRC authors were involved in a process of selection, summary, distillation—which was also necessarily an exercise in exclusion, silencing," in "The Power of Truth: South Africa's Truth and Reconciliation Commission in Context," in *Commissioning the Past,* ed. Posel and Simpson, 15.

**19.** See Reed Brody, "Justice: The First Casualty of Truth?"; and Richard Wilson, "Challenging Restorative Justice," *Human Rights Dialogue* Series 2, no. 7 (2002).

**20.** See Frederick van Zyl Slabbert's measuring of the TRC process against a legal process and finding it wanting, in "Truth without Reconciliation, Reconciliation without Truth," in *After the TRC,* ed. James and Van de Vijver, 69.

**21.** See, for example, A. Neier, "The Nuremberg Precedent," *New York Review of Books,* November 4, 1993.

**22.** See Sanford Levinson, following Osiel, who argues that truth commissions become relevant precisely because courts cannot address the depth and complexity of problems in deeply divided societies: "As Osiel suggests in his important *Mass Atrocity, Collective Memory and Law,* the Durkheimian assumption of an underlying moral consensus that merely need be evoked by the formal criminal law is belied by the circumstance that, as a practical matter, generates the need for truth commissions in the first place, which is the presence within a given social order of deep divisions over basic political questions." "Trials, Commissions and Investigating Committees: The Elusive Search for Norms of Due Process," in *Truth v. Justice: The Morality of Truth Commissions,* ed. Robert I. Rotberg and Dennis Thompson (Princeton, NJ: Princeton University Press, 2000), 220.

**23.** The UN Security Council created the ICTR by Resolution 955 of November 8, 1994, under Chapter VII of the United Nations Charter. The ICTR was established for the prosecution of persons responsible for genocide and other serious violations of international humanitarian law committed in the territory of Rwanda between January 1, 1994, and December 31, 1994. It may also deal with the prosecution of Rwandan citizens responsible for genocide and other such violations of international law committed in the territory of neighboring states during the same period. Resolution 955 specified that the purpose of this measure was to contribute to the process of national reconciliation in Rwanda and to the maintenance of peace in the region.

**24.** See Julie Mertus, "Truth in a Box: The Limits of Justice through Judicial Mechanisms," in Amadiume and An-Na'im, *The Politics of Memory*. Martha Minow describes testifying as an ordeal that presents the victims with no opportunity to give their narrative directly, in Minow, "Hope for Healing," in Rotberg and Thompson, *Truth v. Justice*.

**25.** Augusto Pinochet's arrest in London on October 17, 1998, was the result of a *commission rogatoire* (official petition) to question him, filed by Judge Balta-zar Garzón of the Spanish National High Court. Judge Garzón had been investi-gating cases of human rights violations constituting crimes against humanity, committed in Chile under Augusto Pinochet's regime. On October 28, 1998, the British High Court declared Pinochet's detention unlawful on the grounds that he enjoyed immunity from prosecution as a former head of state. An appeal of the High Court judgment was subsequently brought before the House of Lords to ad-dress the legal concerns surrounding the arrest, and on November 25, 1998, the House of Lords reversed the High Court ruling. On January 11, 2000, the British home secretary announced that he was "minded" to halt extradition on medical grounds and invited Spain to make representation. The Spanish government refused to act on Garzón's request for legal action in the British courts.

**26.** Sergio Bitar, a powerful left-wing politician and former cabinet minister for the assassinated Chilean president Salvador Allende, speaks to the agonizing dilemmas of this position: "I can't sleep at night. I'm constantly grappling with this. But as a Chilean, I think what's best for my country is to try to put him on trial here. We are a deeply divided nation because of Pinochet, and it's time we got rid of our ghosts. Chileans are best qualified to do that ourselves." Anthony Faiola, "Pinochet's Arrest Presents His Enemies with Dilemma; Some Want Him Freed and Returned to Chile," *Washington Post*, November 5, 1998.

**27.** See Martha Minow: "The aspiration to develop as full an account as pos-sible requires a process of widening the lens, sifting varieties of evidentiary materi-als and drafting syntheses of factual material that usually does not accompany a trial. . . . The sheer narrative project of a truth commission makes it more likely than trials to yield accounts of entire regimes. Trials, in contrast, focus on partic-ular individuals and their conduct in particular moments in time, with decisions of guilt or nonguilt, and opinions tailored to those particular questions of indi-vidual guilt." Minow, "The Hope for Healing," 39.

**28.** The South African Truth and Reconciliation Act offers the concept of *Ubuntu* (I am human through your humanity) in this respect. Chapters in Rotberg and Thompson, *Truth v. Justice,* and in Alex Boraine, Janet Levy, and Ronel Sheffer, eds., *Dealing with the Past: Truth and Reconciliation in South Africa* (Cape Town: Institute for Democracy in South Africa, 1994), make these arguments, as do other books on the subject. Jonathan Allen discusses these claims in the South African context in "Balancing Justice and Social Unity: Political Theory and the Idea of a Truth and Reconciliation Commission," *University of Toronto Law Journal* 49 (Summer 1999).

**29.** The ICTR Web site lists twenty-two persons as currently on trial at the ICTR. Twenty-nine persons are awaiting trial. The tribunal has convicted eight persons and acquitted one. Six of the eight convicts, including former Rwandan prime minister Jean Kambanda, are serving their prison sentences in Mali. For 2002–3 the General Assembly of the United Nations decided to appropriate to the ICTR a total budget of US$177,739,400 and 872 posts (information from International Criminal Tribunal for Rwanda, www.ictr.org, gathered on January 30, 2003).

**30.** Clearly we cannot reduce the question of justice and accountability to a proportionate relationship between prosecutions and number of victims; as Paul Seils and others have argued, often "who" is prosecuted matters much more than "how many." Equally, however, it would be problematic to reduce the question of justice to the identification of those few who had command responsibility. To the extent that our social analysis of the enormously complex "event" of the Rwandan genocide addresses the plurality of enabling conditions and sources of responsibility, our approaches to justice should also address those complex lines of accountability rather than reducing the issue to a simplistic mapping of command responsibility of those state authorities who engineered the violence. Whether the ICTR prosecutions can be shaped to meet this challenge is the question. On the difficult and complex questions that should inform our evaluation of the relationship between the ICTR process and justice and accountability for the Rwandan genocide, see Mahmood Mamdani, *When Victims Become Killers* (Princeton, NJ: Princeton University Press, 2001).

**31.** The International Criminal Tribunal for the Former Yugoslavia (ICTY) was established by UN Security Council Resolution 827. This resolution was passed on May 25, 1993, in the face of serious violations of international humanitarian law committed in the territory of the former Yugoslavia since 1991, and as a response to the threat to international peace and security posed by those serious violations. The ICTY employs 1,248 staff members and has cost $695 million to date (information from International Criminal Tribunal for the former Yugoslavia, www.un.org/icty/latest-e/index.htm, gathered on January 2003).

**32.** From these prosecutions, seventeen sentences have been passed, with a further twelve under appeal. Twenty-four of the indictees remain at large (information from International Criminal Tribunal for the Former Yugoslavia, www.un.org/icty/latest-e/index.htm, gathered on January 30, 2003.

**33.** This case (IT-98-30/1) is currently under appeal. The prosecutor had called for a thirty-five-year sentence for Prcac and his colleague Kvocka. See www.un.org/icty/kvocka/trialc/judgement/kvo-tj011102e-5-7.htm.

**34.** Note the well-known arguments against those who "squander moral capital" on "the mirage of corrective justice" that results only in the "perpetuation of moral arbitrariness and the creation of a new generation of victims," in Bruce Ackerman, *The Future of Liberal Revolution* (New Haven, CT: Yale University Press, 1992), 72–73. Of course, Ackerman does not call for truth commissions as an alternative to such prosecutions of past wrongdoers; rather, his argument is that we should spend that moral capital on forward-looking efforts, preparing the ground squarely for the future rather than looking back at the past.

**35.** See Daniel J. Goldhagen, *Hitler's Willing Executioners: Ordinary Germans and the Holocaust* (New York: Knopf, 1996). Of course, as we note in the section that follows, this is not an indictment of the ability of trials to paint a more complex picture. In fact, in the case of Germany, this was clearly a failure that characterized Nuremberg in particular rather than Nazi war crimes trials per se— for instance, the doctor's trial under Control Council Law No. 10 gave "an account of how the whole medical system was put to the service of the Nazi program, including the complicity of civilian and military elements within the medical profession." See www.ushmm.org/research/doctors/medical.htm (written comments by Paul Seils to the author on a draft of this paper, January 29, 2003).

**36.** See Charles Ville-Vicencio's argument along these lines, with reference to the work of Michael Marrus: "The bigger picture invariably is ignored in courts of law." Villa-Vicencio, "Why Perpetrators Should Not Always Be Prosecuted," 5.

**37.** Commissions are generally characterized by an attempt to paint an overall picture of certain human rights violations over a period of time. See Priscilla B. Hayner, "Fifteen Truth Commissions, 1974 to 1994: A Comparative Study," *Human Rights Quarterly* 16, no. 4 (1994). The South African TRC's *Final Report I*, chap. 5, 71 and 73, claims that the forum of the truth commission allowed for a greater understanding of why these abuses happened. See also Crocker, "Truth Commissions, Transitional Justice, and Civil Society," in Rotberg and Thompson, *Truth v. Justice*; and Martha Minow, *Between Vengeance and Forgiveness: Facing History after Genocide and Mass Violence* (Boston: Beacon Press, 1998), on the ability of truth commissions to address systemic violations. Paul van Zyl has highlighted the role of the TRC's public hearings in shaping the national debate about apartheid (TRC discussion, ICTJ, December 6, 2002).

**38.** The ICTY's Statute Article 7 states that a commander's criminal responsibility can arise in two ways: either directly, under Article 7(1), where he has "planned, instigated, ordered, committed or otherwise aided and abetted in the planning, preparation or execution of a crime referred to in articles 2 to 5"; or indirectly, under Article 7(3), where a commander can be held responsible for the acts of his subordinate "if he knew or had reason to know that the subordinate was about to commit such acts or had done so and . . . failed to take the necessary and reasonable measures to prevent such acts or to punish the perpetrators thereof." The *Celebici* case (IT-96-21) was the first at the ICTY in which command responsibility for failure to act, under Article 7(3) of the tribunal's statute, was considered (ICTY *Bulletin* no. 15/16 10-III-1997). As Paul Seils notes, the Tadic trial (IT-94-1) may be said to go even further than Celebici "in setting the socio-historic context"; moreover, the tribunal's Rule 61 hearings provision allows the "judicial format to bend much more towards the needs of victims, albeit in rather particular circumstances" (written comments to the author on a draft of this paper, Paul Seils, January 29, 2003). For a summary note regarding Rule 61 provisions see www.yale.edu/yjil/v231a4.html.

**39.** Of course, in some cases such trials may have an impact even without such proactive efforts. "The Argentine trials, as far as I know, did not do anything other than deal with the 700 cases of torture and disappearance. There was no community outreach or victim program in connection with the trials, but as Carlos Nino points out, it was the very drama of the trials that captivated the country and contributed to its impact. The process did not prioritize public engagement— it flowed naturally from the event itself" (written comments by Paul Seils to the author on a draft of this paper, January 29, 2003). See Nino's analysis of the Argentinean process in Carlos Santiago Nino, *Radical Evil on Trial* (New Haven, CT: Yale University Press, 1998).

**40.** See Paul F. Seils, "Reconciliation in Guatemala: The Role of Intelligent Justice," *Race and Class* 44, no. 1 (2000): 50.

**41.** Some truth commissions are empowered to name names in making findings. This can be an important way to provide accountability if the circumstances allow. Such circumstances may include the possibility of impartiality and due process in making findings, prospects of either helping or hindering prosecutions, the political tensions attending the process, and so on. When prosecutions are unlikely, the naming of names may be a particularly important way of providing individualized accountability. To the extent that truth commissions are focused on collective acknowledgment and collective responsibility, calling individual perpetrators to account through the naming of individual names may be particularly important.

**42.** The community reconciliation process in East Timor is the most interesting model in this regard. All defendants who are charged with "lesser" crimes are channeled through a community reconciliation process where, if found guilty, they face a community service requirement rather than a criminal sanction. Crimes such as murder or rape are channeled through the special prosecutor's office.

**43.** Two trials following the Greensboro massacre resulted in acquittal, and one in a plea deal, leaving "an awkward silence" over the events. See Nancy H.

McLaughlin, "Group Says Shooting Inquiry Is Needed to Help Clear the Air," *News and Record,* Greensboro, NC, January 17, 2003.

**44.** For instance, plea bargaining is a classic example of how a court may agree to lesser sentences, compromising on its objectives regarding appropriate justice for one defendant in return for his or her cooperation with the prosecutor's office in pursuing justice regarding other perpetrators, in thwarting anticipated crimes, and so on. In an ideal world the court would prefer to pursue all these objectives without the sacrifices of a plea bargain, yet when there are tensions between the courses of action needed to pursue all these objectives, the prosecutor may compromise and settle for a plea bargain.

**45.** As we move forward, many of these questions will be repeatedly revisited in terms of how the complementarity provisions of the ICC are worked out in relation to national truth commissions.

**46.** Peru may be a particularly interesting case because the commission has its own judicialization unit, which takes selected cases arising through the commission for more in-depth investigation, with a view to presenting them to the attorney general's office for prosecution.

**47.** East Timor's Regulation No. 2001/10, "On the Establishment of a Commission for Reception, Truth and Reconciliation in East Timor," para. 44.2, establishes that information shall be provided to the commission on a confidential basis and that the commission shall not be compelled to release information except at the request of the Office of the General Prosecutor (OGP). Paragraph 26 defines the relationship between the Community Reconciliation Process (CRP) and the OGP. Statements may be referred to the OGP from the CRP for investigation where there is credible evidence of a deponent's commission of a serious criminal offense.

**48.** Currently it appears that both institutions have made a de facto decision to proceed without a formal MOU but with some informal understanding that there will not be any information sharing. But it is not clear how such an information firewall can be maintained in all cases—for instance, it is not clear if the firewall would have to be maintained if the TRC should be in receipt of exculpatory information regarding an alleged perpetrator's being investigated or even prosecuted by the court. It is in this context that there have been proposals for a more formal agreement regarding information-sharing protocols that anticipate and address such areas of ambiguity in advance. See Marieke Wierda, Priscilla Hayner, and Paul van Zyl, *Exploring the Relationship between the Special Court and the Truth and Reconciliation Commission of Sierra Leone* (New York: International Center for Transitional Justice, June 24, 2002).

**49.** TRC discussion, ICTJ, December 6, 2002. The most effective functioning of this formula may be tracked by following threads that run between the investigations of the Transvaal AG and the amnesty applications received by the TRC around the time of the De Kock trial in 1996.

**50.** However, there were continued concerns about lack of cooperation regarding information sharing between the AG's office and the investigation unit of the commission; see Piers Pigou, "False Promises and Wasted Opportunities? Inside South Africa's Truth and Reconciliation Commission," in *Commissioning the Past,* ed. Posel and Simpson, 55.

**51.** TRC discussion, ICTJ, December 6, 2002.

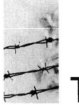

# Truth vs. Justice?
## Commentary

Richard Ashby Wilson

Vasuki Nesiah's excellent deconstruction of the opposition between truth and justice does us a great service by encouraging us to think in more flexible ways about the diversity of truth commissions and criminal justice institutions established in the process of democratization. She is correct to suggest that our evaluation of these institutions requires sensitivity to each individual instance and also to the contexts and histories in which they operate. We should be careful not to make sweeping generalizations about either the opposition or the complementarity of truth commissions and courts, and instead seek to gain a full picture of the complex interactions of these institutions in a number of diverse locales. Nesiah does not go far enough, however, in producing an analytical framework to evaluate truth commissions, and this is a result partly from her conscious decision not to define basic terms such as "justice" and "transitional justice." This omission prevents us from identifying the political vision of the common good or the juridical principles that could guide our assessment of prosecutions and truth commissions. On what common basis are we to evaluate their limitations and achievements? I concur with Geoffrey Robertson, who asserts that "transitional justice" is a contradiction in terms, which carries hidden assumptions that truth telling or amnesty or the restoration of social bonds is in itself a form of justice.[1] All these may be necessary or even desirable, but they are not justice, which I understand to be the "non-teleological retributivism" delineated by Robert Nozick.[2]

Nesiah does, however, present us with some intriguing observations that might facilitate a rethinking of the relationship between justice and public truth-telling institutions: that the differences between truth commissions and courts are not enough in themselves to explain the different outcomes produced by the same institutions, or to explain why different institutions produce similar outcomes. It is, of course, true that truth commissions are more centrally concerned with producing a historically accurate account of past mass violations, and courts are more directed toward determining guilt or innocence and punishing offenders. Yet beyond this a number of different results are possible, and this does not always depend on whether the institution is a commission or a court. Some truth commissions, such as the Guatemalan Historical Clarification Commission, have provided historical accounts that aid accountability, understood both broadly, in terms of publicly attributing responsibility, and narrowly, in terms of facilitating criminal trials. Some criminal justice institutions have written broad and contextual histories of conflicts, for example, the International Criminal Tribunal for the Former Yugoslavia in the Tadic and Krstic cases. Some truth commissions have written feeble, incomplete, and deeply flawed histories of conflicts (e.g., Chile, South Africa, Argentina), and some courts (Eichmann in Israel and the Touvier and Barbie cases in France) have not held fast to due process and fair procedure in trying individuals for mass violations.[3]

The question, then, is, why are some commissions and courts more successful than others at writing history or administering justice? Can we create an analytical framework that includes all institutions of justice, history writing, and reconciliation in democratizing countries? Nesiah attends to these issues more in the second half of her paper, and in what follows, I seek to complement her preliminary observations by providing a common explanatory framework for thinking about courts and truth commissions together. My assertion is that two criteria could help us untangle the morass of complexity.[4] In evaluating both truth commissions and courts, first we need to look closely at their constitution within national or transnational bureaucracies, and then we need to ask what legal categories motivate their investigation. I take the view that transnationally constituted truth commissions and courts have tended to be freer of national political imperatives, and this has allowed them to deliver fuller historical accounts and to function in a manner that adheres more closely to principles of fairness. Also, truth commissions and courts that are guided by legal categories that emphasize collective agency, such as genocide and crimes against humanity, tend to write more contextually rich and complex histories of conflicts.[5] I will deal with each of these points in turn.

Truth commissions were initially advocated because prosecutions were deemed impossible or counterproductive and because their proponents felt that courts could not write adequate accounts of mass violations. Yet more than one truth commission has been an abject failure as a history-writing institution, and that is because their historical function has become subordinated to other political imperatives, such as nation building and manufacturing legitimacy for state institutions. The same can be said of some national court processes, which either have turned into show trials (Eichmann and Demjanjuk in Israel) or have become long-winded deliberations on ultimately unknowable questions about "the true identity of the nation" (the trial of Maurice Papon in France). All these courts and truth commissions are nationally constituted; that is, they are set up by, and beholden to, national political elites and, even more narrowly in some cases, the executive branch of the state. In cases of democratic transition from authoritarianism, this places the state in a position of conflict of interest. It asks the state to judge itself and make itself vulnerable to lawsuits of demands for reparations from victims, usually in a context where the former perpetrators or authoritarian politicians are still in positions of power (F. W. de Klerk in South Africa, Pinochet in Chile).

The most successful truth commission so far in terms of furnishing an adequate historical account of a conflict has been the Guatemalan Historical Clarification Commission. Although Guatemalan nationals played an important role, the Guatemalan commission was formulated, funded, and largely administered by the United Nations. Although not free of politics, it was less politically compromised by pressures from national bureaucracies and elites than were commissions in Argentina and South Africa. The Guatemalan truth commission, unlike its national counterparts, wrote a history that provided a great deal of contextualization and structural and historical analysis in its attribution of mass atrocities to, among other things, the Cold War, U.S. foreign policy, economic inequality, political authoritarianism, and racism.

Also, transnationally established courts in the United Nations system, while not without their faults, have demonstrated an adherence to due process, an independence from debates about national identity, and an ability to write history more adequately than national courts do. This latter point is borne out if we look at the Tadic case (IT-94-1-T) of the International Criminal Court of the Former Yugoslavia (ICTY), which, being the first judgment of the ICTY, set out a historical understanding of the conflict in Bosnia-Herzegovina that a historian would recognize: It dealt with the Ottoman and Austro-Hungarian empires, World War II, the death of Tito and the collapse of communism, the rise of ethnonationalism in multiparty elections and in the Belgrade media, and the subsequent violent fragmentation of Yugoslavia along nationalist lines.

If we look closely at the Tadic case at the ICTY and at the Guate-malan Historical Clarification Commission, we will see another similarity beyond their shared transnational constitution, namely, their focus on genocide and crimes against humanity. The Guatemalan Historical Clarifi-cation Commission was the first truth commission to conclude that a gov-ernment had pursued a policy of genocide against a civilian population. It dedicated a whole volume to the origins and causes of the war, to show the structural and collective conditions that constituted the genocidal policies of the state between 1981 and 1983. Genocide is a collective policy of exter-mination carried out by an organized group (the Guatemalan state and mil-itary) against another group (Mayan peasants). It cannot be random or ad hoc. Its systematic nature must be proved through historical and structural documentation and analysis. Asserting that genocide took place requires more contextualization than with an individual violation, since it requires the linking of different sites at different times, under the same policy of extermination.

The same argument applies to the persecution of a civilian population, as in the Tadic case. Disparate individual facts about Tadic's crimes in the Omarska camp in Prejidor, Bosnia, may be known, but they make sense only within a narrative that integrates the facts into a coherent story of ethnic cleansing and genocide carried out by Serb nationalists with the full mili-tary, financial, and ideological support of the Yugoslav government in Bel-grade. For Tadic to be guilty of a crime against humanity, it must be proved that there was a wider plan of persecution that was centrally organized and extensive across a region or country. Doing so requires a wide contextual and historical approach that delineates the main origins, patterns, and methodical plans of a policy of persecution of a civilian population and places Tadic's acts squarely within a joint criminal enterprise. This broader approach is not confined to the Tadic judgment but also characterizes many other judgments of The Hague and Arusha tribunals, and especially those of Krstic at the ICTY and Kambanda and Akayesu at the ICTR.

Thus, we have seen how it is possible to make sense of both truth commissions and court prosecutions within the same analytical frame-work by examining their institutional constitution within the nation-state or transnational bureaucracies such as the UN and by paying attention to the legal categories that motivate their history writing. This allows us to think beyond the sterile dualism of truth versus justice, to understand why some courts and truth commissions have failed or succeeded on their own terms, and to think about in which directions democratizing institutions might go in the future.

# Notes

1. Geoffrey Robertson, *Crimes against Humanity: The Struggle for Global Justice* (London: Penguin, 2000).

2. Robert Nozick, *Philosophical Investigations* (Cambridge, MA: Harvard University Press, 1981).

3. On Argentina, Chile, and Guatemala, see Greg Grandin, "Insoluble Acts and Historical Solutions: Law, History, and Latin American Cold War Terror" (unpublished ms., 2001). On Guatemala, see Paul F. Seils, "Reconciliation in Guatemala: The Role of Intelligent Justice," *Race and Class* 44, no. 1 (2002): 33–59. On the French Holocaust trials, see Richard J. Golsan, ed., *The Papon Affair: Memory and Justice on Trial* (New York: Routledge, 2000); Richard J. Golsan, "History and the 'Duty to Memory' in Postwar France: The Pitfalls of an Ethic of Remembrance," in *What Happens to History: The Renewal of Ethics in Contemporary Thought,* ed. Howard Marchitello (New York: Routledge, 2000); Tzvetan Todorov, "The Touvier Affair," in *Memory, the Holocaust and French Justice: The Bousquet and Touvier Affairs,* ed. R. J. Golsan (Dartmouth, NH: University Press of New England, 1996), 114–21; and Nancy Wood, *Vectors of Memory: Legacies of Trauma in Postwar Europe* (Oxford: Berg, 1999). For a critique of the South Africa Truth and Reconciliation Commission's approach to truth, see Richard Ashby Wilson, *The Politics of Truth and Reconciliation in South Africa: Legitimizing the Post-Apartheid State* (Cambridge: Cambridge University Press, 2001). On the Eichmann trial, see Hannah Arendt, *Eichmann in Jerusalem: A Report on the Banality of Evil* (New York: Viking Press, 1965).

4. There are, of course, others, such as the nature of the transition—whether negotiated or produced through military defeat—but space barely allows me to develop two points.

5. I will not, however, assert that courts trying cases of war crimes or genocide produce "better justice" than courts trying crimes that more usually fall under national domestic law. Nor do they seem to provide witnesses with any less cruel treatment during cross-examination.

# 14

# Promoting the Human Rights of Forced Migrants

Susan Martin and Andrew I. Schoenholtz

By conservative estimates, about fifty million migrants are living outside their home communities, forced to flee to obtain some measure of safety and security. Forced migration is an inevitable and increasing consequence of conflict, especially internal and ethnic conflict. Addressing humanitarian crises involving mass migration is integral to maintaining international security, establishing peace in war-torn societies, and promoting sustainable development and respect for human rights. This is particularly the case since September 11, as it has become apparent that countries such as Afghanistan that experience prolonged humanitarian emergencies can too easily become breeding grounds for terrorism and repression.

The post–Cold War era has seen both improvements and setbacks in protecting the rights of forced migrants. The purpose of this chapter is to offer an overview of the nature of forced migration and to explain how the changing contexts in which displacement occurs present special challenges in protecting the rights of refugees and displaced persons. To this end, the chapter is divided into two parts: First, an overview section reviews (1) definitions and concepts essential to understanding the nature of forced migration today, and (2) the legal framework for promotion and protection of the rights of forced migrants. The second section of the chapter then outlines four of the most pressing challenges to the protection of forced migrants. This section also includes a table of the relevant actors concerned with forced migration.

## Overview of Forced Migration Today

### Essential Definitions and Concepts

This chapter focuses on a range of migrants who share a common situation —they have been forced to flee their homes. Forced migration has many causes and takes many forms. People leave because of persecution, human rights violations, repression, conflict, and natural and human-made disasters. Many depart on their own initiative to escape these life-threatening situations, although in a growing number of cases, people are driven from their homes by governments and insurgent groups intent on depopulating or shifting the ethnic, religious, or other composition of an area.

*Refugees* are a subset of forced migrants who have a special status in international law, coming under the terms of the 1951 UN Convention and Protocol Relating to the Status of Refugees. The UN High Commissioner for Refugees (UNHCR) has special responsibilities as the international organization mandated to protect and assist refugees. UNHCR estimates that about twenty million persons were under its mandate as of January 2002, of whom twelve million were refugees and the remainder fit into other categories of forced migrants.[1] Under the 1951 convention a refugee is a person outside his or her country who has a well-founded fear of being persecuted on returning. Refugee status has been applied more broadly, however, to include persons who are outside their country of origin because of armed conflict, generalized violence, foreign aggression, or other circumstances that have seriously disturbed public order, and who therefore require international protection and assistance.[2]

The number of refugees—that is, persons outside their home country —is at its lowest level in years, not because of a decrease in armed conflict and rights deprivations, but because of reduced opportunity for flight across state boundaries. Thus, the decrease in the number of refugees means not that the number of forced migrants has decreased but only that the majority of those in flight are considered *internally displaced persons* (IDPs) and not refugees. In the late 1990s, the internally displaced outnumbered refugees by two to one. The Norwegian Refugee Council's Global IDP Project recently estimated that there are about twenty-five million IDPs who have fled from conflicts around the world.[3] UNHCR considers about five million of the IDPs to be under its mandate.[4] While there is no international convention similar to the 1951 Refugee Convention for internally displaced persons, the United Nations has promoted Guiding Principles on Internal Displacement, drawn from existing human rights and humanitarian law, to provide a more comprehensive framework for protecting and assisting internally displaced persons. The Guiding Principles describe internally displaced persons as "persons or groups of persons who have been forced, or obliged to flee or to leave their homes or places of habitual residence, in particular as a result of armed conflict, situations of generalized violence, violations of human rights, or natural or human-made disasters, and who have not crossed an internationally recognized state border."

The decrease in the number of refugees reflects a second phenomenon as well: the repatriation of millions of *refugee returnees* to their home countries. During the 1990s, large-scale return to a wide range of countries occurred. In Africa alone, repatriation occurred in Angola, Burundi, Eritrea, Ethiopia, Liberia, Mali, Mozambique, Namibia, Rwanda, and Somalia. Other prominent repatriation destinations were Cambodia, Afghanistan, El Salvador, Nicaragua, Guatemala, and Bosnia-Herzegovina. In some cases, the movements have been voluntary and secure, because hostilities have truly ended and with peace could come repatriation and reintegration. Too often during the past decade, though, refugees as well as internally displaced people returned to communities still racked by warfare and conflict. A range of factors induces such return. Countries of asylum, weary from having hosted the refugees, may place pressure on them to repatriate prematurely; donors may also reduce their assistance in the expectation that return will soon take place.[5] The refugees themselves may wish to restake their claim to residences and businesses before others take them, or they may wish to return in time to participate in elections. Families split by hostilities may be anxious for reunification.

*Statelessness* is both a cause and a consequence of forced migration. Stateless persons generally enjoy fewer rights than those who are citizens of a sovereign state. When they are also distrusted minorities within the country in which they reside, stateless persons often experience discrimination and may be the targets of violence and repression.[6] These factors may cause them to take flight. Statelessness is a consequence of forced migration in situations where refugees lose their former nationality but do not qualify for a new one. This may occur for seemingly benign reasons. For example, the stateless person's country of origin may confer citizenship through "jus solis," birth on its territory, whereas the country of asylum may confer citizenship through "jus sanguine," that is, by descent. The children born to refugees will qualify for neither citizenship, not having been born in their parents' home country and not sharing the nationality of the host country.

Environmental degradation and natural disasters uproot another type of forced migrant. Unlike the refugees and displaced persons described above, *environmental migrants* generally do not need protection from persecution or violence, but like refugees and internally displaced persons, they may be unable to return to now uninhabitable communities. Most environmental migrants move internally, some relocating temporarily until they are able to rebuild their homes, others seeking permanent new homes. Some environmental migrants, however, cross national boundaries.[7]

Development policies and projects may also cause large-scale migration of what are referred to as *development-induced migrants.* Involuntary relocations occur, for example, as a result of the building of dams for irrigation or hydropower, highway construction, and urban renewal. These relocations often raise grave human rights concerns.[8] Some governments have tried to redistribute residents from overpopulated to underpopulated regions, sometimes compelling relocation through force.[9] An important subgroup of these migrants shares the characteristics of refugees and internally displaced persons because aid is withheld based on their nationality, race, religion, or political opinion. Sometimes, the location for a project resulting in mass displacement is chosen to lessen political opposition or to repress a targeted group. For example, rural resettlement projects in Vietnam and Cambodia during the 1970s focused on "unemployed or semi-employed; traders; those who have capital; students who cannot pursue their studies; officers, officials and personnel of the old regime; relatives of those undergoing reeducation; the Chinese; members of religious minorities; and skilled machinery workers."[10] These situations thus may differ little from displacements caused by more overt political factors and conflict.

## The Legal Framework

International legal standards for the protection of forced migrants can be found in refugee, human rights, and humanitarian law. The Universal Declaration of Human Rights, the first modern international document to address rights to move domestically and internationally, exhibits the tension between individual rights and state obligations. First, Article 13 establishes the individual right to move and reside freely within one's own country. That article also declares the right to leave any country, including one's own, and to return to one's own country. The Soviet Union wanted to qualify the right to leave, but the drafting committee determined this to be too statist a position.

Having established a right to leave one's own country, the committee then turned to the problem that to be able to leave one's own country, an individual must enter another one. Member states differed considerably on how to resolve this issue. Some supported a right to asylum, but others, including the United States delegation, led by Eleanor Roosevelt, preferred to limit state obligations with regard to refugees. Article 14 affirms only a "right to seek and to enjoy in other countries asylum from persecution." In a very close vote, states rejected any obligation to grant asylum.

Within just a few years, states addressed this issue again, but in a very different, European-focused context. The 1951 UN Convention Relating to the Status of Refugees and its 1967 protocol emerged in the early days of the Cold War, largely to resolve the situation of the millions of refugees who remained displaced by World War II and fascist/Nazi persecution. At its core, this treaty substitutes the protection of the international community (in the form of a host government) for that of an unable or unwilling sovereign. Defining refugees as persons who were unable or unwilling to avail themselves of the protection of their home countries because of a "well-founded fear of persecution based on their race, religion, nationality, political opinion or membership in a particular social group," the 1951 convention included geographic (Europe) and time (persons displaced before 1951) limitations, which were lifted in the 1967 protocol. Since 1967, the refugee convention has been a universal instrument, applying to refugees worldwide.

The principal obligation of states is quite narrow: to refrain from forcibly returning (refouling) refugees to countries in which they would face persecution.[11] States do not have the obligation to provide asylum or admit refugees for permanent settlement, and they may relocate refugees in safe third countries that are willing to accept them. The convention has been interpreted to require states to undertake status determinations, however, for asylum applicants at their frontiers or inside their territories in order to determine if they have valid claims to refugee protection. While the only legal obligation to a refugee is nonrefoulement, in practice this has often meant admission and asylum in the host country.

The convention drafters recognized that among refugee populations would be found individuals whose actions made them undeserving of international protection. The so-called exclusion clauses of the convention set forth two major kinds of such individuals: human rights violators and serious criminals. Thus, those who have committed a crime against peace, a war crime, a crime against humanity, or a serious nonpolitical crime are excluded from international protection.

The convention also sets out the rights of refugees who have been admitted into the territory of another country. Fundamental human rights such as freedom of religion and access to courts are guaranteed to be at least those accorded to the citizens of the state hosting the refugee. Refugees lawfully residing in a host country are guaranteed public relief in this way as well. Rights regarding employment, property, elementary public education, and housing are accorded to refugees in a manner no less favorable than those accorded to citizens of other countries. In addition, the convention may not be applied in a discriminatory way regarding race, religion, or country of origin.

The limits of a treaty focused on persecution as the cause of forced migration reverberated particularly in the developing world.[12] In recognition of the actual forced movements occurring regularly in Africa, the Organization of African Unity (OAU) adopted the Convention Governing the Specific Aspects of Refugee Problems in Africa, in 1969. While acknowledging the UN Refugee Convention as the basic and universal instrument regarding the protection of refugees, the OAU Convention broadened the definition of "refugee" and set out other important protection provisions. The definition includes anyone who, "owing to external aggression, occupation, foreign domination or events seriously disturbing public order in either part or the whole of his country of origin or nationality, is compelled to leave his place of habitual residence in order to seek refuge in another place outside his country of origin or nationality."[13]

The OAU explicitly forbids states to reject asylum seekers at the frontier. The grant of asylum is declared to be a peaceful and humanitarian act, not to be regarded as unfriendly by other states. The convention also establishes the importance of settling refugees at a reasonable distance from the frontier of their country of origin for security reasons. This regional treaty further states that no refugee shall be repatriated against his or her will. Most African states are parties to the OAU Convention.[14]

The United States and European nations have developed more limited policies on protecting civil war refugees and others covered by the OAU Convention. Before the 1990s, these states generally refrained from returning such refugees but provided them with minimal rights. This situation improved somewhat in the 1990s. Various European states established complementary or subsidiary protection policies in response to movements of large numbers of former-Yugoslavian refugees at different times during the 1990s.[15] UN high commissioner for refugees Sadako Ogata first called upon the international community to grant temporary protection to the tens of thousands of Croats fleeing to neighboring countries during the conflict with Serbia in 1991. Hundreds of thousands of Bosnians fled the civil conflict there, starting in 1992. UNHCR and the Europeans hoped that these wars would resolve themselves quickly and feared that permanent asylum would ratify ethnic cleansing. While those who made it to Germany and other European countries did find safety, they experienced different kinds of treatment in terms of rights. Many were not permitted access to the asylum system. The members of the European Union are working on developing consistent policies on complementary protection for the future.[16]

The 1990s United States version of temporary protection is at once broader and more limited than the European version. Temporary protected status (TPS) covers not only refugees fleeing armed conflict but also those fleeing natural disasters. While this type of protection is established by statute, Congress gave the attorney general significant discretion in determining which nationals qualify for TPS, and these officials have exercised their discretion by selecting for this status only some of the many countries experiencing conflict. Most importantly, even when the attorney general provides TPS to certain nationals, this status is limited to those who have already reached the United States at the time of the attorney general's proclamation. This type of protection regime was not established to handle ongoing mass migration emergencies. On limited occasions, however, an attorney general has moved the qualifying date forward to allow those nationals who arrived after the initial qualifying date to become eligible for TPS. Those protected by this status are allowed to work but are generally not eligible for public assistance.[17]

From the discussion above, it is apparent that the most developed international and regional protection frameworks for forced migrants apply to refugees—persons who have crossed international borders. Only in the past decade has there been serious attention to those who are displaced within their own countries as a result of persecution, conflict, or instability. Two of the principal barriers to protecting internally displaced persons result from the exercise of sovereignty by states unwilling to assist and protect their own citizens, and from the reluctance of governments to infringe on the sovereignty of other governments. This problem exists at both ends of the spectrum. In some cases, the offending states are powerful members of the Security Council, such as Russia and China, who would use their veto if the international community tried to intercede on behalf of those internally displaced from such areas as Chechnya and Tibet.[18] In other cases, such as Somalia and Liberia, there is no effective sovereign authority within the country willing or able to request international assistance.[19]

International human rights and humanitarian law have helped change the meaning of sovereignty to include responsibility for the welfare of the residents of one's territory. To quote Francis Deng, the representative of the UN secretary-general on internally displaced persons, and his colleague Roberta Cohen, in arguing for greater international attention to internally displaced persons:

> Since there is no adequate replacement in sight for the system of state sovereignty, primary responsibility for promoting the security, welfare and liberty of populations must remain with the state. At the same time, no state claiming legitimacy can justifiably quarrel with the commitment to protect all its citizens against human rights abuse. . . . Sovereignty cannot be used as justification for the mistreatment of populations.[20]

As the internally displaced continue to reside in their own country, of course, their rights derive from other international instruments: human rights conventions and, to the extent displacement is caused or affected by war, the Geneva Conventions. Applying these international laws to the situation of internally displaced persons, the Guiding Principles on Internal Displacement, developed in the late 1990s by the secretary-general's representative on internally displaced persons, sets forth the major rights of the internally displaced and the responsibilities of sovereign authorities to such individuals before and during displacement. The Guiding Principles also look to international refugee law by analogy for guidance in certain situations. Although the principles do not have legal force themselves, they set standards that guide governments and rebel groups regarding their conduct toward civilians before, during, and following displacement. This consolidation and focusing of international law regarding the internally displaced has been adopted into domestic law by such nations as Colombia and Georgia. Important gaps in the protection framework for internally displaced persons continue to exist, however, because the human rights laws and the Geneva Conventions are laws of general applicability that were not specifically designed to address the full range of problems faced by the internally displaced.

## Conflict and Forced Migration: Cause and Consequence

Conflict is both a cause and a consequence of forced migration and the efforts to address it. The majority of the world's refugees and internally displaced persons have fled conflicts, largely civil wars that target civilian populations. Major countries of origin include Afghanistan, Angola, Burma, Burundi, Colombia, the Democratic Republic of the Congo, Indonesia, Sierra Leone, and Sudan.[21] Some of the conflicts have lasted for decades, along with the displacements that they produced. Others have been settled recently, but return and reintegration of the forced migrants is not complete.

Migration can also be a cause of conflict and instability, which then produces still more displacement. To use Indonesia as an example, transmigration policies adopted by the government exacerbated tensions that then erupted into violence in several islands. Transmigration generally involved movements of settlers from densely populated to less populous islands, often without consultation with the local population. According to the U.S. Committee for Refugees, "In Kalimantan, tribal clashes between Madurese on one side and Dayaks and Malays on the other resulted largely from Indonesia's transmigration policy—a factor in the other conflicts as well. In Papua, as in Aceh, transmigration and the control of natural resources fuel a separatist movement based on a view of the Javanese as neo-colonialists. In Java and elsewhere, transmigrants who for decades have lived on other islands are returning to a home that is no longer a home, adding to the ranks of the displaced."[22]

The forced migrants may themselves be parties to conflict. In their seminal work *Escape from Violence*, Zolberg, Suhrke, and Aguayo coined the term "refugee warriors" to describe militants who used refugee camps as a base for military operations back in their home countries.[23] Examples included mujahedeen soldiers operating from refugee camps in Pakistan, and Cambodian resistance groups operating from camps along the Thai-Cambodian border. In some cases, the warriors have kept civilian populations hostage in these camps, as occurred in the camps in eastern Zaire dominated by Hutu militia who had committed genocide in Rwanda. More often, the civilians are the wives, mothers, and children of the warriors and support their military objectives.

The conflicts that cause forced migration can also spill over to neighboring countries along with the refugees. Conflict in West Africa began in Liberia but soon spread to Sierra Leone, Guinea, and Côte d'Ivoire as cross-border clashes intensified. The Hutu-dominated camps in eastern Zaire became launching points for attacks on Rwanda as well as for fighting in Congo itself.

Most often the relationship between conflict and forced migration is murkier than in these examples, raising a host of questions about the extent to which international assistance to refugees and displaced persons fuels conflicts. Some argue that by providing aid to the families of combatants, the international community is in effect subsidizing conflicts that would not otherwise be sustainable.[24] While some humanitarian organizations have withdrawn assistance when they concluded that the aid did more harm than good,[25] for the most part, these agencies hold that their prime imperative is to provide neutral and impartial aid to persons in need, without second-guessing the ramifications of that aid on conflict.[26]

Regardless of the role that humanitarian aid may play during conflicts, resolving the situation of refugees and displaced persons is necessary to resolving the conflicts that caused the displacement in the first place. The transitions from war to peace and from relief to development are generally far from the smooth paths that one would hope for these societies. From the very beginnings of peace negotiations, the impact of forced migration must be taken into account. Often the only UN presence in a war-affected country is the humanitarian agencies, but those agencies' staff may not be consulted or participate in the peace negotiations even when they have a better sense of the situation on the ground than political figures do. Certainly, peace agreements themselves must include realistic frameworks for addressing displacement, including plans for return and reintegration of refugees and internally displaced persons. In developing different plans and scenarios for peace, the negotiators should examine the impact of displacement, as well as the effects of various displacement scenarios, on the likelihood that peace will be achieved.

Forging closer cooperation between the humanitarian and political regimes has risks, however. Humanitarian agencies are already vulnerable to attacks by military and political forces that doubt their impartiality or neutrality. At times these attacks are violent, leading to some of the security risks discussed above. Even agencies whose mandates require them to be neutral in dealing with all parties to a conflict, such as the International Committee for the Red Cross, have been subject to such attacks. Should peace negotiators be seen as tipping toward one side over another, or should the United Nations as a body impose sanctions against warring parties or rights abusers, humanitarian agencies that are perceived, even unfairly, as engaged in these political processes may be targeted or refused access to civilian populations. Nevertheless, finding long-term solutions to the causes of forced migration may well justify the risks.

The plight of forced migrants is directly related to the situations that cause their flight. Finding durable solutions to forced displacement requires solutions to the conflict, repression, instability, and other causes of mass migration. However, it must be kept in mind that political changes, including an end to conflict, though necessary, are not sufficient to resolve large-scale displacement. Forced migrants, along with the communities they reside in, must have access to economic opportunities, permanent shelter, and other necessities of life. Forced migrants also need assurances of legal and property rights. Where property cannot be recovered, some form of compensation should be negotiated. For those living in war-torn societies, solutions mean a transition from dependence on relief to reconstruction and then longer-term development.

A durable solution means that forced migrants have been integrated into the place they reside, or reintegrated the communities to which they

have returned. At a minimum, integration implies that there are no significant differences between this population and the existing local population
in terms of their rights and legal status. In difficult times, the entire population may be in a situation of isolation, misery, and insecurity, and in this
case the humanitarian assistance and development aid should logically be
targeted at the community level.

## Central Challenges to Protecting
## the Rights of Forced Migrants

Barriers to protecting the rights of refugees and other persons displaced by
conflict fall into three principal areas: (1) absence of secure environments
in which to protect forced migrants; (2) gaps and inconsistencies in institutional responses to forced migration; and (3) threats to first asylum. This
section discusses each of these in turn.

### Insecurity of Forced Migrants
### and Humanitarian Workers in Conflict Zones

Insecurity is by far the biggest impediment to securing the rights of forced
migrants, particularly when the displaced are still within their own countries
or remain under the control of military forces in a country of refuge.[27] Insecure conditions impede access to vulnerable populations for delivery of aid,
create protection problems for aid workers as well as their clients, and make
it impossible to monitor and evaluate the effectiveness of aid operations.
Because of attacks on humanitarian aid operations and their consequences,
forced migrants too often end up "out of sight and out of mind" of the very
humanitarian system that is designed to assist and protect them.

A professional security assessment should be made at the start of each
complex humanitarian emergency and repeated periodically thereafter.
The vulnerabilities of forced migrants to attack and exploitation are key
issues to cover in such assessments, as are the vulnerabilities of humanitarian aid workers seeking to bring assistance and protection to these populations. The assessments should recommend ways to increase access to and
protection of forced migrants and to reduce risk to aid workers.

Peacekeepers can play an important role in securing access to and
protecting displaced populations, although their involvement is limited.
The decision to intervene with military forces even when loss of life is a
risk, and to commit peacekeeping troops to maintain security, is a difficult
one that political leaders are generally loath to make.[28] Nevertheless,
humanitarian interventions occurred with some regularity during the
1990s, and peacekeepers are likely to continue to be deployed during

humanitarian emergencies. Military forces, such as those of NATO and Australia, have also been called on to assist with logistics, construction, and other aspects of humanitarian aid in such places as Kosovo and East Timor. The peacemaking and peacekeeping forces should have clear mandates to protect civilian populations and humanitarian relief operations in such situations. They should have adequate human and financial resources to fulfill this security mandate, and they should negotiate terms of reference for cooperation with humanitarian agencies. Better training of military forces that are likely to come into contact with civilians, particularly displaced persons, could also help improve security for IDPs, returnees, and other war-affected populations.

At the same time, civilian capabilities to protect forced migrants should be developed. A welcome step is the decision by the United Nations in January 2002 to provide funding out of the regular budget for staff safety and security activities. The United Nations Security Coordinator (UNSECOORD) was provided with a core budget to deploy one hundred field security officers (FSOs) in crisis areas. Many times the threat to relief operations comes from bandits and criminal elements or loosely organized militias rather than actual military forces. In such situations, civilian policing may be the appropriate way to gain greater security for displaced persons and humanitarian workers. Many agencies maintain rosters of emergency professional personnel who can be called up for short-term assignments. Such a roster of police may be useful in broadening access to the expertise needed both for assessing security problems and for identifying and implementing appropriate remedies. Given the scale of insecurity, though, it may be necessary to develop a standing international police force that is explicitly mandated to protect the humanitarian operations. The UNSECOORD FSOs may form the core of such a group.

Humanitarian organizations must also look to their own programs to reduce the vulnerability of forced migrants to attacks, abuses, and exploitation. Reports of the sexual exploitation of refugees and displaced children in West Africa highlighted problems that have long been known or suspected. Dependency on humanitarian aid creates vulnerability to exploitation by unscrupulous officials, military, police, and aid workers. If the aid is insufficient and no legitimate economic opportunities are available, women and children will be forced to take other measures, including prostitution, in order to feed themselves and their families. These problems arise in all settings, affecting refugees and displaced persons in camps and spontaneously settled in rural and urban areas. Growth in the population of street children in cities may be one indicator that the humanitarian response is failing to provide adequate security for a highly vulnerable group.

## Gaps and Inconsistencies in Institutional Responses

Dozens of international, national, and private agencies play important roles in providing food, shelter, health care, and other services to refugees, returnees, and internally displaced persons (see tables 1 and 2). Despite—and in some cases because of—the vast number of agencies, there are serious gaps, particularly in protecting the rights of forced migrants. This is particularly the case when people are displaced within their own countries.

In most refugee situations, the host government requests the assistance of UNHCR in helping to ensure adequate assistance and protection. UNHCR in turn works with implementing partners that include government ministries as well as nongovernmental organizations. UNHCR's ability to operate effectively can be seriously eroded if the national government is uncooperative, hostile to the presence of refugees, or unwilling or unable to control other actors who disrupt aid operations. UNHCR nevertheless has a clear mandate in such cases to bring the problem to international attention as a barrier to refugee protection and assistance.

Ensuring the protection of IDPs is even more problematic. National governments retain the principal responsibility for protecting their citizens. But even though progress has been made in setting out protection standards through the Guiding Principles on Internal Displacement, violations of these guidelines are rampant.[29] Unlike in refugee situations, where UNHCR's mandate is clear, there is no comparable institutional locus of responsibility for international protection of IDPs when sovereign states are unwilling or unable to fulfill their responsibilities.

Recognizing that effective humanitarian aid and protection of internally displaced persons is still inadequate, OCHA formed a unit specifically responsible for IDPs, which began work in January 2002. But as a small office within a larger bureaucratic structure, the unit faces serious challenges to its ability to carry out its mission. While the unit may develop effective strategies to protect, assist, and find durable solutions for IDPs, it relies on the willingness of other UN agencies to take on the operational responsibility to implement the strategy.

When he was U.S. ambassador to the United Nations, Richard Holbrooke recommended that full responsibility for IDPs be assigned to UNHCR. He pointed out that IDPs were in fact internal refugees. Given UNHCR's extensive experience in assisting and protecting international refugees, it would have the greatest capacity for undertaking similar efforts

**Table 1.** The Major UN Actors

The **UN High Commissioner for Refugees** is mandated to assist and protect refugees. It exercises this authority with refugees defined under the 1951 Convention and its 1967 protocol, the OAU Convention. It also exercises its good offices to assist and protect refugees and displaced persons at the request of the UN General Assembly, the secretary-general, and national governments. UNHCR also exercises its mandate on behalf of the internally displaced, using its discretion in determining if and when to do so unless specifically requested by the General Assembly.

The **UN Office for the Coordination of Humanitarian Affairs** (OCHA), created in 1997 to replace the Department of Humanitarian Affairs (DHA), coordinates humanitarian agencies. The undersecretary-general for humanitarian affairs, who is also the emergency relief coordinator (ERC), heads OCHA and chairs the Interagency Standing Committee (IASC), which brings together all major humanitarian, development, and human rights bodies and the Executive Committee for Humanitarian Affairs (ECHA).

The **Office of the High Commissioner for Human Rights** supports the work of the **representative of the secretary-general for internally displaced persons.** Appointed in 1992 at the request of the UN Commission on Human Rights, the representative is mandated to monitor displacement problems worldwide, undertake country missions, establish dialogues with governments, develop an international legal framework, promote effective institutional arrangements at the international and regional levels, identify

on behalf of those who were internally displaced. UNHCR fears, however, that countries of asylum will refuse admission to refugees if they believe that UNHCR is protecting the internally displaced, further eroding what UNHCR sees as its primary mandate: to maintain first asylum and protect refugees from refoulement (forced return) to situations in which they may be endangered.[30]

ICRC would be another possibility for taking on explicit responsibility for protection of IDPs, building on its responsibilities under the Geneva Conventions for civilians in armed-conflict situations. As with UNHCR, ICRC has the experience and expertise to undertake protection activities on behalf of IDPs, many of which already come under its mandate. ICRC's role is quite limited, however, when internal displacement comes from causes other than armed conflict. An expansion of ICRC's protection activities to

**Table 1.** The Major UN Actors *(cont.)*

preventive and protection strategies, focus attention on the needs of internally displaced women and children, and publish reports and studies in an effort to increase international awareness of the problem.

The **United Nations Children's Fund** (UNICEF) executive board reaffirmed in 1992 that UNICEF should "continue providing emergency assistance to refugee and displaced women and children, particularly those living in areas affected by armed conflict and natural disasters."

The **United Nations Development Program** (UNDP) describes itself as having three key roles in reference to mass exoduses: prevention, coping, and recovery.

The **World Food Program** (WFP) aims "to save lives in refugee and other emergency situations; to improve the nutrition and quality of life of the most vulnerable people at critical times in their lives; and to help build assets and promote the self-reliance of poor people and communities, particularly through labor-intensive works programmes."

UN-authorized peacekeeping operations, supervised by the **Department of Peacekeeping Operations** (DPKO), play a role in protecting forced migrants. Some peacekeeping operations have a specific mandate to protect displaced persons, as in Rwanda and the former Yugoslavia, or are mandated to protect the delivery of humanitarian assistance by UN agencies and other organizations, as in Somalia and the former Yugoslavia.

include at least those displaced by generalized violence and ethnic tension would seem consistent with its mandate, however.

A further possibility would be the UN High Commissioner for Human Rights (UNHCHR). UNHCHR has broad responsibility for preventing, and protecting victims of, human rights abuses. The agency already provides support to the secretary-general's representative on internally displaced persons, who routinely investigates and reports on protection problems facing IDPs and who developed and presented the Guiding Principles on Internal Displacement. UNHCHR has had a weak field presence, however, and has not generally taken on operational responsibilities. In recent years, though, UNHCHR has established field offices in a number of countries with large numbers of displaced persons, including Afghanistan, Angola, Burundi, Colombia, the Democratic Republic of the Congo, and Uganda.

**Table 2.** Other Major Actors

The **International Committee of the Red Cross** (ICRC) is an "impartial, neutral and independent organization whose exclusively humanitarian mission is to protect the lives and dignity of victims of war and internal violence and to provide them with assistance." It directs and coordinates international relief activities in situations of conflict and promotes adherence to humanitarian law and universal humanitarian principles. ICRC's activities derive from the 1949 Geneva Conventions and Protocols, the principal instruments of humanitarian law. Since most conflicts today are within states, Article 3, common to the four Geneva Conventions, is particularly pertinent.

The **International Organization for Migration** is involved in all phases of complex forced migration emergencies, providing technical and operational expertise in such areas as transportation, health, and other services for migrants. Typical projects include assistance to vulnerable returnees, including elderly, women, and children, reinsertion of demobilized combatants, registration of returnees, tracing and family reunification, migration information and referral services, and support for microeconomic development activities for affected communities.

Regional organizations respond in various ways to forced migration. The **Organization of African Unity** (OAU) adopted its own convention, which broadens significantly the definition of a refugee to include not only those fearing persecution but also those fleeing other dangerous situations. The **Economic Community of West African States** (ECOWAS) deployed the Eco-

The secretary-general could assign responsibility on a case-by-case basis, judging which agency has the field presence and capacity in specific countries. This process would be flexible, but the agency requested to undertake protection in a particular situation would not necessarily have the resources or will to accept the responsibility. A more formal and permanent process would give the explicit mandate for protection of IDPs to one of the agencies listed above. Going further, responsibility for all assistance and protection of forced migrants, refugees and IDPs alike, could be consolidated into a single organization, perhaps a "UN High Commissioner for Forced Migration."

Regardless of the institutional arrangements, funding will be a major factor in determining whether forced migrants receive adequate protection and assistance. Inadequacies in funding have undermined efforts to protect forced migrants. By midyear, only 29 percent of the 2002 requests through

---

**Table 2.** Other Major Actors *(cont.)*

nomic Community Monitoring Group (ECOMOG) to serve as a peacekeeping force and ensure delivery of humanitarian assistance in Liberia and Sierra Leone. The **Inter-American Commission on Human Rights** has taken the lead regarding internally displaced persons, appointing a special rapporteur, a voluntary position that marked the first such appointment at the regional level. The **Council of Europe** appointed a special rapporteur on internal displacement in Europe, and the **Organization for Security and Cooperation in Europe** (OSCE), a major player in human rights in Europe, has added programs on forced migration.

**National governments** and, in some cases, insurgencies have the principal responsibility for assisting and protecting persons forced to leave their homes because of conflict, natural disasters, or other reasons, but major gaps remain in their ability and willingness to carry out these activities.

**Nongovernmental organizations** (NGOs) are the operational arm of the humanitarian system for assisting and, to a lesser degree, protecting forced migrants. They play an important advocacy role as well. International and local NGOs provide a wide array of services, including food delivery, health and mental health care, sanitation, shelter, nutrition, education and training, income generation programs, and social services.

The **forced migrants** themselves are important actors on their own behalf. They provide assistance and protection to their own communities.

---

the Consolidated Inter-Agency Appeals for Complex Humanitarian Emergencies had been met, excluding the response to Afghanistan. Even counting Afghanistan, which garnered considerable, though now flagging, donor attention, fewer than 40 percent of the appeals were met. Additional problems include a serious maldistribution in funding by country, by types of forced migrants, and by functions. Existing funding mechanisms contribute to maldistribution through short funding cycles, bilateral rather than multilateral funding, and donor preference for certain elements of humanitarian appeals.

## Challenges to First Asylum

The vast majority of persons fleeing conflict try to find protection and assistance in the developing world. According to the *World Refugee Survey 2002*, between thirteen and fourteen million of the almost fifteen million refugees worldwide reside in Africa, the Middle East, and Asia. While only a limited number of refugees from these regions reach Europe, North America, or Australia, the asylum policies and practices in the developed world seriously affect the protection of the large numbers of refugees who remain in their regions.

**Refoulement and Denial of Access.** When states in the developed world violate the core protection obligation provided by the Refugee Convention and Protocol—nonrefoulement—states in the developing world imitate their misbehavior. During the two-year period from 1992 to 1994, the official policy of the United States was to interdict Haitians on the high seas and return them directly to Haiti without considering any protection needs and rights they might have.[31] This was a period of political repression in Haiti, when the democratically elected government had been overthrown by a military coup. It was no surprise in 1996, then, when Côte d'Ivoire officials denied entry to a boat, the *Bulk Challenge,* carrying several thousand Liberian refugees. Despite a long tradition of generosity toward refugees from Liberia, Côte d'Ivoire did not hesitate to turn this boat away, knowing full well that a key supporter of UNHCR had recently refouled thousands of Haitians on boats.[32]

Even when developed nations stop short of such open refoulement but deny entry to their territory, the message is clear: find protection elsewhere. Australia adopted a new policy to address boat arrivals of asylum seekers in late August 2001, not long before national elections were to be held. Under this policy, Australia refuses to allow such arrivals into Australian territory and sends them to other countries in the Pacific, where their refugee claims are assessed. After the number of boat arrivals increased in the late summer, Australia refused entry to a Norwegian freighter, the *Tampa,* carrying some 430 persons, most of whom claimed to be Afghans. The Australians negotiated temporary refuge for the passengers with the tiny Pacific nation of Nauru and with New Zealand. Australia provided Nauru with an aid package worth the equivalent of 10 million Australian dollars in return for hosting the asylum seekers. New Zealand said it would assess the asylum claims of those brought to its territory. The Nauru government asked UNHCR to screen the asylum seekers taken to Nauru, and UNHCR eventually agreed, but only for the group sent to Nauru. UNHCR expressed serious concern that Australia's actions could send a negative message to impoverished nations closer to conflict zones, which often take in hundreds of thousands of refugees.[33]

Roadblocks to asylum have become the rule rather than the exception in developed countries beginning in the 1980s. Visa requirements, carrier sanctions, safe country of origin and safe third country rules, expedited processing and removal, filing deadlines, detention, and pre-inspection discourage or bar asylum seekers from receiving protection in developed countries. Visa requirements imposed by Croatia and other European states, for example, seriously inhibited the ability of Bosnians to flee their country during the civil war. Many analysts believe that such tools lead asylum seekers into the hands of smugglers, making escape and protection far more risky.[34] Such roadblocks are being adopted as well by countries just now developing individualized asylum systems. Developed countries such as Germany and the United States have advised countries such as Poland and South Africa how to replicate the developed-country asylum system.

**Detention and Lack of Representation.** Detention of asylum seekers has been adopted by states purportedly to discourage arrivals and ensure compliance with legal proceedings. In general, it is used with respect to asylum seekers arriving in boats or at the border. European states, Australia, and the United States employ this policy, but no systematic study has evaluated the deterrent effects of detention. No doubt, detention ensures compliance with legal proceedings, but a major study has shown that detention at the outset is not an effective or humane use of a limited resource, except in the case of those persons deemed security or public safety risks. For asylum seekers with legitimate claims, the study showed, supervised release—an approach more in keeping with the humanitarian nature of asylum—results in compliance at a much lower cost than detention.[35]

Detention has a deleterious effect on the ability of asylum seekers to assert a good claim for protection, by making it very difficult to obtain effective representation.[36] Given the complexity of asylum law and its proceedings, as well as linguistic and cultural barriers for most asylum seekers, representation plays a major role in setting forth a good claim for protection. Asylum seekers are four to six times likelier to be granted asylum if they are represented.[37] Two of every three asylum seekers in the United States are unrepresented in the first instance (before an asylum officer), and still one of every three lacks representation in formal proceedings before immigration judges.

**Expedited Processing.** European nations were the first to create rapid asylum procedures, which were practiced in the major countries there by 1994. These procedures were aimed particularly at identifying "manifestly unfounded" applications at the airports and other ports of entry. Applicants arriving from "safe states" (discussed more fully below) are screened out of the regular asylum process and into an accelerated determination system. In Germany, for example, the asylum seeker in this situation has forty-eight hours to apply.[38] Rejected asylum seekers are given three days to file an appeal with an administrative court. In the United Kingdom, asylum seekers from "safe" countries are returned within twenty-four hours.[39]

In the United States, the Illegal Immigration Reform and Immigrant Responsibility Act of 1996 created an expedited removal procedure upon entry for those with fraudulent documentation or no documentation. Under these procedures, asylum seekers must demonstrate that they have a credible fear of persecution in order to continue with their asylum application. The law mandates that the "credible fear" determination be made swiftly and requires that the immigration judge's review of that determination be completed in no more than one week. Detention is mandated during this period of time.[40]

The effects of expedited processing are not clear. In Germany, most asylum seekers who use the three-day airport procedure or the rapid border procedure are unsuccessful. At the border, this is particularly because of the "safe third country" policy (discussed below). Yet some 90,000 asylum seekers on average lodged applications in Germany each year from 1998 to 2001. In many cases, apparently, applicants tell the German authorities that they do not know what route they took to reach the interior of Germany.[41] In the United States, more than 90 percent of those placed in expedited proceedings meet the credible fear requirements and are then placed in the full hearing proceedings before an immigration judge.

**Safe Third Country and Safe Country of Origin.** Most developed nations have adopted the general principle in their asylum laws that the first safe haven country to which a refugee flees should be the one in which he or she seeks asylum.[42] This is often qualified when an asylum seeker is trying to join family members in a particular safe country. European countries developed the "safe third country" policy initially to prevent asylum seekers from "shopping" for asylum: being denied in one European state, then trying again in another. The Dublin Convention and the Schengen Implementation Treaty both identify the country responsible for making the one and only asylum determination on behalf of all signatories, a determination that all other signatories then pledge to respect. The assumption made in these arrangements is that all EU countries are safe. Some states actually name safe third countries in their asylum laws. For Germany, all EU and European Free Trade Association states, as well as Poland and the Czech Republic, are named. Most states provide general criteria for assessing whether a third county is to be considered safe. Austrian law states that all countries that apply the refugee convention are to be considered safe third countries. More than 140 nations have signed the refugee convention or the refugee protocol, including known human rights violators.

**Independent Review.** Developed nations' asylum systems have traditionally permitted some degree of review of the initial asylum decision. This practice, however, is changing, particularly in the United States. The trend in the United States, in terms of both administrative and judicial review, has been to limit very significantly the role of the review function in the asylum system. The 1996 U.S. law Illegal Immigration Reform and Immigrant Responsibility Act of 1996 (IIRIRA) made the Immigration Court the final arbiter of the merits in "credible fear" proceedings.[43] These determinations cannot be appealed to the Board of Immigration Appeals (BIA) or the federal courts, both of which have traditionally had significant review authority over the lower administrative court.

In 1999, the U.S. attorney general authorized major changes in the BIA review process in order to address an increasing caseload and backlog, including authority to issue summary affirmances, that is, decisions without any analysis, in certain circumstances.[44] Changes initiated by a new attorney general in 2002 went considerably further in order to speed up adjudication at the BIA in such drastic ways that some experts believe they will render the appeal process meaningless. The attorney general required the BIA members to clear their current backlog of about 55,000 cases within 180 days—so fast that each appellate judge had to decide thirty-two cases every workday, or one every fifteen minutes.[45]

While these policies that limit first asylum directly affect a small proportion of refugees worldwide, they send a very strong signal to countries around the world. The intended message is clear: If you're fleeing conflict or persecution, do not try to escape to a developed country. The unintended consequence is equally clear: The states that created the refugee convention to correct the inadequate responses to those fleeing Nazi Germany are no longer strong supporters of refugee protection. They may talk to developing nations as if they were, trying to persuade those nations to protect and assist the vast majority of forced migrants in the world, but developing countries see what is really going on, and act accordingly.

## Conclusion

Years after exuberance about the end of the Cold War prompted the UN High Commissioner for Refugees (UNHCR) to declare a "decade of voluntary repatriation," conflict continues to force millions of people to flee, seeking safety outside their home communities. Some manage to escape their countries and find temporary or permanent refuge abroad, while an alarmingly large number remain trapped inside or are forced to repatriate before the home country's conditions change in any significant way. Too few find truly durable solutions that allow them to regain secure and dignified lives. Given the large-scale suffering and loss of life, both real and potential, addressing the challenges to protection set out in this chapter must be a priority for the entire international community.

## Notes

1. UN High Commissioner for Refugees, *2001 Statistical Yearbook* (Geneva: UNHCR, 2002).

2. The UN General Assembly and secretary-general have asked the UNHCR to use its good offices to assist and protect refugees from conflict as well as from generalized violence. For the evolution of UNHCR's role, see UNHCR, *State of the World's Refugees* (Oxford: Oxford University Press, 2000).

3. Global IDP Project, *Internally Displaced People: A Global Survey* (London: Earthscan Publications, 2002).

4. UNHCR, *Statistical Yearbook.*

5. The rapid return of refugees from Pakistan to Afghanistan occurred, at least in part, because of pressure from Pakistan, tired of having hosted millions of refugees for more than two decades, as well as encouragement from donor countries. See David Turton and Peter Marsden, "Taking Refugees for a Ride? The Politics of Refugee Return to Afghanistan," Afghanistan Research and Evaluation Issue paper, December 2002, at www.areu.org.pk/.

6. "Denial or removal of the rights of citizenship can be a means comprehensively to deny a population a broad range of human rights. Short of physical extermination or expulsion from one's country, this denial of civil rights reduces a population to the most extreme vulnerability to abuse and exploitation." Human Rights Watch, "Racism, Nationality, Statelessness, and the Rights of Citizenship" (statement to the First Preparatory Committee for the World Conference Against Racism, Racial Discrimination, Xenophobia and Related Intolerance), www.hrw.org/campaigns/race/hrw-statement1.htm.

7. Refugee Policy Group, "Migration and the Environment," (Geneva: International Organization for Migration, 1992).

8. For ways to reduce human rights violations, see World Bank, "Operational Policy on Involuntary Resettlement," OP 4.12 Involuntary Resettlement, December 2001; and World Bank, "Bank Procedure on Involuntary Resettlement," BP 4.12 Involuntary Resettlement, December 2001. Both at lnweb18.worldbank.org/ESSD/sdvext.nsf/65ByDocName/Policy.

**9.** Susan Forbes Martin, "Development and Politically Generated Migration" in *Determinants of Emigration from Mexico, Central America, and the Caribbean,* ed. Sergio Diaz-Briquets and Sidney Weintraub (Boulder, CO: Westview Press, 1991).

**10.** Quoted in W. Courtland Robinson, *The Causes, Consequences, and Challenges of Development-Induced Displacement* (Washington, DC: Brookings Institution, 2003), www.brookings.edu/dybdocroot/fp/projects/idp/articles/didreport.pdf.

**11.** According to the UN High Commissioner for Refugees, "There is no universally accepted definition of 'persecution,' and various attempts to formulate such a definition have met with little success. From Article 33 of the 1951 Convention, it may be inferred that a threat to life or freedom on account of race, religion, nationality, political opinion, or membership in a particular social group is always persecution. Other serious violations of human rights—for the same reasons—would also constitute persecution." From *Handbook on Procedures and Criteria for Determining Refugee Status under the 1951 Convention and the 1967 Protocol Relating to the Status of Refugees,* 1992, www.unhcr.ch/cgi-bin/texis/vtx/publ/opendoc.pdf?tbl=PUBL&id=3d58e13b4.

**12.** See Louise W. Holborn, *Refugees, a Problem of Our Time: The Work of the United Nations High Commissioner for Refugees, 1951–1972* (Metuchen, NJ: Scarecrow Press, 1975).

**13.** 1969 OAU Convention Governing the Specific Aspects of Refugee Problems in Africa, www.africa-union.org/Official_documents/Treaties_%20Conventions_%20Protocols/Refugee_Convention.pdf.

**14.** In a similar vein, the Cartagena Declaration on Refugees expands the definition of protected refugees in the Latin American region. Like the OAU definition, it supports the 1951 Convention and adds protection to those who have fled their country "because their lives, safety or freedom have been threatened by generalized violence, foreign aggression, internal conflicts, massive violation of human rights or other circumstances that have seriously disturbed public order." It emphasizes that repatriation of refugees must be voluntary, and embodies principles for their protection, assistance, and reintegration. Although a nonbinding instrument, the declaration has been endorsed by the General Assembly of the Organization of American States, and most states in Latin America apply the Declaration's broader definition of a refugee as a matter of practice. Some have incorporated this definition into their own national legislation.

**15.** Susan Martin and Andrew I. Schoenholtz, "Temporary Protection: U.S. and European Responses to Mass Migration" (working paper, Institute for the Study of International Migration, Georgetown University, Washington, DC, 2000).

**16.** See "Scoreboard to Review Progress on the Creation of an Area of 'Freedom, Security and Justice' in the European Union," Brussels, 13.4.2000 COM(2000) 167 final/2, http://europa.eu.int/eur-lex/en/com/pdf/2000/com2000_0167en02.pdf.

**17.** Susan Martin, Andrew I. Schoenholtz, and Deborah Waller Meyers, "Temporary Protection: Towards a New Regional and Domestic Framework," *Georgetown Immigration Law Journal* 12 (1998): 543.

**18.** See country pages, Internal Displacement Monitoring Centre, www.internal-displacement.org/.

**19.** Ibid.

**20.** Roberta Cohen and Francis Deng, *Masses in Flight: The Global Crisis of Internal Displacement* (Washington, DC: Brookings Institution, 1998).

**21.** See U.S. Committee for Refugees, World Refugee Survey 2002 for statistics on the countries of origin of the major refugee and internally displaced populations.

**22.** U.S. Committee for Refugees, *Shadow Plays: Refugees and Internally Displaced Persons in Indonesia* (Washington, DC: U.S. Committee for Refugees, 2001).

**23.** Aristide Zolberg, Astri Suhrke, and Sergio Aguayo, *Escape from Violence: Conflict and the Refugee Crisis in the Developing World* (New York: Oxford University Press, 1989).

**24.** See, for example, Ben Barber, "Feeding Refugees, or War?" *Foreign Affairs* 76, no. 4 (July–August 1997): 8–14.

**25.** For example, the International Rescue Committee and Médecins Sans Frontières withdrew from the camps in eastern Zaire when they concluded that their aid was reinforcing the hold of the *génocidaires* on the civilian population.

**26.** See the Humanitarian Charter adopted by humanitarian aid agencies, at www.sphereproject.org/handbook/hc.htm.

**27.** This section is based largely on the authors' participation in a three-year collaborative project on barriers to effective assistance and protection for forced migrants. The study team conducted field visits in Burundi, Sri Lanka, Colombia, East Timor, and Georgia. The case studies consistently revealed insecurity to be the principal barrier to assistance and protection, particularly when humanitarian aid operations were the target of military activities. Preliminary findings were presented at the biannual meeting of the International Association for the Study of Forced Migration, at Chiang Mai, Thailand, 2003.

**28.** Based on the authors' own participation in meetings called by the National Security Council to discuss military intervention in Kosovo and ways to deal with the resulting humanitarian response to forced migration.

**29.** See country pages, Internal Displacement Monitoring Centre, at www.internal-displacement.org/.

**30.** See UNHCR, "Internally Displaced Persons: The Role of the United Nations High Commissioner for Refugees," March 6, 2000, www.unhcr.ch/ cgi-bin/texis/vtx/excom/opendoc.pdf?tbl=EXCOM&id=3ae68d150.

**31.** Martin, Schoenholtz, and Waller, "Temporary Protection," 543.

**32.** U.S. Committee for Refugees, *World Refugee Survey, 1997* (Washington, DC: USCR, 1997).

**33.** U.S. Committee for Refugees, *World Refugee Survey, 2002* (Washington, DC: USCR, 2002).

**34.** See, for example, European Council on Refugees and Exiles, "The Promise of Protection: Progress towards a European Asylum Policy since the Tampere Summit," December 2001, www.ecre.org/research/popwhole.pdf.

**35.** Vera Institute of Justice, "Testing Community Supervision for the INS: An Evaluation of the Appearance Assistance Program," www.vera.org/publication _pdf/aapfinal.pdf.

**36.** Andrew Schoenholtz and Jonathan Jacobs, "The State of Asylum Representation: Ideas for Change," *Georgetown Immigration Law Journal* 16, no. 4 (2003).

**37.** Ibid.

**38.** Susan Martin and Andrew I. Schoenholtz, "Asylum in Practice: Successes, Failures, and the Challenges Ahead," *Georgetown Immigration Law Journal* 14 (2000): 589, 602.

**39.** Ibid.

**40.** Immigration and Nationality Act (INA), Section 235(b)(1)(B)(iii)(IV).

**41.** Martin and Schoenholtz, "Asylum in Practice," 589, 603.

**42.** Ibid., at 606–7.

**43.** INA Section 235(b)(1)(B)(iii)(III).

**44.** 64 FR 56135 (October 18, 1999).

**45.** 67 FR 54878 (August 26, 2002); Lawyers Committee for Human Rights, "New Regulations Threaten to Turn Board of Immigration Appeals into Rubber Stamp," August 28, 2002.

# 15

# Human Rights Education and Grassroots Peacebuilding

Janet E. Lord and Nancy Flowers

At the inception of the United Nations, the essential link between peace and human rights was explicit and unquestioned. The United Nations Charter proclaims the maintenance of peace and the promotion of human rights among the organization's prime purposes. Article 55 of the charter declares,

> With a view to the creation of conditions of stability and well-being, which are necessary for peaceful and friendly relations among nations . . . the United Nations shall promote: . . . universal respect for and observance of human rights and fundamental freedoms for all without distinction as to race, sex, language, or religion.

The Preamble to the Universal Declaration of Human Rights (UDHR) reiterates this link even more succinctly: "Recognition of the inherent dignity and of the equal and inalienable rights of all members of the human family is the foundation of freedom, justice and peace in the world."

Subsequent international instruments address both the right to education and corresponding duties on the part of governments to provide certain types of education in various contexts. The United Nations and its specialized agencies took the lead in specifying objectives for member states in the area of human rights and peace education, with UNICEF and UNESCO playing leading roles.

Nonetheless, during the past fifty years a distinction between education for peace and education for human rights has evolved that is reflected both in international documents and in the practice of educators. Broad educational goals relating to the strengthening of human rights and the promotion of peace appear as separate and distinct categories in international documents, a differentiation often reflected in the practice of human rights education (HRE) and peace education. Only since the end of the Cold War has the link between peace education and HRE begun to be acknowledged again in international documents, and the goals and methods of the fields begun to converge in practice.

This chapter begins with an analysis of the relationship between HRE and peace education as expressed in the right to education under international human rights law and in international documents. It then reviews how peace education and HRE, respectively, have been defined and differentiated in practice and discusses their convergence in recent years. We then offer criteria for transformative HRE and peace education programming and conclude with the application of these criteria to three case studies.

## The Right to Human Rights Education and Peace Education

International human rights law defines a right to education that encompasses not only the right to receive an education and the right to educational freedom but also rights regarding the standard, quality, and content of education. Thus, Article 26 of the UDHR, in addition to providing for access to education, also proclaims that education

> shall be directed to the full development of the human personality and to the strengthening of respect for human rights and fundamental freedoms and, further, that education shall promote understanding, tolerance and friendship among all nations, racial or religious groups, and shall further the activities of the United Nations for the maintenance of peace.

The Universal Declaration thus recognizes that the right to education encompasses both education to strengthen human rights and education to promote peacebuilding. These appear, however, as two separate and distinct concepts in the provision on the right to education. This acknowledgment that the rights to education include human rights– and peace-oriented content features also in subsequent international human rights documents, though they also maintain the implicit distinction between the two. Thus, for example, the International Covenant on Economic, Social, and Cultural Rights, in Article 13, reaffirms the substantive right to education and provides direction for content of education, acknowledging its role in strengthening respect for human rights on one hand and in promoting peace between nations and minority groups on the other.[1]

Specialized international human rights conventions and nonbinding declarations have also recognized the role of education both in promoting peace and in building respect for human rights and fundamental freedoms. Typical is the provision in Article 7 of the International Convention on the Elimination of All Forms of Racial Discrimination, which obligates states to introduce measures "in the fields of teaching education, culture and information, with a view to combating prejudices which lead to racial discrimination and to promoting understanding, tolerance and friendship among nations and racial or ethnic groups."[2] Again, however, educational goals are twofold and introduced as separate and distinct categories: first for education toward the realization of the main human rights objective of the convention, namely, nondiscrimination; and second for education toward the promotion of tolerance and friendship among nations and racial and ethnic groups. Likewise, Article 29 of the Convention on the Rights of the Child provides that the education of the child "shall be directed to . . . the development of respect for human rights and fundamental freedoms, and for the principles enshrined in the Charter of the United Nations,"[3] and further to "the preparation of the child for responsible life in a free society, in the spirit of understanding, peace tolerance, equality of sexes and friendship among all peoples, ethnic, national and religious groups, and persons of indigenous origin."

For decades UN organizations perpetuated this division found in international documents. The 1978 International Congress on the Teaching of Human Rights, convened by UNESCO, mandated that "equal emphasis be placed on economic, social and cultural, civil and political rights" with "human rights education and teaching based on the principles" of international human rights documents. The congress also recognized the connection between human rights and peace, while the distinction between the two in the context of education was maintained:

> Care should be constantly taken to create awareness about the close relationship between human rights, on the one hand, and development and peace, including inter alia disarmament, on the other hand. UNESCO should make it a priority task to promote analysis and understanding of this relationship.[4]

In addition, the congress recommended the development of new approaches in HRE that emphasize "the interrelationship between Human Rights teaching and the other major problems of mankind."[5] In the context of recognizing the rights of the child, the congress recommended HRE in formal and informal sectors and also included a separate recommendation, according to which the director-general of UNESCO would "promote the teaching of non-violent alternatives and strategies for the peaceful resolution of conflicts."[6]

## Peace Education Defined in Practice

The understanding of such "non-violent alternatives and strategies" for peace has been evolving for more than a century. Peace education as an educational movement has its roots in the nineteenth century, when the forerunners of today's peace educators advocated ethical education for children and the education of individuals for citizenship.[7] Betty Reardon has traced the modern development of peace education along three general chronological tracks.[8] First, during the years following World War II, peace education entered into a reform phase, in which it focused on negative peace, or the prevention of war and the control of arms races. The main thrust of peace education programming during the reform era was to change the behavior of citizens and states, depending on which nonviolent alternatives would contribute to war prevention. The reconstructive phase of peace education, developed during the 1960s, reflected broader agendas and sought to address international structures with the aim of abolishing war and achieving complete disarmament. Peace education under this model tended to focus on institutional change and addressed the role of global institutions in resolving conflicts and making peace. Finally, the transformational phase of peace education, still in progress, combines objectives of both negative peace and positive peace and therefore encompasses an ever-broadening agenda. The rejection of all forms of violence, including structural violence, is sought under what Reardon refers to as a "comprehensive peace education."

As currently defined in practice, "peace education" is an umbrella term that captures many program models, all with some link to peace and conflict resolution. In some cases, organizations with peace education programs acknowledge in explicit terms the connection between human rights and peace and may include some coverage of human rights material in trainings. In other cases, organizations offer peace education programs that feature conflict resolution skills building and make no explicit connection to human rights, though some refer to "social justice" as a goal.

The Peace Education Foundation provides a definition of peace education that is typical of more narrowly focused programs that stress conflict resolution without any clear human rights orientation. Its model is "based on a comprehensive body of research related to teaching social competency skills, reducing disruptive behavior and creating a positive learning environment." Its peace education programs include community-building skills; rules for fighting fair; understanding conflict, perception, and diversity; the management of anger, and other emotions; and effective communication skills, but make no reference to human rights standards and advocacy skills.[9]

During the past ten years there has been a move within some organizations with peace education programming to bridge the divide between peace and human rights education curricula. Thus, for example, peace education as defined by the American Friends Service Committee (AFSC) recognizes the role of human rights in creating a peaceful world. However, the tools of HRE, and in particular international human rights standards, are not identified as a central part of its peace-building initiatives. The Peace Education Program at the AFSC "works towards the abolition of war and fulfillment of human rights as essential to creating a nonviolent world order in which all may live together"[10] and develops peace education curricula "devoted to the promotion of peace, global justice, and international understanding."[11] Peace education is part of AFSC's Peacebuilding and Demilitarization Program, which engages in, among other things, peace education with the aim of (1) understanding the root causes of war and violence; (2) exploring peaceful alternatives to war and violence; (3) building awareness of immediate peacebuilding issues and concerns such as nuclear weapons, missile defense systems, and small-arms proliferation, budgetary and social impact of military spending, and the use of economic sanctions as a weapon of war; (4) strengthening youth involvement in peacebuilding work; and (5) supporting and building a new peace movement.[12] Of its four peace education program areas, its Middle East Program addresses human rights violations facing Palestinians and Israelis, and its Latin American/Caribbean Program includes human rights monitoring.

Among organizations with peace education programming, UNICEF comes closest to an integrated understanding of HRE and peace education but nonetheless maintains a distinction between the two. The Peace Education Working Group at UNICEF defines peace education as

> the process of promoting the knowledge, skills, attitudes and values needed to bring about behavior changes that will enable children, youth and adults to prevent conflict and violence, both overt and structural; to resolve conflict peacefully; and to create the conditions conducive to peace, whether at an intrapersonal, interpersonal, intergroup, national or international level.[13]

As understood in UNICEF's definition, the term "peace" encompasses an understanding of the components of negative peace—the absence of overt violence—and positive peace, or the presence of social, economic, and political justice: "Peace education must address the prevention and resolution of all forms of conflict and violence, whether overt or structural, from the interpersonal level to the societal and global level."[14]

Significantly, UNICEF's approach to peace education does recognize its important role in rights-based work and links its role in peace education to its mandate to work for children's rights: "Peace is a fundamental precondition without which rights cannot be realized, while at the same time the ensuring of basic rights is essential to bringing about peace."[15] While UNICEF takes the view that child rights and HRE and peace education are "closely linked activities that complement and support each other," they remain separate and distinct in the organization's categorization of its educational programming. A distinguishing feature of HRE according to UNICEF is learning about the content of international human rights documents, the impact of violations, and the development of skills to enable children to act in ways that will promote rights. As shown above, peace education, on the other hand, "must address the prevention and resolution of all forms of conflict and violence, whether overt or structural, from the interpersonal level to the societal and global level." While peace education may well incorporate human rights into its areas of coverage, UNICEF sees HRE as narrower in focus.

In the years immediately following the 1999 Hague Appeal for Peace Conference, some peace education programs around the world started to give more explicit recognition to the link between human rights and peace and have included human rights issues in their curricula. For example, the International Peace Bureau (IPB), the oldest international peace network, defines peace education as "a participatory process which changes our way of thinking and learning for peace and justice"[16] and, noting the "continued development of weapons of mass destruction, conflicts between states and ethnic groups, the spread of racism, community violence, the huge and widening gap between the rich and the poor throughout the globalized economy, massive violations of human rights and the degradation of the environment,"[17] presents peace education as a mechanism to challenge such global problems. The recommended content of peace education in this model should include "human rights, development and environmental education, human and security issues, reconciliation, conflict prevention/resolution training, critical media awareness, gender studies, nonviolence and international relations."[18] Similarly, the Global Campaign for Peace Education, launched in May 1999 at the Hague Appeal for Peace Conference, defines peace education as "a holistic, participatory process that includes teaching for and about human rights, nonviolent responses to conflict, social and economic justice, gender equality, environmental sustainability, disarmament, and human security."[19] Its methodology is intended to facilitate "reflection, critical thinking, cooperation, and responsible action" and promote multiculturalism and "is based on values of dignity, equality and respect."

Finally, since 1997, the Centre for Conflict Resolution, in Cape Town, South Africa, has made human rights an integral part of its approach to conflict resolution training, designing exercises intended to bring out the relationship between human rights and conflict management through an examination of the causes of conflict and basic human needs.[20] This approach is based on the following premises: (1) that all human rights relate to one or more human needs; (2) that human rights are important for the management of conflict because their implementation provides for the basic satisfaction of human needs; (3) that conflict leads to human rights violations, and the denial of human rights leads to conflict; and (4) that human rights documents are important tools of conflict management, and their implementation is in the interests of all people. A paper published by Michelle Parlevliet in the center's *Track Two* journal, "Bridging the Divide: Exploring the Relationship between Human Rights and Conflict Management," underlines the need for much deeper integration between the fields of conflict management and human rights through dialogue among practitioners.[21]

## The Development of Human Rights Education

HRE as a specialized field effectively began with the adoption of the UDHR in 1948. To fulfill the UDHR's charge to "strive by teaching and learning to promote respect for these rights and freedoms," the UN General Assembly resolved, on the occasion of its adoption, that "the text of the Declaration should be disseminated among all peoples throughout the world" and encouraged its translation into as many languages as possible.[22] As a result, the UDHR today holds the *Guinness Book of Records* title for the document translated into the greatest number of languages.

The UN General Assembly further recommended that member states use

> every means within their power solemnly to publicize the text of the Declaration . . . [and] to cause it to be disseminated, displayed, read and expounded principally in schools and other educational institutions, without distinction based on the political status of countries or territories.[23]

Mere dissemination of human rights principles was frequently all that was required of human rights education by early international human rights documents. Indeed, in the first decades after the adoption of the UDHR in

1948, HRE was essentially confined to dissemination. Even the adoption of the International Covenant on Civil and Political Rights and the International Covenant on Economic, Social and Cultural Rights in 1966, and their entry into force in 1976, inspired little educational response beyond courses in international law. It was during this period that HRE came to be identified principally with law schools. Even leading human rights NGOs such as Amnesty International invested few resources in education beyond what was then called "human rights awareness," drawing attention to specific cases of violation in order to mobilize action. Only the Council of Europe was promoting systematic HRE, principally to promulgate the European Convention of Human Rights; as a result, only in Europe were human rights being integrated into the formal educational establishment of individual countries.

This legal orientation and focus on violations contributed to the growing separation of HRE and peace education. However, powerful voices such as Martin Luther King Jr. and Pope John XXIII, in his encyclical 1963 "Pacem in Terris,"[24] continued to insist on the essential interdependence of the two, and people in many parts of the world were combining human rights principles and nonviolent tactics in their struggles to challenge dictators, racist policies, and colonial oppression.

During the 1960s and 1970s, against the background of the Cold War, the extension of nuclear capability, and the war in Vietnam, peace education became firmly established in European and U.S. educational institutions. While education for human rights was becoming more narrowly focused on international law, education for peace found vast new popular audiences and practical relevance among antiwar and antinuclear movements. Although peace education may have suffered some disparagement by identification in the popular imagination with "flower children," "peaceniks," and liberal movements of the 1960s, it benefited from the contemporary insistence on the integration of personal ethics with global movements for peace and social justice.

In contrast, HRE did not come of age until the late 1980s and early 1990s, and as with peace education, this maturing was stimulated by immediate need and practical application. Activists in countries such as Chile, South Africa, and the Philippines developed grassroots HRE methodologies in order to build movements for change. The more people became aware of the complexities of global interdependence in such areas as economics and ecology, the more they realized the value of the universal norms and standards of human rights as tools for advocacy. As the former Soviet Union began to dissolve, governmental and nongovernmental institutions

saw in HRE an important tool to foster democracy in the newly independent states of central and eastern Europe. European and North American
governments, foundations, and NGOs expanded funding for HRE projects
around the world.

Seemingly overnight, HRE was in demand, especially where peacebuilding and social stability were called for. In the 1980s, however, HRE
lacked the developed theoretical and methodological foundations that had
already been established for peace education. Because human rights were
not part of anyone's basic education or of teachers' preservice training, most
early practitioners were self-taught, cobbling together theory and practice
from the work of educators such as Paolo Freire with examples from the
Philippines and Latin America, as well as from such related fields as environmental education, gender studies, global education, and peace education itself. A particular challenge was overcoming the long-established law-
and-legal-violations approach and relating human rights to positive values
and action at the personal, family, and community level. Especially in
Europe and North America, where most funders were located, HRE was
regarded as a means of addressing "problems happening somewhere else,"
rather than as a positive value system to apply in one's own society.

## Reintegrating of Human Rights Education and Peace Education

A pronounced shift occurred during the 1990s as HRE and peace education
began to converge under the umbrella of democracy and peacebuilding
activities. Education became increasingly identified in international documents as an important component of the peacebuilding agenda, although
interestingly, references are generally to HRE, which is broadly defined.[25]

UN secretary-general Boutros Boutros-Ghali's 1992 "Agenda for
Peace"[26] sets forth proposals for the response of the United Nations and
the international community to contemporary conflicts and identifies four
major areas of activity: preventive diplomacy, peacemaking, peacekeeping,
and postconflict peacebuilding. The UN Security Council began to give support to HRE as one among many mechanisms for institutional change,
democratization, and reconstruction, marking a departure from peacekeeping practices before the late 1980s. Thus, El Salvador, Haiti, and Cambodia
peacekeeping operations all included HRE components, signaling the start
of a pattern that continues today in peacekeeping operations.

By the time of the 1993 United Nations World Conference on Human Rights, HRE was explicitly linked to the goals of peace. The Vienna

Declaration thus recognizes that HRE is "essential for the promotion and achievement of stable and harmonious relations among communities and for fostering mutual understanding, tolerance and peace."[27]

In 1994, on the strength of endorsements by the Vienna Declaration, the UN General Assembly proclaimed 1995–2004 as the United Nations Decade for Human Rights Education, giving huge new impetus to the field. International documents concerning the proclamation define HRE in very broad terms, extending well beyond the dissemination of human rights principles to include objectives linked to democracy, peace, and conflict resolution. For the purposes of the Decade for Human Rights Education, the United Nations defines HRE as

> training, dissemination and information efforts aimed at the building of a universal culture of human rights through the imparting of knowledge and skills and the molding of attitudes, which are directed towards:
>
> - The strengthening of respect for human rights and fundamental freedoms;
> - The full development of the human personality and the sense of its dignity;
> - The promotion of understanding, tolerance, gender equality and friendship among all nations, indigenous peoples and racial, ethnic, religious and linguistic groups;
> - The enabling of all persons to participate effectively in a free society;
> - The furtherance of the activities of the United Nations for the maintenance of peace.[28]

At the same time, key actors such as the Office of the High Commissioner for Human Rights and Amnesty International established their first full-time staff positions for HRE. In addition, many international conferences and trainings on HRE were held,[29] new NGOs dedicated to HRE were founded (such as the Asian Regional Resource Center for Human Rights Education, the People's Decade for Human Rights Education, and Human Rights Education Associates), and books, articles, and curricula on HRE began to appear from all parts of the world.[30]

Definitions of HRE currently in use continue to vary in emphasis, with NGOs drawn to its potential for advocacy, governmental organizations stressing its role in building stable and just societies, and academics inclined to see its educational role as a practical value system.[31] However, almost all programs combine knowledge of the international human rights system and its underlying principles with skills to promote and protect human rights and behavioral change to reflect human rights principles.

## HRE and Peace Education Today

Now, at the start of the twenty-first century, HRE is recognized as an established field, but its distinction from closely related fields, especially peace education, remains ill defined. Betty Reardon has made the most significant effort to clarify the distinction and similarities between the two, declaring, "Human rights is as fundamental and constitutive to peace education as human rights are to peace."[32] She sees both as transformative for society and for the individual alike and credits human rights with the potential for

> providing the basis for a prescriptive, holistic yet particularized approach that would make peace education not only more comprehensive but also far more comprehensible. The actual human experiences that comprise much of human rights education are more readily understood than the theoretical and analytical content of peace education.[33]

This statement underscores an important distinction between HRE and peace education, namely, the tendency of content, especially law and current events, to dominate in HRE, and process, especially methods of dealing with conflict, to dominate in peace education. Michelle Parlevliet has analyzed this at once complementary and contradictory nature of the practice of human rights and conflict management: "Human rights actors are generally concerned with the application of objective standards to determine issues of justice and establish the extent to which parties have upheld or violated such standards. Conflict management practitioners, on the other hand, seek to reconcile the needs, interests, and concerns of disputant parties in a constructive way, rather than trying to determine who is right and who is wrong."[34] She argues that conflict management practitioners should be trained in human rights awareness and instruments in order to understand the relationship between rights and conflict, the nonnegotiable nature of fundamental human rights, and the long-term ramification of agreements that do not maintain human rights standards. Human rights actors and agents of humanitarian agencies should be trained in conflict management skills such as crisis intervention; negotiation; facilitation; and problem-solving, communication, and confidence-building approaches to mediation.

Certainly both fields benefit from a holistic approach that integrates rather than divides. HR gives a concrete justification for seeking and maintaining peace in the real world, while peace education provides a process for creating the kind of peaceful environment without which human rights can never be attained.

**Table 1. Human Rights Education and Peace Education Compared**

| | Human Rights Education | Peace Education |
|---|---|---|
| **Goals** | ■ Behavior change, both personal and societal<br>■ Promotion and protection of human rights<br>■ Creation of a culture of human rights | ■ Behavior change, both personal and societal<br>■ Create and maintain peace, avoid conflict<br>■ Creation of a culture of peace |
| **Audience** | ■ All societies<br>■ Entire community | ■ All societies<br>■ Entire community |
| **Setting** | ■ Formal, informal, nonformal education | ■ Formal, informal, nonformal education |
| **Knowledge Content** | ■ Human rights principles and responsibilities<br>■ UDHR and specific human rights documents<br>■ Evolution of human rights<br>■ Mechanisms for human rights advocacy | ■ Human rights principles and responsibilities<br>■ The nature of conflict and peace<br>■ Conflict analysis<br>■ Community mechanisms for building peace, resolving conflict |
| **Values and Attitudes** | ■ Respect for self and others<br>■ Respect for difference, bias aware, gender equity<br>■ Personal responsibility for human rights<br>■ Empathy, solidarity<br>■ Personal transformation, social transformation | ■ Respect for self and others<br>■ Respect for difference, bias aware, gender equity<br>■ Personal responsibility for peace<br>■ Empathy, solidarity<br>■ Personal transformation, social transformation |

|  | | |
|---|---|---|
| **Skills** | ■ Conflict resolution/transformation<br>■ Critical thinking<br>■ Analysis of human rights dimension of situations<br>■ Leadership<br>■ Participatory democracy<br>■ Methods to uphold, protect, advocate for human rights<br>■ Integration of human rights principles into personal awareness and behavior | ■ Communication: active listening, self-expression, reframing<br>■ Critical thinking, problem solving<br>■ Conflict resolution/transformation<br>■ Mediation, negotiation, facilitation<br>■ Crisis intervention<br>■ Cooperation<br>■ Assertiveness, leadership<br>■ Self-control, dealing with emotions, tolerance of change |
| **Learning Methodologies** | ■ Participatory, interactive, collaborative<br>■ Takes place in a context of respect for HR | ■ Participatory, interactive, collaborative<br>■ Takes place in a context of peace |
| **Formal Education** | ■ Integrated into curriculum and learning environment<br>■ Not a separate subject<br>■ Reinforced by pre-service and in-service training of educators | ■ Integrated into curriculum and learning environment<br>■ Not a separate subject<br>■ Reinforced by pre-service and in-service training of educators |
| **Potential Challenges** | ■ Reaction to human rights violations vs. Tool for creating social justice<br>■ Human rights values conflict with community/cultural values | ■ Reaction to conflict vs. Tool for creating and maintaining peace and social justice<br>■ Peace values conflict with community/cultural values |

Indeed, when the fundamentals of both fields are compared, their commonalties far surpass their differences. Although table 1 summarizes the fields in broad strokes, it shows their principal distinctions to lie in emphases, not in goals or methods. Although most peace education stresses building skills and changing attitudes, whereas HRE focuses more on application of a body of knowledge, both are ultimately directed toward building and maintaining just and peaceful societies.

## Criteria for Transformative Education

Good practice in both HRE and peace education combines a knowledge-based approach with a skills-and-attitude approach. Whether designated HRE or peace education, any program that seeks social transformation through education needs to include three critical components: planned flexibility, a long-term commitment, and a community base.[35]

### 1. Planned Flexibility

Regardless of good funding, critical need, or excellent intentions, HRE and peace education projects ultimately succeed or fail on their ability to plan for and respond to constantly shifting political and societal circumstances.

The language of peace accords and mandate statements is usually vague in the extreme regarding HRE, for example, "fostering an environment in which human rights shall be ensured." The specific goals and concrete plan of action to fulfill that mandate are too often developed by international experts in isolation from the people whom the program is intended to serve. Incorporating local people is usually the most neglected aspect of planning because it is the most difficult to achieve, especially in postconflict situations, where planners often cannot safely enter a country until the program is to be implemented. As a result, the most successful HRE programs are designed to anticipate change, actively seek out local partners, and adapt with their help to the local environment.

In recommending such an evolving approach to HRE planning, Paul Martin describes five stages with changing actors, topics, arenas of learning, goals, and methods: stage one, prepeace and settlements; stage two, negotiations; stage three, beginning transition and early reconstruction; stage four, midstream and actual reconstruction; stage five, sustainability, self-sufficiency, and the termination of external action.

Planned flexibility does not eliminate the need for certain fixed goals and assumptions. From the outset, programs must assume their success and anticipate how to build on it. The more effective the HRE, the more demand for administrative, educational, and field support for the educators who deliver it. If strong administrative structures are planned and established in the beginning, they will have the capacity to serve the expanding project.

Because no program dependent on outside money and personnel will survive for long, every HRE program must also plan for its ultimate sustainability. The keys to sustainability are (a) proven value and effectiveness such that local people want to keep the project going, (b) well-trained local personnel with the skill and commitment to keep it going, and (c) methods adapted to local needs and resources. To accomplish these, a program must start strong and prove itself quickly, developing a methodology, training a team of local educators, and building a reputation within the first years.

Whether or not a program eventually sustains itself, outside organizations must also assume and plan from the start for their eventual withdrawal. In situations of active conflict, contingency plans should also include temporary suspensions of the program.

## 2. Long-Term Commitment

Although factual knowledge may be conveyed in a short course, transforming attitudes and mastering skills require time, repetition, and reinforcement. The first few months of a program are critical for establishing credibility, but the most significant accomplishments are made over long periods of continued learning. Therefore, effective human rights and peace education must be sustained and sustainable over a period of years, not months.

In formal education, HRE and peace education should begin with the first grade and continue throughout schooling, not taught as a separate subject but integrated into all aspects of school life. To accomplish this requires systematic training of teachers and school administrators, development of materials, and evaluation of existing policies and curricula.

In formal and informal education, repetition and follow-up are essential to solidifying learning. Learning must be both immediately relevant and consistently, convincingly useful; otherwise, few adults will continue to participate. Adults need to participate in their own learning, receive it in manageable installments, and test learning against reality, all of which requires years, not months.

## 3. Community Base

Outsiders may be involved in planning and supporting programs at their inception, but ultimately human rights education and peace education need to be grounded in local people and local needs.

HRE and peace education address local concerns. They may be put into perspective by global norms and standards and analyzed and addressed by peace-building skills, but education starts with the issues that affect people's daily lives.

For human rights and peace education to take root in a community, the people who deliver it must be indigenous to that community. Thus, one of the first and most important tasks of any human rights or peace education project is to train a team of trainers and reinforce initial trainings with periodic follow-up workshops. Only local people can effectively analyze local conditions or adapt materials and methodologies to the local culture and values. To further ensure both sustainability and genuine local ownership, existing organizations and institutions need to be brought into collaboration as early as possible. In this way program sponsors become facilitators and supporters of others who are developing training in human rights and peace building for their own communities.

Programs must choose their initial audiences strategically, but the ultimate audience for human rights and peace education is the whole community. This means deploying a wide variety of educational approaches and outreach techniques, and constant self-evaluation for inclusiveness.

## Applying the Criteria

These components for successful HRE and peace education combine lessons learned from practical experience; however, few if any programs meet all these criteria. The following examples illustrate not only the importance of careful planning, sustainability, and a community base, but also the difficulty in achieving all three.[36]

## 1. The Example of Cambodia, 1991–93

**The Situation.** The Paris Peace Agreements of 1991, which brought an end to the conflict in Cambodia, established the United Nations Transitional Authority in Cambodia (UNTAC) and called specifically for "the development and implementation of a programme of human rights education to promote respect for and understanding of human rights"[37] during the transition period of October 1991 to September 1993. This unprecedented task of carrying out large-scale HRE at all levels and of all types in a country still reeling from years of war and extreme oppression fell to the Human Rights Component of UNTAC.

**The Program.** In his article "HRE in UN Peace Building,"[38] Stephen Marks describes the six-step process the Human Rights Component used to develop and implement a specific strategy and plan of action for this program:

- *Identifying target audiences* for both formal and informal education, including UNTAC staff, existing administrative structures (e.g., police, teachers, judges), and civil society (e.g., journalists, monks, health professionals, human rights and women's associations).

- *Determining content expectations* appropriate for each identified audience. For example, a three-month course for law students stressed critical thinking and analysis of real-life situations from a human rights perspective. A UNESCO course for journalists aimed at skills development, with many sessions dealing with human rights aspects of current events in Cambodia and, in particular, with freedom of expression. This stage of the program also involved the printing of teaching materials and training of educators from the formal sector:

- *Assembling required human and financial resources,* including training provincial human rights officers with responsibility for education, training, and information at the provincial level.

- *Setting a timetable for each of the projects,* a task with special urgency given the extremely short time allowed the mission. Most courses were one to two weeks in duration.

- *Implementing the projects,* which also had heightened urgency from the awareness that the present resources and political will were unlikely ever to exist again.

- *Evaluating the program,* a process that varied in quality and thoroughness from one project to another.

**Evaluation.** This HRE program in Cambodia, like all educational efforts conducted in the context of conflict, had special constraints imposed by the particular situation. Foremost of these was the limited time established by the terms of the Paris Peace Agreement, which was exacerbated by bureaucratic delays. As a result, the criterion of a long-term commitment was virtually impossible. Marks observes that "HRE during the presence of a UN mission can only be the first step in a much longer process of systematic training."[39]

The absolute limit of two years to prepare and implement the program also imposed severe limitations on the quality of planning and evaluation. However, despite working in a country where approximately 80 percent of students with higher education had been killed or forced to flee, and where even interpreters were rare, UNTAC's project was very successful at building a community base, training trainers, and working with local institutions whenever possible.

As Marks explains, despite inherent limitations in the program, the lessons learned in the Cambodia HRE effort are universally applicable. He points to the importance of mobile teams for mass education, the effectiveness of interactive methodologies, the potential influence of promoting human rights through religious communities, and the need for official codes of professional conduct for civil servants. Above all, he stresses that long-term support for the groups who received training and continuing development of trainers is essential to laying foundations for humane governance.

In the years since UNTAC's efforts in Cambodia, such support has indeed been ongoing, principally from international NGOs such as the Asia Foundation. When Marks returned to Cambodia in 1998 to evaluate the development of civil society, he found many thriving and effective indigenous human rights NGOs: "Proof positive that UNTAC's investment in HRE had paid off."[40] He noted, however, that many of these NGOs showed little evolution of their strategies and methods since their initial training. Richard Pierre Claude reported the same vitality in 1999, when he worked with Cambodian NGOs to develop interpersonal HRE pedagogies for reaching grassroots populations. He observed, "These NGOs see the value of HRE and are committed to it as an integral part of their work."[41]

## 2. The Example of Southern Sudan, 2000

**The Situation.** In 2000, UNICEF initiated an HRE program in southern Sudan that sought to prepare people in this region for a new era of peace after nearly thirty years of active warfare. Nearly two million people had died in the civil war between the Khartoum government supporters and opposition forces, principally made up of the Sudan People's Liberation Army (SPLA), but in early 2000 the end of armed conflict and a new regional government, if not a new nation, seemed attainable. The Bahr el-Ghazal humanitarian cease-fire between the government and the SPLA permitted the United Nations and relief agencies operating under the umbrella organization Operation Lifeline Sudan (OLS) to provide food and medicine to civilian populations in the south, and the SPLA had officially agreed to uphold the UDHR and the CRC.

**The Program.** Although the project addressed specific problems immediately related to UNICEF's mandate (e.g., child soldiers and discrimination against women and girls), the overarching goal was to make human rights principles and standards known in the general population as a basis for rebuilding their society.

At the heart of UNICEF's program was the development of grassroots rights awareness teams, local men and women trained in human rights and popular education methodologies who could provide HRE to widely scattered rural populations. Supported by southern Sudanese coordinators in the central villages of the two pilot districts, Rumbeck and Yambio, these teams had responsibility for educating villagers in their areas. Although the project description did not explicitly link human rights and peace, it held up the human rights principles found in the UDHR and CRC as a basis for rebuilding communities and maintaining peace. In the absence of any functioning legal system, the human rights framework provided standards against which to evaluate local problems and solutions.

The project was designed to be long term and sustainable, with UNICEF providing training and support to the rights awareness teams, but no financial incentive beyond a bicycle to enable them to travel to distant villages. Although all members of the population were included, these trainings sought in particular to convince village women that the whole community benefited when human rights, especially those of its children, were protected. Decades of warfare had eroded traditional family structures and given these women new roles of influence and responsibility that made them agents for positive social change.

**Evaluation.** As planned, the rights awareness team project met most of the criteria for a good transformative education program, combining knowledge with action in ways designed to engage the mostly rural, nonliterate population. It was planned for long-term sustainability, expansion, and flexibility; it worked in alliance with local church and educational organizations; it trained local people to develop training methods and materials appropriate to local cultures and concerns. If brought to fruition, it might have provided an unusually clear example of the union of HRE and education for peacebuilding. Ironically, however, the failure of peace put an end to the project. Only months after the accomplishment of its initial stages of training trainers, and the beginning of rural trainings, the cease-fire was broken, and renewed armed violence forced UNICEF to abandon this promising project. Although at the end of 2004 peace in southern Sudan again seems eminent, the project has not been resurrected, nor is any evaluation available with which to assess how it might have succeeded.

## 3. The Example of Serbia, 1994–2003

**The Situation.** In late 1994, when the Federal Republic of Yugoslavia was still actively at war in Bosnia and Croatia, the regional office of UNICEF for the former Yugoslavia held a conference in Belgrade on the rights of the child. Although the political situation did not permit the conference explicitly to promote peace, it did examine conflict as a barrier to the realization of children's rights. On the success of this initial conference, the next year UNICEF made a commitment to a variety of grassroots NGO projects that promoted peace and HRE. Because the government viewed UNICEF as a neutral agency, many of these projects were able to work in the state schools, where NGOs were effectively forbidden.

In October 2000, when these projects were already well established, the Milosevic government fell, the opposition came to power, and many of the coordinators of these peace and human rights projects assumed positions in the Ministry of Education. Although there was still caution among NGO activists, who feared that peace education might become just another governmental dogma, the Ministry of Education allowed NGO projects to operate more freely in schools and began considering ways of incorporating promoting human rights and the interactive methodologies they both employ throughout the state school system.

These programs received an unexpected emphasis in the summer of 2001, when the Serbian Orthodox Church influenced the Serbian parliament to pass legislation allowing religious education in schools for the first time since World War II. In response, progressive educators in the Serbian Ministry of Education immediately put forward an alternative course based on democratic and civic education. Because they had only months to develop this alternative curriculum, they drew on existing programs already proven successful in schools, many of which had been supported by UNICEF. Thus, the human rights and peace education content that was once marginalized was suddenly incorporated into the national curriculum.

**The Program.** In the 2001–2 academic year Serbian students in the first year of primary and secondary school had a "voluntary choice": religious education, civic education, or neither. The primary civics curriculum was derived from an NGO project, "Non-violent Communications," also known as Giraffe Language, and the UNICEF-supported "Smile Keepers" project, which focused on psychosocial skills for improving communication and helping children deal with violence, both in their personal lives and in that of their postwar country. Both source projects were based on interactive methodologies and skill-building techniques typical of peace education. The secondary curriculum was taken from the UNICEF-supported "Goodwill Classroom" project, which focused on conflict resolution skills, and an NGO project from the Yugoslav Child Rights Centre, which had developed a curriculum based on the Convention on the Rights of the Child, called "How Can We Do It Together?"

During the 2002–3 school year both the religious and the civic education programs were extended to include the first and second years of primary and secondary school. This year, however, students faced a "compulsory choice" between religious education and civic education. Whereas the first year the majority of students opted for neither course, now the number opting for civic education doubled in the primary grades and jumped from 5 percent to 70 percent in secondary school. Unfortunately, however, when first introduced, civic education had been labeled the "alternative subject" in the popular media and depicted as in opposition to religious education, which was scheduled at the same time. Evaluators and teachers from both subjects would have liked to see the two courses scheduled at different times so that those students who wished could choose both.

Despite the urgency with which these courses were created, they proved extremely successful. A thorough evaluation, published in September 2002 for the Ministry of Education by UNICEF, UNESCO, the Open Society Institute, and the Fund for an Open Society–Serbia, found that children loved the curriculum because it uses interactive methods unknown in the standard curriculum. Teachers were equally enthusiastic about the methodology but felt more comfortable using it with conflict resolution than with children's rights at the secondary level. Apparently because the human rights material seemed more legal and serious, teachers were inclined to fall back on traditional teaching methods, despite systematic training with the new materials and methodologies. Evaluators also noted an interesting pattern in the application of HRE beyond the classroom as teachers began to take the initiative to address what they now recognized as children's rights issues in the community. For example, to combat harsh corporal punishment both at school and at home, teachers organized parent-teacher workshops on the human rights of children.

**Evaluation.** These human rights and peace education projects in Serbia are unusual not only in terms of the special circumstances that moved them from the margins into the mainstream of formal education but also for the long-term nature of their development. By the time they were moved into the state curriculum, they had been developed, tested, and refined locally for six years, and many hundreds of teachers had been trained in their content and methodology. Although the incorporation of these projects into the national curriculum was not foreseen by UNICEF or its partner NGOs when the projects were first developed, UNICEF must be credited with recognizing the value of sustained support, and the program directors with having the flexibility to adapt to opportunities. The Ministry of Education hopes to add additional years of civic education, but curriculum developers are still struggling to catch up with the rapid expansion of the program.

While still probationary and dependent on sustained government support and goodwill, those programs now included in the national curriculum will clearly be sustained and systematically evaluated for the near future. However, the future of NGO projects not included in the civic education curriculum is less clear. UNICEF's capacity to fund these projects is gradually being reduced. In order to have access to schools or continue to operate through school clubs, parent groups, and after-school programs, they must seek funding though local school authorities or other agencies.

Evaluators have recommended preservice education on interactive methodologies, human rights, and peace. Though such training is still to be added to teacher education institutions, the methodology used in these courses has already found perhaps greater support than the content itself, and teachers are trying to apply it to other subjects, including religious education.

The Serbian example, like every other, is a hybrid of local situations, needs, and opportunities with the special concern of the funders, in this case the rights of the child. In Serbian schools HRE is merged with peace education and delivered in the name of "civic education." Serbia illustrates clearly the importance of long-term commitment and a community base, for without established programs and experienced teachers already in place, the new civics curriculum could never have succeeded. It also serves to emphasize the necessity of winning popular support in order to endure. Students, parents, and especially teachers have found the civics course meaningful for their lives and communities. As one teacher remarked to evaluators, "Nobody should be a teacher who doesn't know the rights of the child."

## Merging Human Rights Education and Peace Education

The foregoing case studies must, of course, be considered in the context of the conflict and peacebuilding that gave them impetus. However, each illustrates how the components of planning, a firm grounding in the community, and, most importantly, long-term commitment to implementation are tied to its success or failure. All three also show the role of chance (e.g., the collapse of the Sudan cease-fire), the value of adaptability (e.g., the need to quickly create a formal civics curriculum out of existing programs in Serbia), and the importance of persistence (e.g., that the human rights component did not immediately find ways to reach Cambodian health professionals and the Buddhist community, which eventually proved to be critical agents for implementing HRE). These examples also demonstrate the essential relatedness of peace education and HRE. Regardless of what the programs were officially called, all three were aimed at establishing knowledge, skills, and attitudes needed to further human rights and build peace.

In the study *HRE for Peace Building,* Paul Martin argues for the inclusion of HRE in standard international peacebuilding operations. This important study, based on research carried out on HRE in conflict and post-conflict situations, recognizes the high effectiveness of HRE as a tool for peacemaking but emphasizes that it is poorly prescribed and rarely understood by those who negotiate and implement a peace. For example, Martin points to two lengthy reports on peacebuilding (a 1998 report for the UN Research Institute for Social Development titled "Rebuilding after War," and also "Laying a Durable Foundation for Post-conflict Societies," based on a conference held in June 2002) that make no explicit reference to HRE. Martin's case studies in El Salvador, Guatemala, Liberia, Mexico, and Sierra Leone confirm the conclusion, drawn from the examples given above, that even when officially mandated, HRE programs almost never receive the resources or time they need to succeed.

Martin never differentiates HRE from peace education or even comments on their complementarity. While acknowledging that HRE programs may include other forms of education (e.g., civic education to prepare for elections, conflict resolution techniques for mediating daily interactions, advocacy skills for addressing authorities, and legal literacy for seeking justice through the law), he clearly sees HRE as synonymous with education for peace.

While Parlevliet regards HRE and conflict resolution as separate fields, she is emphatic that conflict resolution is imperative to effective HRE:

> Building people's knowledge of rights and enhancing their capacity to identify rights is not necessarily sufficient to ensure that they will be able to enjoy those rights. They also need to gain the capacity and confidence to exercise those rights.[42]

She suggests that human rights educators need conflict resolution skills to manage the tensions and resentments that arise when people's stereotypes and prejudices are challenged. In fact, she advises that it is often preferable to avoid framing issues in terms of human rights and to approach them indirectly, in terms of "human dignity" or "basic human needs."

## Conclusions

All the available evidence suggests that no program of HRE for peacemaking has ever been thoroughly implemented or thoroughly successful. UN bodies, governments, NGOs, and educators seem convinced that HRE can contribute to peacebuilding, but this opinion is grounded mostly in optimism and partial results. The reasons for inconclusive results are many, but the prevailing one points to failure to give HRE programs the resources and time required to change behaviors and attitudes, especially in an environment of hostility and mistrust. Funders and project planners know the outcome they want, but they need to understand better the process of HRE and peace education and what it takes to achieve them.

In the meantime, human rights educators and peace educators must collaborate to overcome the perceived division between them and acknowledge and build on their interdependence. HRE gives credible substance to peace education. Peace education provides HRE with well-developed theory and process. Alone, neither can claim to be completely effective. In fact, most HRE programs contain elements of peace and conflict resolution, and most peace programs introduce HR principles, though they are usually generalized as "social justice." In the absence of solid research that establishes the advantages of integration to both human rights education and peace education, they are likely to continue to evolve along separate tracks, thereby reinforcing the historical divide and discouraging collaboration among human rights educators and peace educators. This would be a setback for the progressive development of both fields.

## Notes

1. International Covenant on Economic, Social, and Cultural Rights, G.A. Res. 2200A (XXI), 21 UN GAOR Supp. (no. 16), at 49, UN Doc. A/6316 (1966), 993 UNTS 3, entered into force January 3, 1976. For General Comment 13 of the Committee on Economic, Social, and Cultural Rights, see E/C.12/1999/10, 1999 (on the aims of education, including the goals to which states are obliged to direct education). See also Article 13(3) of the Additional Protocol to the American Convention on Human Rights in the Area of Economic, Social, and Cultural Rights, adopted at San Salvador, El Salvador, November 17, 1988 (not yet entered into force): "Education should be directed towards the full development of the human personality and human dignity and should strengthen respect for human rights, ideological pluralism, fundamental freedoms, justice and peace. They further agree that education ought to enable everyone to participate effectively in a democratic and pluralist society and achieve a decent existence and should foster

understanding, tolerance and friendship among all nations and all racial, ethnic or religious groups and promote activities for the maintenance of peace"; Article 11(2) of the African Charter on the Rights and Welfare of the Child, adopted July 11, 1990, entered into force November 29, 1999, provides that the education of the child shall be directed to, among other things, "fostering respect for fundamental freedoms" and "the preparation of the child for responsible life in a free society, in the spirit of understanding, tolerance, dialogue, mutual respect and friendship among all peoples and ethnic, tribal and religious groups."

**2.** International Convention on the Elimination of All Forms of Racial Discrimination, 660 UNTS 195, entered into force January 4, 1969, Article 7.

**3.** Convention on the Rights of the Child, G.A. Res. 44/25, Annex, 44 UN GAOR Supp. (no. 49), at 167, UN Doc. A/44/49 (1989), entered into force September 2, 1990, Article 29(1)(d).

**4.** Principles of the International Congress on the Teaching of Human Rights, adopted on September 12–16, 1978, Vienna, Austria. Part 1, para. 5, reprinted in OHCHR, Human Rights Education and Human Rights Treaties, 1999, UN Doc. HR/PUB/DECADE/1999/1, at 7.

**5.** Malta Recommendations, para. 2.3, reprinted in OHCHR, Human Rights Education and Human Rights Treaties, 1999, UN Doc. HR/PUB/DECADE/1999/1, at 7.

**6.** Ibid.

**7.** See generally Aline M. Stomfay-Stitz, *Peace Education in America, 1828–1990* (Metuchen, NJ: Scarecrow Press, 1993).

**8.** Betty A. Reardon, *Comprehensive Peace Education* (New York: Teachers College Press, 1988), xi.

**9.** See Catherine H. Diekman, *Research-Based Effectiveness of the Peace Education Foundation Model* (Miami: Peace Education Foundation, 1999), available at www.peaceeducation.com.

**10.** www.afsc.org/peacprog2.htm.

**11.** www.afsc.org.

**12.** Ibid.

**13.** Susan Fountain, *Peace Education in UNICEF* (UNICEF, June 1999), 6, available at www.unicef.org/programme/education/peace_ed.htm.

**14.** Ibid.

**15.** In its study on peace education, UNICEF notes the links between teaching about the Convention on the Rights of the Child and peace education, making the case that teaching about the convention provides opportunities to reinforce concepts central to peace education. See UNICEF, Peace Education in UNICEF (June 1999), 38, available at www.unicef.org/girlseducation/files/PeaceEducation.

**16.** www.ipb.org.

**17.** Ibid.

**18.** Ibid.

**19.** www.haguepeace.org.

**20.** http://ccrweb.ccr.uct.ac.za.

**21.** Michelle Parlevliet, "Bridging the Divide: Exploring the Relationship between Human Rights and Conflict Management," *Track Two* 11, no. 1 (March 2002), available at http://ccrweb.ccr.uct.ac.za/two/11_1/.html.

**22.** See UN Archive/Geneva, SOA, Box 365, Files 373/1/01/04, and 06.

**23.** G.A. Res. 217 D (III), December 10, 1948, reprinted in OHCHR, Human Rights Education and Human Rights Treaties, 1999, UN Doc. HR/PUB/DECADE/1999/1, at 7.

**24.** See Pope John XXIII, *Pacem in Terris*, April 11, 1963, in *The Papal Encyclicals*, 5 vols., ed. Claudia Carlen Ihm (Raleigh, NC: McGrath, 1981), vol. 5, 107–29.

**25.** Notably, the International Congress on Human Rights Teaching, Information and Documentation, convened by UNESCO in 1987, recommended, among other things, that "the Director-General highlight . . . the relationship to be established between education for Human Rights and fundamental freedoms on the one hand, and education for peace and international understanding on the other," and the development of new HRE approaches that emphasize "the interrelationship between Human Rights teaching and the other major problems of mankind." In the context of recognizing the rights of the child, the congress recommended HRE in formal and informal sectors, and the promotion of "the teaching of nonviolent alternatives and strategies for the peaceful resolution of conflicts." Malta Recommendations, para. 3.7, reprinted in OHCHR, Human Rights Education and Human Rights Treaties, 1999, UN Doc. HR/PUB/DECADE/1999/1, at 7. This movement toward integration is repeated in other international documents, including the 1993 UNESCO World Plan of Action on Education for Human Rights and Democracy (the Montreal Declaration), which makes a strong association between HRE and the goals of democratic peace.

**26.** United Nations, report of the secretary-general pursuant to the statement adopted by the Summit Meeting of the Security Council on January 31, 1992, "An Agenda for Peace, Preventive Diplomacy, Peacemaking and Peace-Keeping," UN Doc. A/47/277-S/24111, June 17, 1992.

**27.** Vienna Declaration and Program of Action, World Conference on Human Rights, Vienna, June 14–25, 1993, UN Doc. A/CONF.157/24, para. 78.

**28.** OHCHR, Human Rights Education and Human Rights Treaties, 1999, UN Doc. HR/PUB/DECADE/1999/1, at 1.

**29.** The first international NGO conference on HRE was held in New York City in October 1992, sponsored by the People's Decade for Human Rights Education, the Center for the Study of Human Rights at Columbia University, and the Friedrich Ebert Foundation.

**30.** For the most current and complete international HRE resource lists, see the Database on Human Rights Education, Office of the High Commissioner for Human Rights: http://193.194.138.190/hredu.ns; and Human Rights Education Bibliographies, Amnesty International: http://web.amnesty.org/pages/hre_bib1.

**31.** For a discussion of definitions of HRE, see Nancy Flowers, "What Is Human Rights Education?" in *International Perspectives in Human Rights Education,* ed. Viola B. Georgi and Michael Seberich (Guetersloh, Germany: Bertelsmann Foundation Publications, 2004.), also available at www.HREA.org.

**32.** Betty A. Reardon, *Educating for Human Dignity* (Philadelphia: University of Pennsylvania Press, 1995), 4.

**33.** Betty A. Reardon, "Human Rights as Education for Peace," in *Human Rights Education for the Twenty-first Century,* ed. George J. Andreopoulos and Richard Pierre Claude (Philadelphia: University of Pennsylvania Press, 1997), 22.

**34.** Parlevliet, "Bridging the Divide."

**35.** Based on the authors' cumulative experience of HRE programs, these criteria agree on many points with similar standards set out for peace education in John Paul Lederach, *Preparing for Peace: Conflict Transformation across Cultures* (Syracuse, NY: Syracuse University Press, 1995); and Paul Martin et al., *Human Rights Education for Peace Building: A Planning and Evaluation Handbook* (New York: Center for the Study of Human Rights, Columbia University, 2004).

**36.** For additional examples of human rights and peace education projects, see Kent Arnold, "The Challenge of Building Training Capacity: The Centre for Conflict Resolution Approach in Burundi," in *Peacebuilding: A Field Guide,* ed. Luc Reuchler and Thania Paffenhola (Boulder, CO: Lynne Rienner, 2001), 227–90; Johan Svensson, "Designing Training Programs: The Life and Peace Institute Approach in Somalia," in *Peacebuilding: A Field Guide,* 291–300; Fountain, *Peace Education in UNICEF;* Asian Regional Resource Center, "Report on Southeast Asia Human Rights Education: Training of Trainers for Peace Building," October 2001, available at www.arrc-hre.com/publications_frameset.html; Croatian Commission for UNESCO, *Peace and Human Rights for Croatian Primary Schools Project* (Zagreb: Vedrana, 2000); Martin, *Human Rights Education for Peace Building;* John Prendergast, "Applying Concepts to Cases: Four African Case Studies," in *Building Peace: Sustainable Reconciliation in Divided Societies,* by John Paul Lederach (Washington, DC: United States Institute of Peace Press, 1999), 153–80.

**37.** Agreements on a Comprehensive Political Settlement of the Cambodia Conflict (Paris, October 23, 1991), Annex 1 (UNTAC Mandate), Section E (Human Rights), available at www.c-r.org/accord/cam/accord5/acc_cont.shtml.

**38.** Stephen Marks, "Human Rights Education in UN Peace Building: From Theory to Practice," in *Human Rights Education for the Twenty-first Century,* ed. George J. Andreopoulos and Richard Pierre Claude (Philadelphia: University of

Pennsylvania Press, 1997), 33–50; see also Allen S. Keller et al, "A Cambodian Human Rights Education Program for Health Professionals," 345–58, and Donna Hicks, "Conflict Resolution and Human Rights Education: Broadening the Agenda," in *Human Rights Education for the Twenty-first Century*, 80–95.

    **39.** Marks, "Human Rights Education," 46.

    **40.** Marks, telephone interview, May 2, 2003.

    **41.** Richard Pierre Claude, telephone interview, May 6, 2003.

    **42.** Parlevliet, "Bridging the Divide," 16.

# 16

# Building a Democratic Middle Ground

## Professional Civil Society and the Politics of Human Rights in Sri Lanka's Peace Process

Alan Keenan

With the signing in February 2002 of a Norwegian-brokered cease-fire agreement between the Sri Lankan government and the Liberation Tigers of Tamil Eelam (LTTE, or Tamil Tigers), the people of Sri Lanka gained a desperately needed respite from war. Raging off and on with increasing ferocity for more than twenty years, the separatist war led by the Tamil Tigers against the Sri Lankan state had, at the time of its suspension, killed an estimated 65,000 people on an island of fewer than twenty million people. Upward of two million others have been displaced or injured, lost family members, or otherwise been devastated by the armed conflict.

The period since the signing of the cease-fire has seen the longest sustained stretch without active warfare in Sri Lanka for twenty years. Sri Lankans of all ethnicities have reaped substantial benefits from the cessation of armed hostilities, even as more lasting peace dividends are still awaited. In the southern, predominantly Sinhala areas of the country, there has been relief from the absence of LTTE bombings and the security restrictions imposed to prevent them, as well as appreciation for the thousands of soldiers' lives that have been spared by the cessation of fighting. There has been increased freedom of movement throughout the country, especially for Tamils who were subject to restrictions imposed on them by either the government or the LTTE, or both. Tamils in the south are, for the moment at least, no longer vulnerable to arbitrary arrest and brutal treatment at the

459

hands of "antiterrorist" police. In the north and east of the island, which the LTTE claims as the "traditional Tamil homeland" and where the bulk of the fighting and destruction have taken place, the government lifted a crippling economic embargo, and many civilians have begun, very slowly, to rebuild their lives as best they can, returning to their villages, reconstructing houses, and starting new businesses. Initial hopes ran high that large amounts of financial support promised by international agencies and donors might begin to translate into real changes on the ground, and that the shattered economies throughout the island might begin to be rebuilt.

With the LTTE's withdrawal from peace talks in April 2003, however, and with its refusal to take part in the much-heralded international donor conference in Tokyo in June 2003, the peace process entered a prolonged state of uncertainty and stalemate. The LTTE's sweeping proposals for an "interim self-governing authority" in the northeast of Sri Lanka, announced with much fanfare in late October 2003, have still not been taken up for discussion.[1] After months of negotiations and bitter dispute between President Chandrika Kumaratunga and her rival prime minister, Ranil Wickremasinghe, the president dissolved parliament in February 2004 and called new elections for early April.[2] Following a campaign in which the government's security concessions made to the LTTE as part of the peace process were a topic of heated debate, a coalition between the president's Sri Lanka Freedom Party (SLFP) and the leftist and Sinhala nationalist People's Liberation Front (JVP) defeated the prime minister's United National Party (UNP). With the support of smaller parties, the SLFP-JVP alliance was eventually able to gain a majority of seats in parliament, but major policy disagreements between the two main partners—especially with regard to the peace process—largely crippled the new government. With the JVP blocking any moves toward accommodation with the LTTE, President Kumaratunga was unable to reach agreement with the LTTE on an agenda for new negotiations.

The uncertain political situation was further complicated in March 2004 when the LTTE's military commander for the Eastern Province, known by his nom de guerre, Karuna, declared his autonomy from the main wing of the LTTE, based in the north of Sri Lanka. After his forces in the east were attacked by the northern LTTE in April 2004, Karuna's fighters began waging a low-intensity guerrilla war against the LTTE—with assistance from the Sri Lankan military, the LTTE has repeatedly charged. With the LTTE facing a serious threat to its hold on the Eastern Province and unable to force the government to negotiate on its terms, there were signs by the end of 2004 that war was imminent.

The devastating arrival of the South Asian tsunami on December 26, 2004, seemed at first to change the political equation. Initial cooperation between civilians across ethnic lines, and even between ground-level LTTE and Sri Lankan security forces, however, quickly faded in the face of a renewed power struggle between the Tigers and the government. With the various parties all attempting to exploit the situation for their own political gains, negotiations to devise a "joint mechanism" to distribute the billions of dollars of international relief and reconstruction assistance were protracted and politically divisive. The president's eventual agreement with the LTTE —six months after the tsunami—led to the JVP's withdrawal from the government, in protest at what it saw as dangerous and unnecessary accommodations to the "terrorist" LTTE. The supreme court's decision soon thereafter to strike down major portions of the agreement, however, effectively rendered it inoperable, further undermining any lingering faith the LTTE might have had in the potential for negotiations with the government.

The August 2005 assassination of the Sri Lankan foreign minister, Lakshman Kadirgamar—an ethnic Tamil long considered a traitor by the LTTE—threw the peace process into even deeper crisis. Following as it did a period of increased attacks by the LTTE on Tamil opponents and Sri Lankan police and military personnel who, it claimed, were in league with Karuna, the assassination led to universal international condemnation—including a ban on travel by LTTE representatives to the European Union—and further inflamed Sinhala nationalist opposition to negotiations with the Tigers.

It was in this context that Sri Lanka held an unexpected election for president in November 2005, following another decision by the supreme court. The SLFP's candidate and sitting prime minister, Mahinda Rajapakse, running on a platform largely dictated by his alliance with the JVP and a smaller Sinhala nationalist party, argued against giving the LTTE any role in the distribution of tsunami relief and reconstruction funds, defended the "unitary" state against proposals for a federal constitutional solution to the conflict, and criticized what he saw as the structural bias of the cease-fire agreement in favor of the LTTE. Rajapakse won a narrow victory over the UNP's Ranil Wickremasinghe, the former prime minister and architect of the Norwegian-backed peace process. He was helped by an LTTE-enforced "boycott" by Tamil voters in the areas they control—expressing the Tigers' apparent desire for the victory of the more hard-line candidate. One of Rajapakse's first acts as president was to call for a fundamental reworking of the peace process so as to prevent further human rights abuses and cease-fire violations by the Tigers and to protect the sovereignty and unitary nature of the Sri Lankan state. The LTTE responded by saying that its patience was wearing thin and suggesting that it was contemplating a return to warfare in the near future if the new government failed to address quickly the fundamental aspirations of the Tamil people.

The election of Rajapakse effectively marks the end of Sri Lanka's nearly four-year-old peace process, while leaving great uncertainty as to whether a new mode of engagement between the Sri Lankan state and the LTTE can be devised before escalating tension and low-intensity conflict explode into war. Given how charges and countercharges of human rights violations have played a major role in undermining trust on all sides of the conflict, the moment offers a useful vantage point from which to reflect on the role that human rights protections might play as part of conflict resolution efforts in Sri Lanka.[3] This chapter will explore the challenges facing civil society activists and organizations that want to make human rights principles an integral part of any negotiated settlement between the government and the LTTE.

Efforts to ensure effective human rights protections during the peace process have, from the very beginning, run counter to the basic thrust of the conflict resolution strategy being pursued at the level of the formal "track one" negotiating process. This has become even more pronounced since the Tigers' withdrawal from negotiations. With no sign that the major players are likely to integrate human rights protections into the peace process of their own accord, the task of pushing a human rights agenda and broadening the nature of peacebuilding has largely fallen to the set of local organizations, intellectuals, and activists known as "civil society." This has been, in part, a role assigned them—at least in public discourse—by the foreign governments and international donors that provide Sri Lankan civil society organizations with virtually all their funding. With donor governments and institutions themselves reluctant—especially after the LTTE withdrawal from direct negotiations—to push very hard for a rights-based approach to the peace process, they have preferred instead to assign this task to "civil society." The vision of local civil society as the defender of human rights and as a popular agent of peacebuilding is one that local groups and activists themselves are generally happy to promote. Indeed, there is a powerful normative ideal of civil society to which both donors and local organizations regularly pay homage, one in which local NGOs and citizens' groups are seen as a source of independent political initiatives— ideally emerging from relatively free and open public discussion—in defense of basic liberal and democratic rights and values.

So far, however, the practice of those organizations and activities that claim the mantle of Sri Lankan civil society—those that I will be referring to as "professional civil society"—falls short of this demanding democratic and liberal ideal.[4] The first three and a half years of cease-fire have revealed Sri Lankan civil society to be severely damaged from thirty years of ethnic and class conflicts, during which it was itself a target of combatants from all sides. In particular, civil society groups committed to human rights and to a negotiated and just settlement to the war have proved to be divided over the proper relation to take toward human rights violations during the peace process. In part as a result of these divisions, they have so far been unable to generate significant or coordinated actions to promote human rights norms as a central aspect of the peace process, despite the wide consensus in favor of such efforts and despite the courageous efforts of many individuals.

Such difficulties are in many ways not surprising, given that Sri Lanka's conflicts and the dilemmas involved in trying to solve them are themselves rooted in undemocratic structures of power and, crucially, the lack of space for independent, nonethnicized political work. Nonetheless, close consideration of the difficulties that civil society groups and activists have faced in being effective defenders of human rights during the peace process raises more general—and troubling—questions about the capacity and role of "civil society" in sustaining and deepening the peace.

My analysis also aims to bring out the democratic deficits of Sri Lankan human rights discourse and of the peace process itself as it has been constructed and enacted to date. Organized almost exclusively as a deal between two politico-military entities—the Sri Lankan state and the LTTE— that have shown scant respect for basic human rights, the achievement of "peace" has been understood by its chief architects and by many of its civil society and international supporters as being at odds with any serious acknowledgment of past human rights violations and with attempts to institute effective safeguards against ongoing and future abuses.

However, as developments during the first three and a half years of the peace process have made clear, there are powerful arguments to be made that without a stronger emphasis on the ongoing protection of basic human rights and on negotiating a settlement that addresses the basic injustices and rights violations that have fueled the conflict, any "peace" will rest on dangerously weak foundations. With a basic tension between human rights and the official peace process now firmly established, however, developing effective civil society interventions in defense of human rights and a just peace will require great skill and perseverance.

To begin to overcome these obstacles, civil society organizations, together with their international donors and supporters, must consciously work to cultivate more deeply democratic conceptions and practices of human rights and of "peacebuilding," or conflict resolution. For these efforts to prove successful, "civil society" must first begin to democratize itself. What is generally understood today in Sri Lanka by the term "civil society" —especially in the discourse and funding practices of international donors— is a relatively small set of well-established organizations, mostly based in the capital city, Colombo, and staffed by the English-speaking, generally cosmopolitan middle class and elite. Because of its centrality to the public discourse on "civil society," the work of this professionalized segment of civil society will be this chapter's primary focus. However, professional civil society can hope to challenge the entrenched forms of power and inequality that underpin systematic violations of human rights only by broadening its base of support and mobilizing deeper democratic energies and influence. Democratization, in this sense, means the creation of more inclusive, representative, and egalitarian organizations and forms of civil society practice.

Such democratic transformations will be possible, however, only by initiating processes of collective self-questioning within and between civil society groups. The willingness to entertain and respond more openly to criticisms of their own work not only offers resources for developing more effective forms of practice but also promises to open up new lines of dialogue among civil society groups and between such groups and the larger Sri Lankan public. Of particular importance here would be the possibility of building stronger ties among human rights groups and activists presently divided in complex ways along ethnic and ideological lines, particularly over the appropriate stance to take in relation to the human rights violations of the LTTE.

Finally, given the central role of international donors in funding and defining the programmatic agenda of Sri Lankan civil society, no democratization of the latter is possible without some democratization of its relationship to the former. Strengthening the ability of Sri Lankans to intervene independently and effectively in defense of human rights and peacebuilding will require serious efforts to create more transparent, equal, and mutually accountable relationships between local groups and their international funders, built on a free exchange of information, ideas, and criticism.

## A Very Short History of Sri Lanka's Postcolonial Conflicts

At the heart of the protracted war between the LTTE and the Sri Lankan state is a more-than-fifty-year failure of Sri Lankan political elites to work out an equitable and mutually acceptable distribution of power between the Sinhala majority and the Tamil minority.[5] Almost immediately upon independence from Britain in 1948, Sri Lankan Tamils found themselves on the receiving end of a delayed assertion of Sinhala majoritarian nationalism.[6] Regardless of whether it was controlled by the Sri Lanka Freedom Party or its chief competitor, the United National Party, any government that attempted to accommodate the peaceful demands for political autonomy in the Tamil-speaking-majority regions of the north and east found its efforts thwarted by the party in opposition, which never failed to invoke the threatened rights of the Sinhala majority.[7] No party in power has ever found itself strong enough or committed enough to define the Sri Lankan state in more pluralist and inclusive terms.[8] Eventually, the repeated failure of Sinhala political leaders to meet the legitimate aspirations of Tamils for equal citizenship fueled more radical demands for a separate state of "Tamil Eelam." A vicious cycle of state and counterstate violence and mutually hardening nationalisms finally exploded into full-scale war following the massive state-sanctioned anti-Tamil violence in July 1983. Since then, the LTTE has proved to be a ruthless and extraordinarily disciplined political and military antagonist. Itself a product of the terror of the Sri Lankan state, it has eventually crushed or incorporated its various military and political rivals and emerged as a deeply antidemocratic counterstate, controlling much of the north and east of Sri Lanka and maintaining tight political control among Tamils across the island and in the international diaspora.

But Sri Lanka has suffered through far more than a simple "ethnic conflict" between the mostly Hindu Tamil minority and the mostly Buddhist Sinhalese majority. For more than three decades now it has been the site of multiple and overlapping violent conflicts. These include two uprisings, one in 1971, the other in 1987–90, by left-wing Sinhala youth of the People's Liberation Front (known, according to its Sinhalese initials, as the JVP), both of which were ruthlessly crushed by government and government-supported vigilante forces, at the total cost of an estimated 50,000– 60,000 lives. The better-known war, between the Sri Lankan state and Tamil militant forces, has gone through many phases and starred many protagonists. After the withdrawal of Indian peacekeeping forces in 1990, the ethnic conflict eventually developed into an increasingly conventional war between government forces and fighters of the LTTE. A number of former Tamil militant groups, which had joined the democratic process as political parties, continued to maintain paramilitary wings that ended up fighting alongside government police and army units against the Tigers, while also engaged in their own illicit moneymaking and "policing" activities.[9] In 1990 long-standing tensions between the LTTE and largely Tamil-speaking Muslims living in the north and east of the island took more violent forms, with LTTE massacres of Muslim civilians and the expulsion of an estimated 90,000 Muslims from the LTTE-controlled northern Jaffna peninsula.[10] This drove deeper a wedge of anger and suspicion between many Tamils and Muslims, hardening the sense of separate identity among many Muslims and complicating peacemaking efforts in Sri Lanka to this day.

The past three decades of civil conflict have thus left a legacy of massive violence from which virtually all Sri Lankans—Tamil, Sinhalese, Muslim, Buddhist, Hindu, Christian—have suffered to different degrees. The particular forms the violence has taken have also meant that there are no innocent political groups or actors, despite the attempts of many to present their group as innocent victims of someone else's injustice. The violence, discrimination, human rights violations, and antidemocratic repression have come from self-proclaimed "representatives" of all the major communities (though certainly not from all Sri Lankans). Moreover, much of the violence has been *within* ethnic communities. This intracommunal bloodshed includes the often violent political rivalry between the two major Sinhala-dominated political parties, the United National Party (UNP) and the Sri Lanka Freedom Party (SLFP); the brutal violence between the JVP and the Sinhala-dominated government; and the vicious infighting among competing Tamil militant groups, which continues to this day as the LTTE attempts to make its political hegemony among Tamils complete.[11] Among other things, the complexity of Sri Lanka's recent history of collective violence teaches us that the war between the LTTE and the Sri Lankan government cannot be brought to a peaceful end without involving other actors. This includes other communities, the most important being Muslims, as well as competing elements among both Tamils and Sinhalese.

## Re-engaging with the Tigers: The Road to Peace?

Despite this complex history, the Norwegian-facilitated peace process has been almost entirely focused on the government-LTTE relationship—more specifically, on satisfying the political needs of the LTTE for long enough to convince it of the benefits of becoming part of "mainstream" politics, and of the excessive costs of going back to war. The current Norwegian-led effort began in 2000 as an initiative under the government of the SLFP-dominated People's Alliance (PA) and President Chandrika Kumaratunga, and its first two years contrasted sharply with the basic strategy of the PA government during its seven years in office.[12] The PA and President Kumaratunga, elected in 1994 on a platform of peace and negotiations, initiated an eight-month period of negotiations, de-escalation, and humanitarian relief for the northern and eastern regions of Sri Lanka. In response to the LTTE's decision to break off negotiations in April 1995 and return to war, claiming that the PA government wasn't negotiating in good faith, the government developed a double strategy that it called "war for peace." While attempting to weaken the LTTE militarily, the government simultaneously tried to address what it considered the "core issues" of the conflict through groundbreaking constitutional proposals. These issues centered on recognizing the legitimacy of Tamils' political grievances through the devolution of significant power to a combined Northeastern Province, within the structure of a federal but united Sri Lanka. The idea was to address the root causes of the Tamil people's political alienation and oppression, thereby weakening the need—and support—for the violent militancy of the LTTE. The LTTE, naturally, was less than enthusiastic about the government's attempt to distinguish between it and the Tamil people. What from one angle was an important attempt to increase democratic space for the articulation of less militant, nonseparatist Tamil political voices can be seen from another angle as a typical divide-and-rule strategy, especially given the failure of all earlier attempts by non-LTTE political parties to win fair treatment and equal rights for Tamil people.

The PA and Kumaratunga's strategy ultimately proved a failure, because of both the LTTE's successful military responses and the Tamil population's growing alienation from the government as a result of the heightened intensity of the war. This included the terrible suffering of Tamil civilians caught in the war zones of the north and east, but also the indirect effects on the large number of Tamils living outside the north and east, especially in Colombo, who were constantly subjected to harassment by the police and other security forces in search of "terrorist suspects." The decision of the United National Party (UNP) to oppose the PA's constitutional proposals in August 2000, even after the autonomy provisions for Tamils had been significantly watered down in response to UNP and Sinhala nationalist pressure, was also a crucial factor in the failure of the PA policy.

The UNP, under Ranil Wickremasinghe's leadership, had for the previous several years proposed a very different strategy, and its return to power in the December 2001 elections gave it the chance to put that strategy into practice. Rather than try to weaken and isolate the LTTE, and without proposing its own long-term solution to the central political and ethnic issues at stake, the UNP government chose to accommodate many of the Tigers' central needs and demands, at least in the short term. These included, first of all, the cease-fire agreement, the terms of which have allowed the LTTE to consolidate its administration in the northern Wanni region and expand its political influence into the Eastern Province and Jaffna peninsula.[13] Equally important was the UNP government's agreement in principle to establish an interim administration in the north and east that would be largely under the control of the LTTE.

Indeed, the underlying idea of the Norwegian-brokered peace process has been to offer the LTTE greater political legitimacy in the international arena, access to international resources and money for reconstruction, and increased political control of the north and east—short of a formal state— in exchange for an end to the fighting, the chance at economic reconstruction of the south, and the hope of eventually bringing the Tigers into the constraints of world-system and "mainstream" democratic politics. While the LTTE agreed in principle, during the initial rounds of talks, to negotiate a political settlement along federal lines, these negotiations have yet to take place, and neither the Tigers nor the UNP government with whom they had talks expressed any real interest in directly addressing the fundamental political issues at stake in the conflict.[14] Throughout its first three and a half years, even after the SLFP-JVP alliance took over the reins of government, the official peace process has been dominated by a specific model and discourse of conflict resolution. It is one that emphasizes the importance of "trust building" between official "partners"—almost entirely limited to the government and the Tamil Tigers—and the urgency of solving humanitarian needs, a concern that effectively endorses the LTTE's demand that "normalization" of life in Tamil areas precede any discussion of long-term solutions to the war and the ethnic injustice and distrust. Rather than emerging from a desire to address the needs, rights, and aspirations of the Sri Lankan people—most especially the Tamil people—the LTTE-government negotiations of 2002–3 were rooted almost solely in the narrow political and economic interests of the two negotiating parties. For various reasons, neither side was eager to address the complex political and legal issues that underlie the armed conflict. Nor were they working to strengthen connections and mutual understanding between the different communities.[15] The UNP, whether in government or in opposition, has yet to offer any serious proposals to address the underlying grievances of the Tamil people. This avoidance of issues of justice and accountability has extended beyond the complex issues of constitutional reform and the exact nature of a federal solution to Tamil demands for self-determination. It includes a reluctance to initiate any public discussion of the causes of the war and of how the now well-established patterns of mutually reinforcing group hostility can be reduced. Despite the critique of the UNP's approach to peace offered by the

SLFP-JVP alliance, the JVP's rejection of any engagement with the LTTE prevented the alliance from doing any better.

## Human Rights Violations: A Threat to the Peace Process

The approach to peace dominant throughout the peace process has allowed little or no room for making human rights protections an integral part of the negotiating and peace processes. Indeed, even as the track one negotiations were making initial headway, the process was overshadowed by human rights–related concerns. By the first anniversary of the cease-fire, the frequency and volume of complaints of human rights violations, together with worries about their possible impact on the peace process, had increased noticeably. Specific allegations by various groups, as well as official findings of cease-fire violations by the Sri Lanka Monitoring Mission (SLMM)—the team of Norwegian monitors established to maintain adherence to the cease-fire agreement—have been made against both negotiating parties. The issue that has generated the greatest public concern has been the ample evidence of the LTTE's recruitment—often forced—of child soldiers. This has continued despite repeated promises by LTTE leadership that no recruitment would take place and that any underage soldiers in its ranks would be released immediately.[16] Also of major concern has been the systematic assassination, abduction, and "disappearance" of members of Tamil political parties opposed to the LTTE, including many Tamils who had acted as informants for the Sri Lankan army and police. Other human rights criticisms of the LTTE have centered on its practice of demanding large "contributions" (or "taxes") from individuals and businesses throughout the north and east of the island, as well as various forms of economic pressure and even violent attacks on Muslims throughout the east coast. The cumulative effect of these actions has been the marked shrinking of any space for dissent, or for democratic politics, in the north and east of the island and within Tamil society in general, virtually all of which is now under the effective control of the LTTE, which has come about in part through threats and intimidation and in part through widespread allegiance to the Tigers' nationalist goals.[17] While Karuna's split from the main faction of the LTTE initially created some room for dissenting voices in the Eastern Province, the frequent killings of Tamils of both sides that followed has only further reduced the space for Tamils throughout the island to engage in independent political activity.

Although the overwhelming majority of cease-fire violations officially verified by the SLMM have been committed by the LTTE, the government has been judged by the SLMM to be guilty of its own cease-fire violations. These have ranged from the security forces' continued occupation of temples, schools, and private homes in the north and east, to a number of deadly police shootings of Tamil protesters, and continued acts of harassment against Tamils in the north and east.[18] Since the commencement of Karuna's guerrilla campaign in the east against the main faction of the LTTE, the Tigers have consistently complained that the Sri Lankan military is lending logistical and intelligence support to Karuna's fighters, in their opinion a direct violation of the cease-fire agreement. The Tigers have responded to the killings of their members by escalating attacks on Tamil political opponents and Sri Lankan military and police intelligence officers of all three ethnicities.

The response by the various parties involved in the official peace process to these violations has so far been very weak. While the Sri Lanka Monitoring Mission was expected by many to act as a de facto human rights monitor, this is a role that the SLMM is neither comfortable with nor well equipped to undertake. In addition to the lack of any enforcement mechanism for its rulings, the SLMM has repeatedly made clear that it views its mandate as preserving the cease-fire agreement—even if this means ignoring or downplaying human rights violations by both sides (which, in the context of the cease-fire agreement, have mostly been by the LTTE).[19] When the SLMM has ruled against the LTTE, particularly with respect to the forcible recruitment of child soldiers, its rulings have been largely ineffectual. Indeed, while the LTTE has made repeated public commitments that it will cease all recruitment of children, the practice has continued throughout the duration of the cease-fire. In addition, the LTTE has refused SLMM monitors access to its training camps, has threatened parents of abducted children in the presence of SLMM monitors, and continues to deny access by either the SLMM or the ICRC to its well-known but hidden prisons, which are estimated to house hundreds of detainees. In addition to their failures to investigate their own questionable actions, the police and government security forces have been criticized for not taking action to prevent or investigate LTTE violence and harassment against civilians (primarily other Tamils and Muslims), even when the facts of the case are well known. The government, even under the SLFP-JVP alliance, has generally tried not to antagonize the LTTE, even at the cost of its obligations to its own citizens, whether Tamil, Muslim, or Sinhala.

The widespread nature of such violations, particularly those of the LTTE, together with the ineffectiveness of the monitoring and legal mechanisms now in place, have been a cause of great worry for both supporters and opponents of the present peace process. Particularly worrisome is the effect that such violations have had on popular support for the peace process. The evident inability or unwillingness of the LTTE to respect even the most basic liberal and democratic rights of those living in areas it effectively controls, together with its efforts to strengthen itself militarily through continued recruitment and rearmament, have lent credence to a number of disaster scenarios put forward by opponents of the peace process. According to these scenarios, the LTTE is using the peace process merely as a means to strengthen itself militarily and politically in order to better attain its ultimate goal of a separate state of Tamil Eelam. Indeed, the fact that the LTTE's own antidemocratic activities feed into Sinhala nationalist fears and suspicions, and thus make a Sinhala political consensus harder to achieve, is interpreted by some as a deliberate aspect of the LTTE's politico-military strategy. The LTTE's human rights violations, antidemocratic practices, and continued military buildup have been seized on by individuals and groups opposed to the peace process. These have ranged from sections of the Sri Lanka Freedom Party (SLFP) to the nationalist JVP and smaller, explicitly Sinhala parties and nationalist groups, including segments of the Buddhist clergy, some of whom were elected to parliament in April 2004 under the banner of the Jathika Hela Urumaya (JHU), or National Heritage Party.

However, it is not only unprincipled "spoilers" or other opponents of a negotiated settlement between the government and the LTTE that see LTTE violations as a cause for concern. The most sustained, detailed, and in many ways sophisticated critiques of LTTE actions, and of the structural weaknesses of the Norwegian-sponsored peace process, have come from the University Teachers for Human Rights, Jaffna (UTHR-J). Since the late 1980s UTHR-J, a small but influential group of Tamil activists originally based at the University of Jaffna, has offered detailed bulletins and reports analyzing the human rights situation throughout Sri Lanka, with a particular emphasis on the north and east of the island. UTHR-J's reports have been noteworthy for offering sharp criticisms of all parties to the conflict, whether the government, the LTTE, other Tamil paramilitary groups, or the Indian Peace Keeping Force, which occupied the north and east of the island from 1987 to 1990.[20]

For UTHR-J, the central weakness of the peace process has been its purely pragmatic basis. UTHR-J argues that the initial priority that the

Norwegians and the UNP government gave to keeping the LTTE happy has had the effect of placing under even greater pressure whatever fragile ethnic and political middle ground among the public that might have survived the war. By acquiescing in the LTTE's violent assertion of its status as "the sole representative of the Tamil people," all the while offering the Tamil people nothing substantive in the way of increased rights that might weaken the LTTE's hold on Tamil politics, the peace process threatens to ratify the equation—both in appearance and in fact—between Tamils and the LTTE. Given the unwillingness of the government or the Norwegian mediators and the SLMM to hold the LTTE in check—allowing the Tigers to strengthen their antidemocratic grip on the north and east, terrorizing their "own" people while asserting hegemony over the local Muslim population and frightening Sinhalese—this approach gives support to the dangerous belief among many Sinhalese and Muslims that "the Tamils" are being given too much, at the expense of Sinhalese and Muslim rights. LTTE violations and frequent refusals to abide by SLMM rulings, in turn, have helped legitimize the intransigence of sections of the Sinhala-dominated government bureaucracy, whose resistance to working out administrative arrangements with the LTTE in the north and east were one factor in the LTTE's April 2003 decision to pull out from talks. After years of ferocious and bitter fighting with the LTTE, large sections the Sinhala-dominated police and security forces feel they are now being prevented, in the name of "peace," from carrying out their duties regarding LTTE violations, creating the real risk of an explosion of anger and violence against Tamil civilians should the cease-fire break down.

## Civil Society to the Rescue?

The work of UTHR-J continues to be very controversial. Despite its willingness to criticize rights violations and antidemocratic practices on all sides of the conflict, the organization's reports are seen by many, particularly other Tamil political activists, as biased in the government's favor. Nonetheless, although UTHR-J's reports are frequently criticized as unduly negative toward the peace process and those who are trying to make the most of it, many, if not most, civil society activists would endorse the idea that the ability and willingness to criticize all human rights violations, no matter who commits them, is a crucial element for a sustainable peace. This view is based in part on pragmatic considerations: By holding all parties accountable to a single set of human rights standards, a major weapon in the arsenal of "extremists," or "spoilers," seeking to undermine the peace process would be removed. More important, however, such a broad-based approach to the peace process would also assist in the creation of a political middle ground for accommodation and, perhaps eventually, reconciliation across and within the various ethnic communities. With the initiation of a process of collective self-criticism, in which people could begin to accept that wrongs have been committed in their name by their own "representatives," space would be created for democratic political action that is more independent of the major players and their violent methods.[21] Many within organized civil society have thus argued for the importance of expanding participation in the peace process, both to make it more inclusive and sustainable and to ensure that whatever "peace" emerges is as democratic and rights-friendly as possible.[22]

The first three and a half years of the cease-fire have certainly seen numerous pronouncements from almost all corners of Sri Lankan civil society to the effect that respect for basic human rights is essential to lasting peace.[23] In an attempt to instantiate these sentiments in a formal document, there was an early effort among some civil society activists to produce a draft human rights agreement that could be presented to the two negotiating parties for their ratification.[24] There have also been a number of small-scale civil society initiatives in support of human rights "on the ground." These have included a handful of independent fact-finding missions to investigate particular sites of recent intercommunal violence,[25] a fact-finding and network-building mission by Colombo-based women's groups in the north and east,[26] and various ad hoc attempts to build links between civil society groups in the south and those in the north and east.[27]

In this context, many civil society groups welcomed the announcement, at the end of the fifth session of peace talks in February 2003, that the Sri Lankan government and the LTTE had agreed to be bound, throughout the remainder of the peace process, to a set of human rights standards to be formulated by the independent human rights advisor Ian Martin. Planning began for a variety of different civil society human rights monitoring schemes, based partly on hopes of exploiting the opening provided by Martin's official role at the track one level and by the apparent interest of Sri Lanka's international financial donors in seeing that their reconstruction and development assistance is used in ways that strengthen democratic rights and lay the foundations for a sustainable peace. The hope was that civil society monitoring might help strengthen and make meaningful any official monitoring mechanism established by the government and the LTTE. Unfortunately, Martin's proposals were rejected by the LTTE and the government in the final session of talks before the LTTE's withdrawal from negotiations in April 2003. With the collapse of the human rights track at the level of formal negotiations, and the subsequent withdrawal of strong international pressure in support of human rights monitoring, Sri Lankan human rights groups have been faced with the even more formidable task of establishing their own independent monitoring programs, with no particular success to date.

## The Challenge of Bringing Rights Back In

To date, then, while civil society groups have generally argued that human rights protections must be made an integral part of the peace process, they continue to have trouble putting this belief into action. Very few concrete or coordinated actions have been taken, or even forceful statements made (other than those published by UTHR-J), in response to specific violations of those rights or to the underlying structures that make them possible. There continues to be great reluctance throughout Sri Lankan civil society to translate the general commitment to human rights norms into effective action in defense of rights.[28]

The rest of this essay will try to explain the complex factors behind the lack of forceful human rights interventions by civil society groups in the Sri Lankan peace process. The obstacles to establishing independent civil society interventions in defense of basic human rights touch on the very nature of Sri Lanka's professional civil society, and perhaps on contemporary "civil societies" more generally. The difficulties testify to the basic reluctance of people and organizations throughout Sri Lankan civil society to talk about, much less challenge, established relations of power. While the rhetoric of Sri Lankan politicians and political parties is often quite violently oppositional, the language and approach of those organizations and individuals who dominate the agenda of professional civil society tend to be quite mild and often indirect in their criticisms of those in power. The underlying assumption of most professional civil society interventions in the political domain seems to be that relations of unequal or unaccountable power are best approached quietly or through indirect means, if not simply ignored.

Given the ongoing threat of violence from the government and armed groups, especially the LTTE, and more recently from the breakaway faction of the LTTE led by Karuna, it is obvious that fear plays a large role in keeping more forceful public criticism to a minimum. Such fear is in part the product of decades of political violence, in which independent political and citizens' groups were often the direct target of organized violence, both by the Sri Lankan state and by armed militant groups (and even by the Indian Peace

Keeping Force that occupied the north and east in the late 1980s). Since the early 1970s, the modern Sri Lankan state, regardless of which political party happens to be in power, has repeatedly shown its willingness to violently repress any countervailing political force, whether it be independent trade unions, members of opposition political parties, or ethnic minorities.[29] It has in large part been the systematic willingness of the Sri Lankan state to resort to illegal violence that has spawned the particularly brutal nature of its violent opposition, whether the massive antistate violence of the JVP in the early 1970s and late 1980s, or the ultimately much more disciplined and effective violence of the LTTE. Given this history and the LTTE's continued willingness to bully and murder its critics, especially other Tamils, into submission, it is not surprising that most Sri Lankans, even those who are politically educated and active, prefer to avoid direct confrontations with the holders of political power. Even among those Tamils who will criticize the LTTE's actions forcefully in private, few within Sri Lanka are willing to do so publicly. That the LTTE has used the peace process to gain virtually complete control over all "civil society" organizations in the north and east of the country has increased the climate of fear and thus further shut down what space might have existed for articulating criticisms of LTTE actions.

But it is not only fear, however deep or well founded, that discourages more forceful civil society interventions against both the government's and the LTTE's human rights violations. Despite a basic consensus on principle, Sri Lankan civil society organizations concerned with political issues are in fact quite divided along what might be called ethno-ideological lines, in particular over the proper position to take regarding rights violations and antidemocratic practices of the LTTE.[30] The result is a general reluctance among all but UTHR-J and a handful of individual activists to offer forceful and sustained criticisms of the LTTE. Not surprisingly, this reluctance is particularly true of those human rights organizations staffed by Tamils and oriented toward the defense of Tamil people's rights. Such organizations virtually never criticize the actions of the LTTE, generally seeing their role instead as defending the rights of Tamils against the oppression of the Sinhala-dominated state.[31] While it is clear that much of this approach is due to deeply held political beliefs—including, for many activists, a deeply held Tamil nationalism and a well-founded distrust of the Sri Lankan state —it is also clear that the historical and continuing threat of LTTE violence against Tamil politicians and political activists critical of the LTTE dissuades some who might otherwise speak up.

Political divisions over the proper response to human rights violations by the LTTE do not follow strictly ethnic lines, however.[32] While the reluctance to criticize the LTTE is strongest among Tamils, it also exists among Sinhala activists. Many Sinhala activists and predominantly Sinhala organizations that work on human rights and conflict issues are reluctant to appear anti-Tamil or insufficiently "progressive" on ethnic issues.[33] Like most of their Tamil counterparts, many Sinhala peace and human rights activists fear that criticism of the LTTE will distract attention from, and weaken criticisms of, what they see as the more fundamental problem of Sinhala racism and majoritarianism. In this sense, differences over whether to criticize publicly the human rights and cease-fire violations of the Tamil Tigers often result from largely unarticulated disagreements over which agent is seen to be the greatest threat to human rights and democratic values: the state or the Tigers. Of particular concern to many Sinhala peace and human rights activists is the desire not to repeat what they see as the mistakes of the past, in particular the way in which the People's Alliance government, once spurned at the negotiating table by the LTTE, launched a "war for peace" that targeted the LTTE not only militarily—with incalculable suffering for ordinary Tamil people—but also rhetorically and ideologically, with the effect of strengthening the position of hard-line anti-Tamil Sinhala groups.

For these reasons, civil society organizations and activists have grown reluctant to press too vigorously on human rights issues. Given that violations of fundamental civil and political rights during the cease-fire have been most publicly and systematically committed by the LTTE, it has been difficult to criticize such violations without seeming to offer political ammunition to opponents of a negotiated solution with the LTTE. There has also been a continuing worry among many in civil society that raising human rights concerns "too forcefully" might in a more general sense have disruptive rather than productive effects on the peace process.[34] Such fears are not totally unwarranted, given that the peace process has been structured almost entirely as a deal between the Sri Lankan government and the LTTE, neither of which is known for its open and democratic relationship with "its" people. A strong human rights agenda, were it to be pushed vigorously as an integral part of the peace process, would seem likely to increase the costs for both parties to any negotiated settlement. And the inevitable failure of the parties to live up fully to human rights standards could lend support to those opposed to the peace process, whichever "side" they happened to be on.

In light of the rejection of Ian Martin's human rights proposals, the LTTE's subsequent withdrawal from the peace talks, and the growing public condemnation of the LTTE's systematic assassination of political opponents and continued recruitment of child soldiers, some prominent members of professional civil society, together with many in the powerful "donor community," have argued that the need for "constructive engagement" with the LTTE militates too forcefully against pressing human rights issues. This is in part a natural response to the practical realities of the LTTE's political and military strength, and to the fact that no peace process is possible without the LTTE's cooperation. The discourse of constructive engagement, however, also tends to make much of the need to understand the sensitivities of the LTTE. Respecting its desire for recognition as an equal partner with the government and as a potentially legitimate member of the international community is seen as necessary to maintaining the LTTE's commitment to a peaceful transformation of Sri Lanka's ethnic crisis. Pushing the Tigers too hard on their continued violence and antidemocratic practices is seen as likely only to lead to their further withdrawal from what is seen as the potentially moderating influence of negotiations and involvement with the international community (particularly in the form of development and reconstruction assistance). The danger of withdrawal is especially high according to this argument, given the moralism that characterizes much of the human rights criticism of the LTTE, some of which seems to denounce any engagement with the LTTE before its full democratic and liberal transformation.[35]

The emergence of public debates over how and on what terms to engage with the LTTE has offered a rare window on divisions within professional, Colombo-based civil society. Given their potentially explosive nature, disagreements between those who publicly criticize the LTTE and those who don't have not typically been articulated in the open. To be publicly pro-LTTE, especially for Tamil activists, can be a dangerous thing, as was made clear with the May 2005 assassination of Dharmaratnam Sivaram, Sri Lanka's most prominent pro-LTTE journalist. It could easily become dangerous again. Equally important, to accuse another human rights or peace activist, whether Tamil or Sinhala, of being "soft" on the LTTE has generally been considered bad form, at least within the world of Colombo civil society organizations. Thus, liberal critics of the LTTE are normally loath to make public their unhappiness with their less critical civil society colleagues. Unfortunately, both the existence of these disagreements and the continued hesitation about openly discussing them (or their psychological and ideological sources) have hindered the building of a strong democratic movement against abuses by all sides. Instead, the existence of such rarely articulated but widely known divisions has the effect of ratifying the severe limits that characterize civil society politics in Sri Lanka.

In what follows, we will explore in more detail a set of three mutually reinforcing barriers that prevent civil society organizations from playing a stronger role in defending human rights as part of a commitment to a just and sustainable peace. These are the relationships between (1) the political divisions that exist over the meaning and practice of human rights, (2) the democratic deficits of the peace process, controlled as it is by organizations (the government, the LTTE, and international donors and foreign governments) that are, in different ways, deeply resistant to democratic accountability, and finally, (3) the democratic deficits of the liberal, cosmopolitan forms of professionalized civil society political activity that have developed over the past two decades of war, in large part through international sponsorship. My analysis will suggest the need for advocates of human rights and of a peaceful, negotiated settlement to Sri Lanka's long-running war to rethink the nature of all three categories—civil society, conflict resolution or peacebuilding, and human rights—and to begin to refashion their practice in more fully democratic ways.

## Democratizing Human Rights

The divisions within Sri Lankan civil society over the proper role of human rights principles and advocacy during the peace process need to be understood in light of the ambiguities and complexities that characterize the discourse on human rights more generally. The highly politicized, often ethnically defined differences over human rights issues, especially over the proper position to take on LTTE abuses, are sustained in part by the difficulty of defining and practicing the universality and reciprocity characteristic of enlightenment concepts of human rights. Debates that often seem to be between those *in favor* of giving a central role to human rights issues in the peace process (which generally has meant criticizing the actions of the LTTE) and those *opposed* to such a role can also be read as debates about the best or most appropriate definition of human rights, or about which *kind* or set of rights is most in need of protection. It is possible to draw out of the contemporary debates over human rights and the peace process three major lines of argument, which, depending on one's dominant political principles—and at times one's partisan allegiances—give emphasis to different strands of the larger (though rather fractious) family of human rights.

For instance, critics of the lack of strong human rights protections during the peace process, and of the lack of effective civil society outcry and action on these issues, generally focus on the standard collection of liberal civil and political rights. These include most directly the right to life, the right against arbitrary arrest and imprisonment, the right to due process of law, freedom of political association, and related political rights. Such "negative rights" attach to the *individual* and either protect against encroachment by the state or other groups into a "space" considered as belonging to the individual or else guarantee the tools for individuals to be active citizens and political participants. Violations of these sorts of rights by the LTTE have dominated the public discussion of the human rights situation in Sri Lanka today. (Before the cease-fire, violations of these same rights by the government took center stage among those concerned with human rights issues.)

Another major strand of human rights evoked in contemporary debates is those rights to basic dignity that often come under international humanitarian law: the right of refugees to shelter, food, and protection against attack, and, today, their right to return to their properties and to be provided with the basic social infrastructure necessary to a decent existence —land free of mines, roads that can be driven on, schools with roofs, hospitals with medicines and doctors. These rights, while endorsed in principle by all parties to the conflict, are emphasized most strongly today by the LTTE and its supporters in their demands for a speedy "return to normalcy" for the millions of people in the north and east of the island whose lives have been disrupted by decades of war—and more recently by the tsunami of December 2004. Addressing these "humanitarian" concerns through an explicit language of *rights* has increasingly become the choice of the LTTE, following its long use by local and international humanitarian agencies that work with victims of the war.

The preferred language of rights of the LTTE and its Tamil-nationalist supporters and sympathizers centers on the right to "self-determination" for the Tamil people. This is the fundamental right that the LTTE says it has been struggling for from its beginning. Unlike the previous sets of rights, whether humanitarian or civil and political, the right to self-determination attaches not to individual Tamils but to the Tamil "people" as a whole. It is the right of the Tamil people, or "nation," to rule themselves as they see fit, free from interference by other communities. One can argue that it was in part the long history of gross violations of Tamils' *individual* rights—to life, property, equal opportunity—by successive Sri Lankan governments that reinforced the belief among many Tamils that neither individual nor "minority" rights are sufficient to guarantee their freedom and equal dignity. From this perspective Tamils are a nation, not just a minority, and deserve recognition as such. This is in part to guarantee the fundamental democratic right to an equal and active role in one's own governance (which has been denied in practice due to the majoritarian characteristics of the Sri Lankan political system), as well as for pragmatic reasons of collective self-protection.[36]

The discourse of "human rights," then, is used in the present Sri Lankan context to defend very different political projects and to take very different positions on the peace process. Despite the understandable concerns of those frustrated at the lack of action to stop the widespread rights violations by the LTTE, it is useful to recognize that from the perspective of the LTTE—and, more crucially, from the perspective of its supporters and sympathizers—its struggle is a human rights struggle. Thus, while it is indisputable that the LTTE has systematically violated the first set of civil and political rights, LTTE officials and supporters can plausibly (though incompletely) argue that they are in fact committed to a human rights agenda. Indeed, they are fighting for nothing else but the achievement of these rights, whether through a sovereign state of Tamil Eelam or through some form of confederation or federalism.

However, the issue cannot simply be left there. Central to the appeal of the Tamil nationalist struggle and the goal of self-determination is a *democratic* ideal: the ideal of the Tamil people ruling themselves, governing their own affairs, freed from Sinhala domination. For that struggle to be a truly democratic one that leads to a democratic outcome, however, not all means are permissible. The collective rights of the Tamil people don't trump or do away with individual rights; in fact, they actually need those rights in order to make (democratic) sense. Certain basic civil and political rights have to be respected even for the collective right of self-determination to be internally consistent.[37]

Central to the democratic ideal is the notion that the powers given to political representatives and officeholders are (1) given only on trust and (2) never given completely. Instead, they must be supplemented by the people's active involvement in their own governance, through monitoring, challenging, advising, and ultimately, when necessary, *replacing* those who temporarily make use of the people's power. A democratized conception of human rights, then, would include (1) the right of individuals to organize themselves and to act politically, independent of, and even in opposition to, the government or quasi-governmental powers; (2) the right to hold those in power and the institutions of the state accountable, both making sure that the wishes and interests of the majority and of the common good are respected, and preventing abuses of rights and excesses of power; and (3) all the specific liberal rights necessary to achieving these general democratic rights: rights of speech and publication, political association, bodily integrity, and so on. In short, the establishment and preservation of independent spaces for citizen power are definitive of democratic politics. For this reason, when the LTTE and Tamil nationalists sympathetic to their struggle argue that they are fighting for the human rights of the Tamil people, it is incumbent on them to show that the democratic rights of *all* Tamils, and all others within the reach of their power and authority, are or can be respected.

Were such an explicitly democratic conception of human rights to be adopted, then, it would seem in principle to hold out hope for reducing, if not fully overcoming, the tension between the traditional liberal set of civil and political rights and the idea of a collective right to national self-determination. For the latter vision of Tamils' collective rights to make sense, the former set of individual rights must also be respected. And from the evidence of history, respect for the liberal rights supposedly guaranteed to all Sri Lankan citizens would seem, in practice, to require some form of collective autonomy for the Tamil people living in the north and east of the island.

Embracing a more explicitly and consistently democratic conception of human rights should also enable Sri Lankan human rights activists of different ethnic identifications and political allegiances to discover greater common ground. It would offer a basis for the consistent critique of the violation of Sri Lankans' democratic rights, whatever their ethnicity, and by whatever party (whether LTTE, Sri Lankan army or police, JVP, or Tamil paramilitaries). By doing so, and by articulating a perspective that could honor the shared suffering from human rights violations that members of *all* Sri Lankan communities have experienced, such a conception of rights could build trust across ethnic divides and help lay the groundwork for a cross-ethnic coalition of activists and organizations, beyond Colombo-based organizations, that is committed to more complete democratization of Sri Lanka as a whole. More specifically, a critique of the antidemocratic practices of both the LTTE and the Sri Lankan state would create greater space for democratic, nonviolent political activity by Tamils, who would find themselves no longer forced quite so absolutely to sacrifice their liberal and democratic principles to the defense of their collective rights as Tamils.

As this last point suggests, however, even as a democratized practice of human rights advocacy would stress the importance of consistently applying basic principles to all parties in the conflict, it would by no means be politically neutral. Instead, a consistently democratic approach to human rights issues is itself a particular—and controversial—political project, one that directly challenges both the political program of the LTTE (and certain other forms of Tamil nationalism) and the underlying institutions and exclusionary practices of the Sri Lankan state and the Sinhala nationalism that underpins them. For instance, any attempt to create greater space for nonviolent, democratic Tamil political activity, perhaps in common with predominantly Sinhala or Muslim political groups, would be a direct threat to the LTTE's violent claim to be the sole representative of the Tamil people. And those undertaking such a political program, especially to the extent that their criticisms of the Sinhala-dominated state were actually embraced by progressive elements of the Sinhala polity or the state itself, would surely be denounced as traitors to the Tamil cause and as agents of a classic divide-and-rule policy.

## Democratizing the Peace

A more explicitly democratic approach to human rights advocacy, then, would face difficulties not just from the psychological dynamics and ethnopolitical identifications discussed above but also from the entrenched political realities that help sustain them. Indeed, it is precisely these basic political realities, against which the task of developing a more democratic conception and practice of human rights must struggle, that are ratified and strengthened by the Norwegian-sponsored peace process and the dominant ideas of conflict resolution embedded within the process. As we have already seen, the interests and officials of the LTTE and the Sri Lankan government (as well as the less obvious interests of the "international community") have almost completely dominated the process so far. Given that neither party has displayed any serious commitment to human rights principles, the most obvious effect of these restrictions, as we have already seen, is to marginalize human rights concerns as the province only of "spoilers."

Equally worrisome, however, is the nature of the "peace" that has been built on the foundations of the government–LTTE–international community triad. With the emphasis almost solely on "trust building" between the two negotiating parties, there has been very limited space or encouragement for independent civil society initiatives in favor of a negotiated settlement and accommodation across communities.[38] This is true in the south but even more so in the north and the east, where NGOs and civil society organizations over the course of the cease-fire have been forcibly consolidated into LTTE-controlled consortia. The effect of this lack of free space has been to obstruct any serious attempts at independent trust building or reconciliation at the local or national level. Indeed, the dominant conflict resolution model followed in Sri Lanka has been characterized by a fundamental paradox: Trust building at the "track one" level has effectively prevented sustainable trust building at other layers of society. Given the troublesome political issues that might be raised, and the challenges that open discussion and free political activity would pose to the sources of both government and LTTE power, independent efforts to engage with and ultimately transform the conflicting perceptions and experiences of Sri Lankans of different ethnic and political affiliations have been discouraged. With the UNP-led government committed, not to any principled long-term solution or even to a set of interim reform policies that might slowly weaken Sri Lanka's polarized ethnic attitudes and affiliations, but solely to keeping the peace process going until the economic and social benefits of the lack of war become irreversible, their central strategy has simply been to do whatever is necessary to keep the LTTE happy and within the process.

With so little space for independent political contact between Tamils, Sinhalese, and Muslims, the divergent conceptions of "peace" that exist among most members of these three groups have, largely speaking, been further ratified rather than brought into contact in a way that makes them more susceptible to mutually beneficial transformation. For most Tamils who publicly express political opinions, "peace" means the chance to win back the political rights they lost to the Sri Lankan state. The peace process, then, is a forum in which their many years of suffering, and the anger it has produced, can finally be expressed. But peace certainly hasn't meant accepting that wrongs have been committed on all sides, or acknowledging the role that the LTTE's own violence has played in hardening many Sinhala and Muslim hearts. Among many, perhaps most, Sinhalese, there is a strong belief that "peace" should really mean "peace and quiet," rather than the outcome of a process of political, constitutional, and social changes necessary for Tamils to be treated as equal citizens. For many Muslims, finally, peace means a chance to return to the homes and lands from which they have been forcibly displaced and to live their lives in security, no longer harassed or politically manipulated by the competing claims of Tamil and Sinhala nationalism. For the more politicized Muslims, peace increasingly means having a political unit of their own, in and through which they are free to determine their own affairs. Unfortunately, the way in which the peace process has been so dominated by the concerns and actions of the government, the LTTE, and international donors merely strengthens these divergent conceptions of peace, rather than challenging them and leading to their democratic transformation.

For the international community, in turn, "peace in Sri Lanka" has meant an opportunity for its financial and development agencies to lay the foundations for renewed economic liberalization and "growth" and for the social stability that is seen both as one of its effects and as one of its causes. Unfortunately, this has proved to be a largely technical and bureaucratized vision of peacebuilding, and its effects on the capacity of local civil society to do effective peace and human rights work of its own are far from obviously beneficial. From the advent of the formal government-LTTE-Norwegian peace process, there has been a flurry of new activity by the established international players in Sri Lanka: UN agencies (UNHCR, UNICEF, UNDP), the World Bank, the Asian Development Bank, bilateral (i.e., government) aid agencies (e.g., USAID, NORAD, DFID, CIDA, SIDA), and smaller international nongovernmental agencies such as Care International, Oxfam, FORUT, Save the Children, and many others. Their activity has involved numerous "needs assessments," much project planning, the formation of working groups and special subcommittees, the drafting of complex rules and legal arrangements for the disbursement of reconstruction monies, and, as an essential part of this, endless liaising between the various agencies, governments, and INGOs involved, and between them and the relevant LTTE and Sri Lankan government officials. (The complex and time-consuming nature of such work only increased with the massive influx of international aid workers, INGOs, and volunteer groups in response to the December 2004 tsunami.)

The problem with this approach to peacebuilding is not only the inefficiency of such large amounts of time spent coordinating between the different bureaucracies but, more fundamentally, the highly technical approach to Sri Lanka's complex social and political challenges that it involves. Highly paid conflict and development "experts" are brought in for short-term consultancies, with little knowledge of the particularities of Sri Lanka's politics, cultures, and histories, and with little likelihood (if recent history is any guide) of systematic follow-up by those better versed in local knowledge. Instead, the assumption seems to be that Sri Lanka's problems are similar enough to other "ethnic conflicts" that they can be addressed through largely technical means, without deep knowledge of the complexities of the political and social context or of the social problems to be addressed —displacement, land disputes, poverty, exclusivist ethnic identifications— which are embedded in long-standing and complex structures of undemocratic power. Even the longer-term international workers remain in Sri Lanka for only two or three years. By the time they have begun to gain a better understanding of the specific nature of Sri Lanka's challenges, they are on their way out. Local groups, academics, and activists, many of whom have spent years developing careful political and social analyses of Sri Lanka's overlapping conflicts, are primarily assigned the job of implementing the projects determined by international consultants and the resident staffs of donor governments and agencies. The peacebuilding and reconstruction agendas are largely set by the international donors; local organizations and activists have very little space to question or refine the agendas set by others, much less to determine the agenda themselves or to hold the donors accountable in any systematic way.[39] Even the creation by bilateral donors of a number of different "peace funds," designed explicitly to support the role of civil society groups in the peace process and to develop the overall peacebuilding capabilities of Sri Lankan civil society, has not yet succeeded in transforming this dynamic to any considerable extent.

## Toward a More Democratic Civil Society

The inability of Sri Lanka's professional civil society to carve out, in the peace process, an agenda and space independent of the government and the LTTE as well as of its international donors, is symptomatic of a more basic, structural weakness of civil society as a whole. For citizens' groups and civil society organizations to be effective at pressing human rights concerns, holding those in power more accountable, and opening up spaces for independent trust-building initiatives, new, more democratic forms of political organizing and institution building will have to be developed. For Sri Lankan civil society to become a more effective agent of democratization, it will itself have to undergo a significant degree of democratization.

The existing democratic deficits of Sri Lankan civil society begin from the very way in which it is generally understood and addressed. In political discussions in Colombo, especially among international donors, "civil society" primarily refers to those highly professionalized, Colombo-based institutions—research centers, human rights and peace groups, development-oriented NGOs—that are staffed by English-speaking, highly educated, liberal-minded, cosmopolitan intellectuals, lawyers, or activists. "Civil society" can also refer to smaller, community-based groups outside Colombo that have established recognizable institutions that are stable and well enough organized to be funded according to the standard rules of donor bureaucracies (that is, using project proposals written in English, standardized accounting procedures, regular status reports, and so on).[40] "Civil society" thus refers to those groups that international donors can easily work with and identify with, and with whom they are in broad ideological agreement.[41]

Less often included in the working definition of "civil society" are those political groups and institutions that do not depend on foreign donors for their activities and that do not follow today's dominant liberal, cosmo-politan set of political positions. These groups include, for example, trade unions, professional organizations, student groups, certain other, less lib-eral religious groups, and the more nationalist wing of the Colombo elite.[42] Their exclusion from the working definition of "civil society" is in part a re-sult of the fact that many such groups have been and continue to be politi-cized in partisan, or ethnicized, ways and at times have engaged in or jus-tified "uncivil" behavior (e.g., the violence attributed to student groups affiliated with particular political parties, trade unions used by political par-ties to intimidate their opponents, and the often strident opposition articu-lated by large parts of the Buddhist clergy to devolution of state power).

While it is understandable that donors would be less inclined to offer support to groups that do not share their liberal, multicultural, free-market ideology, it is perhaps unwise to write them out of the working definition of "civil society" from the very start. For one thing, doing so makes it harder to see the value and possibility of building bridges and maintaining channels of communication between the different wings of civil society— channels that might enable one to discover areas of common ground or com-promise that would otherwise go unnoticed.[43]

Even more important, the tendency to equate professionalized, cos-mopolitan, Colombo-based groups—and, to a lesser extent, those profes-sionalized groups outside Colombo—with "civil society" makes it easier to ignore the unrepresentative and largely undemocratic nature of such groups. This oversight inadvertently ratifies elite control of Sri Lankan society more generally. Indeed, the very factors that make possible their strong connec-tions with international funders are what tend to cut these groups off from the rest of Sri Lanka. For even as such elite-based groups are prone to speak in the name of Sri Lankan civil society and the Sri Lankan people as a whole, Colombo-based groups in particular are, generally speaking, quite isolated from the vast majority of Sri Lankans on the basis of class, language ability (few Sri Lankans outside the small elite speak English), and political ideol-ogy. The elite nature of the best-established and most prominent civil soci-ety organizations explains in part the lack of emphasis placed on issues of socioeconomic rights and class inequality.

Colombo-based elite, cosmopolitan groups, and activists thus cannot automatically be assumed to represent the needs, interests, or political views of most Sri Lankans. All the less so, given that there are no significant mechanisms established among such groups to ensure their accountability to the larger Sri Lankan community in whose name they speak. Indeed, in many ways Colombo civil society groups have much the same relationship to their rural or non-English-speaking fellow citizens as international donors have to the Colombo-based recipients of their aid. While Colombo-based groups do frequently venture outside Colombo to work with other non-English-speaking Sri Lankans, the work tends to be sporadic, not very well coordinated, and rarely followed up in systematic ways. The agenda is almost always set by the Colombo groups, and the actual interactions between the groups often reinforce hierarchical power relations, with those at the grassroots level being the objects of training or skills building, but rarely being treated as equals from whom the trainers themselves could learn. There is generally no space within the activities sponsored by these groups for such power relations to be addressed or questioned. This lack of political accountability is not merely a normative, or ethical, failing. It also has negative strategic political effects, because it cuts off Colombo and other elite civil society groups from larger political energies and possible sources of knowledge and inspiration that might come from non-Colombo and nonelite constituencies. This isolation, in turn, prevents such groups from establishing the local-level political support, and thus the political leverage, necessary to have effective influence over national-level political leaders.

The democratic deficits of professional, donor-sponsored civil society groups are not, however, primarily the fault of the individuals involved, many of whom are quite aware of, frustrated by, and struggling against the institutional and social constraints just described. The problems are instead more structural and have much to do with the financial dependence of such groups on international donors. The heavily bureaucratized form of so much of the work done by Sri Lankan civil society groups, especially Colombo-based research and advocacy groups, is largely a response to the needs and demands of their donors. Since most of their funding is short term and project based, a large proportion of available time is spent on the necessities of constant fund-raising and the paperwork that comes with it: the preparation of project proposals, maintenance of records, completion of evaluations, and writing of annual reports. Indeed, maintaining the institution itself in some ways becomes the rational priority, with competition between groups (for funds and for the public recognition that leads to funds) being more common than cooperation. As a result of funding patterns, activities tend almost entirely to take the form of short-term projects rather than long-term, sustained campaigns. This leads to frequent shifts of direction within organizations and constant loss of institutional memory, which are one cause of the lack of coordination between different groups who would seem to have much to gain from one another. Finally, staff members are recruited primarily for their ability to perform specific useful tasks rather than for their political knowledge or commitment and generally show little interest in using their employment as a source or occasion for political education. Thus, civil society organizations tend to be characterized by a careerist rather than an activist mindset, with many members joining out of a not-so-surprising desire for a safe, relatively well-paying job. This helps explain some of the cynicism that NGOs and those who work for them provoke among growing numbers of the Sri Lankan people—a cynicism that undermines the credibility and thus the political effectiveness of such groups.

What results from this combination of institutional, funding, class, and ideological dynamics is a quite cautious form of political activity, aimed at a very restricted audience rather than toward more active and challenging forms of popular mobilization. Thus, there are frequent seminars and workshops, as well as reports and publications, oriented toward the political elite and intellectual class and therefore conducted and written in English. Those training and capacity-building programs that are oriented toward nonelite and non-Colombo audiences tend to be of a highly technical sort. Thus, for instance, a wide array of "human rights education" courses and workshops catalog the various categories of rights granted Sri Lankans through international covenants and national law, but they rarely foster any discussion of how these rights might relate to the specific history of human rights abuses in Sri Lanka's recent past and to their various social and political causes. The most politically challenging forms of civil society politics consist of public interest lawsuits and legal litigation in particularly acute cases of individuals' rights being violated (e.g., illegal detention, disappearances, rapes by security forces, and cases under the Prevention of Terrorism Act). While such legal actions often require real courage and can involve real risk, they also reinforce a generally legalistic approach to human rights concerns, with more structural political issues, and what would be needed to challenge them, left unaddressed.[44]

However valuable such political activity is in the abstract, and would be in a social context of a well-functioning liberal democracy with a strong judiciary and a political culture that generally respects fundamental rights, such a context is not Sri Lanka's. The dominant forms of political work characteristic of professional Sri Lankan civil society are ill equipped to challenge the democratic deficits of the peace process or, more generally, the entrenched forms of power and conflict from which Sri Lanka has suffered for so long. Thus, the political work of professional civil society rarely names or challenges undemocratic or unaccountable power as such, nor does it organize people to recognize, criticize, and challenge it. As suggested above, this reticence is partly born of the need to defend and protect one's existing institution and is thus a cost incurred by what is in other ways the strength of Sri Lankan civil society: its highly organized and professional nature. It is also a product of dependence on international donors, especially foreign governments, few of which are willing to support politically controversial civil society initiatives.[45] Caution also clearly comes from the basic liberal and elite ideological dispositions of civil society leaders. This is ultimately linked to the particularly strong disinclination among Sri Lankans of all classes to challenge established authorities and hierarchy. Some degree of discomfort, even fear, at the risks such challenges might entail is certainly understandable, and given its deep roots, it is not going to disappear soon. Yet it is striking to notice just how little elite civil society does to challenge this tendency, even in its own operations or its relations with its external donors.

The point of this analysis is not to blame or condemn Sri Lanka's elite, professionalized civil society for the democratic deficits of its political work. Such deficits are largely the result of long-standing historical developments, over which individual activists and civil society leaders have little control. The point, rather, is that for civil society to become anything like the force for lasting peace and human rights that its leaders and its donors wish it to be, the democratization of civil society must become a conscious political project for everyone involved. What is most worrying about the present state of donor-funded civil society in Sri Lanka is the absence of any space where these issues can be discussed and debated. As far as a process of democratization *within* local civil society—both within elite, Colombo-based organizations and between them and their nonelite constituencies—there is virtually no discussion or awareness of the issue, and little evident interest within the leadership of elite civil society organizations in producing more egalitarian, representative, and self-questioning forms of political practice.

As for relations *between* local civil society organizations and their international financial supporters, there is frequent, well-founded grumbling from local activists, but no forum for discussing the mutual expectations and responsibilities of each to the other.[46] The donations of international agencies and foreign governments are generally presented and accepted as acts of generosity rather than aspects of deeply political relationships that bring with them certain responsibilities, including the willingness of donors to be held accountable to local constituencies. With such issues largely off the table even within local civil society discussions, it has been left to nationalist "spoilers" of various kinds to raise them. It has generally only been Sinhala nationalists (joined more recently by Tamil nationalists and the LTTE itself) who have dared criticize the unaccountable forms of power involved in the kinds of international support afforded to Sri Lankan civil society (and in other projects carried out directly by INGOs and multi-laterals). In similar ways, it is often only the nationalist wings of the political left, that is, the JVP and its supporters, who articulate any kind of class analysis and critique of the elite dominance of Sri Lankan civil society.[47]

## Conclusion and Recommendations

In light of the difficulties sketched out above, it will clearly take some time before Sri Lankan civil society becomes anything like the strong force for peace and human rights that it is sometimes theorized and often hoped to be. Whatever fate awaits Sri Lanka—further stalemate, a return to war, or renewal and deepening of the LTTE-government-Norwegian peace process—stronger and more democratic forms of civil society are needed if human rights are to be better protected. While it is too much to expect that Sri Lankan civil society organizations and activists will be democratizing the Sri Lankan state, the LTTE, or the sphere of formal politics anytime soon, it is not too much to expect that democratic habits—of equal treatment and equal voice, of questioning authority, of allowing as wide and active participation as is practically possible—can begin to be cultivated more widely within civil society groups and between them and their various publics. In this, the international community could play a crucial role, by advocating for and helping to subsidize such democratic transformations. But for this to happen, international funding bodies must be willing to open themselves up for public questioning and investigation as well. Transparency and accountability, key words in the donor vocabulary of good governance, must apply to donors, too.

The following is meant to suggest what such a process of democratization might look like, and how it might strengthen the ability of Sri Lankan civil society organizations to act in defense of basic democratic and human rights. While born of an analysis of the specific challenges facing Sri Lanka's civil society organizations, the following recommendations would also likely be useful for other situations of protracted social conflict, and even beyond.

1.  *Create spaces in which to discuss and strategize ways beyond the present political and social limitations of professional, liberal, cosmopolitan civil society.*
    (a) Such spaces for discussion and debate would aim, in the broadest sense, to cultivate habits of collective self-questioning and critique. In this way, the target of professional civil society's critical energies would move beyond those of the state, militant

groups, and nationalists of various sorts to include the democratic deficits in its own institutions and political practices. This would require Colombo-based, cosmopolitan civil society groups to give up their claims to speak for civil society and to accept instead that they constitute specific, partial, and not always democratic versions among other possible forms of civil society. Among other things, such a change in self-understanding might make it more possible to open up lines of communication between the liberal cosmopolitan groups that international funders prefer and the more nationalistic, even chauvinistic, elements of Sinhala civil society, which often have strong democratic and even rights-based commitments of their own despite their being generally excluded from the standard conception and discourse of "civil society."

(b) Cultivating habits of collective self-critique would open up space to debate ways of challenging and moving beyond the deeply rooted social and class limitations of established civil society. Professional civil society can hope to challenge the entrenched forms of power and inequality that underpin systematic violations of human rights only by broadening its base of support and mobilizing deeper democratic energies and influence. This will require Colombo-based groups not only to work at making their own organizations more representative and less hierarchical but also to cultivate sustainable connections to groups outside the capital and to other forms of civic organizations, such as trade unions, professional organizations, and student groups, which go beyond the standard nongovernmental organizational model of institutions.

(c) Finally, and especially important, the conscious creation of spaces for collective civil society debate would aim to stimulate discussion of the often ethnicized ideological and strategic disagreements that currently complicate civil society interventions in defense of human rights. It would be crucial here to create spaces in which disagreements over the very meaning of "human rights" and "peace" could be openly articulated and more safely debated, however difficult this might be today.

2. *Establish practices through which the complex politics of the relationship between international donors and their local civil society "partners" can be brought out into the open and debated.*

(a) The aim would be first of all to clarify as much as possible the different political agendas that shape donors' funding choices and the ways these go on to structure not only the programs but also the larger political and social imagination of local civil society groups. Here the point would be to foster stronger accountability in both directions—just as donors are right to ask their local recipients of aid for greater clarity about both the means and the ends of their work, so, too, civil society organizations have the democratic right (and obligation to their Sri Lankan publics) to contribute to formulation of the overall political vision for the transformation of Sri Lankan society that drives the projects they carry out.

(b) To build such a strengthened relationship, however, would require opening up discussion about the *form* of donor support, and the political limitations that short-term, project-oriented, and bureaucratically managed programming places on the ability of Sri Lankan civil society groups to effect the kind of democratic social change that both donors and recipients say they wish to see. While many among local groups as well as donors are frustrated with the limitations that such funding brings with it, there is no space in which these frustrations can be publicly discussed, and ways beyond them imagined. Yet it is hard to see how Sri Lankan civil society can act effectively to counter human rights abuses without developing more directly political and challenging forms of practice.

Were something like the above practices of democratic debate, dialogue, and collective self-critique to be consciously and carefully cultivated —within civil society organizations, between different segments of civil society, and between local civil society and its foreign donors—the realities of violence, unaccountable power, and gross social and economic inequalities that presently plague Sri Lanka would not suddenly come to an end. But powerful seeds of democratic thinking and practice would have been planted, the ultimate fruits of which might someday surprise even the most cynical of political observers.

## Notes

This essay is based on three years of field research in Sri Lanka, initially sponsored by a generous postdoctoral fellowship from the Solomon Asch Center for Study of

Ethnopolitical Conflict, at the University of Pennsylvania. Research was also facilitated by a visiting fellowship at the International Centre for Ethnic Studies, Colombo, Sri Lanka, and by a grant from the American Institute for Sri Lankan Studies. I would like to thank all three institutions, as well as the many people in Sri Lanka who patiently gave of their time and opinions in response to my never-ending requests for assistance, for their help in making this essay possible. I would also like to thank audiences in Colombo and at the University of Pennsylvania, as well as Jeff Helsing, Ian Lustick, Clark McCauley, Brendan O'Leary, and Camilla Orjuela, for their helpful comments and critiques on earlier versions of this essay

1. Expressing frustration at the lack of tangible improvements in conditions for Tamils in the north and east more than a year after signing the cease-fire, the LTTE demanded that the Sri Lankan government propose arrangements for an interim administration in the northeast capable of effectively disbursing promised international reconstruction assistance. Ultimately rejecting three successive government plans, the LTTE finally announced its own "interim self-governing authority" (ISGA) proposal on October 31, 2003. The ISGA plan would have given the LTTE effectively uncontestable control over the Northern and Eastern provinces for a period of five years and was thus not something any Sri Lankan government could possibly accept without major amendments. Nonetheless, reactions from the United National Party government, from much of professional civil society, and from representatives of foreign governments and international agencies were generally positive, arguing that the proposal could form the starting point for a return to direct negotiations. The president's Sri Lanka Freedom Party and her soon-to-be coalition partner, the People's Liberation Front (known by its Sinhala initials as the JVP), denounced the ISGA proposal as a stepping-stone to a separate Tamil state and the division of the island. Just a few days after the publication of the ISGA proposals, President Chandrika Kumaratunga threw politics in the southern, Sinhala-dominated parts of the island into confusion and paralysis when she used her constitutional powers to retake control of the defense and other crucial ministries from the government of her longtime rival, Prime Minister Ranil Wickremasinghe. She cited as one of her central motivations the threats she saw to national security from the LTTE's growing military strength and unchecked cease-fire violations.

2. Under Sri Lanka's constitution, the president and the parliament are elected separately. President Kumaratunga was elected to a second six-year term in December 1999. With the election of Ranil Wickremasinghe's United National Party as the lead member of a coalition government in December 2001, Sri Lanka entered a period of difficult "cohabitation" between the president and the prime minister, who are bitter personal and political rivals. Thus, the roughly two years of the UNP-led peace process were constantly overshadowed by the difficulties of this relationship.

**3.** Just as the many cease-fire and human rights violations by the LTTE have played a part in raising Sinhalese and Muslim fears about the nature of any negotiated settlement with the Tigers, so there is similar, and well-founded, skepticism felt by most Tamils about the likelihood that the Sri Lankan government will ever offer a fair settlement to nearly sixty years of discrimination and ill treatment. The government has generally behaved well with respect to the basic civil and political rights of Tamils during the period of the cease-fire and has thus recently come under much less censure for human rights violations than the Tigers. This, however, should not obscure the fact that the continued occupation of Tamil lands by Sinhalese security forces, and the continued lack of tolerable living conditions throughout much of the north and east of the island, constitute major infringements on basic human rights. Nor can one ignore the likely complicity of at least some sections of the Sri Lankan military in the attacks by Karuna's and possibly other Tamil militant forces against LTTE cadres and civilian sympathizers.

**4.** By "professional" civil society, I am referring to the range of institutionalized and professionalized research, lobbying, and advocacy groups, primarily located in Colombo, that both think of themselves as constituting and frequently speak in the name of civil society. These organizations generally share a liberal, cosmopolitan worldview, draw their staffs and audiences from the educated, English-speaking Colombo upper middle class and elite, and have close connections with foreign governments and donor agencies, whose rhetoric and funding further promote these organizations as *being* civil society. This segment of civil society is to be distinguished from those organizations and political groups, such as trade unions, student groups, professional societies, and organizations of the non-Christian clergy, that don't generally speak in the name of civil society. Instead, they typically speak for their membership, for the working class, or perhaps "for the good of the nation."

**5.** For three distinctive stories of Sri Lanka's fall into fratricidal and ethnicized warfare, see Rajan Hoole, *Sri Lanka: The Arrogance of Power* (Colombo: University Teachers for Human Rights, 2001); K. M. de Silva, *Reaping the Whirlwind: Ethnic Conflict, Ethnic Politics in Sri Lanka* (London: Penguin, 1998); and A. J. Wilson, *Sri Lankan Tamil Nationalism* (Vancouver: UBC Press, 2000). The most interesting recent scholarship in Sri Lanka consciously attempts to historicize and pluralize the dominant ethnic categories. See in particular Neluka Silva, ed., *Hybrid Island* (Colombo: International Centre for Ethnic Studies, 2002).

**6.** This included, most famously, the "Sinhala only" policies begun in 1956, which mandated the use of Sinhala for government business. It also later included other discriminatory policies meant to make up for what many Sinhalese saw as the disproportionate number of Tamils in universities and the civil service.

**7.** The most famous of these attempts was the so-called Bandaranaike-Chelvanayakam Pact, signed in 1957 by the SLFP prime minister S. W. R. D. Bandaranaike and the Tamil leader of the Federal Party, S. J. V. Chelvanayakam.

Bandaranaike, who came to power in 1956 on the platform of "Sinhala only," was assassinated in 1959 by a Buddhist monk for daring—unsuccessfully—to reverse himself and recognize the collective rights of Tamils. The fact that changes to the Sri Lankan constitution currently must be approved by a two-thirds majority of parliament—a majority that the present electoral system makes it virtually impossible for one party or coalition to achieve on its own—helps to sustain the tradition of interparty rivalry on the ethnic question and remains a major stumbling block to any negotiated settlement.

**8.** The UNP government that was elected in 1977 did in fact maintain a two-thirds majority in parliament, but it was by that point unable or unwilling to use its power to grant the concessions necessary to bring the violent Tamil militancy to an end.

**9.** For a valuable analysis of the emergence of a "dirty war" aspect to Sri Lanka's conflicts, ones that are no longer rooted in ethnic identifications, see Darini Rajasingham-Senanayake, "The Dangers of Devolution: The Hidden Economies of Armed Conflict," in *Creating Peace in Sri Lanka: Civil War and Reconciliation,* ed. Robert Rothberg (Washington, DC: Brookings Institution Press, 1999).

**10.** The LTTE saw Muslims as undermining their national struggle by their willingness to cooperate with the Sri Lankan security forces, particularly in the Eastern Province. There are also long-standing economic and social tensions between Muslims and Tamils, despite their common suffering from Sinhala and Buddhist majoritarianism.

**11.** For an excellent analysis of the multiple and overlapping conflicts that complicate efforts to end the war between the LTTE and the Sri Lankan government, see Ram Manikkalingam, "Political Power over Ethnic Identity," *Frontline* 19, no. 13 (June 22–July 5, 2002). For a helpful discussion of the class character of much of Sri Lanka's recent civil violence, see Jayedeva Uyangoda, "Sri Lanka's Left: From Class and Trade Unions to Civil Society and NGO's," in *Sri Lanka: Global Challenges and National Crisis,* ed. Rajan Philips (Colombo: Ecumenical Institute for Study and Dialogue and Social Scientists Association, 2001).

**12.** There are numerous analyses of past negotiations and peace processes aiming to end the Sri Lankan civil war. Among the most useful are Godfrey Gunatillike, *Negotiations for the Resolution of the Ethnic Conflict,* Marga Monograph Series on Ethnic Reconciliation 1 (Colombo: Marga Institute, 2001); Kethesh Loganathan, *Sri Lanka: Lost Opportunities* (Colombo: CEPRA, 1998); Liz Philipson, *Negotiating Processes in Sri Lanka,* Marga Monograph Series on Ethnic Reconciliation 2 (Colombo: Marga Institute, 2001); and Kumar Rupesinghe, ed., *Negotiating Peace in Sri Lanka: Efforts, Failures and Lessons* (London: International Alert, 1998).

**13.** For the text of the cease-fire agreement, see www.peaceinsrilanka.org.

**14.** There were signs that this might have begun to shift when the Tigers presented their proposal for an "interim self-governing authority" in late October

2003. With President Kumaratunga's assertion of control over the defense, interior, and media ministries just a few days later in November 2003, and the confusion into which the peace process was then thrown, no talks could be held on the ISGA. Although any discussion of the powers to be held by an LTTE-dominated interim administration in the north and east would necessarily touch on many of the substantive issues at stake in the conflict, the Tigers remain committed to considering questions on interim arrangements before making any attempt to reach a long-term solution. This issue is at the heart of the stalemate that prevented a resumption of talks with President Kumaratunga and the UPFA government in mid-2004, with the new government insisting that any interim administration must be considered in tandem with discussion about longer-term solutions.

15. Any significant program of cross-ethnic dialogue and trust building would clearly involve a large amount of collective self-critique, as the causes of the war and the suffering it brought emerge for public discussion. The government's reluctance to embark on this course probably stems from the anger and defensiveness that such a process would provoke among many Sinhalese, as well as from the various skeletons that would likely emerge from the closets of earlier UNP-led regimes. The LTTE's reluctance is likely based on the fear that such cross-ethnic openness would weaken its hold on the Tamil people by weakening Tamils' sense of grievance and of being under threat.

16. Recruitment, including forcible conscription of children as young as twelve, and public demands that every Tamil family contribute at least one son or daughter to the LTTE have continued despite a 2003 "Action Plan" agreed to by UNICEF and the LTTE-controlled Tamil Rehabilitation Organization (TRO). The Action Plan called for the LTTE to demobilize all underage recruits and to have those demobilized move through a system of "transit centers," run jointly by the TRO and UNICEF, before returning to their families. The plan has come under heavy criticism, both by Sinhala-centric newspapers and by rights activists, for its lack of independence from the LTTE and for its inadequate protections of the rights of the children involved. The first fifty children were demobilized to a transit camp in early October 2003. Only a handful of others have since been formally released to the camps. Meanwhile, UNICEF itself has acknowledged that the LTTE continues to recruit children. Roughly 1,000 underage fighters, more girls than boys, were among the forces disbanded by the renegade LTTE leader Karuna in April 2004 as he came under attack from forces loyal to overall LTTE leader Prabhakaran. The LTTE eventually rerecruited many of these boys and girls, despite stiff resistance from them and their families in the Eastern Province. There has also been ample evidence that the LTTE continued to recruit children after the 2004 tsunami, including some children who were removed from tsunami refugee camps (see, for instance, the report from Human Rights Watch available at http://hrw.org/english/docs/2005/01/14/slanka10016.htm). For a long and detailed analysis of LTTE child soldier recruitment and the failures of international attempts to prevent it, see Human Rights Watch, "Living in Fear: Child Soldiers and the Tamil

Tigers in Sri Lanka," available at http://hrw.org/english/docs/2004/11/10/slanka9651.htm.

**17.** For two interesting articles that suggest the degree of LTTE control over Tamil "civil society" organizations in the Northern and Eastern provinces, see Amantha Perera, "Iron Grip of the Tiger," *Sunday Leader,* June 22, 2003; and Sinha Ratnatunga, "Tigers Await Interim Rule in Northeast," *Gulf News Online,* August 10, 2003. Col. Karuna's decision in March 2004 to break off from the "Wanni Tigers" and form the "Batticaloa-Ampara Tigers" and the ensuing division and violence have complicated this picture somewhat. Even after the apparent military defeat of Karuna's forces, the northern LTTE leadership has had trouble restoring full control over the Eastern Province. There was initially a substantial amount of popular resistance to the LTTE's attempt to rerecruit the soldiers—especially children—disbanded by Karuna, and to efforts to reestablish the LTTE's systems of taxation and political control. Unfortunately, this has been accompanied by political assassinations and intimidation from both sides of the LTTE split. A number of assassinations of high-ranking LTTE military and political officials in the east in the spring and summer of 2005, which the LTTE argues could only have been carried out with the complicity of the Sri Lankan military, put the cease-fire, and the peace process built on it, under severe pressure.

**18.** The worst incident of this sort took place in the eastern town of Kanjirankuda in October 2002 and was followed by the failure of police to stop retaliatory attacks shortly thereafter by Sinhala crowds on Tamil demonstrators in nearby Trincomalee.

**19.** For the SLMM's statistics on cease-fire violations, see www.slmm.lk. By the summer of 2003, complaints about the "pro-LTTE" bias of the SLMM had become a central preoccupation of Sri Lankan journalists and political commentators. With the LTTE repeatedly refusing to abide by SLMM rulings against it, the international monitors have also gained a reputation as being relatively powerless. In the first of what have now become many such criticisms by different human rights groups, Human Rights Watch and Amnesty International released complementary reports in July 2003 that were sharply critical of the LTTE for its wave of political assassinations of Tamil opponents, and that called on the SLMM to broaden its interpretation of its mandate to include the protection of civilians and their basic human rights. In response to these criticisms, the deputy head of the SLMM, Hagrup Haukland, was quoted as maintaining that the SLMM is not mandated or equipped to investigate political assassinations. "There is police to do this job and it is for them to go after the killers," he was quoted as saying. See Dilip Ganguly, "European Cease-Fire Monitors Say They Are at Difficult Job in Sri Lanka," Associated Press, August 8, 2003. The inability of the SLMM to stop the escalation of political killings by the LTTE and, to a lesser extent, by anti-LTTE forces associated with Karuna, has only increased public perception of its powerlessness.

**20.** UTHR-J has now published many reports that have been increasingly critical of the peace process. All its publications, stretching back nearly fifteen years, are available at www.uthr.org. For an interesting article that describes UTHR-J's work and the conditions under which it is forced to work, see Martha Ann Overland, "Fighting for Human Rights," *Chronicle of Higher Education*, February 28, 2003.

**21.** In an earlier essay I have attempted to sketch out the broad outlines of how human rights concerns could be more effectively integrated into the peace process. See "Democratizing Human Rights, Strengthening Peace: Sri Lanka's Historic Challenge," *Tamil Times* 22, no. 3 (March 15, 2003).

**22.** See, for instance, the important document produced by five prominent civil society activists and intellectuals working on peace issues in Sri Lanka: Tyrol Ferdinands, Kumar Rupesinghe, Paikiasothy Saravanamuttu, Jayadeva Uyangoda, and Norbert Ropers, "The Sri Lankan Peace Process at the Crossroads: Lessons, Opportunities and Ideas for Principled Negotiations and Conflict Transformation" (Colombo, January 2004), www.cpalanka.org/research_papers/Sri_Lankan_Peace_Process.pdf. For my critique of the "Crossroads" argument, see Alan Keenan, "Critical Engagement or Constructive Engagement? Sri Lankan Civil Society at the Crossroads of Politics and Principle," *Lines* magazine, May 2004, www.lines-magazine.org.

**23.** For a representative statement of Sri Lankan liberal civil society concerns about the absence of human rights protections within the peace process and about the generally closed nature of the process, see the statement published in the *Daily Mirror*, May 6, 2003, and later republished as "The Peace Process and Human Rights," *Tamil Times* 22, no. 5 (May 15, 2003). That statement, as well as all the statements published by the "Peace Support Group," can be found on the Web site of the Centre for Policy Alternatives, www.cpalanka.org.

**24.** This effort, chaired by the well-respected legal scholar Deepika Udagama, was organized by the Sri Lanka Foundation Institute, a quasi-governmental research institute.

**25.** The reports of fact-finding missions to the sites of violence in Valaichchenai and Puttalam, jointly undertaken by the Centre for Policy Alternatives and INFORM, can be found at www.cpalanka.org.

**26.** An "International Women's Mission to the North and East of Sri Lanka" took place October 12–17, 2002. See Social Scientists Association, "Women's Concerns and the Peace Process," *Pravada* 8, no. (2002), for the final report and recommendations.

**27.** A convention of civil society activists, jointly organized by the National Peace Council, the Japanese Centre for Conflict Prevention, and Seva Lanka, was held in the northern town of Vavuniya in March 2003.

**28.** A potential exception to this rule is the initiative of the international grassroots organization Nonviolent Peaceforce (www.nonviolentpeaceforce.org/

english/srilanka/slpintro.asp). Working in partnership with the Sri Lankan election monitoring group PAFFREL, Nonviolent Peaceforce (NP) has deployed about a dozen international human rights and peace "monitors" in four different geographical locations, three of them in the north and east. During and after the April 2004 fighting between rival LTTE factions in the Eastern Province, NP monitors were involved in offering protection and assistance to civilians, as well as to underage soldiers released by Karuna's faction but under pressure from the northern LTTE leadership to rejoin its ranks. Another partial exception here is the work of the Asian Human Rights Commission (www.ahrchk.net/index.php). The Hong Kong–based group has succeeded in building a network of local Sri Lankan activists who report primarily on abuse and torture by Sri Lankan police. Unfortunately, the work of the AHRC is limited almost entirely to the Sinhala areas of the island and generally has not addressed the human rights issues raised by the peace process. That both these initiatives are cooperative efforts between Sri Lankan and international groups is worth noting. A particularly notable local human rights initiative was the Collective for Batticaloa, which investigated and reported on the situation in the Eastern Province after Karuna's forces were militarily defeated by the northern LTTE. Its report from the summer of 2004 is available at www.lankademocracy.org/documents/batticollective.html. For an article that discusses and analyzes the group's work, see Alan Keenan, "No Peace, No War," *Boston Review* 30, nos. 3–4 (Summer 2005): 31–37; www.bostonreview.net/BR30.3/Keenan.html.

**29.** For a history of political violence in Sri Lanka running into the early 1990s, see Jagath Senaratne, *Political Violence in Sri Lanka, 1997–1990: Riots, Insurrections, Counter-Insurgencies, Foreign Intervention* (Amsterdam: V. U. University Press, 1997).

**30.** For further discussion of some of the complex dynamics between peace, human rights, and ethnic identification in Sri Lanka, see the essays by Jehan Perera, Jeevan Thiagarajah, and Alan Keenan in *Human Rights Dialogue* 2, no. 7 (Winter 2002). An interesting discussion of similar dilemmas that exist in Northern Ireland and Palestine/Israel can be found in Eitan Felner and Michael Ignatieff, "Human Rights Leaders in Conflict Zones: A Case Study of the Politics of 'Moral Entrepreneurs'" (2003), www.ksg.harvard.edu/cchrp/pdf/Felner.2004.pdf.

**31.** Some politically active Tamils have argued that the primary—perhaps the sole—job of human rights defenders is to challenge *state* power rather than the power of nonstate entities such as the LTTE. Whatever legitimacy this argument may have had, it has become less persuasive the more the LTTE's statelike character has grown.

**32.** These political differences are due in part to the Tamil human rights activists' greater degree of identification with the LTTE than any similar identification by Sinhala activists with the Sri Lankan state. This difference is an understandable effect of the history of the conflict and the power imbalances between the Sri Lankan, Sinhala-dominated state and the Tamil people and their political representatives. In one sense, then, there are no real equivalents of Tamil human rights groups among Sinhalese. To the limited extent that it makes sense to speak of Sinhala-dominated human rights groups, they are without exception committed to a negotiated settlement based on a recognition of Tamil people's just demands and equal rights. The dominant discourse of Sinhala nationalists, on the other hand, unlike that of Tamil nationalists, is not that of human rights, at least not of the liberal-democratic sort. This claim nevertheless requires qualification and raises important political and methodological issues. There are at least two strands of specifically Sinhala political discourse and activism that do invoke certain forms of human rights.

First, there is the attachment of many Sinhala political activists to the People's Liberation Front (JVP). While the Sinhala nationalist elements of the JVP's ideology would be mixed much more strongly with the rhetoric and emotional power of left-wing, class-oriented analysis than is the case with the LTTE, there is nonetheless a parallel antagonism toward the Sri Lankan state. During the years of terror in the late 1980s and early 1990s, when the violence of the second JVP uprising was in full swing and JVP activists and reported sympathizers were disappearing or being killed by agents of the state, Sinhala groups were organized to defend the rights of Sinhala victims of state repression. Indeed, at that point the most important independent political and human rights groups in Sri Lanka (e.g., the Movement for Interracial Justice and Equity, and the Civil Rights Movement) were explicit in their defense of the civil and political rights of both Tamils and Sinhalese. The possibility of building common political ground between Tamils and Sinhalese based on their shared suffering from both state and counterstate power, however, though ripe in theory, remains largely unexplored in practice. The difficulties of building such common ground are also due to the class differences between the largely rural and working-class nature of JVP supporters, and the middle-class and urban nature of the professional civil society and human rights groups dominant in today's political context.

There is a second Sinhala discourse of "human rights." Overlapping at times with the JVP's fear of a loss of Sri Lanka's sovereignty, and the division of the country through the establishment of Tamil Eelam, there is the discourse of neglected "Sinhala rights." For many Sinhala nationalist activists, the "rights" of the majority are being neglected because of pressure from international forces and their cosmopolitan agents in Sri Lanka. Thus, while Sinhala nationalist parties and activists—many of whose leaders are from the same educated, English-speaking middle class as their cosmopolitan opponents—struggle to identify with the Sri Lankan state, they are unable to do so in the state's present form, given that the Sri Lankan government is seen to have failed to defend Sinhala rights against foreign invasions and Tamil "racist" separatism.

There are, therefore, specifically Sinhala discourses of human rights, which in many ways parallel those of Tamil nationalism and support for the LTTE. This raises the following important methodological point: My analysis in this paper is primarily concerned with those civil society (whether "peace" or "human rights") groups that accept that basic injustices, both individual and collective, have been committed by the Sri Lankan state against Tamils and that there is an urgent need to rectify these injustices. Such groups and their criticism of Sinhala majoritarian hegemony are not yet dominant politically throughout Sri Lanka (in part for reasons to be discussed at length below). And yet, in large part because of their cosmopolitan nature and connection to international media and money, these groups have established and control the dominant framework for defining and addressing human rights issues in Sri Lanka. It remains important to note, however, that they do not have a complete monopoly on the discourse or definition of "human rights." Unfortunately, there is a disturbing unwillingness of Colombo cosmopolitan civil society groups to engage in critical debates over the defining terms of their own existence, that is, what constitutes "human rights." For their own political good, however, it would be wise to try to engage with pro-Sinhala groups and noncosmopolitan, even nonliberal civil society groups in an attempt to take into account their positions, interests, and fears, if only to undercut the appeal of Sinhala nationalist rhetoric and positions to the larger Sri Lankan public.

**33.** Muslim civil society activists, especially those based in the Eastern Province, generally feel no such inhibitions about criticizing the Tigers. Many share a strong fear of what life would hold for them under an LTTE-controlled interim administration.

**34.** It is worth noting that all these concerns are more pronounced with respect to criticisms of rights violations by the LTTE. This is due in part to the fact that the LTTE's hold on power depends today more directly on brute force, psychological manipulation, and terror than does that of the Sri Lankan state. On the other hand, the fact that there is greater fear among Tamils about the negative politicization of human rights criticisms is also a sign of the asymmetries of *symbolic* power between the Sri Lankan state, with its established institutions, majoritarian support, and international legitimacy, and the LTTE, which, despite its proven military power, remains relatively isolated internationally, and economically and institutionally quite weak.

**35.** What remains missing from this argument, at least in its present forms, is any criterion for judging when engagement with the LTTE would be constructive and when it would merely legitimize antidemocratic political structures and practices. For an interesting collection of essays that attempt to think through such issues, with some reference to the case of Sri Lanka, see Conciliation Resources, "Choosing to Engage: Armed Groups and Peace Processes," *Accord* 16, (2005), available at www.c-r.org/accord/engage/index.shtml.

**36.** For others, the recognition of the Tamil nation is a matter of basic moral respect, rooted in a particular belief about Tamil "nationness" and an attachment to what is taken to be an essential collective identity.

**37.** Moreover, the collective rights of the Tamil people in no way trump the democratic rights of those Sinhalese and Muslims who happen to live in areas of the north and east that are considered by Tamil nationalists to be part of the Tamil "homeland." Their democratic rights must be equally respected. The exact means by which the democratic rights of local minorities within any area to be ruled by "the Tamil nation" should be respected is immensely complex and has been at the heart of struggles over various proposed constitutional reforms during the past two decades. It is not actually clear whether it is wise to approach the issue through the language of the right to self-determination, which raises the practically and conceptually difficult question of how to integrate the democratic rights to "self-determination" of other communities, the most important being the Muslims of the Eastern Province. While of fundamental importance to the resolution of Sri Lanka's protracted crisis of the state, these questions are beyond the scope of this paper. For a classic statement of the Sri Lanka liberal cosmopolitan position on these issues, see Neelan Thiruchelvam, "The Politics of Federalism and Diversity in Sri Lanka," in *Autonomy and Ethnicity: Negotiating Competing Claims in Multi-ethnic States*, ed. Yash Ghai (Cambridge: Cambridge University Press, 2000).

**38.** As Sumanasiri Liyanage suggests in an essay written just after the LTTE withdrew from the peace talks in April 2003, the danger of the way in which the UNP-led process was structured was not only that the LTTE might take advantage of the process to forcefully establish Eelam, but that even if they do not, the process might never be deepened (i.e., allowed to deal with the substantive political issues at stake) or "widened" (i.e., allowed to involve a broader range of stakeholders and issues). See Sumanasiri Liyanage, "What Went Wrong?" *Lanka Academic*, June 6, 2003, www.theacademic.org.

**39.** For an excellent analysis of the overly technicist and depoliticizing nature of Sri Lanka's dominant model of conflict resolution, see Vasuki Nesiah, "Editorial: Conflict Resolution Talk: Talks about Talks," *Lines* magazine, August 2002, www.lines-magazine.org. For a related critique of the first two years of the Norwegian-led peace process, see Keenan, "Critical Engagement or Constructive Engagement?"

**40.** "Grassroots" groups have been the preferred beneficiaries of funding from the four "civil society peace funds" created by various bilateral donors since the beginning of the peace process. This choice seems to have been part of a conscious decision by donors to move beyond the confines of Colombo-based elite civil society. So far, however, the funding focus on non-Colombo groups has not led to any noticeable shift in the overall dynamics of civil society political activism. Nor has it involved any significant change in the donors' vision of civil society, which is still largely expected to support the peace process as defined and controlled by the government, the LTTE, and international actors, rather than have a meaningful and independent role in defining the nature of and means to achieve peace in Sri Lanka.

**41.** That Sri Lankan groups might promote policies approved and even formulated elsewhere is not in itself disturbing. That autonomous political agendas and forms of political organizing tend to be displaced by the need to maintain international funding, however, is quite worrisome for those interested in building stronger and more democratic forms of civil society politics. Indeed, at least in the form recently popularized by international donors, the very idea of "civil society" is part of a larger political and ideological project pursued by global powers to shrink state powers and public institutions and replace them with private enterprise and "nongovernmental" organizations. For an excellent analysis of the contemporary complexities, theoretical and practical, of "civil society," see Neera Chandhoke, *The Conceits of Civil Society* (New Delhi: Oxford University Press, 2002). The deep dependence of Sri Lanka's professionalized civil society on foreign donors raises a basic question about whether democracy can, in fact, be built from "the outside," especially by unaccountable, socially disconnected, and short-term agents. For an excellent analysis of the paradox of "democratization from outside," see Jude Howell, "Making Civil Society from the Outside: Challenges for Donors," *European Journal of Development Research* 12, no. 1 (June 2000): 3–22. An excellent analysis of the obstacles that Sri Lankan civil society organizations face when lobbying for a peaceful settlement to the war can be found in Camilla Orjuela, "Building Peace in Sri Lanka: A Role for Civil Society?" *Journal of Peace Research* 40, no. 2 (2003): 195–212. See also Jonathan Goodhand and Nick Lewer, "Sri Lanka: NGO's and Peace-Building in Complex Political Emergencies," *Third World Quarterly* 20, no. 1 (1999): 69–87. For general analyses of the politics of Sri Lankan civil society organizations, see Nira Wickramasinghe, *Civil Society in Sri Lanka: New Circles of Power* (New Delhi: Sage Publications, 2001); and Udan Fernando, *NGO's in Sri Lanka: Past and Present Trends* (Colombo: Wasala Publications, 2003).

**42.** A clear indication of the professionalized conception of Sri Lankan "civil society" relied on by donor agencies is offered in the "Tokyo Declaration on Reconstruction and Development in Sri Lanka," a document published by the host governments and multilateral aid agencies at the conclusion of the Tokyo development aid conference in June 2003. In the paragraph titled "Inputs from Civil Society Organizations and Private Enterprise," the publishers state, "The Conference welcomes the inputs from the civil society meetings held in Colombo on 26–27 April, 2003, and in Tokyo on 8 June, 2003. The conference is of the view that the intensity and continuity of involvement on the part of civil society organizations are essential to achieve success in the challenging task undertaken by the parties. The conference is encouraged by the dynamic role played by private enterprise. The conference also recognizes the contribution of academic communities, trade unions, professional groups, religious organizations and others." Thus, academics, trade unions, professional associations, religious organizations, and others are apparently not considered "civil society organizations." The "civil society meetings" referred to were workshops and meetings involving select members of Colombo's prominent, professionalized research and advocacy groups.

**43.** One notable exception to this general rule is the concept paper written as part of the development of the British- and German-supported peace fund known as FLICT, "Facilitating Local Initiatives in Conflict Transformation." Part of FLICT's founding concept was the explicit recognition that Sri Lanka's civil society includes many more actors besides those liberal, cosmopolitan, professionalized organizations usually funded by international donors. With this recognition in mind, FLICT was designed to be able to fund a larger and more representative range of civil society actors. Unfortunately, while FLICT has been able to fund many smaller and nonelite groups outside Colombo, it has yet to succeed in finding civil society "partners" that don't follow the basic NGO or CBO model of organization or that expand significantly into new, nontraditional peace constituencies such as local business consortia, the Buddhist clergy, trade unions, or student groups. The text of the FLICT concept paper can be found at www.flict.org.

**44.** As Vasuki Nesiah and I argue elsewhere, developing a more democratic conception of human rights would require challenging and transforming what we call the "dominant human rights framework" in Sri Lanka. This framework, rooted in liberal individualist conceptions of rights, focuses on specific cases of human rights violations and the legal prosecution of specific perpetrators and ignores more systemic analysis that holds the potential to foster more democratic and inclusive forms of political organizing by situating such violations in a larger social and political context. Among other things, the liberal and legalistic bias of most human rights work in Sri Lanka obstructs serious organizing by Colombo-based professional civil society organizations around socioeconomic rights and thus makes it more difficult to build bridges to nonelite groups and potential activists. See Vasuki Nesiah and Alan Keenan, "Human Rights and Sacred Cows: Framing Violence, Disappearing Struggles," in *From the Margins of Globalization: Critical Perspectives on Human Rights,* ed. Neve Gordon (New York: Lexington Books, 2004).

**45.** Some of the structural impediments to a politically independent Sri Lankan civil society were brought out clearly in the spring of 2003 with the public distribution of an exchange of e-mails between the Colombo representative of the Australian Agency for International Development and a director of a Sri Lankan NGO. The exchange revealed that AusAID routinely submits local NGO project proposals for approval by Sri Lankan government officials. Donor caution about funding politically controversial civil society initiatives has increased noticeably in the context of the peace process.

**46.** See Darini Rajasingham-Senanayake, "The Post/Conflict Rituals, the Needs of Multilateral Agencies, and Cycles of War: Local-Global Information Asymmetries," *Daily Mirror,* June 5 and June 9, 2003, www.dailymirror.lk. Reprinted as "The International Post-conflict Industry: Myths, Rituals, Market Imperfections and the Need for a New Paradigm," *Polity* 1, no. 3 (July–August 2003).

47. While such critiques have contained much that is true and important, they have grown increasingly crude and intolerant as frustrations with the course of the peace process have grown among many Sinhala activists. By the end of 2003 and early 2004, a powerful (if not always coherent) discourse had emerged articulating a common sense of threat from the Norwegians, other facets of "the international community," Christians, Tamil nationalists, global capital, and the cultural invasion of "foreign" products and values. The power of this discourse explains in large part the surprising success of the JHU and its slate of Buddhist monks in the April 2004 parliamentary elections. The anti-international, anti-Christian, and anti-NGO discourse has only grown more powerful since the post-tsunami arrival of massive numbers of international relief and voluntary groups, many of them sponsored by Christian groups, some of which combine their relief work with evangelism.

# Conclusion

# Toward a More
# Integrated Approach

Julie A. Mertus and Jeffrey W. Helsing

At a meeting between conflict resolution practitioners and human rights advocates a few years ago, a human rights worker pointedly remarked in stressing the focus of international humanitarian law, "My organization does not do peace. We believe that conflict is sometimes necessary—so fight, but respect rights and fight within the laws of war. . . . [Our role is] to denounce those who fight in violation of those laws."[1] Some years earlier, an anonymous United Nations official wrote in *Human Rights Quarterly*, "To end the war is the primary responsibility of the peace negotiator . . . . The human rights fact-finder cannot expect to be an integral part of the peace negotiations. The work of the fact-finder is relevant, but should not become disruptive of, the process of negotiating peace."[2] Another perspective was articulated by Jean Arnault of the UN Mission in Guatemala, who declared that "human rights was central not only to the peace process, but to the very legitimacy that made the peace process possible."[3]

These three statements seem to indicate a belief that the fields of human rights, international humanitarian law, and conflict resolution are discrete disciplines. However, the contributors to this book show that there is a growing awareness of the complementarity of these fields. The success of those working to prevent, manage, or resolve conflict is enhanced by incorporating human rights advocacy into their efforts. At the same time, efforts to secure greater respect for human rights and humanitarian norms are furthered when coordinated with efforts to build peace by laying the foundations for a society that is not only just but also stable.

As the chapters in this book indicate, international humanitarian law, human rights, and conflict resolution cannot be disentangled and treated as dissimilar disciplines that complement and contribute to one another only occasionally and under certain conditions. All three are critical components of the process of creating a lasting and sustainable peace. It is not that the human rights worker quoted above *should* "do peace" but that he or she *must* do peace. Any actions taken to preserve human rights, resolve conflict, or protect the victims of war must consider how such efforts will help ensure that violations, violence, and death and suffering do not recur.

In this concluding chapter, after first considering the role of international humanitarian law vis-à-vis human rights and conflict resolution, we examine both the tensions and the complementarities in the dynamic and complex interrelationship between these three fields. Finally, we touch on the growing influence of nonstate actors in the conflict resolution arena.

## Humanitarian Law as a Bridge between Conflict Resolution and Human Rights

The violations of human dignity that occur during violent conflicts cannot be resolved by any unitary approach that isolates human rights, conflict resolution, or humanitarian law from the other approaches. International humanitarian law is always focused on armed conflict and the need to mitigate the suffering of those touched by it; however, it does not deal with the causes of war or with questions of whether one conflicting party or the other is right. The focus in international humanitarian law is on the conduct of the fighting and on the effects of the war. Human rights law, in contrast, focuses on the condition of all people under all circumstances, not just in wartime. Moreover, the lack of human rights is itself often a source of violent conflict, making efforts to ensure respect for human rights critical to achieving long-term peace and stability.

International humanitarian law can serve as a bridge between peace negotiators and human rights advocates. Humanitarian law provides a vehicle to get human rights concerns on the table. It is a human rights and legal tool that peace negotiators can use to reduce suffering and build confidence among victims. The successful implementation of humanitarian law can strengthen a peace process or agreement without necessarily disrupting the creation of a sustainable peace, by enhancing the legitimacy of that peace. Humanitarian law cannot easily be politicized—it does not take sides. Thus, a sense of equity is possible in securing peace, because the parties to a conflict will ideally see that the application of the law is blind and punishes perpetrators regardless of what side they are on or whether they are part of the state structure.

Also, as the nature of contemporary violent conflict increasingly shifts from a contest between nation-states to fights among substate actors, human rights advocates must move beyond a nation-state orientation and focus also on individuals and parastatal groups. In doing so, international humanitarian law becomes a critical tool for human rights. Humanitarian law may be used in addressing state misappropriations of assistance and may serve as both carrot and stick to substate groups. Further, establishing humanitarian cease-fires may be a valuable tool in peacebuilding.

## Tensions and Conflicts

The interests of those who promote human rights, international humanitarian law, and conflict resolution are fundamentally complementary, especially when viewed over the long term. Yet, unfortunately, they can often come into conflict when short-term or narrowly focused objectives take center stage. For example, human rights principles can act as a lever for conflicting parties to come to normative agreements in peace negotiations, but human rights interests can also present a major obstacle to peaceful resolution of conflict in the short term: They may exacerbate existing differences between parties and contribute to the rejection of an agreement because a principle of human rights is considered more important than the immediate concerns of halting violence or securing a peace agreement. That was the case, or so a UN official claimed, in September 1993 when the human rights community scuttled a potential Bosnian peace agreement.[4]

As another example, international humanitarian relief efforts may exacerbate conflict or become an obstacle to achieving long-term peace. In the 1990s humanitarian organizations such as UNHCR were criticized for their neutrality, particularly in the case of Rwanda. If basic human rights are to be upheld, those guilty of war crimes or human rights violations must be brought to account and not feel that they can seek refuge in the neutrality of humanitarian groups. Critics urged UNHCR to become judgmental, distinguish between right and wrong, and point fingers when necessary. UNHCR and other humanitarian organizations were accused of providing momentum for the continuation of the war. Some argued that the UNHCR's focus on assisting Hutus in Congo who had escaped from Rwanda risked undermining the efforts of the government to unify Congo and gain legitimacy, thus contributing to continued conflict and violation of human rights (by all sides).

While human rights advocates generally promote using trials to establish postconflict justice and accountability, this shorter-term measure may not ultimately serve the longer-term shared goals of achieving both human dignity and security. Holding trials may reinforce the perceived victory or dominance of one group over another, but in many internal conflicts what may be best for the nation or community is not that one side win but that both sides find a way to live together. Human rights must be a critical component of such a shared future, but a truth commission may be more conducive to achieving a lasting peace between two or more groups.

As many conflict resolution practitioners have increasingly emphasized, and as the case of Sierra Leone demonstrates, the peace resulting from agreements is dynamic and unpredictable. Once fighting stops, it is possible, and often desirable, to launch new efforts that will create better conditions for a sustainable peace. In Sierra Leone, as in a number of other conflicts, amnesties were key to getting a settlement and an end to fighting. Then, later, some amnesties were rescinded, or key violators of human rights were still brought to justice once conditions changed. Thus, peace agreements may serve as catalysts and frameworks for further societal reconciliation and human rights efforts, rather than being ends in themselves. In Guatemala, human rights efforts became effective only after real security was created and civil society institutions, the judiciary, and police were functioning independently.[5]

Two examples of peace agreements that have been sustained for more than a decade are in Mozambique and Namibia. Yet neither settlement included human rights. On the other hand, the implementation of the agreements and the postconflict transition phase incorporated human rights into the constitutions; as a result, human rights became embedded in these societies. In contrast, human rights concerns were critical to ending the violence in El Salvador and Guatemala and were incorporated into the peace settlements there. Some analysts of the conflict pointed out that government adherence to the human rights conditions in the peace agreement helped enhance confidence in the peace process and isolate spoilers. After civilian massacres in Xaman, the human rights provisions in the Guatemalan peace accord enabled the civilian leadership to assert greater control over the military, helping to strengthen peace and democracy there.[6]

Thus, peace agreements, once the sine qua non of interest-based conflict resolution and crisis diplomacy, are not sufficient for sustainable peace. In defending the 1995 peace agreement ending the war in Bosnia, General Wesley Clark asserts, "Dayton was the best agreement we could get at the time. It stopped the war."[7] Robert Myers, who worked with Workers Aid, a British NGO in Bosnia and Kosovo, has argued that neutrality on the part of the United Nations and NATO in fact "directly assist[ed] the ethnic cleansers."[8] His point is that neutrality undermined those who wanted to promote a multiethnic society, because the international community constantly defined the conflict as intercommunal and forced those interested in building peace into nationalist camps. In particular, the arms embargo had a terrible effect on moderate, multiethnic political forces in Bosnia. Some Bosnians have gone so far as to equate such neutrality with collaboration, according to Myers. As Jonathan Moore notes, citing the situation in Afghanistan, a results-based humanitarianism will often trump a rights-based humanitarianism; withholding humanitarian relief without immediately establishing women's rights was counterproductive. In short, compromises are necessary, and in Moore's words, "[B]eing serious about translating the humanitarian imperative into duty means we must make agonizing choices."

As Christine Bell points out, the primary mechanism by which conflict is addressed is peace agreements, whether the conflict is internal or external in nature. The prospects for securing human rights depend on negotiations that create a sustainable peace that will not be rejected easily by one party or the other down the road. For negotiators and conflict resolution practitioners, compromise is often at the core of such negotiations, just as it is often the turning point in the transition from violence and in the development of legal and political institutions.

Conflict resolvers tend to see human rights as an instrument of peace, a tool to help achieve a better—that is, more sustainable—peace. Many human rights advocates see human rights as a necessary condition of peace. No agreement will work—because it will not be just—if it does not include human rights. Yet human rights cannot always be at the front of all efforts to make peace, nor can they be the only objective of postconflict efforts. No human rights advocate or organization should opt for human rights at the exclusion of peace or conflict resolution. This is a false choice. Peace efforts that incorporate the respect for and preservation of human rights will be more far-reaching; those that do not incorporate human rights will be less effective and sustainable. Inclusion of group as well as individual rights and social and cultural rights, along with political rights and liberties, will yield an environment more prone to sustaining peace. Human rights advocates who do not work with a view to the larger needs in building a sustainable peace will be much less effective, as in the case of Sri Lanka.

Institutionalized respect for human rights and the establishment of the rule of law are two primary means of conflict prevention. Efforts to protect and implement human rights are essential to the constructive management of conflict. Justice cannot be traded away in a peace process; how and when to push for and implement human rights can have a significant bearing on the prospects for successful peace negotiations, humanitarian assistance, and conflict prevention. Humanitarian law and a focus on crimes of war can be an immediate and effective way to reduce or resolve high-intensity violent conflict. The message of the authors in this book is that a complementary dynamic between peacebuilding and human rights and international humanitarian law must be created; human rights will be strengthened only if peace is viewed as more than a nonviolent state of human interaction or merely an environment in which human rights and laws of war can be better supported.

An issue related to the role of human rights in peacebuilding is the need to incorporate the impact of refugees and displaced persons, in Uganda and elsewhere, into the long-term prospects for peace and stability. Those displaced by conflict are not simply collateral damage; they are consequences of conflict and, as such, will be greatly affected by peace agreements. They may even contribute to the spread of conflict elsewhere. The needs of such refugees must be incorporated into peace agreements to help prevent further conflict. As Susan Martin and Andrew Schoenholtz emphasize, "[P]eace agreements themselves must include realistic frameworks for addressing displacement, including plans for return and reintegration of refugees and internally displaced persons. In developing different plans and scenarios for peace, the negotiators should examine the impact of displacement, as well as the effects of various displacement scenarios, on the likelihood that peace will be achieved."

## Intervention May Lead to the Violation of Human Rights

There is a critical ethical dilemma, as many authors in this volume note: Humanitarian intervention can both prevent and cause deaths. The peace process cannot ignore human rights and be concerned solely with ending violence; at the same time, human rights advocates must consider ending violence and beginning the process of peace as critical to embedding human rights in a society in transition from war to long-term peace.

In fact, human rights may be violated in the name of humanitarian intervention. Richard Falk focuses on Kosovo because it had a resounding impact on both the human rights and the conflict resolution fields. There was no consensus on whether intervention in Kosovo was justified by the claim that genocide or ethnic cleansing had to be prevented. For many, the intervention was not conducted on the basis of international law or of human rights. Richard Falk and Tom Weiss, while acknowledging both the potential merits of humanitarian intervention and the need to adhere to certain moral standards—much along the lines of just-war theory—come to different conclusions about whether humanitarian intervention was justified. Ram Manikkalingam makes another point about risks:

> So universal standards and campaigns may be drawn up that inadequately consider the concerns of the very groups they apply to. This may lead to standards that are inappropriate for particular circumstances, however thoughtful or well intentioned they may be. Compelling adherence to these standards can disrupt the lives of people living in vulnerable communities. The sense that HR standards disrupt lives can also be shared by weaker subgroups such as women within a community, who may be the purported beneficiaries of these universal standards. If indeed groups as a whole reject standards that ought to apply to them, HR as a political project risks becoming a coercive project imposed on those it is meant to benefit.[9]

In grappling with the critical issues of how war is waged while protecting civilians, John Cerone cites international humanitarian law as an increasingly accepted and growing tool that governs military intervention and other uses of force. In some ways, Cerone's arguments serve as a bridge between Falk and Weiss, because humanitarian law provides a framework for the use of force under conditions that protect the civilian population. But Falk also makes the point that intervention cannot simply be the use of force to halt another's use of force. A needs-based approach focuses on conflict *transformation,* not just conflict management, by dealing with people's need for economic and social development as well as their need for justice. Outside intervention must give strong consideration to the long-term consequences of such actions. This applies equally to military intervention, human rights advocacy, humanitarian relief, and third-party mediation. Efforts that do not address needs or work to create long-term sustainability may be counterproductive and, from Falk's perspective, immoral. Jordan Paust builds on this ethical dilemma, demonstrating that responses to terrorism can present another form of intervention and effort at conflict prevention. However, ignoring human rights can contribute to conditions that spawn violence and terrorism.

## International Law versus National Sovereignty

One facet of the emerging international public order is the growing sense of entitlement of the international community to act on behalf of human rights anywhere in the world. But such a right of intervention is a hotly contested issue, especially given the sacredness of sovereignty within small countries with a history of colonization. As the nature of conflict and combatants has changed, so, too, have the means of response to conflict. International humanitarian law has evolved as a result; with it, the sophistication and reach of human rights protection and advocacy have advanced, as have methods of preventing, resolving, and transforming conflict. Still, questions remain about the degree to which prospects for ensuring human rights and peacebuilding are limited by the continued central role of states. Currently states have only sporadically shown goodwill toward promoting human rights and peacebuilding.

The International Criminal Court (ICC) provides an example of the codification and enforcement of human rights that represents a leap forward in international law. The ICC also represents an extension of international law's reach to nonstate actors, but the lack of cooperation and recognition by many state actors may erode its effectiveness and credibility. In 2004, an interesting dilemma emerged in Uganda: Does an ICC investigation of war crimes hinder attempts at securing a peace agreement between the Ugandan government and the Lord's Resistance Army?

With the rise of intrastate conflicts and a greater focus on the rights of individuals, the role of the state comes into question, and the pressure on states to ensure rights and peace increases. Ultimately, will peace, humanitarian assistance or protection, and the safeguarding of human rights remain in the hands of the state? At some point, responsibility for the security and rights of the local people will fall on the shoulders of a state and its governmental apparatus, regardless of the interventions of nonstate actors. Still, one can argue that ultimately human rights cannot be protected without sovereignty, unless they are provided (along with food, shelter, and so on) at the global level. Peacemakers and human rights advocates must be aware of the need to build up the capacity of state institutions responsible for ensuring peace, rights, and security, while working to ensure a strong regime of international human rights.

## A Human Right to Peace?

The conflict resolution worker worries that some degree of peace is necessary in order for human rights to be embraced. But is peace, as Abdul-Aziz Said and Charles Lerche claim, a right? If peace is a prerequisite for human rights, then should we put more resources into peacebuilding and less into human rights, because the immediate priority must be peace and only then can human rights follow? As Jack Donnelly notes, "Many human rights are protected and enjoyed even in times of war, let alone in the (sometimes rather lengthy) intervals of peace (understood as absence of war) we are able to enjoy."

Where there is peace, human rights are more likely to be enforced. Where human rights are upheld, peace is more likely to be achieved. Donnelly adds, "The fact that we have not yet recognized a human right to peace does not mean that it might not be done in the future. There is no logical reason why peace could not become an internationally recognized human right. To establish a human right to peace, however, would require major changes in our moral, legal, and political practices." Until then, as the chapters in this book demonstrate, the achievement of peace will make the enforcement of human rights easier, more likely to last, and stronger. Incorporating human rights into peace processes will greatly increase the likelihood that an agreed-on peace is sustainable and that conflict is resolved and transformed rather than simply managed or contained.

## Justice, the Rule of Law, and Sustainable Peace

International humanitarian law can be more than a powerful deterrent for future behavior in a conflict; it can also help to create an environment that allows for the development of the rule of law, a necessary condition if a society is to move toward reconstruction and, potentially, reconciliation. As Susan Martin and Andrew Schoenholtz note, if the rule of law does not develop, terrorism and repression may instead replace it. This is particularly likely if impunity for criminals persists, a sense of injustice endures, and humanitarian emergencies continue in postconflict settings. Also, conflict resolution efforts must address the needs of internally displaced persons and refugees, while human rights and humanitarian law are critical to their protection and assistance.

For outside actors especially, how they work to bring about justice or punish perpetrators profoundly affects the prospects for sustainable peace. Each intervention, whether it involves mediating a peace agreement, providing shelter and relief, or establishing a truth and reconciliation commission, has a ripple effect throughout the affected society.

For instance, the decision to hold war crimes trials either within the society where the crimes occurred and where the victims and perpetrators live or outside the society (as with the trials in The Hague of accused Bosnian war criminals) can have a significant impact on the outcomes of conflict resolution efforts. Local communities need to see justice at work rather than just hear about justice in some distant—and foreign—capital. International justice should not be in competition with national or local justice processes, as, for example, in the competing agendas of the International Criminal Tribunal for Rwanda (ICTR) and the Rwandan-based *gacaca* process.

Richard Wilson raises the issue of whether a truth commission is more effective and less political if established transnationally rather than as a local entity. On one hand, the history and facts of the conflict can be established more objectively and contextually if the commission is established as a transnational entity; on the other hand, the long-term prospects for a sustainable peace will be hurt if there is no sense of ownership of the process among the population of the affected society. Vasuki Nesiah notes that "the alienation of the Hague proceedings from civil society and the war's enduring fissures in the Balkans" cast doubt on the likelihood of such trials inspiring long-term peace and reconciliation in the former Yugoslavia. As she notes, transitional justice is complex; there are many ways to seek justice for victims and to punish perpetrators. Those choices make a difference in long-term peace and stability.

A peace agreement that includes an amnesty may significantly impede creation of a sustainable peace if it allows perpetrators to escape justice in the larger cause of ending violence. Reconciliation is less likely under such circumstances. As Lisa Schirch writes, human rights monitors and humanitarian laws can play a very powerful role in helping to prevent or reduce violence in the midst of conflict and war, by putting a spotlight on the behavior of combatants or state and nonstate institutions and organizations. But those focused on conflict resolution, such as Ellen Lutz, Alan Keenan, and Michael Lund, caution that human rights NGOs can become, or at least be viewed as, parties or stakeholders in a conflict. The NGOs often want to see a particular outcome, but such an objective can create situations that hamper conflict resolvers' efforts to engage conflicting parties in a meaningful process of peace. Human rights advocates, often using international humanitarian law tools, can, as Lutz argues, "serve to harden parties' positions, thereby making it more difficult for them to explore their real interests." Lund contends that one cannot truly prevent conflict and achieve sustainable peace if violent conflicts are viewed as morality plays between good guys and bad guys.

## From Tension to Harmony: Complementarity

The tensions that clearly exist at the intersection of conflict resolution, humanitarian law, and human rights should not blind us to the numerous complementarities that are also present. Each of the three fields has matured in the past two decades and has much to contribute to the others. The international conflict resolution field has moved beyond a focus primarily on negotiations (and hence beyond states as the only actors) to the promotion of different phases of conflict management, from conflict prevention to conflict transformation. Conflict and peace are therefore viewed and analyzed from a more comprehensive and long-term perspective. Peacebuilding is much more than the ending of hostilities and the start of negotiations. Sustainable peace is dependent on the implementation of an agreement as well as on postconflict reconstruction and reconciliation. Security must be ensured, civil society strengthened, the rule of law built or enhanced. New institutions and processes of governance must be built or rebuilt, and economic needs must be addressed. Whether in trying to prevent conflict or rebuild after conflict, addressing the root causes of conflict becomes very important.

The contributors to this volume illustrate many of the ways in which harmony exists between the work of human rights advocates and that of conflict resolution experts. Lisa Schirch notes that a growing awareness of competing ideas, criticism, and potential coordination between human rights and conflict transformation practitioners "is a good sign of growth for both fields. Each field needs the challenging questions raised by the other, for frustration and challenge are the mothers of innovation and improvisation." Many in the conflict resolution field acknowledge that human rights have been incorporated into peacebuilding plans on a regular basis, and practitioners or scholars who work with conflict resolution NGOs ignore human rights at their peril.

As the conflict management field moves increasingly toward an emphasis on "conflict transformation," justice and peace are viewed by some as critical to moving from conflict to sustainable peace. Still others may view justice as merely a subjective concept. As Vasuki Nesiah illustrates, there are different approaches to justice in the human rights field itself: retributive versus restorative, punitive versus nonpunitive. These create significant disparities in approaches to peacebuilding. Retribution and punishment may be important for the victims of abuses and necessary for a society to put abuses and inequalities into a process of healing, but they may also make resolution of conflict more difficult. Restorative justice may make it more possible to transform conflict.

Many of the authors also acknowledge that human rights law and humanitarian law are increasingly valuable tools for mitigating the worst excesses of conflict. As Christine Bell comments, international humanitarian law and human rights can contribute to a more sustainable peace when used to help shape a peace agreement or certain conditions of implementation. And as Kevin Avruch notes, human rights are not just tools but form an important part of a universal discourse that can in turn help shape peaceful outcomes. The expansion of human rights dialogue to include cultural and indigenous rights has led conflict resolution practitioners to focus on important sources of many of the violent intrastate conflicts of the past fifteen years. Yet discussions of human rights may not be fruitful. In Sri Lanka, divisions have emerged within the local human rights community, often revolving around issues of ethnic and religious identity. Thus, human rights norms have not become a central component of the Sri Lankan peace process despite strong consensus to make them so. The inability to cooperate on human rights, and for human rights advocates to make themselves relevant to the ongoing peace process, has led to the marginalization of human rights in Sri Lanka. As many authors stress, human rights must be a significant part of attempts to create a sustainable peace, but at the same time human rights advocacy can, from a conflict resolution perspective, complicate attempts to build peace.

## Nonstate Actors and the Widening of Conflict Techniques

In some phases of violent conflict and peacemaking, states may have the only tools necessary to end violence—through agreed-on cease-fires and peace treaties—but nonstate actors often play roles in preventing violence, securing peace, and embedding it in a community or society. Many of the chapters in this volume address the role of civil society and, specifically, human rights and humanitarian NGOs. These groups may not be able to resolve violent interstate or intrastate conflicts, but they can contribute to alleviating structural causes of conflict, facilitating communication among parties to the conflict, and bridging gaps between them. They may also help reduce the effects of war and violence, through humanitarian relief efforts and by bearing witness to crimes of war, ideally serving as deterrents as well. It is in this arena that the intersection of human rights, international humanitarian law, and conflict resolution is growing.

Even though human rights and conflict management efforts increasingly complement each other, differences in approaches and priorities remain. Each approach has a different (intended and unintended) impact on power dynamics. Human rights advocates often prefer a "rights-based" rather than an "interest-based" approach to resolving conflict. For many practitioners, a sustainable peace is possible only when all parties to a conflict see that ending violent conflict is in their respective interest. Interest-based approaches to conflict resolution often are premised on a need to find common ground between the parties, whereby an end to violent conflict is perceived to be in the interest of all parties and agreement that will meet their interests is possible. Negotiation, cooperation, and compromise often form the basis of such an approach. Rights-based tactics depend much more on law and treaties to help sort out who is right or wrong. Some scholars charge that this means searching for a "right" or true, perhaps even "perfect," peace. The challenge for human rights advocates is to show the conflicting parties that the protection of human rights is in their mutual interest. Mohammed Abu-Nimer and Edy Kaufman illustrate that this can be done and that striving for human rights may lead to finding common ground.

The widening range of conflict resolution techniques has been matched by an expansion of the range of actors interested in the intersection of human rights and conflict. Some authors included in this volume, such as Richard Falk, Tom Weiss, Julie Mertus, and Maia Carter Hallward, address debates over the role of the United Nations and powerful states willing and able to act unilaterally; others address the role of nonelite contributions to peace—education, as analyzed by Janet Lord and Nancy Flowers, and humanitarian assistance, as discussed by Susan Martin and Andrew Schoenholtz. Alan Keenan emphasizes that to achieve long-term peace and justice, civil society must be restored or developed, and that enlisting the efforts of grassroots advocates is often critical to that task.

The effectiveness of nonstate organizations, however, depends a great deal on what the state and society allow them to do. Hugo Slim argues that NGOs need to cultivate a sense of humanitarian duty in both state and nonstate actors so that political will includes a humanitarian approach. NGOs have been successful in mobilizing public opinion in certain areas, particularly with respect to land mines and debt relief. The combination of publicity campaigns and measures for increased accountability complements the desires of those in the conflict resolution field who want to see more open, transparent peace processes or negotiations. Such transparency forces negotiators to embrace elements of society that will have to live with, and have a stake in, any cease-fire or peace agreement. Incorporating human rights into peacebuilding mechanisms helps attract new and important voices to the peace process.

Many nonstate actors, from the human rights and conflict resolution fields alike, have become involved in some aspect of preventing or managing violent conflicts that arise because of human needs that governments cannot or will not meet. Such NGOs reason that as long as needs are unmet, there is always the potential for renewed conflict. In undertaking to address unmet human needs, NGOs are concerned with their own obligations, moral duty, accountability, evaluation, and best practices. This affects not only what should be done but *how* it is done. Many NGOs are now following codes of conduct that establish certain duties and obligations in how to provide humanitarian assistance. These efforts bridge the gap between conflict resolution and human rights, and they are having an impact on how humanitarian relief and peacebuilding are conducted.

Education and training programs at the local level can be a way to familiarize participants with international human rights standards, impressing on local actors and civil society organizations the importance of human rights practice and principles. Because there are internationally accepted norms regarding human rights, even individuals living in societies where they cannot enjoy their rights today are at least made aware of what those rights are and the legal basis from which they derive. As Janet Lord and Nancy Flowers make clear, the success of peace and human rights education depends on programs that belong to local communities and address their long-term needs.

Increasingly, humanitarian and democratization NGOs are including human rights programs in their mandates. Human rights organizations, both indigenous and international, play a critical role in rapid response and in reporting human rights violations, even in the face of oppression and government denial. They raise concerns about peace agreements lacking human rights provisions and can inform diplomats and conflict resolution practitioners about cultural practices and understandings of peace, justice, and reconciliation. In many conflicts, the only international presence in a war-affected country are the humanitarian agencies, but often their staffs are not consulted about peace negotiations, and their experiences regarding the local situations are ignored. Too often, the sources behind systematic human rights violations (which often contribute significantly to the violent conflict itself) are not investigated or understood. Those sources must be uncovered, and options to prevent such violations in the future must be developed, if a sustainable peace is to be built. This is a critical intersection of human rights, international humanitarian law, and conflict resolution interests, because many of those same root causes must be addressed if a particular conflict is to be resolved, a stable peace created, and human rights secured.

An equally important role for the human rights and humanitarian law fields lies in the implementation of peace agreements or cease-fire agreements. The need to monitor compliance is often fulfilled in part by human rights groups or by individuals who work to ensure that human rights are upheld by the combatants. Former NATO commander General Wesley Clark noted that for the NATO peacekeeping mission in Bosnia, "human rights are the greatest weapon we have—not just legally but in terms of shaping people's expectations."[10]

Not only have emerging human rights organizations in societies in conflict been involved in rights promotion and enforcement; they have also served a crucial function as civil society organizations. By their mere existence and operation, all civil society organizations, including those focused on human rights, can be integrated into a society. Through participation in civil society, interest groups demonstrate their respect for the rule of law and the civil resolution of conflicts. In particular, human rights institutions can provide a paradigm and foster relationships that are conducive to conflict prevention.

## Conclusion

A major goal of this book has been to lay out differences and commonalities within and between the fields of human rights, humanitarian law, and conflict resolution. The book introduces many of the practical issues and ethical dilemmas that policymakers, diplomats, aid and humanitarian workers, advocates, and even soldiers, peacekeepers, and civilian police face in conflict situations. For the people on the front lines of human rights advocacy and humanitarian relief as well as those involved in peacemaking and peacebuilding, ethical dilemmas are not an abstraction but a daily reality. In this regard, the role of culture, education, humanitarian aid and intervention, and a democratic civil society, as well as the challenges of armed intervention, terrorism, war crimes, and displaced persons, all point to the need for more cooperative efforts in managing conflict and building sustainable peace.

Much more remains to be done to explore human rights in conflict situations. Human rights accountability on the part of enforcers and non-state armed groups is an important and, we think, underresearched issue of concern. The role of the media warrants greater attention, given the increased ability of reporters to be on the front lines of conflicts and the differentials in transparency of communication in different states. It would be interesting to analyze how diplomats raise human rights issues during negotiations (both for cease-fires and for peace agreements). Another noteworthy dimension of analysis is the role of human rights investigations in a peace process and settlement. Much more could be done to examine the gender dimensions of conflicts as well as the role of people with disabilities in conflicts. As the fields of human rights and conflict resolution draw closer together, the ways in which transnational crime creates challenges requiring different strategies from those used by the human rights community should also be explored.

This book is an initial contribution to what we hope will be a much wider and deeper discussion about the interrelationship between conflict resolution, human rights, and international humanitarian law in conflict situations. The relationship between conflict and human rights is complex and dynamic, and it demands an equally dynamic response from those who work to protect human rights and who strive for peace.

## Notes

1. Joe Saunders, "Bridging Human Rights and Conflict Resolution: A Dialogue between Critical Communities" (report on a Carnegie Council on Ethics and International Affairs workshop, July 16–17, 2001), www.carnegiecouncil.org/viewMedia.php/prmTemplateID/1/prmID/161.

2. Anonymous, "Human Rights in Peace Negotiations," *Human Rights Quarterly* 18, no. 2 (May 1996): 256.

3. Jean Arnault, *How Can Human Rights Be Better Integrated into Peace Processes?* conference report (Washington, DC: Fund for Peace, 1998), 18.

4. Anonymous, "Human Rights in Peace Negotiations"; for an excellent discussion of how the protection and enforcement of human rights can lead to conflict, particularly in the South Africa case, see Michelle Parlevliet, "Bridging the Divide: Exploring the Relationship between Human Rights and Conflict Management," *Track Two* 11, no. 1 (March 2002): 8–43.

5. See Tonya L. Putnam, "Human Rights and Sustainable Peace," in *Ending Civil Wars,* ed. Stephen Stedman, Donald Rothschild, and Elizabeth Cousens (Boulder, CO: Lynne Rienner, 2002), 248.

6. For further analysis of the Guatemala case, see Kristine Höglund, Negotiations amid Violence: Explaining Violence-Induced Crisis in Peace Negotiations Processes, *Interim Report IR-04-02* (Laxenburg, Austria: International Institute for Applied Systems Analysis, January 2004).

7. Wesley Clark (speech, Woodrow Wilson Center for International Scholars, Washington, DC, June 13, 2000).

8. Robert Myers, "The Fallacy of Neutral Humanitarianism in Bosnia," *Human Rights Dialogue* 2, no. 5 (Winter 2001): 20.

9. Ram Manikkalingam, "Culture, Relativism, and Human Rights—Commentary," this volume, p. 126.

10. Clark (speech at Woodrow Wilson Center).

# Index

# United States Institute of Peace

The United States Institute of Peace is an independent, nonpartisan federal institution created by Congress to promote the prevention, management, and peaceful resolution of international conflicts. Established in 1984, the Institute meets its congressional mandate through an array of programs, including research grants, fellowships, professional training, education programs from high school through graduate school, conferences and workshops, library services, and publications. The Institute's Board of Directors is appointed by the President of the United States and confirmed by the Senate.

# Human Rights and Conflict

This book is set in Slimbach; the display type is Bell Gothic. The Creative Studio designed the book's cover. Helene Y. Redmond designed the interior and made up the pages. The text was copyedited by Michael Carr and proofread by Karen Stough. The index was prepared by Sonsie Conroy. The book's editors were Nigel Quinney and Amy Benavides.